OKANAGAN COLLEGE LIBRARY

03780046

P9-DTJ-038

Gender Development

OKANAGAN COLLEGE
LIBRARY
BRITISH COLUMBIA

Gender Development

Judith E. Owen Blakemore
Indiana University–Purdue University Fort Wayne

Sheri A. Berenbaum
The Pennsylvania State University

Lynn S. Liben
The Pennsylvania State University

Psychology Press
Taylor & Francis Group

New York   London

Cover design by Lynn Liben; photographs by JeongMee Yoon, The Pink and Blue Project (www.jeongmeeyoon.com). We express our gratitude to Ms. Yoon for permission to reproduce these photographs.

Psychology Press
Taylor & Francis Group
270 Madison Avenue
New York, NY 10016

Psychology Press
Taylor & Francis Group
27 Church Road
Hove, East Sussex BN3 2FA

© 2009 by Taylor & Francis Group, LLC

Printed in the United States of America on acid-free paper
10 9 8 7 6 5 4 3 2 1

International Standard Book Number-13: 978-0-8058-4170-1 (Hardcover)

Except as permitted under U.S. Copyright Law, no part of this book may be reprinted, reproduced, transmitted, or utilized in any form by any electronic, mechanical, or other means, now known or hereafter invented, including photocopying, microfilming, and recording, or in any information storage or retrieval system, without written permission from the publishers.

Trademark Notice: Product or corporate names may be trademarks or registered trademarks, and are used only for identification and explanation without intent to infringe.

Library of Congress Cataloging-in-Publication Data

Blakemore, Judith E. Owen.
  Gender development / Judith E. Owen Blakemore, Sheri A. Berenbaum, Lynn S. Liben.
     p. cm.
  ISBN 978-0-8058-4170-1
  1. Gender identity. 2. Sex differences (Psychology) 3. Parent and child. 4. Identity (Psychology) and mass media. 5. Mass media and sex. 6. Family in mass media. I. Berenbaum, Sheri A. II. Liben, Lynn S. III. Title.

HQ1075.B545 2008
305.3--dc22   2008019279

Visit the Taylor & Francis Web site at
http://www.taylorandfrancis.com

and the Psychology Press Web site at
http://www.psypress.com

Contents

Preface

It is obvious to those of us who do research and teach on the topic of children's gender development that there has long been a need for an advanced textbook and reference work in the area. We hope that this book will fill that need. Our goal was to provide a textbook for advanced undergraduate and graduate courses in gender development, as well as a book that could serve as a resource for scholars in the area.

There are many textbooks devoted to the topics of sex and gender, and in particular, to the psychology of women, but their focus is rarely developmental. As an advanced-level book focused on the gender development of children and adolescents, this text is unique. There have been a few gender development texts in the past (none for more than a decade), but even those few were at an introductory level. Thus we believe this book will fill an important niche for both teachers and scholars. It is our hope that it will also serve as a stimulus to increase the teaching of courses on gender development at both the undergraduate and graduate levels. To make the book accessible to students, a glossary of significant terms, boldfaced when first introduced, is included at the end of the book. Every chapter begins with a quote, often from literature, about a topic related to gender and children. We have also included many lively anecdotes about children's gender-related experiences, ideas, and behaviors, such as Michael Messner's (2000) delightful story about the Barbie Girls and the Sea Monsters.

The book is organized into four parts. The first introductory part contains two chapters. Chapter 1 introduces the field, and chapter 2 outlines its history, beginning before the 20th century and continuing through the time of the publication of Maccoby and Jacklin's *Psychology of Sex Differences* in 1974.

The second part concerns differences between the sexes. This includes the basic biology of sex in chapter 3, and two chapters organizing research on behavioral sex differences. Chapter 4 addresses motor and cognitive behaviors, and chapter 5 addresses personality and social behaviors.

The third part focuses on contemporary theoretical perspectives on gender development. We consider biological approaches in chapter 6, social and environmental approaches in chapter 7, and cognitive approaches in chapter 8.

The fourth part addresses the social agents of gender development, beginning with children themselves as agents of their own gender development in chapter 9, followed by family, peers, the media, and schools as agents of gender development in chapters 10, 11, 12, and 13, respectively. We follow chapter 13 with a brief epilogue.

We have included the most recent research on gender development. For example, in chapter 6 we show how genes and hormones affect the behavioral development of males and females, including the most recent findings about causes of gender identity, and we consider the significance of very recent findings about brain sex differences. In chapter 9 we look at the most recent research on children's cognitions about gender, including new work on the development of gender constancy. In chapter 11 we examine research on sexual minority youth as they negotiate romantic and sexual relationships in adolescence. In chapter 12 we look at the impact of new technologies such as video games and Internet use on the development of boys and girls, and in chapter 13, we look at the impact of single sex schools.

We have taught courses on this topic, both to upper-level undergraduates and to graduate students, and we believe this book has appealing features for both groups of students. This is an inherently interesting subject matter to students. We think all will find that the integration of stories and examples enriches the material and connects it to their lives. The depth and variety of the research and theoretical models presented will provide a foundation for undergraduates and graduate students alike. Graduate students in particular should be able to use the cited works as a base for further examination of the literature in almost any area of gender development work.

This book is a collaboration among three authors. Although we have each contributed to the whole book through collectively planning the organization, content, and some basic themes, we have each taken responsibility for writing individual chapters. One of us, Elaine Blakemore, wrote the majority of the chapters (1, 2, 4, 5, 7, and 10–13), and as indicated by footnotes in the relevant chapters, the other two of us wrote two chapters each: Sheri Berenbaum chapters 3 and 6 and Lynn Liben chapters 8 and 9. Throughout the writing process, we each commented on one another's chapters and occasionally wrote sections for chapters that were not our primary responsibility. We made an effort to blend our writing styles, but we each have a somewhat different voice and some different perspectives on the field. Our different perspectives enrich our coverage of the material and reflect the diversity in the field. This means, however, that occasionally a perspective or point taken in one chapter may vary somewhat from the perspective found in another chapter. We believe that a book with different voices and perspectives is a better reflection of this rich and diverse (but sometimes controversial) field than a book with a single author would be.

In many places, we draw links among the individual chapters (e.g., referring to later and earlier discussions of similar points and sometimes even descriptions of the same studies for different purposes). Although chapters have been designed to be read sequentially, each chapter covers particular topics and perspectives that are not always related in a linear fashion to topics in the preceding or subsequent chapters. Therefore, we provide full citation authorship the first time a reference is used within an individual chapter rather than only the first time it is used within the entire book. This procedure should make it easier for instructors who wish to assign chapters in a different order than they appear in the book and ensure that individual chapters are useful for advanced scholars who may wish to use only parts of the book to review or learn about a particular content area.

We know that a book gets to print not only through the efforts of its authors, but also through the contributions of many other people behind the scenes; this book is no exception. We begin by acknowledging the contribution of one of our (and we know, others') heroes in this field—Eleanor Maccoby—to whom we have collectively dedicated this book. It is Eleanor more than any other scholar who legitimized the study of sex differences in developmental psychology, in part by the ground-breaking book that she edited in 1966, *The Development of Sex Differences*, and in part by the many related books and articles that she has authored or coauthored since then. She has also trained a steady stream of outstanding graduate students, although sadly none of us is numbered among them. Nevertheless, we have each benefitted from her student progeny, some of whom have become collaborators with one or more of us, and some of whom have provided input and encouragement to us as we wrote this book. And, more directly, Eleanor has also offered us her wisdom and support throughout this project. We are deeply grateful.

We would also like to acknowledge with our sincere thanks to those colleagues who reviewed portions of this book in its varied stages: Rebecca Bigler, Kristina Bryk, Barbara Bulman-Fleming, Jeanette Clausen, Susan Gelman, Carol Lawton, Susan McHale, Carol Lynn Martin, Diane Ruble, Margaret Signorella, and the reviewers engaged by Erlbaum Associates/Psychology Press: Rebecca Bigler, the University of Texas at Austin; Yvonne Caldera, Texas Tech University; Campbell Leaper, University of California–Santa Cruz; and Richard Lippa, California State University–Fullerton. Although they should not be held responsible for the final form of this book, they certainly should be thanked for their help in its reaching a final form. We also acknowledge the students in our classes and in our laboratories at Indiana University–Purdue University Fort Wayne and The Pennsylvania State University who read early versions of some of the chapters and provided helpful comments. So, too, we would like to thank our editors at Taylor & Francis, Debra Riegert and Richard Tressider. Debra supervised this book from the time we first brought the idea to Lawrence Erlbaum Associates to the time it reached print, and Richard handled the production process with efficient expertise. We have appreciated the patience, wisdom, and responsiveness they have shown throughout the process. We also thank Roberta Shadle for her assistance with illustrations and artwork.

Finally, we would each like to add our individual acknowledgments to some important influences from beyond the academy. First, to Tom Blakemore in gratitude for more than 35 years of feminist partnership, and to Greg and Neil Blakemore, whose childhood experiences provided many examples and stories used throughout this book. Second, to Edith and Charles Berenbaum, for providing the right genes and the nurturing environment for their optimal expression, and for enacting their beliefs that girls can do anything. Third, to the memories of Florence Gettenberg Liben and Jay Liben, who are, respectively, the doctor of the anecdote that opens chapter 9 and the person who—with pride—never tired of correcting those who assumed that he was the one with the medical degree. We will welcome the day that such corrections are unnecessary.

Introduction

1

Boys ran around in the yard with toy guns going kksshh-kksshh, fighting wars for made-up reasons and arguing about who was dead, while girls stayed inside and played with dolls, creating complex family groups and learning how to solve problems through negotiation and role playing. (Keillor, 1993, p. 12)

Gender is one of the fundamental ways in which the social life of human beings is organized. Indeed, one of the first questions people ask when they hear of a birth is whether the child is a boy or a girl. From infancy onwards, parents often think that boys and girls are very different. For example, a few years ago, a newspaper columnist wrote about his young son (Weasel, 2001). His son is messy, leaves grape juice stains on the counter, and has Oreo rings around his mouth. He doesn't like to take afternoon naps, he plays with "boy stuff," and is obsessed with monster trucks. Weasel noted that his daughters have very different interests and behaviors than his son. More than likely many readers found the column charming, and agreed that boys and girls really do seem like different kinds of beings.

However, we might wonder why parents, or people in general, are inclined to emphasize the differences between boys and girls, rather than the similarities. If you consider the entire context of behavior from the routine (e.g., eating) to the highly complex (e.g., using language and sophisticated cognitive processes), surely human female children are more similar to human male children than they are different. On the other hand, if there are differences between boys and girls, what are they, how large or important are they, and where do they come from? Are such differences inevitable? Do you find them in all situations and cultures, or do they come and go as the situation changes? Is it better to encourage children to adopt gender roles, or better to eliminate them as much as possible?

Worldwide there are few factors that influence the lives people lead from birth to death as much as the person's sex or gender. Gender matters from the trivial to the most profound aspects of a human being's life. Whether a child is born a boy or girl determines the name the child is given, the way the child is talked to, the color of the child's clothing, and the toys and objects that are provided to the child. It influences who their playmates will be and how they will interact with those playmates. In some cultures it influences what or how much education children receive (Schulz & Schulz, 1999). Once children grow up, gender continues to play a major role. Male and female adults have different clothing and hairstyles, occupations, life roles, responsibilities for the upbringing of children, different household and other chores, and different interactions with others every day of their lives.

Yet, in many respects, perhaps gender is becoming less important. Compared to many periods in human history, boys and girls today have many similar experiences and are expected to do many of the same things, especially in modern industrialized societies. They often receive identical or at least similar educations, and many adopt the same occupations. In some instances, males and females care for the children and do domestic tasks equally. So, although there is a long history of gender being extremely significant in human lives, we can also ask whether that significance is now diminishing.

In this book we will examine the role that gender plays in the behavior and experiences of children. In part I we introduce you to the study of gender development and explore its early history. In part II we describe basic biological and behavioral differences between the sexes. In part III, we discuss the major theoretical approaches to the study of gender development. In part IV, we explore agents of gender development—how family, peers, the media, schools, and children themselves influence the process. Finally, we close the book with a short epilogue suggesting how these factors work together in the process of gender development.

As we begin, we urge you to consider gender development as representative of development in general, and not as a unique developmental process. The development of boys and girls is certainly affected by both biological and social processes, and is influenced by interactions with parents, peers, school, and the culture at large. However, the same is true of any aspect of children's development. So, although our focus is gender development, it is important to recognize that the developmental processes that affect gender are by no means unique. The study of gender development therefore has the potential of helping us to understand many aspects of development. Finally, we note that, although gender is studied in many disciplines (e.g., anthropology, sociology), the examination of gender in this book is from the perspective of developmental psychology.

In this chapter we introduce the study of gender development. We begin with several different terms, issues, and controversies associated with the study of sex and gender in psychology in general, and in developmental psychology in particular. An examination of all of these issues at one time may seem a bit overwhelming, but we urge you not to panic. We will return to them throughout the book, and we do not expect you to fully understand them at this point. Rather, we want you to realize that there are many facets of gender development, including some that you may not have ever stopped to think about. Our goal here is to begin with an overview of the field, and we hope that a brief examination of these many terms and issues is a helpful part of that overview. As we reach the end of chapter 1, we move on to a brief introduction to children's gender development and to the theoretical perspectives that organize the field.

THE MANY COMPONENTS OF SEX AND GENDER

Many people seem to think that all aspects of sex and gender are consistent. They may assume that a person is definitely biologically male or female, definitely heterosexual or homosexual, definitely masculine or feminine, and that all of these aspects of sex and gender are likely to be consistent. However, qualities like these are much more complex than they may seem on the surface. Although most children are born unambiguously biologically male or female, some are not. The biological aspects of being male or female (chromosomes, hormones, genital structures, etc.) are sometimes inconsistent within a single person, and they certainly vary from person to person. The cultural aspects vary even more. Not all girls are especially feminine, at least as typically defined by the culture in which they live, and they may be feminine in some ways but not in others. A teenage girl may love sports and may be a fiercely competitive basketball player. She may also love dressing up and wearing makeup and nail polish. When thinking about her future plans, she may waver between being a nursery school teacher or a computer programmer. She is very likely not to question or doubt that she is a girl, or even think about it much. She simply accepts that she is a girl. On the other hand she may certainly question certain aspects of feminine gender roles. Perhaps she is a lesbian, although she may not be sure of that until she is well into adulthood. Sexual orientation is not always easily tied to masculinity and femininity. Although many boys who have exceedingly feminine interests in childhood do grow up to be gay men (Bailey & Zucker, 1995), others do not, and the majority of tomboys are heterosexual as adult women. Issues of sex, gender, gender identity, gender role, and sexual orientation are not simple. To clarify some of these issues, we begin with definitions of some of the terms we will be using in this book.

"Sex" or "Gender": What's the Difference?

Until the 1970s, the term **sex** was the most commonly used term to refer to boys and girls and men and women, and *sex roles* was the most commonly used term to refer to adopting cultural definitions of masculinity and femininity. More recently the term **gender** has often been used to refer to these same things.

We hear about sex differences in behavior, and about gender differences in behavior, about sex roles, and about gender roles (Pryzgoda & Chrisler, 2000). But are these terms appropriately used as synonyms? Do they have different meanings, and if so, what are they?

The use of the term "gender" rather than "sex" to refer to males and females began its modern usage with psychologist John Money's adoption of the term **gender roles** (Money, 1973) to distinguish between "genital sex," and all other aspects of being a male or female person. Money devoted his professional life to the study of sex, gender, and sexual orientation, especially in cases of people who had various anomalies of sex chromosomes and hormones. When he adopted the use of the term "gender," he used it to refer to external components of gender (which later came to be called "gender roles"), and internal components (which are now called **gender identity** and **sexual orientation**).

How are the terms "sex" and "gender" used now? Actually, there is no convention for the use of these terms that is accepted by all scholars of sex and gender, even within a single discipline like psychology. Some scholars rarely use the word "sex" except to refer to sexuality, and others rarely or never use the word "gender." Some call boys and girls the "two sexes," and others call them the "two genders." Some refer to "sex differences" in behavior, others to "sex-related differences," and still others to "gender differences." Some talk of "sex roles" and others talk of "gender roles." It is possible to read a single issue of a journal and find all of these terms used by different authors.

One common scheme used by many psychologists is to use the term "sex" for the biological aspects (e.g., hormones, chromosomes, genitals) of being male or female, and "gender" for the social or cultural aspects (Unger, 1979; Winstead, Derlega, & Unger, 1999). However, it is not always easy to know what is biological and what is learned, and many behaviors may be influenced by several different factors. Another widely used scheme developed by social psychologist Kay Deaux (1984) is to use the term "sex" to refer to the categories of male and female, and "gender" to refer to any judgments about the nature of differences between males and females, about roles, and about masculinity and femininity. Using Deaux's terminology, one would refer to boys and girls as the "two sexes," not the "two genders," whereas terms such as "gender identity," "gender roles," and **gender stereotypes** would be consistent with her scheme.

What terminology can you expect in this book? The use of the term "sex" to refer to sexual behavior and sexuality (e.g., sexual orientation) and clear biological phenomena (e.g., sex hormones, sex chromosomes) is essentially universal. In addition, the use of the terms "gender identity," "gender stereotypes," and "gender roles" has also been very consistent in recent years. We will most certainly use the term "sex" to refer to sexuality and to biological phenomena such as hormones, and we will use the terms "gender roles" and "gender stereotypes" rather than "sex roles" or "sex stereotypes." Following Deaux's convention, we will ordinarily call boys and girls "the sexes." With respect to behavioral differences between boys and girls, we will usually refer to "sex differences," but not necessarily always. Choosing the use of the term "sexes" to refer to boys and girls and talking about "sex differences" does not imply that we believe that social or cultural forces are unimportant. On the contrary, we will take the position that many factors influence gender development: biological, cognitive, social, and cultural. In short, be warned that in this book—as in the literature at large—there is no simple formula for interpreting the words "sex" and "gender," and thus you will need to examine the full context (the sentence, paragraph, or even the entire chapter) to interpret meaning accurately.

The "Sexes" or the "Genders": How Many Are There?

The majority of children are born unambiguously male or female, but a small number of children, probably less than 2% of live births (Fausto Sterling, 2000), are born with **intersex** conditions. This refers to a situation in which a child's sex chromosomes and one or more of their genital structures are not completely consistent. These conditions include those who have both ovaries and testes (or one of each) and some portions of the internal and external genitals of both sexes, and those who have only one type of gonad (either ovaries or testes), but whose external and/or internal genital structures do not fully match their gonads. Biologist Anne Fausto Sterling (1993) once argued that if one considers people with such conditions, biological sex could be seen as a continuum, and depending on where one divides the continuum into categories, there could be five or more biological sexes. Although she may not have been entirely serious about there being five sexes, she continues to stress that the basic biology of sex can vary a great deal among individuals: "on close inspection, absolute dimorphism disintegrates even at the level of basic biology. Chromosomes, hormones, the internal sex structures, the gonads and the external genitalia all vary more than most people realize" (Fausto Sterling, 2000, p. 19).

Certain aspects of gender also vary along a continuum. Boys, for example, might range from very masculine to very feminine in their interests and personalities. But even if both the biological underpinnings of sex and the social and cultural aspects of gender vary, contemporary Western culture only allows for two categories. Socially and culturally, a child can only be a boy or a girl—there isn't a third or fourth category. Fausto Sterling (1993) points out that since the Middle Ages, people with intersex conditions in Western cultures have been socially and legally required to choose to be either male or female. Children born with intersex conditions are usually assigned to one gender or another, and have often undergone genital surgery to match their genitals to their gender of rearing. For example, this may involve surgery to reduce the size of an enlarged clitoris that resembles a penis (Lightfoot-Klein, Chase, Hammond, & Goldman, 2000). In recent years, advocacy groups such as the Intersex Society of North American (see www.isna.org) have advocated the elimination of reconstructive surgery on infants and young children (unless medically necessary) until they have reached an age when they can decide for themselves, both about their gender category and genital reconstructive surgery. Not surprisingly, this has been a very controversial topic, with strong opinions on both sides of the issue.

Are there always only two gender categories in every culture? Although not usually related to having intersex characteristics, Native American cultures (Fulton & Anderson, 1992) have often been reported to have a **third gender** category of adult roles for both males and females, sometimes called a **berdache**. These were typically men or women who wore the clothing and lived the social roles of the other sex, including having a marriage partner of the same biological sex as they were. In Samoa (Mageo, Fulton, & Anderson, 1992), there is a third gender category consisting of males who dress in women's clothing, and who have different social rules for their behavior than either males or females. In Albanian culture, still continuing today in rural northern Albania, are people called **sworn virgins**—women who live, dress, and work as celibate men (Young, 2000). Thus, it is not always the case that there are only two gender categories. Nonetheless, in most cultures, and certainly in most modern Western cultures, there are two social categories, male and female. When a child is born, (or with the growing use of prenatal testing, even before) we want to know if the child is a boy or a girl.

Having Gender and Doing Gender

Consider the following story told by sociologist Michael Messner (2000), who writes about his 5-year-old son's first season of playing organized soccer. On the first day of soccer season in a middle class Los Angeles suburb, thousands of parents and their 4- to 17-year-old children congregated on the grounds of a high school awaiting the opening ceremonies. A group of 4- and 5-year-old boys, the Sea Monsters, waited to play their very first soccer game. They had chosen their name at a meeting some weeks before, after having been given their uniforms in the team colors of green and blue. As they waited for events to begin, parents were chatting and getting to know one another while watching their children. Beside the Sea Monsters was a team of similar-aged girls, the Barbie Girls. Both teams had banners, but the Barbie Girls had something better: a red wagon with a 3-foot-tall Barbie doll dressed in a cheerleader outfit in their team colors, green and white, rotating on a pedestal. Barbie's hair was streaked with green and she had a green bow in it, as did many of the girls. A boom box played Barbie music and several girls sang along, holding hands, walking around the Barbie float. Soon the Sea Monsters noticed the girls:

At first, the boys are watching as individuals, seemingly unaware of each other's shared interest.... I notice slight smiles on a couple of their faces, as though they are drawn to the Barbie Girls' celebratory fun. Then, with side-glances, some of the boys begin to notice each other's attention on the Barbie Girls. Their faces begin to show signs of distaste. One of them yells out, "NO BARBIE!" Suddenly, they all begin to move—jumping up and down, nudging and bumping one another—and joining a group chant: "NO BARBIE! NO BARBIE! NO BARBIE!" (Messner, 2000, p. 768)

In his discussion of these events Messner confronts the contrast between "doing gender" versus "having gender." Having gender refers to gender as an inherent characteristic of individuals—children are boys or girls, and their gender affects their behavior—it makes them different. The parents he writes about seem to think that their children have gender. The parents argue that the children are so different; there seems to be something about the nature of being a boy or a girl that produces that difference. Doing gender, on the other hand, refers to choosing to match one's behavior to a set of gender-related ideals. One does a gendered performance to match one's own behavior to those cultural ideals. Messner notes that, although the soccer-playing behavior of the young boys and girls was indeed overwhelmingly similar, he never heard parents point out the similarities, only the differences. This emphasis on difference by the parents is an instance of doing gender.

But the children in this example also do gender. Messner tells of several instances of the children choosing gendered activities and being supported in these choices by their parents and the other adults involved in the league. For example, he classified the children's choices of the names for their teams into four categories: sweet names (e.g., Blue Butterflies, Barbie Girls), neutral names (e.g., Team Flubber), paradoxical names in which there was a mix of power and vulnerability (e.g., Little Tigers), and power names (e.g., Raptor Attack, Sea Monsters). As might be expected, there were notable differences in the names that boys and girls chose for their teams, especially at the youngest ages, with boys being more likely to choose power names and girls being more likely to choose sweet, paradoxical, or neutral names. Indeed, the entire structure of the soccer league (e.g., coaches, girls' and boys' teams, the colors of the uniforms provided to the children) was arranged along gender lines. It is not very difficult to find other examples of people doing gender in ways such as these.

We are so embedded in the social processes of gender that most of these processes are invisible to us. We usually think in terms of having gender; boys are boys and girls are girls. Although we may realize that many factors influence the behaviors and characteristics of boys and girls, we still tend to think of those characteristics as residing in the child. However, it is useful to consider that a person's sex or gender influences many complex processes of daily interaction involving choices that people make for their behavior and actions in the context of social relationships, as well as responses that others have to them. Every day, boys, girls, men, and women choose certain clothing, hairstyles, toys, and behaviors, and people respond to them in predictable ways when they do. The reactions of others further influence a person's behavior and choices. Messner and others argue that gender is best seen in terms of these interactional processes, rather than in terms of stable characteristics, traits, or roles. In other words, having gender puts the emphasis on the characteristics of the individual, whereas doing gender puts the emphasis on ongoing social interaction.

Gender Identity

Gender identity is a term that has been used somewhat differently by different theorists. Later in the book, especially in chapters 8 and 9, we will discuss these uses in more detail, but for now it is fine to think of the term as referring to individuals knowing that they are either a male or female person. In children, this is associated with their being able to reliably answer the question: "Are you a boy or a girl?" The research suggests that most children can do so around 2.5 years of age (Etaugh, Grinnell, & Etaugh, 1989; Fagot & Leinbach, 1989). Some developmental psychologists (Egan & Perry, 2001; Zucker, 2000) have included other aspects of a child's knowledge and feelings as part of gender identity. In addition to knowing whether one is a boy or a girl, these have included feelings of similarity to others of one's gender, contentedness with being that gender, and a sense of pressure to follow that gender's roles.

One issue related to gender identity concerns one's comfort with the gender category that was assigned at birth. Most people don't even think about or question their sex or gender, but a small number do. The *Diagnostic and Statistical Manual* (DSM-IV, American Psychiatric Association, 1994) includes a category called **gender identity disorder** that is used as a diagnosis for children. Gender identity disorder includes the following elements: "a strong and persistent cross-gender identification (not merely a desire for any perceived cultural advantages of the other sex)"; "a persistent discomfort with his or her sex, or a sense of inappropriateness in the gender role of that sex"; and "clinically significant distress or impairment in social, occupational, or other important areas of functioning" caused by the disorder. Finally, a child must not have an intersex condition to be said to have gender identity disorder (Zucker, 2000, p. 674, from the DSM-IV). Although there is some debate about whether this relatively rare condition should be considered a disorder at all (Bartlett, Vasey, & Bukowski, 2000), there are certainly some children who, from a very young age, show discomfort with their gender category.

Sexual Orientation and Sexual Identity

Sexual orientation refers to feelings of sexual attraction or arousal or to sexual behavior with partners of the same sex, the other sex, or both sexes; and **sexual identity** refers to whether people identify themselves as predominantly heterosexual, homosexual, or bisexual (Ellis & Mitchell, 2000). Same-sex attractions and behavior are believed to have occurred throughout human history. However, lesbian, gay, and bisexual identities were not generally found before the end of the 19th century (Patterson, 1995), and the number of people identifying themselves as lesbian, gay, or bisexual increased substantially during the 20th century.

Certainly sexual orientation and sexual identity are much more central in the lives of adolescents and adults than they are in the lives of children, nonetheless sexual feelings and romantic attraction arise sooner than many people may think. Although sexual feelings are experienced even in early childhood, research suggests that most children have their first erotic attractions and feelings around the age of 10, probably as sex hormones are being produced by the maturing adrenal glands (McClintock & Herdt, 1996), and many individuals recall their first crushes and sexual attractions around this age. Developmental researchers have been interested in studying the childhood and early developmental roots of adult sexual orientation. They have asked questions about biological and childhood influences on sexual orientation, and how these influences are related to other aspects of children's gender-related behavior. Three general issues have been studied: an examination of the genetic and early hormonal influences on sexual orientation; the study of the relationship between family configurations and sexual orientation; and a study of the relationship between childhood gender roles or behaviors and eventual sexual orientation (Bailey & Zucker, 1995; Rieger, Linsenmeier, Gygax, & Bailey, 2008). This is a topic we will return to in later chapters, but for now it seems sufficient to say that the developmental factors that influence male and female sexual orientation may be different (Baumeister, 2000; Diamond, 1998; Veniegas & Conley, 2000).

Sex or Gender Differences

Here we ask to what extent do boys and girls (or men and women) differ in some aspect of physical development or behavior. For example, are boys stronger or taller than girls, and if so, at what ages? Do girls have better fine motor skills than boys, or are they better behaved or more polite? Are boys messier and girls kinder or gentler? If so, to what extent do these differences exist, and is there overlap between the genders. Are some girls messy and some boys gentle? Does the circumstance, situation, or culture matter?

Much of the early research conducted by developmental psychologists on gender development in children was focused on the question of sex differences in behavior (Terman, Johnson, Kuznets, & McNemar, 1946; Terman & Tyler, 1954; Wellman, 1933). There were many thousands of studies on behavioral differences between boys and girls during the 1900s, but until around 1960 much of that research did not have a strong theoretical focus. That is, researchers examined differences between boys and girls but did not systematically address the reasons for these differences. Even if a difference is found consistently, information about its causes must be studied separately. Such causes may include biological factors, childhood experiences and socialization, social roles, status and power, and the expectations of others in social interaction. Just because you may know that boys are consistently more physically aggressive than girls doesn't mean you know why they are.

In the second half of the 20th century, the research on sex differences improved in at least three ways: the methodology was better, the theoretical underpinnings of the research were stronger, and the tools available to analyze findings were better. In particular, research on gender was helped enormously by a statistical procedure called **meta-analysis** (Johnson & Eagly, 2000). Meta-analysis involves quantitatively pooling the results of many studies. For example, studies on sex or gender differences in a particular behavior (e.g., aggression or self-esteem) may be combined to reach a conclusion about whether there is a consistent difference between males and females in that behavior and how large the difference is.

There is now an extensive research literature on sex and gender differences in many characteristics and behaviors, including physical (e.g., height, perceptual speed), cognitive (e.g., math, spatial skills), and social (e.g., aggression, empathy). This research clearly demonstrates that there are some consistent average differences between the sexes in several behaviors, but it also shows that there is a great deal of overlap in the distributions of characteristics, skills, and abilities in boys and girls. There really is not a case of a sex difference in which all girls are better than all boys (or vice versa) in some domain.

There is also an increasing focus on the reasons for as well as the implications of such differences. For example, if on average, girls have better verbal skills than boys, does that mean all of the best poets are women? Or if, on average, boys have better spatial skills than girls do, does that mean more girls get lost finding their way around? Questions of causality and implications are clearly much more important than simply cataloguing such differences. We will return to the study of sex and gender differences in behavior in detail in chapters 4 and 5, and questions about the causes and importance of such differences will be discussed throughout the book.

Gender Stereotypes

The term **stereotype** was originally used by a journalist to refer to learned belief systems that are shared by members of a culture (Lippman, 1922). The term is now widely used in the social sciences to refer to beliefs about members of a particular group simply because they are members of that group (Biernat & Kobrynowicz, 1999). Social psychologists have devoted much effort to the study of stereotyping, finding that it is very common, automatic, and has many potential influences on social interaction (Fiske, 1998). It is also the case that children typically learn **gender stereotypes** before they learn stereotypes about other groups (Fiske, 1998; Zemore, Fiske, & Kim, 2000). Some of the mechanisms for the development of these stereotypes and reasons that gender might be particularly salient are suggested by the developmental intergroup theory (Bigler & Liben, 2006, 2007) discussed in Chapter 8.

Gender stereotypes are beliefs about the characteristics of males and females. There are many components to gender stereotypes, including personality characteristics, physical attributes, roles, occupations, and possibly assumptions about sexual orientation (Biernat & Kobrynowicz, 1999; Deaux & Kite, 1993; Zemore et al., 2000). For example, men are more likely to be seen as strong, rugged, and broad shouldered, whereas women are more likely to be seen as dainty and graceful (Deaux & Kite, 1993). With respect to personality characteristics, men are more likely to be seen as competent, confident, and independent, and women are more likely to be seen as warm, kind, and concerned about others' feelings (Deaux & Kite, 1993; Zemore et al., 2000). The traits associated with male competence have often been called **agentic** or **instrumental** characteristics, and the traits associated with females' concern for others have been called **communal** or **expressive**. Agentic and communal characteristics are generally positive, but there are also negative attitudes about men and women. On the minus side, men may be seen as aggressive, arrogant, or selfish, and women as overly emotional (Zemore et al., 2000). Nonetheless, some recent research has found that stereotypes about women are generally viewed more positively than those about men (Kite, 2001), at least in terms of being warm, kind, or nice. Men, on the other hand, may not be seen as being as nice as women, but they are seen as being more competent, powerful, and having higher status.

Some recent research (Prentice & Carranza, 2002) has also examined the extent to which these stereotypes are seen as prescriptive or obligatory. That is, should men and women each have certain characteristics, and at the same time, not have others? These researchers reported that college students believed that women ought to have characteristics such as being friendly, cheerful, compassionate, patient, and emotionally expressive, while not being intimidating, arrogant, self-righteous, stubborn, or domineering. According to these same students, men ought to be ambitious, assertive, aggressive, rational, athletic, and leaders with strong personalities, while they ought not to be emotional, naive, gullible, approval seeking, or weak.

In terms of children's knowledge and attitudes about these stereotypes, there is a large amount of research on this topic that we will explore in chapter 9. It is clear that children begin to learn this knowledge at an early age, and that even fairly young children see girls and women as nicer, and boys and men as more competent (Liben & Bigler, 2002; Ruble, Martin, & Berenbaum, 2006).

Gender Roles

Some years ago one of us asked a 3-year-old family friend what she wanted to be when she grew up. She answered that she wanted to grow up to be a princess or a Barbie. Clearly, she had learned something about gender roles. Social psychologist Alice Eagly and her colleagues define gender roles as "shared expectations that apply to individuals on the basis of their socially identified sex" (Eagly, Wood, & Diekman, 2000, p. 127). Gender roles certainly overlap with gender stereotypes, but stereotypes are attitudes about members of a group, and roles are behaviors that people engage in, characteristics or attributes that they possess, or positions they hold in a society.

Among the most basic of gender roles are the roles of homemaker and economic provider. Related to these roles are the communal and agentic personality characteristics discussed above under the topic of stereotypes. Eagly and others have pointed out that communal personality characteristics (e.g., care and concern for others) serve one well in the role of caretaker for children and other family members; whereas agentic personality characteristics, such as independence and competence, are well adapted to the world of work (Eagly, Wood, & Diekman, 2000). Eagly and her colleagues also argue that if women are predominantly occupying the homemaker role, then it would be reasonable that during childhood the experiences and education of girls would prepare them for this role, and if men are the primary economic providers, boys might be expected to learn skills to prepare them for this adult role. It probably does not surprise you to learn that researchers have found that household tasks such as cooking, cleaning, and child-care are more frequently allotted to girls, whereas tasks such as mowing the lawn are more often assigned to boys (Coltrane & Adams, 1997). Cross-cultural research has found that girls are often more likely to be socialized to be nurturant, obedient, and responsible, whereas boys are more likely to be socialized to be self-reliant and achieving (Best & Williams, 1997).

Although homemaker and economic provider are among the most basic of the gender roles, most adult women and many men in modern Western societies do both of these roles, at least to some degree (Barnett & Hyde, 2001; Coltrane, 2000). However, even though both men and women are in the world of paid employment, they nevertheless often work at different occupations or different job assignments (U.S. Department of Labor, 2006). Therefore, occupations can be considered in the category of gender roles as well. Female-dominated occupations have more extensive nurturing, homemaking, and care-taking components to them, whereas many male-dominated occupations are associated with physical strength, aggressiveness, and agentic personality characteristics (Eagly et al., 2000), although in actuality it is sometimes difficult to disentangle what characteristics are linked to the jobs themselves versus what characteristics are assumed to be linked to jobs as a function of their being held predominately by men versus women (Liben, Bigler, & Krogh, 2001).

Other than the homemaker and provider roles, certain occupations, and the personality characteristics and occupations that are related to those roles, other aspects of gender roles include physical appearance such as clothing, hairstyles, and other items related to dress such as items to place in or on the hair and jewelry. Gender roles also include leisure interests, codes of social etiquette and self-presentation, and rules for sexual behavior (Twenge, 1999). For children we can also include play with certain "gender-appropriate" toys (Liben & Bigler, 2002), as well as various activities, including sports, the arts, and academic domains such as mathematics or literature (Eccles, Freedman-Doan, Frome, Jacobs, & Yoon, 2000).

Social scientists including sociologists, anthropologists, and psychologists have also examined gender roles across cultures (Best, 2001; Best & Williams, 1997; Gibbons, 2000; Williams, Satterwhite, & Best, 1999). Although all cultures make distinctions between male and female roles, the particular content of what is assigned to men and women can vary from culture to culture (Wade & Tavris, 1999). For example, in some cultures women may do the marketing or weaving, whereas men do so in other cultures. Cultures vary in how much emotion men and women are expected to show, whether women in particular are expected to remain sexually chaste before marriage, and how much contact men and women can have on a daily basis. Cultures also vary in the extent to which the genders are expected to be different at all. Wade and Tavris (1999) give the example of Tahiti as one of the least gender-differentiated cultures; there are few differential expectations for the behaviors of men and women. Even their language lacks gender pronouns, and most names are used for either males or females.

Although certain aspects of gender roles vary greatly from culture to culture, other aspects are often similar. Williams and Best and their colleagues (Williams & Best, 1990; Williams et al., 1999) have studied university students' attitudes about gender-related personality traits in 25 countries from all over the world. They have found a remarkable degree of consistency in the traits assigned to males and females in these 25 countries, like the instrumental and expressive characteristics already discussed. For example, in these various countries, males were consistently seen as active, adventurous, aggressive, independent, strong, logical, and unemotional. Women, on the other hand, were consistently seen as affectionate, emotional, fearful, submissive, talkative, timid, weak, and whiny.

There is also cross-cultural similarity among the genders in aspects of production tasks. In many societies men are more likely to hunt large animals, do metalworking, and do lumbering, whereas women are more often found carrying water, cooking, laundering, and gathering vegetables (Eagly et al., 2000; Wood & Eagly, 2002). These differences seem to arise, in part, from women's reproductive roles and men's greater physical strength. Of course, one of the most consistent differences between males and females cross-culturally is that women participate in more childcare (Geary, 2000; Kenrick & Luce, 2000).

There are also cross-cultural similarities in gender roles related to dating and mating, with men choosing younger women, less powerful partners, and more partners than women (Buss, 2000; Kenrick & Luce, 2000); and in interpersonal violence in that men engage in more violence against other males than females do against other females, and partner violence is typically related to males' attempts to control their female partners (Smuts, 1995; Wilson & Daly, 1996).

In childhood, there is a great deal of cross-cultural consistency in rough and tumble play, with boys doing more, and in the phenomenon of gender segregation in which children play predominantly with children of their own sex (Best & Williams, 1997; Geary & Bjorklund, 2000). In these groups, boys are more concerned with dominance and social status, whereas girls are more intimate and communal. In addition, across many cultures, but not all, boys are also more aggressive than girls, and girls are more likely to care for younger children (Best, 2001; Edwards, 2000; Munroe, Hulefeld, Rodgers, Tomeo, & Yamazaki, 2000).

Gender and Status

No discussion of gender roles would be complete without a discussion of the differential power and status of males and females. As adults, men in general have more legal, economic, and political power and higher social status than women in general, although there are some obvious exceptions. The economic provider role has more power and status than the homemaker role, and female-dominated occupations are generally lower in status, power, and pay than male-dominated occupations (Eagly et al., 2000). Men control more economic resources worldwide, and are found in far more positions at the highest levels of authority in government, business, and the professions. Women, on the other hand are found more often among the poor in almost all countries across the world (Goodwin & Fiske, 2001). Children are aware of men's higher status around the age of 10, and probably before (Levy, Sadovsky, & Troseth, 2000; Liben et al., 2001).

An important question for us is whether this kind of power or status differential is relevant to children. Do boys have higher status than girls? In some cultures there are dramatic differences in status, as in the extreme example of the Taliban rule in Afghanistan, where girls were not permitted to go out in public, be educated, or even to learn to read (Schulz & Schulz, 1999). As one indicator of status, in many developing nations worldwide parents show a preference for having male children (Ataca & Sunar, 1999; Haughton & Haughton, 1996; Hortacsu, Bastug, & Muhammetberdiev, 2001; Khanna, 1997; Wen, 1993; Winkvist & Akhtar, 2000). In China and India in particular, parents are more likely to abort female fetuses and give up female babies for international adoptions in their quest to have sons (Bandyopadhyay, 2003; Evans, 2001; Van Balen, 2005). Ironically, these practices eventually lead to a shortage of women for their sons to marry.

What about in contemporary Western societies? If girls and boys were equal in status or value, there would be no reason for parents or potential parents to prefer to have a son or a daughter. Research through the 1970s (see Williamson, 1976) found that both men and women preferred boy children if they could have only one sex, or boys as firstborns, and that families would keep trying to have another child if they had not yet had a boy. This is clearly less the case today. Recent research with American, Canadian, and Australian parents suggest that a very common preference is to have one child of each sex or to have no preference one way or the other. There is still some tendency for people to prefer sons as firstborns, with a substantial number of men still preferring sons, but women are much less likely to express a preference for either, or to prefer daughters (Marleau & Saucier, 2002; McDougall, DeWit, & Ebanks, 1999; Pollard & Morgan, 2002; Swetkis, Gilroy, & Steinbacher, 2002). These findings suggest that in societies such as these, there is now much less of a tendency for parents to value male children over female children, although some preference remains, especially for men.

In terms of their interactions with each other, children also appear to act as though boys have higher status. Even as preschoolers, girls are less able to influence boys to respond to their requests than boys are to influence either boys or girls (Jacklin & Maccoby, 1978; Serbin, Sprafkin, Elman, & Doyle, 1984). In elementary school boys are much less willing to allow girls into their peer groups than girls are to allow boys into their peer groups (Maccoby, 1998), and boys are very avoidant of appearing feminine. It is not entirely clear why boys are less able to be influenced, are more exclusive, and are so unwilling to appear feminine, but all of these phenomena are consistent with boys having a higher status than girls, even as children. Campbell Leaper, a researcher who has studied boys' and girls' peer groups in childhood, has argued persuasively that boys' childhood peer groups show evidence of being higher status groups than girls' (Leaper, 2000 , 1994b) in that boys are more likely to maintain their groups' boundaries, and they are more likely to behave punitively towards other boys who initiate contact with girls or who behave in a feminine way. Girls, on the other hand, are more likely to cross gender barriers and to adopt masculine roles or behaviors, and are more willing to permit boys to play in their groups. Leaper argues that these patterns are consistent with the general finding that members of a lower status group are willing to adopt the characteristics of a higher status group, whereas the higher status group members are not willing to adopt those of the lower status group.

Changing Gender Roles

It is clear that adult gender roles have undergone great change in the last several decades, especially in the developed world (Barnett & Hyde, 2001; Cole, Zucker, & Duncan, 2001; Diekman & Eagly, 2000). One of the major sets of changes has to do with increasing education for women, and concomitant increases in the number of women in the paid labor force. For example, in the United States about 34% of women (compared with 86% of men) older than 16 were in the paid labor force in 1950, whereas in 1998 the comparable figures were 60% of women and 75% of men. Comparable changes have taken place in many other countries. The United Nations (2000) reports that women now constitute more than one third of the paid labor force in all areas of the world except in northern Africa and western Asia, and that many women in the world work while they have young children. However, although more women work, they make less money than men, and often work in occupations that are dominated by women (U.S. Department of Labor, 2006; United Nations, 2000). Nonetheless, an increase of women in the labor force is clearly a major change of the last half century.

Changes in work force roles also impact family roles, leading to a reduction in men's decision-making power in the family and an increase in their participation in childcare and other household tasks (Barnett & Hyde, 2001; Coltrane, 2000; Hoffman & Youngblade, 1999; Zuo & Tang, 2000). There are positive benefits of these changes, for both men and women, but especially for women (Barnett & Hyde, 2001; Coltrane, 2000; Gutierrez-Lobos, Woelfl, Scherer, Anderer, & Schmidl Mohl, 2000). Both men and women who have multiple roles (i.e., labor force participant, spouse, parent) have fewer mental and physical health problems and greater life satisfaction. Women in particular have fewer mental health problems when they are involved in the labor force and are more satisfied with their marriages when they and their husbands share more of the household tasks.

Women's employment is also linked to their attitudes about gender roles, with employed women, and typically their husbands and children as well, having more nontraditional attitudes about gender roles (Hoffman & Youngblade, 1999; Zuo & Tang, 2000). In general, more egalitarian attitudes about gender roles and norms is another consistent change in the second half of the 20th century (Eagly et al., 2000; Twenge, 1997a, 1997b), although egalitarian attitudes are stronger in women than in men. There is also research showing that women have become more likely to adopt male personality traits and to become more assertive as their status and roles have changed (Twenge, 1997b, 2001); however, men have not generally shown analogous changes.

There is very little research examining these kinds of historical changes in children's gender role behaviors or attitudes. In one study in Africa (Munroe & Munroe, 1997), the researchers observed that in the period between 1967 and 1978 there was a notable decrease in girls' responsibility for the care of younger children because they were more likely to be in school. Boys were also more likely to be in school, although the increase was not as great as for girls because more boys were in school in the 1967 observation. However, boys showed a small increase in responsibility for younger siblings during the same period. On the other hand, cross-cultural studies have reported that as societies have become more modernized, and role expectations have changed, there has been little change in children's learning of gender norms (Best & Williams, 1993). Interestingly, as is the case among adult women, in many contemporary cultures girls have more egalitarian attitudes about gender roles than boys do, even among preschoolers (Best & Williams, 1993; Signorella, Bigler, & Liben, 1993).

Are Gender Roles Desirable for Children?

One obvious change with respect to the study of children's gender roles is the position that developmental researchers have taken about their desirability. Science, especially when it takes human behavior as its focus of study, is rarely value-neutral. It is difficult, perhaps impossible, for scientists to remove themselves from the values that shape the culture in which they live and work, and issues of sex and gender are among the most contentious and value-laden of any topic we study. Attitudes about gender roles changed in Western cultures during the second half of the 20th century, and researchers' perspectives were affected by that change. Up until the 1970s the developmental psychologists who studied children's gender development usually expressed the idea that raising boys to be masculine and girls to be feminine was a desirable outcome that was necessary for normal development (e.g., Kagan, 1964). Now it is much more common, although certainly not universal, for researchers, teachers, and others to see gender roles as limiting and restricting, perhaps even harmful (Bailey, 1993; Bem, 1983; Bigler, 1999; Katz, 1996), and to advocate raising children to be less gender differentiated. When we discuss the influence of parents, teachers, and the media on children's gender development, we will return to a consideration of those factors that promote less stereotyping and greater gender flexibility in children's development, as well as some of the advantages of these kinds of experiences for children.

What changed this situation? Why did a substantial number of people change from seeing gender roles as normal and desirable to seeing them as limiting and restrictive? There are obviously many factors involved, but one of the major factors was the women's movement and the resulting influence of feminism in both society and academia.

FEMINISM AND FEMINIST CRITIQUES OF SCIENCE

Feminism is a word that carries much emotional meaning beyond the actual definition of the word itself, so much so that even people who hold generally feminist views are reluctant to call themselves feminists (Liss, O'Connor, Morosky, & Crawford, 2001; Twenge & Zucker, 1999). What is feminism? A feminist perspective has at its core two issues (Unger, 1998). First, feminists believe that males and females are and ought to be equally valuable. There is recognition that in many cultures in the world females and the feminine have been valued less than males and the masculine. Feminists take the position that the devaluation of girls and women is wrong and should be opposed. Part of this perspective is a commitment to equal opportunities for boys and girls, and hence the elimination of restrictions that gender roles and stereotypes pose for both, but especially for girls. The second key aspect of feminism is a commitment to social activism towards the goal of full equality of males and females.

However, there is a difference between feminism as a philosophy of life and feminism as a theoretical basis for scholarship. There are many psychologists who study issues of sex and gender who would call themselves feminists, but who are not feminist scholars (e.g., see Smuts, 1995). Although feminism influenced the shift in how gender roles are viewed, and that many people who do research on children's development would say they are feminists, explicitly feminist scholarship has not been very common in the study of children's gender development (Leaper, 2000).

There are many different forms of feminist scholarship (Rosser & Miller, 2000). In spite of the differences among them, one of the key influences of feminism has been to call into question that the scientific process is value-neutral. Feminist scholars have pointed out that values shape the research process at many levels, and that values have led to certain kinds of biases. For example, scientists' values have shaped the kinds of research questions that have been asked (e.g., asking how children have been harmed by their mothers' employment as opposed to how they have benefited from it or been harmed by their fathers' employment). Gender-based bias has existed in the design of the research when researchers did not think they needed to examine a group of males when studying the impact of hormonal cycles or fluctuations on behavior, or when only males were tested in a study, and yet the findings were generalized to both males and females. Values have also affected researchers' interpretations of research findings (Wilkinson, 2001). When we study the history of the research on children's gender development in the next chapter, the values that shaped this research will be very evident.

Feminist critiques of science in general, and of psychology in particular, have usually been of three different types (Riger, 1992; Wilkinson, 2001). The first type of feminist critique is often called **feminist**

empiricism (Riger, 1992; Wilkinson, 2001) or liberal feminism (Rosser & Miller, 2000). Proponents of this view argue for elimination of gender bias in the research process at all levels from the questions asked through the interpretations of the results. It is this kind of feminist scholarship that can be found most frequently in psychology in general, and in the study of children's gender development in particular. It is this kind of research that has shown that traditional gender roles are often harmful to adults' mental and physical health, life satisfaction, marital satisfaction, and economic well being, for either men or women or both (Barnett & Hyde, 2001). Researchers thought it was important that they ask these questions to find the answers.

The second feminist approach that can be found among psychologists, but is not as common as the first, is **feminist standpoint epistemology** (Riger, 1992; Wilkinson, 2001). In this view, knowledge, including scientific knowledge, is influenced by the perspective of the person producing the knowledge, particularly by their position in the social hierarchy. An example of this approach in psychology that is that of Carol Gilligan's study of moral development in girls and women (Gilligan, 1982; Gilligan, Lyons, & Hanmer, 1990). Gilligan reported that girls and women were more likely to emphasize caring about the impact on other people in their lives when faced with moral dilemmas, whereas boys and men were more likely to emphasize abstract principles of justice. Feminist standpoint critics would argue that these ways of viewing the world arise out of males' and females' status or position in the social world—their standpoints. They would also argue that science is not complete without knowledge generated from many standpoints.

The third type of feminist critique of scientific research in psychology, also less common than feminist empiricism, is **feminist postmodernism** (Riger, 1992; Rosser & Miller, 2000; Wilkinson, 2001). Riger (1992) points out that this approach is often very difficult for traditional psychologists to understand, because the perspective is so different from the typical scientific view. Psychologists, like other scientists, have traditionally accepted without question that there is a factual world to discover. Postmodern views, which are quite prevalent in the humanities and some of the other social sciences, argue that science does not really discover the world, but that it creates it, and there are multiple versions of reality. In psychology, postmodernist views are often called social constructionism (K. J. Gergen, 2001; M. Gergen, 2001), also having the perspective that knowledge is not discovered, but is socially constructed. We will discuss postmodernism and social constructionism further in chapter 7 when we address social and cultural theories of gender development.

Where do we—the three authors of this book—fit within the types of academic feminism? We do consider ourselves to be feminists, and we are committed to the ideal that boys and girls and men and women are of equal value. We recognize that scientists have not always been committed to that ideal. Nonetheless, we are equally committed to the ideals of science and to the belief that we must be willing to be open to letting the data be examined, regardless of what they show. We do not think that research findings should be judged by any political standards, but instead by the rigor of the data gathering, analysis, and interpretation. At the same time, we recognize that theoretical positions or world views (Overton, 2006; Pepper, 1942) affect the ways that questions are asked, the kinds of data that are judged to be relevant, and the ways that data are interpreted. We find it difficult to state a label that neatly applies to us, but if any one of the labels described above would fit us, it would be that of feminist empiricists.

CHILDREN'S GENDER DEVELOPMENT

In this book we will consider gender from a developmental perspective. Two-year-olds do not have the same gender knowledge, roles, or behaviors that 15-year-olds do. Most of the issues introduced earlier in the chapter undergo developmental change, often under different conditions and with different timetables. It is also the case that gender development is complex—it has many different components, and there is often a lack of simple relationships among these various components (Antill, Cotton, Russell, & Goodnow, 1996; Ruble et al., 2006; Serbin, Powlishta, & Gulko, 1993; Spence & Hall, 1996). What follows is a brief set of highlights of some of the things we can consider about children's gender development.

Certainly one of the central questions of research on sex and gender is that of sex or gender differences. How are boys and men different from girls and women? What are the differences, when do we see them, and what influences them? We will certainly devote considerable attention to sex differences in chapters 4 and 5 of this book, and to the questions of cause and influence throughout the book. But these are not the only questions of gender development.

One way that gender development has been conceptualized is through the process of **sex typing**. Sex typing (sometimes also called **gender typing**) has been defined as "the mapping of objects, activities, roles, and traits onto biological sex such that they follow prescriptive cultural stereotypes of gender" (Liben & Bigler, 2002, p. 5). These terms (sex typing or gender typing) have been used in two broad ways. First, they have been used to refer to the process by which this mapping occurs, and second, to the extent that children show the results of this mapping (e.g., Maccoby, 1988). Thus, one might say that various processes occur to sex or gender type children, who then may be described as sex (or gender) typed, and that much of gender development can be seen in these terms.

In terms of their own understanding of gender, children begin the process of gender development with the ability to identify males and females, including eventually, themselves. Somewhere in the first year of life children are able to respond differently to pictures of males and females, and to male and female voices (Leinbach & Fagot, 1993; Miller, 1983). This is the very beginning of children's understanding of gender. However, they do not usually identify boys and girls using gender labels until a little after age 2 (Etaugh et al., 1989).

By the middle of the preschool years, children acquire knowledge of some basic gender stereotypes, especially for familiar objects like toys (Blakemore, LaRue, & Olejnik, 1979; Martin, Wood, & Little, 1990; Perry, White, & Perry, 1984; Weinraub et al., 1984). In time they also come to identify the gender-related aspects of certain activities (e.g., sports, household tasks) as well as adult occupations and the gender-related aspects of personality characteristics. Such knowledge increases during the preschool and elementary years (Carter & Patterson, 1982; Etaugh & Liss, 1992; Levy et al., 2000). In chapter 9, we will look at the research on children's cognitions about gender in much more detail.

Children also come to prefer the toys, activities, and objects associated with their gender (Lobel & Menashri, 1993; Moller & Serbin, 1996), sometimes even before they know that the toys are gender stereotyped (Aubry, Ruble, & Silverman, 1999; Blakemore et al., 1979; Perry et al., 1984). Indeed, this is one of the most reliable aspects of gender development from early childhood through adulthood—males and females often have quite different interests, and those interests are often linked to gender roles.

Boys' and girls' social relationships also differ. There is a notable tendency for boys and girls to play in same gender groups in childhood (Leaper, 1994b). Indeed, by school age children are spending about 60–70% of their free time with playmates of the same sex, and most of the rest of the time in mixed sex groups (Maccoby, 1998), spending very little time in the exclusive company of the other sex.

Boys and girls play quite differently in their same-sex peer groups, so much so that some have said that they grow up in different peer cultures (Leaper, 1994a; Thorne & Luria, 1986). For example, in their peer groups, girls' communication styles are more collaborative, cooperative, and reciprocal, whereas boys' are more individualistic and focus on dominance. These differences are believed to foster interpersonal closeness and social sensitivity in girls, and independence, shared action, and dominance in boys (Kyratzis, 2001; Leaper, 1994a; Maccoby, 1998).

These styles also change developmentally. Although 3-year-old girls may be more reciprocal than 3-year-old boys in their social interactions, it is probably obvious that 15-year-olds of both sexes can have much more sophisticated social interactions than 3-year-olds. Another important developmental change in social interactions and relationships comes when, in adolescence, young people begin to spend much more time with friends of the other sex, eventually moving into heterosexual dating. We will cover more about peer relationships in chapter 11.

This very brief overview of some of the features of gender development is, of course, incomplete. We will be examining all of these issues in much more detail as we progress through the book. We will also examine biological, cultural, social, and cognitive influences on the gender developmental process.

Influences on Gender Development: Theoretical Perspectives

There are several major theories that organize the study of gender development, and to those theories we now turn. To begin, it is valuable to understand what a scientific **theory** is, as well as its purpose. Sometimes people think that a theory is the opposite of fact. The implication is that theory is simply conjecture, or a hypothesis that hasn't been confirmed. Such a view is incorrect. Scientific theories incorporate factual information as well as an interpretation of those facts. A scientist is not content to simply collect more and more data; scientists want to decide in some structured way what kinds of data they collect as well as how to interpret those data once they are collected (Anastasi, 1992).

In a description of the nature of the process of building knowledge about human development, Willis Overton (1998) uses an analogy of building a house: the house is like the knowledge we gain about human development. In Overton's analogy the empirical investigators—the researchers who collect and analyze data, and who publish their research—are like the building contractors. Their skills are necessary to build the house, but they wouldn't think of building it without a plan. The theorists, on the other hand, are like the architects who design the plans that direct the building process. Having a theory gives organization and meaning to the knowledge construction process.

Thus, the purpose of theories is twofold: to organize knowledge that already exists, and to direct researchers as they seek additional knowledge (Leahey, 1994). The first purpose of scientific theories is to organize the data collected by researchers using some general principles, and the simpler and more straightforward the principles are, the better. The second purpose of scientific theories is to generate further research about a topic. Having a theoretical model to generate research produces a more organized scientific process. As the theory guides the new research, one critical feature is that it be falsifiable—that the new research has the potential to demonstrate if the theory is in error. If that happens, the theory needs to be modified, or perhaps eventually abandoned. But even if it is abandoned, it served its functions. It organized the information that was known at the time, and it generated further research. A particular theory may be an excellent way to organize the information at a particular point in history, but eventually it may outlive its usefulness.

Using Overton's analogy should also help clarify that one theory is not necessarily the only way to organize knowledge, nor is one always better than another. There are many viable theories that guide the research on children's gender development. Some theories organize certain areas of research better than others, and some have more to say about certain aspects of the process, but it is not necessary to reject one to accept that another has value. Like the plans of various architects, theories have strengths and weaknesses, but each may have something important to say about the process, and knowing about several theoretical views is enormously helpful in coming to understand all of the factors that impinge on children's gender development.

Theories of Gender Development

One of the key questions for developmental psychology in general is the "nature-nurture" question. That is, to what extent is behavioral development influenced or controlled by biological factors such as genes or hormones; to what extent is it influenced or controlled by experiential factors, such as the way parents may praise some behaviors and criticize others; and how do these factors interact with each other? In the area of children's gender development the nature-nurture question has been very evident, although there is also a third general view. The approaches to gender development can be summarized as the biological (nature), socialization (nurture), and cognitive views (Ruble et al., 2006).

The **biological view of gender development**, which we will discuss in detail in chapter 6, examines the influence of genes and chromosomes, sex hormones, and brain organization on sex differences in physical functioning and behavior (Hoyenga & Hoyenga, 1993). For example, during prenatal development male and female children are exposed to a different hormonal environment over several months of their development. Researchers ask how these hormones impact physical development, both of the genitals and in the brain, and how the resulting differences in the brain affect later behavior (Collaer & Hines, 1995). Of particular interest are children who have been exposed to atypical levels of prenatal hormones for their sex, such as girls with **congenital adrenal hyperplasia** (CAH). In this rare genetic condition, girls with CAH are exposed to high levels of masculinizing hormones (androgens) produced by their own adrenal glands during prenatal development. As children, they have been found to show some behaviors that are more typical of boys, such as greater interest in boys' toys, higher activity levels, greater aggression, and less interest in interacting with infants (Berenbaum, 1999; Berenbaum & Hines, 1992; Berenbaum & Resnick, 1997; Berenbaum & Snyder, 1995; Leveroni & Berenbaum, 1998).

Also included in the biological view is **evolutionary theory**, which examines the influence of human beings' evolutionary history on sex differences in behavior (Buss & Kenrick, 1998; Kenrick & Luce, 2000). The evolutionary view is especially interested in sex differences that are very consistent across cultures such as behaviors involved in childcare and mating, and less interested in differences that are limited to particular cultures or historical periods.

The **socialization approach** emphasizes the differential treatment of children by parents, other family members such as grandparents or siblings, peers, as well as treatment by teachers in school and by other adults outside of the family (Fagot, Rodgers, & Leinbach, 2000; Ruble et al., 2006). The socialization approach is rooted in the tradition of **learning theory**, which examines the influence of reinforcements, punishments, and observational learning on behavior (Bandura, 1977). An example of how learning mechanisms might be powerful comes from a recent study (Mondschein, Adolph, & Tamis-LeMonda, 2000) in which mothers of 11-month-old infants estimated their babies' abilities to crawl down an inclined ramp. The crawling abilities of the boy and girl babies were measured, and, on average, were no different; boys and girls were equally good crawlers and attempted to crawl down ramps of equivalent slope. However, mothers of sons estimated that their babies could crawl steeper slopes, and would be more willing to attempt to crawl down more difficult slopes than did mothers of daughters. This is likely to have significant consequences if parents are substantially more likely to underestimate the capabilities of girls and to overestimate the capabilities of boys.

The socialization perspective also includes the investigation of gender-related influences of the media, including books, television, movies, and now video games (Huston & Wright, 1996; Kinder, 1999). There are two general issues with respect to the media and gender role socialization (Ruble et al., 2006). The first is that males are portrayed in the media much more frequently than females, and the second is that the roles and behaviors that are displayed in television, movies, and books are often gender stereotyped.

A new theoretical approach in the environmental tradition, but more common in sociology and the humanities than in developmental psychology, focuses on the social construction of gender (Leaper, 2000; Messner, 2000). **Social construction theory** is a postmodern theory of gender that proposes that knowledge can never be removed from social time and place; that gender norms, roles, and behaviors are constructed; and that these constructions affect behavior, cognitions, and social interactions. There are now some developmental psychologists who are beginning to study how children, their parents, and others construct gender, and we will cover more about this approach in chapter 7.

The third theoretical perspective that guides the research on the origins of gender development is the cognitive approach. **Cognitive theories** focus on children's knowledge about gender, gender stereotypes, and norms and how this kind of knowledge influences children's thinking about gender as well as their gender-related behavior.

There are two general types of cognitive theories of gender development. The first, **social cognitive theory** (Bussey & Bandura, 1999), can be seen as a transition between the environmental and cognitive approaches. It comes from the tradition of social learning theory but has shifted away from traditional learning theory's sole emphasis on the environment to an equivalent focus on how children's knowledge and thinking influences their behavior.

The other cognitive theories can be grouped under the term **developmental constructivist theories**. The most important constructivist theory in developmental psychology's history is Piaget's (Piaget, 1970). Piaget believed that children create or construct their own knowledge through their interactions with the physical and social world, and that these constructions serve as the foundation for developmental change.

The first constructivist approach to gender development was Kohlberg's **cognitive developmental theory** (Kohlberg, 1966). Kohlberg emphasized that children's knowledge about gender progresses through three stages, and that children come to guide their own gender development because of valuing things in the environment that they perceive to be for them (e.g., a boy comes to like playing with trucks because he comes to think that trucks are for someone like him—a boy).

Today, **gender constructivism** theorists in developmental psychology are concerned with the way in which children's cognitions about gender change as they develop (Liben & Bigler, 2002). One constructivist theory is developmental **gender schema theory** (Martin, 2000; Martin & Halverson, 1981; Martin, Ruble, & Szkrybalo, 2002). This theory emphasizes children's increasing knowledge of gender stereotypes and values, known as **gender schemas**. Gender schema theorists ask how and when children learn gender schemas, what kind of information they learn, and how their knowledge influences their behavior. A later variant of gender schema theory, the dual-pathway gender schema theory (Liben & Bigler, 2002), also addresses the way that children's idiosyncratic interests and experiences may in turn influence children's more general gender schemas.

The last group of constructivist approaches we cover stems from intergroup theories that originated in social psychology (Tajfel & Turner, 1986). At the core of intergroup theory is the belief that people's need for positive self-regard leads them to feel that the groups to which they belong (in-groups) are superior to other groups (out-groups). Developmental psychologists have addressed how intergroup processes might lead children to develop and maintain group stereotypes and prejudices (Levy & Killen, 2008; Rutland, Cameron, Milne, & McGeorge, 2005). Later in the book we describe in detail the way that **developmental intergroup theory** has been applied to gender in particular (Bigler & Liben, 2006, 2007).

As we will see, all of these theoretical approaches have an important role to play in understanding the roots of children's gender development. We should not regard one as right, or better than the others, nor should they be seen as necessarily in conflict with one another (Maccoby, 2000). It may be the case that some aspects of gender development have their roots in evolutionary processes, some in the effect of hormones on the developing brain, some in the reinforcement provided by parents and others, some in the interaction of children's peer groups, some in the observation and imitation of gendered behavior and roles in the child's experience and the media, some in cognitive constructions, and some because of social interaction with others. There is no reason to think that biological, social, and cognitive factors are not all involved in the process of children's gender development.

CHAPTER SUMMARY

In this chapter, we introduced the study of children's gender development. Several terms were defined, including the very basic terms "sex" and "gender." "Sex" often is used to refer to the biological aspects of being male or female, whereas "gender" is used to refer to the social and cultural aspects of being male or female. We also discussed gender identity, sexual orientation, sexual identity, gender stereotypes, gender roles, and feminism, as well as several other terms. We emphasized that gender development is very complex, and there are often no simple relationships among its various components. Finally, we highlighted several theoretical perspectives that emphasize different parts of the process of gender development and that we will discuss later in the book.

History of the Study of Gender Development

2

It is utterly impossible without injury to hold girls to the same standards of conduct, regularity, severe moral accountability, and strenuous mental work that boys need. (Hall, 1906, p. 291)

There is perhaps no field aspiring to be scientific where flagrant personal bias, logic in the cause of supporting a prejudice, unfounded assertions, and even sentimental rot and drivel, have run riot to such an extent as here. (Woolley, 1910, p. 340)

In this chapter we will examine the scientific study of children's gender development from the late 1800s through the mid 1970s. There are three reasons why we have included this chapter in the book. First, it is sometimes difficult to realize that the science of psychology is more than a century old, and that many questions that people are still researching today have a long history. The writings of philosophers served as the foundation for the science of psychology, and philosophers concerned themselves with the issues of sex and gender since the time of Plato and Aristotle (Salkever, 1990; Saunders, 1995). Sex differences have been studied scientifically since the 1600s (Graunt, 1662), and were examined by several scientists during the 1800s (Galton, 1883, 1894; Geddes & Thomson, 1897; Quetelet, 1830/1969). Many of these early philosophers and scientists saw males and females as opposites, and often found girls and women to be inferior to boys and men.

The second reason that we would like to include a brief coverage of the history of the field is to demonstrate that issues and problems may be studied for a period, then abandoned, and then later returned to but studied in a new way. Crutchfield and Krech (1962) refer to this as the "spiral of history." It is not necessarily the case that scientific study in some domain is steady and progressive, always building on old knowledge and becoming closer to the "truth." Rather, people may return to study problems that were examined and abandoned decades earlier, and may not even be aware that the older research exists. Scientific study is affected by many factors, including the ideological climate at any given time, the social needs of the culture that a scientist is in, new technological advances that permit the advanced study of an issue, as well as by coincidence and accident (Crutchfield & Krech, 1962). For example, as we have already pointed out, the study of issues related to sex and gender increased enormously once the feminist movement arose in the 1970s. What may not be nearly as obvious now is that feminist scientists were studying sex and gender as early as 1900.

The third reason that we want to include a history of the field is to explore the role that theory plays in guiding research. Much of the early scientific study of sex and gender was atheoretical—it lacked the guidance of well-constructed theories. That leads to a situation in which researchers simply collect more and more data, but are not able to organize and understand the findings very efficiently. They also duplicate efforts—people may collect the same data as others have previously, but the field advances little. An examination of the early history of the field can show us how the field changed when it began to be organized by theory.

THE EARLY STUDY OF SEX DIFFERENCES

Wilhelm Wundt in Germany and William James in the United States are generally credited with being the fathers or founders of modern psychology (Hothersall, 1995). Both of them established their laboratories in 1875 and did most of their work between that time and the early part of the 20th century. The work of these early psychologists was generally focused on the behavior of adults or animals and was not usually concerned with either child development or issues of sex or gender. However, in the early part of the 20th century several psychologists in both Germany and the United States did devote study to differences between the sexes, although little of this work focused on child development. Among the topics that these psychologists discussed were differences in male and female brains, the "maternal instinct" and the concept of **variability**. For a fascinating discussion of the way that values permeated this work, see Shields (1975). Probably not surprisingly, much of it concluded that females were deficient in both intellectual and moral capabilities.

G. Stanley Hall: The Founder of Developmental Psychology

The founder of the scientific study of children's development is usually said to be G. Stanley Hall (Strickland & Burgess, 1965), who began his work on child development with the publication of a report about children's knowledge before they entered school (Hall, 1883). Hall made many contributions to developmental psychology as well as to education. In 1887 he founded the *American Journal of Psychology*, the first psychology journal published in the United States, and was instrumental in founding the American Psychological Association (Hothersall, 1995; Ross, 1972), becoming its first president in 1892. In 1891 he founded *The Pedagogical Seminary*, a journal devoted to child study, which later became the *Journal of Genetic Psychology* (Strickland & Burgess, 1965; White, 1992), which is still published today.

Hall developed the use of questionnaires so that others, primarily teachers and mothers, could collect data from the children, and completed several studies of children during the 1880s and 1890s (Strickland & Burgess, 1965; White, 1992). He also supervised the majority of the doctoral degrees granted to American psychologists prior to 1900 (Hothersall, 1995). After 1890 he and his students (Hall's students included John Dewey, Joseph Jastrow, James McKeen Cattell, Lewis Terman, and Arnold Gesell, among many others) produced a huge amount of scholarship on the emotional, physical, and intellectual development of children (White, 1992). Hall also first used the term "adolescence" (Leahey, 1994), and developed the concept of adolescence as a developmental period (Hothersall, 1995; Ross, 1972).

In some of his writings and work, Hall dealt with differences in the behavior and development of boys and girls (Diehl, 1986; Minton, 2000). One of Hall's most influential books is his two-volume work *Adolescence* (Hall, 1905), which was followed by a shorter book titled *Youth* (Hall, 1906) that covered the same material for a lay audience. Both books contain a chapter on the education of adolescent girls, and the more scholarly *Adolescence* also contains chapters on sexual development (especially in boys) and adolescent love. By today's standards, many of the views that Hall expressed on these topics would be considered at least mildly humorous, if not downright ludicrous. For example, he considered masturbation to be a dangerous practice, the effects of which could include exhaustion, epilepsy, heart murmurs, and lying.

Hall's chapter on the education of adolescent girls is one of the first writings in developmental psychology about the nature of sex differences. Hall claimed girls were more suited to having children than to being educated, therefore their education should prepare them for motherhood. Boys' education and experiences, on the other hand, should allow them the opportunity to express aggression and savage impulses so they could develop masculine strength (Minton, 2000). Girls were more feeling than thinking, more concrete, had slower logical thought, had less patience for science or invention, were more conservative, had a more excitable vasomotor system, were more emotional, more fearful, suggestible, faithful, dependent, reverent, and devoted. Hall said women dress more for adornment than for protection or practical uses; they have long hair, they wear ornaments, they like feathers and flowing garments, as well as pins, powders, and perfumes. He said women go in flocks and are less likely to stand out as individuals. They are best suited for ordinary matters whereas men are best suited for the extraordinary.

Hall took the position, accepted by other influential scholars of the time such as sociologist Herbert Spencer and Harvard Medical School professor Edward Clarke (Rosenberg, 1982), that the more civilized or highly evolved the "races" were, the more the men and women of that race were divergent (Hall, 1905).

He argued that it would be contrary to evolution for women of the most "civilized races" to adopt the characteristics and educational attainments of the men of those races because evolution acted to make men and women more different.

Hall was a vehement opponent of coeducation during high school and college, believing that boys and girls should be educated separately during adolescence for three reasons: so that girls' reproductive organs could develop in adolescence free from the exhaustion of demanding schooling, so that boys could be free to express their more savage adolescent impulses without the presence of girls, and because of his concern that if young men and women interacted with each other in school they would later not be attracted to each other enough to marry (Diehl, 1986). He also had the opinion that higher education could potentially harm women's health (Diehl, 1986; Hall, 1965), a view also common among other scholars of the time (Rosenberg, 1982). Several sections of his chapter on the education of adolescent girls (Hall, 1905) discuss the harm of a college education to the menstrual cycles, reproductive organs, and general health of young women, as well as the greatly reduced potential of college-educated women to marry and have children. Ironically, while Hall was the president of Clark University between 1892 and 1920, about 150 women pursued graduate degrees in several fields there, including several who were his own students (Diehl, 1986). Hall also encouraged African Americans and Asians to pursue doctoral study in psychology at Clark University although he viewed other races as inferior to Whites. The first African American to receive a Ph.D. in psychology, Francis Sumner, was Hall's student (Schultz & Schultz, 1992).

Although Hall played a critical role in the foundation of developmental psychology, he was not known as a careful or meticulous researcher. In fact, the limitations of his positions on sex differences in behavior and coeducation were even recognized by some of his contemporaries. For example, Hall's biographer Dorothy Ross noted in reference to *Adolescence* that "large parts of it were filled with unctuous comments about sexuality" (Ross, 1972, p. 326), a characterization she attributed to the influential psychologist Edward Thorndike, who reviewed it at the time.

The First Scientific Research on Sex Differences

Helen Thompson Woolley and Leta Stetter Hollingworth

As we said earlier in the chapter, scientific study is affected by events in the culture. Between 1880 and 1910 many new opportunities opened up for women in the sciences (Rossiter, 1982), and these women were highly motivated to show that prevalent ideas about the limitations of women were in error. During this period, Helen Thompson (later Helen Woolley) was pursuing her graduate work at the University of Chicago, in a psychology department that was exceptionally supportive of its women graduate students, and one of the few places where one could objectively study the nature of sex differences (Rosenberg, 1982). Although her dissertation (Thompson, 1903) did not involve the study of children, it is often credited as one of the first well-controlled scientific studies of behavioral differences between men and women (Rosenberg, 1982). She studied sensory, motor, and intellectual behaviors, and made every attempt to control variables and match her male and female participants. She devised many of the tests she used herself and was committed to careful and rigorous study of the issue. Today, we would consider such controls to be an essential part of the research process, but they were much less common in the early 1900s. Unlike previous researchers who had simply provided average differences between the sexes, Thompson showed the distributions of males and females and the overlap between them. On some tasks (e.g., mechanical puzzles) she found men did better, whereas on others (e.g., memory) women did better, but the average differences were generally very small. Although there were large differences between individual men and women, on average the men and women she studied were very similar.

After a year of postdoctoral study in Europe, Thompson began her academic career on the faculty of Mount Holyoke College in 1901 (Rosenberg, 1982; Rossiter, 1982). She resigned in 1905 to marry Paul Woolley (a physician who later became a medical school professor), with whom she had two daughters. At that time it was generally impossible for a married woman, especially one with children, to have an academic career; universities would not hire them. The Woolleys lived in Cincinnati for several years where she was active as a child development specialist, suffrage leader, and community activist. During her early years in Cincinnati, Woolley conducted and published research on child development, including some on the topic of sex differences in children and adolescents (Woolley, 1915; Woolley & Fisher, 1914).

Woolley also published two review articles summarizing research on the topic of sex differences (Woolley, 1910, 1914), noting that this field increased dramatically between the two reviews. These reviews considered research on sensory, motor, intellectual, and social behaviors, as well as the topic of variability. In both reviews she despaired over researchers' tendencies to be led by their prejudices rather than by good science. The widely cited quotation at the beginning of this chapter is from the 1910 article. When summarizing the research in 1914, in an attempt to deal with all of the contradictory findings and conclusions, Woolley stated "The general discussions of the psychology of sex ... show such a wide diversity of points of view that one feels that the truest thing to be said at present is that scientific evidence plays very little part in producing convictions" (Woolley, 1914, p. 372). Woolley concluded that most differences between males and females were more than likely of social rather than biological origin.

Later Woolley worked at the Merrill Palmer School in Detroit (later to become the Merrill Palmer Institute, home of the *Merrill Palmer Quarterly*), establishing one of the first experimental nursery schools in the United States to study child development and early childhood education. She left the Merrill Palmer School to take a position at Columbia University Teacher's College in New York, where she also established two experimental nursery schools. Unfortunately, around this time her husband divorced her and she faced both medical and psychological problems. Eventually, Columbia dismissed her, and she was never able to find professional work again. Woolley's granddaughter recently published a poignant biography of the difficulties Woolley faced (Morse, 2002).

Another psychologist who examined issues of sex and gender in the early part of the 20th century was Leta Stetter Hollingworth (Benjamin, 1975; Hollingworth, 1943; Rosenberg, 1982). Hollingworth began her graduate work at Columbia University after her husband, Harry Hollingworth, completed his doctoral degree there and was able to finance her study because scholarships to finance graduate education were not typically given to women. When assisting her husband in a study of the effect of caffeine on behavior, she noted that there was no effect of the women's menstrual cycle on their performance. This finding intrigued her because at this time it was commonly held that women suffered incapacity at certain points in their cycle. She went on to study the impact of the menstrual cycle on behavior for her doctoral dissertation (Hollingworth, 1914a). She did not inform her 23 female and 2 male participants about the purpose of her study, but had the women report information about their cycles, and had both sexes report unusual events and physical symptoms on a daily basis. Most of the participants were given several mental and motor tests every third day for 1 month, whereas eight of them were given the tests every day for 3 months. Two of her participants who experienced pain at the beginning of menstruation performed somewhat less well on one test (the naming of opposites) during those days, but there was no other evidence of the impact of the menstrual cycle on the behaviors she measured.

While a graduate student at Columbia, Hollingworth obtained a position as a mental tester for the city of New York testing children's intelligence primarily for the courts, charitable agencies, and the schools (Hollingworth, 1943). The major purpose of this testing was to diagnose mental retardation. One of the important scientific hypotheses of the time was the variability hypothesis (Benjamin, 1975; Shields, 1975). Essentially the argument was that women and girls were more concentrated around average, and that men and boys were more likely to be found at the extremes on any characteristic. For example, although many men and women would be found with average intelligence, more men than women were believed to be at the extremes of intelligence, both geniuses and mentally retarded. As Hollingworth herself most aptly pointed out, the most important implication of this hypothesis is that females are not likely to be ever found among the gifted (Hollingworth, 1914b). It was also believed that this reflected greater evolutionary progress made by males, as we saw earlier in Hall's position, a view that can be traced back to Darwin (Shields, 1975).

To further examine the variability hypothesis, Hollingworth and Helen Montague (1914) examined 1,000 infants of each sex at birth on ten measures (weight, length, shoulder circumference, and seven cranial measurements), using several different statistical measures of variability and found that the males were slightly larger, but that there were no consistent differences in variability on any of the ten measures. From the vantage point of the 21st century, one is absolutely struck by the thorough and careful research methods used by these psychologists almost a century ago. Hollingworth also published a review of published research on the question of variability (Hollingworth, 1914b) and came to a very strongly worded set of conclusions about the relationship between variability and women not achieving at high levels:

> Surely we should consider *first* the established, obvious, inescapable, physical fact that women bear and rear the children, and that this has always meant and still means that *nearly 100 percent of their energy is expended in the performance and supervision of domestic and allied tasks, a field where eminence is impossible.* Only when we had exhausted this fact as an explanation should we pass on to the question of comparative variability, or of differences in intellect or instinct. Men of science who discuss at all the matter of woman's failure should seek the cause of failure in the most obvious facts, and announce the conclusion consequent upon such search. Otherwise their discussion is futile scientifically. (Hollingworth, 1914b, p. 528, italics original)

Hollingworth also wrote on the topic of sex differences in behavior, publishing three review articles in *Psychological Bulletin* in the years following Woolley's two reviews (Hollingworth, 1916, 1918, 1919). In these reviews Hollingworth dealt with research that was published on the topic of sex differences in "mental traits," which consisted predominantly of measures of intelligence, memory, achievement, and occupational interests. Hollingworth was quite critical of investigators comparing their particular groups of male and female subjects as though they were representative of males and females in general, and of not recognizing differences in opportunities and experiences of the two sexes. She also emphasized the great amount of overlap and similarity between males and females found in many studies.

After the 1920s, Hollingworth's work moved into the arena of giftedness in children as she became a professor of educational psychology at Teacher's College at Columbia University. She later wrote a very influential adolescence textbook that came to replace Hall's as the leading textbook of the time on adolescence (Hollingworth, 1928).

Edward Lincoln: An Early Review of the Research on Children's Sex Differences

One of the first publications to thoroughly examine the issue of sex differences in children's behavior and development was Edward Lincoln's doctoral dissertation in educational psychology at Harvard University, published as a book in 1927 (Lincoln, 1927). In the introduction to the book Lincoln makes the following observation:

> It will be apparent to the reader as he proceeds through the chapters that no comprehensive scientific study of sex differences has ever been made. Various aspects of the problem have been carefully and extensively treated, but few investigators have dealt with more than one or two traits. For the most part, studies of differences between the sexes have been reported incidentally in connection with other problems. I have tried to find the results of the most important of the previous investigations, and to assemble them, together with several contributions of my own, in such a way as to show in the clearest manner possible what sex differences exist, and how significant they may be. (Lincoln, 1927, p. viii)

As an educational psychologist, Lincoln was primarily concerned with the implications of any sex differences to children's performance in school. Although he discussed research on adults to some degree, his summary of the research was focused squarely on children's capabilities and behaviors at various ages. Lincoln summarized sex differences in physical growth and development, sex differences in mental development, sex differences in variability, and the educational significance of these differences. It is clear from his writing that Lincoln was very concerned about the need for objectivity and statistical sophistication and was a believer in equal educational opportunities for all children.

Lincoln first addressed the research on sex differences in physical growth. He reported that boys weighed slightly more and were slightly taller than girls, except for the period between 11 and 14, when girls were slightly taller and heavier because they reached puberty and completed their development sooner. On all other measures of anatomical and physiological development, girls were more mature than same-aged boys. Lincoln concluded: "In general, it seems that the girls are at a stage of development which is from 12 to 18 months in advance of the boys" (Lincoln, 1927, p. 29).

The next issue that Lincoln examined was sex differences in mental development. He reported on several tests of cognitive ability, including measures of general ability such as the **Stanford-Binet intelligence tests**, as well as many measures of individual cognitive skills. Lincoln concluded that there was no evidence of sex differences in general intelligence, but that there were differences in certain individual skills. Girls often performed better on tests measuring verbal or linguistic skills and fine motor performance, whereas boys did better on tests measuring mathematics and visual or spatial skills, although not labeled as such by Lincoln.

Lincoln also examined children's performance in several academic areas in elementary and high school. He concluded that girls are generally better than boys in the "fundamental operations of arithmetic," but boys show better mathematical reasoning and problem solving, although he thought that the differences were not large, but may increase in the later grades. With respect to reading, he concluded that girls were probably better in oral reading and the speed of silent reading, and possibly in comprehension, but the data he cited were somewhat inconsistent, and the differences were small. He concluded that girls had better handwriting, spelling, and composition, but that boys did better in history, especially in the upper grades. Lincoln also examined grades and school progress and concluded that girls get better grades and are less likely to be retained in a grade or to drop out of school. His final conclusion was "a definite superiority on the part of girls in school achievement" (Lincoln, 1927, p. 104).

Lincoln next tackled the issue of variability and concluded that, on some measures and tasks or at some ages boys were more variable, whereas on other tasks or ages girls were, and on still other tasks there was no difference in variability. He stated "It appears, then, that neither sex can be called more variable on the basis of data at present available" (Lincoln, 1927, p. 164).

Lincoln's final chapter dealt with the implications of any differences between boys and girls for educators. He considered it desirable that boys and girls interact with each other and be educated together because they need to learn to live and work together. He argued that women had been entering fields that had previously been reserved for men, and he expected that they would do so increasingly in the future, hence the need for coeducation would be even greater as time went on. However, his most important arguments focused on the amount of overlap between boys and girls on measures of physical development, intellectual capacity, and school performance. He stated that, even if there is a sex difference in some trait, that difference is small in comparison to the range in either sex. He concluded that the most important issue for educators was the existence of large differences in abilities within both sexes, not the small average difference between them. He stated "Boys and girls will then go forward in various phases of school work at various rates of progress, not because they are one sex or the other, but because each is an individual who differs from other individuals in many ways" (Lincoln, 1927, p. 181).

Both before and after his dissertation was published, Lincoln published several papers on intelligence testing and statistics (e.g., Lincoln, 1931, 1934, 1936; Lincoln & Workman, 1935); however, he did not appear to tackle the issue of sex differences again. Although psychologists of the time were definitely interested in methodological rigor, many male psychologists were not as committed to the equality of the sexes as was Lincoln, nor is there much information about why he was. Lincoln's work on sex differences does not appear to have made much impact on the field, although virtually all of his conclusions would still be considered reasonable in light of the data that have been collected in the 75 years since the book was written. Perhaps the time just was not right.

The Middle of the 20th Century: The Handbooks and Manuals of Child Psychology

The handbooks and manuals of child psychology contain chapters that summarize and organize the research on various topics in developmental psychology. They are often considered the definitive work on the status of any particular field in the discipline, and hence are very influential. An examination of the first three handbook chapters on the question of children's gender development allows us to see what issues were considered important to these early investigators and what was known about the field at the time.

The 1930s: The Murchison Handbooks

The first handbook, Carl Murchison's *Handbook of Child Psychology*, (Murchison, 1931), did not contain a chapter directly related to sex differences or gender development. When the second edition of Murchison's handbook was published in 1933, there was a chapter titled "Sex Differences" written by Beth Wellman (Wellman, 1933). Wellman is most known for her work on the environmental effects of deprivation and enrichment on young, orphaned children's intelligence test scores (e.g., Skeels, Updegraff, Wellman, & Williams, 1938; Wellman & Skeels, 1938). As a result of this work, she became one of developmental psychology's early champions of the effects of the environment on behavior.

Wellman pointed out that in the past men were considered to be superior to women in almost every area of achievement, and only occasionally a woman excelled in some arena. However, it had become apparent that achievement was only partly determined by ability, and boys and girls were similar in most kinds of ability. She also stated that males were previously considered more variable, and hence more likely to be found among the gifted, but that belief also had to be abandoned.

Wellman also addressed several weaknesses in the research comparing the two sexes, including samples of participants that were too small or not representative, and inadequacy or bias in testing materials. She also criticized investigators for not distinguishing between the existence of sex differences and the causes of those differences, with many apparently assuming such differences were innate. She said that although there were, at that time, hundreds of studies on sex differences, there was virtually no well-controlled research on why and under what conditions such differences come about.

Wellman's chapter was organized into the following topics: intelligence, specific mental abilities, language development, motor development, personality, and education. She emphasized that sex differences were small, that there was much overlap between the two sexes, and that findings were sometimes inconsistent. With respect to general intelligence, there was possibly a small advantage for girls, but it was not usually statistically significant. More boys were found among the gifted and among the retarded, but the reasons were not clear. She named several specific tests on which boys perform better such as form boards, puzzles, and mazes. She stated that girls were better at memory, color discrimination, and language skills. Girls' motor development was said to be advanced, whereas boys had better mechanical skills.

Wellman reported that boys had more problem behaviors in childhood and girls were more industrious at school, self-controlled, inhibited, persistent, jealous, and possibly had more nervous habits. Boys were said to be more extroverted, and girls more "motherly," and girls scored higher on tests of morality. Boys and girls were interested in different occupations and activities and showed a strong tendency to play with others of their own sex.

Wellman reported that girls got better grades in school, sometimes even in areas in which boys did better on the achievement tests in those subjects. In terms of specific academic subjects, girls did better in language, art, spelling, and handwriting, whereas boys did better in science, history, and mathematics in the later grades. Boys often did better in achievement tests, and there seemed to be more of a discrepancy between achievement test performance and grades for girls.

The 1940s and 1950s: Terman and the Carmichael Manuals

The next editor of the manuals of child development was Leonard Carmichael, and he remained the editor through the 1970s; these important books were referred to as the "Carmichael manuals" for almost half a century. In the 1940s and 1950s, Lewis Terman and his colleagues wrote the chapters on sex differences. The 1946 chapter was written with the assistance of several colleagues (Terman, Johnson, Kuznets, & McNemar, 1946), and the 1954 chapter was coauthored with Leona Tyler (Terman & Tyler, 1954). Terman, a doctoral student of G. Stanley Hall, had a long and prolific career and was especially known for bringing the Binet intelligence tests to the United States (and naming them the Stanford-Binet, after Stanford University, where he spent most of his professional life), as well as for his studies of gifted children, who were sometimes known as "Terman's Termites." With his graduate student and later colleague, Catherine Cox Miles, Terman also developed the first tests of masculinity and femininity (Lewin, 1984; Terman & Miles, 1936).

As had previous summarizers of the sex differences' literature, Terman and his colleagues (Terman et al., 1946; Terman & Tyler, 1954) discussed physical differences between males and females that might have an impact on behavior. They pointed to data showing the differences in height, weight, and rate of maturation. They discussed the differences in the sex ratios at birth, with 103–107 males born for every 100 females, and many more males than females conceived and later miscarried or stillborn. They suggested that homoeostatic mechanisms (e.g., body temperature, blood sugar) fluctuate less and operate in a more narrow range in males. They stated that boys showed more neuromuscular reactivity and motor tension, and also that boys showed several conditions more frequently, including left handedness, stuttering, epilepsy, color blindness, reading deficiencies, and mental retardation, concluding in the 1954 chapter that such findings might indicate "a general biological superiority of the female" (Terman & Tyler, 1954, p. 1066).

With respect to intellectual and cognitive ability differences between males and females, both chapters covered a very detailed set of findings. Terman and Tyler (1954) provided the following set of generalizations, which are certainly similar to some of the earlier reports and, we will find, are predictive of almost all of the subsequent reports on sex differences in cognitive skills and abilities.

1. If there is a difference between the sexes in general intelligence, it cannot be identified by means of our present tests, since some types of problems favor males, others favor females, and there is no satisfactory way to decide which ones constitute more valid indicators of general mental ability.
2. Girls tend to excel on verbal types of problems; boys, on quantitative or spatial.
3. School marks almost universally indicate superior achievement for girls, whereas achievement tests show girls superior in all kinds of language material, boys in science and mathematics.
4. Vocational aptitude tests show boys higher in mechanical aptitudes and girls higher in clerical aptitudes.
5. Ability differences are most apparent at the older age levels in children. Most of them do not show up at the preschool period. (Terman & Tyler, 1954, p. 1068)

Terman and Tyler's 1954 chapter was the first time that a handbook chapter pointed to the male advantage on tests of spatial ability. Although Lincoln (1927) and Wellman (1933) as well as earlier investigators such as Woolley (Thompson, 1903) had mentioned males' better performance on tasks like block design and mazes that clearly measure spatial skills, they did not categorize those skills as spatial. Terman and Tyler also pointed to the work of several investigators who had been studying sex differences in spatial skills in the late 1940s and early 1950s (e.g., Emmett, 1949; Smith, 1948; Witkin, 1949).

In both chapters Terman and his colleagues (Terman et al., 1946; Terman & Tyler, 1954) discussed the sex difference in variability, which they referred to as "dispersion." The research they cited tended to show somewhat greater male variability, although many studies showed no difference and some showed greater female variability. In both chapters they concluded that the fact that men had excelled in so many domains over the years of history was more likely due to differences in motivation and opportunity.

Terman and his colleagues (Terman et al., 1946; Terman & Tyler, 1954) also discussed research on children's interest in various activities such as sports and games. They reported that boys had greater involvement in sports like football and baseball, and that there was a notable decline in girls' interest in any sports in adolescence. They listed numerous activities and games that were more popular with boys (e.g., marbles, wrestling, hunting, fishing, rowing) or girls (e.g., dolls, dressing up, playing house, dancing, sewing, cooking), or equally popular with both (e.g., Red Rover, follow-the-leader, dominoes, cards). They pointed to findings showing that girls had more restricted activities, being more likely to play at home, and that boys had more vigorous and active play, more organized play, and a greater variety of different kinds of play activities.

They discussed children's differential interest in types of reading materials, and in movies and radio programs. They noted that girls read more than boys, and generally preferred novels, milder adventure, and romance, as well as magazines and poetry. Boys were more likely to prefer active and violent adventures and more likely to read about science and sports. The research on radio programs, which was a precursor of today's research on children's television watching, found boys to prefer adventures, war stories, and westerns, and girls to prefer romances and tragedies. The reports of favorite movies showed a similar pattern.

They also examined children's preferences for school subjects, finding that boys were more likely to prefer science, mathematics, and history, whereas girls were more likely to prefer English, languages, art, and music. They noted that such preferences were more common in high school than in elementary school. Studies of occupational interests also showed large differences between boys and girls, in predictable directions for the times. Girls had fewer occupations to choose from and typically indicated interest in teaching, social work, art, journalism, and entertaining. Boys, on the other hand, showed greater interest than girls in science, engineering, farming, operating engines, construction work, and the like.

Terman and his colleagues also examined sex differences in social behaviors. Boys were found to be more aggressive, dominant, and more likely to engage in problem or delinquent behavior, including in the classroom. Girls, on the other hand, were reported to be more able to inhibit impulses, more fearful at all ages, and more emotionally unstable or neurotic, but only after ages 12–14. They also found that, at all ages, girls had lower aspirations for themselves than boys did. They concluded that girls are more interested in people and social relationships. They found girls to be more interested in social than nonsocial games, more concerned about their appearance, more concerned about getting along with others, more angry about being socially slighted, and that they were more likely to show concern for others (Terman et al., 1946; Terman & Tyler, 1954).

They also examined the nature of children's peer groups and reported that boys have more friends, but that girls were more likely to have cliques and to make unfavorable remarks about others not in their group, and that different characteristics were related to popularity for boys (e.g., leader, good at games, takes chances) and girls (e.g., quiet, not a show-off, not quarrelsome; Terman & Tyler, 1954).

In both chapters (Terman et al., 1946; Terman & Tyler, 1954) Terman and his colleagues discussed, for the first time in any of the major reviews that we have examined so far, research findings related to possible cultural and familial influences on sex differences in children's behavior and concluded that there were very many differences in the experiences of boys and girls. They cited such things as clothing, toys and activities, play experiences, restrictions on mobility, and discipline at home and at school.

Finally, Terman and Tyler (1954) discussed the topic of sex roles and some early research on children's knowledge about sex roles, as well as some that compared the sex role behaviors of boys whose fathers were or were not present in the home. Their final conclusion was that it was an important task for future researchers to further investigate children's sex role behaviors and the environmental factors that influence them.

Although this summary has covered the major topics discussed by Terman and his colleagues, it is by no means complete. Many other topics that had demonstrated sex differences (e.g., the subject matter of boys' and girls' drawings, differences in thumb sucking and bed wetting, and responses to the Rorschach) were covered in their review. However, as we will see as we move on to contemporary research on children's gender development, the reports of Terman and his colleagues of half a century ago foreshadow many of the findings of contemporary researchers.

PSYCHOANALYTIC THEORY

At the same time that early developmental psychologists were doing scientific work on sex differences, Sigmund Freud was writing about the psychological development of boys and girls. However these were parallel activities that did not have much influence on each other (Hornstein, 1992; Hothersall, 1995). In the early years of the 20th century experimental psychologists essentially ignored Freud and his theories. By the 1930s to1940s psychoanalytic theory had become so popular that experimentally trained psychologists began to submit the theory to empirical tests (Hornstein, 1992; Sears, 1985), and one can see the impact of Freud's theory on the study of children's gender development by the 1950s.

Sigmund Freud lived and worked in Vienna in the late 1800s and early 1900s. He was trained as a medical doctor, receiving his medical degree in 1881. He developed a form of therapy for neurosis, **psychoanalysis**, and a theory of the causes of human behavior. Freud's primary study was of people who had psychological problems; however he saw his approach as a scientific theory of all human behavior, normal and abnormal.

Psychoanalytic theory focused on the unconscious and its effect on behavior. Freud thought that the unconscious personality was much larger than the conscious personality, rather like an iceberg under the surface (Hall, Lindzey, & Campbell, 1998; Schultz & Schultz, 1992). To examine the unconscious, Freud used psychoanalysis to explore the lives and experiences of his patients, who were people who came to him for help with their psychological problems. These explorations served as the data from which he constructed his theory of personality and behavior. Freud concluded that the human personality consisted of three parts: the **id**, the **ego**, and the **superego** (Waters & Cheek, 1999; Westen, 1990). The id is entirely unconscious and consists of basic instincts such as hunger, aggression, and sex. Early in development, the infant is 100% id. During infancy the ego begins to form; it is partly conscious and partly unconscious. The ego functions in reality and tries to bring satisfaction to the desires of the id while meeting the demands of the superego. The superego, or conscience, is also largely unconscious and consists of moral values and prohibitions, often in contrast to the impulses of the id. The superego develops during the phallic stage, a very important time for the development of gender identity. Eventually, the personality functions as a whole, with three component parts. The id is the biological part of the personality; the ego, the psychological; and the superego, the social (Hall et al., 1998).

Psychoanalytic Theory: Developmental Implications

The Developmental Stages

Freud proposed a series of stages during which the personality was thought to develop. In Freud's view, personality develops as the result of experiences that a person has in the first five years of life, especially experiences in the family. Freud also believed that people's psychological problems originated during these early years, generally as a result of interactions with parents. In each of these stages the child's libido is focused on a particular erogenous zone, and the child's psychological growth depends on whether the child's needs are met or thwarted during each stage (Hall et al., 1998; Schultz & Schultz, 1992; Waters & Cheek, 1999).

The first of Freud's stages is the **oral stage**, which takes place from birth to about the age of a year and a half, and where the center of gratification or source of pleasure is the mouth. In the next stage, the **anal stage**, which lasts until about the age of 3, the center of pleasure is the anus. A critical developmental task for a child of this age is toilet training, and the child needs to begin to control some of his id impulses and meet the demands of society. The third of the early developmental stages is the **phallic stage**, where the child's focus of pleasure is now the genitals: the penis for boys and the clitoris for girls. According to Freud, the child now develops feelings of sexual attraction. By about the age of 5 or 6 the child has completed the period of early development when the personality forms and enters the **latency stage**, which lasts until adolescence. In adolescence the child enters the **genital stage** in preparation for adult life and relationships (Waters & Cheek, 1999; Westen, 1990).

Identification and Its Implications for Gender Development

The concept of **identification** was a critical concept for psychoanalytic theory. Identification is based on attachment with a parent, and through this attachment the child eventually becomes like the parent by internalizing the parent's characteristics. During the oral and anal periods both boys and girls are said to identify with their mothers through a process called **developmental or anaclitic identification**. This is said to happen because their mother is their caretaker, and when they become attached to her they come to fear the loss of her love. By identifying with her they can reduce their fear of losing her love (Bronfenbrenner, 1960; Tyson & Tyson, 1990). Freud (1927) also believed that children have affectionate feelings for their fathers during this period, although those feelings were thought to be less intense.

The phallic period was said to bring a new developmental challenge, the **Oedipus complex**. This term came from the classic Greek myth of a son who grew up to kill his father and marry his mother, although without knowing their identities. To consider the Oedipus complex, we need to look at the development of boys and girls separately. In Freud's view, during the phallic period, a boy's erotic impulses focus on his penis, and he begins to feel sexual attraction. Because of his mother's centrality in his life, this sexual attraction focuses on her, and the boy comes to see his father as a rival for his mother's affections. To complicate matters the boy also feels affection for his father. However, his father is bigger and stronger than he is, and is therefore a potentially dangerous rival (Tyson & Tyson, 1990).

During the phallic period the boy comes to realize that his sisters and other little girls have different genital organs that he does and comes to the conclusion that girls' genital organs have been removed. In other words, the little boy concludes that girls have been castrated, and he believes that the same thing could happen to him. If his rival father discovers that the son is sexually attracted to his mother, perhaps his father will castrate him. This fear is called **castration anxiety**. How does the little boy handle his castration anxiety? The primary mechanism is through a second kind of identification, **defensive identification**, or **identification with the aggressor**. This kind of identification is based on fear, in this case fear of punishment or castration (Bronfenbrenner, 1960). By identifying with his father he identifies both with what he would like to be (his father) and what he would like to have (his mother). Gradually his sexual attraction to his mother, and the anxiety it creates, will recede further into his unconscious and eventually diminish, and his identification with his father will become more important.

In addition to reducing his castration anxiety, this new identification with his father will accomplish at least two other goals. By taking on his father's characteristics as internal to himself the little boy will develop his superego; his father's moral standards will become his own. Secondly, he will develop his masculine gender role. This is why the concept of identification is so important to the psychoanalytic view of gender development. In Freud's view, boys become masculine by identifying with their fathers in order to resolve the Oedipus complex.

The situation for girls during the phallic period is different from that of boys. Girls' erotic feelings now come to center on the clitoris. When they discover the anatomical differences between boys and girls, they are immediately horrified and angry. They believe they have been castrated, and they resent it, leading to a condition Freud called **penis envy**. In Freud's own words "They notice the penis of a brother or playmate, strikingly visible and of large proportions, at once recognize it as the superior counterpart of their own small and inconspicuous organ, and from that time forward fall a victim to penis-envy" (Freud, 1927, p. 136).

Freud thought that there were at least three consequences to penis envy. The first was a **masculinity complex**: a girl's refusal to believe that she has been castrated, resulting in her acting as if she were a man. The second possible consequence of penis envy was an inherent sense of inferiority, and the third was a weakening of the attachment that girls felt to their mothers, because they would typically blame their mothers for their having been castrated.

So, how does a girl resolve her situation and leave the phallic period with a superego and a feminine gender role? Recall that a feminine gender role comes through identification with her mother, whereas a superego results from internalizing the moral standards of whichever parent she identifies with. The situation is complicated because girls enter the phallic period already identifying with their mothers and cannot make the switch to identifying with their fathers, at least not if they are going to be normal girls. Also, because they are already "castrated," they cannot be driven by a motive to avoid it. The development of a girl's superego and femininity cannot be as neatly resolved as they are for boys, and Freud concluded that resolution of these issues was difficult for girls. Some, perhaps many, girls continue to have a lingering masculinity complex.

Freud came to the conclusion that the major way in which girls came to resolve their dilemma was to substitute the wish for a penis with a wish to have a child. A girl then comes to develop an attraction to her father, who could provide this child for her to compensate for her lack of a penis. Her mother now becomes a rival for her father's affections. A girl's attraction to her father and rivalry with her mother has sometimes been called the **Electra complex**, the female analogue to the Oedipus complex, although it certainly is not directly analogous. Perhaps the best thing a girl can hope for if she does resolve her Electra complex is to leave the phallic period with a wish to become a mother. Because the resolution was difficult, in Freud's view one certainty was that the superego in girls would never develop to the same degree that it would in boys (Freud, 1927); therefore girls' sense of morality would inevitably be weaker.

Early Disagreements Among Psychoanalytic Theorists

Even in Freud's own time there were many disagreements between him and his many students and followers (who are often called **neo-Freudians**). If students and followers disagreed too much with Freud's views, they were expelled from the inner circle. Eventually Freud disagreed with almost all of his major followers and ceased to interact with them. Often, when a follower left the fold, a new psychoanalytic camp was established, and even these groups sometimes broke apart (Leahey, 1994). The result was that the psychoanalytic "school" of psychology became fragmented into many different camps.

One of the followers of Freud who broke away was Carl Jung. Jung developed a neo-Freudian theory with particular relevance for gender development (Keehn, 1996; Westen, 1990). Jung broke with Freud in 1913 because he had a very different view of the unconscious, and because he objected to Freud's heavy emphasis on sexuality. In Jung's view the three parts of personality consisted of the **persona**, which was the conscious part, as well as two unconscious parts: the **personal unconscious** and the **collective unconscious** (Keehn, 1996). The personal unconscious consists of elements of the unconscious that are personal to that individual, such as painful, repressed memories. The collective unconscious consists of images or archetypes that are part of the humanity of every person. Jung believed that everyone, male or female, had an unconscious feminine archetype, the **anima**, and an unconscious masculine archetype, the **animus**. Thus he thought that everyone had a masculine and feminine aspect to his or her unconscious personalities.

Some of the neo-Freudians' objections specifically concerned Freud's views on the psychological development of girls and women. During the 1930s and 1940s, two psychoanalytic theorists, Karen Horney and Clara Thompson, particularly objected to Freud's ideas about penis envy (Horney, 1935, 2000; Thompson, 1942, 1943, 1953, 1971). Both Horney and Thompson believed that cultural influences were far more important than biological anatomy in creating envy of men or a sense of inferiority in girls and women. In particular, they emphasized women's subordinate position in society as a critical factor in creating such feelings. They also thought that social and cultural experiences were the major influences on psychopathology in both sexes, and they preferred to emphasize childhood experiences less than Freud did. Horney developed the concept of **womb envy**, stating that men were likely to envy women's ability to have children. Thompson was particularly critical of Freud's belief that girls came to wish for a baby to compensate for not having a penis. As she said, "Childbearing is a sufficiently important biological function to have value for its own sake" (Thompson, 1942, p. 333).

The Impact of Psychoanalytic Theory on the Study of Gender Development

One can certainly find scholarly articles written during the early part of the 20th century examining Freudian views about gender development in children (e.g., Freud, 1927; Jones, 1910, 1933; Klein, 1928; Pearson, 1931; Pfister, 1918; Searl, 1938). However, the majority of such writings were either clinical case histories or theoretical arguments, and not the kind of empirical studies that are the foundation of developmental psychology. By the 1930s or 1940s there were some reports of empirical studies on Freudian topics (e.g., Isaacs, 1933), especially on the topic of identification with same sex parents (e.g., Bach, 1946; England, 1947; Robinson, 1946). However, one is hard pressed to find much evidence that Freudian theory played a major role in guiding the research done by developmental psychologists on the topic of children's gender development until the work of Robert Sears (Grusec, 1992; Sears, 1950, 1985; Sears, Maccoby, & Levin, 1957).

The Learning Theorists and Empirical Tests of Psychoanalytic Theory

Learning theory influenced psychologists who wanted to experimentally test psychoanalytic notions. The major goal of these psychologists was to translate Freudian concepts into learning terms and then to study them experimentally. Sears and his colleagues were interested in studying the effects of child rearing on personality development (Sears, 1950, 1985; Sears et al., 1957), and they used psychoanalytic theory, translated into learning terms, to guide that research. This was the first time in the study of gender development when theory was systematically guiding research.

Identification

For the study of children's gender development, the most important theoretical concept was identification (Sears, 1957, 1985). When a boy comes to identify with his father, he is said to internalize his father's masculine role, as well as his father's moral values and other aspects of his father's personality. When the boy identifies with his father he becomes like him. A comparable process was proposed for girls and their mothers (Bronfenbrenner, 1960; Kagan, 1964; Mussen & Distler, 1959). Most psychologists at the time thought that identification with one's same sex parent and the adoption of sex roles was desirable, healthy, and a primary goal of socialization (e.g., see Parsons, 1958; Parsons & Bales, 1955). Parents were to follow sex roles so that their children could develop normally. Consider the following statements:

> If the dominant parent is the opposite sex of the child this should strengthen cross-sex identification, and may retard the development of normal sex role preferences. This disruption in identification and sex role preferences should be particularly marked in boys from mother-dominant homes since the acquiescing father supplies a socially inappropriate model for the son. (Hetherington, 1965, p. 189)

> Boys who have a stronger identification with mother than with father tend to be more dependent and prone to anxiety in threatening situations. Moreover, the occurrence of maternal dominance over a passive father, together with maternal rejection of the child, is frequent in the histories of schizophrenic males. (Kagan, 1964, p. 148)

During the period from about 1950 until the early 1970s there were many studies examining children's identification with their parents (e.g., Baxter, Horton, & Wiley, 1964; Block & Turula, 1963; Emmerich, 1959; Hartley, Lynn, Sutton-Smith, & Lansky, 1964; Heilbrun, 1965a, 1965b, 1965c; Hetherington, 1965; Johnson, 1963; Levin & Sears, 1956; Mussen & Distler, 1959; Sears, Rau, & Alpert, 1965). This work examined parental qualities (e.g., whether they were cold, distant, aggressive, and punitive, or warm, accepting and nurturant), and hypothesized relationships between these parental qualities and behavior in the children. In gender research the focus was on the degree of similarity between children and their parents of the same sex, and the extent to which parents followed and children adopted their appropriate sex roles.

One topic of particular interest was whether children would be differentially likely to identify with or be similar to a nurturant mother or father, or to a powerful, harsh, or non-nurturant mother or father, and if such processes would be different for boys and girls. Did children of both sexes identify with the nurturant parent, or the powerful one, or both? Or did boys do one thing and girls another? As it turned out, there were few simple answers to these questions. Another question that researchers examined in identification research concerned the effects of father absence (e.g., Barclay & Cusumano, 1967; Leichty, 1960; McCord, McCord, & Thurber, 1962). Naturally, if a child was expected to learn sex roles from a father and mother, and if boys especially needed a father with whom to identify, researchers wondered what happened to sex roles when the parents had divorced or the father had died.

As researchers studied these issues, failures of the hypotheses generated by identification theory became very common. Researchers frequently were unable to find that children were like their same-sex parent, or that sex role behaviors were influenced predominantly by identification with parents (e.g., Mussen & Rutherford, 1963; Rosenberg & Sutton-Smith, 1968). Sometimes hypotheses would be confirmed for one sex but not the other (e.g., Emmerich, 1959; Hetherington, 1965). In a major study on identification, Sears and his colleagues (Sears et al., 1965) concluded that it was difficult to find much support for the predictions of identification theory in their data on sex typing and gender roles. It became obvious that several gender-related behaviors in children (e.g., toy and game preferences) had little or nothing to do with parents' characteristics and behaviors, and that siblings and other children played a major role in the process of sex typing (Brim, 1958; Mischel, 1970; Rosenberg & Sutton-Smith, 1968).

Sex role identification

At the same time that researchers were examining children's identification with their parents, the concept of **sex role identification** was proposed (e.g., Lynn, 1962). In addition to identifying with their parents, children were also thought to identify with and internalize their sex role. In this way they were said to come to adopt the general cultural aspects of male and female characteristics and roles, above and beyond the specifics of identifying with their own parents. A common measure of sex role identification used at this time was the **IT scale** (Brown, 1956, 1957). Like other measures developed from the psychoanalytic framework, the IT scale was a projective test. Children were thought to project their unconscious personalities onto "IT," who was a stick figure not identified as a boy or girl. The test asked the children for IT's preferences for several sex-linked toys, objects, and activities. Several studies using the IT scale found boys to have stronger masculine preferences than girls had feminine ones (Brown, 1956, 1957; Hall & Keith, 1964), until it was discovered that young children thought IT was male (Brown, 1962; Dickstein & Seymour, 1977; Endsley, 1967; Sher & Lansky, 1968). The children, especially girls, apparently were not projecting their own preferences onto IT at all. Gradually, the IT scale was abandoned and other measures and conceptions of gender development came to be used (e.g., Brinn, Kraemer, Warm, & Paludi, 1984; Edelbrock & Sugawara, 1978; Slaby & Frey, 1975).

As researchers had increasing difficulty with the concept of identification (e.g., Bronfenbrenner, 1960; Kagan, 1958; Lynn, 1962; Sanford, 1955; Sears et al., 1965), there were several attempts to change the concept, define it better, or to study the conditions under which it might operate. Soon, however, there were calls from the learning theorists to abandon the concept of identification entirely. In a particularly important article, Hill (1960) argued that the terminology of learning theory was sufficient to explain the processes of personality development, and that the concept of identification and similar terms derived from psychoanalytic theory, such as **internalization** and **introjection**, were unnecessary and confusing. Very shortly thereafter, social learning theory (Bandura, 1969; Bandura & Huston, 1961; Bandura & Walters, 1963; Mischel, 1966, 1970) became the major theoretical model guiding research on social development and socialization. The perspective of social learning theory was that the processes of learning (reinforcement, punishment, and especially observation and imitation) played the major roles in the acquisition of social behavior and personality characteristics, and that sex typing was no different in that regard from any other form of social learning.

Eventually, the research on identification as a critical aspect of children's development in the family, gender-related or otherwise, faded away. The major reason for this was the repeated failures of the research to find that children were necessarily more like their same-sex parents, or that the idea of identification added much to our understanding of how gender development takes place. Most researchers came to agree with writers like Hill, Bandura, and Mischel (Bandura, 1969; Bandura & Huston, 1961; Hill, 1960; Mischel, 1966) that the psychoanalytic concepts were unnecessary, and that the learning concepts did a better job of explaining the pattern of results found in the research.

Of course, one remaining question is why psychoanalytic views of identification persisted as long as they did. Again, we can return to the influence of values. Psychoanalytic theory was very influential in the culture, much more so than the research done by empirically oriented developmental psychologists. When a view holds so much sway, it takes a great deal of research to move it from center stage.

TRANSITION TO THE CURRENT RESEARCH: CHANGES DURING THE 1960s AND 1970s

By the 1960s to 1970s, psychological research had become increasingly methodologically sophisticated, theoretical models were more prevalent, and the second wave of the feminist movement arose on the scene (Marecek, Kimmel, Crawford, & Hare-Mustin, 2003). All of these influences can be seen in the work we are about to consider.

Three major works were published on children's gender development in the 1960s and 1970s, and it is useful to examine them as we end our discussion of historical influences on the research of children's gender development. They are Eleanor Maccoby's edited book, *The Development of Sex Differences*, published in 1966; Money and Ehrhardt's 1972 book, *Man and Woman, Boy and Girl*, on the development of gender identity, especially in children with intersex conditions; and Maccoby and Jacklin's 1974 book, *The Psychology of Sex Differences*.

Eleanor Maccoby: The Development of Sex Differences

Eleanor Maccoby, who collaborated in some of her earlier work with Robert Sears (e.g., Sears et al., 1957), has been one of the 20th century's most influential developmental psychologists. She has studied several topics in developmental psychology including parental socialization, the impact of television, perceptual development, the effects of divorce, and of course, gender development (American Psychological Association, 1996; Maccoby, 1989; O'Connell, 1990). The publication of her book *The Development of Sex Differences* in 1966 (Maccoby, 1966a) marked a major turning point in the study of children's gender development. In the early part of the 20th century much of the research on children's gender development did not have a clear theoretical foundation but was focused on the study of sex differences with little systematic examination of the roots of such differences. By mid-century, learning theorists' translations of psychoanalytic theory generated much research, but the predictions of the theory did not find consistent support. The time was right for new theoretical models.

Maccoby's 1966 book was the result of a 3-year faculty seminar at Stanford University devoted to understanding the nature of the development of sex differences. It consisted of six chapters written by various authors, as well as an annotated bibliography of research on the topic (Oetzel, 1966). The chapters included Maccoby's own chapter on sex differences in intellectual skills (Maccoby, 1966b), an anthropologist's contribution focusing on the impact of cultural institutions on sex differences in behavior (D'Andrade, 1966), and a summary chapter written by a sociologist (Dornbusch, 1966). The key aspect of this book is its focus on possible reasons for sex differences, rather than on the differences themselves. From the perspective of the future theoretical work on children's gender development, three chapters were fundamental: a chapter on hormonal influences on sex differences in behavior (Hamburg & Lunde, 1966); one on **social learning theory** (Mischel, 1966); and one on an entirely new theoretical view,

cognitive developmental theory (Kohlberg, 1966). To this day, these remain among the major theoretical models that guide the research on children's gender development.

Hamburg and Lunde (1966) reviewed the research on possible biological, especially hormonal, influences on sex differences in behavior. They discussed the timing of puberty and possible effects on behavior of sex hormones in infancy and childhood, but especially after puberty. They also discussed some of the work on children with endocrine abnormalities and concluded that, if there was a discrepancy, sex of assignment and rearing was more important in establishing gender role than was chromosomal sex.

Mischel's chapter on social learning theory began with a definition of sex-typed behaviors as those that "elicit different rewards for one sex than the other" (Mischel, 1966, p. 56), and sex typing as "the process by which the individual acquires sex typed behavior patterns" (Mischel, 1966, p. 57). Mischel then discussed the use of the Freudian construct of identification, noting that what psychoanalytic theorists called identification, experimental psychologists called imitation. He concluded that the time had come to stop using the Freudian terms altogether. The bulk of Mischel's chapter dealt with research findings related to sex-typed behavior in which the learning principles of reinforcement and punishment (including reinforcement delivered by the self), as well as imitation and observational learning could account for those differences.

Lawrence Kohlberg had already formulated his well-known theory of moral development when he wrote the chapter on a cognitive approach to sex role development in Maccoby's book (Kohlberg, 1966). Moral development continued to be the major focus of Kohlberg's work until his death in 1987 (Hayes, 1994; Oser, 1990). In his work in both moral and gender development, Kohlberg was influenced by Piaget, and by the idea that children's thinking about some aspects of their social life was a critical factor in their behavioral development.

Kohlberg argued that children's understanding of their social world changed as their cognitive capabilities became increasingly sophisticated. With respect to issues of sex and gender, he said there would be universal changes in children's understanding of sex role concepts because of universal developmental changes in cognitive skills. He proposed three stages of children's understanding of gender, concluding that understanding of gender concepts would precede children's gender stereotyped behavior.

In his chapter, Kohlberg argued against a social learning or reinforcement view of gender development, concluding that these factors were less important than children's own cognitive understanding of gender. Beginning with their hearing of the labels "boy" and "girl," children eventually come to know their own gender. Then they come to associate various items with their gender, and to value those items and choose to adopt them. In time, Kohlberg's view came to be called a self-socialization view of gender development. In his chapter, he reviewed the research available at the time demonstrating children's increasing knowledge of gender-related concepts, and evidence that direct reinforcement was not necessary to produce this understanding. Of course, culture and learning were certainly involved because they provided the content of the knowledge that children came to adopt.

Kohlberg took issue with both social learning and psychoanalytic theorists' emphasis on the centrality of parents. He said that there are too many cultural forces that influence gender concepts to believe that this kind of development depended solely or primarily on parental identification or imitation. In later chapters we will learn more about Kohlberg's theory and the huge impact that the cognitive approach has had on the contemporary study of children's gender development.

Money and Ehrhardt: Man and Woman, Boy and Girl

Another influential work published around this time was John Money and Anke Ehrhardt's *Man and Woman, Boy and Girl* (1972). Money's life work was devoted to the study of the interaction of biological and environmental factors in the development of people's gender identity and the implications for many other gender-related issues, particularly sexual orientation. Ehrhardt was Money's colleague and research associate at Johns Hopkins University in Baltimore between 1966 and 1973 while the work for this book was completed. Money and Ehrhardt's book was focused primarily on individuals with endocrine disorders, intersex conditions, and individuals who had extremely small or absent genitalia. The book was devoted to the topic of the formation of gender identity and gender role. To them, gender identity was defined as personal, private, and internal—one's experienced sense of gender role. Gender role was defined as the public manifestation of gender: everything that a person says or does to indicate that one is male or female, including sexual behavior.

Money and Ehrhardt argued that it was outmoded to ask questions about biological versus environmental influences on gender identity and gender role. Instead, its development unfolded with a series of interacting influences. Particularly important among these influences was prenatal development, especially differences in gonadal hormones during prenatal life, which affected both the genitals and the brain. Once a child was born, the child's behavior and experiences, including treatment by important others such as parents, played critical roles in the development of gender identity and role. Another crucial time was puberty, with the influx of pubertal hormones. Money has been criticized for being too biological in his views about gender (Rogers & Walsh, 1982), and for not being biological enough (Diamond & Sigmundson, 1997), but it is very clear that he and Ehrhardt emphasized both factors. The study of the gender development of individuals with various biological disorders could shed light on the role played by both factors and their interaction.

Maccoby and Jacklin: The Psychology of Sex Differences

The final work we will consider in the history of the study of children's gender development is Maccoby and Jacklin's 1974 book, *The Psychology of Sex Differences*. Maccoby and Jacklin reviewed the results of more than 1,600 studies that compared males and females on some behavior or psychological characteristic. They did not deal with biological differences such as size, strength, or developmental timetable, but rather focused predominantly on behavior. The book cannot be said to be focused on sex differences, because Maccoby and Jacklin were as interested in similarities as differences, and that is perhaps the most critical difference between their work and many of the previous reviews of the material.

Maccoby and Jacklin pointed out that one of most the serious problems with the research on sex differences was that when sex differences were not found, the information about the lack of difference was usually not published. Therefore, if a handful of studies on some topic found a difference between males and females, and published such a difference, the finding would be repeated in textbooks and other sources for years, yet there might be many more studies that did not find such a difference that did not enter published scholarship.

Therefore, Maccoby and Jacklin undertook the incredibly time-consuming task of finding all of the recent published scholarship they could locate that measured some behavior that had both male and female subjects taking part. They focused more on research involving children and adolescents, but included work on adults as well. The book contained 86 summary tables comparing the results of these studies on some behavior or characteristic. Each study cited in one of these tables was put into one of three categories as demonstrating: a statistically significant difference ($p < .05$) indicating that one sex or the other scored higher on that measure, or showed more of that behavior; a trend towards such a difference ($.05 < p < .10$); or no difference between the sexes. Recognizing that some studies are more powerful than others, they also reported sample sizes, as well as ages of the subjects in each study in the table. They also pointed out that any conclusion they would make about there being no difference between the sexes on some behavior was really a conclusion that a difference had not been clearly or consistently demonstrated at that time, because future research might find a difference.

The book was organized into three sections: (a) intellect and achievement, (b) social behavior, and (c) origins of sex differences. In the section on intellect and achievement, Maccoby and Jacklin discussed research on perception, learning, memory, achievement and ability testing, and achievement motivation. They concluded that the basic processes of perception, learning, and memory were very similar in males and females. With respect to specific skills, they concluded that girls had better verbal skills and boys had better spatial and mathematical skills, but differences were not consistently found in these domains until adolescence. They tackled the variability issue and concluded that there may be greater male variability in spatial or mathematical skills, but not verbal skills. As others had reported for decades, they found that girls got better grades, but female achievement is much less than that of males after the years of schooling are over. As far as motivation to achieve, after an examination of a variety of issues that might be linked to these findings, their only strong conclusions were that girls have less confidence in their ability to do a variety of tasks, less confidence in their ability to control events that affect them, and are more likely to invest themselves in social relationships.

In their examination of social behavior, Maccoby and Jacklin pointed out that it was much more difficult to examine these kinds of behaviors than the cognitive domain, especially in terms of issues such as motives and feelings. Nonetheless, they examined a very large number of such behaviors. They reported that boys were more likely to be found to have a higher activity level, although not under all conditions. Group play with other boys was especially likely to stimulate high activity levels. After the toddler period, boys displayed more anger. Girls might be more anxious, although observational studies had not found it to be the case, and the finding might be due to girls' greater willingness to report anxiety on self-report measures.

They noted that the quality of social relationships with peers was somewhat different, with more rough and tumble play and fighting among boys and smaller, more intense or intimate friendships among girls, but that overall social relationships and interactions were very similar. Males of all ages and in similar species were consistently more aggressive, especially in terms of direct, physical aggression. Girls might be more likely to direct their aggression by being "catty." Boys were more competitive in athletics, but not necessarily in other domains. Girls were more likely than boys to comply with the requests of adults, but there was little evidence of a sex difference in compliance in other situations, and little consistency in the findings on dominance.

Maccoby and Jacklin also examined many possible reasons for the sex differences they discussed. Throughout each of the chapters they looked at research on sex differences in other species and across cultures, when available or relevant. They also discussed studies that suggested biological or social influences on the differences. The last section of their book was devoted to findings about sex-typed behavior and to research on the role of imitation, modeling, and parental socialization in creating any of the differences between the sexes. They concluded that there was little evidence that children were more likely to imitate their same-sex parent, or same-sex models in general. Children were exposed to and could imitate all kinds of behavior, gender-appropriate or not. An important factor was what they chose to imitate. That is, Maccoby and Jacklin pointed to the idea of self-socialization: children have a role in the adoption of their own gender-related behavior.

They reported that in the family, boys' motor behavior was accepted and stimulated more than girls', and that some evidence suggested that parents might enforce demands that they make on preschool boys more strongly, or that they might restrict them more, but the evidence was mixed. Boys were consistently more likely to be physically punished and there was some evidence that indicated they might receive more praise. They concluded that parents, especially fathers, were more likely to accept cross-sex behavior in girls than in boys. Otherwise, parents treated boys and girls very similarly.

They also examined parents' beliefs about sex differences in their children. Although they treated them similarly, and that there were few consistent differences in the capacities of boys and girls, parents clearly thought they were different (e.g., boys were thought louder and messier, and girls were thought more likely to cry or be frightened), but the qualities desired by parents differed little for boys and girls.

When it was first published, the book had a huge impact on people's thinking about sex differences and socialization, and it is fair to say that the book shaped the research on gender development for the next generation. One way in which the impact of a publication is measured is to determine how many other researchers cite it in their own writings. In a recent search of the Social Science Citation Index, Maccoby and Jacklin's book was reported to have been cited in more than 3,500 other works since it was published, and the rate of citations has not changed much since its publication; researchers are still actively citing it more than 30 years since it was published.

Despite its impact, not everyone accepted Maccoby and Jacklin's (1974) perspectives without question. The conclusions about sex differences and about parental socialization were challenged immediately (O'Connell, 1990), especially by Jeanne Block (1976; 1983), who had studied children's gender development for some years. Block particularly disagreed about Maccoby and Jacklin's conclusions that there were few differences in parental socialization of boys and girls, believing that there was evidence for several important differences in how girls and boys were treated by their parents.

CHAPTER SUMMARY

This chapter has been a survey of the study of children's gender development by developmental psychologists, almost exclusively American, from the early 20th century until the early 1970s. We began with three reasons for including this chapter in the book. First, we included this historical chapter to demonstrate that many questions about sex differences and gender development have a long history and do not always show a simple progression in which new research builds on prior research and in which recent work is necessarily more sophisticated than earlier work. Although one would hope to see these progressions, the path is not always a smooth one. For example, this historical review shows that researchers examined the question of more variability among males than among females for more than a century, making various pronouncements over the years but never really developing a clear set of conclusions. Indeed, it will become clear as we move into later chapters that this topic is still with us.

Related to this particular question about variability is the second reason for including this chapter: what Crutchfield and Krech (1962) have referred to as the "spiral of history." Scientific study is not necessarily steady and progressive, but waxes and wanes as a function of various factors such as the ideological climate of the time, increasing methodological sophistication, as well as coincidence or accident. We can certainly see how factors related to the values of the time influenced the study of gender development over the years of the 20th century.

Our third reason concerns the role that theory plays in guiding research. Few theoretical models existed in the early part of the 20th century. By mid-century, much research on children's gender development was guided by psychoanalytic theory as interpreted by learning theorists. Once the failure of the research to support the predictions of the theory became more evident, the theory was supplanted by several other theoretical models that remain with us today: biological theories, social learning theory, and cognitive developmental theory. In the chapters that follow, we will be reviewing contemporary theories as well as the empirical research that has been conducted to evaluate and extend them.

Biological Foundations of Sex and Gender[1]

3

I never felt out of place being a girl. I still don't feel entirely at home among men. Desire made me cross over to the other side, desire and the facticity of my body....Biology gives you a brain. Life turns it into a mind. (Eugenides, 2002, p. 479)

Many of us spend a lot of time thinking about the ways in which boys and girls and men and women are different (and some of us write books about it). But, few of us spend time wondering how we got to be men or women in the first place. As we show in this chapter, sex is not simply defined by any single criterion, and there is not a straightforward link between sex and gender.

WHAT MAKES SOMEONE A BOY OR GIRL, MAN OR WOMAN?

Think for a minute about two questions: What makes someone a boy or girl? How do you know that you are a woman or a man? You may be thinking these questions are strange or perhaps that the answers are self-evident. But as will become evident in this chapter (and later ones), the answers to these questions are complex and critically involve understanding biological foundations of sex and gender.

Now consider some possible answers. As you will see, most answers are inaccurate or incomplete, and we will explain the reasons for this later in the chapter.

- "A penis makes someone a boy and a vagina makes someone a girl." So, is a person without a penis always a girl? It turns out that there are some boys who do not have a penis.
- "A Y chromosome makes someone a boy and two X chromosomes make someone a girl." So, is a person with a Y chromosome always a boy? It turns out that there are some people who have a Y chromosome and who look like (and feel just as feminine as) people with two X chromosomes.
- "Testosterone makes someone a man and estrogen makes someone a woman." So, is a person with high testosterone (or low estrogen) always a man? Is a person with low testosterone never a man? It turns out that there are some women who have high levels of testosterone and some men who have low levels.

The question gets even trickier when you ask what makes someone masculine or feminine. Do the same factors that contribute to categorizing a person as girl or boy, woman or man, contribute to variations in physical or psychological characteristics that are related to sex? If you are a (heterosexual) man, how do you decide if a prospective partner is "feminine" enough for you? Certainly you do not look at someone's chromosomes or hormones. Do you look at physical appearance? Do you look at how she behaves? If you do, what characteristics do you examine? And what causes those variations?

The question we asked—"What makes someone a boy or girl, man or woman?"—and the potential answers to it are our way of introducing you to the fact that there are many levels of sex and gender (see Table 3.1), in essence constituting many steps in what are called the processes of **sex determination**

---

[1] Sheri Berenbaum was the primary author of chapter 3.

TABLE 3.1   Levels of Sex

Chromosomal (genetic) sex

Gonadal sex

Hormonal sex

Internal reproductive organs

External genital appearance

Assigned sex/sex of rearing

Gender identity

Source: Adapted from Money, J. & Ehrhardt, A.A., *Man and woman, boy and girl,* Baltimore: Johns Hopkins, 1972; and Grumbach et al., in *Williams textbook of endocrinology* (pp. 842–1002), Philadelphia: W.B. Saunders, 2003.

and **sex differentiation** (Grumbach, Hughes, & Conte, 2003). And it should now be clear to you that there is not a single criterion that might be used to decide whether someone is a boy or girl, man or woman—something that was not well understood until about 50 years ago (Money & Ehrhardt, 1972) and that continues to be the subject of much research (e.g., Berenbaum, 2006; Hughes, Houk, Ahmed, Lee, & LWPES/ESPE Consensus Group, 2006; Meyer-Bahlburg, 2005b). Sex determination and differentiation involve many steps, from chromosomes and genes to gonads, to reproductive structures and external genitals, to physical appearance at birth, which determines social sex ("It's a boy!" "It's a girl!")—and then to psychological aspects of sex and gender. These steps are regulated by at least 50 different genes that work in several different ways, including the formation of specific organs in the body (including the brain), hormones that control bodily functions, and receptors that allow those hormones to affect organs. For most of us, all of the steps work together to produce consistency among the components of sexual differentiation, so it is easy to say "I am a woman" or "I am a man." But for some of us (maybe 1 in 4,500), there is a mismatch (discordance) among the levels, and these people are considered to have **disorders of sexual development (DSDs)**. As discussed later in the chapter and in chapter 6, people with these conditions tell us a lot about the ways in which biology affects gender development.

The goal of this chapter is to introduce you to the biological foundations of sex, that is, the processes of sex determination and sexual differentiation. This information will be revisited in chapter 6 when we consider ways in which these biological processes also play a role in gender development. The chapter is divided into five sections. The first and longest section concerns the ways in which physical appearance is shaped by chromosomes, by genes on those chromosomes, and by hormones before birth; it also includes discussion of the ways in which these processes can go awry. The second section includes information about changes in physical appearance at adolescence that are under the control of hormones at puberty. The third section is about sex differences in physical growth that are particularly relevant to gender development. The fourth section is a brief description of brain structure and how the brain underlies behavior. The final section addresses the evolutionary processes thought to underlie the physical and psychological differences between the sexes.

EARLY BIOLOGICAL PROCESSES OF SEX DETERMINATION AND DIFFERENTIATION

We start with very early development, what happens well before birth. As you will see, all bodies are wired with the same basic plan, and the path to becoming a boy or a girl is initiated by a gene on one of the chromosomes. But—and this is something that you will hear again in this book—there is not always a perfect correspondence between a person's genes and the consequences of those genes. This is what is known as the relation between **genotype** (genetic make-up, the specific genes a person has) and **phenotype** (measurable characteristics). Phenotypes can be physical (e.g., height, blood pressure, brain size) or psychological (e.g., spatial ability, sociability). There is not always an absolute association between genotype and phenotype, because genes may be modified by other genes or by the environment. This applies to both physical and psychological phenotypes.

Genes and Chromosomes

Before we discuss the genetics of sexual differentiation, we digress for a brief primer on basic genetics for those of you who need a refresher. If you already have a good understanding of genetics, you might want to skip ahead to the next section.

Some Basic Genetics

All of our genetic material is contained on 23 pairs of chromosomes. One chromosome in a pair comes from the mother and the other from the father. Chromosomes contain many different genes, in physical locations called loci (the singular is **locus**). An important feature of chromosome pairing is that the genes at a given locus are also paired, so that individuals inherit one gene from the mother and the other gene from the father. The gene may have different forms called **alleles**. If the allele is the same on each chromosome pair (the same form of the gene is inherited from both parents), the individual is called **homozygous** for that gene (or at that locus). If the alleles are different at a given locus, because different forms of the gene were inherited from the mother and the father, the individual is called **heterozygous** for that gene (or at that locus).

Genes produce proteins, and the product of the gene at a given locus depends on the alleles that are present. In some cases, the alleles have additive effects, so the product is simply the sum of the products of the two alleles. In other cases, the alleles have unequal effects, with one allele **dominant** over the other allele; the nondominant allele is called **recessive**. In those cases, individuals who inherit one dominant and one recessive allele will have the same phenotype as individuals who inherit two dominant alleles, and both will have a different phenotype from individuals with two recessive alleles.

The overwhelming majority of genetic material—the 22 autosomes and their associated genes—is the same in males and females. But one of the 23 pairs of chromosomes—the sex chromosomes—differs in males and females, with females having two X chromosomes and males having one X and one Y.

Chromosomal and Genetic Sex

Genetic sex is determined at conception. The mother donates an egg, which contains 22 autosomes and one sex chromosome, in this case an X chromosome. The egg is fertilized by sperm from the father, which also contains 22 autosomes and one sex chromosome, which can either be an X chromosome or a Y chromosome. The **zygote** resulting from the fertilization of the egg by sperm carries 23 pairs of chromosomes, 22 pairs of autosomes (numbered 1–22) and one pair of sex chromosomes, either XX or XY, the 23rd pair. The specific profile of the chromosomes is called a **karyotype** and standard notation is to indicate the total number of chromosomes, normally 46, followed by the two sex chromosomes. If the sperm carries an X chromosome, the karyotype of the resulting zygote will be 46,XX, a chromosomal female; if the sperm carries a Y chromosome, the karyotype will be 46,XY, a chromosomal male.

The X chromosome is substantially larger and contains many more genes than the Y chromosome, and these genes, like those on the autosomes, are involved in many biological functions. But the Y chromosome contains a specific and unique gene, called *SRY* (for sex-determining region of the Y chromosome) that starts the program for "maleness." People who have *SRY* proceed down the pathway to be a boy, and people who do not have *SRY* proceed down the pathway to be a girl. In many ways, it seems amazing that the switch to determine whether someone is male or female is a single small piece of genetic material residing on the smallest chromosome. But maybe it is less shocking when we consider that human beings and chimpanzees share 98% of their genetic material.

Consequences of Sex Differences in Karyotype

There are other consequences of the sex difference in sex chromosome complement (composition), particularly of the fact that females have two X chromosomes and males have one X and one Y.

Effects of genes on the Y chromosome

Only males have a Y chromosome; therefore, genes on the Y chromosome are expressed only in males. Because many of these genes have no counterpart on the X chromosome (or autosomes), expression of these genes is limited to males. For a long time, it was thought that the main genes on the Y chromosome were *SRY* and a few others with little importance (e.g., "hairy ears"). But recent studies show that the Y chromosome carries genes involved in basic biological functions and that defects in these genes may lead to infertility in men (Lahn & Page, 1997).

X-linked inheritance

The sex difference in the number of X chromosomes means that there is a change in the typical pairing of the chromosomes and a corresponding change in the genes possessed by males and females. Females have a matched pair of (X) chromosomes and thus matched pairs of genes at each locus (with each gene having a counterpart on the other chromosome). Males have only one X chromosome and most genes on that chromosome do not have matches on the Y chromosome, so males have only one gene at each locus. This means that females have twice as many X-chromosome genes as do males, and this results in sex differences in traits coded by those genes. This is called **X-linked inheritance** and the traits affected by these genes are called **X-linked traits**. Recessive genes on the autosomes are expressed equally often in males and females, but recessive genes on the X chromosome are expressed much more often in males than in females. This is because females need two recessive genes to express the trait (one on each X chromosome i.e., one from each parent). In contrast, in males a recessive gene on the X chromosome will lead to the expression of that trait because (in most cases) there is no corresponding gene on the Y chromosome. This means that there is no second gene that can potentially dominate (obscure) the one on the X chromosome. Color blindness is an example of an X-linked trait, because it is caused by a recessive gene on the X chromosome. For girls, there is likely to be a normal gene on the second X chromosome that prevents the expression of the recessive trait of color blindness. For boys, there is no matched gene on the Y chromosome, and hence color blindness is expressed. This results in a sex difference in the incidence of color blindness: approximately 10% of males are color blind, whereas very few females are.

X-inactivation

There are some mechanisms to compensate for the fact that females have twice as much X-chromosome material as do males, to prevent females from producing twice as much as males of whatever information is coded by genes on the X chromosome. (This does not happen for the autosomes, because both males and females have two chromosomes.) Through a process called **X-inactivation**, one of the two X chromosomes in each cell is randomly turned off during a girl's early embryonic development. But this does not happen until after at least some of the genes have been expressed because, as we will see below, two X chromosomes are necessary for complete female development. Interestingly, however, about 10–15% of genes on the X chromosome appear to "escape" X-inactivation, and the resulting differences in gene product have been hypothesized to be responsible for some of the differences between males and females (Willard, 2000).

Imprinting

An exciting discovery concerns the fact that the expression (manifestation) of a gene depends on whether it is inherited from the mother or from the father, a process called genomic imprinting, or simply **imprinting**

(Tilghman, 1999). Imprinting on autosomal genes is not likely to have different effects on male versus female offspring, because autosomes are transmitted equally to the two sexes. But imprinting of genes on the X chromosome may result in phenotypic sex differences. Boys necessarily inherit the X chromosome from the mother, which is all she has; they necessarily inherit the Y chromosome from the father. (If the father had contributed his X chromosome, he would have had a daughter, not a son.) Thus, girls inherit one X chromosome from the mother and one from the father. X-linked genes from the father thus have the potential to affect traits in daughters but not in sons. This means that if a gene on the X chromosome is imprinted, it matters for girls which parent transmits the gene, but it does not matter for boys ("matters" in the sense that the trait influenced by that gene will differ). We will provide some examples of this in chapter 6.

Sex-Limited Inheritance

Sex differences in a trait may result from differential expression of genes in males and females, due to sex differences in other aspects of physiology, such as sex hormones; this is called **sex-limited inheritance**. The genes involved in baldness, for example, are on the autosomes, but their expression requires the presence of high levels of testosterone. Many people think that baldness comes through mothers and is transmitted only to sons (i.e., X-linked), but it turns out that baldness is likely due to many genes, including ones that come equally from the mother and the father and are passed on equally to sons and daughters. Then why are men much more likely than women to be bald? It's because of **gene expression**, which in this case means that the expression (or display) of the gene (being bald) happens only when the person also has high levels of testosterone (Otberg, Finner, & Shapiro, 2007). This happens much more often in men than in women. This is an example of some other aspect of a person's biology affecting whether a gene is expressed. So, you can see that sex differences in some aspects of biology might change the expression of genes that are found equally in males and females.

Sex differences in environmental exposure might also affect gene expression (Wizemann & Pardue, 2001). For example, sex differences in rates of skin cancer might be due to modification of gene expression by sex differences in sun exposure; for example, men likely to be exposed to the sun by working outside, or women revealing their bodies while sunbathing. It is easy to think of examples in which sex differences in hormones or environmental exposure might modify the expression of genes that do not differ in frequency in males and females, but it is more difficult to demonstrate when and how these effects actually occur. Furthermore, gene expression is not just restricted to physical traits, but also applies to psychological traits.

Gonads and Genitalia: The Crucial Role of Hormones

The two sexes start out with the same sets of structures that differentiate into male or female gonads, internal reproductive organs, and genitals (for detailed review, see Grumbach et al., 2003). Because development can go either way, the initial structures are called indifferent. The path that is taken depends on which substances are present at specific points in development. This means that we all start out able to become a male or a female (called **bipotentiality**). As we discuss in detail below, there are three parts to this development. First, males and females start out with the same basic structures, the indifferent **gonads** (there are two of them, one on each side of the body) that become either testes or ovaries, which produce sperm and eggs, respectively. Second, there are two sets of **genital ducts**, with only one developing and the other disappearing [**Müllerian ducts** can become the uterus and fallopian tubes, whereas **Wolffian ducts** can become the epididymis, vas deferens (ejaculatory ducts), and seminal vesicles]. Third, the **external genitalia** (or genitals) are initially identical in males and females and have the capacity to develop into a penis and scrotum or into a clitoris, labia, and lower part of the vagina. The physical process of masculinization is formally called **virilization**. Before we describe the three main steps in normal sexual differentiation, we need to talk about hormones, particularly **sex hormones**.

Sex Hormones

A hormone is a chemical substance that is produced by an organ of the body or cells in an organ and is transported through the blood to have an effect on (regulate the function of) another organ or parts of that organ. Hormones vary in amount (level) or concentration across people and even within a person across time of the day, month, year, or lifetime. Sex hormones are those that differ in concentration between males and females and are involved in the differentiation of the body into male and female and in completely normal reproductive function (i.e., the ability to engage in sexual activity and produce offspring). Sex hormones are produced mainly by the gonads, but other organs also produce hormones with similar effect.

The main sex hormones are **androgens** and **estrogens**. Androgens are produced by the testes (the male gonads), by the ovaries (the female gonads), and by the **adrenal glands** in both males and females. Estrogens are produced directly by the ovaries in females and by the placenta during gestation of both males and females and are produced indirectly by being converted from androgens in both males and females. This means that both males and females produce and respond to both androgens and estrogens, but they do so at different concentrations at many, but not all, stages of the lifespan. Both androgens and estrogens come in several forms. The forms of androgens that have the most effect on the body and behavior are **testosterone**, **dihydrotestosterone**, and **androstenedione**. The form of estrogen that has the largest effect is called **estradiol**. There is another hormone, **progesterone**, which is produced in the ovaries, and it plays a large role in reproduction, but a small role in behavior, so we will not discuss it much in this book.

Three Main Steps in Sexual Differentiation

We now return to the three main events in sexual differentiation: development of the gonads, development of the genital ducts into the internal reproductive system, and development of the external genitalia.

Development of the gonads

The first event is the development of the testes or ovaries. The initiator of the move from our bipotential or indifferent state to differentiation resides on the Y chromosome. The *SRY* gene is the main determinant of sex, and it is responsible for the development of the indifferent gonads into testes at about weeks 6–7 of gestation, although several other autosomal and X-linked genes are necessary for complete testes development. In the absence of *SRY*, and with the involvement of other genes, the indifferent gonad develops into an ovary at about 3 months of gestation. Female-typical development is generally considered to be the "default" process (or a passive process), that is, it occurs when *SRY* is not present, but it is important to note that completely normal female development does require other genes. If the indifferent gonads have not become testes by a specific time in prenatal development, around 8 weeks of gestation, the default mechanism operates, and the gonads become ovaries *if* all other aspects of development are proceeding normally. If testes develop, they produce two substances important for further development of the male body, androgens and **Müllerian inhibiting substance** (MIS, also called anti-Müllerian hormone).

Development of the internal reproductive system

The second event in the differentiation of a male or a female is the development of the internal organs involved in reproduction from what are called the genital ducts. There are two sets of genital ducts, with only one developing and the other disappearing. In typical development, the sexes develop a different set of genital ducts, with the amount of androgens and MIS present during the third month of fetal life determining which set of genital ducts develops and which set disappears, as shown in Figure 3.1. Specifically, high levels of androgens stimulate the development of the Wolffian ducts into the male genital system, and high levels of MIS destroy the Müllerian ducts so that a female genital system cannot develop. When testes are present and functioning (and therefore there are high levels of androgens and MIS), the result is the degeneration of the Müllerian structures and the stimulation of the Wolffian ducts into the epididymis, vas deferens (ejaculatory ducts), and seminal vesicles. When testes are absent, there is insufficient androgen to stimulate the development of the Wolffian ducts, so they degenerate, and there is no MIS to destroy the

Müllerian structures, so they develop into the uterus, fallopian tubes, and upper part of the vagina. Again, female-typical development is the default, proceeding in the absence of androgens and MIS. The fetal ovary has no documented role in the differentiation of the female genitalia (Grumbach & Auchus, 1999).

Development of the external genitalia

The third event in the differentiation of a male or a female is the development of the external genitals, and this also depends on androgen. The amount of androgen that is present at about 7–8 weeks of gestation determines whether the undifferentiated genitalia develop into those characteristic of a boy or those characteristic of a girl, as shown in Figure 3.2. The specific form of androgen that is important is dihydrotestosterone (DHT); it is produced directly from testosterone through the action of an enzyme, **5-α-reductase**. (You will see later in this chapter and again in chapter 6 why this detail is important.) High levels of DHT cause the development of three aspects of male-typical genitalia, whereas absent or low levels result in female-typical development. The first is the erectile tissue, becoming a penis when DHT is high, or a clitoris when it is low. The second is the labioscrotal swelling, fusing to form the scrotum and

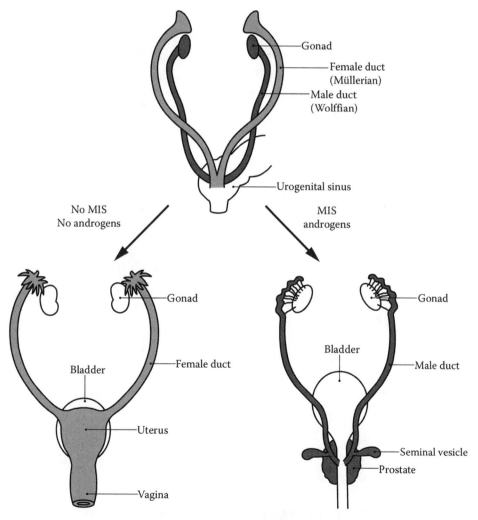

FIGURE 3.1 Development of female (left) and male (right) internal reproductive structures from common tissue. (Modified from Migeon, C.J. et al., Syndromes of abnormal sex differentiations, Baltimore: Johns Hopkins, 2001. http://www.hopkinschildrens.org/intersex. With permission.)

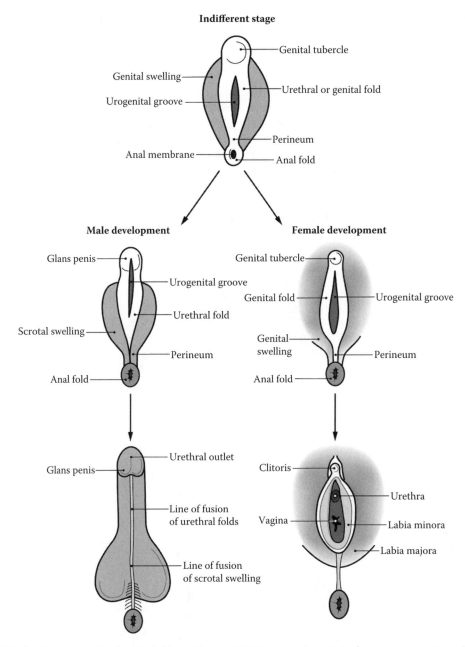

FIGURE 3.2   Development of male (left) and female (right) external genitalia from common tissue (top).

covering of the penis when DHT is high, or remaining separate to form the labia majora when it is low. The third is whether there is a single opening for urine and sperm (urogenital sinus) that forms when DHT is high, or separate vaginal and urethral canals when it is low.

The Importance of Timing of Hormone Exposure

As indicated above, male-typical gonadal and genital development depends on high levels of androgens, which is probably why androgen is considered a male hormone. Figure 3.3 shows the levels of testosterone

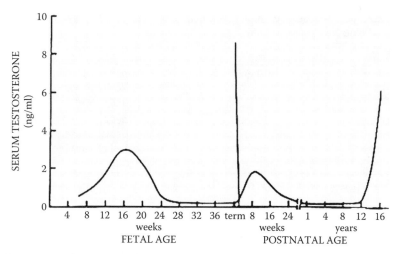

FIGURE 3.3 Time course of testosterone in males. (From Smail, P.J. et al., in *Pediatric andrology* (pp. 9–19), The Hague, Netherlands: Martinus Nijhoff, 1981.)

for males from early in gestation into adolescence; the levels for females are low throughout this period and so are not shown. As is apparent, males do not always have high levels of testosterone. They do have high levels (and therefore there are large sex differences in testosterone) starting at weeks 7–8 of gestation, after the testes have developed, and the levels remain high until well into the second trimester of gestation. It is this surge that is responsible for differentiation of the male reproductive system and external genitals and most likely affects other aspects of physical development, including brain development, and thus behavior. Note that testosterone levels in males decrease later in gestation, although they do remain somewhat higher than those in females through birth. Testosterone levels in males increase again for a short while in months 1–5 after birth (the significance of this increase is not well understood), and then return to low levels—and not different from those of females—until puberty, when they increase substantially. Testosterone levels remain high in males from puberty throughout adulthood, although they do decline in middle age and beyond. In fact, this decline in androgens in men is now termed "andropause." Although some have considered andropause to be a parallel to the decline in estrogens experienced by women in menopause in middle age, they are not quite the same. Men experience a more gradual decline in androgen than women experience in estrogen, that is, menopause is an abrupt process, whereas andropause is a gradual one.

The ovaries in the female fetus do not produce significant amounts of estrogens (Grumbach & Auchus, 1999), but fetuses of both sexes are exposed to high levels of estrogens coming from the placenta. This suggests a reason why estrogen does not play a large role in prenatal development. Anything that is influenced by estrogen would affect males and females equally because they both receive estrogens from the placenta. Therefore, it seems unlikely that estrogen would play a role in prenatal sexual differentiation.

So, males, on average, have considerably higher androgens than females during early and mid-prenatal development, again in the early postnatal period, and then again beginning in puberty and continuing throughout the rest of the life span. Females, on average, have considerably higher estrogens than males at some later point in fetal development (and this is not well known), and then again beginning in puberty and continuing to menopause. Imposed on these between-sex differences is, of course, within-sex variability, but there is very little overlap between males and females. The woman with the highest testosterone still has levels lower than those of the man with the lowest testosterone (unless one or both of them has a hormonal disorder). And imposed on this is within-person variability, the most well known of which is menstrual cycle variation in women. Typical hormone levels in men and women are shown in Table 3.2.

TABLE 3.2   Range of Sex Hormone Levels in Adults (Measured in Nanograms per Deciliter of Blood)

HORMONE	MEN	WOMEN
Estrogen	1.0–5.0	*Varies across menstrual phase* Follicular phase: 3.0–10.0 Luteal phase: 9.0–16.0
Progesterone	10–50	*Varies across menstrual phase* Follicular phase: ≤50 Luteal phase: 300–2,500
Testosterone	265–800	10–40

Hormone levels from Diamond and Bercu (2004).

Hormone Levels and Responsivity

We have focused on the importance for physical development of the levels (concentrations) of sex hormones that are present. If androgens are present in high concentrations, then development proceeds in a male-typical direction, whereas low or absent concentrations of androgens allow development to proceed in a female-typical direction.

But development requires more than high levels of hormones. Those hormones must be recognized by the cells that depend on them for their development. Hormones exert their effects through **receptors** on the body's cells. For a hormone to be effective, there must be functioning receptors for the hormone. Much is now known about androgen receptors (Quigley et al., 1995), and it is clear that normal androgen receptors are necessary for complete masculine development. We will return to this later in the chapter.

Disorders of Sex Development

Given the many steps involved in sexual differentiation—from sex chromosomes to genes, to gonads and hormones, to genital ducts and external genitalia—it is not surprising that sometimes the process does not go completely as it should. Such errors are called disorders of sex development (DSDs, formerly called **intersex** conditions) and include alterations in sex chromosome complement, gonads, or anatomy. Some of these disorders represent a true mismatch among the levels of sex listed in Table 3.1, that is, one level is male-typical and the other is female-typical. Other disorders are not so much a mismatch among levels of sex as they are incomplete development at one level. Some DSDs are not readily apparent and are discovered when a teenage girl fails to menstruate or when an adult male is found to be infertile as part of a medical work-up to find out why he and his partner cannot conceive a child. Others disorders are apparent when a child is born with **ambiguous genitalia**, that is, external genitalia that do not look like those of a typical girl or a typical boy.

These disorders certainly have implications for the person affected, and they also provide us with important scientific and clinical information. For example, the discovery of the *SRY* gene came about through studies of people who had two X chromosomes but who looked like normal men, because through an error during cell division, *SRY* was added to one of the X chromosomes. From a scientific perspective, people with DSDs represent natural variations of factors that we could never manipulate intentionally because of ethical and practical reasons, and are therefore called **experiments of nature**.

We will talk more about DSDs in chapter 6 when we show how an understanding of gender development has been advanced by studies of individuals with these conditions, a field pioneered in the 1950s by John Money and his colleagues (Money & Ehrhardt, 1972; Money, Hampson, & Hampson, 1957; Zucker, 1999). To give you a taste of what is to come, we describe some DSDs here and ask you to think about what they mean for understanding gender development and in relation to the question we posed at the beginning of the chapter: What makes someone male or female? As you will see, genes on the sex chromosomes and sex hormones are hypothesized to affect behavior, and in chapter 6 we will present the evidence to support that hypothesis.

Nomenclature to Describe DSDs

There has been controversy about the terms used to describe DSDs, with particular concern that traditional terminology has been based less on medical and scientific knowledge than on old-fashioned attitudes and prejudices (such as paternalism and stigma) (Hughes et al., 2006). Current classification is based on objective description of the condition, including etiology (cause) if it is known. Some children are known to have DSDs on the basis of clinical features such as ambiguous genitalia, but a specific cause for the disorder cannot always be ascertained with current knowledge.

The current system classifies DSDs into three general categories: (a) sex chromosome DSDs; (b) 46,XY DSDs, including disorders of gonadal (testicular) development, disorders in androgen synthesis or action, and others (primarily defects in the development of the penis); and (c) 46,XX DSDs, including disorders of gonadal (ovarian) development, disorders of androgen excess, and others (primarily defects in the development of the reproductive system). Although the system makes use of karyotype for classification, emphasis is on description of the condition rather than on the chromosomes. This is particularly important when there is a mismatch between sex chromosome complement and physical appearance, such as a child with a Y chromosome who looks like and is reared as a girl, as described below.

Sex Chromosome DSDs

Disorders of chromosomal sex occur when the zygote does not have two sex chromosomes, but rather has only one X (and no other sex chromosome) or more than one X and one Y (such as XXY, XYY). (Notice that there is no disorder with one Y chromosome and no X chromosome, because the Y chromosome alone is not enough for life.) These **aneuploid** conditions (abnormal number of chromosomes) result from an error in the formation of egg or sperm, or from an error when cells divide in the zygote itself, so that the zygote has cells that are either missing a sex chromosome or contain extra ones. Abnormalities of sex chromosomes are less likely to result in spontaneous abortions (miscarriages) than are abnormalities of the autosomes, probably because the sex chromosomes carry less genetic information than the autosomes and because X-inactivation works on multiple X chromosomes (and therefore an unusual number of them has fewer harmful consequences). Therefore, the incidence of sex chromosome abnormalities is not trivial—approximately 1 in 500 live births. The most common abnormalities of the sex chromosomes include XO (**Turner syndrome**), XXY (**Klinefelter syndrome**), XXX, and XYY.

Turner syndrome

Turner syndrome (TS) results from an absence of or abnormality in one X chromosome (for reviews and additional information, see Davenport & Calikoglu, 2004; Grumbach et al., 2003; Kesler, 2007; Migeon, Berkovitz, & Brown, 1994). It occurs in approximately 1 in 1,900 female live births. TS is characterized by several abnormalities in physical development, including short stature (for which individuals often receive growth hormone treatment), webbing of the neck, cardiac problems, and failure of gonadal development and subsequent hormone deficiency (see below). Some females with TS have only one X chromosome in all of their cells (45,X karyotype), some have one X chromosome in some cells and two X chromosomes in other cells (this is called a **mosaic karyotype** because it is composed of two different types of cell lines, each with a different karyotype, and this is denoted as 45,X/46,XX), and still others have both X chromosomes, but one of them is abnormal. These variations in karyotype are associated with variations in the clinical features noted above, with the most severe condition associated with complete absence of the second X chromosome.

Although, as discussed above, individuals with two X chromosomes usually have one X chromosome inactivated, this process does not take place immediately after conception, and individuals with TS make it clear that both X chromosomes are necessary for completely normal development. Because a Y chromosome is necessary for male-typical development, and individuals with TS do not have a Y chromosome, they are female—they do not have testes, and the absence of testosterone causes the external genitalia to develop in a female-typical fashion, including clitoris, labia, and separate urethral and vaginal openings. Individuals with TS have **gonadal dysgenesis**, meaning they do not have normal gonadal development. Some individuals with TS develop ovaries that degenerate during fetal life. Because of the abnormal gonads, individuals with TS cannot produce hormones such as estrogen. In the overwhelming majority of TS patients, estrogen production is very low or absent, and life-long estrogen replacement therapy is initiated in adolescence to stimulate growth and secondary sexual characteristics (such as breasts) and to maintain bone health.

TS represents an opportunity to examine whether any of several factors involved in physical aspects of sexual differentiation are also involved in psychological sexual differentiation. Thus, psychological studies of TS (to be discussed in chapter 6) consider the effects of a missing or abnormal X chromosome, of reduced ovarian hormones early in development, and of increasing estrogens with treatment at puberty.

Klinefelter syndrome

Klinefelter syndrome (KS) results from an extra X chromosome in a karyotypic male, so the karyotype is 47,XXY (for reviews and additional information see Bojesen & Gravholt, 2007; Grumbach et al., 2003). It is the most common chromosomal disorder in males, occurring in approximately 1 in 500–1,000 male live births. Males with KS have decreased testicular volume, low sperm count, low testosterone, and other signs of **undervirilization**, or reduced physical masculinization). They are tall and have long limbs. An interesting question is whether there is also reduced psychological masculinization, an issue to be explored in chapter 6.

46,XX DSD

This category of DSDs concerns individuals who are born with a normal karyotype, including two X chromosomes, but whose physical appearance is masculinized (virilized) in some respects. These conditions can arise in several ways. In some cases, the fetus itself produces masculinizing hormones, usually because of a genetic disorder. In other cases, the fetus is exposed to masculinizing hormones from the mother; this might occur because the mother took medications with masculinizing effects, or because the mother developed a tumor that produced high levels of these hormones. We focus on the most common type of 46,XX DSD.

Congenital adrenal hyperplasia

Congenital adrenal hyperplasia (CAH) is a condition in which the amounts of sex hormones that are produced are not typical for female fetuses (for reviews and additional information, see Grumbach et al., 2003; Speiser, 2001b). In particular, females with CAH produce high amounts of androgen beginning early in gestation. CAH is one of the most common causes of ambiguous genitalia, occurring in approximately 1 in 10,000–15,000 live births. It is inherited in a recessive fashion, and the defect is in a gene called *CYP21*. *CYP21* is on chromosome 6 and encodes an enzyme normally present in the adrenal gland called **21-hydroxylase (21-OH)**. Individuals with CAH due to 21-OH deficiency are unable to produce enough **cortisol** to suppress the release of adrenocorticotropic hormone (ACTH). This results in an accumulation of products that normally become cortisol, which in turn results in increased production of androgen from the adrenal gland. This excess androgen has many of the same effects as testosterone produced by the testes in males.

CAH occurs in males and females with equal frequency (consistent with the fact that it is inherited in an autosomal fashion), but the major effects of having higher-than-normal levels of androgen are for individuals with two X chromosomes. Remember that external genitals of males and females start from the same structures, and that they develop in a masculine direction in the presence of high levels of testosterone. In females with CAH, the excess androgen from their own adrenal glands acts like testosterone from the testes of males, causing the genitals to become virilized. The extent to which this happens varies, but it is common for a girl with CAH to have a large clitoris and to have her labia partially fused, beginning to look like scrotum. Of course, the scrotal sac is empty because there are no testes (because there is no Y chromosome and no *SRY*—and therefore ovaries will have developed). In extreme cases, girls with CAH may have external genitals that are similar to those of boys, with a clitoris that is so large that it resembles a penis, and the separate urethral and vaginal openings are not present, but there is a single opening that has moved to the large phallic structure. (Surgery is usually performed in early childhood to make the genitals look like those of a typical girl.) But the internal reproductive structures of females with CAH are normal: they do not produce MIS (they have no testes) and apparently not enough androgen in the local area of the genital ducts to cause the Wolffian structures to develop, so the Müllerian ducts develop normally into a uterus and fallopian tubes, and, as a result of female-typical chromosomes and normal autosomal genes, they have ovaries.

The *CYP21* gene has been well studied (Speiser, 2001a; Wedell, Thilén, Ritzén, Stengler, & Luthman, 1994), with clear evidence for an association between the type of genetic defect (genotype) and clinical aspects of the disorder (phenotype). For example, girls for whom this gene is completely nonfunctional (and produce no 21-OH enzyme) have more virilized genitalia than do girls with genes that function poorly (and produce some enzyme). We will revisit the relation between genotype and phenotype in chapter 6 when we discuss behavior of girls with CAH.

Females with CAH provide an opportunity to look at ways in which behavior is affected by androgens and by rearing. Females with CAH are reared as girls, so, to the extent that behavior is influenced by social factors, they should be similar to females without CAH. However, they have higher-than-average levels of androgens during fetal development, so to the extent that the brain, and ultimately behavior, is influenced by the same hormones that affect the body, females with CAH should be masculinized in their behavior. We will discuss the evidence from females with CAH in chapter 6.

46,XY DSD

This category of DSDs concerns individuals who are born with a normal karyotype, including one X and one Y chromosome, but who do not develop a completely male-typical appearance, so are considered undermasculinized (undervirilized). These conditions can arise in several ways. In some cases, the fetus itself does not produce enough masculinizing hormones or is insensitive to the hormones that are produced, usually because of a genetic disorder. In other cases, the fetus is exposed to typical levels of hormones, but the genitalia are altered because of an anatomical defect or accident. We describe several types of 46,XY DSD.

Androgen insensitivity syndrome
Androgen insensitivity syndrome (AIS) represents a case in which hormone levels are fine, but there is a problem with a hormone receptor, specifically the receptor for androgen (for reviews and additional information, see Grumbach et al., 2003; Hughes & Deeb, 2006). The defect is inherited in an X-linked recessive fashion, which means that only individuals with a 46,XY karyotype are affected; the gene is rare, so it is extremely unlikely that there would be females who would inherit both recessive genes. The gene for the androgen receptor has been well studied (McPhaul, 2002; Quigley et al., 1995), and it is clear that mutations in the gene cause a range of abnormalities of male sexual development. In the most extreme case—called **complete androgen insensitivity syndrome** (CAIS, formerly called testicular feminization)—individuals are completely unable to respond to androgen that is produced by the body. CAIS is rare, and there are not good data on its incidence, with estimates ranging from 1 in 20,000 to 1 in 99,000 individuals with 46,XY karyotype.

The development of individuals with CAIS can be predicted from what we know about the process of sexual differentiation. They have a Y chromosome, the *SRY* gene, and therefore normal testes producing normal amounts of testosterone throughout development, including prenatally. But the body does not respond to that testosterone. Because the development of the penis and scrotum depends on the response of the tissues to high levels of androgen, individuals with CAIS—who are unable to respond to androgen, no matter how high the level—will develop female external genitalia (the default) even with a Y chromosome and testes. Their internal reproductive structures are also affected. The testes of individuals with CAIS work normally to produce both testosterone and MIS. They have enough MIS to cause the Müllerian ducts to degenerate, but their insensitivity to testosterone prevents the development of the Wolffian ducts (just as if the testes were absent). This means that individuals with CAIS do not have either female-typical or male-typical internal reproductive structures. In many ways, individuals with CAIS are extremely feminine in appearance, because they have very little body hair, and because the androgens they have are converted to estrogens, which promote breast development at puberty.

Individuals with CAIS provide an opportunity to examine the ways in which psychological characteristics are affected directly by the Y chromosome. Gender development would be expected, in most respects, to be female-typical in individuals with AIS, because their tissues do not respond to androgen and because they look like and are reared as girls. But, because they have a Y chromosome, any genes on that chromosome that directly affect psychological development would cause females with AIS to be masculinized in their behavior. We will look at the evidence on this issue in chapter 6.

We have described the extreme condition in which the androgen receptor is not functioning at all (which is why it is called Complete Androgen Insensitivity), but there is a spectrum of androgen insensitivity, caused by mutations in the androgen receptor gene, that make the androgen receptor function less well than it should. This is called **partial androgen insensitivity syndrome** (PAIS). As you might imagine, people with PAIS have varying degrees of undervirilization, ranging from relatively mild (such as low fertility) to moderate (such as very small penis causing them to be considered to have ambiguous genitalia). It is reasonable to speculate that these people might also be less masculine in their behavior, and we will mention this again in chapter 6.

5-α-reductase deficiency

Earlier in the chapter, we mentioned that DHT is the specific hormone responsible for the masculinization of the external genitalia, and that it is produced from testosterone by the action of the enzyme 5-α-reductase. It turns out that some individuals have defects in that enzyme, a condition that is called **5-α-reductase deficiency** (5αRD) (for reviews and additional information, see Grumbach et al., 2003; Imperato-McGinley & Zhu, 2002). This means that they cannot convert testosterone into DHT, so males with 5αRD do not have enough of the hormone they need to masculinize the external genitalia. You might then expect that, because their genitalia look like those of girls or are ambiguous, they might be reared as girls. And that, in fact, is what happens (at least some of the time). But the story gets a bit more complicated at puberty; these individuals begin to virilize because they are able to take advantage of the very high testosterone present to convert some to DHT (primarily using another enzyme) and because physical development at puberty is primarily mediated by testosterone itself. So, males with 5αRD develop a penis at puberty. They also develop other physical features usually affected by testosterone at puberty, such as a beard and male physique. You can imagine how disconcerting it would be to change from a girl into a boy at age 12. Although this condition is very rare, it happens to be common in some communities in the Dominican Republic, and the communities are now aware of it and are not surprised when some girls start to develop male characteristics. Because of the frequency of the condition in these communities, it is now common for children with ambiguous genitalia due to 5αRD to be reared as boys from the beginning. But this is not true in other communities (including the United States), in which the condition is rare and often undetected until puberty.

Individuals with 5αRD have a male-typical internal reproductive system—that is, Wolffian structures of epididymis, vas deferens, and seminal vesicles. Their testes produce normal male-typical MIS, which prevents the development of a uterus and fallopian tubes.

You may be wondering what happens to these children if they are reared as girls and then virilize at puberty, and that is exactly the question scientists have asked. If gender-related behavior is influenced by rearing, then these children should remain girls without much trouble—assuming that their testosterone production is stopped so they do not start to develop a masculine physical appearance, something that can be done by removing their testes. But, if gender-related behavior is affected by any kind of androgen other than DHT, then they should behave like boys. In chapter 6 we describe the evidence that helps us to decide between these alternatives. Interest in this condition is not just confined to scientists; the novel *Middlesex* is about an individual with 5αRD whose feelings are quoted at the beginning of the chapter (Eugenides, 2002).

Idiopathic Hypogonadotropic Hypogonadism

The condition called **Idiopathic Hypogonadotropic Hypogonadism** (IHH) is caused by a deficiency in **gonadotropin-releasing hormone** (GnRH) from the **hypothalamus** (for reviews and additional information, see Grumbach et al., 2003; Layman, 2007). (The term "idiopathic" means that the cause of the condition is unknown.) Because GnRH stimulates production of sex hormones by the gonads, males with IHH are undervirilized. They have small testes, reduced fertility, and incomplete or partial pubertal maturation. Most boys with IHH are diagnosed when they fail to develop at puberty. It is unclear exactly when the defect begins to manifest, but it is assumed that sex hormones are low early in development. This suggests that males with IHH might be exposed to lower than average testosterone during sensitive periods of brain development and thus are behaviorally demasculinized, a topic we consider again in chapter 6.

Micropenis

Sometimes a child with a Y chromosome is born with a penis that is normally formed but very small (for additional information, see Grumbach et al., 2003). It is generally caused by a hormonal problem (often originating in the hypothalamus or the pituitary gland in the brain) that occurs after the first trimester of fetal development. The penis is formed early in development, but then fails to grow normally. Normally, the length of a newborn boy's penis is 2.8–4.2 cm (about 1.1–1.7 in.). The penis is measured by carefully stretching it and measuring from the tip of the penis to its base. When the penis is shorter than 1.9 cm (3/4 in.), it is considered **micropenis**; this is more than 2.5 standard deviations below the average. In the past, boys with micropenis were reassigned to be girls for the following reasons (Meyer-Bahlburg, 1998; Money, Hampson, & Hampson, 1955; Zucker, 1999). It was assumed that boys with micropenis would have a difficult life: They would be subject to teasing by other children, they would not be able to urinate in a standing position, and they would not be able to have satisfactory sexual relations with women. It was also assumed that they would do well as girls, because everyone was considered to be "psychosexually neutral" at birth and able to identify as male or female if reared that way. We now know that the outcome for boys with micropenis is quite fine with male rearing (e.g., Mazur, 2005), as described in chapter 6, and that gender identity is more complicated than sex of rearing, as discussed below and in chapter 6.

Boys without a penis

Although it is unusual, it sometimes happens that a boy is lacking a penis. Early in this chapter, we said that some people might use the presence of a penis as the main criterion to decide that someone is a boy, but by now it is clear that there are many other aspects of physical development that determine "maleness." So, a boy without a penis represents a case in which the external genitalia are different from all other aspects of male physical development, including chromosomes, genes, gonads, and hormones. There are two primary situations in which a boy might lack a penis. The first results from a very rare congenital defect called **cloacal exstrophy**, in which the bladder and external genitalia are not properly formed. Although it occurs in both sexes, the effect is most pronounced in males, because an affected boy is born without a penis but has otherwise completely normal male-typical physical development; that is, Y chromosome, *SRY* gene, testes that produce androgens and MIS, tissues that respond to both substances, and therefore Wolffian ducts and epididymis, vas deferens, and seminal vesicles. The disorder is usually detected at birth. The second situation in which a boy might lack a penis results from an accident after birth, such as a mishandled circumcision. This is called **ablatio penis**. So, are these children boys or girls? Should they be reared as boys or girls? These children have become the focus of heated discussion and controversy over the past few years, and a questioning—or at least a re-examination—of standard medical practice.

The family of a boy without a penis and health professionals treating him are confronted with a difficult decision. Should the child continue to be reared as a boy, but without a normal-looking penis? (Although some surgical correction could be done, the penis would never look or function as a normal penis.) Or should the child be reared as a girl, with surgery done to make a vagina so her genitals would look like those of a normal girl?

Until recently, the decision was influenced by scientific and medical ideas formulated in the 1950s, which consisted of two important principles (and some evidence, but mostly from clinical cases and not as systematic as would be expected now) (Money & Ehrhardt, 1972; Money et al., 1957; Zucker, 1999). First, gender identity was believed to be determined exclusively by the rearing environment. This means that children reared as boys would identify as boys, and children reared as girls would identify as girls, regardless of chromosomes, genes, gonads, genitalia, or hormones. Second, gender identity was considered to be established by age 2, so it was deemed inappropriate to make changes to a child's sex assignment after that age. Third, the development of satisfactory gender identity and overall psychological adjustment was assumed to depend on a match between genital appearance and **social sex** (the sex to which the child was assigned and in which the child was reared). This means that a boy without a penis was considered to be in danger of psychological problems. For example, the argument went, other boys in the locker room would tease the child and ostracize him, and the child would be distressed if he could not urinate standing up.

Therefore, for most boys with cloacal exstrophy and boys with accidental loss of the penis before age 2, the child's social sex was changed, and the child was reared as a girl. However, this treatment has come under serious scrutiny in the past few years primarily on the basis of scientific and popular reports about one child born a boy but raised as a girl (Colapinto, 2000; Diamond & Sigmundson, 1997). The child, like his twin brother, was reared unequivocally as a boy until his penis was accidentally damaged during a circumcision at age 7 months. Following the accepted treatment at the time, the family was counseled to reassign the child as a girl. After much consideration and discussion, the reassignment was made in the child's second year of life, although the final surgery to construct a vagina was not completed until the child was 21 months old. We will consider outcome in this case in chapter 6 when we examine the theories and evidence regarding biological influences on gender development.

Most DSDs that were described above are considered experiments of nature—they allow us to examine biological influences on gender development, because variations in biology allow separation of components of sex that usually go together. This last case represents the other side of the coin—an **experiment of nurture**—because it is a manipulation of the environment that results in a separation of components of sex. In chapter 6 we will return to these conditions and their importance for understanding gender development.

So, What Makes a Boy or Girl?

If you now go back to the question we asked at the beginning of the chapter, you may have a different answer than when you started the chapter. But, you are taking a course in psychology, so you may think that you still cannot answer the question because you do not yet have all the information you need. In fact, we hope that you are thinking that you need to defer your answer until you know more about how behavior and psychological characteristics are affected by chromosomes, genes, and hormones, which is the focus of chapter 6.

PUBERTY

We have just described the initial processes of sexual differentiation, ones that are key for determining how a child is reared. But the process of typical sex development is not complete until **puberty**, which is the term for the physical changes that enable the person to become a sexually mature adult (Marshall & Tanner,

1986). The term **adolescence** was formerly used to mean the same as puberty, but it is now more often used to refer to the psychological changes that accompany the biological changes that take place at puberty.

Overview of Puberty

Puberty involves the development of **secondary sex characteristics** (adult height, pubic hair, underarm hair, and adult genital status, which means full-grown testicles and a penis in boys, and breasts in girls), and the achievement of reproductive capacity (ovulation and menstrual cycling in girls and fully mature production of sperm, known as spermatogenesis, in boys).

The control of the onset of puberty involves the **hypothalamic-pituitary-gonadal axis**. This refers to the fact that two regions of the brain, the hypothalamus and the pituitary gland, work together and exert effects on the gonads (testes and ovaries) and, in turn, receive feedback from the gonads. Puberty starts when the hypothalamus releases GnRH. GnRH acts on the pituitary to release two hormones (called **gonadotropins**) that jumpstart sexual development, **luteinizing hormone** (LH) and **follicle-stimulating hormone** (FSH), which in turn stimulate the gonads (ovaries and testes). Under these gonadotropins, the gonads get to work, producing sex steroid hormones and gametes. The sex hormones produce major physical changes, prepare the body for its reproductive role, and help it to maintain that role. As all of you who have experienced puberty know, it is not a single event that occurs all at once, but a series of events that occur gradually across several years. In general, there is an orderly progression of physical changes, with almost all children going through the changes in the same order, but at different ages, and with different speed. Boys start and end puberty later than do girls, with the physical changes usually happening in girls between the ages of 10 and 14 and in boys between the ages of 12 and 16.

Pubertal Processes

The Signs of Puberty

The first obvious sign of puberty in both sexes concerns changes to secondary sex characteristics. In girls, the breasts begin to develop (starting with **breast buds**, which are elevations of the breast and surrounding area) at the average age of 9.5–10 years, with most girls having fully developed breasts at age 14. In boys, the earliest physical evidence of puberty is an increase in the size of the testicles, with the average sometime before age 12. Subsequent changes in both sexes are in the growth of body hair, particularly in the pubic area and armpits, and the development of acne. In boys, puberty continues with growth in muscles, deepening of the voice, and development of facial hair. In girls, puberty includes first menstruation, or menstrual period. Contrary to most people's conceptions of puberty, first menstruation appears late in puberty (the average age is about 12), and is generally the last change to occur. Boys do not have a similar single event that can be easily used to indicate puberty, but the process is actually gradual in both boys and girls. Both boys and girls experience marked increases in body size during puberty, with girls experiencing their growth spurt earlier in the pubertal process than do boys; this will be discussed in more detail a bit later in the chapter. Estrogen is responsible for breast and reproductive development in females, and for bone growth in both sexes. Androgen is responsible for physical development in males, and for pubic and underarm hair in both sexes.

Components of Puberty

As you might have realized from the description above, puberty is really several processes. In girls, puberty involves both the development of breasts, which is called **thelarche**, and the onset of menstruation, which is called **menarche**. Both thelarche and menarche make up what is called **gonadarche**. In boys, gonadarche involves the development of the genitalia. Gonadarche is what most people think about what they think about puberty, and it is the process that begins at the ages indicated above and earlier in girls than in boys. In addition to gonadarche, both boys and girls experience **adrenarche**, which involves the production of androgens from the adrenal gland (and from the ovaries in girls), which, in turn, are responsible for the onset of sexual hair (what is called **pubarche**). Adrenarche starts several years earlier than gonadarche, and at similar ages for boys and girls.

Measuring Pubertal Development

The development of each feature of puberty—height spurt, pubic hair, girls' breast development, and boys' testicular and penile development—can be described by reference to standards called **Tanner stages**, named after John Tanner, a pediatrician who conducted many of the key studies that document the changes that occur during puberty (Tanner, 1978). Tanner 1 is prepubertal, that is, no detectable pubertal development, and Tanner 5 refers to complete adult levels of development. Figure 3.4 provides drawings of each Tanner stage.

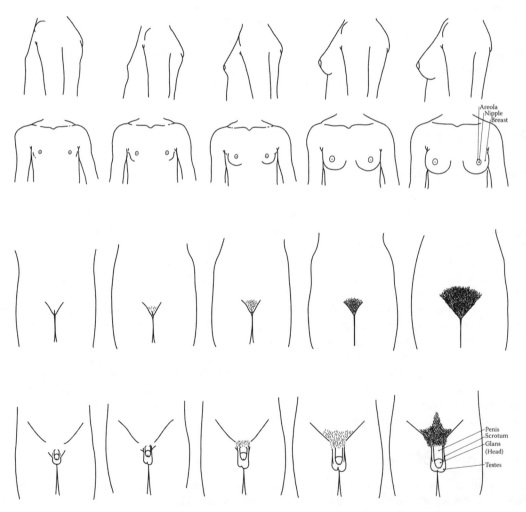

FIGURE 3.4   Schematic drawings of Tanner stages of pubertal development. (From Tanner, J.M., *Foetus into man*, Cambridge, MA: Harvard University Press, 1978.)

Tanner staging is considered the gold standard measure of pubertal development, both for scientific studies of pubertal development (including psychological studies, as discussed in chapter 6) and for clinical practice (pediatricians who track children's growth to make sure that it is proceeding normally). The most accurate determination of pubertal staging is based on a physical examination by a health professional with expertise in pubertal development. But, the most accurate measures are not always the easiest to obtain, so researchers sometimes rely on reports of Tanner stages made by teenagers themselves or by their parents (Brooks-Gunn, 1987; Dorn, Dahl, Woodward, & Biro, 2006). This might involve individuals comparing themselves (or parents comparing their children) to the pictures shown in Figure 3.4 or to verbal descriptions that correspond to the pictured stages. Although this is not as good as having physical development evaluated by health professionals, it is a reasonably good approximation, especially if the interest is in whether the teen is on-time, early, or late (rather than in nailing down a specific age for specific physical changes).

There are three points to note about using Tanner stages to mark pubertal development, and they reflect the fact that pubertal onset is not a single, abrupt event. First, a variety of physical features change at puberty, and not all at the same time. Which features should be measured depends, in part, on the question being asked. For example, if we want to know whether teenagers' pubertal development influences the way that they are treated by their teachers or friends, we would want to measure an aspect of puberty that is visible to other people, such as a growth spurt or breast development in girls. Second, these physical features reflect the actions of the main sex hormones, estrogen in girls and testosterone in boys, and it might seem easiest to measure the hormones directly. But hormones fluctuate in a lot of ways, especially in teenagers, so hormones can be imperfect measures. Third, the variations in the components of pubertal development, and the limitations of the different methods for measuring it, mean that there is not a single best way to measure it (Dorn et al., 2006).

Variations in Pubertal Development

Individual differences

Although the progression described above is typical, and most children go through these events in the same sequence, there are exceptions to this pattern; for example, about one third of girls have pubic hair before they have breast buds (Tanner, 1978). There is a lot of variation in the age at which children start puberty (what is called pubertal onset) and the pace at which puberty progresses (what is called the tempo or rate of puberty). There is much more known about variations in pubertal onset than in tempo, because it is easier to measure the first than the second. Measuring tempo means studying the whole course of puberty across several years of extensive—and impractical—assessments. If some children go through the different pubertal stages very quickly, then they would need to be examined every month or more often, but this is difficult and expensive, and what teenager wants a stranger examining her or his body so often? And, such repeated exams would be especially unpleasant—and unproductive—for adolescents who take a long time going through puberty, because they would not show any changes for several assessments in a row.

Even measuring pubertal onset is not as simple as it seems, as noted above. What part of puberty is of most interest? Most researchers study menarche, the age at which a girl has her first menstrual period, because this is a salient and easily marked event. But, menarche is fairly late in puberty and does not really indicate when puberty started. Furthermore, there is no parallel indicator of pubertal development for boys. Better indicators of pubertal onset might be development of specific features (e.g., breasts or testicles), but that requires a bit more subjective judgment. As we noted, such judgments are best made by health professionals who are trained and experienced in making the judgments, but it is not easy to incorporate such measures into a typical study; they are time-consuming to do and arouse objections from the schools in which much research is done, from parents who are reluctant to have unknown adults examine their children in the nude, and, of course, from teenagers themselves, many of whom are not yet comfortable with their developing bodies. This is why researchers often rely on adolescents' self-reports of their pubertal development.

Group differences

Added to the variations among people in pubertal timing are ethnic and racial differences and changes across time. African American girls enter puberty first, followed by Mexican-American girls, and then white girls (Wu, Mendola, & Buck, 2002). Puberty has been starting earlier over the past century. There is some indication that this change across time—what is termed a **secular trend**—is continuing but at a slower pace (Herman-Giddens et al., 1997), and some of the earlier onset might be due to obesity because, as noted below, fat plays a role in puberty (Kaplowitz, Slora, Wasserman, Pedlow, & Herman-Giddens, 2001), and to environmental pollutants, which can change people's hormones (and are thus called endocrine-disrupting chemicals) (Bourguignon, 2004).

Disorders of Pubertal Development

As noted above, there is considerable variation in the ages at which children start puberty and the rate at which they pass through the different stages. There are also more marked variations in pubertal development, which, in extreme cases, represent disorders that require medical treatment. Mild variants of normal development include premature thelarche (breast development) and adrenarche (mild androgen effects, such as pubic hair); these variants generally do not involve activation of the hypothalamic-pituitary-gonadal axis and therefore do not require any intervention. However, some children have very early or very late pubertal development, and in many of these cases, they receive medical treatment to delay or initiate their development. Both mild and extreme variations in pubertal timing are relevant for issues discussed throughout this book. Gender development at adolescence has been linked to the onset of puberty, both through direct effects of hormones on the brain and behavior, and through indirect effects of physical appearance and changing expectations on the teen's transactions with the social environment. This will be discussed in chapter 6.

Precocious puberty

Precocious puberty is a very early onset and rapid progression of puberty, reflecting physical changes and abnormal hormones at a younger age than is considered normal for pubertal onset (Lee & Kerrigan, 2004). It occurs about 10 times more often in girls than in boys. Children with precocious puberty are usually treated because there are adverse consequences of experiencing puberty at a very early age. These include accelerated growth but ultimate short stature (because growth is completed prematurely), early sexual and reproductive capacity, and potential for engaging in age-inappropriate behavior; the latter will be discussed in chapter 6. Treatment involves suppression of gonadotropic secretion with **gonadotropin-releasing hormone analog (or agonist**; GnRHa). In essence, this treatment stops puberty for the time being, until the child is considered the appropriate age to begin pubertal development. Precocious puberty is usually diagnosed in girls who have a rapid progression of puberty before age 8 (and in boys before age 9), but there is some controversy about whether the age of diagnosis should be earlier in girls, given the evidence for secular changes in puberty and the potential consequences of unchecked early puberty, and whether there should be different criteria for white and African American girls given the earlier development of the latter (Kaplowitz & Oberfield, 1999; Ritzén, 2003).

Delayed puberty

Delayed puberty refers to the situation when children fail to begin puberty well beyond the typical onset. Because of the earlier typical development in girls than in boys, delayed puberty can be diagnosed in girls at age 13 and in boys at age 14. Most of these adolescents have a simple delay of puberty (what is called "constitutional delay") and do eventually experience puberty and have complete sexual maturation (Achermann, 2004); some may receive sex hormone treatment to induce puberty because of psychological concerns about delayed development. But, some children may fail to undergo puberty at all for a variety of reasons, including genetic defects (including DSDs discussed above), tumors, and metabolic diseases. Some, but not all, of these conditions can also be treated medically.

What Causes Puberty and Its Variations?

Genetic initiators of puberty

Surprisingly, there is still a lot that is unknown about the factors that trigger the hypothalamic-pituitary-gonadal axis and initiate puberty. Where does the signal to the hypothalamus originate? Some recent work has implicated a gene called *GPR54* as a crucial signal for the beginning of puberty because children who have defects in the gene do not enter puberty normally (Seminara et al., 2003). *GPR54* was discovered through parallel studies in people and mice—the former from a family with a condition mentioned above, IHH, a rare inherited disease in which sexual development is incomplete or absent because not enough GnRH is released from the hypothalamus, and the latter from mice that were experimentally engineered to lack the gene and failed to develop sexually. There is a lot of exciting work associated with *GPR54*, but it is only one of many genes involved in pubertal onset.

Environmental initiators of puberty

A variety of signals from inside the body and from the external environment appear to be necessary for the onset of puberty, probably by ensuring that the appropriate genes are turned on (Bourguignon, 2004). Nutrition plays a key role in puberty, and there may be a link between fat mass or body size and the onset of puberty (so overweight girls start puberty earlier than normal weight girls). Illness, physical activity, and adverse physical and psychological events can depress the hypothalamic-pituitary-gonadal axis and disrupt puberty. For example, teenage girls who engage in intense sports activity and girls with anorexia have disruptions in their menstrual cycling, probably due to their low body fat.

Social factors likely also play a role in pubertal timing. This has been clearly demonstrated in other species. For example, in female rodents, puberty is accelerated in females housed with males, and delayed by rearing with other females; these effects are mediated by what are called **pheromones**, chemical signals emitted by one animal and causing a change in other animals (e.g., Vandenbergh, 1983). In girls, puberty has been related to a variety of aspects of the family environment, as described next.

Family factors in girls' pubertal onset

In the early 1990s, Belsky and his colleagues used an evolutionary approach to socialization to hypothesize that early experiences "set the stage" for a child's reproductive strategy. They proposed the following theory:

> A principal evolutionary function of early experience—the first 5–7 years of life—is to induce in the child an understanding of the availability and predictability of resources (broadly defined) in the environment, of the trustworthiness of others, and of the enduringness of close interpersonal relationships, all of which will affect how the developing person apportions reproductive effort. (Belsky, Steinberg, & Draper, 1991, p. 650)

The theory focuses on girls, because the mechanisms involved—an individual's trade-offs between physical growth and production of offspring—are more relevant to girls than to boys, and because pubertal timing can be more easily marked in girls than in boys (menarche has no corresponding measure in boys). Thus, girls who experience an adverse environment in early-to-middle childhood were hypothesized to have an earlier puberty than girls who experience a supportive environment. The theory has been the subject of considerable research for two primary reasons. First, the predicted association between early family environment and pubertal timing is uniquely derived from evolutionary perspectives on socialization and cannot fit into traditional socialization approaches (discussed in chapter 7). Second, because early puberty in girls increases risk for a variety of psychological problems (discussed in chapters 6 and 11), any factor that is shown to accelerate puberty might be a potential target of intervention to reduce psychological problems.

There is a considerable amount of evidence to confirm the hypotheses of Belsky and his colleagues. Early puberty in girls is associated with a variety of aspects of the child's early environment, including fathering (e.g., an absent father, a father who is not involved in his daughter's life), and parenting generally (e.g., poor parenting) (for details and reviews, see Belsky et al., 1991; Ellis, 2004). Nevertheless, it is important to note that these effects are not large, so it is not possible to make strong predictions for individual girls. This probably helps explain the fact that some females had an early menarche but a good supportive family, whereas others females had a late menarche but grew up without a father at home. It also explains the fact that findings are not entirely consistent across studies.

PHYSICAL SEX DIFFERENCES OF IMPORTANCE FOR GENDER DEVELOPMENT

Up to this point in the chapter, we have considered the basic processes of physical development in boys and girls, both early in development when the two sexes are formed, and at puberty when they reach sexual maturity. The factors that lead boys and girls down different physical paths also cause the sexes to differ in aspects of physical development. This includes differences in height and weight, bone and muscles, and in vulnerability to genetic and environmental hazards. It is to these differences that we now turn.

Physical Growth

Height

There are sex differences in height early in development, but the differences become dramatic during puberty. As shown in Figure 3.5, boys are slightly longer than girls at birth (19.68 vs. 19.41 in.) and continue to be slightly taller throughout childhood until the beginning of the **adolescent growth spurt**. In Figure 3.5, you can see the overlapping heights of American boys and girls of various ages. By the age of 5, the average height of boys is 42.99 in. tall, and the average height of girls is 42.52 in.; by 10, boys are 54.65 in., and girls are 54.41 in. (National Center for Health Statistics, 2000). It should be obvious that the sex differences are very small.

Weight

Sex differences in weight are similar to those in height. At birth, American boys weigh about 7 lb. 12 oz. on average, whereas girls weigh about 7 lb. 8 oz., again a very small difference. By age 5, boys weigh about 40.75 lb. on average, and girls weigh 39.73 lb. By age 10, girls weigh slightly more, an indication that their adolescent growth spurt is beginning (boys' weight = 70.74 lb.; girls' weight = 72.89 lb.). For a few years girls are slightly taller and heavier than boys, because, as noted above, they go through puberty about 2 years earlier on average (Marshall & Tanner, 1986). At age 13, girls average about 5 ft. 1.9 in. tall and weigh 101.4 lb., whereas boys average 5 ft. 1.6 in. tall and weigh about 101 lb. But, by adulthood, men are substantially taller and heavier than women (adult males = 5 ft. 9.1 in. and 180 lb. and adult females 5 ft. 3.7 inches and 152 lb., National Center for Health Statistics, 2001).

Adolescent Growth Spurt

As noted earlier, puberty includes an adolescent growth spurt, a period of time, generally lasting about 1–2 years, when the rate of growth of the skeleton, muscles, and internal organs speeds up dramatically, and then slows down again until final growth is reached. The average age of the beginning of this increased growth rate in Western countries is about 10.5 years of age for girls, and 12.5 years of age for boys (Marshall & Tanner, 1986). During the growth spurt, children of both sexes gain between 2.5 and 5 in. in height, although girls tend to gain somewhat less than boys do. These changes can be dramatic, and are sometimes known to wreak havoc with clothing budgets. When there is widespread poverty and

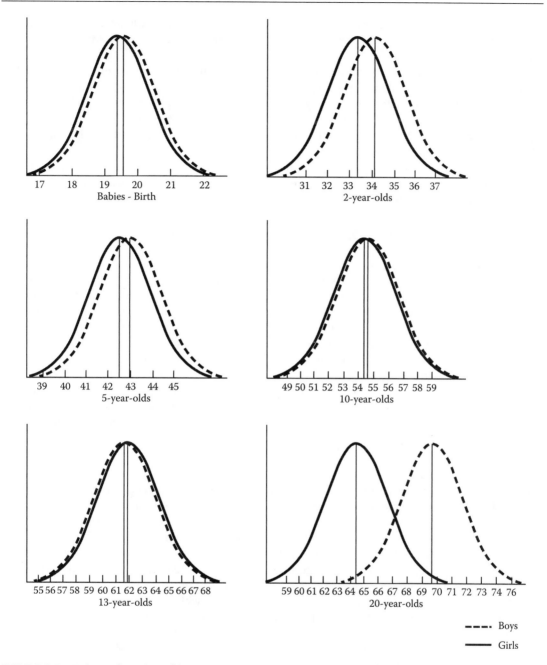

FIGURE 3.5 Estimated overlap of boys' and girls' heights at various ages (adapted from National Center for Health Statistics, 2000).

malnutrition, both boys and girls begin their pubertal period at later ages, and children's ultimate heights and weights are less (Eveleth & Tanner, 1990).

Because boys have 2 additional years of childhood growth rates by the time they begin the adolescent growth spurt, they usually begin the growth spurt at an already taller height, about 3.5 in. taller on average. A consequence of this increased period of childhood growth is that boys' legs are ultimately longer than girls' legs relative to the size of their trunks. There are pubertal differences in the growth rates of various parts of the body, with girls having relatively more growth in the hip area, and boys in the shoulders. But the longer forearms of boys relative to those of girls are due to differential growth rates during prenatal development and childhood, not during adolescence (Geary, 1998; Marshall & Tanner, 1986; Tanner, 1978).

Because girls reach puberty earlier than boys, their ultimate period of growth is shorter, and on average they reach the end of their growth period at a younger age than boys do. Typically, girls do not increase in height after the age of 16, but boys can continue to gain height up to the age of 19 or beyond (Overfield, 1985). It is not unknown for boys to continue to gain height while they are in college. The basketball player, David Robinson, grew 7 in. while he was at the Naval Academy during his college years (National Basketball Association, 2005).

It is sometimes claimed that girls develop faster than boys (e.g., Garai & Scheinfeld, 1968; Geary, 1998). Girls do reach puberty and physical maturity sooner than boys do, but it is not clear whether their faster developmental pace applies throughout childhood or to all areas of development (Tanner, 1978).

Components of Growth That Show Sex Differences

Finger length

A fascinating but quirky sex difference concerns fingers. Girls usually have a longer index finger on their right hands and a longer ring finger on the left, while boys have the opposite pattern (Tanner, 1978). Beginning sometime in childhood, there is a sex difference within each hand in the ratio of the index (second) finger to the ring (fourth) finger (what is called the **2D:4D ratio**). The ratio is lower in boys and men than in girls and women because boys and men typically have a longer ring (fourth) finger than index (second) finger, whereas girls and women tend to have both fingers about the same length, or have slightly longer index fingers (Manning, Stewart, Bundred, & Trivers, 2004). These differences are found in several different ethnic groups, with the ethnic differences sometimes larger than the sex differences (McIntyre, Cohn, & Ellison, 2006). The 2D:4D ratio has been considered to reflect prenatal androgen exposure, but the supporting evidence is thin (Cohen-Bendahan, van de Beek, & Berenbaum, 2005).

Otoacoustic emissions

There is also a sex difference in characteristics of the auditory system called **otoacoustic emissions** (OAEs). OAEs are sounds *produced* by the ear and are related to hearing sensitivity (McFadden & Mishra, 1993); they come from the cochlea and can be recorded with a miniature microphone inserted into the external ear canal (for review, see Kemp, 2002; Probst, Lonsbury-Martin, & Martin, 1991).

There are two types of OAEs. Spontaneous OAEs (SOAEs) represent sounds that are spontaneously and continuously produced by most normal-hearing ears. Click-evoked OAEs (CEOAEs) are sounds produced in response to a brief acoustic stimulus and vary in strength (amplitude). OAEs show sex differences across the life span (from infancy through adulthood), with females having more SOAEs and stronger CEOAEs than males (McFadden, 1998; McFadden & Pasanen, 1998). The differences are moderate-to-large in size; mean differences are about 0.6-1 standard deviation (Loehlin & McFadden, 2003), about 75-85% of females but only 45-65% of males have at least one SOAE (McFadden, 1998). OAEs have been hypothesized to reflect prenatal exposure to androgens, but the relevant evidence is not strong (Cohen-Bendahan et al., 2005).

Growth of the Bones and Muscles

Growth of the skeleton consists of increases in size and **ossification**, the maturing of cartilage into bone that takes place from prenatal development until adolescence. Bone development is typically measured by the degree to which the bones are ossified. Girls have more mature skeletal development early in life. By the middle of the prenatal period, female fetuses are 3 weeks ahead of male fetuses in bone development, by birth they are 4–6 weeks ahead, and they continue to show more mature bone development through the years of childhood (Tanner, 1978; Taranger et al., 1976). Girls eventually reach adult levels of bone development up to 2 years ahead of boys (Jimenez-Castellanos, Carmona, Catalina-Herrera, & Vinuales, 1996; Nguyen et al., 2001; Tanner, 1978). Therefore, in terms of rate of bone development, there is clear evidence that girls are ahead of boys. It is also the case that once developmental maturity is reached, the bones of women are not as dense as those of men (Overfield, 1985).

There is little evidence that girls are advanced in terms of the development of their muscle tissue, and, in fact, boys show the advantage here. Children acquire most of their muscle fibers during prenatal development and during the first 4 months after birth. Most muscular development, then, consists of an increase in size of the muscle fibers, not an increase in the number of fibers. The muscle fibers of boys and girls are very similar in size and number during infancy and early childhood (Malina, 1986), but by at least the age of 6 boys have somewhat more muscle tissue than girls do (Arfai et al., 2002; Wang et al., 1999). By puberty the difference is quite striking, especially in the upper body—the trunk and arms. For example, boys' arm muscles increase almost twice as much as girls' do over the adolescent years; their leg muscles increase only slightly more than girls'.

Related to the development of muscles is physical strength. Very small differences in strength, at least on some measures, are found even in the first 3 years of life (Jacklin, Maccoby, Doering, & King, 1984). For example, newborn boys can hold up their heads slightly longer than newborn girls can. Boys and girls both increase in muscle strength over the years of childhood, but after the age of 13, muscle strength increases much more in boys (Malina, 1986; Sartorio, Lafortuna, Pogliaghi, & Trecate, 2002), and the sex difference in upper body strength is most notable from that point into adulthood. This pattern of small differences in childhood, with a large increase during adolescence, can be seen for a measure of grip strength (which is considered to be the best indicator of overall strength, Sartorio et al., 2002) in Figure 3.6.

Although growth of the muscles is a basic aspect of physical development, it is also affected by practice, especially by resistance weight training (Malina, 1986). This kind of increase in muscle size can certainly take place in adulthood as well as in childhood, as those who take regular trips to the weight room at the gym hope. In fact, there is evidence that children are less able to produce the same kinds of muscle increases with weight training that adults can, and it is also the case that adult women cannot achieve the same degree of growth that men are able to.

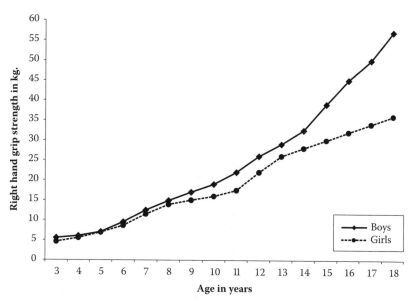

FIGURE 3.6   Grip strength as a function of age and sex (adapted from Malina, 1986).

Biological Vulnerability

For the most part, up to this point we have discussed growth under ideal conditions of health and nutrition, but conditions are not always ideal. During development, the growth and development of boys is more vulnerable than is that of girls to harm from environmental hazards such as disease, malnutrition, and exposure to harmful drugs (Overfield, 1985; Reinisch & Sanders, 1992). This vulnerability is first noticeable during prenatal development. The **primary sex ratio**, the number of males conceived relative to the number of females conceived, is difficult to determine, but all estimates agree that substantially more males than females are conceived—at least 120 males for every 100 females (Overfield, 1985). By birth the ratio is about 105 males for every 100 females born, a figure known as the **secondary sex ratio**. Clearly more males die prenatally. More males die in infancy and early childhood and adolescence as well, so that by around age 30 years in Western countries the sex ratio is equal. However, after that age, females begin to outnumber males, because more males continue to die at younger ages. There are many reasons for this phenomenon, most beyond the scope of this book because they involve the behavior and health of adults. In childhood, the two most relevant factors are biological vulnerability and risk taking, a topic we will return to in chapter 5.

With respect to biological vulnerability in the early years of development, not only are boys more likely than girls to die from the effects of malnutrition and diseases, their physical growth and development is more likely to suffer under this kind of physical stress. As we have seen, males are taller and stronger than females under ideal conditions, but under conditions of substantial malnutrition, female development is less harmed. For example, when children grow up without adequate nutrition, height is generally affected in all children, but the heights of males are affected more, such that when they reach adulthood, their heights are more similar to the heights of similarly malnourished females (Overfield, 1985). There are a number of other ways in which the greater biological vulnerability of males can be seen.

Sex Similarities in Physical Development

Because this is a book on gender development, we have focused on the ways in which male and female bodies are different, and the factors that produce those differences. But we would be remiss if we did not remind you of the many ways in which the bodies of the two sexes are similar. Barring genetic disease or accident, we all have two arms, two legs, and the same basic body plan, including a heart, a liver, two kidneys, and so on. Those body parts may function differently in the two sexes as we have noted, and in other ways. For example, women appear to have a more aggressive immune response than do men to infectious challenge, but are also more likely than men to develop autoimmune disease. Men and women experience heart attacks with different symptoms. Women appear to be more sensitive than men to the adverse effects of toxins in cigarettes (Wizemann & Pardue, 2001). But we should not lose sight of the many ways in which the sexes are similar to each other.

BRAIN UNDERPINNINGS OF SEX AND GENDER

We have talked about the many ways in which the bodies of boys and men are different from the bodies of girls and women, and the factors that create those differences. We now turn to the question of whether the brain differentiates in a parallel fashion to the body. Many cartoons—not to mention apparently credible books—would have us believe that the brains of girls and women are dramatically different from the brains of boys and men. But, from what we know so far, the brains of the two sexes are not strikingly different from each other. Perhaps this is not surprising in light of the fact that the bodies of the two sexes are also similar in many ways.

We divide our discussion of the brain into two sections. In this chapter, we provide basic information about the brain and suggest how our knowledge of the brain might help us to understand gender development. In chapter 6, we consider brain theories of gender development and the evidence that supports or refutes them.

A Primer on Brains

The brain is usually described in terms of terms of geography. The description that follows is necessarily simplified. Details related to behavior can be found in neuropsychology books (e.g., Banich, 2004).

Structure of the Brain and Implications for Function

The **cerebral cortex** (outer part) is the part of the brain primarily involved in higher-order thought. It is divided into two hemispheres (left and right) joined by the **corpus callosum** (a bundle of fibers that help to transmit information between the hemispheres), and each hemisphere consists of four lobes (**frontal lobe**, **temporal lobe**, **parietal lobe**, and **occipital lobe**). Each hemisphere is divided into the four lobes, so there are actually two of each type of lobe, that is, left frontal lobe, right frontal lobe, left temporal lobe, right temporal lobe, left parietal lobe, right parietal lobe, left occipital lobe, and right occipital lobe. The two hemispheres and the four lobes play relatively distinct roles, although the different brain areas work collaboratively to generate thought, emotion, and behavior. The left hemisphere plays a key role in language, sequencing, and analytical thought, whereas the right hemisphere has its major role in synthesis and in simultaneous processing (including spatial skills). The different functioning of the hemispheres is referred to as **hemispheric specialization** or **lateralization**.

The four lobes have relatively specialized functions: The occipital lobes are primarily involved in processing of visual information; the temporal lobes in processing of auditory information (including language) and memory (particularly the hippocampus in the temporal lobe); the parietal lobes in integrating sensory information and in visuospatial processing; and the frontal lobes in reasoning, judgment, planning, and regulation of emotion. The corresponding left and right lobes are specialized along the lines of the left and right hemispheres. For example, the left temporal lobe is primarily involved in processing language-related and sequential auditory information and verbal memory, whereas the right temporal lobe is primarily involved in processing spatial and simultaneous auditory information and nonverbal memory.

To get all the brain tissue enclosed inside the skull, the brain is folded. The raised parts are called **gyri** (singular, gyrus) and the grooves are called **sulci** (singular, sulcus) or fissures. The sulci serve as anatomical landmarks and divisions within the brain. For example, the **central sulcus** separates the frontal and parietal lobes. Specific gyri are considered to play important roles in cognitive function. For example, **Heschl's gyrus** in the temporal lobe plays a role in language processing. Although the same general pattern of gyri and sulci is found across all brains, there is variability across individuals.

The inner part of the brain is concerned with basic maintenance functions (such as control of body temperature and monitoring of hunger and thirst) and with emotion. Of particular interest in this inner part is the **limbic system**, which is key to perceiving, processing, and responding to emotional signals. A limbic structure that has received considerable attention for its role in emotion is the **amygdala**.

Brain tissue consists of **gray matter** and **white matter**, so called because they have different coloring. Gray matter consists of nerve cell bodies, dendrites, glia (cells that support and nourish the cells) and vasculature (blood supply). White matter consists of the myelin sheath that covers the axons of neurons, facilitating transmission of nerve impulses.

Methods for Studying Linkages Between Brain and Behavior

Much of our early knowledge about the different roles of different areas of the brain came from clinical studies of people who had brain damage that was restricted to one region or one side of the brain, or who had their corpus callosum cut in a last-ditch effort to control epileptic seizures that did not respond to any other treatment (so-called "split-brain" patients; Gazzaniga, 1967; Gazzaniga, 1970; Sperry, 1964). In the 1960s, it also became possible to study lateralization in normal individuals using clever experimental techniques that involved restricting stimulus presentation and processing to one hemisphere. These studies revealed **perceptual asymmetries**; that is, differences between the hemispheres in the ways in which they perceive and process language and spatial tasks (the left being better at the former and the right at the latter). These differences in the functions of the two halves of the brain are paralleled by differences in their anatomical structure. For example, there is a region called the **planum temporale** that is larger on the left side than on the right side. The planum temporale is a region of the temporal lobe that is involved in language, known because people with damage to that area of the brain (from a tumor or stroke) have language problems.

Knowledge about the neural substrates of behavior has exploded in the past decade or so with the advent of imaging technology—primarily **magnetic resonance imaging (MRI)**—that allows scientists to observe the brains of living people. Structural MRI allows observation of fine-grained details of brain anatomy, whereas **functional magnetic resonance imaging (fMRI)** provides a measure of the brain at work, showing how different parts of the brain are activated in response to specific tasks, such as looking at emotional pictures or solving a language problem.

Sex Differences in the Brain

A key question concerns sex differences in the anatomy and function of the brain, and the relation between brain sex differences and psychological sex differences. We will discuss this topic in chapter 6, but we point out now that it is not simple to make inferences about the causes of any associations between brain sex differences and psychological sex differences. Many people (including respected researchers) argue that psychological sex differences result from brain sex differences, but it is also possible that psychological sex differences cause brain sex differences. The brain is a flexible organ, changing in response to environmental input (that's how we learn, for example), so what we do changes what our brain looks like and how it works.

EVOLUTION: WHY SEX DIFFERENCES?

Thus far in this chapter, we have focused on the factors that lead an organism to become male or female, and some physical consequences of being male or female. Such immediate causes are called proximal because they are "close" in time to the characteristics of interest, in our case characteristics that differentiate boys and men from girls and women. **Proximal explanations** of sex differences involve factors such as genes, hormones, and brain structure; they also involve factors that will be discussed later in the book, such as socialization. An equally important and interesting question concerns the reason for sex differences in the first place; that is, why do members of our species come in two forms with different karyotypes and different sex hormones leading to different bodies? This question concerns distal factors; that is, factors that are removed in time from (do not immediately precede) the characteristic we are studying. Explanations involving distal factors are called **distal explanations**. In our case, distal explanations relate to the **evolution** of characteristics related to sex and gender; that is, to changes in these characteristics that are genetically transmitted across generations.

So, we shift now to asking about factors in our ancestral history that caused the sex differences, in essence asking what caused the two sexes to look and behave in somewhat different ways. To do that, we first discuss some basic principles of evolution.

Basics of Evolution

The fundamental principle of evolution is that species change across time as a result of genetic changes that are transmitted across generations. We provide a brief description of mechanisms of evolution as they relate to our understanding of sex and gender.

Natural Selection

There are differences across organisms (including human beings) in how long they survive and how well they reproduce. Some of these differences may be due to environmental circumstances, such as a natural disaster that wipes out a large community. Some of those differences reflect characteristics of organisms that are **heritable**; that is, transmitted through genes across generations. **Natural selection** refers to the variability (across members of a species) in survival and reproduction that depends on an organism's heritable characteristics; that is, on characteristics that are influenced by genes that are transmitted from parents to offspring. Note that selection does not occur directly on the genes, but on the manifestation of the genes, or the phenotype (the observable characteristics).

Consider the following example from the web site of the University of California Museum of Paleontology, Berkeley (University of California Museum of Paleontology, 2006). Imagine a population of beetles in which there is variation in the characteristic of color, with some beetles colored green and some colored brown. Because environmental resources are limited, not all individuals are able to reproduce to their full potential, so here, green beetles are more likely to be eaten by birds and less likely to survive to reproduce than are brown beetles. The surviving brown beetles have brown baby beetles because the characteristic of color is heritable. Beetles with the advantageous (brown) color characteristic have more offspring than beetles with the disadvantageous (green) coloring, and thus brown coloring becomes more common than green coloring in the population. If this process continues, eventually, all individuals in the population will be brown. So, evolution by natural selection operates if there is variation in the characteristic in the population, variation in reproduction, and a genetic basis to the characteristic. There is good evidence for the role of natural selection in the evolution of a variety of characteristics.

It is important to note that natural selection applies to psychological characteristics as well as physical ones. Many aspects of behavior are important for survival and reproduction, and many aspects of behavior are influenced by genes (Carey, 2003), so behavior is subject to natural selection. Among the behavioral characteristics that are subject to natural selection are mating rituals in birds and dances in bees (University of California Museum of Paleontology, 2006). It is clearly more difficult to document natural selection for psychological characteristics in human beings than in other species, but evolutionary psychology is an active scientific subdiscipline of psychology (e.g., Gaulin & McBurney, 2004).

Sexual Selection

A special case of natural selection is especially relevant to gender development. It is called **sexual selection** and involves characteristics that increase the likelihood that an organism will obtain a mate and reproduce. There are numerous examples of what animals do to obtain mates: peacocks maintain elaborate tails, fruit flies perform dances, and animals in some species deliver fancy gifts. Sexual selection is so important that it sometimes results in features that are actually harmful to the organism's survival. For example, extravagant and colorful tail feathers may attract predators as well as members of the opposite sex.

Whereas natural selection relates to characteristics that vary in a population without regard to sex, sexual selection concerns characteristics that show sex differences, particularly those directly related to increasing the likelihood of mating and reproducing. As in natural selection, any inherited characteristic that increases an individual's reproductive success will increase in frequency in subsequent generations. In sexual selection, these characteristics are specific to one sex and lead some members of that sex to reproduce more successfully than other members of that sex. Reproductive success is defined not just in terms of the number of offspring that are produced, but in the number that live to reproductive age and can reproduce themselves; this is called **fitness**.

Male and female animals (including human beings) have different roles in mating and reproduction, with females gestating and nurturing offspring. The nature and consequences of this difference have been well studied in nonhuman species and the principles applied to our own species. Females invest a lot of time and energy in reproduction, so they are choosy in selecting mates. This maximizes the likelihood that their offspring will have good genes and that there will be sufficient resources to rear the offspring until they themselves can reproduce. Males must compete with other males to be chosen by females, so they are more showy. Males have also have evolved other strategies to reflect the fact that they cannot be certain of paternity (that they are, in fact, the genetic father of offspring they help to rear). The situation with females being the choosy sex and males the showy sex is the most common across species, although the sex difference is reversed in some species.

Evolution and Gender Development

To recap, evolution means that heritable characteristics that facilitate reproduction and survival are likely to be passed on across generations and therefore to become more common. Evolution acts on both physical and behavioral characteristics. In light of the different reproductive tasks of females and males, it is easy to see how the sexes have evolved different genital anatomy, both internal reproductive structures and different external genitalia. An interesting question is whether human males and females have also evolved different behavioral strategies to facilitate their different reproductive tasks, and how those evolved behaviors might be relevant to the gender-related behaviors that are the focus of this book. We will return to this topic in chapter 6.

CHAPTER SUMMARY

The determination of sex—female or male—is a multistep process, from chromosomes (XX or XY) and genes (primarily absence or presence of *SRY*) through gonads (ovaries or testes) and hormones (primarily low or high levels of testosterone) to internal reproductive structures (uterus, fallopian tubes, and upper part of the vagina or epididymis, vas deferens, and seminal vesicles) and external genitalia (clitoris, labia, and lower part of the vagina or penis and scrotum), to sex assignment and sex of rearing, and finally to psychological and behavioral sex. The latter is the main topic of this book and, as you will see, is not just the endpoint of a series of genetic and hormonal processes, but the result of the interplay between those factors and environmental experiences. The process of typical sex development is not complete until puberty, which generally occurs during adolescence and involves the development of secondary sex characteristics and the achievement of reproductive capacity. The factors that lead boys and girls down different physical paths also cause the sexes to differ in aspects of physical development. Behavior is subserved by the brain, with different regions of the brain important for different psychological functions, and we are beginning to learn about the specific ways in which the brain influences gender development. The processes of sexual differentiation have evolved to facilitate reproduction and survival of our species. Biological theories of gender development are built on the notion that the same factors that account for physical sexual differentiation also account for psychological sexual differentiation. The specifics of these theories and the evidence to support them are the subject of chapter 6.

Motor Development and Cognition

4

It is about as meaningful to ask "Which is the smarter sex?" or "Which has the better brain?" as it does to ask "Which has the better genitals?" (Halpern, 1997, p. 1092)

In the current and next chapter, we present research findings demonstrating sex and gender differences in development and behavior, including what is now known about how boys and girls differ in motor skills, cognitive abilities, personality, social behaviors, interests, and psychopathology and adjustment. In these two chapters, we focus primarily on the differences themselves. For the most part, we wait until later chapters to discuss the theories and empirical research that attempt to understand the reasons for these differences. In the epilogue we will return briefly to the consideration of how biological, social, and cognitive forces work together in the gender developmental process.

All normal children develop motor, language, and cognitive skills, and most of these developmental accomplishments are similar for boys and girls. Children also differ from one another and many of these differences are not related to gender, nor do they violate gender stereotypes. For example, one of us was recently helping to look after several toddlers and preschoolers. One 3-year-old boy was diligently working with puzzles, carefully taking them apart and putting them back together. Later we read a story several times over. He didn't move from the area for more than half an hour. While he was sitting there, a 3-year-old girl was repeatedly jumping off the top of a slide to the floor quite rambunctiously, despite the fact she was wearing a dress and patent leather shoes. Are these children typical of boys and girls? Certainly they are, despite the fact that these two children (at least during this half hour) seemed to defy the generalization that boys are more active than girls. Gender has such power to influence the way we think about children's behavior that it is sometimes easy to overlook the fact that either boys or girls could demonstrate almost any behavior or characteristic, and that children of both sexes show a range of behavior.

Over the years, probably the most common approach to sex differences has been one that emphasizes them, a perspective that has been called the **alpha bias** (Hare-Mustin & Marecek, 1988). People taking this approach have generally contended that the natures of males and females are very different. (As an example, think back to chapter 2 where we discussed G. Stanley Hall's long lists of stereotypical differences between males and females.) In the past (although far less so today), people who maximized sex differences often argued that males had an inborn superiority. Because of that offensive history, it is not surprising that many researchers have ambivalent feelings about the study of sex differences (e.g., see Bem, 2000).

A common response has been to minimize sex differences, a perspective that has been called a **beta bias**. People who minimize differences argue that the differences are small, inconsistent, and artifactual (e.g., see Hyde, 2005). It is almost as though some people seem to feel that differences between males and females must be minimized to avoid judging males as superior. However, as we will see, not all sex differences are small or inconsistent. Furthermore, as others have noted (Kimball, 2001), even small effects may have practical significance (e.g., even if men are only slightly more likely to take risks while driving, the increased number of deaths is still important), and even large effects may not always matter (e.g., males' greater height and strength are not relevant to classroom performance, nor to many of the occupational roles in modern society).

WHAT IT MEANS TO SAY THERE IS A SEX OR GENDER DIFFERENCE

There are two common assumptions about sex differences, sometimes called "dangerous assumptions" (Caplan & Caplan, 1999). The first is assuming that a sex difference in some behavior means that all males behave one way and all females behave another, and the second is assuming that the finding of a difference between males and females implies that the difference is biologically based, and that a biological influence on a behavior means that the behavior is unchangeable (Eagly, 1995; Halpern et al., 2007). Both of these assumptions are very common and both are wrong.

When scientists measure or observe a behavioral sex difference, they most often report differences in terms of average scores of the males and females who took part in that particular study. One classic example of a clear sex difference concerns height. As you know, males are generally taller than females, although the difference is much more noticeable after puberty than it is in childhood. At birth, the average boy infant is about 19.7 in. long, whereas the average girl is 19.4 in., obviously not much of a difference (National Center for Health Statistics, 2001). The average height for adult men in the United States is 69.1 in. (about 5'9"), and the average height for women is 63.7 in. (about 5'4"), a much larger difference, but still there is overlap in the male and female distributions (National Center for Health Statistics, 2001). You undoubtedly know some women who are taller than the average man, and some men who are shorter than the average woman. We will return to the question of physical characteristics such as height shortly, but for now, our purpose is simply to point out that when one group, on average, scores higher on some measure than a second group, it does not mean that every individual member of the first group scores higher on the measure than does every given member of the second group.

As an example of how psychologists measure sex differences in the behavioral realm rather than the physical one, we can look at the data collected in a study conducted some years ago examining children's and young adults' interactions with a 1-year-old baby (Blakemore, 1981). There were 60 participants, equally divided into males and females in three age groups: preschoolers (4- and 5-year-olds), middle school children (fifth and sixth graders), and college students. Each participant was videotaped alone with the baby for about 7 minutes, during which time the participants could interact with the child in any way they chose (including not at all).

Twelve behaviors involved in interacting with the baby (e.g., touching, tickling, talking, singing, kissing, bouncing, and entertaining with a toy) were coded from the videotapes, and the frequencies of all behaviors were summed to produce a total interaction score. The total interaction scores ranged from 0 to 150. A person scoring over 100 would have been actively interacting with the baby throughout the entire period (because multiple behaviors could be scored simultaneously), whereas a person scoring 0 would never have interacted with the baby at all, instead spending the entire time sitting, playing with toys, or reading.

There was an overall difference in means between the sexes, with males averaging about 48 behaviors versus about 74 for females. This sex difference was found in each of the three age groups, although the older participants interacted more than the younger ones did. The average scores of the males and females in each of the age groups are shown in Figure 4.1.

For our present discussion, it is important to note that the results from this study not only illustrate the average difference between male and female participants; they also illustrate the overlap between them. Some of the girls and women interacted very little with the baby, and some of the boys and men interacted a great deal. The individual scores from these study participants can be found in Table 4.1.

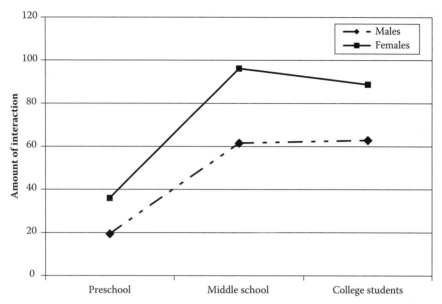

FIGURE 4.1   Interaction with a baby by males and females of different age groups. Data from Blakemore (1981).

Distributions, Central Tendencies, and Standard Deviations

At this point, we will review some basic statistical terms that we will be using in some detail through the rest of this chapter and chapter 5. Following this brief discussion, we will return to our discussion of the research on sex differences.

The term **distribution** refers to a set of scores on some measure, task, or characteristic. In the study we have just been discussing, the distribution of scores is shown Table 4.1. There are 60 scores, and they range from 0 to 150. Again we can see that the male and female distributions overlap, and that many of the scores are in the same range.

As you may remember from your statistics class there are three measures of the **central tendency** of a distribution: the **mean**, the **median**, and the **mode**. The mean, also called the **arithmetic mean**, is obtained by adding all the scores and dividing by the number of scores (i.e., the measure that we used above when stating the average score). The median is the score that is in the middle of the range of scores in the distribution, and the mode is the most common or frequent score. In the study we just described, the mean score, averaging over all participants, is 60.8, and the median is 69.5. The mode, on the other hand is 0, because 7 participants did nothing with the baby, and no other score was as common. If you look at Table 4.1, you will see that the mean, median, and mode are all higher in the case of females, and that this pattern exists separately for each age group as well. No matter how you measure it, in this study the females interacted more with the baby than the males did.

When many participants are measured on some trait or characteristic, the scores are commonly (although not always) **normally distributed**. In a normal distribution, most of the scores cluster around the mean, and the farther one gets away from the mean—either above or below it—the fewer scores there are. Normal distributions are also symmetrical, which means that there is roughly the same number of people scoring at various points above and below the mean. A good example of a normally distributed characteristic that shows a sex difference is height, as illustrated in Figure 3.6 in chapter 3, which shows heights by sex from birth through age 20 (National Center for Health Statistics, 2000). Both males' and females' heights are normally distributed. The two groups' heights are very similar in early childhood and show a high degree of overlap. Then, around puberty, the girls are a bit taller on the average than the boys.

TABLE 4.1   Scores Measuring Interaction With a Baby

	PRESCHOOL	MIDDLE SCHOOL	COLLEGE
Males	0	5	0
	0	17	0
	0	28	34
	0	37	47
	0	50	60
	1	68	73
	1	71	81
	52	74	87
	54	131	111
	86	134	136
Mean	19	62	63
Median	0.5	59	66.5
Mode	0	None	0
Females	0	13	38
	7	80	68
	10	83	77
	11	90	88
	18	91	89
	18	96	91
	30	106	101
	77	110	101
	83	142	114
	106	150	121
Mean	36	96	89
Median	18	93.5	90
Mode	18	None	101

Summary statistics
Mean: 60.78 (males: 47.93; females: 73.63; mean difference: 25.7)
Standard deviation: 44.86 (males: 44.16; females: 42.45)
Median: 69.5 (males: 48.5; females: 85.5)
Mode: 0 (males: 0; females: several duplicate scores from 18 to 106)

Source: From Blakemore, J.E.O., *Child Development*, *52*, 386–388, 1981.

By age 20, the men are much taller than the women, and the distributions no longer show much overlap. In adulthood there are relatively few men who are shorter than the average woman, and few women who are taller than the average man.

In all of the measures we have been looking at, there is **variability** in the distributions of the scores—not everyone scores the same. Variability refers to how much the scores are spread out or clustered together. For example, you could have two sets of scores with a mean of 100, and both could be symmetrical, but in one case the scores could vary from 80 to 120, and in the other case they could vary from 10 to 190. They both vary, but in the second case the variability is much greater. One common measure of variability is the **standard deviation**, which is based on the average difference between the individual scores and the mean. If the scores are more spread out, then many of the scores differ a great deal from the mean score, and the standard deviation will be larger. In a normal distribution, about 68% of the scores fall within 1 standard deviation above and below the mean, and about 95% of the scores fall between 2 standard deviations above and below the mean.

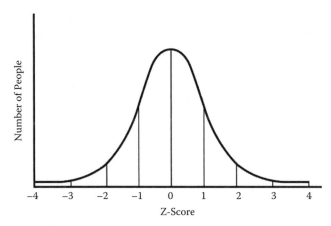

FIGURE 4.2   Standard normal distribution.

In chapter 2, we discussed historical hypotheses about sex differences in variability. The usual perspective of the time was that males were more variable. The implication is that, even when the average difference between the sexes is very small, there can be a large difference at the high or low end of the distribution when one sex is more variable than the other. In the example above, in which one set of scores ranges from 80 to 120 and the other set ranges from 10 to 190, it is obvious that there are more very low and very high scores in the second set. As we will see, this issue continues to be relevant today when comparing the performance of males and females on cognitive tasks.

It is also useful to understand the concept of a **standard normal distribution**. This is a distribution in which the scores have been transformed to have a mean of 0 and a standard deviation of 1. The scores that are used with this distribution are called **z-scores**, each unit of which refers to the number of standard deviations above or below the mean. A z score of 1 is 1 standard deviation above the mean, a z-score of −3 is 3 standard deviations below the mean, and so on. A standard normal distribution can be seen in Figure 4.2.

Another statistic that is important to understand as you are reading this book is Cohen's *d* **statistic** (Cohen, 1969). Essentially *d* is a measure of the standardized **effect size**, or a measure of how far group means are apart in standard deviation units. In research on sex and gender differences there is a common convention that the female mean is subtracted from the male mean. Thus, if male scores are higher, *d* is positive, and if female scores are higher, *d* is negative (Hyde, 1986, 1994). In the study we have been using as an example (see Table 4.1), the mean difference between males and females is 25.7 points (with the female score higher) and the average standard deviation is 43.31, so *d* is −0.59 (25.7 ÷ 43.31 = 0.59). In other words, the average female score is more than half a standard deviation greater than the average male score.

Finally, it is useful to know the conventions used for categorizing differences between groups as small, moderate, or large. One convention that is often used is that a *d* of 0.20 is small, a *d* of 0.50 is moderate, and a *d* of 0.80 is large (Cohen, 1969). There are several other ways that people use to estimate how large a difference is (Johnson & Eagly, 2000). One is called the CL, or **common language effect size index** (McGraw & Wong, 1992). The CL refers to the percent of time that a member of one of the groups would be expected to outscore a member of the other.

For example, the difference between the height of adult males and females is an example of a large difference. As you can see in Figure 3.6, they are about 2 standard deviations apart (*d* ≈ 2.00). This is so large that more than 90% of the time, if a male and female are paired at random, the male will be taller. If *d* were 0 (no difference), the male of the pair would be taller than the female of the pair 50% of the time, and the female would be taller than the male the other 50%. In the case of the convention discussed above, a small *d* (0.20) would translate into a CL of the male being the taller one about 55% of the time; for a moderate *d* (0.50), the male would be the taller one about 65% of the time.

Height is a physical difference, but as developmental psychologists we are primarily interested in differences in behavior. There are few behavioral gender differences that are anywhere near as large as the 2-standard-deviation difference in height between adult men and women. Behavioral differences are usually less than 1 standard deviation, and often less than half a standard deviation. However, as was pointed out above, even small effects may have practical significance, and when one group is more variable, the differences among the number of male or females among the very highest or lowest scorers can be quite large indeed.

Meta-Analysis

For most of the 20th century, psychologists summarized findings on sex differences by **narrative reviews**, in which they read and organized the research and tried to make sense of the pattern of the findings. Illustrative were the reviews of sex difference research by Maccoby and Jacklin (1974) discussed in chapter 2. Although narrative reviews are still being done, another important technique was developed in the late 1970s called **meta-analysis**. Meta-analytic reviews of research on sex differences began to appear in the 1980s and have continued in contemporary work (Hyde, 1986, 1994; Johnson & Eagly, 2000; Kimball, 2001).

Meta-analysis is a statistical technique that permits a researcher to combine the results of many studies quantitatively. To do a meta-analysis of the research on a sex or gender difference on a particular topic (e.g., verbal skills or aggression) the reviewer must first try to locate all studies that include data relevant to that topic. This process is not as easy as it might sound, because not all completed studies have been published, and importantly for examining sex differences, the published studies are likely to differ from those that were not. In particular, studies that do not find significant sex differences are less likely to be published than are studies that do find sex differences. Thus, using only published studies may tilt the direction of findings unfairly. In short, it is important to include as much well-designed research as possible because a meta-analysis is only as good as the research that goes into it.

After locating as many studies as possible, the reviewer then calculates an effect size for each study, usually d, and then calculates an average of all of the effect sizes. Next, the reviewer calculates whether all of the effect sizes are similar, or **homogeneous**. In most, if not all, of the meta-analyses of sex and gender differences, the data show that effect sizes are not homogenous. Instead they are **heterogeneous** (Kimball, 2001), which means that among the studies reviewed, some effect sizes were small and others large. Researchers then try to determine what factors might have led to the different effect sizes. Perhaps the studies varied with respect to what constructs or factors the tests were actually measuring, the context in which the data were collected (e.g., the laboratory vs. the natural environment), or in some other methodological detail. Perhaps, though, differences between boys and girls really are different across age periods (as in the example of changing patterns of sex differences in height described earlier). Researchers continue to divide the full set of studies into subsets that have similar effect sizes and then try to see what differentiates the groups of studies that produce large versus small effects.

To conclude, this has been a brief overview of some of the statistical and methodological issues affecting research on sex and gender differences. Throughout this chapter and the next we will discuss mean differences, standard deviations, effect sizes, narrative reviews, and meta-analyses as we discuss the findings of research on sex and gender differences in behavior.

MOTOR DEVELOPMENT AND MOTOR SKILLS

Motor skills are skills involving the movement of muscles. Gross motor skills consist of movements of the arms, legs, feet, or whole body (e.g., running or throwing). Fine motor skills involve small or fine-tuned movements, often involving the hands and fingers (e.g., cutting with scissors). As children go through the first years of infancy and the toddler period, motor skills are a very important part of their developmental progression. In the first year of life babies develop the ability to roll over, sit up, crawl, and walk. In the second year these skills become much more fine tuned, and by the age of 2 children can walk efficiently and do such fine motor tasks as open drawers and build towers three or four blocks high.

There are few, if any, sex differences in these early developmental accomplishments. Although boys are slightly heavier and taller, and—as we will see shortly—more active, boys and girls develop skills such as reaching, sitting, crawling, and walking at similar ages (Adolph, 1997; Adolph & Avolio, 2000; Adolph, Vereijken, & Denny, 1998; Bayley, 1965; Bertenthal & Clifton, 1998; Capute, Shapiro, Ross, & Wachtel, 1985; Mondschein, Adolph, & Tamis-LeMonda, 2000). There are no sex differences in the motor decisions that young children make (e.g., which body part to move to do a task), in their ability to undertake risky motor activities, or in the degree of risks they take in these physical arenas as infants and toddlers (Mondschein et al., 2000).

After the first year or two of development, sex differences begin to appear in the development of physical skills. Some tasks that depend on underlying neurological development but do not reflect muscular strength (e.g., eye-motor coordination) seem to be accomplished at somewhat younger ages by girls (Karapetsas & Vlachos, 1997; Pollatou, Karadimou, & Gerodimos, 2005; Thomas & French, 1985). There is also some research showing that girls accomplish toilet training at a slightly younger age on average than boys do (Martin, King, Maccoby, & Jacklin, 1984). A series of studies of neuromotor development, involving such tasks as repetitive finger movements, side-to-side jumping, walking on toes or heels, or maintaining balance were recently completed on more than 600 Swiss children between 5 and 18 years of age (Largo, Caflisch, Hug, Muggli, Molnar, & Molinari, 2001; Largo, Caflisch, Hug, Muggli, Molnar, Molinari et al., 2001). This research revealed very few small sex differences, with girls developing certain skills sooner, especially fine motor skills and upper body tasks. However, boys did better on skills requiring rapid movement, and there were no sex differences on several other tasks. Other research has also failed to find sex differences in fundamental movement skills during the elementary years (Arceneaux, Hill, Chamberlin, & Dean, 1997; Cleland & Gallahue, 1993; Crum & Eckert, 1985), and thus it is probably safe to conclude that any differences in these kinds of neuromotor skills are probably small and inconsistent.

Other kinds of motor skills are more clearly related to muscular strength, and on these tasks boys often do better. Thomas and French (1985) conducted a meta-analysis of studies of sex differences in children and adolescents' performance on 20 physical skills by children and adolescents between the ages of 3 and 20. They found that five of the tasks fit the pattern that we saw in Chapter 3 for grip strength (see Figure 3.7). This is a typical age-related pattern of sex differences in strength-dependent motor or physical tasks. Specifically, these tasks showed small differences in favor of boys in early childhood ($d = 0.25$ to 0.50), increasing differences through middle childhood ($d = 0.50$ to 1.00), and large differences in adolescence ($d = 1.00$ to 2.00). Another group of tasks showed essentially no difference in childhood, and moderate to large differences ($d = 0.50$ to 1.00) after puberty, again with boys having better performance. Boys were substantially better at catching a ball in both preschool and adolescence ($d = 0.75$), but only slightly better ($d = 0.25$) during elementary school. Some additional tasks showed sex differences that were not related to age. That is, either boys or girls were always better at these tasks, but the differences did not increase or decrease as they got older.

Throwing speed and throwing distance were found to have a still different pattern, with large sex differences even among preschoolers. For example, d for throwing distance was 1.5 by the age of 2 years, and was just as large for throwing speed by age 4. By adolescence, both throwing speed and distance were at least 3 standard deviations greater in boys. That means that by adolescence the distributions of boys' and girls' performance no longer overlap, so that the girl with the best throwing skills for girls is still likely to throw a ball a shorter distance at a slower speed than the boy who has the worst throwing skills of the boys. For example, some researchers have reported that college women throw a comparable distance to elementary school boys (e.g., see Butterfield & Loovis, 1993). It certainly brings meaning to the expression "throwing like a girl." The results of Thomas and French's meta-analysis are summarized in Table 4.2.

TABLE 4.2   Differences Between Boys' and Girls' Performance on Motor Tasks

TASK	APPROXIMATE EFFECT SIZE[a] (d)			
	PRESCHOOL	ELEMENTARY SCHOOL	ADOLESCENCE	OVERALL
Small differences in childhood increasing with age to moderate to large differences in adolescence				
Dash[b]	0.25–0.50	0.50–1.0	1.0–2.0	0.63
Grip strength	0.25–0.50	0.50–1.0	1.0–2.0	0.66
Long jump	0.25–0.50	0.50–1.0	1.0–2.0	0.54
Shuttle run[c]	0.25–0.50	0.50–1.0	1.0–2.0	0.32
Situps	0.25–0.50	0.50–1.0	1.0–2.0	0.64
No difference in childhood, with moderate to large differences by adolescence				
Balance	0.00	0.00	1.00	0.09
Pursuit-rotor tracking[d]	0.00	0.00	0.75	0.11
Tapping	0.00	0.00	0.50	0.13
Vertical jump	0.00	0.00	>1.00	0.18
Large effect sizes at all ages, but increasing with age				
Throwing a ball – distance	1.5		3.0	1.98
Throwing a ball – velocity	1.5		3.5	2.18
Sex differences not related to age				
Agility				0.21
Anticipation timing[e]				0.38
Fine eye-motor coordination[f]				−0.21
Flexibility				−0.29
Reaction time				0.18
Throwing accuracy				0.96
Wall volley				0.83
Other tasks				
Catching a ball	0.75	0.25	0.75	0.43
Arm hang[g]	0.00	0.00	0.00	0.00

Source: From Thomas, J.R. & French, K.E., *Psychological Bulletin, 98,* 1985, 260–282.

[a] Not all effect sizes were provided.

[b] A short run (e.g., the 50-yard or meter, or 100-yard or meter dash).

[c] A run in which the person runs back and forth between two lines 20 m apart in time to recorded beeps. It is sometimes called the "beep test," and is a measure of endurance or aerobic fitness.

[d] A task in which a person must track a small moving target with a stylus or a computer mouse.

[e] A task in which a child must anticipate when an event will take place and then respond appropriately. An example is watching a baseball pitch in anticipation of when to swing the bat.

[f] This was a set of tasks including hole punching, peg shifting, manual dexterity, turning a screw, etc.

[g] A task in which a child maintains flexed arms while holding on to and hanging on a bar, supporting themselves for as long as possible.

Research conducted since Thomas and French's (1985) meta-analysis has been consistent with this pattern of findings (Aponte, French, & Sherrill, 1990; Butterfield & Loovis, 1993, 1994; Loovis & Butterfield, 1993, 1995, 2000). For example, Butterfield and Loovis and their colleagues examined such skills as throwing, catching, kicking, skipping, and striking in elementary school children. They reported that boys' performance exceeded that of girls in most of these tasks, with some differences being large at all ages (e.g., throwing), whereas others were much smaller and significant only at some ages (e.g., kicking), and still others not different between boys and girls (e.g., skipping). In all cases, the development of these skills was related to participation in sports, although the amount of participation in sports did not completely account for the sex differences.

It is clear then, that there are sex differences in some motor and physical skills, and that both underlying physical development and the opportunity to practice are related to these differences. When skills may reflect underlying neurological maturity, or measure fine motor skill, girls may do slightly better. When the skills depend on substantial muscle strength, boys are likely to do better. Thomas and French (1985) concluded that many of the small differences between boys' and girls' skills in childhood (i.e., not the large ones such as throwing speed and distance), were more likely related to experience and gender role socialization than to differences in the physical capacities of boys and girls. Consistent with that view, one analysis of the possible impact of small differences in height and arm length in childhood on throwing, running, and balance concluded that the difference in the boys' and girls' sizes could not account for the difference in their performance of these skills (Clark & Phillips, 1987). Sex differences in tasks that depend on strength that are measured after adolescence are a different matter. After puberty, sex differences in many strength-dependent physical skills are clearly related to the inherent muscular and aerobic capacity of males relative to females.

The Impact of Practice

Although underlying physical development forms the basis for the development of physical and motor skills, it is important to understand that deliberate and extensive practice is critically important in the development of expert levels of performance in these areas (Ericsson & Charness, 1994). People do not develop high levels of performance in the physical arena without a great deal of effort and practice, generally accompanied by equivalently high levels of motivation to do so. For example, one of us recently read a newspaper article (Burlage, 2002) about a high school basketball player who had just made the record as the all-time greatest scorer in Indiana girls' basketball. She was on the way to possibly becoming the top scorer in either girls' or boys' basketball, quite an undertaking in a state where basketball comes close to being a cultural obsession. This young woman had been invited to an Olympic trial while still a high school sophomore. At the time, her soon-to-be college coach pointed out that someone just does not develop that degree of skill without hours and hours of practice. This is a very important factor to keep in mind as we consider sex differences in physical and athletic skills.

Self-Confidence in Physical Skills

Some research has examined gender differences in self-confidence in performing physical and athletic tasks, and this research has also been subjected to meta-analysis (Lirgg, 1991). Lirgg's meta-analysis reported that males were more confident in their ability to do physical tasks ($d = 0.40$), especially when the tasks were stereotypically masculine ($d = 0.65$), such as playing football. Her meta-analysis only reported on confidence in one feminine task, ballet, and females were more confident in that study ($d = -1.02$). However, males were also more confident than females on neutral tasks ($d = 0.50$), suggesting that the stereotyped nature of the tasks does not tell the whole story.

Masculine and Feminine Movement Styles

One final area of motor development is moving, sitting, or standing in a gendered fashion. This refers to styles of movement that are marked as masculine or feminine, such as crossing one's legs at the knees rather than the ankles while sitting, or walking with longer or shorter strides or with masculine or feminine motion of the shoulders or hips. Adults are certainly capable of distinguishing between men and women on the basis of such cues (Johnson & Tassinary, 2005). Children have been found to perform these gendered movement patterns more frequently the older they are, so that adolescents are much more likely to move and sit in a gendered fashion than are children in kindergarten or early elementary school (Hayes & et al., 1981). Such differences are first found in sitting styles, later in walking, and finally in standing. Also, if asked to change these motor patterns to those of the other sex, children are readily able to do so, although this ability also increases between the elementary and high school years.

ACTIVITY LEVEL

Activity level can be defined as a child's energy expenditure through movement, and it includes behaviors such as squirming, rolling away, climbing, fidgeting, or running. Activity level can be measured in three ways: by parents or others who know the child completing rating scales, by direct observations of activity levels made by trained observers, or by using a motion-sensing device known as an **actometer** or an **accelerometer**. Meta-analyses have also been performed on several studies of activity level in infants, children, and even on a handful of studies in fetuses (Campbell & Eaton, 1999; Eaton & Enns, 1986).

These meta-analyses have found consistent, but relatively small activity level differences in infants ($d = 0.20$), and larger differences during the preschool ($d = 0.44$) and elementary ($d = 0.64$) age groups, with boys being more active. The differences were more likely familiar, low-stress situations, and when peers were present. This difference was found with objective measures and observations, and interestingly, the effect sizes were actually somewhat smaller when measured by parents' observations. The research on fetuses ($d = 0.33$) did not have a large enough set of studies to produce a significant effect size, but the finding was in the same general direction, and later research has also found more activity in males prenatally (Almli, Ball, & Wheeler, 2001).

This pattern of data presents a picture of slightly higher activity levels in infant boys as compared to infant girls, with the difference being greater as children grow older, and in contexts of free play with peers (Campbell & Eaton, 1999; Eaton & Enns, 1986). Eaton and Yu (1989) also did research to determine whether sex differences in activity level during elementary school were related to girls' more rapid or mature development. They did find a relationship between maturity and activity level, but even when developmental maturity was accounted for, boys were still more active than girls. Research conducted since these meta-analyses using an accelerometer worn by children for 3 consecutive days found boys to be consistently more physically active than girls from the ages of 8–16 years (Santos, Guerra, Ribiero, Duarte, & Mota, 2003). The authors of this study were concerned about the implications of their findings for the physical fitness of girls, a topic to which we will return in the next chapter.

INTELLECTUAL AND COGNITIVE SKILLS

General Intelligence

When intelligence or IQ tests were originally constructed, they were intentionally designed to avoid producing any overall differences in male and female performance (Hyde & McKinley, 1997; Snow & Weinstock, 1990). Despite the difficulty in looking for sex differences using tests specifically designed not to have them, careful analyses of the issue have concluded that there is no difference in overall performance of intelligence tests between males and females (Flynn, 1998; Halpern & LaMay, 2000), nor is there a difference in the early development of intellectual skills (Bayley, 1965). Rather, there is a pattern

TABLE 4.3   Differences Between Boys and Girls in Cognitive Skills

TASK	APPROXIMATE EFFECT SIZE (d) WHEN AVAILABLE
Tasks girls and women perform better	
Detection of tones, odors, taste, touch	Small
Perceptual speed	−0.21 to −0.62
Memory	Small
Overall verbal skills	−0.11
Early language development	Small or not known
Speech production	−0.33
Reading comprehension	−0.002 to −0.30
Essay writing	−0.09 to −0.61
Dyslexia and stuttering	Large
Phonological processing	−0.50 to −1.00
Verbal fluency	−1.00 or larger
Mathematical computation	−0.14
Tasks boys and men perform better	
Visual acuity	Small
Analogies	0.22
Spatial perception	0.40
Mental rotations	0.40 to 1.00
Mathematical problem solving	0.08 to 0.29
SAT-M (mathematics)	0.40

Sources: From Arceneaux, J.M. et al., *Perceptual and Motor Skills, 83*, 1996, 1211–1215; Born, M.P. et al., *Journal of Cross-Cultural Psychology, 18*, 1987, 283–314; Halpern, D.F., *Sex differences in cognitive abilities* (3rd ed.). Mahwah, NJ: Erlbaum, 2000.

of difference such that boys are somewhat better at some tasks and skills (e.g., spatial tasks and mathematical problem solving), and girls are somewhat better at others (e.g., verbal fluency, writing ability, and perceptual speed; Arceneaux, Cheramie, & Smith, 1996; Born, Bleichrodt, & Van der Flier, 1987; Halpern, 2000). We will be discussing these differences below, but you can also find them summarized in Table 4.3.

Although there is no difference in ability in general intelligence, there does appear to be a difference in the speed of taking tests that measure it. One recent study (Camarata & Woodcock, 2006) examined the performance of more than 4,000 participants ranging in age from 2 to 90 years who took part in the standardization studies of the Woodcock-Johnson (W-J) series of cognitive and achievement batteries during the 1970s and 1980s. The W-J is a widely used measure of intelligence and general cognitive abilities. In addition to general intelligence, it measures seven other general abilities and skills (verbal ability, visual-spatial thinking, auditory processing, fluid reasoning, long-term retrieval, processing speed, and short-term memory), as well as subsets of each of those broader domains. It also contains measures of achievement in math, reading, and writing.

As expected, no difference in general intelligence was found. There were some small to moderate differences in some of the specific domains (males had higher scores on general academic knowledge and verbal skills, overall $d = 0.20$ and 0.13, respectively; and females had higher reading fluency and writing achievement scores, overall d values on the timed test of about $−0.33$ and $−0.44$, respectively). A very striking finding, however, was that females had faster processing speeds across almost all of the timed tests and at most ages, although the difference was especially noticeable during adolescence. The d values ranged from about $−0.20$ to about $−0.55$, the latter during the high school years. This report of females having faster speeds on standardized measures of intelligence and cognitive abilities has not been widely reported before now, and thus additional research will be needed before it will be possible to judge whether this finding is replicable.

Sensation and Perception

Some research has shown small sex differences in sensory and perceptual abilities and skills. There are no available meta-analyses of this research, but narrative summaries (Baker, 1987; Halpern, 2000) conclude that females are somewhat better at the detection of pure tones, odors, and tastes, and are more sensitive to touch, whereas males have better visual acuity. So far as we know, these differences are very small.

Another skill in the perceptual domain is called **perceptual speed** (Halpern, 2000; Hedges & Nowell, 1995). These kinds of skills involve being able to perceive details and shift attention quickly, although some measures involve fine motor skills as well. Females typically do better at these kinds of tasks in both childhood and adulthood, although Feingold (1988) concluded that more recent research demonstrates smaller differences ($d = -0.34$) than older research ($d = -0.62$).

Memory

At this point there are no meta-analyses of sex or gender differences in memory in children; however, narrative reviews have concluded that, on many measures, girls and women have somewhat better memories than boys and men do (Halpern, 2000; Hedges & Nowell, 1995; Kimura, 1999; Stumpf & Jackson, 1994). Girls and women have more accurate recall for tests involving the learning of facts or material that they read, they learn lists of words more readily, and they have better recall for lists of common objects like animals, food, furniture, and appliances. One study of children between the ages of 5 and 16 (Kramer, Delis, Kaplan, O'Donnell, & Prifitera, 1997) found girls of all ages to perform better on verbal memory tasks and to use better memory strategies such as clustering meaningful words together. Other research has shown that girls and women have better recognition memories (McGivern et al., 1997), better episodic memories (Davis, 1999; Herlitz, Nilsson, & Baeckman, 1997), better memories for the spatial location of objects (Eals & Silverman, 1994), and they recall the dates of events more accurately (Skowronski & Thompson, 1990). Girls' earliest recollections also occur at a slightly younger age (Mullen, 1994). The effect sizes in studies of memory have generally been small to moderate, on the order of -0.20 to -0.50.

Language Development and Verbal Skills

There are many different kinds of verbal and language-related skills. For example, consider vocabulary size, use of correct grammar, reading, doing anagrams, and following verbal instructions. These are clearly different skills. One of the most obvious places to start in an examination of the verbal domain is to look at early language development. Do girls or boys learn to talk earlier? Is the language use of young boys and girls different? Does one sex have more language-related problems such as stuttering or dyslexia?

Early Language Development

In a very comprehensive report on children's early language development (McCarthy, 1954), published over half a century ago, girls were reported to be slightly ahead of boys on a several measures of language development including age at first word, first combinations, average sentence length at various ages, and grammatical correctness. Two decades later Maccoby and Jacklin (1974) reported that girls learned to talk slightly earlier than boys did, but that these differences were very slight and often not statistically significant, and any differences had disappeared by the age of 3 years.

Some more recent studies have shown that girls to be slightly ahead of boys on some measures, especially vocabulary growth (Berglund, Eriksson, & Westerlund, 2005; Fenson et al., 1994; Galsworthy, Dionne, Dale, & Plomin, 2000; Morisset, Barnard, & Booth, 1995; Rome-Flanders & Cronk, 1995). For example, one study (Huttenlocher, Haight, Bryk, Seltzer, & Lyons, 1991) reported that, on average, girls knew 13 more words than boys at 16 months of age, 51 more words at 20 months, and 115 more words at 24 months. One very extensive study (Bornstein, Hahn, & Haynes, 2004) examined children between 1 and almost 7 years of age on several different measures of language development (e.g., maternal and teacher reports, standardized measures of language skill, analysis of transcripts of spontaneous speech). These investigators found girls to be consistently ahead of boys on almost all of these measures between the ages of 2 and 6, but not before or after. This suggests that girls' language development is advanced in early childhood, but that boys eventually catch up.

Verbal Skills

Meta-analyses of verbal skills (Feingold, 1988; Hyde & Linn, 1988; Hyde & McKinley, 1997) have examined several measures of verbal and language skills in children (mostly 4 and older), adolescents, and adults. When children who have language disorders are eliminated from study, the differences between boys and girls in several verbal skills generally favor females, but are often very small. The measures of effect size in Hyde and Linn's (1988) meta-analysis were as follows: $d = -0.11$ for overall verbal skills; -0.20 for general verbal ability tests; -0.02 for vocabulary; -0.03 for reading comprehension; -0.09 for essay writing; -0.33 for speech production; and 0.22 for analogies (note for this one measure, boys were better). There is disagreement among researchers as to whether differences of this size have any practical significance. Some conclude that they are so small that males and females have essentially identical verbal skills (Caplan & Caplan, 1999; Hyde & Linn, 1988; Hyde & McKinley, 1997), but others assert that the evidence continues to support a conclusion that there are better verbal and language skills among girls and women (Geary, 1998; Halpern, 2000; Kimura, 1999; Lippa, 2002).

One recent review of sex differences in several important cognitive skills in adolescents was neither a traditional narrative review nor a meta-analysis. Hedges and Nowell (1995) examined six very large studies that used nationally representative studies of high school students between 1960 and 1992. They looked at performance on several cognitive skills including reading, writing, memory, reasoning, perceptual speed, spatial skills, mathematics, social studies, science, and some vocational and mechanical skills. They calculated average differences (using the d statistic), as well as differences in variability between the sexes. Hedges and Nowell did, in fact, find greater variability among the males on most of the skills they measured, although the differences were generally very small, with males between 3 and 15% more variable. We will refer to the results of this study again when we consider spatial skills, mathematics, and science.

With respect to verbal skills, the results of Hedges and Nowell's analysis demonstrated that adolescent girls had better reading comprehension (d values from -0.002 to -0.30 depending on the sample), and notably better performance in writing (d values from -0.53 to -0.61). Given the importance of reading and writing to almost any kind of academic achievement, Hedges and Nowell expressed great concern about the number of males near the bottom of the distribution of both reading comprehension and writing skill. In fact, of all the academic skills that they examined, the sex difference in writing was the largest.

Sound Frequency: Pitch

After puberty the vocal chords lengthen so that adolescent and adult males speak at a lower frequency. However, males speak even lower than the physical structure of their vocal chords would naturally produce, and females speak higher, and these differences are larger in some cultures than others. More strikingly, pitch differences exist in children. That is, even though there are no differences in the structure of the vocal chords in childhood, boys speak with a lower pitch than girls do. This difference is probably related to children's unconscious matching of their voices with gender norms (Gleason & Ely, 2002).

Speech and Language Disorders

Girls have fewer speech disorders such as dyslexia and stuttering (Halpern, 2000; Hyde & McKinley, 1997). Stuttering is 3–4 times more frequent in boys, and **dyslexia**, a disturbance in the processing of the sounds of language leading to difficulties with reading in particular, is found 2–10 times more frequently in boys. The more serious dyslexia is, the more likely it is to be found in boys.

Verbal Fluency

At least in adulthood, women perform better than men on a variety of tasks involving processing the sounds of letters (Majeres, 1997, 1999), and are much better ($d > -1.00$) at tasks requiring them to generate a list of words that sound alike or that begin with a particular letter (Halpern, 1997; Kimura, 1999), a skill called **verbal fluency**.

Language Use

As a final consideration in language development, we would like to consider language use. Even preschool children are aware that males and females speak differently (Gleason & Ely, 2002). When they pretend to be a male puppet, a "daddy," or another male figure, children are more likely to use lower pitches, make more demands, and talk about stereotypically male topics such as those related to the world of work. When pretending to be female they are more likely to use polite requests, higher pitch, and more exaggerated intonations. They are even more likely to speak in a more demanding way to another child if that child is pretending to be "the mother," and more politely to the child pretending to be "the father."

Sometimes people think that girls and women talk more than boys and men, but in adulthood the evidence shows that, although some people are much more talkative than others, on average men and women use about the same number of words each day (Mehl, Vazire, Ramirez-Esparza, Slatcher, & Pennebaker, 2007). In childhood, one recent meta-analysis (Leaper & Smith, 2004) found that girls were very slightly more talkative in general ($d = -0.11$), but noticeably more talkative between the ages of 1 and 3 ($d = -0.32$), probably because of more advanced language development during this age period. This same meta-analysis reported that boys were very slightly more likely ($d = 0.11$) to use assertive speech such as being directive or critical, and that this held across the age groups. Finally, these authors found a small difference in affiliative speech ($d = -0.26$), with girls being somewhat more likely to do such things as express agreement or offer support to their conversational partners. This type of speech was also much affected by the children's age, with preschoolers ($d = -0.51$), 10- to 12-year-olds ($d = -0.36$) and 12- to 17-year-olds ($d = -0.26$) having greater differences than elementary-aged children.

Judgments About the Duration of Events

These skills relate to judgments about how long various events last. People may be asked to hold down a button for what they think is some length of time, say 60 seconds. Alternatively, they may be asked how long they think a certain event lasted. In some studies they are told in advance that they will have to make this judgment, and in other studies they are not. Judgments about the duration of events have relevance to cognitive processes such as attention and short-term memory.

Research in this area has also been subjected to meta-analysis (Block, Hancock, & Zakay, 2000), producing a small difference between males and females (d ranging from 0.06 to 0.27, depending on the particular analysis). Although the effect sizes were small, the meta-analysis also determined that females judge that events last about 10% longer than males do, and are more likely to overestimate how long the events actually last. For example, according to Block and his colleagues "females verbally estimate a 100-second duration as 110 seconds, but males estimate the duration as 98 seconds" (Block et al., 2000,

p. 1340). However, this effect is usually limited to situations in which they do not know in advance that they will have to make such a judgment. When they are told in advance that they will have to make a judgment, males and females perform similarly. Most of the research used adolescent or adult participants, and therefore little can be said about developmental changes in these kinds of skills.

Spatial Skills

You probably know instantly what we mean when we talk about "mathematical" or "verbal skills," probably in part because these are skills are directly taught and tested in school settings. You may be somewhat less familiar with the term "spatial skills." Even though schools do not typically teach and test spatial skills directly, they are probably just as central to educational, intellectual, and daily life. For example, spatial skills are needed to understand the maps used in history or geography lessons, or the three-dimensional models used in chemistry, as well as to find one's way around in the environment.

Spatial skill is generally defined as the ability to encode, generate, retrieve, or mentally manipulate visual images (like internal pictures) in some way. The kinds of items that are generally included in the spatial domain include mazes, paper-folding tasks, embedded figures, determination of vertical and horizontal, and imagining the rotation of objects in two or three dimensions (Newcombe, Mathason, & Terlecki, 2002). In everyday life, when one does something like imagining how to move or rotate suitcases to fit them into a car trunk, one is using spatial skills. However, spatial skills can be evident in nonvisual modalities as well. For example, spatial skills can be kinesthetic rather than visual, as when one is traveling through large environments and senses that they should have already reached the destination.

Three Research Traditions in the Study of Spatial Skills

Within developmental psychology, there have been three major research traditions in the study of spatial skills, and each has revealed interesting and persistent sex-related differences. We will describe each very briefly, and then amplify each in turn, offering examples of empirical research that has shown sex differences.

The first research tradition is rooted in the theoretical account of children's developing spatial concepts offered more than half a century ago by Jean Piaget and his collaborator, Barbel Inhelder (1956). Although their work was aimed at describing universal aspects of development rather than at studying individual or group differences, empirical research based on their work has revealed surprising and dramatic sex differences in performance that have continued to intrigue researchers.

The second is rooted in the psychometric testing movement (Eliot, 1987) that began in the early part of the 20th century. For the most part, this kind of testing was used to make decisions about educational or occupational pathways for individuals. For example, testing was used to decide which potential immigrants should be allowed to enter the United States, which children should be guided into vocational versus academic educational programs, who should be accepted into the armed services and in what capacity (e.g., for training as a pilot), and so on. As tests of this kind were given to more and more people, the large data sets that emerged led investigators to see different patterns of performance among various groups, including differences between males and females.

The third research tradition relevant to sex differences in spatial skills comes from another subfield of psychology—environmental psychology. This area is focused on understanding how people use and represent the large-scale environments in which they live and work (e.g., neighborhoods, cities, recreational areas), and on how they are able to negotiate their way through those environments. As in the other two traditions, researchers in this tradition did not set out to study sex differences, but many have ended up doing so because they could not help but notice that persistent sex differences exist.

Piaget

We turn first to the developmental account offered by Piaget and Inhelder (1956). They proposed that children gradually develop systematic spatial concepts that are used to represent abstract spatial ideas (e.g., the **Cartesian coordinate axes** used in mathematics) as well as concrete objects and phenomena encountered in the physical world (e.g., understanding relations among landmarks in one's neighborhood). In particular, they suggested that by interacting with their environment, children gradually construct three kinds of spatial representations: topological, projective, and Euclidean.

Topological concepts concern the property of being connected or bounded. Thus, key topological ideas are those that are related to proximity (nearness) in some way, such as the ideas of "next to," "on," or "between." Topology ignores distance and angle. Thus, someone having only topological concepts would not differentiate between shapes of different sizes or shapes. For example, topological concepts would allow someone to identify when a circle was next to versus on top of a square, but not to differentiate between a small square and either a large square or rectangle (because the latter two distinctions depend on differentiating side lengths).

Projective concepts can be thought of as "point of view" concepts—that is, the spatial relations that depend on one's viewing perspective or vantage point. Thus, for example, consider how a landscape looks to two people who approach it from opposite directions. A barn that appears to the left of the house when approaching the scene from one direction appears to be to the right of the house when approaching the scene from the opposite direction. Or, consider how a round dinner plate looks when you view it from straight overhead (a perfect circle) versus when you view it from an angle while seated on a chair at the table (an ellipse).

Finally, **Euclidean concepts** can be thought of as "metric" or "measurement" concepts. These are spatial relations that establish some frame of reference (such as a starting place) and that provide some specific system for measurement over the space. An example is using a coordinate grid to locate a point on a map (e.g., the lines of longitude and latitude), or using a plumb line to establish the true vertical.

Topological concepts emerge very early (during the preschool years) and there have not been reports of sex differences on these concepts. Projective and Euclidean concepts develop far more gradually during early and middle childhood, and research using the tasks developed by Piaget and Inhelder to measure these skills has revealed dramatic and persistent sex differences. To illustrate the kinds of sex differences that have been found in projective and Euclidean concepts, we describe findings from research using the "water-level task" (see Figure 4.3). In this task, respondents are shown a drawing of an empty container such as a glass or bottle, and they are asked to draw where the water will be when the container is tipped at various angles. The task was designed as a Euclidean assessment because it taps children's ability to use a general system of horizontal and vertical coordinate axes to observe and represent the horizontals and verticals that occur in the everyday physical world. In the case of water, gravity's effects force liquid to remain parallel to the ground no matter what the position of the container. Children who do not have a fully developed conceptual grid system of horizontals and verticals find it difficult to ignore the immediate sides of the container and thus even notice that the water line remains in an invariant horizontal position. Thus, as long as the bottom of the container is parallel to the liquid line (in other words, as long as the container is upright), children can draw the line correctly. When the container itself is tipped, however, some children have serious problems in perceiving or drawing the line as horizontal.

In their original research, Piaget and Inhelder described stages that children traversed as they went from the preschool years through middle childhood. As may be seen in Figure 4.3, at first young children do not even realize that liquid forms a planar surface. Once they do, they think that the water stays parallel to the bottom of the container, perhaps even stuck on the base even if the container is entirely inverted. A bit later they come to recognize that there is some change in the water's orientation relative to the sides of the container, but fail to recognize the liquid remains parallel to the floor or the ground outside the container. Eventually they should come to recognize that the water remains parallel to the horizon, and that the tipped angle of the container is irrelevant.

Although the original description of this developmental progression implied that all normal children would master a Euclidean system and thus perform correctly on the water level task by middle or

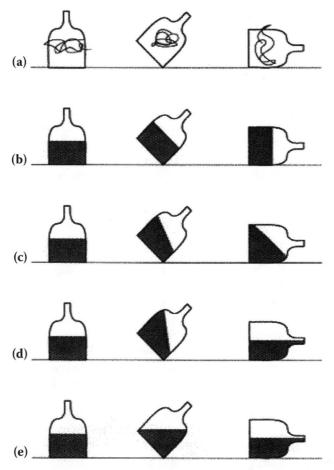

FIGURE 4.3 Stages in the water-level task, adapted from Piaget and Inhelder (1956), including (a) failure to recognize a planar surface, (b) assumption that liquid remains consistently parallel to the base, (c) recognition of some movement relative to the sides of the container, (d) understanding the water line as horizontal when it parallels the long axis of the container, and finally (e) invariant horizontality in all positions. (From Downs, R.M. & Liben, L.S., *Annals of the Association of American Geographers*, *81*, 304–327, 1991. With permission.)

late childhood, several researchers—beginning as early as the 1960s (e.g., Rebelsky, 1964)—began to notice that even college students often performed badly on the water level task, and—particularly relevant here—that a disproportionate number of those having difficulty were women. This finding has been replicated numerous times over the years, even when participants have the opportunity to observe half-filled tipped bottles (Barsky & Lachman, 1986; Liben, 1978; Sholl, 1989; Thomas, Jamison, & Hummel, 1973), and even when examples and verbal rules are given to help them (Liben & Golbeck, 1984). Often as many as 40% of college women err on this task!

This work with adults led investigators to ask whether sex differences would also be evident in children, and indeed they are. For example, Thomas and Jamison (1975) tested individuals from preschool through college age using cardboard disks inside the bottle to represent the water level. They found that when the bottle was upright, errors disappeared by the fifth grade. However, when the bottle was tilted, errors continued through college age, especially in girls and women. People had difficultly even when an abstract "tipped rectangles" version of the task was used (Liben & Golbeck, 1980).

Psychometric testing and spatial skills

The second tradition takes a more "data-driven" approach. It generally begins by giving people many different kinds of intellectual tasks or tests (e.g., subscales of IQ tests), and then examines what kinds of patterns emerge from the various tests. A particularly common way to examine the data from this research tradition is to use the statistical procedure of **factor analysis**. The purpose of a factor analysis is to determine which tasks or items seem to tap the same skill, knowledge, or "factor." The items or tasks that elicit similar kinds of responses are said to measure the same underlying factor. Thus, if a particular person tends to perform well (or badly) on one kind of task within a given factor, that person also tends to perform well (or badly) on another kind of task that measures the same factor.

Within the domain of spatial skills, **psychometricians** have long used factor analysis to try to determine whether there are some identifiable factors among the many different spatial tasks that have been developed (e.g., Ekstrom, French, & Harman, 1976; Eliot, 1987). Of even more relevance to our interests here are analyses that have been concerned more specifically with the emergence of sex differences in various types of spatial skills (or factors). Marcia Linn and Anne Petersen (1985) conducted the seminal work in this area.

Linn and Petersen's work combined two analytic approaches. First, they used "task analyses," in which they logically analyzed what kinds of demands various spatial tasks appeared to place on respondents. Second, they used meta-analysis to reveal underlying patterns in the data. Of particular importance is that they used their meta-analyses to determine whether the patterns in the data were similar among all people, or instead, whether patterns differed for different subgroups defined by age and sex of respondents. This process allowed them to identify (a) subsets of spatial skills, (b) whether each did or did not reveal sex differences, and (c) in cases in which there were sex differences, how large the differences were, and how early in development the differences emerged. Having good descriptions of the timing of sex differences may help investigators to generate hypotheses about the factors that might be responsible for those differences. For example, if a sex difference in some skill emerges at puberty, it would be reasonable to explore the possibility that hormonal changes associated with puberty might play a role.

Linn and Petersen's meta-analysis revealed consistent overall differences between males and females in spatial tasks. This general finding was replicated in a later meta-analysis by Voyer, Voyer, and Bryden (1995), who reported an overall effect size of $d = 0.39$ and by Hedges and Nowell (1995) who reported d values between 0.13 and 0.25 favoring males. Hedges and Nowell also found notable differences in variability in spatial skills, suggesting that more than twice as many males as females are found in the highest ranges of spatial ability.

Linn and Petersen (1985) further identified three major subcategories of spatial ability: spatial perception, mental rotation, and spatial visualization. The first, **spatial perception**, refers to an individual's ability to identify spatial relations with respect to one's own bodily location or position in relation to something in the external space. The water-level task described earlier as part of the discussion of the Piagetian work on spatial concepts fits within this category because the horizontal orientation of the water line can be judged readily in relation to the vertical orientation of the body. A second well-known example of a spatial perception task is the "rod and frame task," designed to study **field dependence/ independence** (Witkin & Goodenough, 1981). In this task, a person is asked to adjust a luminous rod to a vertical position when it is embedded in a luminous tilted frame. Because the room is darkened, the horizontal and vertical cues that would normally be available by sight cannot be used, and thus respondents need to rely on perception of their own vertical bodily position (gravitational upright) to solve the problem. The more that people are affected by the surrounding frame, the more they are said to be "field dependent." Field-independent individuals are more able to rely on their own bodily position to make this judgment.

Both the meta-analyses conducted by Linn and Petersen and by Voyer and his colleagues found a sex difference of $d = 0.44$ for spatial perception, a degree of difference that would be referred to as moderate. Both meta-analyses also found that the effect size increased with age, with small or no sex differences under the age of 13, more consistent or larger differences between ages 13 and 18, and the largest and most consistent differences after age 18. Particularly striking was Linn and Petersen's finding of that for those older than 18, d was 0.67.

The second component, **mental rotation**, refers to the ability to imagine a figure or object as it is moved in some way in two- or three-dimensional space. Probably the best-known mental rotation test is the block design task by Vandenberg and Kuse (1978). This task uses drawings of block-constructions (illustrated in Figure 4.4) first designed by Shepard and Metzler (1971) to study the speed with which people rotate images mentally. Respondents are first shown a particular block array as the model or standard. They are asked to look at additional block drawings to decide whether it depicts the identical block construction but in a different position, or it is instead an entirely different block construction. Because respondents are given only a relatively brief amount of time to work on the problems, the ease with which one can rotate images mentally is reflected in the total number answered correctly. If there were no time limit, most people would eventually get the right answers.

The results from meta-analyses on mental rotation skills show a consistent advantage for males (in the meta-analysis of Linn & Petersen, $d = 0.73$; in that of Voyer et al., $d = 0.56$). Research with preschool and elementary-aged children has reported boys to do better at rotating objects in two and three dimensions as early as 4 years of age, and throughout elementary school (Ehrlich, Levine, & Goldin-Meadow, 2006; Johnson & Meade, 1987; Kerns & Berenbaum, 1991; Levine, Huttenlocher, Taylor, & Langrock, 1999; Vederhus & Krekling, 1996) although the childhood difference is often reported as somewhat smaller, around 0.40. There is also evidence that girls and women have relatively worse performance on tasks requiring rotation in three dimensions (such as the Vandenberg and Kuse block figures) than on those requiring rotation in two dimensions (such as rotating a letter of the alphabet, or the pieces in the game Tetris). Linn and Petersen (1985) found the d for three-dimensional tasks to be 0.97, almost a whole standard deviation better for males than females, clearly a large difference. In one study of preschool children, there was no difference between boys and girls in solving tasks involving rotation in two dimensions, but the young boys were consistently better than girls in three-dimensional rotation (McGuinness & Morley, 1991).

Finally, the third component skill identified by Linn and Petersen (1985) was **spatial visualization**, which is measured by several different tasks such as embedded and hidden figure tasks, block design, and form boards. These tasks may involve manipulating spatial information in several steps. Some of the steps may require different strategies; therefore, the tasks may involve more than one kind of skill. We can use as an example a task from this third category—the paper folding task developed by the Educational Testing Service (Ekstrom et al., 1976). In this task, the initial figure for each item shows a piece of paper that is folded in a series of steps, and then one or more holes are punched through the folded paper. The response choices offer drawings of five unfolded pieces of paper that contain holes, and the task is to select which unfolded paper shows the correct pattern of holes. To solve the problem, one might use mental rotation strategies or verbal reasoning. Because of the possibility of alternative and varied strategies, spatial visualization is less clear-cut or unidimensional than either mental rotation or spatial perception. In fact, some researchers view this as a "wastebasket" or "grab-bag" category, containing those spatial tasks that do not fall neatly within either of the other two categories and thus argue that it is not really a useful grouping (Johnson & Meade, 1987; Voyer et al., 1995). Perhaps given the potential utility of various solution

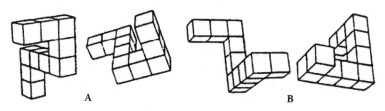

FIGURE 4.4 Sample mental rotation task. The task is to determine if the two figures labeled A and the two figures labeled B could be made identical by rotating them in space. (From Halpern, D.F. et al., *Psychological Science in the Public Interest*, 8, 1–5, 2007. Reproduced with permission of Blackwell Publishing.)

strategies, it may not be surprising that this is also the one component of spatial skills for which there has not been strong evidence for sex differences. Neither meta-analysis found males to be consistently better than females at these tasks (Linn & Petersen's meta-analysis, $d = 0.13$; meta-analysis of Voyer et al., $d = 0.19$).

One important question about spatial skills like mental rotation and spatial perception relates to the implications of having strong skills in these domains. It is quite clear that strong language and writing skills influence academic success and eventual job performance in many modern occupations. But what about spatial skills? There has been research examining the role of spatial skills in performance in mathematics, and we will consider that a bit later. One might also ask whether strong spatial skills relate to performance in educational programs and occupations that might reasonably depend on spatial skills (e.g., engineering or architecture). There is strong correlational evidence that students in occupations or educational programs like these do have relatively high spatial skills, in part because spatial skills are sometimes used as a criterion for selecting students into such programs (e.g., dental school admissions tasks). For example, Shea, Lubinski, and Benbow (2001) have linked spatial ability to educational tracks and occupations such as engineering, architecture, physics, chemistry, and medical surgery. Furthermore, training in spatial skills has been shown to have a positive impact on performance in engineering (Sorby & Baartmans, 1996, 2000) and chemistry (Small & Morton, 1983).

Environmental psychology and spatial skills: wayfinding

The third research tradition in the spatial domain has obvious practical applications. This research tradition has addressed sex-related differences in spatial skills that are concerned with people's ability to navigate their environments, as well as to remember the locations of places or objects in the world. Indeed, the topic of finding one's way around the environment (known as **wayfinding**) often serves as the focus of many jokes and cartoons about the sexes (e.g., that women cannot read maps and that men are unwilling to ask for directions).

The scholarly research on wayfinding has been conducted in outdoor, indoor, and virtual (computer) environments. A typical research paradigm is one in which participants are taken out into an unfamiliar environment, led to various locations, and asked to point (e.g., with a telescope or some other pointing device) to locations seen earlier. Or, participants may be led along a real or virtual route for one or more times and then asked to navigate it themselves, perhaps to navigate the return trip, or to create some kind of representation (e.g., a sketch map) of the route. Data from these tasks suggest that males tend to do somewhat better overall (Kallai, Karadi, & Kovacs, 2000; Lawton, 1994, 1996; Lawton, Charleston, & Zieles, 1996; Malinowski, 2001; Malinowski & Gillespie, 2001; Moffat, Hampson, & Hatzipantelis, 1998; Schmitz, 1999), especially in unfamiliar outdoor environments. The research also finds that males and females tend to use somewhat different strategies for finding their way around.

Men are more likely to rely on **cardinal directions** (Dabbs, Chang, Strong, & Milun, 1998; Montello, Lovelace, Golledge, & Self, 1999; Sholl, Acacio, Makar, & Leon, 2000), geometric information inferred from movement (e.g., Galea & Kimura, 1993), perhaps even by updating from vestibular body cues (Sholl & Bartels, 2002). Women are more likely to rely on landmarks (e.g., "turn right at the church") both when finding their own way (e.g., Dabbs et al., 1998; Galea & Kimura, 1993) and when giving directions to others (Ward, Newcombe, & Overton, 1986). Research with children between the ages of 5 and 18 (Fenner, Heathcote, & Jerrams-Smith, 2000; Gibbs & Wilson, 1999; Schmitz, 1997) finds similar differences between boys and girls in orientation, pointing accuracy, wayfinding anxiety, and landmark use.

Research that tests people's skills in identifying another kind of spatial location—locations of specific objects within smaller spaces—has generally shown better performance among females. That is, females have been shown to remember the locations of objects and to identify missing objects from an array better than males (Cherney & Ryalls, 1999; Eals & Silverman, 1994; James & Kimura, 1997; Montello et al., 1999; Silverman & Eals, 1992). So, we can say that the data available seem to suggest that males have an advantage in remembering and navigating to distant locations in large spaces, whereas females have an advantage in remembering detailed information and locations of objects in small, nearby spaces.

Spatial skills: integrating the three traditions
Research is still underway to try to understand the relations among the kinds of skills studied under each of the research traditions discussed above. Some of the concepts studied by Piaget are easily integrated into the three-component analysis of spatial skills offered in the psychometric literature. For example, as already noted, the water-level horizontality task fits solidly within the spatial perception component identified by Linn and Petersen (1985). Similarly, many of the tasks designed by Piaget and Inhelder to assess projective spatial concepts are easily categorized as tests of individuals' skill in mental rotation. Other studies have tried to relate success on wayfinding tasks to success on paper and pencil spatial ability tasks and generally have found some, but limited, connections (Hegarty, Montello, Richardson, Ishikawa, & Lovelace, 2006; Malinowski, 2001). A factor that is likely to diminish the connection is the potential availability of many different strategies that can be used to find one's way around (e.g., geometric inference; landmark use). Additional research is needed to clarify whether the observed sex differences in large-scale spatial tasks go beyond (or merely reflect) the sex differences in specific spatial skills that appear to be useful for wayfinding tasks (e.g., Hegarty et al., 2006; Liben, Myers, & Kastens, 2008).

Quantitative Reasoning, Arithmetic, and Mathematics

As is the case with verbal and spatial skills, there are many different kinds of mathematical or quantitative abilities and skills. For example, there are more routine abilities such as counting, and the simple operations of arithmetic such as addition and subtraction. There are the different areas of mathematics such as algebra and geometry, and there are applications such as statistics. There is most certainly a difference between **computation** (calculating the correct answer without making errors), and **problem solving** (determining the correct procedure to use, and then using the procedure to find a solution to a problem that is often stated in words).

When children learn the earliest quantitative skills (e.g., counting) during the toddler and preschool years, there is no evidence that either sex performs better than the other (De Lisi & McGillicuddy-De Lisi, 2002; Ginsburg, Klein, & Starkey, 1998). Once children enter school, the picture changes. Girls get better grades in arithmetic and mathematics classes throughout the school years, including during the college years (De Lisi & McGillicuddy-De Lisi, 2002; Felson & Trudeau, 1991; Halpern, 1997; Kimball, 1989); however, their good grades are not limited to math—they get better grades in all subjects, a topic we will return to when we examine the issue of gender in the schools in chapter 13.

Although their grades are better than those of boys, girls do not generally perform as well as boys do on standardized tests measuring mathematics knowledge and skills (e.g., the SATs). For example, the average math SAT (SAT-M) score of male high school seniors in 2004 was 537 and of female seniors was 501 ($d = 0.31$), although their verbal scores (SAT-V) were essentially the same (512 and 504, respectively, $d = 0.07$); Snyder & Tan, 2005). Today girls take almost the same number of math classes as boys do (Royer, Tronsky, Chan, Jackson, & Marchant, 1999; Snyder & Tan, 2005), although in the past they did not. When researchers have examined the sex difference when the number of math classes was accounted for, boys still performed better on standardized tests (Bridgeman & Wendler, 1991). However, this finding does not apply everywhere in the world where such mathematics performance has been tested. This sex difference in mathematical performance was not found in recent studies in Great Britain, and in one study of eighth graders in 38 countries, the gender difference among students of high ability was found in only three countries, and one of those was the United States (Freeman, 2003; Mullis et al., 2000).

A meta-analysis of sex differences in mathematics performance (Hyde, Fennema, & Lamon, 1990) found no overall sex difference ($d = -0.05$) in mathematics performance, but a different pattern depending on what skill was being measured. If the measure was understanding of mathematical concepts taught in schools, again there was no difference ($d = -0.03$). In measures of computation, girls performed better, especially during elementary and middle school ($d = -0.14$). For measures of mathematical problem solving, males performed slightly better ($d = 0.08$), but the effect was quite dependent on age. There was essentially no difference between males and females during the lower grades, but the older the children became, the better males became relative to females on problem solving, so that by high school $d = 0.29$. Consistent with the findings of the meta-analysis, more recent research has also found that girls are generally better at computation, whereas boys are better at problem solving (De Lisi & McGillicuddy-De Lisi, 2002), but these differences are not large. Standardized tests like the SAT-M, however, do produce larger effect sizes, typically around 0.40 (De Lisi & McGillicuddy-De Lisi, 2002; Hyde, Fennema, & Lamon, 1990).

Variability

The question of variability has also been raised regarding sex differences in mathematics (Hedges & Nowell, 1995), and males do indeed seem to be more variable. A consequence of a small average difference with males getting higher scores on measures like the SAT-M or problem solving tests, combined with greater male variability, would result in many more males than females performing at the highest levels on these measures. Hedges and Nowell (1995) found that there were about twice as many males as females scoring above the 95th percentile on tests such as the SATs.

Mathematically precocious youth

One group of researchers has spent several years following very mathematically talented children and adolescents (Benbow, 1988; Benbow, Lubinski, Shea, & Eftekhari-Sanjani, 2000; Shea et al., 2001). This research is part of the Study of Mathematically Precocious Youth (SMPY), originated by Julian Stanley at Johns Hopkins University in the 1970s (Benbow & Stanley, 1980). For more than 30 years, talent searches have taken place throughout the United States to identify mathematically skilled children in seventh grade. Children in participating schools are invited to take part in the study if they score in the top 3% on achievement tests that their schools routinely give. When the children take part, they are given the SATs as seventh graders, usually before they have studied the material that the SATs specifically test. By now, more than 1 million children have participated (Benbow et al., 2000).

This research has found that many more boys than girls score at the highest end of the SAT-M while still in middle school in every year that the search has taken place, whereas the SAT-V scores do not differ between boys and girls. The average scores on the SAT-M are usually around 30 points higher for boys in these talent searches, but the most dramatic differences are at the uppermost part of the range. Scores on the SAT-M range from 200 to 800 points, and it is worth remembering that high school seniors average around 500. A score above 700 is an outstanding score for a graduating senior, let alone for a 12-year-old. In 1988 Benbow reported that about twice as many boys as girls among these talented 12-year-olds score higher than 500, about 4 times as many boys score higher than 600, and about 12–13 times as many boys as girls score higher than 700. Interestingly, some recent reports have found that this ratio is declining, and that between 2 and 4 boys in this age range now score above 700 relative to each girl (Halpern et al., 2007). Nonetheless, that is still notably more boys than girls. Also, some researchers have studied mathematically talented children at younger ages, and found boys scoring higher than girls as early as the preschool years (Mills, Ablard, & Stumpf, 1993; Robinson, Abbott, Berninger, & Busse, 1996).

Relationships Between Mathematics and Spatial Skills

Several researchers (e.g., Halpern, 2000; Linn & Petersen, 1986; Shea et al., 2001) have wondered whether there is a relationship between math performance and spatial skills—that is, whether spatial skills are part of the reason for the sex difference in mathematics. It is important to keep in mind that people who are intelligent in general may have strong skills in several cognitive domains—verbal, spatial, mathematics, memory, and so on—so general intelligence should be accounted for before examining this relationship. Several studies suggest that there is such a relationship, in that spatial skills have been found to be related to mathematics performance, even after the impact of general intelligence has been statistically controlled (Casey, Nuttall, & Pezaris, 1997; Casey, Nuttall, Pezaris, & Benbow, 1995; Friedman, 1995; Geary, Saults,

Liu, & Hoard, 2000). Interestingly, at least one study has found that preschoolers who have good spatial skills have better mathematical skills than other children some years later (Assel, Landry, Swank, Smith, & Steelman, 2003). However, the relationship has not always been found in all groups studied (e.g., see Casey et al., 1995), and it has been found more consistently for girls than for boys in virtually every study that has examined the issue. That is, having good or poor spatial skills seems to influence girls' performance in mathematics more than it does boys'.

It is important to keep in mind that spatial skills are only one factor that may relate to performance in mathematics. Friedman (1995) conducted a meta-analysis of correlations between performance on mathematics and spatial tasks. A meta-analysis using correlations is somewhat different from the meta-analyses we have discussed thus far. The unit of measurement here is a correlation (the degree of relationship between two variables) rather than the average difference in score between two groups (e.g., between males and females). Friedman did report a relationship between performance in mathematics and spatial skills, especially for girls, and especially among the most talented groups. However, Friedman also measured the relationship between verbal skills and performance in mathematics and found that the relationship between verbal skills and math was even greater than for spatial skills and math. She concluded that there was little evidence that the sex difference in spatial skills was the only or the major reason for the sex difference in math performance, although it did seem to contribute.

Speed of Recall of Basic Mathematical Facts

One interesting possible contribution to the gender difference in math performance on standardized tests versus classroom grades is a difference in the speed of recall of basic mathematical facts (Royer, Tronsky, Chan et al., 1999; Royer, Tronsky, Marchant, & Jackson, 1999). This research provides support for the idea that girls get higher grades whereas boys get better achievement test scores because somewhat different skills are needed for doing well in these areas. In the classroom the rapid solution of problems is likely to be less important than it is when taking tests such as the SATs, which are heavily speeded and solving each problem a little more quickly will have substantial benefits over the whole test. Their research shows that after around the middle of elementary school, the most skilled boys (in math) are faster at retrieving math facts than the most skilled girls are, and that this difference helps the boys do better in the testing situation. Also, as we know, the difference between boys and girls is most often found when high ability or more select groups are tested, such as those students who take the SATs (i.e., college-bound seniors), or groups like those studied in the SMPY studies. Royer and his colleagues also suggest that the boys with the worst academic performance (for boys) get even poorer grades than girls with the worst academic performance (for girls), and hence they will drag the boys' average grades downward. An important question is why do the highest scoring boys have faster retrieval times? Royer and his colleagues suggest that the reason may be practice, especially practice outside of school because of their interest in the subject matter.

Problem Solving and Strategy Use

Research has also examined how boys and girls solve math problems, and whether differences in strategies could partially account for differences in standardized test scores and grades. As was already noted, the strategies that work to get good grades may not work as well with standardized tests. On standardized tests, girls are more likely to do well on problems that are familiar and well defined and are more likely to use strategies that have been taught to them by their teachers (Gallagher & De Lisi, 1994; Gallagher et al., 2000; Stumpf, 1995). Boys, on the other hand, are more likely to do better on problems that require using a less well-defined solution strategy, and more on figuring the problem out at the time, or on using novel strategies. Using strategies that depend more on memory, or are more conventional, are also related to having more negative attitudes about math, and to being less confident in one's math ability. One needs to be quite confident in one's math ability to try out unconventional approaches, and it seems that boys, especially high-ability boys, have more confidence in their ability to try out such strategies. Boys and girls have been shown to use different strategies as early as the first grade (Carr & Jessup, 1997; Carr, Jessup, & Fuller, 1999).

Attitudes and Anxiety

What about attitudes towards and interest in math, anxiety about it, and confidence in one's ability? It is clear that males do take more math course work in college, and are more likely to earn degrees in mathematics, especially graduate degrees, suggesting that more boys and men find math useful and interesting (Snyder & Tan, 2005). Anxiety about their performance in math is more common among girls, even in cultures like Japan where mathematics performance is generally high (Satake & Amato, 1995). However, the differences between males and females may not be very large. A meta-analysis of such attitudes (Hyde, Fennema, Ryan, Frost, & Hopp, 1990) found that most gender differences in attitudes toward math were small, on the order of $d = 0.15$ or less. There were some exceptions to this general trend. Females did have noticeably more math anxiety than males ($d = -0.30$) in low ability groups, but to a lesser degree in average or high ability samples (d between -0.09 and -0.18).

Relationships between anxiety and performance

There have also been studies of the relationship between attitudes and anxiety and actual mathematics performance. The **structural equation modeling** analysis by Casey and her colleagues (1997) discussed above found that math self-confidence was related to SAT-M performance, although less so than was spatial skill. A series of meta-analyses (Ma, 1999; Ma & Kishor, 1997a, 1997b) examining relationships of attitudes, confidence, and anxiety to performance in mathematics among children in elementary and high school found that these factors did predict performance in math, but that the relationships were similar for boys and girls.

Stereotype Threat

One attitudinal factor that may have particular implications for gender and performance on difficult math tests has been called **stereotype threat** (Steele, 1997). This refers to a phenomenon in which people's performance is affected by stereotypes about their group as being poor in some domain—like women and math. The effect seems to be most powerful when people are good at that domain, and when they care about their performance in it. Research has examined the impact of racial and ethnic stereotypes on academic performance, showing that when stereotypes operate, they can both increase (e.g., Asians and math), and decrease performance (e.g., African-Americans and general academic performance). In the case of gender and math, high-ability women perform more poorly when they think a particular test measures ability, and when they think that it is a test in which men generally outperform women. That is, their performance is degraded when they are faced with a negative stereotype about their group's performance on such a test.

In one study of stereotype threat, a group of Canadian researchers (Walsh, Hickey, & Duffy, 1999) found that women college students performed more poorly on a subset of SAT-M questions when they thought the questions measured male-female differences than when they simply thought it was to compare the performance of Americans and Canadians (about which there is no negative stereotype, at least for math). In another study (Spencer, Steele, & Quinn, 1999) stereotype threat was more likely to affect the performance of high-ability women than women of more average ability, and only on difficult tests. Interestingly, these researchers also found that when no information about the math task was given to participants, the men scored better, but when participants were told that men and women did equally well on this test, there was no difference between the men's and women's performance on the same items. That is, even when not primed by the researchers, the stereotype was in operation, just as it is likely to be in the everyday lives of male and female students. This is potentially of very serious concern when tests like the SATs are used by competitive colleges and universities to make admissions decisions. We know that girls and young women get higher grades and at the same time lower scores on tests such as the SATs.

However, if selective colleges rely on both tests and grades, and especially if they weigh the tests more heavily, fewer women are likely to be admitted (Leonard & Jiang, 1999).

The impact of stereotype threat on ethnic and gender differences in performance in mathematics has also been found to affect children's performance in math (Ambady, Shih, Kim, & Pittinsky, 2001). In a study of Asian-American girls between kindergarten and eighth grade, Ambady and her colleagues activated the girls' Asian identity, their gender identity, or neither. Both the oldest (sixth through eighth grades) and youngest (kindergarten through second grades) girls performed best when their Asian identity was activated, and worst when their gender identity was activated, and intermediate when no identity was activated. Girls in the middle elementary grades, however, actually performed best when their gender identity was activated. The researchers also measured knowledge of stereotypes about ethnic identity and gender as they relate to performance in math. When asked to point to a picture of the best math performer, they found that the youngest and oldest groups thought boys were better, whereas the middle group (the ones who actually performed better when gender was activated) thought girls were better at math. In a second study of Asian boys, the boys performed better when both their gender and their Asian identities were activated.

Applications of Mathematics

Researchers have also studied gender differences in applications of math such as the use of statistics and computers. Meta-analysis and narrative reviews of attitudes towards, anxiety about, and use of computers (Chua, Chen, & Wong, 1999; Miller, Schweingruber, & Brandenburg, 2001; Morahan-Martin, 1998; Schumacher & Morahan-Martin, 2001; Whitley, 1997) both in children and adults have found higher levels of anxiety about, less positive attitudes towards, and less computer use among girls and women. However, the more recent studies have found this to be less so with the most recent groups, especially in the use of computers for schoolwork and email. We will consider more about the involvement of children with computers, especially computer games, in chapter 12.

Interest, Involvement, and Performance in Science

The last of the cognitive areas we will consider is science, which is most certainly not a single skill, but nonetheless is worth examining for evidence of the impact of gender on interest, attitudes, and performance. As we already know, girls get better grades in school, and their grades in science are no exception (Weinburgh, 1995). But again, we can see boys doing better on standardized tests. In their review of six large studies of high school students between 1962 and 1990, Hedges and Nowell (1995) included measures of general science ability. They found consistently better performance by boys (d between 0.11 and 0.50), greater variability, and very high ratios of males to females at the highest levels of ability (e.g., up to 7 times as many males as females above the 95th percentile). These ability differences clearly parallel their findings in the math and spatial areas, although the science findings were generally larger than both.

As is the case in mathematics, women are less likely than men to earn college degrees in the physical sciences and engineering. In the report published by the National Center for Education Statistics in 2005 (Snyder & Tan, 2005), in 2003 women earned 19% of the bachelor's, 21% of the master's, and 17% of the doctoral degrees in engineering. In the physical sciences they earned 41, 37, and 28% of the bachelor's, master's, and doctoral degrees, respectively. However, the situation is quite different in the biological, medical, and social sciences. During the same period women earned 64, 69, and 78% of the bachelor's degrees in biology, anthropology, and psychology, respectively, and 46, 61, and 66% of the doctoral degrees in these fields, as well as 45% of the degrees in medicine. The number of women in the biological, social, and medical sciences has, of course, increased in the last few decades.

Gender differences in children's and adolescent's attitudes about science have also been studied. A meta-analysis of such attitudes (Weinburgh, 1995) examined differences between boys' and girls' evaluative beliefs about various scientific fields, relationships between their attitudes and their achievement, as well as changes over time and differences among various scientific fields. She found that boys had somewhat more positive attitudes about science (overall $d = 0.2$), but that attitudes depended on the kind of science. The meta-analysis separated scientific fields into biology, physics, earth science, and general science, finding larger differences in attitude in earth and general science ($d = 0.34$ in both cases), smaller in physics ($d = 0.12$), and essentially no difference in biology. As is clear by now, none of these differences is large. The relationship between attitudes and achievement in science was positive (correlation = .50 for boys and .55 for girls), demonstrating that children with more positive attitudes about science achieved at a higher level. There was no evidence of change over time in either attitudes or the relationship between achievement and attitudes.

CHAPTER SUMMARY

In this chapter, we examined the nature of the study of sex differences, including the use of both narrative review and meta-analysis to explore the results of many studies at the same time. We emphasized that, even when there is a consistent difference between the average performance of males and females in some area, there is almost always substantial overlap between groups of males and females.

We first examined motor development and found that most of the early developmental milestones are accomplished at similar ages in boys and girls. After the first few years of life, girls are typically somewhat more skilled at tasks requiring fine motor and upper body movements, whereas boys do somewhat better at skills requiring muscle strength, but during childhood most of these differences are small. One exception is throwing speed and distance, at which boys do much better, even during the preschool years. After adolescence, skills that depend on muscular strength are performed substantially better by males. However, the opportunity to practice these skills plays a very important role in their development in both boys and girls.

The final domain we examined in the physical arena was activity level, and boys have been found to have somewhat higher activity levels, especially when playing in groups of other boys.

We also examined the cognitive skills of boys and girls. The sexes are equally intelligent, but may show different patterns of strengths and weaknesses. Girls and women tend to have slightly better verbal skills, although in some verbal areas such as verbal fluency, phonological processing, and writing skills, the differences are larger. They also do better on tasks measuring perceptual speed and have better memories on several different measures of memory. Boys and men have better spatial skills in some areas, especially mental rotation and spatial perception, the largest differences being in the area of rotating objects in three dimensions. Girls do better at math computations and get better grades, but boys do better on standardized tests. In the math domain, girls do better on problems that have been taught to them, whereas boys do better at the use of novel or creative strategies to solve problems that are unfamiliar to them.

One important question is whether there is something consistent—a kind of cognitive process—that underlies these differences. One suggestion made by Halpern (2000) is that girls do well at tasks that require rapid access to long-term memory, whereas boys do well at tasks that require them to manipulate new and unfamiliar information, especially visual displays, and that many of the sex differences in cognition may be related to these general patterns. Whatever research may eventually reveal about the causes for the various differences reviewed in this chapter, it is clear that sex differences exist in a wide range of physical and cognitive domains, as well as in the social and psychological domains, the topics to which we now turn.

Personality and Social Behaviors

5

Q: What would you do if a dragon tried to kidnap you?
A1: I would get a hose and blow the fire right out of his mouth. (Bryan, age 4)
A2: Well, I wouldn't let him catch me, but if he did I'd just kick him in the nuts. (Travis, age 6)
A3: I would just have to get a sword and chop his head off. (Jimmy, age 5)
A4: I don't know. I'd probably hide in my sleeping bag. (Mandy, age 4)
A5: I'd just trick him. I'd climb up high and then he wouldn't get me. (Ann, age 4)
A6: First, I'd tickle him until he dropped me. And then I'd pull his tail off. (Cathy, age 6) (question and
answers from Bailey, 1993, p. 54)

Just looking at the responses above to the question that preschool teacher Karen Bailey (1993) asked her students certainly gives one the impression that boys and girls behave differently. Compared to the girls, the boys sound considerably more aggressive or at least active in defending themselves. Most of us can probably come up with similar examples. One interesting exercise you might undertake is to ask children similar questions to the one that Bailey asked her students. Alternatively, you could ask parents who have children of both sexes how they think the boys and girls are different. Do they think children of one sex are easier to raise, or more aggressive, or more easily frightened? Consider how their answers are related to gender stereotypes.

In this chapter we will examine social behaviors and personality characteristics of boys and girls. There are a huge number of possible behaviors that could be considered here, but we will try to limit our discussion to behaviors that have been studied in children, and those for which there is solid evidence of a difference between boys and girls, although we will sometimes include information about adults. When people consider the differences between boys and girls, they may think about specifically gendered activities: that girls wear dresses and bows in their hair and play with toys such as Barbie dolls, whereas boys wear shirts and jeans and play with toy trucks. It is certainly clear that boys and girls do have such gendered appearances and interests, but they will not be the major focus of this chapter. In later chapters we will discuss children's toys, clothing, and other activities that are associated with the gender roles of boys and girls as part of the socialization process.

As in chapter 4, we will discuss the results of individual studies, narrative reviews, and meta-analyses. Again we will use d as a measure of effect size. Recall that a d of 0.20 is small, a d of 0.50 is moderate, and a d of 0.80 is large (Cohen, 1969), and also that a small effect size may have an important impact on peoples' lives, whereas a large one may not. Also, again keep in mind that there is enormous overlap between males and females in almost any measure of behavior, and an average difference between the sexes does not necessarily inform us about a particular male or female person.

We also remind you that we are not including much information in this chapter about reasons for these differences between the sexes. In later chapters, we will be exploring many potential influences on behavioral sex differences. As we noted at the beginning of chapter 4, we will return to a brief look at factors that influence sex differences in the epilogue. It is certainly worth remembering that the existence of a sex difference tells us little about why it occurs.

EMOTIONS

Is one sex more or less emotional than the other, and if so, does such a difference exist among children as well as adults? Emotional expressiveness has often been seen as a key aspect of femininity, whereas masculinity often is thought to involve the suppression of emotion (Fischer & Manstead, 2000), with the exception of the expression of anger. In a review of the research some years ago Leslie Brody (1985) discussed the pervasiveness of the cultural belief that women were more emotional than men. At the time she had recently read several letters to the editor in *Time* magazine that expressed the view that a woman could not be vice president because women were too emotional (e.g., "Women are emotional. They are also unaware of the exigencies of life, and they lack objectivity," Brody, 1985, p. 103). People may even have these beliefs about themselves. Brody also told of a 6-year-old girl she knew who was convinced that she was afraid because she was a girl. Perhaps some of these stereotypical beliefs have lessened in recent years, but they certainly have not gone away.

Expressing Emotion

We have been discussing emotion and emotional expression as though they were the same thing, and of course they are not. What people actually feel is not always expressed. Because scientists are only able to study what is observable, or what people report on questionnaires, people's felt emotions are very difficult to study. The bulk of the research on the question of emotion is therefore focused on **emotional expression**. However, the study of emotional expression is complicated by the degree to which it is a gendered activity. People are likely to display certain emotions consistent with their positions in society (e.g., pride and lack of vulnerability for males; warmth, happiness, and fear for females), so it is very difficult to know whether, in fact, females are more emotional than males (Brody & Hall, 2000).

Emotional expression has been measured in three ways: observations; self-reports or reports by others like parents and teachers; and physiological measures of emotional arousal. When others observe or report about the emotional behaviors of others, or even when one completes a questionnaire about one's own emotions, the effects of stereotypes can influence what is found (Brody, 1985; Whissell, 1996), and stereotypes about emotions certainly exist.

Self-Reported Emotion

Self-reports, in which people complete questionnaires about their own emotions, are very commonly used in the study of adult emotions. Fischer and Manstead (2000) examined self-reported emotional expression in adults in 37 countries from across the world, including countries from North, Central, and South America; Europe; Asia; Africa; and the Middle East. The emotions that they studied included joy, fear, anger, sadness, disgust, shame, and guilt. The countries varied on several dimensions, including on the traditionality of gender roles. Despite these variations, the research consistently found that women reported more emotion on three dimensions: they reported more intense emotions, they expressed emotions more openly, and they indicated that their emotions lasted for a longer time. However, there were also effects of culture. In more individualistic Western cultures, despite the fact that these cultures are often more liberal or "modern" with respect to gender roles, the differences between the sexes was greater, especially in emotions like sadness and fear, but even for joy, anger, and disgust. Fischer and Manstead proposed that "males who grow up in individualistic societies are encouraged in the course of sex-role socialization to learn to avoid situations that could give rise to emotions that pose a threat to their status as independent males who are (or should be) in control of the situation" (Fischer & Manstead, 2000, p. 90).

Other reviews of the self-report research have also concluded that, in adulthood, women are more emotionally expressive (Brody, 1985; Brody & Hall, 2000). There are few studies of self-reported emotions in young children, given that filling out questionnaires is not something that small children are usually asked to do. Sometimes parents are asked to complete such measures about their own children. One such study of preschool children's temper tantrums (Einon & Potegal, 1994), a very common emotional expression in toddlers and preschoolers, did not report any greater frequency of such behavior in either sex. Boys, however, were reported as hitting more often when having a tantrum, and as having more facial expressions of anger.

Elementary school age children can be interviewed or asked to complete self-report measures of emotion. With respect to anger, sometimes boys report more anger, sometimes girls do, and sometimes there are no differences between them (Brody, 1984; Brody, Lovas, & Hay, 1995; Buntaine & Costenbader, 1997; Wintre, Polivy, & Murray, 1990; Zahn-Waxler, Cole, Welsh, & Fox, 1995). On the other hand, girls often reported fear and sadness more frequently from early elementary school age onwards.

Observational Studies of Emotion

There are also observational studies of emotional expression. Usually such research depends on ratings of people's facial expressions of emotion or other behaviors (e.g., smiling or crying) that can be used to indicate emotion. In adulthood, women usually are found to display more facial and gestural expressions of emotion (Brody & Hall, 2000), except that men may display anger more than women do.

Observational studies of emotional behavior in boys and girls have found few consistent differences in emotional expression during the first two years of life (Brody, 1985; Eisenberg, Martin, & Fabes, 1996; Malatesta, Culver, Tesman, & Shepard, 1989). As we have already discussed, infant boys are more active (Campbell & Eaton, 1999; Eaton & Enns, 1986), and when differences are found in emotionality and temperament, they tend to show that boys are more difficult, fussier, harder to soothe, or have higher rates of arousal, express more intense emotions, or are more emotionally expressive (Brody, 1996; Weinberg, Tronick, Cohn, & Olson, 1999).

During the preschool and early elementary years, again the findings from observational studies are not especially compelling or consistent, but some researchers have found boys expressing more anger and less fear and sadness than girls (Eisenberg et al., 1996; Hubbard, 2001; Kochanska, 2001; Zahn-Waxler et al., 1995) by the preschool years. There are no meta-analyses of this research, and the size and consistency of the sex differences do not really allow any strong conclusions about whether boys or girls are more emotional during childhood. More convincing is evidence that boys come to purposefully hide emotions like sadness and fear (Fuchs & Thelen, 1988; Larson & Pleck, 1999; Zeman & Garber, 1996), especially in the presence of peers. One interesting study of 3- and 4-year-olds whose "emotion talk" was followed for a year in their preschool peer groups found that these very young boys had already begun to associate certain emotions such as fear with girls, and hence to show derision towards boys who showed them: "Roger's afraid of a dirt claw. He's a girl." (Kyratzis, 2001, p. 363). Kyratzis also demonstrated that over the course of the year these 3- and 4-year-old boys became increasingly negative about anything associated with girls or femininity, not just emotions.

One important issue concerns children's tendency to demonstrate negative emotions as compared to their ability to hide such emotions, if motivated to do so. This contrast lies at the heart of the difference between experienced emotion and emotional expression. Perhaps boys are motivated to hide certain emotions, and girls are motivated to hide others. In one interesting study (Davis, 1995), first and third grade children were asked to rank the desirability of various toys and objects, some of which were clearly more interesting to children in this age range (e.g., magic markers that smelled or glow-in-the-dark Super Balls) than others (e.g., plastic spoons and teething rings). The children were told that after they did a task they would receive a gift for their help. The first gift the child received was one that had been ranked highly as to its desirability. The child was then asked to help with a second task, for which the gift was one that was ranked as undesirable (called the "disappointing gift" by Davis). The children's reactions to the desirable and disappointing gifts were videotaped. Following these two tasks, the children were asked to play a game in which they would trick a researcher by hiding their reactions to the displays of two prizes (also previously ranked as desirable or not) in boxes that the researcher could not see. If the child's facial expression indicated that both of the prizes were equally desirable, then the child could keep them both, but if the researcher could tell from the child's facial expression that the child liked one more than the other, then the child would not get to keep either of them. Davis called this the "game" task. Note that in the disappointing gift task, the children's actual reactions were recorded, whereas in the game task their abilities to hide their real emotions were being studied. Davis found that the boys and girls did not differ in their reactions to the desirable gift, but girls expressed less negativity when receiving the disappointing gift. That is, the girls were hiding their disappointment consistent with norms of politeness. Davis suggested that the socialization of girls puts more pressure on them to "act nice." In the game task, both boys and girls showed much less negativity when viewing the less desirable prize than they had when receiving the disappointing gift, but boys were still not as effective at hiding their facial expressions as girls were, leading to the conclusion that girls are more practiced at this skill. As we have already seen, boys are likely to have more practice hiding emotions associated with vulnerability rather than ones that might signal impoliteness.

Later in this chapter we will consider aggression and antisocial behavior, and we will see that high levels of physical aggression and antisocial behavior, although infrequent, are much more common in boys than in girls. It is very likely that differences in regulating the emotion of anger are at least partly related to antisocial behavior in children and adolescents. In an examination of this question, one group of researchers (Cole, Zahn-Waxler, & Smith, 1994) explored 5-year-old children's reactions to a disappointing prize, similar to the procedure we discussed above in Davis' study. In this study, some of the children were identified as high risk for developing clinical behavior problems (they were already showing aggressive and hard-to-manage behavior), some were at moderate risk, and some were at low risk (their behavior was in the normal range and not indicative of any problems).

Cole and her colleagues wanted to see how the different groups of children reacted to receiving an undesirable prize. They brought the children to the lab where they first ranked a set of prizes and were told by a research assistant that they would get their top-ranked prize after they did some "work." Some of the prizes were broken or otherwise undesirable. The first research assistant left and another research assistant administered some cognitive tasks, briefly left the room, and returned with the least preferred prize. The children's responses to her and the prize were videotaped. The assistant left the room again, leaving the child alone with the undesirable prize, and again the child's behavior was videotaped. Finally, the first research assistant returned, and asked the child how the tasks went, whether they liked the prize, how they felt when they got the prize, whether the other assistant knew how they felt, and if no, how they kept her from knowing how they felt. She then told them that there had been a mistake and gave them the prize they preferred.

When they got the undesirable prize boys were more likely than girls to display negative emotions like anger; however, that depended on whether the experimenter was absent or present, and the boys' risk status. Children at low risk for behavior problems, both boys and girls, were much more likely to display negative emotion when alone, whereas moderate and high risk boys did so whether the research assistant was there or not. Moderate and high-risk girls showed less negative emotion than similar boys in all the settings, in fact even less than low-risk girls when they were alone. These findings indicated that boys at low risk for behavior problems (like such girls) were able to inhibit their negative emotions even as preschoolers, whereas boys at risk for such problems were much less able to. Although some of the other children said that the prize "wasn't right," only the at-risk boys spoke angrily or rudely to the experimenter when they didn't get the prize they expected. From a gender development perspective, the fact that at-risk preschool girls did not show anger in these settings, even when they were alone, suggests that they are not like at-risk boys in their inability to hide negative emotions, but neither are they like low-risk girls, who did display anger once they were alone. In the authors' words:

> One possibility is that these disruptive young girls were over-regulating the expression of negative emotion. They may have learned that anger is undesirable in girls and may cope with the emotional demands of their lives by minimizing the expression, and perhaps the experience, of anger or distress....[This] contributes to a picture of these girls as coping by becoming quiet and withdrawn. At-risk girls may be more emotionally reactive or under more emotional duress but may modulate their anger and distress at the expense of appropriate expression and instrumental coping. (Cole et al., 1994, p. 844)

Smiling and crying

One particular form of emotional expression that has been studied in some depth is smiling. As adults, women have also consistently been found to smile more than men do (Hall, Carter, & Horgan, 2000). One meta-analysis of smiling (LaFrance, Hecht, & Paluck, 2003) included research on males and females from age 13 onward and found that girls and women smiled more often, with differences being largest in the late teen years and early young adulthood (see Table 5.1). A meta-analysis of sex differences in smiling during infancy and childhood (Else-Quest, Hyde, Goldsmith, & Van Hulle, 2006) reported few consistent

TABLE 5.1 Sex Differences in Social Behaviors

BEHAVIOR	EFFECT SIZE[a] ($d = $)
Behaviors with higher scores in girls and women	
Prosocial behavior (children)	−0.20
Observational studies	−0.26
Laboratory studies	−0.14
Being kind and considerate	−0.42
Comforting	−0.17
Giving help	−0.14
Sharing or donating	−0.13
Sympathy and empathy (children and adults)	−0.34
Self-report measures	−0.60
Observational measures	−0.29
Empathic accuracy (adults)	−0.26
Self-report	−0.56
Observational studies	−0.04
Interest in babies	Not known
Emotional expression (measured by self-report and observation)	Not known
Crying	Large
Smiling	−0.41
Age 13–17	−0.56
Age 18–23	−0.45
Age 24–64	−0.30
Decoding nonverbal cues	
Overall	−0.40
Visual	−0.32
Auditory	−0.18
Visual plus auditory	−1.02
Decoding facial expressions	
Infants	−0.18 to −0.92
Children and adolescents	−0.13 to −0.18
Moral orientation centering on care	−0.28
Childhood	−0.08
Adolescents	−0.53
College students	−0.18
Young adults	−0.33

(continued)

TABLE 5.1   *(Continued)*

BEHAVIOR	*EFFECT SIZE*[a] (*d* =)
Resistance to temptation (forbidden objects tasks)	(*r* = −0.11 to −0.20)
Temperament	
Effortful control	−1.01
Negative affectivity (fear only)	−0.12
Personality	
Anxiety	−0.28 to −0.31
Gregariousness	−0.15
Trust	−0.25
Tender-mindedness	−0.97
Neuroticism	−0.51
Agreeableness	−0.59
Extroversion	−0.29
Behaviors with higher scores in boys and men	
Rough and tumble play	Large[b]
Risk taking[c]	
Hypothetical choice	
Choice dilemma[d]	0.07
Framing[e]	0.05
Other	0.35
Self-reported behavior	
Smoking	−0.02
Drinking/drug use	0.04
Sexual activities	0.07
Driving	0.29
Other	0.38
Observed behaviors	
Physical activity[f]	0.16
Driving	0.17
Informed guessing[g]	0.18
Gambling	0.21
Risky experiment[h]	0.41
Intellectual risk taking[i]	0.40
Physical skills[j]	0.43
Other	0.45
Antisocial behavior	0.25
Temperament	
Surgency	0.50
Cheating	
Attitudes about	0.35
Actual cheating behavior	0.17
Helping (adults, public assistance, especially to strangers)	0.34

(continued)

TABLE 5.1   *(Continued)*

BEHAVIOR	*EFFECT SIZE[a] ($d =$)*
Moral orientation centering on justice	0.19
Children	Not known
Adolescents	0.22
College students	0.00
Young adults	0.40
Personality	
Assertiveness	0.50
Global self-esteem	0.14–0.21
Age 5–10	0–0.16
Age 11–13/14	0.12–0.13
Age 14/15–18	0.04–0.33
Adulthood	0.07–0.18
Older adulthood	0
Body image	0.50

[a] References in text.
[b] No meta-analyses available.
[c] These data are taken from Table 2 in Byrnes, J.P. et al., *Psychological Bulletin*, *125*, 367–383, 1999.
[d] A task in which a person was asked to indicate how much risk they would take in making a choice.
[e] A hypothetical dilemma in which a certain risk is presented to a risk that has some probability but is not certain.
[f] For example: playing in the street, riding an animal, or trying out gymnastics equipment.
[g] Tasks for which a person could earn points or money for correct choices but lose points or money for incorrect ones.
[h] Willingness to take part in an experiment in which a person could be harmed.
[i] Tasks in which a person could decide the level of difficulty of intellectual tasks (like math) that they would be willing to take part in.
[j] Tasks like ring toss or shuffleboard.

differences, although it is possible that girls start to smile more than boys in the elementary years. Of course, the meaning of smiling as a measure of emotion is not entirely straightforward, because smiling may be a social display to other people, and people with less social power are often more inclined to smile than those with more (LaFrance et al., 2003).

Another kind of emotional expression that is consistently associated with gender is crying. In North America and Europe, adult women have consistently been found to cry more than men (Lombardo, Cretser, & Roesch, 2001; Vingerhoets, Cornelius, Van Heck, & Becht, 2000; Vingerhoets & Scheirs, 2000). Vingerhoets and Scheirs (2000) also reviewed the few studies that they could locate on sex differences in rates of crying in children. They concluded that infant boys and girls cry at similar rates, or that boys may cry somewhat more frequently. This state of affairs continues until the age of at least 2 years. After the age of 2, little is known about the developmental progression of this sex difference until adolescence.

Not only do girls and women smile and cry more and display more facial expressions of emotion, people are also more accurate at determining the expressed emotion when looking at girls' and women's emotional expressions than when looking at boys' and men's (Brody, 1985; Hall et al., 2000). You could say that their facial expressions are more accurate indications of the genuine emotion, or are easier to read.

Physiological Studies of Emotion

The third general way that emotion has been studied is by using physiological measures such as blood pressure, heart rate, skin conductance, and the presence of stress hormones in the blood. Such measures can be used as indications of physiological arousal, but it is difficult to use them as indications of particular emotions, because people can be physiologically aroused in the presence of any strong emotion. Physiological measures taken during stressful situations have typically shown that men and women are aroused by different stressors and that they show different patterns of physiological arousal, with some showing greater reactivity by males and others by females (Brody, 1999; Manstead, 1992). Similar findings have been reported from infancy to adolescence. Sometimes researchers have shown boys with higher reactivity (Fabes et al., 1994; Lundberg, 1983), sometimes girls with higher reactivity (Zahn-Waxler et al., 1995), and sometimes different patterns of reactivity with some measures higher in boys and others higher in girls (Davis & Emory, 1995). So, again, it would be hard to conclude on the basis of this kind of evidence that one sex is more emotional than the other.

Interest in Emotional Issues

One final issue related to emotion is the extent to which children are interested in emotional issues. The evidence generally shows that by the preschool years girls talk more about emotions than boys do (Adams, Kuebli, Boyle, & Fivush, 1995; Cervantes & Callanan, 1998; Fivush, Brotman, Buckner, & Goodman, 2000; Kuebli, Butler, & Fivush, 1995). It is also the case that when recalling their childhoods, women remember more about childhood emotional states (Davis, 1999). There is also good evidence that parents talk to girls more about emotions, especially about emotions like sadness, although they are more likely to discuss anger with sons (Brody, 1999; Dunn, Bretherton, & Munn, 1987; Fivush et al., 2000; Kuebli & Fivush, 1992). We will examine this topic when we discuss gender socialization in the family. Given these kinds of conversations between parents and children, it is probably not surprising that even as preschoolers, children associate sadness with women and anger with men (Karbon, Fabes, Carlo, & Martin, 1992).

Emotion: Conclusions

In conclusion, there is a persistent stereotype that women and girls are more emotional than men and boys. When emotional expression is measured by self-report and observation, there is some evidence in support of this view, but the differences are not especially large or consistent, especially in children. What does seem to be the case is that both boys and girls learn to display the emotions that are consistent with their gender roles and learn to hide others. When emotional arousal is measured physiologically, there is little evidence supporting the idea that women and girls are more emotional.

Coping With Emotional Distress

Researchers who have studied coping with emotional distress and other forms of stress in adulthood have identified two broadly different ways of coping: **problem-focused coping** and **emotion-focused coping** (Saarni, Mumme, & Campos, 1998; Vingerhoets & Scheirs, 2000; Whissell, 1996). Problem-focused coping is acting to try to get rid of the things that are causing emotional distress. Emotion-focused coping, on the other hand, is an attempt to reduce or regulate the intensity of the emotions themselves. Some emotion-focused coping could involve attempts to modify thoughts (cognitive distraction), whereas other such coping could involve distraction with activities like exercise. Even crying can be a form of coping with emotional distress (Vingerhoets et al., 2000).

There is no clear evidence that either sex in childhood or adulthood copes more effectively with emotional distress (Altshuler & Ruble, 1989; Whissell, 1996). Some research suggests that they use different strategies to cope, with girls or women using emotion-focused strategies or seeking social support, and boys using distraction with activities like exercise (Bernzweig, Eisenberg, & Fabes, 1993; Porter et al., 2000; Saarni et al., 1998), although from middle childhood on, boys and girls use both kinds of strategies (Compas, Malcarne, & Fondacaro, 1988). In a review of the relationship between gender and coping, Whissell (1996) concluded that differences in coping strategies were often very small and dependent on the situation. Reasonably consistent with that conclusion were the findings of a meta-analysis (Tamres, Janicki, & Helgeson, 2002) of the research on gender and coping in children and adults. Tamres

TABLE 5.2 Sex Differences in Coping Styles

COPING BEHAVIOR	EFFECT SIZE (r)	INTERPRETATION
Problem-focused		
Active	−0.13	Women more
Planning	−0.04	Marginal women
Seek instrumental social support	−0.07	Women more
General problem focus	−0.12	Women more
Emotion-focused		
Seek emotional social support	−0.20	Women more
Avoidance	−0.03	Women more
Denial	0.00	No difference
Positive reappraisal	−0.03	Women more
Isolation	−0.03	No difference
Venting	−0.03	Marginal women
Rumination	−0.19	Women more
Wishful thinking	−0.13	Women more
Self-blame	−0.01	No difference
Positive self-talk	−0.17	Women more
Exercise	−0.04	Marginal women
Other		
Seek nonspecified support	−0.10	Women more
Religion	−0.07	Women more

Source: Adapted from Tamres, L.K. et al., *Personality and Social Psychology Review*, 6, 2–30, 2002. With permission. When the same effect size is significant in some instances and not others, it is due to there being a larger sample size, less variability, or both.

and her colleagues found that women and girls used 11 of the 17 coping strategies that were examined (some were emotion-focused and some were problem-focused) more than men and boys did, but the effect sizes were small (generally less than −0.15), as can be seen in Table 5.2. However, whenever there was a consistent sex difference, females used the strategies more than males did. For three strategies (seeking social support as an emotion-focused strategy, **rumination**, and positive self-talk) the effect sizes were between −0.15 and −0.20, still relatively small.

Responding to and Decoding the Emotions of Others

How do boys and girls respond to or decode the emotions of other people? There has long been a stereotype that girls and women are more skilled at responding to the feelings of others, a stereotype that has often been labeled "women's intuition" (Graham & Ickes, 1997). When researchers have studied these issues, they have divided them into two general areas: decoding others' emotions, especially from facial expressions and other nonverbal cues; and vicariously responding to the emotions of others with empathy or sympathy.

Processing and Comprehension of Facial Expressions and Other Nonverbal Cues

There are some instances when it's difficult to classify a set of behaviors as either cognitive or social, and this is certainly an example of that. We have chosen to include this kind of skill among the social behaviors, but it is really a form of **social cognition**—a cognitive skill that has impact on social relationships.

The behaviors in this category involve being able to accurately decode or understand the facial expressions and other nonverbal behaviors of other people. Certainly this skill would be important in social relationships, because the ability to easily interpret the meaning of other people's nonverbal cues ought be an asset in relating to others. Some years ago Hall (1978) published a meta-analysis showing that girls and women performed better than boys and men at decoding nonverbal cues ($d = -0.40$). When the nonverbal cues were separated into visual, auditory, and combined cues, girls and women performed better in each of these areas. The effect sizes can be seen in Table 5.1.

Decoding facial expressions
A more recent meta-analysis (McClure, 2000) examined a very specific kind of nonverbal information processing: the processing of facial expressions of others' emotions. McClure examined this skill in infants, children, and adolescents to determine whether girls are always better than boys at this skill, or whether the sex difference changes as children grow older. One of the most interesting aspects of this meta-analysis is the inclusion of studies of this skill in infancy. You may wonder how one can test whether infants can understand other people's facial expressions. Obviously, with older children and adolescents one can ask them what emotion is being demonstrated by a pictured face, and that is exactly what researchers typically do. But what do you do with infants who cannot use language? Generally this research uses two procedures for young infants, and a third for somewhat older infants. The procedures used with young infants are known as **visual preference** and **habituation**. In preference studies, infants are shown pictures of more than one facial expression to see if they show a preference for one or the other. If they do, we assume that they are able to tell the difference between them. In habituation studies, infants are shown a picture of a facial expression repeatedly. After they have seen a picture several times, they typically look at it for much less time than they originally did, and they are said to have habituated to it, that is, they are no longer interested in it. Then, if you show them a new facial expression, and they look much longer at the new picture, we assume that they can tell the difference between the two expressions. When they are a little older, around a year or so, infants are able to use the facial expressions of others as a source of information about what they should do, a skill known as **social referencing**. They have been found to approach their mothers when they are smiling, and to respond to fearful expressions by halting the behavior they are engaging in (Klinnert, Emde, Butterfield, & Campos, 1986; McClure, 2000).

McClure (2000) found that from infancy through adolescence, girls were better at decoding the facial emotions of others than boys were, but the effect sizes were generally small ($d = -0.13$ to -0.18), except in infancy, when they were moderate to large ($d = -0.70$ to -0.92). Although the effect sizes beyond infancy were small, their range suggests that between 56 and 70% of girls would perform above average on these tasks, whereas only 30 to 44% of boys would do so.

Sympathy and Empathy

Researchers have also examined sex and gender differences in **sympathy** and **empathy**: expressions and feelings of concern about the misfortune of others. Summaries of this research (Eisenberg, Spinrad, & Sadovsky, 2006; Lennon & Eisenberg, 1987) have reported that females in both childhood and adulthood demonstrate more empathy, especially in self-report measures and when it is obvious that it is being measured. Interestingly, self-report measures show a larger sex difference in empathy between older children and adults than in younger children, suggesting that it is quite possible that increasing knowledge of gender-related expectations has an effect on these kinds of measures. In support of such a conclusion, physiological measures such as heart rate and measures of arousal in response to the distress of others do not show much of a difference. A meta-analysis (Eisenberg & Fabes, 1998) of sympathy and empathy in children and found an overall effect size favoring girls ($d = -0.34$), and a larger effect with self-report measures ($d = -0.60$) than with observational measures ($d = -0.29$), and no difference between boys and girls on physiological measures.

Two reviews by Graham and Ickes, one narrative and one a meta-analysis, examined the issue of empathic accuracy in adults—that is, how accurately men and women were perceiving others' emotional states (Graham & Ickes, 1997; Ickes, Gesn, & Graham, 2000). If the researchers asked men and women to estimate how good they were at perceiving the emotional states of others, women reported better skills than men did ($d = -0.56$), but if the researchers simply measured how accurate they were, men and women did not differ ($d = 0.04$). They concluded that the difference is one of motivation to match the gender stereotype, and not one of genuine ability to accurately perceive other people's emotional states.

To conclude, studies of people's abilities to decode the emotional responses of others, or to respond to them with sympathy or empathy, generally find that girls and women are somewhat more sympathetic, empathic, or accurate at decoding emotions, but that the differences are usually small. They also tend to disappear when measured physiologically rather than by self-report.

OTHER FORMS OF SOCIAL COGNITION

As we noted earlier, social cognition skills are cognitive skills that impact social relationships. Up to this point we have considered social cognition that was largely emotionally focused, but now we move on to forms of social cognition that are more broadly based.

Theory-of-Mind

One widely studied social cognitive skill has been labeled **theory-of-mind**. Theory-of-mind concerns young children's developing ability to understand that other people have thoughts, feelings, and wishes— that they have minds. Much of the theory-of-mind research has focused on the "false belief" task, in which a correct response requires that the child recognizes that another person holds a belief that the child knows to be untrue (Wellman, Cross, & Watson, 2001). The ability to distinguish between one's own thoughts and another's demonstrates that the child appreciates that others have separate beliefs, desires, and knowledge—that is, their own minds.

Research on theory of mind has generally been concerned with the ages at which this type of knowledge develops, what affects its development, and how knowing that others have minds and feelings affects other aspects of social relationships. The relationship to gender has not been a central focus, but some researchers have examined it. There is some evidence that girls develop theory-of-mind skills at somewhat younger ages than boys do (Charman, Ruffman, & Clements, 2002; Walker, 2005), and that they are more likely to talk about the mental states and feelings of others (Hughes & Dunn, 1998). These have been reported as relatively small effects.

Perspective-Taking

Another such skill is **perspective-taking**. Much as it sounds, perspective-taking skill concerns children's ability to understand or take another's point of view. Coming out of cognitive developmental research generated by Piaget's theory, some perspective-taking research concerns rather concrete abilities, such as a child's ability to know that there is a different physical viewpoint when looking at a three-dimensional scene. However, children also develop the ability to consider the emotional points of view of others, sometimes called affective **perspective-taking** (Hughes & Dunn, 1998). Here, children are asked what emotions other people are feeling, sometimes using stories or scenarios acted out by puppets.

Many reports find no difference in boys' and girls' perspective-taking abilities, especially in younger children (e.g., Hughes & Dunn, 1998). But there are also reports that girls are more skillful at or able to understand the emotional perspectives of other people, particularly once they have reached older childhood or adolescence (Ittyerah & Mahindra, 1990; Schonert-Reichl & Beaudoin, 1998).

There is reasonably good evidence that social cognitive abilities are related to general social competence, especially in dealing with peers (Litvack-Miller, McDougall, & Romney, 1997). Here also, there is some evidence that young girls may have somewhat better skills in socially competent behavior such as entering groups of unfamiliar peers, in dealing with peer behaviors that are annoying or provoking, and at social skills such as sharing or taking turns (Walker, Irving, & Berthelsen, 2002).

To conclude, although there is some evidence of relationships among social cognition, social competence, and gender, the relationships of such skills to sex and gender have not been studied in much depth, and there are no meta-analyses available. However, the pattern of findings certainly suggests that such skills may be a little better in girls.

PROSOCIAL BEHAVIORS

The general category of **prosocial behaviors** consists of behavior that is voluntarily done to assist or help others (Eisenberg & Fabes, 1998). Are boys or girls, and men or women more likely to give assistance or nurturance to others who need help or care, or show concern for the plight of the less fortunate?

Helping Others

Eagly and Crowley (1986) used meta-analysis to examine gender and helping behavior in adults. They pointed out that there are different kinds of helping, and that they were gendered. For example, women might be expected to care for others' emotional needs, whereas men might be expected to save others from harm in a protective or heroic way. Most of the studies in the meta-analysis were short-term episodes of helping strangers, which are more consistent with the masculine form of helping. Indeed, men were found to be more helpful ($d = 0.34$) and women to receive such help more often ($d = -0.46$). Men were also more likely to have the skills to provide help (e.g., changing a tire) and less likely to be fearful of the potential repercussions of helping an unfamiliar stranger in public.

A more recent meta-analysis of children's (average age about 8 years old) helping and other prosocial behavior was done by Fabes and Eisenberg (as cited in Eisenberg & Fabes, 1998) and produced a different finding: girls were more prosocial ($d = -0.20$). However, their measures of helping were quite different that the ones reported in Eagly and Crowley's meta-analysis. Fabes and Eisenberg found that the difference was greater for measures of being kind and considerate ($d = -0.42$) than for giving help ($d = -0.14$), sharing or donating ($d = -0.13$), or comforting ($d = -0.17$). They reported larger differences in observational studies ($d = -0.26$) than in experimental or laboratory studies ($d = -0.14$). Finally, they reported that the sex difference increased as children grew older, but the age of the participants was confounded with the studies' methods (e.g., more observational studies of older children), so at this point we do not really know what happens to this difference developmentally.

Children's Thoughts About Helping

Although researchers have examined behaviors like sharing, helping, and demonstrating concern, one interesting question concerns what children think about these kinds of behaviors. Greener and Crick (1999) asked boys and girls in third through sixth grade to describe what other children do when they want to be nice to someone. They found that boys and girls named such things as including the others in their groups and letting them play, being friends with them, avoiding being mean to them, and sharing with them. The most common responses were to be friends, to include the other child in the group, and to share with them. There was no difference between boys and girls in the in the percentage of time they chose each of these ways to be nice. As the researchers pointed out, both boys and girls named including them in the group as the most important way to demonstrate prosocial behavior to other children.

Interactions With Babies and Toddlers

One important prosocial behavior that is often seen as gendered is nurturance towards those younger than oneself, particularly interest in and care devoted towards infants and toddlers. We know that women and girls are more often responsible for the care of infants and younger children (Berman, 1980; Best & Williams, 1997; Edwards, 2002), and that this is one of the most consistent cultural universals. But what about people's demonstrated interest in interacting with babies and young children? Do girls and women demonstrate more interest in or interactions with babies and very young children, especially when they are not responsible for looking after them?

There are no meta-analyses of this research, and the last comprehensive review of the research was published more than 20 years ago (Berman, 1980). Since Berman's review, several published studies examined interest in and interaction with infants and toddlers. We will consider three areas of research: adults' interactions with unfamiliar infants, children's and adolescents' interactions with unfamiliar infants, and children's interactions with their own infant siblings.

Interactions With Unfamiliar Infants

There are a few studies on adults' interactions with unfamiliar infants. The research has used two procedures: one has been to have a person wait in a waiting room with a mother and her infant (Feldman & Nash, 1978, 1979b), and the other has been to have the person alone with the baby during a short period of interaction (Blakemore, 1981, 1985). Both studies in which the adult and infant were alone found more interaction on the part of women than of men (d about -0.70), whereas the waiting room studies found a sex difference only among parents and grandparents of infants. That is, only when they themselves were parents or grandparents of the infant did women show more interaction with another baby and the baby's mother in a waiting room.

There have been several studies of children and adolescents interacting with unfamiliar infants. Much of this research has found girls showing more interest in and interactions with babies from the preschool years onward, with early adolescence being a time when sex differences are especially likely (Berman, Monda, & Myerscough, 1977; Berman, Smith, & Goodman, 1983; Blakemore, 1981, 1991, 1998; Feldman & Nash, 1979a; Feldman, Nash, & Cutrona, 1977; Frodi, Murray, Lamb, & Steinberg, 1984; Jessee, Strickland, & Jessee, 1994; Lee & Jessee, 1997; Leveroni & Berenbaum, 1998; Reid, Tate, & Berman, 1989). Studies in which the child interacts with a baby in the presence of the baby's mother, as in a waiting room, have been less likely to report sex differences before adolescence (Fogel, Melson, Toda, & Mistry, 1987; Melson & Fogel, 1982; Nash & Feldman, 1981). One group of researchers (Frodi & Lamb, 1978) measured physiological responses in 8- and 14-year-olds to videos of infants crying and smiling, as well as behavioral interactions with live infants. The physiological responses did not differ between boys and girls, but girls interacted more with the babies. Finally, researchers have also asked children about their knowledge about babies (Blakemore, 1992; Melson & Fogel, 1989; Melson, Fogel, & Toda, 1986), and have found no difference between boys and girls in how much they know about babies.

Children's Interactions With Their Infant Siblings

Some research has also looked at children's interactions with their baby siblings. Some of this research has not reported differences between boys and girls in their nurturant interactions with their baby brothers or sisters (Dunn & Kendrick, 1982; Lamb, 1978), and some has found complicated interactions between the sex of the baby and the sex of the older child (e.g., Dunn & Kendrick, 1981), often reporting that older brothers with baby brothers are the least nurturant of the older siblings. However, several studies have shown that older sisters are more nurturant towards baby siblings in general (Abramovitch, Corter, & Lando, 1979; Abramovitch, Corter, & Pepler, 1980; Blakemore, 1990; Kendrick & Dunn, 1982; Kier & Lewis, 1998; Stewart, 1983a, 1983b; Stewart & Marvin, 1984), and especially towards baby sisters.

Interactions with infants: conclusions
So what picture emerges from this research? Clearly, many things are yet to be known about boys' versus girls' degree of interest in and interaction with babies, and the factors that influence it. However, the bulk of the evidence seems to suggest that, from a young age, girls show more interest in and nurturant interaction with babies than boys do, although the degree of difference found is affected by the particular conditions under study. There appears to be no difference in physiological responses to infants.

Some research has also studied boys' and girls' nurturance towards their pets, and has occasionally compared the children's interactions with their pets with their interactions with babies. Most of that research has reached the conclusion that boys and girls are equally interested in caring for pets (Melson & Fogel, 1989, 1996). So the fact that girls show more interest in caring for babies does not necessarily extend towards having more interest in nurturance in general.

PHYSICALLY ACTIVE PLAY, PARTICIPATION IN SPORTS, RISK-TAKING, ACCIDENTS, AND INJURY

Rough and Tumble and Physically Active Play

Three kinds of physical play have been identified: **rhythmic play** in infancy such as foot kicking; **exercise play** during the preschool years, including such activities as running and jumping; and **rough and tumble play** (R & T play) beginning some time during the late preschool period and continuing through early adolescence (Pellegrini & Smith, 1998). The rhythmic play of infancy is equally common in boys and girls, but both of the latter types of physical play, particularly R & T play, are more characteristic of boys.

Exercise play consists of such activities as running, jumping, climbing, chasing, lifting, and pulling (Pellegrini & Smith, 1998). It is common during the preschool years (about 10 to 20% of all play) and declines once children are in elementary school (Pellegrini, 1990; Smith & Connolly, 1980). Preschool boys are somewhat more likely to engage in this type of play than are girls, possibly due to their greater activity level, but it is not certain if boys do it more than girls do during the elementary years.

Rough and Tumble Play

More research has focused on R & T play, which overlaps with active physical play but also includes elements of play fighting and pretend aggression. Children may alternate between being a victim and a victimizer in these kinds of play fights (Pellegrini, 1993), and generally children who engage in this kind of play thoroughly enjoy it. R & T play accounts for about 3–5% of preschool children's free play, increases to 7–8% of early elementary school children's play on the playground at recess, to 10% around the age of 7–11 years, and decreases after that to about 3% of the activity of 14-year-olds (Humphreys & Smith, 1987; Pellegrini & Smith, 1998). There is a very consistent set of findings that boys engage in more R & T play in virtually every culture in which it has been studied (Boulton, 1996; Braza, Braza, Carreras, & Munoz, 1997; DiPietro, 1981; Finegan, Niccols, Zacher, & Hood, 1991; Hines & Kaufman, 1994; Pellegrini, 1990; Pellegrini & Smith, 1998).

It is interesting to note that adults—especially women and particularly teachers—often think that R & T play is aggressive and therefore something to be discouraged (Costabile, Genta, Zucchini, Smith, & Harker, 1992; MacDonald, 1992). One recent study found that teachers often have difficulty telling the difference between play fighting and real fighting, so they see play fights as problematic because they can turn into real fights and children can get hurt (Smith, Smees, Pellegrini, & Menesini, 2002), although that does not actually happen very often. Real aggression is much less common than play aggression (Humphreys & Smith, 1987).

Children, on the other hand, say that they can clearly distinguish between the play activities, which they see as exciting and fun, and real aggression, which is more likely to be seen as potentially harmful or dangerous (Pellegrini, 2002; Smith, Hunter, Carvalho, & Costabile, 1992; Smith et al., 2002). One clear difference between R & T play and true aggression is that play is almost always done with a cooperative partner or group, all of whom are clearly enjoying themselves. In fact, boys are often drawn to such play styles as soon as they see others doing them, whereas girls are more likely to avoid those activities (Jacklin & Maccoby, 1978). It is also the case that socially competent and popular or high-status children are much less likely to become aggressive during R & T play than rejected children are (Pellegrini, 1988, 1994), and that boys use the activities of R & T play to show affection to other boys they care about (Reed & Brown, 2001).

Some physical activities that are part of R & T play are done at similar rates by young boys and girls, but others are much more characteristic of boys. For example, preschool girls and boys are very similar in their rates of jumping (DiPietro, 1981), although girls may take turns using something like a trampoline, whereas boys are more likely to do it together and collapse into play wrestling (e.g., see Maccoby, 1998). One important distinction has been made between R & T play that consists primarily of chasing, and R & T play that is rougher and consists of play fighting and hitting. Most children, both boys and girls, like chasing and participate in it, but fewer children like play fighting, and play fighting is the particular kind of R & T play that boys are more likely to do than girls (Smith et al., 1992).

Participation in Sports

In chapter 4 we considered physical skill differences that might relate to participation in sports. Here we consider sex differences in sports participation itself. Participation in organized sports, particularly during the adolescent years, has typically been more prevalent among boys than girls in many countries across the world, although girls' participation is increasing in many of the Western democracies. In North American high schools and colleges during the past several years, about 40% of the athletes have been girls (Cheslock, 2007; National Federation of State High School Associations, 2006; Sport Canada, 1998). By comparison, in 1971 only about 13% of high school athletes were girls, clearly a huge increase during a 35-year period when gender equity in sports has been an increasingly important concern on the part of athletic associations and schools. In the United States, much of the impetus for the increasing participation of girls and young women in sport is due to the passage of Title IX, a federal law passed in 1972 that prohibited discrimination on the basis of sex in any programs or activities on the part of federally funded educational institutions. Title IX has implications for many activities that take place in schools and universities, but it has had particular impact on opening athletic programs to girls and women.

Despite the increase in girls' participation in recent years, sports and athleticism remain more central to boys' lives than to girls' in many European countries as well as in North America (Finegan et al., 1991; Flammer, Alsaker, & Noack, 1999; Messner, 1990). For example, one recent study in Iceland, a country that is noted for the equality of the sexes, found many more organized sports for boys, and that the coaches and leaders of such programs were much more likely to be men (Vilhjalmsson & Kristjansdottir, 2003). Being an athlete is a key part of masculinity in modern Western cultures (Koivula, 1999; Lantz & Schroeder, 1999; Wheaton, 2000), and athleticism and sport participation is more important to boys' popularity than to girls' (Lease, Kennedy, & Axelrod, 2002). Even children recognize that athletics is an area where boys who participate are held in higher esteem than girls who do so (Solomon & Bredemeier, 1999).

The fact that sport participation is seen as a male domain also affects the probability that girls will continue to participate in it as they grow older, especially in sports that are defined as masculine.

Many children stop participating in sports and become less physically active as they reach adolescence (Bradley, McMurray, Harrell, & Deng, 2000), and such physical inactivity impacts fitness and health for children of both sexes. However, the decrease in sport participation and physical activity is especially likely in girls. Interestingly, girls who are less feminine, who are tomboys, or who play with nontraditional toys, are more likely to continue in such sports through their adolescent and college years (Guillet, Sarrazin, & Fontayne, 2000).

In childhood, boys are more likely to say they enjoy sports and believe that they are good at athletic activities (Eccles & Harold, 1991; Freedman-Doan et al., 2000). Interestingly, parents as well as coaches, teachers, and peers believe that boys are more competent and interested in sports than girls are, and these beliefs have been shown to influence the children's own beliefs and their capabilities (Biernat & Vescio, 2002; Eccles, Freedman Doan, Frome, Jacobs, & Yoon, 2000; Trent, Cooney, Russell, & Warton, 1996), a topic we will return to when we consider gender socialization.

There are certain sports that few girls take part in (e.g., football and wrestling), and others that few boys take part in (e.g., spirit squads, softball, and field hockey), whereas still others are done with similar frequencies by both sexes (e.g., track and field, soccer, and tennis; National Federation of State High School Associations, 2006). Analyses of the characteristics of sports that are associated with females and femininity (e.g., cheerleading, figure skating, gymnastics) include being beautiful and graceful, whereas those that are associated with males and masculinity include danger, risk, and violence, team spirit, speed, and strength (Koivula, 2001). Clearly these are gendered attributes.

Some research also shows that boys and girls have somewhat different reasons or motives for taking part in sports, with boys being more focused on extrinsic factors like becoming popular or gaining status, and on competition, whereas girls are more focused on having fun and becoming more physically fit (Weinberg et al., 2000). Other research has found that although athletic participation is valued more for males in general, participation in gender-appropriate sports is valued much more for both sexes than participation in gender-inappropriate sports (Holland & Andre, 1994). For example, British researcher Michael Gard (2001) interviewed 12- to 14-year-old boys about various aspects of participation in sports. The boys were extremely negative about any sports associated with girls or femininity, referring to them as "gay" or "girlie."

It is also interesting that danger and risk are seen as part of associating masculinity with sports. Indeed, sports like mountain climbing, downhill skiing, snowboarding, car racing, bike racing, skateboarding, rollerblading and the like do indeed carry significant risk of injury. Even sports that take place in school can be dangerous—for example, football. Consider this young British boy's reason for playing rugby: "I like being in a sport, but contact sport, 'cos I like smashing people, and I like getting smashed myself" (Gard, 2001, p. 223). Shortly, we will see that risk taking is more likely to be done by boys in many areas of their lives.

Finally, one concern about gender and sports relates to the extent to which playing in sports has implications for adult roles, independent of physical fitness. Indeed, some researchers have reported that girls' participation in sports in childhood is related to greater self-confidence and more participation in nontraditional careers (Coats & Overman, 1992; Miller & Levy, 1996).

Risk-Taking

In chapter 4 we discussed the fact that there is a higher death rate of boys in childhood and adolescence, and that some of that difference is related to the greater tendency of boys to take dangerous risks. The fact that boys are more likely to take risks is related to accidents and injuries throughout childhood and adolescence, even into young adulthood. It is certainly a stereotype that boys are covered in bumps and bruises, and this is a stereotype that has some basis in fact.

There have been several studies of sex differences in risk-taking. In a meta-analysis of this area of research, one group of researchers (Byrnes, Miller, & Schafer, 1999) divided studies of risk-taking behaviors into three types. The first kind of study was of experimental tasks in which participants were asked to make a choice between two risky alternatives to see how much risk they would tolerate. For example, when presented with a scenario involving the risk of death from an operation, how much risk of death would the participants say they were willing to accept (e.g., 10, 50, or 90%) and still have the operation? These were imaginary or hypothetical scenarios in which they did not really have to face the consequences of their choices. The second type of study was self-reported risk-taking in which people (usually adolescents or older) indicated whether they engaged in risky behavior like taking drugs or having unprotected sex. The third type of study was observational, in which researchers actually observed the risk-taking behavior, such as making observations of drivers in traffic or of children on the playground. Examples of each of these categories can be seen in Table 5.1 (see the section on scores that are higher in boys and men).

Byrnes and his colleagues concluded that boys and men did take more risks, but that the degree of risk depended on age and the particular kind of risk. The effect sizes, all of which are presented in Table 5.1, varied between essentially 0 and 0.43, although half were greater than 0.20. They also found that girls and women were less likely to take risks when outcomes might be harmful (e.g., reckless driving), as well as when they might be beneficial (e.g., taking risks while practicing the SATs). Although the effect sizes were not large, when dangerous or life-threatening activities are involved even effect sizes of this magnitude could result in substantially more male deaths. We do, in fact, know that from childhood through young adulthood males suffer from more injuries, and they experience more injury-related deaths at all ages (Fingerhut & Warner, 1997). This is especially noticeable in death rates due to automobile accidents, in which male drivers are 2–3 times more likely to die than are female drivers (Harre, 2000; Mayhew, Ferguson, Desmond, & Simpson, 2001; Nell, 2002) in many Western countries.

There were also effects of age in the meta-analysis (Byrnes et al., 1999). After age 21 the effect size was very small ($d = 0.05$), with larger differences in childhood and adolescence (d values from 0.10 to 0.26). However, some kinds of risks were not measured in children (e.g., alcohol, driving, sex), whereas others were only evaluated in children (e.g., playing on gym equipment). Nonetheless, it is certainly reasonable to conclude that boys engage in more risk taking over all of the childhood and adolescent years.

Changes in Adolescent Risk-Taking in Recent Years

One interesting finding that Byrnes and his colleagues reported was evidence that the difference in risk-taking was decreasing in recent years. The average effect size in studies published before 1981 was 0.20, but it was 0.13 in studies published after that time. Similar trends have been noted for car accidents (Mayhew et al., 2001), in that young women's accident rates are becoming more similar to young men's, although their fatal car crashes still remain much lower. In addition, although teenage boys continue to abuse illicit drugs at higher rates than girls do, teenage girls are now smoking cigarettes and using alcohol at rates similar to teenage boys (Centers for Disease Control, 2002; Johnson, O'Malley, & Bachman, 2002). For example, among high school and college students binge drinking is now being done to much the same degree by males and females (National Center on Addiction and Substance Abuse, 2002). In a recent article in *Time* magazine a young woman college student was quoted as saying:

> You don't want to be that dumb girly girl who looks wasted and can't hold her liquor. I know it's juvenile, but I've had boys comment how impressed they are at the amount of alcohol I've consumed. To be able to drink like a guy is kind of a badge of honor. For me, it's a feminism thing. (Morse et al., 2002, p. 57)

As we have noted previously, women's gender-related characteristics have been changing in the direction of men's. Although there is much to be applauded about new opportunities for women and girls, it is obvious that smoking, drinking, and driving riskily are hardly to be cheered.

Risk-Taking and Parental Responses in Very Young Children

One group of researchers has specifically examined risk-taking and injuries in very young children (Morrongiello & Dawber, 1998, 1999, 2000). The purpose of their research was to examine parents' reactions to children's risk-taking to see if there is evidence that boys and girls are socialized differently in ways that could help explain their differential injury rates. We will return to a discussion of their research on this topic when we look at parental socialization in a later chapter. However, for now an examination of one of their studies will give us an interesting look at the differential risk-taking that young boys and girls engage in, and tell us a little about how mothers respond to that risk-taking. Morrongiello and Dawber (1998) had mothers and their 2- to 3-year-old children come to the university to take part in a research project. They designed a laboratory to look like an office with a sitting area, told the mothers that the normal waiting room was unavailable that day, and asked them apologetically if they could wait in the "office."

In this office there were 12 "hazards," including three hot substances (e.g., a coffee pot) that might possibly burn the child, three items that might cut the child (e.g., scissors), three possible poisons (e.g., Windex), and three items that might cause a fall if the child attempted to climb on them or touch them. None of these hazards were really dangerous. The hot items were really cold, the scissors were dull, the poisons were colored water or were empty, and the items that might cause a fall were actually very secure. However, the mothers could not know that the objects were not really dangerous.

The mothers were asked to complete questionnaires while waiting in the office. The researchers later observed from videotapes whether the children approached or touched the hazards and how the mothers responded to them when and if they did, and the extent to which the children obeyed their mothers when they were asked not to touch an item. They also took measures of the child's previous history of risk-taking and injuries.

In the research setting boys approached hazards almost twice as frequently as girls did (boys approached 9.1 of the 12 items on average, whereas girls approached 5.6) although they did not approach other kinds of items any more frequently. Boys and girls also behaved differently with respect to the hazards. For example, girls were more likely to point at the burn hazards such as the coffee pot, whereas boys were more likely to actually touch them or pick them up. On questionnaires, the mothers also reported that sons had been more likely to take risks and to have had injuries in the past.

The mothers also behaved differently with sons and daughters. Mothers of girls were more likely to ask them to stop, whereas mothers of boys were more likely to use physical strategies such as moving them away from the items. Interestingly, the children also responded differently when their mothers attempted to make them stop interacting with a dangerous item. The researchers found that daughters complied with their mothers' requests 99% of the time, whereas sons complied only about 25% of the time. When sons did not comply, mothers often removed the item.

We have seen, then, that from a very young age boys are more likely to take risks and to be injured. Throughout life, males are more likely to face early death from injuries as a result of risk-taking, and so this is a very significant aspect of male behavior. However, some recent research suggests that the gender difference in risk-taking, at least in adolescence and early young adulthood, may be diminishing.

AGGRESSION

Children have certainly been known to aggress against others in a variety of ways, and some forms of aggression are highly gendered. Every day, children in elementary and secondary schools the world over are taunted by the classmates and called names like "creeps," or "faggots," or told they are ugly or stupid. As an example, one researcher told the story of a group of girls at a school in California who repeatedly and purposefully excluded one of their peers, teased and tormented her, and treated as if she was not really there (Goodwin, 2002). They made her life at school a misery. Children also take part in direct physical attacks on others. For example, in the local newspaper of a medium-sized American city, it was recently reported that a 15-year-old boy was attacked in the middle of the afternoon on the grounds of a local high school by four other similar-aged boys and was beaten until he was bloody and required plastic surgery to repair the damage to his face (Eaton, 2003). These kinds of episodes, although horrible to think about, are a regular part of some children's lives.

Aggression is typically defined as behavior that is intended to hurt or harm another, or that is perceived by the victim as hurtful (Coie & Dodge, 1998). It may include physical aggression such as hitting or kicking, verbal aggression such as insulting someone or calling them names, or fantasy aggression such as pretending to harm another, or thinking or dreaming about behaving aggressively (Maccoby & Jacklin, 1974). There is also aggression in which people harm others my manipulating their social relationships. Social or relational aggression consists of behaviors that damage another person's self-esteem, social relationships, or social standing (Crick & Rose, 2000; Underwood, Galen, & Paquette, 2001). It can include gossiping, spreading rumors, or the purposeful exclusion of others.

Direct Physical and Verbal Aggression

When Maccoby and Jacklin (1974) summarized the research on sex differences in their comprehensive book, they concluded that aggression was the most consistently found social behavior that differed between males and females. Furthermore, they concluded that the difference was found as soon as children were capable of behaving aggressively, and that although aggression itself declined with age, the sex difference continued into adulthood. They also concluded that the difference was found across cultures and in similar species. In addition, boys and men were found to be the targets of aggression more often than were girls and women.

Recent Meta-Analyses

Since Maccoby and Jacklin published their book there have been several meta-analyses of the sex difference in direct aggression (Archer, 2004; Bettencourt & Kernahan, 1997; Bettencourt & Miller, 1996; Eagly & Steffen, 1986; Hyde, 1984, 1986). These meta-analyses have consistently reported that boys and men are more aggressive than girls and women. Hyde (1984, 1986) reported the overall difference between males and females was about half a standard deviation ($d = 0.50$); but the difference was greater in children ($d = 0.58$ in preschoolers) than in adults ($d = 0.27$). She also reported that the difference was affected by the kind of aggression, being greatest in the case of physical and fantasy aggression. It was also greater when observed in naturalistic settings than in the laboratory. The degree to which the gender difference was affected by various characteristics of the study can be seen in Table 5.3.

A more recent meta-analysis of sex differences in aggression (Knight, Fabes, & Higgins, 1996) was careful to control several characteristics of the studies used in the meta-analysis (e.g., observational versus self-report or peer-report). Knight and his colleagues concluded that the sex difference in aggression was very stable ($d = 0.5–0.6$), with the largest differences in physical aggression observed directly ($d = 0.8–0.9$). Unlike Hyde, Knight and his colleagues found that the difference was larger as people became older, rather than smaller. They concluded that Hyde's finding of a decrease in the difference with age was affected by the kind of study (e.g., observations as opposed to self-reports); however, they also judged that the data available at the time did not allow them to determine that the size of the difference either increased or decreased with age. However, there is other research that suggests that at least between birth and approximately the age of 4, boys do become more aggressive relative to girls (Sanson, Prior, Smart, & Oberklaid, 1993).

Another recent meta-analysis (Archer, 2004) examined aggression in real-world settings rather than aggression measured in the laboratory. The measures of aggression were self-report, other report (e.g., peers and teachers), and direct observation. They reported an overall d of 0.42 for aggression. For physical aggression measured by self-report, d ranged from 0.33 to 0.84 using various measures (see Table 5.3), and for verbal aggression d ranged from 0.09 to 0.55. Comparing children to adults, the size of the sex difference tended to be largest in young adulthood (ages 18–30). They also examined several different industrialized countries (e.g., North American and European countries, Australia, New Zealand, and Japan) and found no instances where the sex difference was in the other direction (girls more than boys), although the size of the difference varied.

TABLE 5.3   Comparison of the Degree of Difference Between Male and Female Aggression in Various Types of Studies or with Various Measures

STUDY FEATURE	EFFECT SIZE ($d =$)	
	HYDE (1986)	ARCHER (2004)
1. Design		
Experimental	0.29	
Naturalistic/observational	0.56	0.42
2. Method of Measurement		
Direct observation	0.51	0.53 (physical)
Self-report	0.40	0.39 (physical)
Parent or teacher report	0.48	0.40 (physical)
Projective	0.83	
Peer report	0.63	0.84 (physical)
3. Kind of Aggression		
Mixed (physical + verbal)	0.43	0.42
Physical	0.60	0.39 (self-report) to 0.84 (peer report)
Verbal	0.43	0.14 (observation) to 0.51 (peer report)
Fantasy	0.84	
Willingness to shock, hurt	0.39	
Imitative	0.49	
Hostility scale	0.02	
Other	0.43	

Sources: Adapted from Hyde, J.S., in *The psychology of gender: Advances through meta-analysis*, J.S. Hyde & M.C. Linn, eds. (pp. 51–66). Baltimore: Johns Hopkins University Press, 1986; and Archer, J., *Review of General Psychology*, 8, 291–322, 2004.

Most of the remaining meta-analyses that have followed Hyde's have not focused on children; however, they do provide additional information about the conditions under which a gender difference is likely to be found among adults (Bettencourt & Kernahan, 1997; Bettencourt & Miller, 1996; Eagly & Steffen, 1986). These meta-analyses have confirmed that the gender difference in aggression in adults is larger for physical ($d = 0.40$) than psychological aggression ($d = 0.18$), and larger when it is freely chosen than when it is required in an experimental setting (Bettencourt & Kernahan, 1997; Bettencourt & Miller, 1996; Eagly & Steffen, 1986). Also, when people are provoked by being insulted or aggressed against, the sex difference is smaller ($d = 0.17$). When violent cues are present (e.g., pictures of guns, violent videos, bumper stickers with violent messages), both sexes are more likely to be aggressive (Bettencourt & Kernahan, 1997).

Some have wondered how early the sex difference in physical aggression begins. Although not a meta-analysis, one recent study examined a large, representative sample of children born in the Canadian provide of Québec (Baillargeon et al., 2007). Almost 3,000 children were followed longitudinally for nearly 3 years. The authors reported that, although high levels of aggression were not especially likely in these young children, by 17 months of age and continuing to 29 months of age, boys were found among the very aggressive children much more often than were girls.

Other Cultures

Cross-cultural research (Frey & Hoppe-Graff, 1994; Fry, 1992; Munroe, Hulefeld, Rodgers, Tomeo, & Yamazaki, 2000) consistently shows greater male aggression in many different settings, although there are some cultures in which females are quite physically aggressive (e.g., see Cook, 1992 for a description of very aggressive women among the Margariteños in Venezuela), and some where practically no aggression is seen in either sex (e.g., see Lepowsky, 1994 for a description of a small island society near New Guinea). Nonetheless, the norm is greater aggression among boys and men. A study of naturally occurring aggression among 3- to 9-year-olds in four non-Western cultures, Belize, Kenya, Nepal, and American Samoa (Munroe et al., 2000), observed physical aggression and assault, roughhousing, and verbal aggression such as insults, and found that boys were more aggressive than girls in all four cultures, although the difference between them was greater in the two **patrilineal** cultures (Kenya and Nepal). In these two cultures the amount of aggression in general was also greater. Overall, boys were aggressive in about 10% of their social behaviors, whereas girls were in only 6%. Neither sex was likely to aggress against adults, and as would be expected, aggression decreased as children grew older. Aggression, especially physical, was less likely to be found when adults or parents, especially mothers, were present. Boys' aggression was most likely to be found when they were playing in large groups of other boys.

Attitudes About Targets of Aggression

There are also several attitude differences between men and women, most of which are quite suggestive of the influence of gender socialization. Women are more likely than men to think that their aggression would harm the person being aggressed against, that they would feel guilty if they behaved aggressively, and they are more fearful than men of being retaliated against or harmed by the person they might aggress against (Bettencourt & Miller, 1996; Eagly & Steffen, 1986). Children have shown similar differences in attitude in that boys have more positive attitudes about aggression (Huesmann, Guerra, Zelli, & Miller, 1992).

Finally, there are differences in men's and women's targets: women are more likely to aggress against women than against men, and men are more likely to aggress against other men than against women. Bettencourt and Miller (1996) suggest that fear of retaliation is an important factor in limiting women's aggression against men, but there is a "norm of chivalry" that prevents many men from aggressing against women.

Aggression in the Context of Close Relationships

Some researchers have reported that one kind of interpersonal violence is similar in males and females once they reach adolescence: violence in interpersonal relationships. That is, males and females are equally likely to hit or attack a dating partner or family member, although it is important to keep in mind that a minority of individuals of either sex strike their partners. Estimates suggest that fewer than 20% of partners shove, slap, hit, punch, kick, throw something, or use a weapon to threaten or to injure a partner. On the other hand, parents of both sexes are very likely to strike children, especially children younger than 5, in which the rates are above 90% for both parents. Siblings of both sexes are also very likely to hit one another (Straus, 2001).

The authors of one extensive longitudinal study of childhood and adolescent aggression and antisocial behavior concluded that there is "an extremely robust finding that inside intimate relationships and the privacy of the home, females are just as physically aggressive as males" (Moffitt, Caspi, Rutter, & Silva, 2001, p. 69). A meta-analysis of the same phenomenon (Archer, 2000) among adolescent and adult heterosexual partners found that females were slightly more likely to engage in physical aggression against their partners ($d = -0.05$), a degree of difference that is very close to zero. Males were more likely to inflict damage on their partners, but the difference was small ($d = 0.15$).

The idea that females are just as aggressive as males towards their partners is a hotly debated issue (e.g., see Straus, 1999), and whether males or females are found to aggress more against their partners does depend on what kinds of samples are studied and how serious the aggression is. If the couple involved is older, married or cohabiting (as opposed to dating), if the aggression leads to injury or even death, and if it is reported as a crime, it is more likely that males are found to be the more aggressive (Archer, 2000;

Moffitt et al., 2001). If the couple is dating and the aggression is milder (e.g., slapping, shoving, throwing something), females seem to be either equally or slightly more likely to do it. One factor to keep in mind is that many men are very reluctant to hit women, and women may think that violence against their male partners is trivial because they do not think they are especially likely to injure them. Also, because many men are reluctant to retaliate physically against their partners, women are not especially likely to fear retaliation from these partners. There seems to be two kinds of aggression here. Some aggression (even murder) may arise out of some men's motivation to control their female partners or to prevent them from leaving (Daly & Wilson, 1998). Other aggression, mild or serious, can result from people losing control of themselves when angered by a partner, sibling, or child, and it is this latter type that appears to be equally common in both sexes.

Physical Aggression: Conclusions

What can we conclude about sex or gender differences in direct physical or verbal aggression? It seems quite clear that in natural environments in childhood, boys are more aggressive than girls, especially in peer groups where other boys are present. Physical aggression decreases with age, but it is not clear if the sex difference increases or decreases. In family and dating relationships, several researchers have reported that girls and women are as aggressive as boys and men. It is much less likely for there to be a sex difference in the amount of aggression in adulthood when people are provoked by the person they aggress against, especially if the aggression is not physical, and the threat of dire consequence is small. There are several differences between males and females in attitudes or beliefs about aggression. With peers and in public settings, boys think aggression is more acceptable than girls do, and boys and men are less likely than girls and women to feel guilty or anxious about aggressing and less likely to be fearful about someone retaliating against them. In intimate relationships, by adolescence both males and females think that male violence against females is worse than the reverse.

Social or Relational Aggression

Is there a kind of aggression that is done more by girls than by boys? As early as the 1940s or 1950s developmental psychologists reported that girls were more likely to make unkind remarks about other children outside of their social group than boys were (Terman, Johnson, Kuznets, & McNemar, 1946; Terman & Tyler, 1954). Two decades later, in their discussion of gender and aggression, Maccoby and Jacklin (1974) also reported that girls were more likely to be "catty" with each other. By the 1990s the systematic study of these issues began in earnest (Björkqvist, Lagerspetz, & Kaukiainen, 1992; Crick & Grotpeter, 1995; Galen & Underwood, 1997).

Social or relational aggression might well be summarized by the first part of a title of a paper by Finnish researcher, Kaj Björkqvist, and his colleagues: "Do girls manipulate and boys fight?" (Björkqvist, Lagerspetz, & Kaukiainen, 1992), or in the following quote: "Boys may use their fists to fight, but at least it's over quickly; girls use their tongues, and it goes on forever" (Galen & Underwood, 1997, p. 589). Social or relational aggression consists of behaviors that damage another person's self-esteem, social relationships, or social standing (Crick & Rose, 2000; Underwood et al., 2001). It can include gossiping, spreading rumors, or the purposeful exclusion of others. This kind of aggression has also been called **indirect aggression**, because it often occurs outside of the presence of the victim (Björkqvist, Österman, & Kaukiainen, 1992), but it is clear that all of these terms refer to the same general kind of aggressive behavior (Archer & Coyne, 2005). Some examples include purposefully not inviting another child to a birthday party or making negative comments about another so as to break up a friendship. For example, one of us once observed her son playing with a neighbor girl who whispered conspiratorially about two boys who lived down the street: "Let's not let them play with us." These kinds of actions can be incredibly hurtful to their victims, and girls especially tell stories of painful childhood memories of such events (Crick, 1995; Crick & Grotpeter, 1996; Owens, Slee, & Shute, 2000). A very interesting qualitative study of relational aggression in teenage girls found that girls often use relational aggression to alleviate boredom, for something fun to do, to bring importance to themselves by excluding others, and to cement their own place in a peer group, especially the "right" group (Owens, Shute, & Slee, 2000). What is especially interesting about this is that boys use play fighting for very similar reasons: to have fun and to establish dominance among peers (Pellegrini, 2002).

Researchers report that girls are more likely to be socially or relationally aggressive, although to some extent it depends on how it is measured and the context in which it occurs (Björkqvist, Lagerspetz et al., 1992; Crick & Grotpeter, 1995). Underwood and her colleagues (Galen & Underwood, 1997; Paquette & Underwood, 1999) have found similar degrees of disdainful facial expressions (e.g., rolling one's eyes) and gossip among boys and girls in childhood and early adolescence. In an experimental study involving annoying behavior by an unfamiliar peer, both boys and girls made rejecting remarks about the child when the child was not in the room, but boys were actually more rejecting of the annoying peer when the child was present (Underwood, Scott, Galperin, Bjornstad, & Sexton, 2004). However, in general, cross-cultural research has found that indirect or social aggression is somewhat more common in girls and women in many cultures of the world (French, Jansen, & Pidada, 2002; Fry, 1992; Hines & Fry, 1994; Olson, 1994; Österman et al., 1998), but not always (e.g., Tomada & Schneider, 1997). Even as preschoolers, girls are often found to be more relationally aggressive (Ostrov & Keating, 2004). Preschoolers are also able to identify relational aggression as being associated with girls and physical aggression with boys (Giles & Heyman, 2005).

At this point, there is only one meta-analysis examining sex differences in this type of aggression (Archer, 2004). Archer reported generally smaller sex differences in relational aggression (d values from approximately 0 to about -0.20) than those he reported for physical and verbal aggression, except in the case of observational studies ($d = -0.74$), but there were only four such studies that were included in his meta-analysis. There were larger effects during the teenage years (d approximately -0.10 to -0.30), with girls engaging in more of such aggression, but essentially no difference between boys and girls in childhood or once they reached adulthood.

Girls are also found to be the victims of this kind of aggression more often than boys (Crick & Bigbee, 1998), as early as the preschool years (Crick, Casas, & Ku, 1999). Girls also report that social or relational aggression hurts them more than physical aggression does, whereas boys think that physical aggression hurts more (Galen & Underwood, 1997; Paquette & Underwood, 1999). It is also the case that girls think relational or social aggression is not as bad as physical aggression, whereas boys think the reverse (Crick & Werner, 1998; Galen & Underwood, 1997). That may seem contradictory, but what it seems to suggest is that girls feel especially hurt by relational aggression, yet still think it is more socially acceptable for a person to roll their eyes, gossip, or exclude others than to hit them, whereas boys show the opposite pattern. Children who engage in atypical forms of aggression for their gender (e.g., physically aggressive girls and relationally aggressive boys) have been found to be more poorly adjusted than children who use more typical forms of aggression, although highly aggressive children are more poorly adjusted in general than their less aggressive peers (Crick, 1997).

Social Aggression and Developmental Change

One of the interesting contrasts between social aggression and physical aggression is that social aggression may increase with age as compared to physical aggression, which decreases (Björkqvist, Lagerspetz et al., 1992). There are certainly social constraints against older children's and adults' physical attacks on others, but there may be fewer such constraints against activities like gossip or social exclusion. Also, it takes some degree of cognitive sophistication to manipulate social relationships. Preschool children do tell others that they will not be their friends or cover their ears in an attempt to ignore a peer (Crick & Rose, 2000), but relational aggression is more prevalent by the age of 11 or 12 and older. It seems to be a key aspect of the social relationships of young adolescence (Crick et al., 2001). As noted above, Archer's meta-analysis (2004) showed that the sex difference was essentially nonexistent in childhood, increased through adolescence, and then disappeared by early adulthood. Some have suggested that boys and men become more likely to use this form of aggression when they enter late adolescence and young adulthood, that they may learn it in their relationships with girls and women, and that they come to use it in these relationships in particular (Björkqvist, Österman, & Lagerspetz, 1994; Crick & Rose, 2000; Richardson & Green, 1999).

Björkvist and his colleagues have examined the relationships among empathy, social intelligence, and aggression, and have proposed an explanation of how these factors change developmentally (Björkqvist, Lagerspetz et al., 1992; Björkqvist, Österman et al., 1992; Björkqvist, Österman, & Kaukiainen, 2000). They suggest that the earliest aggression that children show is physical, and that boys do it more than girls. Later, children can use direct verbal aggression, which they report is similar in both sexes. Finally, social manipulation and other forms of indirect aggression become more common in adolescence, and girls are more likely to use it. On the positive side, children also develop in their ability to use conflict resolution to solve disagreements. Björkvist and his colleagues have linked the decreased use of physical and the increased use of indirect aggression and conflict resolution to developmental increases in social intelligence, or the ability to analyze others' social behaviors. That is, it takes more social intelligence to use verbal aggression as compared to physical, and more still to use indirect aggression and to resolve conflicts by peaceful means. Girls are more likely to use indirect aggression and to be skilled at resolving conflicts. Interestingly, empathy (which we will see shortly also has a relationship to gender) has a strong effect on these relationships. When children and adolescents have more empathy towards others they are very unlikely to use physical aggression, and much more likely to choose nonaggressive strategies to resolve interpersonal difficulties with others.

In conclusion, girls are more likely to use social, relational, or indirect aggression than are boys, at least through adolescence. It is not entirely clear whether men come to use it as much as women do in adulthood, but there is some evidence that they may. Social intelligence and empathy affect the degree to which such aggressive strategies are used, and socially intelligent and empathic adolescents are more likely to avoid the use of any type of aggression as a means to resolve their disputes with others.

MORALITY

We just completed a discussion of aggression, and earlier in this chapter we discussed prosocial, nurturant, and empathic behaviors. Both of these types of behaviors have often been included in the category of morality, as has the ability of children to resist **antisocial behavior** such as doing damage to others or property, or breaking rules or laws (Coie & Dodge, 1998). Of course, there are many realms of behavior that people would consider moral (or immoral) beyond violence, aggression, or criminality, and for that matter beyond prosocial behavior as well. Parents and social scientists alike are interested in the extent to which children have traits such as honesty, responsibility, courage, perseverance, and a commitment to values (Turiel, 1998). Psychologists have often studied these kinds of issues by examining children's moral thinking or their moral judgments in addition to their behavior. In this section we will consider both antisocial behavior and moral judgments.

Antisocial Behavior

We have already shown that boys are more likely to behave aggressively, which is one form of antisocial behavior. In fact, it is well known that boys and men are more likely to engage in most forms of serious violent and criminal behavior (Coie & Dodge, 1998; Daly & Wilson, 1998; Knight et al., 1996; Moffitt et al., 2001). The number of individuals who engage in such activities is, of course, small, and the fact that boys and men are more likely to do so does not mean that most boys and men behave this way. Nonetheless, this is a sex difference that is clear and obvious to most people. In a review of the research on antisocial behavior and crime in young people in several Western nations, Rutter, Giller, and Hagel (1998) concluded that there were four main differences between males and females in criminality: (a) the biggest difference between males and females was in young adulthood, (b) crimes involving force or violence were especially associated with males, (c) females were less likely than males to be repeat offenders, and (d) women's "criminal careers" were likely to be shorter.

In a longitudinal study of children between the ages of 3 and 21 in New Zealand (Moffitt et al., 2001), the researchers measured such behaviors as having irritable tempers, fighting, bullying, lying, stealing, being truant, running away, setting fires, destroying property, and being cruel to animals. In adolescence they also measured criminal activities like vandalism, shoplifting, car theft, alcohol and drug use, assaults, and carrying a weapon. On most measures, (except alcohol and drug use and violence against partners and family members), boys were consistently more antisocial than girls at all ages (overall $d = 0.25$, with d values of 0.42 and 0.48 at ages 18 and 21, respectively). On all measures of contact with the criminal justice system, from being arrested to being convicted and sentenced, boys were more likely to have done so than girls.

Homicide

The most serious of all criminal acts is, of course, homicide. Children rarely commit homicide. For example, in the United States in 2005 there were more than 16,000 murders reported by the Federal Bureau of Investigation for that year (Federal Bureau of Investigation, 2006). Of that total, children or adolescents under the age of 17 committed fewer than 500, and most of those were committed by 13- to 16-year-olds. Only 11 murders were committed by children between the ages of 9 and 12, and none by children younger than that. However, although child murderers were rare, most were boys. Of the 11 murders committed by children between the ages of 9 and 12, boys committed 7. Of the 467 murders committed by 13- to 16-year-olds, boys committed 426 (91%).

Conduct Disorder and Rule Breaking

Antisocial behavior in childhood or adolescence can be considered to be **conduct disorder**, which may include aggression as well as antisocial behavior such as stealing, lying, running away from home, harming animals, setting fires, or destroying property (American Psychiatric Association [APA], 1994). It is quite well established that conduct disorder is more common in boys (Eme & Kavanaugh, 1995; Maughan, Rowe, Messer, Goodman, & Meltzer, 2004; Rutter et al., 1998), and when it does happen in girls, it develops at a later age and is less likely to be chronic or long lasting (O'Keefe, Carr, & McQuaid, 1998). It is generally the case that about half of children (most of whom are boys) who engage in persistent and serious misconduct as children progress to criminal acts as adolescents and adults (Moffitt et al., 2001). This is especially true when the misconduct in early childhood consists of physical aggression (Broidy et al., 2003).

Milder forms of misbehavior, especially in toddlers and young children, are much less likely to predict such later difficulties, and it is also not as clear that they are done more by boys. A meta-analysis of studies of both children and adults of resistance to temptation generally found little difference between boys and girls, particularly with respect to cheating in academic and other domains. The only consistent sex difference was on a series of tasks called the forbidden-objects tasks (Silverman, 2003). These involved telling children that they should not look at, touch, play with, or eat various objects. On those tasks, girls of all ages were less likely to do so ($r = .11$ to .20).

Another common form of milder rule breaking is lying. Adult women seem to be more likely to lie to avoid hurting other people's feelings (DePaulo, Epstein, & Wyer, 1993; DePaulo & Kashy, 1998), and the research we discussed earlier regarding the responses of children to the disappointing gift are consistent with the idea that girls and women do not want to hurt other people's feelings, but it is not very reasonable to call such behavior antisocial. Studies in which adults rate children's tendencies to lie typically report that boys lie more than girls (e.g., Gervais, Tremblay, Desmarais-Gervais, & Vitaro,

2000; Stouthamer-Loeber, 1986), but observational studies do not always agree. For example, one study of 3-year-olds (Lewis, Stanger, & Sullivan, 1989) who were instructed not to peek at a toy when the experimenter left the room (most peeked, of course) found that boys were more likely to tell the truth than girls were when asked if they had peeked. A second study (Nigro & Snow, 1992), using a similar procedure, had the adult who asked the children if they peeked either smile at the children or stare at them when she asked. Girls were much more likely to admit peeking to the smiling adult, consistent with the idea that girls are more likely to lie so as not to be embarrassed or ashamed by breaking norms.

To conclude, boys are clearly more likely to engage in serious misconduct and antisocial behavior as children and adolescents, and this kind of activity in childhood predicts becoming involved in criminal activity as adults. The evidence for lesser forms of antisocial behavior is not as clear.

Moral Cognition and Moral Judgments

One of the most extensively researched issues in the study of moral development concerns children's and adolescents' moral judgments or moral decision-making (Turiel, 1998). The major reason for the extensive study of children's moral thinking is the influence of cognitive theories of moral judgments such as Piaget's (Piaget, 1965) and Kohlberg's (Colby, Kohlberg, Gibbs, & Lieberman, 1983; Kohlberg & Puka, 1994), especially Kohlberg's. In Kohlberg's approach the child is said to develop through three levels of moral decision-making (premoral, conventional, and post-conventional or principled); from a self-centered concern (things are right if they turn out well for me) through a concern about moral rules, rights, and justice for others as well as oneself. There are two stages at the premoral level (pleasure and punishment), two at the conventional level (good boy and law and order), and two at the principled level (social contract and universal principles). Kohlberg proposed that the highest levels of moral thinking involve rather abstract **principles of justice** related to treating others fairly (Turiel, 1998).

Kohlberg and Gilligan

Kohlberg's theory was originally based on interviews with boys between 9 and 16 years of age (see Kohlberg & Puka, 1994) who were asked about their responses to various moral dilemmas such as whether one should steal a drug that might save the life of a dying woman. In later research girls and women were asked about their thoughts on such issues. Because they often answered questions about such dilemmas by focusing on the needs of people rather than on principles of justice, girls were sometimes reported as having an average lower stage of morality than boys (Gilligan, 1977; Kohlberg & Kramer, 1969). Carol Gilligan (Gilligan, 1982, 1994) objected to basing a theory of morality on interviews that were only done with boys and then using such a theory to conclude that the moral judgments of girls were not as advanced as those of boys. Gilligan argued that girls and women were concerned about relationships with important people in their lives, and that manifesting care in those relationships is the central feature of morality in their lives. Her position was that a **morality of care** leads to being careful to meet the needs of others with whom one has close relationships and not to exploit or hurt them. A **morality of justice**, on the other hand, emphasizes an independent self and abstract principles of morality. Gilligan called the focus on care rather than justice the "different voice" of girls and women, stressing that it was different, but should not be considered lesser. It is important to make clear how huge the impact of Gilligan's ideas has been; they have been considered among the most significant areas of gender scholarship in the 20th century. For example, Gilligan was named *Ms* magazine's 1984 Woman of the Year, and one of *Time* magazine's 25 innovative Americans in 1996 (Jaffee & Hyde, 2000).

Empirical tests of the morality of justice and of care

After Gilligan proposed her theory of the morality of care as opposed to the morality of justice, researchers began to urge that there be empirical tests of the issue (e.g., Greeno & Maccoby, 1986; Luria, 1986).

One widely cited early review of the issue (Walker, 1984) included both a narrative review and a meta-analysis (although using a somewhat different procedure than is typically done), and examined the data for three developmental periods separately: childhood, adolescence, and adulthood. Walker concluded that there were few differences in the moral reasoning or stage of boys and girls or men and women. His conclusions of no differences were soon disputed (Baumrind, 1986), but he presented a brief updated review and meta-analysis (Walker, 1986), this time providing a measure of the difference between males' and females' stage, a very small one that was not statistically significant ($d = 0.05$). Consistent with that view, a comprehensive study (Dawson, 2002) examining four different sets of data collected by different investigators over a 30-year period found that males had a slightly higher stage at various ages, and females did at other ages, but the effects were very small. In a discussion of Gilligan's notion that the stages of males and females are different, Dawson concluded: "The preponderance of the evidence strongly suggests otherwise" (2002, p. 164).

However, that stages are not different does not necessarily mean that people do not use different kinds of arguments about moral issues. For example, some studies have shown no difference between males and females in stage of morality, but have demonstrated that girls and women do indeed focus more on concern or empathy towards other people in their discussions of moral dilemmas (Gibbs, Arnold, & Burkhart, 1984). A recent meta-analysis of 113 studies comprising more than 2 decades of research on this topic (Jaffee & Hyde, 2000) examined the use of the care and justice orientations. Jaffee and Hyde calculated effect sizes for care and justice orientations, finding a small difference favoring females in the care orientation ($d = -0.28$), and an even smaller one favoring males in the justice orientation ($d = 0.19$). There were also effects of age, which are presented in Table 5.1. The largest effect sizes were during adolescence for the care orientation and for young adults in the justice orientation. Jaffee and Hyde concluded that the results of their meta-analysis thus showed that sex differences in moral orientation were small. They also concluded that both sexes use both moral orientations (care and justice) when discussing their views about moral dilemmas, but that there may be differences in that they prefer to use as a general rule.

PERSONALITY AND SELF-ESTEEM

Temperament

When parents and teachers think that children have different personalities, they are often really considering the children's **temperament**. You can think of temperamental characteristics as being the building blocks of personality. Definitions of temperament generally include such features as activity level, emotionality, self-regulation, and the tendency to approach or avoid new things or new people (Rothbart & Bates, 1998). We have already discussed activity level and emotion, but here we consider temperament more broadly. Several dimensions of temperament in children up to age 13 were examined in a recent meta-analysis (Else-Quest et al., 2006). These authors examined the average level and degree of variability of 35 dimensions and three factors of temperament. The factors they examined were **effortful control** (consisting of dimensions such as distractibility, attention, and task persistence), **negative affectivity** (consisting of dimensions such as intensity, emotionality, fearfulness, anger, and difficulty), and **surgency** (consisting of dimensions such as activity level, sociability, shyness, approach, high intensity, and impulsivity).

The authors of the meta-analysis found a large difference in effortful control ($d = -1.01$) across the years of childhood. Because the ability to regulate attention and control impulses is a very important accomplishment in childhood, they suggested this large difference may reflect greater developmental maturity of girls, but they did not have evidence from older children or adolescents to see boys eventually catch up. Certain dimensions of this temperamental factor of effortful control (e.g., low-intensity pleasure and controlling and shifting attention) also favored girls, but showed smaller overall differences (e.g., d values less than -0.30).

The authors found few differences in negative affectivity, with most effect sizes clustering around zero. The only consistent exception was a slightly higher degree of fear ($d = -0.12$) in girls, and somewhat higher difficulty and intensity of negative affect in boys.

Surgency had several dimensions associated with it that were clearly somewhat different in nature (approach, high-intensity pleasure, smiling and laughing, activity, impulsivity, and lack of shyness). Overall, boys scored higher on surgency ($d = 0.5$). Despite the overall difference favoring boys, and boys' higher scores in the surgency dimensions of impulsivity, activity level, and high-intensity pleasure, girls tended to score slightly higher in the surgency dimensions of positive mood, approach, and shyness.

Overall, the authors concluded that many dimensions of temperament did not differ between boys and girls, and the ones that did were generally relatively small, except for the dimension of effortful control. They also suggested that there was not a clear or obvious link between sex differences in childhood temperament to such differences in adult personality characteristics.

Personality Characteristics

The "Big Five"

There are, of course, many different personality characteristics, and we would not want to look for sex differences in all of them. Instead, we will focus on personality characteristics that have been organized into a group known as "the big five," or the **five-factor theory of personality** (McCrae & Costa, 1999). These five personality factors have come to be seen as the basic structure of human personality, and the structure has been confirmed in many different cultures (McCrae & Costa, 1997). The five factors are: **neuroticism, extroversion, openness to experience, agreeableness,** and **conscientiousness.** Several different personality traits combine into each of the factors; in fact, there are at least 30 such traits. For example, anxiety, depression, and anger/hostility are among the components of neuroticism; gregariousness and warmth are part of extroversion; trust, altruism, and **tender-mindedness** are part of agreeableness; and competence, achievement striving, and dutifulness are part of conscientiousness. Also, people can be open to experience in many different domains such as feelings, fantasy, or intellectual ideas.

Meta-analyses of sex differences in the five factors have generally focused on research done on adults. The first meta-analysis of these factors (Feingold, 1994) found that women were higher in anxiety ($d = -0.28$), gregariousness ($d = -0.15$), trust ($d = -0.25$), and tender-mindedness ($d = -0.97$), whereas men were higher on assertiveness ($d = 0.50$). The second meta-analysis (Costa, Terracciano, & McCrae, 2001) had more research available on several of the traits and was able to make more extensive cross-cultural comparisons of the degree of sex differences. Costa and McCrae found that there were many differences between adult men and women in the traits; however, all tend to be very small (most d values less than 0.25). With respect to the five factors, women were higher in neuroticism ($d = -0.51$ for U.S. adults), agreeableness ($d = -0.59$ for U.S. adults), and extroversion ($d = -0.29$ for U.S. adults). The patterns of the traits that go into neuroticism and agreeableness were consistent: women were higher. With respect to extroversion, the pattern of traits that made up female extroversion consisted of being: "loving, sociable, submissive, cautious, and cheerful" (Costa et al., 2001, p. 327). As Feingold had reported earlier, Costa and McCrae also found that males were more assertive ($d = 0.19$; assertiveness is also a trait on the extroversion factor). There were no differences between males and females in the openness factor, although some of the traits that go into openness did show sex differences. The female pattern was associated with openness to aesthetics (e.g., the arts), feelings, and novelty, and the male pattern was associated with openness to fantasy as well as intellectual ideas. Finally, there was no consistent sex difference of any kind in the conscientiousness domain. Costa and McCrae noted strong cross-cultural similarities in the patterns of sex differences, but the differences between men and women were largest in European and North American countries, and smallest in African and Asian countries.

As pointed out above, little of this research has included children. Feingold (1994) included another meta-analysis of four personality characteristics that had been examined by Maccoby and Jacklin (1974) in their narrative review: self-esteem, anxiety, **locus of control**, and assertiveness. In this meta-analysis research on children was included. Feingold reported that there were no differences in assertiveness between boys and girls in childhood (although there were in adolescence and adulthood; $d = 0.20$); differences in locus of control varied with the instruments used, but there was no overall sex difference at any age; and females were more anxious in childhood, adolescence, and adulthood ($d = -0.24$ in childhood; -0.31 in adolescence and adulthood).

Self-Esteem and Self-Concept

Self-esteem refers to feelings of self-worth, self-respect, or self-acceptance (Major, Barr, Zubek, & Babey, 1999). Some researchers refer to **self-concept** as a more objective appraisal of one's skills or characteristics in particular areas such as academic capabilities, athletic ability, social skills, or appearance (Kling, Hyde, Showers, & Buswell, 1999; Major et al., 1999). Unfortunately, sometimes researchers refer to evaluations of oneself in these areas as self-esteem, such as self-esteem that is focused on appearance or academic work (e.g., Sahlstein & Allen, 2002). It is certainly understandable that there is some inconsistency in this terminology, because there are clearly relationships between people's assessment of their skills and abilities and how they feel about themselves. However, we will adopt the terminology of self-esteem to refer to global feelings of self-worth, and self-concept to refer to evaluations of oneself in particular domains.

Self-Esteem

When Feingold (1994) examined sex differences in children's personality traits, he also examined self-esteem. He found that girls had slightly (but not significantly) higher self-esteem in childhood ($d = -0.11$), whereas adolescent and adult males had slightly higher self-esteem than same-aged females ($d = 0.10$). Since Feingold's review there have been at least three meta-analyses of sex differences in global self-esteem (Kling et al., 1999; Major et al., 1999; Sahlstein & Allen, 2002). Two of the reviews (Kling et al., 1999; Major et al., 1999) provided effect size statistics and an examination of the relationship between sex, self-esteem, and age.

Major and her colleagues found that males had higher global self-esteem than females ($d = 0.14$), with no differences in childhood to age 10, and similar effect sizes for all other age groups (d values between 0.12 and 0.16). Kling and her colleagues conducted two separate meta-analyses. The first was based on an extensive search of the research on the topic. In that analysis they reported that males had higher self-esteem than females ($d = 0.21$), and that there were differences favoring males in all age groups except for adults older than 60 years of age. The largest difference was in high school (ages 15–18; $d = 0.33$), but even boys under age 10 had higher self-esteem than same-aged girls ($d = 0.16$). Cross-national comparisons showed similar degrees of difference between males and females in several Western countries. In their second meta-analysis, Kling and her colleagues examined three large national data sets of longitudinal data collected by the National Center for Education Statistics (NCES), but the age range for that data set was between 13 (eighth graders) and 32; hence, young children were not included. The findings showed that males consistently had higher self-esteem than females, across ages, cohorts (the year the people were born), and years when it was measured. However, the differences were very small, with effect sizes between 0.04 and 0.24, with the youngest groups (13- and 15-year-olds) having larger effects than the older ones.

The fact that these differences are so small conflicts with popular wisdom that girls have much lower self-esteem than boys. In addition, there is not a consistent set of findings about what is the case in childhood (girls greater, no difference, or boys greater). Even the differences in adolescence are not very large. It is also the case that this finding does not apply to every group. Both Major and Kling and their colleagues demonstrated that were no differences in the self-esteem of African American boys and girls even during adolescence, and that African Americans (especially girls) tended to have higher self-esteem than same-sex whites.

Self-Concepts

The self-concepts of boys and girls may also differ as a function of various domains, especially in early adolescence. Physical appearance is often pointed to as a particular concern of girls. A meta-analysis of sex differences in body image among people 12 and older (Feingold & Mazzella, 1998) found that girls and women had less positive body images (overall $d = -0.50$), especially between the ages of 16 and 22, and that this sex difference had increased between the 1970s and the 1990s. One extensive study (Quatman & Watson, 2001) of more than 500 adolescents in grades 8, 10, and 12 examined global self-esteem as well as self-concept in eight separate domains (personal security, home/parents, peer popularity, academic competence, attractiveness, personal mastery, personal permeability or vulnerability, and athletic competence). They found that boys had higher global self-esteem ($d = 0.22$) and more positive self-concepts in six of the eight domains, with no sex difference in the other two (peer popularity and academic competence). Not all research is consistent with this finding though; some have found that girls evaluate their cognitive or academic skills (although not math) more positively than boys do (Sahlstein & Allen, 2002; Wigfield, Eccles, Mac Iver, Reuman, & Midgley, 1991).

A meta-analysis of self-esteem (i.e., self-concept) in more than a dozen different domains in children and adolescents (Wilgenbusch & Merrell, 1999) reported a rather complex pattern of findings depending on the children's age and the domain. These findings are presented in Table 5.4. Consistent with the other research

TABLE 5.4   Sex Differences in Self-Concept in Various Domains, by School Age Group

	ELEMENTARY	SECONDARY	MIXED	TOTAL
1. Global	0.28	0.23		0.24
2. Academic/scholastic	0.27	0.09	−0.07	0.11
Mathematics	0.25	0.29		0.28
Verbal	−0.22	−0.23		−0.23
Musical	−0.46	0.50		0.18
3. Job competence		0.75		
4. Physical appearance	0.16	0.39	0.36	0.37
5. Social	0.18	−0.09	−0.09	−0.04
Close friendship		−0.42		
Romantic appeal		−0.02		
Same-sex peer relationship		−0.38		
Opposite-sex peer relationship		0.00		
6. Family/relations with parents	0.25	0.04	−0.06	0.05
7. Behavioral conduct/bad behavior		0.05		
8. Athletic/psychomotor coordination	0.38	0.37		0.39
Tumbling	−0.79			
Throwing	−0.29			
9. Emotional/affect		0.32	0.14	0.29
Freedom from anxiety		0.64		
Happiness/satisfaction		0.02		
10. Honesty		−0.39		
11. Competence			−0.05	
12. Health		−0.15		
13. Religion		−0.23		

Source: Wilgenbusch, T. & Merrell, K.W., School Psychology Quarterly, 14, 101–120, 1999. With permission.

we have discussed, boys had higher global self-esteem ($d = 0.24$) and more positive self-concepts in mathematics, physical appearance, emotional well being, and athletics. Girls, on the other hand, had more positive self-concepts in verbal skills, close friendships, and same-sex peer relationships. As can be seen in Table 5.4, almost all of the effect sizes were small. There may be particular domains that are especially important to one sex or the other; for example, appearance and thinness for girls, and athletics for boys (Kling et al., 1999; Major et al., 1999). Girls who come to believe that they are not pretty or thin enough or boys who lack athletic skill may find the adolescent years especially difficult in terms of self-esteem or self-concepts.

One influential proposal has linked male and female self-concepts (self-construals) to sex differences in other social behaviors (Cross & Madson, 1997). Cross and Madsen proposed that females have interdependent self-construals and males have independent ones. That is, girls and women see themselves in relation to others, whereas boys and men see themselves as unique individuals with a unique set of characteristics that influence their behavior. These differences are, of course, similar to the instrumental and expressive personality characteristics that we discussed in chapter 1, and to Gilligan's view of moral orientations. However, Cross and Madsen went on to provide empirically based evidence that these different self-construals are related to many other differences in behavior between males and females, both cognitive and social (e.g., emotional expression and decoding others' emotions, prosocial behavior, and aggression). They also provided evidence that girls' self-esteem was more damaged by problems in their relationships (e.g., not being forgiven by a friend), whereas boys' self-esteem was more likely to be damaged by unflattering information about their skills and abilities.

To conclude, there are very consistent findings that from early adolescence through at least young adulthood males have higher global self-esteem than females do, but the differences are rather small. Whether boys or girls (or neither) have higher self-esteem in childhood is not at all clear from the research. It is also the case that girls evaluate their appearance and their athletic skill more negatively than boys do, but other findings are mixed. Finally, the self-construals of boys and girls may differ in the degree to which they emphasize interpersonal versus independent aspects of the self.

TOYS, ACTIVITIES, AND INTERESTS

If you were asked to pick a single psychological characteristic that differentiates boys and girls, you could not do better than the toys and activities that engage them. Studies in many parts of the world (e.g., Blakemore, LaRue, & Olejnik, 1979; Goldstein, 1994; Marcon & Freeman, 1996; Martin, Eisenbud, & Rose, 1995; Nelson, 2005; Serbin, Poulin-Dubois, Colburne, Sen, & Eichstedt, 2001; Servin, Bohlin, & Berlin, 1999; Turner, Gervai, & Hinde, 1993) have documented the differences: girls like and play more than do boys with dolls and doll accessories (clothes, furniture, food), arts and crafts, kitchen toys, fashion and make-up, whereas boys like and play more than do girls with military toys and guns, sports-related toys, transportation toys, electronics, blocks, and complex building sets such as Legos and Construx. The differences are seen no matter how they are measured: in observations of children's play at home, in school (or preschool), and in the laboratory, in reports of children's play (as reported by themselves and by their parents), in children's stated preferences for pictures of toys, and in children's requests for toys. The degree of association between toys and gender is so large and so consistent that certain toys have come to be called "boys' toys" or "girls' toys" (Blakemore & Centers, 2005).

Developmental Course of Sex Differences in Interests in Toys and Activities

Sex differences in children's toy preferences emerge in the toddler years and maybe even earlier. When observed with toys, both at home and at preschool, by age 2 girls prefer dolls and doll accessories and boys prefer vehicles such as cars and trucks (Caldera, Huston, & O'Brien, 1989; Campbell, Shirley, & Caygill, 2002 ; Fagot, Leinbach, & Hagan, 1986; O'Brien, Huston, & Risley, 1983; Weinraub et al., 1984). If asked what they prefer, generally by using pictures of toys or actual toys and asking the child to point or otherwise indicate which ones they like, boys demonstrate preference for boys' toys as early as age 2, and girls by at least age 3 (Blakemore et al., 1979; Perry, White, & Perry, 1984).

Some researchers have used **preferential looking** techniques to examine toy preferences in young infants before they can be asked to choose or point to a preferred toy. Preferential looking is simply a measure of how long children look at one of two pictures presented at the same time. In particular, do they look at one of the two longer, in which case, it can be said to be preferred. In the case of toy preferences, these are pairs of pictures of boys' toys and girls' toys presented together, and the infant's preferred looking time is measured. Using this procedure, some researchers have reported that babies prefer to look at gender "appropriate" toys somewhere in the second year of life (Campbell, Shirley, Heywood, & Crook, 2000; Serbin et al., 2001).

Much interest surrounds the exact age at which these sex differences appear, because of its relevance for theories about the causes of the differences (Martin, Ruble, & Szkrybalo, 2002; Ruble, Martin, & Berenbaum, 2006). One critical issue is whether toy preferences emerge before or after children develop certain kinds of knowledge about sex and gender. This is critical because if children do not know if they are boys or girls, or that toys are identified as being for boys or for girls, they cannot be using this information to guide their toy preferences. So it is important that some researchers have reported that some sex-typed toy preferences are found before children can consistently identify their own sex and before they have any idea that toys are associated with gender, and that is especially so for boys (Blakemore et al., 1979; Campbell et al., 2002; Fagot et al., 1986; Perry et al., 1984; Weinraub et al., 1984). We will discuss the relationships between such cognitive variables and toy preferences in more detail in chapter 9.

The extent and magnitude of sex differences in toy and activity play increases during the preschool years, as documented in many empirical studies of children's observed behavior, their stated preferences, and parents' reports of their children's activities (Blakemore et al., 1979; Carpenter, 1983; Dunn & Hughes, 2001; Maccoby, 1998; Nicolopoulou, 1997; Ruble et al., 2006). By age 5, children show very clear preferences for gender-typed toys, although boys still do so more strongly than girls do. Girls continue to play with dolls and kitchen sets, and to have fantasy play that involves relationships, household roles, and romance; they also spend more time in chores than do boys beginning at ages 3 to 4. Boys continue to play with cars and trucks, as well as blocks and video games, and to have fantasy play that involves superheroes, danger, and aggression. Young boys are more avoidant of play with cross-gender toys than are young girls (Bussey & Bandura, 1992; Fagot et al., 1986).

Sex differences in toys, activities, and interests continuing into middle and late childhood and adolescence are large and varied, including household chores, interests, activities, and as we have already discussed, involvement in sports. As children move out of the early grades, it is not easy to observe their everyday activities, so studies have used several different methods to study the sex-typed nature of activities and interests across age, including questionnaires about children's preferences completed by the children themselves or by their parents (Antill, Cotton, Russell, & Goodnow, 1996; Antill, Russell, Goodnow, & Cotton, 1993; Eccles, Wigfield, Flanagan, Miller, & et al., 1989), preferences for pictured objects (Brinn, Kraemer, Warm, & Paludi, 1984), analysis of letters to Santa Claus (Almqvist, 1989; Downs, 1983; Marcon & Freeman, 1996; Pine & Nash, 2002), and daily reports of time use (McHale, Kim, Whiteman, & Crouter, 2004; McHale, Shanahan, Updegraff, Crouter, & Booth, 2004).

Sex differences in activities expand in scope as children move through adolescence (McHale, Kim, et al., 2004; McHale, Shanahan, et al., 2004; Richards, Crowe, Larson, & Swarr, 1998; Richards & Larson, 1989). Girls spend more time than do boys in relationship-oriented activities, personal care, and household chores, whereas boys spend more time than do girls in sports and male-typical activities (e.g., building things, hunting). Similar gender-typed themes underlie these interests, with girls preferring to write affectionate themes and to read about relationships, romance, adventures, ghost/horror, animal and school-related themes, and boys preferring to use aggressive themes in writing and to read science fiction, fantasy, sports, war, spy books, and comic and joke books (Armstrong, 2001; Finders, 1996; Langerman, 1990; Willemsen, 1998).

Occupational Preferences

Another important domain of interests as children grow older is related to occupations. What kind of job or career do young people want to prepare for in adulthood? As we already know, men and women are often in different occupations (U.S. Department of Labor, 2005). Not surprisingly, children and adolescents often aspire to the same sort of gender-stereotyped occupations that adults occupy (Bobo, Hildreth, & Durodoye, 1998; Helwig, 2002; Liben, Bigler, & Krogh, 2001; Watson, Quatman, & Edler, 2002; Wigfield, Battle, Keller, & Eccles, 2002), and these occupations are predictably related to certain characteristics. Female-dominated jobs are associated with appearance (e.g., fashion, beauty, or hairdressing), art, nurturing (e.g., social work or education), homemaking, and caretaking of children and the elderly. On the other hand, many male-dominated occupations are associated with mechanical, mathematical or scientific skills, physical strength, aggressiveness, and risk taking. The associations between these occupations and the toys and activities we have already discussed should be obvious.

Conclusions

There have been no published meta-analyses of sex differences in play, interests, and time use. Nor has there been any formal analysis of the way that the differences change across development from infancy through adolescence and across adulthood: that is, whether the differences between the sexes in interests and activities increase over time, stay relatively stable, decrease, or even disappear, or, more likely, whether the differences increase at some ages but decrease at others. Some of the "neglect" regarding meta-analysis may reflect the lack of controversy about whether the differences exist—although there is certainly controversy about what causes them and how they develop. But the lack of analysis of developmental change probably reflects the difficulties involved in comparing sex differences in activities across age. Developmental changes in children's activities are very difficult to study because the specific toys and activities that appeal to children change with age. This is apparent to anyone who has seen children play. For example, adolescent girls no longer play with dolls, just as preschool girls do not have much opportunity to shop for clothes or use make-up. The examination of developmental change presents a challenge for all aspects of development (both psychological and physical) in which the phenomenon changes as organisms mature, but it presents more of a challenge in this sphere than in some others because the activities of younger and older children are often so different.

PSYCHOPATHOLOGY

There are more than 100 mental disorders listed in the *Diagnostic and Statistical Manual of Mental Disorders* (DSM-IV, APA, 1994). Just by chance alone one would expect that males and females would differ in the rates of some of them, and in fact they do (Hartung & Widiger, 1998). In Table 5.5 we have presented various disorders for which rates differ among boys and girls in infancy, childhood, and adolescence.

One of the most notable findings about rates of psychopathology and gender is that boys have many more disorders in childhood than do girls, whereas girls and women have more disorders than boys and men in adolescence and adulthood (Hartung & Widiger, 1998). However, that is at least partly because different disorders are associated with childhood than with adulthood. Certain childhood disorders (e.g., attention deficit hyperactivity disorder, conduct disorder, oppositional defiant disorder, reading disabilities) have often not been recognized as disorders or treated in adults, whereas others (e.g., anxiety, depression) are much less likely to have been identified and treated in children.

TABLE 5.5   Sex Ratios in Mental Disorders in Childhood and Adolescence

BEHAVIOR	RATIO, IF KNOWN
Disorders with higher rates in girls	
Rett's syndrome[a]	Primarily girls
Separation anxiety disorder	
Selective mutism[b]	
Disorders with higher rates in boys	
Mental retardation	1.5 to 1
Reading disorder	1.5–4 to 1
Expressive language disorder	
Phonological disorder[c]	
Stuttering	3 to 1
Autism	4–5 to 1
Asperger's syndrome[d]	
ADHD	4–9 to 1
Conduct disorder[e]	
Oppositional defiant disorder[f]	
Tourette's disorder[g]	1.5–3 to 1
Encopresis[h]	
Enuresis[i]	

Source: Adapted from Hartung, C.M. & Widiger, T.A., *Psychological Bulletin*, *123*, 260–278, 1998.

[a] An X-linked genetic condition leading to mental retardation. Most affected male fetuses die before birth.
[b] A condition in which a child does not speak in certain social settings because of anxiety.
[c] A disorder associated with difficulty learning the sounds needed for speaking, reading, and spelling.
[d] A disorder of social and communication skills, similar to autism, but usually without mental retardation.
[e] A serious childhood disorder involving defiance, rule breaking, often involving harm to people, animals, or property, and eventually criminal behavior.
[f] Irritability and defiance. Deliberately annoying. Similar to conduct disorder, but usually less serious. Usually does not harm animals or people or destroy property.
[g] A disorder involving involuntary movements (tics) and vocal outbursts.
[h] Lack of control of the bowels.
[i] Lack of bladder control; bed-wetting.

Internalizing and Externalizing

One important distinction is between **externalizing disorders** and **internalizing disorders**. Externalizing disorders are those in which a person acts in a way that may harm others, or breaks society's (or parents' or teachers') rules (e.g., conduct disorder), whereas internalizing disorders are those in which a person experiences internal symptoms or could be said to act internally or against the self (e.g., depression or anxiety). Externalizing disorders are more common in boys, whereas internalizing disorders are more common in girls (Zahn-Waxler, 1993). One reason that boys may be brought to treatment more often in childhood is that externalizing problems cause more difficulty for adults than internalizing problems do, and it is adults who bring children into treatment (Keenan & Shaw, 1997). For example, a child who is defiant and aggressive causes parents and teachers more grief than a child who is anxious and dependent, although, ironically, anxiety is rather common in children. Therefore, girls' internalizing problems may not be identified in childhood. However, it should also be noted that there are few differences in rates of externalizing problems in early childhood—infancy and the toddler years—until boys begin to show more externalizing problems than girls do around the age of 4 (Keenan & Shaw, 1997). It is possible that early socialization directs difficult temperament in different directions in boys and girls—boys into conduct disorder and girls into anxiety.

Mental Retardation and Pervasive Developmental Disorders

There are many different kinds of and causes of **mental retardation**, which is defined as having an IQ below 70 and substantial problems in daily social functioning that must have begun in childhood (APA, 1994). A discussion of these different forms of mental retardation are well beyond the scope of this book. For our purposes, it is important only to point out that mental retardation is about 1.5 times more common in boys as in girls (Hartung & Widiger, 1998).

Pervasive developmental disorders (PDD) are disorders that involve social skills, communication skills, and the presence of stereotyped behaviors or interests (Tsai, 1998). The most well-known of these disorders is **autism**. In addition to social and communicative skill problems, those with autism often lack language skills and are also frequently mentally retarded (Travis & Sigman, 2000; Tsai, 1998). Another disorder in this category is **Asperger's syndrome** (sometimes called mild autism), in which the children typically have normal language skills and IQs (indeed some are very bright and talented) but have the other characteristics of PDD such as stereotyped behaviors and poor social and communicative skills (Tsai, 1998). Boys are much more likely to have both autism and Asperger's syndrome, with ratios reported to be as high as nine boys to every girl with the disorders (Hartung & Widiger, 1998).

A third disorder in this category is **Rett's syndrome**. With this disorder, a child is born as normal, but by about 18 months of age begins to show a loss of motor skills, speech, and reasoning, and usually displays a set of characteristic movements such as wringing the hands. Almost all children who have Rett's syndrome are girls, but that is because is caused by a dominant gene on one of the two X chromosomes, and male embryos that carry the gene on their single X chromosome do not usually survive to birth (Schanen, 2002).

Conduct, Oppositional Defiant, and Attention Deficit Hyperactivity Disorders

We have already noted that conduct disorder (CD) is more common in boys throughout childhood and adolescence. Similar to CD is **oppositional defiant disorder** (ODD; APA, 1994), which consists of a pattern of irritable temperament, defiance, and aggression, but does not usually involve harm to property, stealing, or vandalism (Lahey, McBurnett, & Loeber, 2000). As with CD, ODD is also much more common in boys than in girls. There is also overlap among CD, ODD, and **attention-deficit hyperactivity disorder** (ADHD), which is from 4 to 10 times more frequent in boys than in girls (Gaub & Carlson, 1997; Hartung & Widiger, 1998; Hartung et al., 2002). ADHD consists of a pattern of inattention and distractibility in which such children have difficultly paying attention and can be easily pulled off task. The children may also be disobedient and exceptionally active relative to others their age. They often fidget, squirm, and talk excessively.

There is great concern that either ADHD or ODD may develop into CD, which is much more serious. One analysis of the data on these conditions (Lahey et al., 2000) suggests that the main components of ADHD that may put a child at risk for developing CD are the components associated with ODD (e.g., defiance as compared to inattention). It is difficult to tell if such a conclusion applies equally to boys and girls, because much of the research on ADHD, ODD, and CD is done only on boys. However, there is reason to assume that girls and boys with ADHD are somewhat different from each other, and that girls with ADHD are both less likely to have ODD and less likely to progress to CD. Meta-analyses (Gaub & Carlson, 1997; Gershon, 2002) comparing the characteristics of boys and girls who had been diagnosed with ADHD found that, as compared to diagnosed girls, boys with ADHD were more hyperactive ($d = 0.15$ in Gaub & Carlson, and 0.29 in Gershon), inattentive ($d = 0.19$ and 0.23), were more likely to be diagnosed with conduct disorder ($d = 0.14$), to be aggressive towards peers ($d = 0.35$) and to have other externalizing disorders ($d = 0.17$ and 0.21). One of the meta-analyses (Gaub & Carlson, 1997) found ADHD boys more likely to have internalizing ($d = 0.10$) conditions, whereas the other (Gershon, 2002) found girls to have more internalizing conditions ($d = -0.12$). Girls with ADHD, as compared with diagnosed boys, were also found to have lower IQs in both meta-analyses (d values ranging between 0.17 and 0.49 for full-scale, verbal, and performance IQs). A similar relationship between IQ has been found for conduct disorder, in that girls with conduct disorder have lower IQs than boys with conduct disorder (O'Keefe et al., 1998).

Eating Disorders

In our discussion of self-esteem and self-concept, we noted that adolescent girls and young women were much more dissatisfied with their bodies than were boys and young men (Feingold & Mazzella, 1998). Such dissatisfaction may evolve into an eating disorder such as **anorexia** or **bulimia**, disorders that are from 10 to 20 times as common in females as compared to males (Tyrka, Graber, & Brooks-Gunn, 2000). Although eating disorders usually do not begin until adolescence, dissatisfaction with weight often happens as early as elementary school. More than half of girls between the ages of 7 and 13, and up to two thirds of girls in middle school and high school feel dissatisfied with their weight and would like to lose some, usually through dieting. About one third of adolescent girls are dieting at any given time, and about 10% do so persistently. In addition, somewhere between 1 and 10% of adolescent girls use purging behaviors like vomiting, or use laxatives or diuretics (Tyrka et al., 2000). Anorexia consists of the loss of body weight (less than 85% of expected weight), fear of weight gain, lack of menstruation (which happens when body fat drops too low), and disturbed body image (APA, 1994). Girls with anorexia may continue to believe they are overweight when they are dangerously thin. Bulimia consists of binge eating (eating large amounts during a short period, often of high-calorie foods like cookies or ice cream) and a set of behaviors, known as purging, intended to prevent weight gain (APA, 1994). The purging behaviors may include excessive exercise, the use of laxatives or enemas, fasting, or induced vomiting.

Depression

Among the characteristics of **depression** are depressed mood, disturbances of sleep, feelings of worthlessness, loss of pleasure in daily activities, and thoughts of suicide (APA, 1994). Although children can become depressed, the rate of depression in children is much lower than in adolescents and adults: about 1% of preschoolers; up to 2.5% of elementary-aged children; and up to 5–6% of adolescents and adults at any given time (Garber, 2000). Although the rate of depression is about twice as high for adult women as men in many countries of the world, before adolescence there is no difference in the rate of depression in boys and girls, or boys may have slightly higher rates (Culbertson, 1997; Garber, 2000; Garber, Keiley, & Martin, 2002; Nolen-Hoeksema, 2001).

A recent meta-analysis of the children's depression inventory (Twenge & Nolen-Hoeksema, 2002) reported rates for boys' and girls' depression between the ages of 8 and 16. Up until age 12, the d values were essentially zero (between 0.02 and 0.06), although all were in the direction of boys having slightly higher rates. At age 13 girls had slightly higher rates of depression ($d = -0.08$), and at ages 14–16, girls had higher rates ($d = 0.22$, 0.22, and 0.18 for ages 14, 15, and 16, respectively).

Anxiety Disorders

The major categories of anxiety disorders are **specific phobia**, **social phobia**, **panic disorder**, **generalized anxiety disorder** (GAD), **obsessive-compulsive disorder** (OCD), **and posttraumatic stress disorder** (PTSD; APA, 1994). Anxiety disorders are among the most common disorders of childhood, occurring in between 12 and 17% of children at any given time (Vasey & Ollendick, 2000). Many of these disorders (e.g., OCD, specific phobias, social phobias) occur well before puberty, and young children can be very anxious about such things as separation from parents, unfamiliar situations, the dark, or even of being invaded by aliens (Muris, Merckelbach, Mayer, & Prins, 2000).

Girls have more anxiety disorders throughout childhood and adolescence, and women do in adulthood, although the differences in the rates of boys and girls having these disorders depends on the particular disorder. Girls seem to be much more likely than boys to experience GAD, panic disorder, and specific phobias (ratios from 2:1 to 3:1), and are slightly more likely to experience PTSD, whereas similar numbers of boys and girls experience social phobia and OCD (Vasey & Ollendick, 2000).

Conclusions

Boys are more likely to be mentally retarded, autistic, and to have Asperger's syndrome. They are also more likely to have ODD, CD, and ADHD. Girls, on the other hand, are more likely to be anxious, and in adolescence and beyond are more likely to be depressed and to have eating disorders. Psychologist Carolyn Zahn-Waxler referred to the relationship between gender and psychopathology as being about "warriors and worriers" (Zahn-Waxler, 1993), a very apt description of the differences between the forms of psychopathology that are characteristic of the two sexes.

CHAPTER SUMMARY

In this chapter we discussed sex differences in social behaviors, personality characteristics, and psychopathology. Most of the differences we discussed in this chapter are relatively small, and whether one finds them or not is often dependent on children's ages, or the way the behavior is measured, or the situation in which it is observed.

Boys are often more physically aggressive than girls, although boys and girls or men and women may be equally aggressive with family members (siblings or relationship partners). Boys are more likely to engage in R & T play, especially when play aggression or fighting is involved. Serious antisocial behavior (stealing, vandalism, etc.) is more characteristic of boys from the age of about 4 onward, but the information about milder misbehavior is not so clear. Boys may be somewhat more likely to think in terms of abstract principles of justice with respect to morality, rather than the feelings and needs of other people.

Adult men are more likely to help those in need of assistance, especially strangers in public settings, where help may sometimes be risky. Indeed, in general boys and men take more risks than girls and women and are consequently injured more frequently. However, the differences in risk taking are decreasing, especially in activities like driving, drinking, and using drugs as adolescents. Boys are also more likely to be identified as having psychopathology in childhood, including mental retardation and PDDs such as autism, as well as externalizing disorders like CD, ODD, and ADHD. In terms of personality characteristics, men (not as much is known about children) are more assertive and open to fantasy and intellectual ideas. Boys and men are consistently found to have slightly higher self-esteem, certainly in adolescence and beyond, and perhaps also in childhood.

Girls and women are more likely to engage in social or relational aggression, harming others through their social relationships rather than hurting them physically. They also express emotions more openly and intensely, especially emotions that signal vulnerability such as fear and sadness, and they smile and cry more, but are perhaps less likely to express anger. Their emotional displays are more easily read by other people. From infancy onward, girls and women are more skilled at reading the emotions of others. They are also more likely to express sympathy and empathy with others' distress, more likely to behave prosocially, and they display more interest in and nurturance towards infants and toddlers. However, physiological measures of emotional intensity, sympathy and empathy, and interest in babies are much less likely to detect such differences between the sexes.

Girls' and women's moral orientations are somewhat more likely to focus on care for others than on abstract principles of justice, but they can use both orientations when needed (as can boys and men). The personality characteristics of girls and women suggest higher levels of anxiety and neuroticism in general, agreeableness, extroversion (especially extroversion that consists of being loving, sociable, submissive, cautious, and cheerful), and open to feelings and the arts. Girls are less likely to be identified as having psychopathology in childhood, but that is partly because the internalizing conditions that are more characteristic of girls are less likely to come to the attention of adults. In childhood, as throughout life, girls are more likely to suffer from several anxiety disorders, and once they reach adolescence, are more likely to suffer from depression and eating disorders.

Biological Approaches to Gender Development[1]

6

> The Guerilla Girls think the world needs a new weapon: The estrogen bomb. Imagine: you drop it on an area of violent conflict and men throw down their guns, hug each other, apologize, say it was "all their fault" and then start to clean up the mess. (Guerilla Girls, 2002)

How much of the psychological differences between the sexes discussed in chapters 4 and 5 are related to the biological differences between them discussed in chapter 3? Is our behavior related to our hormones, so that we could make men more like women if we gave them estrogen, and women more like men if we gave them testosterone? How much of the differences between the sexes can be traced back to the differences in their sex chromosomes? These and related questions are the focus of this chapter.

Why should we expect genes and hormones to affect behavior, including gender-related behavior? Put simply, the brain is part of the body and the brain underlies behavior, so it should not be surprising that the same factors that govern sexual differentiation of the body also govern sexual differentiation of the brain and thus behavior. Furthermore, the process of physical sexual differentiation is essential to the survival of our species—reproduction depends on all of these processes working normally. Given their importance, it seems reasonable to theorize that these processes also play a role in psychological sexual differentiation—and, in fact, this is the basis for biological theories of gender development. A role for biology in gender development will not be surprising to those of you who have taken courses in biology, neuroscience, and biologically oriented psychology courses. But, for a long time some social scientists were resistant to the idea that biology could affect behavior, in part because they assumed that biology was equivalent to "determined." We know now that there is almost nothing about biology that is determined, that is, many biological processes are affected by what we do and the physical and social environment in which we live. It will help to keep this in mind as we describe biological influences on gender development.

Biological theories of gender development are generally not as formally developed as are the social or cognitive theories that we will discuss in later chapters and thus they might be better called biological approaches or biological perspectives. Biological approaches provide explanations of gendered psychological characteristics using the same biological processes that explain sex-related physical characteristics. As discussed in chapter 3, this includes immediate or proximal causes—sex chromosomes, genes, and sex hormones—and historical or distal ones—evolutionary processes.

Distal explanations of gender development concern the evolutionary basis of characteristics that differ between the sexes, particularly characteristics that increase the likelihood that an organism will obtain a mate, reproduce, and rear offspring who themselves reach reproductive age. Those characteristics are most important in adolescence and adulthood, so evolutionary perspectives on gender development primarily concern psychological sex differences in adulthood. For this reason, we will not devote as much space to these perspectives as we will to other biological perspectives. **Proximal explanations** concern mechanisms that are thought to be immediately responsible for the characteristics of interest. For gender development, the proximal biological mechanisms are the sex chromosomes, genes, and sex hormones.

---

[1] Sheri Berenbaum was the primary author of chapter 6.

In this chapter, we discuss the major biological perspectives on gender development, tying gender development back to the basic biological processes we discussed in chapter 3. We begin with a brief discussion of evolutionary perspectives. We follow this with discussions of proximal mechanisms hypothesized to play a role in gender development, including genes, hormones present during early development, hormones present later in life, and brain structure and function.

EVOLUTIONARY PERSPECTIVES ON GENDER DEVELOPMENT: SEX DIFFERENCES IN BEHAVIOR ARISE FROM EVOLUTIONARY PRESSURES

Evolutionary psychologists view our behavior as the result of adaptive pressures, so that our brains—and, therefore, our behaviors—evolved to solve problems faced by our ancestors, and effective solutions enabled them to survive and reproduce. Many of our current behaviors are a byproduct of behaviors that evolved to enable our ancestors to survive and reproduce. Because they were able to reproduce successfully, the genes that influenced their behaviors were selected for and continued in the gene pool of their descendents. Although it is beyond the scope of this book to discuss evolutionary psychology in great detail, it is worthwhile to consider some aspects of the approach that have frequently been applied to contemporary sex differences (for additional information, see Buss, 2000; Geary, 1998, 1999; Zuk, 2002).

Background to Evolutionary Perspectives: Sexual Selection

As we discussed in chapter 3, sexual selection is a type of natural selection. Whereas natural selection relates to characteristics that vary in a population without regard to the organism's sex, sexual selection concerns characteristics that directly increase the likelihood of mating, reproducing, and rearing offspring until they become reproductively mature—and some of these characteristics are related to sex. From an evolutionary perspective, human males and females have evolved in different ways, showing different psychological characteristics, to facilitate their different reproductive tasks.

Basics of Evolutionary Perspectives

The key to **evolutionary perspectives (approaches)** is that the survival of the human species (and, in fact, of all species) depends on successful reproduction, and that we have evolved to maximize the survival of the species. This means that the goal of every human being is to reproduce, although this goal is not necessarily conscious and active; it just means that our species has survived only because human beings have successfully achieved this goal in each generation.

According to evolutionary perspectives, males and females have, over the long course of evolution, been subjected to different adaptive pressures related to their differences in reproduction. In most species, females choose mating partners and males compete for female mates with other males, and these different strategies are thought to arise from the sex difference in the level of parental care (the time and effort devoted to caring for offspring) (Geary, 1998).

Evolutionary psychologists theorize that the sex differences in reproductive strategies have resulted in some of the psychological sex differences we see in contemporary society (Buss, 2000; Geary, 1998). The different reproductive tasks of men and women are hypothesized to be associated with different psychological strategies. Through natural and sexual selection, psychological strategies that increase reproductive success will become increasingly common. There are different specific challenges for men and women related to their different roles in reproduction, so, according to evolutionary psychologists, sex differences in reproductive tasks result in psychological sex differences (Trivers, 1972).

The challenge for women is that they have a greater physical burden of childbearing than do men; they are the ones who gestate and nourish offspring through pregnancy and lactation. Women, therefore, can have only a limited number of children, so they want to be sure that each child is "high quality" and will survive to reproduce him or herself. This would lead women to be fussy about their partners, both in terms of the partner's genes and the likelihood that the partner will help in child rearing. This has been interpreted to account for women's preferences for men with characteristics likely to reflect "good genes" and the ability to provide resources. This would also lead males to compete for female mates with other males, leading to the selection in males of certain traits that are attractive to females, because such traits are thought to reflect good genes.

The challenge for men is not in physical cost, but in uncertainty about paternity: they can never be certain that they are, indeed, the father of their partner's child. This has been interpreted to mean that it would be to men's advantage to try to have as many offspring as possible, and, thus, to account for men's preferences for multiple partners.

Evolutionary Explanations for Specific Gender-Related Characteristics

There are several other aspects to evolutionary approaches, and these, combined with those described above, have been used to explain a variety of sex differences in behavior that occur in many species and, within the human species, across most cultures. We describe some examples here to illustrate the breadth of characteristics that have been considered. But, for several reasons, our coverage of this topic is more limited than our coverage of other biological perspectives considered later: Evolutionary perspectives focus on characteristics in adults, whereas our focus in this book is on children and adolescents; these perspectives have not been tested as well as proximal perspectives described below, in part because they are relatively new, and are difficult to test; they have generated more controversy than other biological perspectives and, to do complete justice to the different sides in the controversy, we would have to have a more detailed and more technical discussion than is feasible.

Gender-typed social behaviors

Females' greater interest in babies is considered to arise from their unique role in childbearing; that is, their greater investment in reproduction because they have to devote more resources than do men to producing and maintaining offspring, including the 9 months spent in pregnancy and the time and caloric energy devoted to breastfeeding. Males' greater aggression is considered to result from their competitions with each other for mates (associated with the fact that females do the choosing).

Emotion

From an evolutionary perspective, emotions serve adaptive functions. One of the best examples of this is fear. Fear protects us from danger by energizing escape from harmful situations. The traditional biological response to fear and chronic stress is the **fight-or-flight** response (Cannon, 1932). This response is thought to have evolved to protect people from harm. Those who escape from harm are more likely to live to reproduce, and hence the fight-or-flight response has been selected through evolution.

Recent work by Taylor and her colleagues has called attention to another kind of response to fear, and especially to chronic stress, which they have termed the **tend-and-befriend response** (Taylor et al., 2000). This response is hypothesized by Taylor and colleagues to be a characteristic response of women, whereas the fight-or-flight response is hypothesized to be a characteristic response of men (although women also experience it). This sex difference in response to chronic stress is proposed to result from different evolutionary pressures on the sexes and is mediated by hormones and the central nervous system. In particular, women's behavior under conditions of chronic stress is considered to be motivated by their greater parental investment compared with men, and women's behavior is affected by the hormones associated with pregnancy and lactation; it is part of the attachment system that evolved to support the bonds between infants and their caregivers, who are largely female. Females, it is argued, act to "create, maintain, and utilize these social groups, especially relations with other females, to manage stressful conditions" (Taylor et al., 2000, p. 411). Fighting or fleeing can be dangerous for a pregnant woman and to the young children for whom women are often responsible. Thus, the tendency to look after dependent children and to form coalitions with other women against threat are suggested to have evolved as better protective mechanisms from danger or chronic stress for women and their children than are fighting or fleeing. A woman who protects her offspring from danger will be more likely to have offspring who reach adulthood and reproduce, hence carrying into future generations the genes that influence these behavioral tendencies.

There are no sex differences in the physiological stress response, but rather in its manifestation in behavior. Furthermore, stress hormone levels may be affected by other circulating hormones that show sex differences. One such hormone is testosterone. At least after puberty, men's high levels of testosterone may make them likely to fight in response to danger and stress. Another such hormone is oxytocin, which is associated with many physiological processes in both sexes, playing a particularly important role in lactation and exerting a calming effect during times of stress.

Evidence from nonhuman animals shows that females produce more oxytocin than do males in response to stress, and that high levels of estrogen seem to make oxytocin especially effective in reducing stress-related anxiety (Taylor et al., 2000). Mounting evidence shows a role for oxytocin in human social affiliative behaviors. For example, oxytocin during pregnancy was found to be associated with postpartum maternal bonding behaviors (Feldman, Weller, Zagoory-Sharon, & Levine, 2007); temporary increases in oxytocin (accomplished through nasal sprays) increase trust (Kosfeld, Heinrichs, Zak, Fischbacher, & Fehr, 2005).

Cognitive abilities

Sex differences in spatial ability have traditionally been explained by the nature of the work done by the two sexes, with males hunting and females gathering. An intriguing alternative hypothesis for the sex difference instead invokes the importance of good spatial skills for males' ability to traverse large territories and encounter a lot of females, and therefore have a lot of opportunities to mate and produce offspring (Gaulin, 1995; Gaulin & Fitzgerald, 1989). Evidence in support of this hypothesis comes from studies in voles (a type of rodent): sex differences in spatial learning are found only in species of voles that are polygynous (males have multiple sex partners and must travel to find those mates) and not in species of voles that are monogamous (males have a single sex partner, so do not wander in search of mates). It will be interesting to see if these findings on spatial ability in voles are confirmed in people, thus providing support for an evolutionary explanation of sex differences in spatial ability.

Evaluation of Evolutionary Perspectives

There are many appeals to an evolutionary approach to behavioral sex differences. It places behavior on an equal footing with other (physical) traits, correctly conceptualizes behavior (as other traits) as an adaptation to problems faced by our ancestors, and provides a single explanation for a range of behavioral sex differences. There is some evidence that evolution has acted to produce physiological and neurochemical differences between the sexes that underlie differences in psychological characteristics.

Nevertheless, as noted above, evolutionary theories are very controversial as scientific explanations of psychological sex differences (e.g., Eagly & Wood, 1999; Newcombe, 2007). This controversy reflects several concerns. First, it is difficult to make inferences about the adaptive significance of behavior; a specific behavior may have evolved because it was adaptive or merely because it is a byproduct of another trait that was crucial to survival.

Second, it is difficult to test evolutionary explanations empirically, especially with respect to human gender development. Although the predictions from evolutionary theory fit some of the data, they do not fit all of the data and there are other theories that also fit the data. With respect to data that cannot be explained, not all men and all women behave in ways that are predicted by evolutionary theory.

For example, not all men desire multiple partners, and some women have high spatial ability. With respect to the nonunique prediction from evolutionary theories, sociocultural factors explain some of the sex differences just as well. For example, sex differences in interest in babies or interest in multiple sex partners might arise from modeling. Most of the people who children observe taking care of babies are women; the media glamorize male celebrities who father children with multiple women, especially younger women, but they are not very kind to female celebrities who have many partners or younger ones.

Third, sexual selection is more complex than initially suggested. Data from nonhuman species show that there is sexual competition among females as well as males, and males may also be choosy about mating partners (Clutton-Brock, 2007). Fitness depends not just on the number of offspring produced, but on the number that survive to reproduce themselves, so both sexes need to invest in their offspring.

Concerns about the limitations of evolutionary perspectives have led to the development of an alternative perspective, which focuses on the origin of sex differences in the different placements of women and men in the social structure, rather than in evolved dispositions (Eagly & Wood, 1999). This alternative has been called a biosocial approach (Wood & Eagly, 2002). According to this perspective, sex-typed mating preferences are not universal (contrary to claims made by evolutionary psychologists) but instead vary across cultures, and sex differences derive from the interaction between the physical specialization of the sexes, particularly female reproductive capacity, and the economic and social structural aspects of societies. Thus, according to the biosocial approach, the psychological characteristics of the sexes are seen to emerge from evolved characteristics of women and men, their developmental experiences, and their roles in society (Wood & Eagly, 2002). This approach is covered in detail in Chapter 7.

Summary: Evolutionary Perspectives on Gender Development

Evolutionary perspectives on gender development focus on the forces of natural and sexual selection as the reasons for psychological sex differences. In particular, the different reproductive tasks of men and women are hypothesized to be associated with different psychological strategies, and those strategies that increase reproductive success will be selected and will increase in frequency. Evolutionary perspectives are appealing, and some evidence is consistent with evolutionary explanations of psychological sex differences. But, there is a need for additional supporting evidence and tests of competing alternative perspectives. We expect that such evidence will be forthcoming as evolutionary perspectives mature. Perhaps the most important message to take home about evolutionary explanations is that they are intriguing, worthy of additional study, and that we would like to see additional evidence to support them.

In any event, evolutionary perspectives are only part of the story, and we need to go beyond them for two other reasons. First, evolutionary theories are distal explanations for sex differences, that is, they explain forces that existed in the past that resulted in the behaviors we see today. But they are not very satisfying if we want to know in specific and tangible ways what accounts for the fact that boys and girls behave differently—that is, the proximal mechanisms underlying gender development. Second, evolutionary explanations are generally concerned with factors that apply to all members of a group—that is, factors that make all boys and men similar to each other and different from all girls and men. But we know that there is usually as much (and often more) variation within sex as there is between the sexes. It is for these reasons that we look for other biological explanations of psychological sex differences.

Moving From Distal to Proximal Biological Mechanisms of Sex-Related Behavior

Proximal biological explanations of gender development correspond to the steps in physical sexual differentiation, invoking as causes genes and hormones (those present early in life and those present at puberty and beyond) as well as brain structure and function. It is not easy to study these explanations, because we cannot manipulate people's genes or hormones. Therefore, much of what we know about this topic comes from people with the **disorders of sex development** (DSDs, formerly called intersex conditions) that we discussed in chapter 3. They provide **experiments of nature**—nature has manipulated one and only one aspect of the typical pattern, resulting in inconsistencies (also called discordance) among the different components of sexual differentiation. Although this type of work has been conducted since the 1950s (Money & Ehrhardt, 1972; Money, Hampson, & Hampson, 1957; Zucker, 1999), it has become much more visible to the general public over the past few years because of a few prominent cases and the political activism and advocacy efforts of people with DSDs (Berenbaum, 2006).

GENETIC PERSPECTIVES ON GENDER DEVELOPMENT

It is clear that there are physical consequences of the fact that males and females are not exactly the same genetically, but could these genetic differences account for psychological differences? **Genetic theories** of gender development focus on precisely this question and are associated with testable hypotheses about the behavioral effects of differences in the number and type of **sex chromosomes** and in the genes contained on those chromosomes, as well as on the possibility that the effects of genes on the **autosomes** may vary by sex.

Direct Genetic Effects

If we believe the popular media and the many cartoons that make their way to us over electronic mail, we might conclude that differences between the sexes result directly from genes on the sex chromosomes. As with many jokes, there is a kernel of truth in those cartoons, as we will discuss in the next section.

Genes on the Y Chromosome

The Y chromosome plays the major role in determining a person's sex, and people have wondered if it plays a role in determining a person's gendered behavior. One of our favorite cartoons explaining a man's behavior in terms of the Y chromosome is shown in Figure 6.1 (created by Jane Gitschier; Flam, 1993).

Studying Y-chromosome effects on behavior
What would it mean for behavior to be influenced by a gene (or several genes) on the Y chromosome? Remember, only boys and men have a Y chromosome, so any characteristic that is influenced solely by a gene on the Y chromosome would be present only in boys and men. There are not many characteristics— besides testes and penis—that are present only in males and not in females. The only behavioral trait that comes close is male gender identity, but even that is not absolute. There are people with XX chromosomes who look like and are reared as females but who feel as if they are males. They are **gender dysphoric**, that is, unhappy as females, identify as males, and want to become males; these people are called **transsexual** or **transgendered**. Both males and females can be gender dysphoric.

Evidence regarding Y-chromosome effects on human behavior
The evidence we have so far paints a picture of a human Y chromosome without any direct genes for behavior. We know this primarily from studying people with **androgen-insensitivity syndrome** (AIS). Remember, these are people with a normal and fully functional Y chromosome, containing a normal and fully functional *SRY* **gene**, producing normal and fully functional testes that make normal levels of androgen, which—and here is the crucial part—their bodies cannot respond to (because their androgen receptors are not working), so they develop a female body and are reared as females. If genes on the Y chromosome affect gender-related behavior, then people with AIS should behave like males.

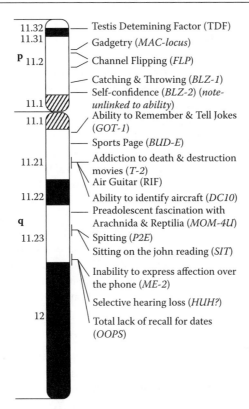

FIGURE 6.1 Cartoon of genes for behavior on the Y chromosome. (From Flam, F., *Science*, *251*, 679, 1993. Created by Jane Gitschier. Reproduced with permission of Jane Gitschier.)

Although individuals with AIS have not been studied extensively, every way that they have been studied shows that they are just like females, not males. For example, in two recent studies (Hines, Ahmed, & Hughes, 2003; Wisniewski et al., 2000), individuals with AIS were found to be similar to control females on measures of gender role (such as recalled childhood activities), sexual orientation, gender identity, and marital status. There were three main limitations to those studies that temper our conclusions. First, the studies had relatively small samples, making it difficult to detect differences that might be present in the population. Second, many individuals with AIS did not participate in the studies either because they could not be contacted or because they declined to participate. This raises the possibility that people who did participate were different in some ways from those who did not; for example, perhaps nonparticipants were more masculine in behavior than participants. Third, behavioral assessments were limited, insofar as the researchers did not directly observe people's behavior and they did not include measures of potentially important aspects of sex-typed behavior such as aggression and spatial ability.

Thus, although it is clear that more studies are needed, the most reasonable conclusion based on the existing data is that people with AIS are behaviorally feminine. This means that, as far as we know thus far, genes on the Y chromosome do not appear to play a major independent role in gender development, at least with respect to the social behaviors that have been studied; we cannot make inferences about cognitive abilities because they have not been well studied.

As we will discuss below, the female-typical behavior of individuals with AIS also tells us about other factors that affect gender development. Because they are reared as females, their female-typical behavior might result from their socialization. But, if androgen affects gender-related behavior, they would also show female-typical behavior. Although they have normal levels of androgens, their body cannot respond to it, so any areas of their brains that are affected by androgens should be like those of females.

Thus, the behavior of individuals with AIS is consistent with either social or hormonal influences on gender development, and later in this chapter we will describe other evidence about hormones.

Evidence regarding Y-chromosome effects on nonhuman sex-typed behavior
The studies in people suggesting that genes on the Y chromosome have no effect on gender development are a bit surprising in light of some recent data from rodents, which suggest that Y-chromosome genes do have a direct effect on the brain and behavior. Some of these data come from mice that have been manipulated to directly examine the effects of the gene that is equivalent to the human *SRY* gene (called *Sry* in mice) and other genes on the X and Y chromosomes. Mice that differ only in the form of the *Sry* gene have been found to differ in a few aspects of brain and behavioral traits, including social exploration (De Vries et al., 2002). Mice that have male sex chromosomes but female hormones have been found to behave like males in two ways—showing more aggression and some indicators of less caretaking of mouse pups (babies)—but like females in other ways—other indicators of parenting and response to the scent of other mice (an indication of sexual interest) (Gatewood et al., 2006). Furthermore, several genes are expressed differently in the brains of male and female mice very early in development, before sex hormones exert their influences (Dewing, Shi, Horvath, & Vilain, 2003). These studies show that genes on the Y chromosome do have direct effects on the brain and behavior in rodents, but it took a lot of careful and extensive investigation to find them. This leaves open the possibility that parallel effects may be found in people if we look hard enough.

Genes on the X Chromosome

It has also been hypothesized that gendered behavior might be influenced by genes on the X chromosome. In light of the disparity in size of the two sex chromosomes, it seems likely that there will be many more behaviorally relevant genes on the X chromosome than on the Y chromosome. Remember that females have two X chromosomes and males have one, so a trait that is influenced by a recessive gene on the X chromosome will be expressed with different frequency in males and females. One of the first biological hypotheses about sex differences in spatial ability concerned a recessive gene on the X-chromosome (Stafford, 1961). This hypothesis has turned out to be not so simple as a recessive X-linked pattern of inheritance, but there is some evidence to suggest that genes on the X chromosome do play a role in some aspects of behavior that show sex differences.

Studying X-chromosome effects on behavior
Much of what we know about X-chromosome genes and behavior comes from females with **Turner syndrome** (TS), in which, as we described in chapter 3, X-chromosome material is either missing or not oriented properly. Additional evidence comes from another condition, **Klinefelter syndrome** (KS), which, as mentioned in chapter 3, is caused by an extra X chromosome; that is, the **karyotype** is 47,XXY. The phenotype of KS is male, because it is the presence of a Y chromosome and the *SRY* gene in particular that determines maleness. It is reasonable to speculate that males with KS might be less male-typical than males with a normal karyotype given their extra X chromosome and physical undervirilization.

Evidence from TS regarding X-chromosome effects on human gender development
Many studies show that females with TS (45, X karyotype) have deficits in specific cognitive abilities, although, contrary to early reports, they are not mentally retarded (for reviews, see Ross, Roeltgen, & Zinn, 2006; Rovet, 1990). A hallmark of TS is deficient visual spatial ability. For example, females with TS perform poorly on tasks of direction sense, mental rotation, drawing and object assembly, motor tasks that require spatial skills, and mathematical performance. TS is also typically associated with deficiencies in *executive function*, which is like a master skill—it includes planning, organizing, and generally maintaining control over thinking and emotion. For example, females with TS have problems in attention and organization, adhering to rules, inhibiting behavior, and in working memory, which involves holding information in mind for a very short time. TS is also associated with deficits in cognitive skills applied to

social situations, such as recognizing emotion in faces, and in some social skills; for example, they show immature behavior (McCauley, Kay, Ito, & Treder, 1987).

Interpretation of studies in TS

Because TS is an experiment of nature with respect to the X chromosome, it is tempting to conclude that the deficits observed result from genes missing from the X chromosome–and, furthermore, that these genes ordinarily contribute to behavior in people with a normal karyotype. But TS is also an experiment with respect to hormones, because hormones produced by the ovaries are low or absent, probably starting early in development. Complicating matters even more, there are physical problems associated with TS, such as short stature, hearing loss, and heart problems. This makes it hard to know what causes the behavioral problems observed in TS—it could be the X chromosome itself, specific genes on that chromosome, abnormal levels of early hormones from the ovaries, later hormones, or indirect effects of the physical problems.

There has been some work to determine which of these possible factors account(s) for the deficits in females with TS (Berenbaum, Moffat, Wisniewski, & Resnick, 2003). First, it seems unlikely that physical problems are a cause of the cognitive and social deficits. Although these problems may limit physical activity in patients and potentially inhibit development of visual spatial skills, this seems unlikely for two reasons: females with TS also have deficiency in abilities that do not depend on physical activity, such as planning and memory; and there is no other evidence from other experiments of nature or from normal people that spatial ability depends on physical ability.

Second, some of the spatial problems seem to relate directly to genes on the X chromosome. The most convincing evidence comes from molecular genetic studies that have mapped the visuospatial deficits observed in TS to a specific region of the X chromosome (towards the tip of the short arm of the chromosome) (Ross, Roeltgen, Kushner, Wei, & Zinn, 2000). The details of the study are beyond the scope of this book, but the gist of the work is the following: how well females with TS scored on spatial tests was associated with whether or not they had deletions in that region of the chromosome—that is, whether they were missing specific genes. This suggests that those genes are necessary for good spatial ability, but these studies need to be repeated by others. And an interesting follow-up question is whether these genes are associated with variations in spatial ability in people without TS.

Third, evidence for direct genetic effects of behavior in TS comes from a study that looked at cognitive performance in relation to the parental origin of the intact X chromosome (Skuse et al., 1997). Differences between those who inherited the X chromosome from the father and those who inherited it from the mother would reflect **imprinting**, as discussed in chapter 3. A notable finding concerned social cognition, which refers to thinking about social situations. As we saw in chapter 5, there are sex differences in some aspects of social cognition: females are better than males in reading the emotions of others. In the studies of TS, this was measured by asking a mother to rate her daughter on such things as awareness of other people's feelings and acceptable social behavior, and specific social behaviors such as interrupting conversations, responding to commands, and unknowingly offending people. Girls with TS performed worse than girls without TS on these tasks, and, among girls with TS, those who inherited the single X chromosome from the mother (denoted $45,X^m$) performed worse than those who inherited the X chromosome from the father (denoted $45,X^p$) (Skuse et al., 1997). Because other aspects of TS, especially hormonal abnormalities, are probably similar in $45,X^m$ and $45,X^p$ females, differences between them must reflect direct effects of genes on the X chromosome.

Several scientists are following up on this and studying imprinting effects, and there are some interesting results, such as imprinting effects on verbal memory (Bishop et al., 2000), but also some difficulties in repeating findings of others, so the reliability and significance of this type of research remains controversial. Assuming that these results are repeated, they have some interesting implications for people without TS because of the potential meaning for sex differences in social skills. The studies in TS suggest that some aspects of these skills are worse when a person gets the gene from the mother than when a person gets the gene from the father. Remember that females get two X chromosomes, one from the mother and one from the father, whereas males get only one X chromosome and it comes from the mother.

If there are imprinted genes for social skills on the X chromosome, as suggested in the studies of TS, this means that poor performance is associated with the X chromosome from the mother, so those who have only that chromosome (males) should perform worse than those who have two X chromosomes, one from each parent (females).

Evidence from KS regarding X-chromosome effects on human gender development

As discussed above, the evidence from TS suggests that there are genes on the X chromosome directly influencing gender development, especially spatial ability and social skills. An important question is whether this evidence is confirmed by studies in people with other conditions associated with sex chromosome aneuploidies, particularly KS. There are not as many systematic studies of KS as there are of TS, but the evidence suggests that males with KS are more likely than males without KS to have speech and language deficits, which is not easy to explain in terms of either the X chromosome or sex hormones (Rovet, Netley, Keenan, Bailey, & Stewart, 1996; Simpson, de la Cruz, Swerdloff, Samango-Sprouse, Skakkebaek, Graham, et al., 2003). Thus, the evidence for behavioral effects of genes on the X chromosome is tantalizing, but we need to have more of it before we can draw definitive conclusions.

Genes on the Autosomes

Genes that contribute to gendered behavior might also be found on the autosomes, but their influence would have to be a bit more subtle than that of genes on the sex chromosomes. Autosomal genes would not by themselves produce sex differences in behavior, but they might have different effects in males and females because of sex differences in factors that affect their expression. One of the amazing properties of genes concerns their regulation. **Gene regulation** refers to the fact that genes get turned on and off in different cells, at different points in development, and in different environments. The most obvious example is that all of the cells in our body contain the same genes, but they are not all expressed in all of the cells. This different expression is what makes a liver cell different from a brain cell, it is what makes pubic hair appear at puberty and not before (unless there is an abnormality in development), and it is part of what makes human beings different from chimpanzees despite the fact that we share a very large proportion of our genetic material (about 98% of our genome).

This process of genetic regulation (also called differential gene expression) is also responsible for sex differences in some traits. Many of the genes for baldness are on the autosomes, but they are expressed primarily in the presence of high levels of testosterone, so men are much more likely than women to become bald. It is also possible that some behavioral sex differences are influenced by autosomal genes that are differentially expressed in males and females because of other factors that differ between them. An obvious factor is hormones, but there are other genetic and environmental differences between males and females that might affect gene expression, such as diet and sun exposure. It is thus reasonable to hypothesize that sex differences in gene expression lead to behavioral sex differences, but we currently have no data that provide a good test of the hypothesis.

Summary: Genetic Effects on Gender Development

Although there is good reason to think that genes on the sex chromosomes affect gender development, the issue is not easy to study because there are very few conditions in which effects of those genes can be studied in isolation. There is intriguing evidence from people with TS that the X chromosome plays a role in spatial ability and social skills. There is currently no evidence for human behavioral effects of genes on the Y chromosome, but studies in rodents suggest that such evidence may eventually be found. Genes on the autosomes might also influence behavior differently in males and females, through regulation by hormones or social experiences, but there is little direct evidence on this issue.

HORMONAL PERSPECTIVES ON GENDER DEVELOPMENT: SEX HORMONES AFFECT MORE THAN THE GENITALIA

There is good reason to hypothesize that sex hormones play a role in gender development. Sex hormones are crucial for physical sexual differentiation, and one of the most important biological differences between the sexes is that high levels of androgens are primarily responsible for the establishment of the male physical phenotype. Given that the brain is a physical structure, it seems likely that the brain and the behavior it sub-serves are also affected by sex hormones. Studies in a variety of nonhuman species establish without question that this is true: sexual differentiation of brain structure and function (including behavior) is dependent on the presence or absence of sex hormones, especially androgen. Furthermore, studies in human beings increasingly show the importance of sex hormones for sexual differentiation of behavior. These studies generally test what are called **hormonal theories** of (or **hormonal perspectives** on) sex differences.

How Hormones Exert Their Effects

Androgens and estrogens are generally considered to exert their effects in two ways, each with different timing. These effects are called **organizational** and **activational hormonal effects**. Organizational hormonal effects occur early in life, usually during prenatal or early postnatal life, and produce permanent changes to physical structures of the body (including the brain). Activational hormonal effects occur at any time in life and produce temporary changes to physical functions while the hormone is present in the body. This applies to the body generally and has been studied with respect to the development of the brain and behavior, most extensively in rodents, but also in human and nonhuman primates.

Organizational and Activational Effects

First, consider organizational effects and an example with respect to the body, specifically, the genitals. High levels of androgen must be present at about weeks 7–8 of gestation for a penis and a scrotum to develop. If androgen levels are high at a later time, the clitoris will enlarge, but never enough to be a penis and will never cause the labia to fuse into a scrotum. The same kinds of structural changes happen in the brain (as discussed below). The times when hormones have their major effects are called **sensitive periods**, meaning that the body is most likely to respond (is sensitive) when hormones are present at these times. You have probably heard about sensitive periods before in psychology. For example, the first few years of life are considered to be very important for the acquisition of language; children who are not exposed to language early in life do not ever develop normal language.

Now, consider activational effects. Hormones continue to affect us as they circulate in the body, primarily throughout adolescence and adulthood. They do so by producing temporary alterations to the body, brain, and behavior. For example, high levels of androgen at puberty and beyond are responsible for the development of body hair. A female who begins to produce excess androgen will start to grow a beard, but the beard will diminish when her androgen levels return to normal. The same kinds of temporary changes happen in the brain, as discussed below.

Thus, hormonal theories of gender development have considered the behavioral effects of both organizational hormones (those that are present early in life and produce permanent changes to some brain structures and the behaviors they subserve) and activational hormones (those that are present later in life and produce temporary changes to some brain structures and the behaviors they subserve). But, it is important to note that the distinction between organizational and activational hormone effects is not absolute (Arnold & Breedlove, 1985). For example, hormones that are present later in life may actually produce permanent changes to the brain; we will talk about this later when we talk about hormonal changes at puberty. Therefore, some have suggested that it is helpful to think of hormone effects occurring along a continuum in terms of permanence: organizational effects are at the permanent end of the continuum, involving changes to the structure of the body and brain, whereas activational effects are at the temporary end of the continuum, involving changes that are short-term or transient (e.g., changes to chemical signals in the brain). Our discussion begins with the effects of early organizational hormones and then proceeds to the effects of hormones present at puberty and beyond.

EARLY ORGANIZATIONAL HORMONES

This section focuses on hormones that are present early in life while the brain is experiencing its greatest development. The question is how these early hormones organize the brain to produce permanent changes in behavior during postnatal life.

Early Hormone Effects in Nonhuman Mammals

The studies in people have been guided by a substantial and systematic literature in nonhuman species, starting with the work of Phoenix and his colleagues (Phoenix, Goy, Gerall, & Young, 1959) who showed that female guinea pigs given androgens early in life showed behavior like that of males when they grew up. Many studies in a variety of other animal species have confirmed and extended the work of Phoenix and his colleagues to show that high levels of androgen during sensitive periods early in development are associated with changes in behaviors that show sex differences, as described below.

What Is Gender Development in Nonhuman Animals?

There are many behaviors—both sexual and nonsexual—in nonhuman animals that show sex differences, and hormones affect many of them. In nonhuman species, sexual behaviors of males and females are different in form; that is, males and females engage in behaviors that are different in substance, not just in amount. Behaviors that differ in form between the sexes are called **sex-dimorphic** (literally "two forms"). Males typically display a pattern of motor movements involving physical mounting of females, insertion of the penis into the female's vagina (called **intromission**), thrusting of the penis, and finally ejaculation. Females respond with specific movements that show that they are receptive to the male; for example, arching of the back (called **lordosis**). These male-typical and female-typical behaviors are studied with respect to their frequency of occurrence (how often they occur during a specific observation period), and duration (how long the animal engages in these behaviors). Scientists also study the sex of the target of these behaviors; for example, whether male animals try to mount other males. Some of the characteristics of sexual behaviors in nonhuman species are similar to characteristics in people, such as intromission and thrusting of the penis. But, there are cross-species differences, most notably that males and females of other species engage in different forms of behavior (mounting vs. lordosis), whereas there is less dimorphism in human males and females.

There is a variety of other behaviors that can be observed in rodents and in primates and that show sex differences. Many of these behaviors directly parallel human behavioral sex differences in two important ways: the behaviors themselves are similar, and the sex differences are not in form, but in level; that is, one sex displays more of the behavior than the other sex. These are usually called **sex-related behaviors**. Behaviors that occur more often or at higher levels in males than in females include aggression, rough play, and aspects of spatial learning. Behaviors that occur more often or at higher levels in females than in males include infant care, grooming, and aspects of learning generally unrelated to space.

Before we turn to androgen's effects on these behaviors, it is important to clarify terminology. The behaviors that are examined in relation to androgen exposure are usually called **male-typical** and **female-typical**, and scientists look to see if changes in androgen produce changes in the amounts of these behaviors. Increases in androgen should make behavior more male-typical and less female-typical, and decreases in androgen should make behavior less male-typical and more female-typical. This terminology derives from studies of sexual behaviors in rodents and primates, in which males and females actually engage in behaviors that are different in form, as described above: male rats mount female rats, and female rats display postures reflecting that they are receptive to sexual activity.

The problem with this terminology is that almost all human behavior and most nonhuman behavior does not exist in two separate forms for males and females—the main difference is usually in the amount of behavior that males and females display, or the frequency with which they display the behavior. Therefore, male-typical behavior is generally used to refer to behavior that is higher in level or frequency in males than in females, and female-typical behavior is used to refer to behavior that is higher in level or frequency in females than in males.

There is also another way to describe behavior that has been shifted towards or away from what is typical for a sex. Behavior that is shifted away from what is male-typical is referred to as **masculinized** (more male-typical) or **demasculinized** (less male-typical). Behavior that is shifted away from what is female-typical is referred to as **feminized** (more female-typical) or **defeminized** (less female-typical).

Some of you might be wondering about the difference between masculinized and defeminized. After all, if something moves towards male-typical, it must move away from female-typical. This confusion results from the fact that the terminology originated with behavior that had two forms, so it was possible to be masculinized but not defeminized; for example, for a female to show sexual mounting behavior but also to show lordosis (receptivity to males). But, we end up in trouble because most behaviors exist on a continuum and not in two forms. Therefore, we resort to convention and use masculinized and demasculinized to refer to changes in behaviors that are higher in level or frequency in males than in females (male-typical), such as aggression and spatial ability, and feminized and defeminized to refer to changes in behaviors that are higher in level or frequency in females than in males (female-typical), such as infant care and grooming.

Methods for Studying Hormone Effects on Nonhuman Sex-Related Behavior

Now that we have clarified the behaviors being discussed and the language used to describe whether they are influenced by hormones, we can turn to the ways in which we study hormone effects on these behaviors. Most studies involve direct manipulations of hormone levels, but there are also studies involving naturally occurring variations in hormones.

Experimental manipulations

The timing of the manipulation is crucial, because the studies are designed to change hormones when the brain is developing. In rats and mice, most of brain development takes place after birth, so hormones are manipulated in the **neonatal** (newborn) period. In guinea pigs and monkeys, most of brain development takes place before birth (as also occurs in human beings), so hormones are manipulated during the **prenatal** period when the animal is in its mother's uterus. For females, manipulations involve injections of male-typical hormones, such as testosterone. For mice and rats, these injections are given in the first few days after birth, whereas for guinea pigs and primates the injections are given to the pregnant mother during the period when brain development is known to be occurring. For males, manipulations involve either injections of chemicals that counteract the effects of testosterone (what are called anti-androgens) or removal of the testes (castration). For mice and rats, it is possible to do injections or castration; for primates and guinea pigs, anti-androgen injections are the manipulation of choice because it is difficult to castrate an animal while it is in its mother's uterus. All of these studies include controls; that is, animals that received a fake manipulation, so we can be sure that the behavior we measure is directly caused by the hormonal manipulation and not by injections or surgery alone. This control condition is equivalent to a human placebo condition and involves a manipulation that is similar to the real one in most ways, but does not contain the active agent. Controls for injections with androgen or anti-androgen would be injections with a substance that has no hormone action; controls for castration would be surgery but no removal of the testes. Whatever the manipulation, the behavior—and often the brain—of the animal are studied when it is older, usually as a juvenile (the animal equivalent of child), adolescent, or adult. Studies measure outcomes in a variety of behaviors that show sex differences. Early studies focused on sexual behaviors, but later studies also examined nonsexual behaviors.

Naturally occurring variations

It is also possible to see the behavioral effects of androgens in the natural world of animals (e.g., mice, rats, gerbils, and sheep) without injecting animals with androgen. This is because some female animals are exposed to higher-than-typical androgen levels because they were littermates of males; specifically, they were gestated in the uterus near males. Rats and mice usually produce several offspring (called pups) in each litter. This means that each animal occupies a space in the uterus next to another animal, what is called **intrauterine position** (IUP). And, all except two animals at each end of the uterus have two neighbors, one on each side. The two neighbors might both be males, both females, or one of each sex— the IUP in these situations is denoted as 2M (or 0F), 2F (or 0M), and 1M (or 1F), respectively. As you will see below, there are long-term consequences of a rodent's prenatal neighborhood, and this has been well studied in mice, rats, and gerbils (Clark & Galef, 1998; Ryan & Vandenbergh, 2002).

Evidence for Organizational Hormone Effects on Nonhuman Sex-Related Behavior

There is overwhelming and compelling evidence from other species that sex-related behaviors are largely influenced by androgens that are present early in life when the brain is developing (for reviews, see Baum, 2006; Becker, Breedlove, Crews, & McCarthy, 2002; Breedlove, 1992; Goy & McEwen, 1980; Wallen, 2005). These effects are observed in a variety of species, from birds to primates, and we focus here on mammalian species with the most relevance to human beings.

Evidence from experimental studies in rodents

In rodents, females that are injected with high doses of androgen in the newborn period show behavior more typical of males than of other females, and males that are deprived of androgen because of castration or injections with drugs that block the effects of androgen (anti-androgens) show behavior more typical of females than of other males (for reviews, see Becker et al., 2002; Breedlove, 1992; Goy & McEwen, 1980). Consider some examples. Female rats that were injected with androgen when they were newborns show adult sexual behavior similar to males: they try to mount other females and are not particularly responsive to overtures by males. Female rodents injected with androgen as newborns also engage in more rough play when they are juveniles, are more aggressive as adults, and perform better in mazes on which males typically excel. Conversely, male rodents that were deprived of androgen when they were newborns do not mount females, engage in less rough play, are less aggressive, and perform worse in those mazes than do normal males.

It is interesting to look specifically at maze performance because these studies are nice parallels for human spatial ability. In rats, there are sex differences in performance in a maze that is called the radial-arm maze. In this task, the maze looks like a wheel with a hub and several spokes. There is food at the end of the spokes, and the rat's task is to get all of the food that is there. For a rat, that means remembering where it has been and not wasting time going back to a place already visited. Male rats usually get more of the food and do so more quickly than do female rats. But, female rats that are given masculinizing hormones early in development learn the maze as well as normal males, and better than normal females. Male rats that are castrated in the newborn period perform more like normal females. Furthermore, rats that do well use different strategies than rats that do not do well. Males and females exposed to masculinizing hormones (high scorers) use geometric rather than landmark cues (Williams, Barnett, & Meck, 1990; Williams & Meck, 1991). These effects seem to be due to changes in areas of the rat's brain that are involved in learning of spatial skills, including the **hippocampus**; these regions are also changed by the hormones (Juraska, 1991; Roof & Havens, 1992; Williams & Meck, 1991).

Evidence from experimental studies in monkeys

We see the same effects of androgen in monkeys, although we have less data here because the topic is harder to study in primates than in rodents (Wallen, 2005). As we noted, most brain development in primates (including human beings) takes place in prenatal life, making it difficult to manipulate hormones in primates. Scientists cannot inject the animal itself, but must treat the pregnant mother. Furthermore, the entire development of primates takes place in a much longer time span than that of rodents, so the studies take a long time to do, and it is expensive and challenging to create a nurturing and compassionate rearing environment for monkeys. These studies have shown that androgen does, indeed, affect behavior in monkeys as it does in rats and mice, and they have revealed some amazing and exciting complexities as described below.

Female monkeys that were exposed to androgen in utero because their mothers were injected with it during their pregnancies show a variety of masculinized behaviors: compared with control females that were not exposed to androgen, they try to mount other females and engage in more rough play and less grooming (Goy, Bercovitch, & McBrair, 1988). Androgens present early in development also affect both learning abilities that show sex differences in monkeys and the development of the brain areas that are important for these abilities (Bachevalier & Hagger, 1991; Clark & Goldman-Rakic, 1989).

The findings in monkeys do more than replicate the studies in rodents; they show how complex these effects can be. First, they show that timing of exposure matters quite a bit, and that there may be several distinct sensitive periods for androgen effects on behavior, even within the prenatal period. We can see this from the study done by Goy and his colleagues (Goy et al., 1988), in which pregnant monkeys were injected with androgen at different times in their pregnancies (which lasts 168 days). Some monkey fetuses were exposed very early in development (the mothers were injected during days 40–64 of gestation), whereas other monkey fetuses were exposed later in development (the mothers were injected during days 115–139 of gestation) and then the behaviors of the juvenile monkeys were studied at several ages from 3 to 27 months. The monkeys that received androgen early in development also had masculinized genitals because the genitals develop early, but those exposed late in development had normal-looking genitals. Observations showed that some behaviors were masculinized by exposure early (but not late) in gestation, whereas other behaviors were masculinized by exposure late (but not early) in gestation, with some overlap between the two effects. For example, female monkeys exposed to androgen early in gestation showed increased mounting of female peers and mothers as well as less grooming behavior, whereas those exposed late in gestation showed increased rough play and increased mounting of peers but not of mothers.

The second complexity to emerge from the studies in monkeys concerns the environmental context. In brief, whether and how hormones affect behavior depends on the environment that the animal is in; this is what we call an interaction between the hormones and the environment. It has been shown in juvenile monkeys that the social environment modifies the expression of behavior that is influenced by hormones (Wallen, 1996). For example, sex differences in rough-and-tumble play occur in all rearing environments, with the size of the difference affected by the environment, whereas differences in aggressive and submissive behaviors are found only in certain rearing situations. Behaviors that show consistent sex differences across social context are most affected by prenatal androgens.

Evidence from naturally occurring variations in hormones

As we noted above, animals differ among themselves in the extent to which they are naturally exposed to androgens. A major source of this variation results from their place in the uterus, specifically whether they gestated next to an animal of the opposite sex, what is called intrauterine position (IUP). There are long-term consequences of IUP (Clark & Galef, 1998; Ryan & Vandenbergh, 2002). In rodents, females that spent their prenatal lives between two males (2M) are more masculine both physically and behaviorally than females that gestated between two females (2F) or one male and one female (1M) (Clark & Galef, 1998; Ryan & Vandenbergh, 2002). With respect to physical traits, for example, 2M females have somewhat masculinized genitals. This is measured by an index called the anogenital distance, which is greater in males than in females and greater in 2M females than in 2F females. They are also different in some reproductive characteristics: compared to 2F females, 2M females have first estrus at a later age (thus becoming fertile later), fewer litters, and shorter reproductive life. With respect to behavioral traits, for example, 2M females are more aggressive than 2F females and are less attractive to males (receiving less sexual behavior from males), showing that hormones can affect not just the behavior of the animal itself but the social response to the animal.

There are parallel IUP effects in males (Clark & Galef, 1998). For example, male gerbils that were between two females in the uterus (2F) are at a reproductive disadvantage compared to those that were between two males (2M): they sire fewer offspring, primarily because they fail to impregnate female partners. This appears to result from problems in sexual behavior, such as longer time to intromission and ejaculation, which may, in turn, reflect deficits in genital muscles.

These IUP studies teach us three very important lessons about hormones. First, naturally occurring differences in hormones affect behavior, creating some of the differences we see among animals naturally. Put another way, pretty normal variations in hormones are responsible for pretty normal variations in behavior. This suggests that the same thing happens in people. Second, the prenatal environment is an important developmental time for rodents also. We said before that the sensitive period for organizational hormone effects in rodents was during early postnatal life, but these studies show that hormones have their effect when they are present during prenatal life also. Third, it is possible to analyze complex behaviors in terms of constituent elements. For example, we can understand why 2F male gerbils have fewer offspring by going back to their sexual behavior and even the way that their muscles are formed.

Effects of Androgens Versus Estrogens

You may have noticed that we have only talked about androgens and their masculinizing effects. Some of you are probably wondering about the effects of estrogens. Although estrogens do have a role in sexual differentiation of both the body and behavior, their effects are much more subtle and harder to pin down than those of androgens. We already noted that physical development proceeds in a generally female direction even without estrogens (e.g., in AIS and even TS), although completely normal female development does depend on two X chromosomes and intact ovaries. We also noted that the ovaries do not develop until later than the testes, and hormones from the ovaries appear to not play a major role during early development (Grumbach, Hughes, & Conte, 2002). It makes sense in the following way: both male and female fetuses are exposed to high levels estrogens from the mother, so if estrogen affected sexual differentiation in utero, then males would be exposed to a substance that would feminize them. Although the current picture suggests that hormones produced by the ovaries do not seem to do very much early in development with respect to the body or behavior, this may change as we learn more. In particular, it is now clear that female physical development is not just a passive process and estrogen is necessary for complete development. Similarly, it seems likely that estrogen is necessary for a complete female-typical brain and behavior, but that the sensitive period for the organizational effects of estrogens is later than that for androgens and may occur postnatally (Fitch & Denenberg, 1998).

Moving From Nonhuman Animals to People

Thus far, we have seen that the amount of sex hormones—androgens, in particular—present at key periods of development affect the sex-typed behaviors of rodents and monkeys. We hope that you are asking whether the same thing happens in people. The short answer is yes. The long answer is the focus of the next sections of the chapter. The following section includes a discussion of the methods we use to answer the question, and the section after that includes a discussion of the evidence obtained from those methods.

Methods for Studying Early Organizational Hormone Effects on Human Gender Development

It is obvious that the scientists who study hormonal influences on human behavior cannot manipulate hormones in people as scientists manipulate hormones in rodents and primates. Even if it were ethical to manipulate hormones (and, of course, it is not), it would not be so easy to do. We would have to inject pregnant women with androgen very early in their pregnancies, before many women even know that they are pregnant. We would have to inject them for an extended period of time during pregnancy. We would have to inject women who are carrying both male and female fetuses even though we would be mostly interested in studying the females, because we cannot know the sex of the fetus until at least 9 or 10 weeks of gestation (the earliest time for doing prenatal testing to know the karyotype of the fetus). We would have to worry about the fact that the injections would also change the genitals of female fetuses, enlarging the clitoris and causing the labia to fuse, perhaps enough to look like a scrotum—this is what happens to girls with **congenital adrenal hyperplasia** (CAH), as described in chapter 3. Thus, scientists studying hormonal influences on human gender development rely on CAH and some of the experiments of nature described in chapter 3.

Experiments of Nature

Individuals with disorders of sex development (DSDs) provide a unique opportunity to examine the behavioral effects of prenatal androgen because they allow us to isolate the components of sexual differentiation and see which ones are most clearly associated with behavior (Money & Ehrhardt, 1972). As discussed in chapter 3, there are many DSDs, and they provide different types of evidence about hormonal effects on gender development.

CAH

Females with CAH are particularly valuable to researchers because they have an excellent mix of characteristics: They are exposed to moderately high levels of androgen beginning early in gestation and continuing through prenatal life, which is considered to be a key sensitive period for hormone effects on brain development; they have typical (low) androgen levels in postnatal life after the disease is detected and treated; and they are reared as females. Also, CAH is relatively common, allowing scientists to put together a big enough sample for systematic study. Females with CAH represent a mismatch (discordance) between hormonal sex and all other aspects of sex (see Table 3.1). This means that differences between females with CAH and females without CAH are due to differences in hormonal sex, specifically prenatal androgen exposure. Put another way, if human gender development is affected by the levels of androgen present during sensitive periods of development—as behavioral sex differences are in other species—then females with CAH should show behavior that is more male-typical (masculinized) and less female-typical (defeminized) than that of females without CAH (typical females). Ideally, those typical females would be sisters of females with CAH who themselves do not have CAH to control for genetic and family environmental factors that might affect behavior (more about that later).

We will describe below the evidence that females with CAH do, in fact, differ in some aspects of their behavior from typical females. But that does not mean that the differences are necessarily due only to androgens. CAH is not a perfect experiment—we have not actually manipulated hormones leaving everything else constant—so we need to rule out other possible explanations. In particular, females with CAH differ from unaffected females in several ways besides prenatal androgen exposure, and it is important to decide if it is these factors, rather than androgens, that contribute to the behavioral differences. We also need to find other evidence that androgens affect behavior. Our inferences (here, as in all of science) can be much stronger if data from multiple sources all lead in the same direction; this is what is called convergence of evidence. Every method has its own limitations, so we can have more confidence in findings that come from different methods all leading to the same conclusion.

What are the limitations to studying CAH and what are the other methods available to us? The main concern about females with CAH relates to their physical appearance. Remember that they are exposed to androgen early in development, when the genitals are forming, so their genitals usually look different from those of typical girls (although the genitalia of girls with CAH are usually surgically corrected in early childhood). It is possible that this physical difference elicits different responses from other individuals, which in turn cause the behavioral differences. For example, behavioral differences between females with CAH and unaffected females might result from parents treating them differently because their genitals look different (Quadagno, Briscoe, & Quadagno, 1977). Females with CAH also have abnormalities in characteristics besides androgens, and studies try to eliminate these factors as causes of behavior. For example, other hormones, such as progesterone and corticosteroids, are abnormal in CAH, and CAH is a chronic illness, which may itself affect behavior. As we will see later, evidence suggests that these factors are not likely explanations for behavioral differences in females with CAH. But it is really important to find other ways to study androgen's effects on behavior so that we do not rely on a single method for all of our information.

Other DSDs

As we have noted, there are some other experiments of nature that provide information about androgen's effects on behavior. It is desirable to have data from males with especially low androgen, because they would be expected to be as different from their brothers as females with CAH are from their sisters, but in the opposite direction—they would be expected to be less male-typical (demasculinized) and more female-typical (feminized) than their unaffected (control) brothers. It turns out that there are not many good conditions that fit this bill, because it is rare for males to be exposed to low levels of androgens alone; it usually occurs as part of a developmental syndrome, making it difficult to study effects of androgen in isolation. Furthermore, the conditions that represent good experiments are not very common, so it is hard to do a study that has enough statistical power to see differences if they exist, but there are some data that we can examine.

A reasonably good experiment of nature regarding behavioral effects of low androgens in boys is a condition called condition **idiopathic hypogonadotropic hypogonadism** (IHH), as discussed in Chapter 3. Other good experiments include boys with **micropenis** or **partial androgen insensitivity** who are exposed at some early point in development to lower-than-normal levels of androgens (also discussed in chapter 3). There is some evidence about behavior in these boys, but not as much as there is about girls with CAH.

Maternal treatment

Other experiments of nature include people who were exposed to atypical hormones because their mothers were given drugs during pregnancy that had masculinizing effects. This is almost never done these days, because physicians are very careful to avoid prescribing any drugs to pregnant women unless they are sure that the drugs have no ill effects, and most women themselves are careful to avoid drugs while they are pregnant.

Experiments of Nurture

Two other conditions have received much attention with respect to telling us about hormonal influences on behavior. They are called experiments of nurture because they involve study of the behavioral consequences of an unusual change in the social environment (Bradley, Oliver, Chernick, & Zucker, 1998). These were described in chapter 3 and include **cloacal exstrophy** and **ablatio penis**. Some 46,XY individuals with completely normal male-typical prenatal development are reared as females because they lack a penis and because the prevailing view for many years was that gender identity is determined completely by rearing and that boys without a normal penis would grow up to have significant psychological problems (Berenbaum, 2006; Meyer-Bahlburg, 1998; Money, Hampson, & Hampson, 1955; Zucker, 1999). If they do behave and identify as girls, then this suggests that gender development is determined by the social environment. If, instead, they are masculinized in their behavior, then this provides evidence for the importance of biology. Because these children have both a Y chromosome and prenatal androgens, male-typical behavior could result from either one.

Studies in Typical Samples

Given the limitations involved in making inferences from experiments of nature and of nurture, it is important to have data from other sources about hormonal influences on gender development. Importantly, this evidence comes from studies of normal people whose hormones are within the normal range. What these studies do is examine variations in these hormones in relation to variations in behavior. This is, of course, difficult to do, because we are interested in effects of prenatal hormones and it is not easy to measure them in utero.

One approach is to extend the studies of IUP described earlier. Female animals that gestate next to a male are more masculine and less feminine than females that gestate next to another female. In people, the closest parallel is twins. The question is whether, in human beings, females who share the uterus with a male are behaviorally masculinized compared to females who share the uterus with a female. And the answer, as you will see, is that females with a male co-twin are masculinized in some ways, but not in other ways. It is important to note that this is not a perfect experiment either, because the social environment is also different for the two types of twins (and growing up with a brother has different effects than growing up with a sister, as discussed in chapter 11), and we do not know if testosterone from the male twin is transferred to the female twin; that is, whether the rodent model applies to human beings.

Thus, a better way to know whether prenatal androgens affect later behavior is to obtain direct measures of a fetus's androgen levels during the times that are considered to be the sensitive periods for the effects of hormones on the brain, usually considered to be sometime between prenatal weeks 8 and 24; as seen in Figure 3.1, this is the time when testosterone levels peak in boys.

One way to do this is to look at hormone levels in amniotic fluid obtained from a pregnant woman who is having amniocentesis for another purpose and then study the child from that pregnancy as he or she grows up. If hormones affect behavior, we would expect that girls who are relatively masculine in their behavior (play a lot with boys' toys, have high spatial ability, etc.) would have had high levels of testosterone in their amniotic fluid during gestation.

There is another approach to look at prenatal hormones in relation to behavior in typical people. This involves using hormones in the blood of pregnant women to reflect what the fetus was experiencing and examining those hormones in relation to the offspring's gender-related behaviors later in life (Hines et al., 2002; Udry, 1994; Udry, Morris, & Kovenock, 1995).

The Evidence: Early Hormones Affect Human Gender-Related Behavior

As you read in chapters 4 and 5, there are many ways in which boys and girls and men and women are different from each other. (There are also plenty of ways in which the sexes are similar, but we are focusing on the differences in this book.) It seems reasonable to ask whether all of them are affected by androgen. This means asking whether females with CAH are more like males and less like females on these traits, whether girls with a boy co-twin are more masculine in behavior than girls with a girl co-twin, whether, within the normal range, girls who had high testosterone when they were in the womb show more masculine behavior than girls who had low testosterone at that time. Researchers have really only begun to scratch the surface here, but so far there is good evidence that androgens do affect some—but not all—behaviors. The main behaviors that have been studied in this regard are activities and interests, including the toys with which children play, aspects of social behavior (especially aggression and interest in babies), cognitive abilities, sexual orientation, and gender identity.

Androgen Effects on Activities and Interests

Some people, especially those who are interested in gender development, assume that differences between boys and girls in their play must be due to socialization. After all, as detailed in chapters 7–13, the social worlds of boys and girls can be quite different. For example, boys and girls are dressed differently, they have different friends, different role models, and so on. Some people assume that it is these factors that cause the behavioral differences. But maybe society is a reflection, rather than a cause, of differences. Data from girls with CAH give us evidence to indicate that gender development depends on more than the social environment, and accruing evidence from other sources confirms these findings, as detailed below.

Early studies of girls with CAH
Studies of girls with CAH in the 1960s and 1970s were the first to give us a hint about the role of hormones in gender development. Money and his colleagues pioneered these studies, recognizing that girls with CAH provide an excellent experiment of nature paralleling the experimental studies done in nonhuman animals. Their early studies showed that girls with CAH were different from girls without CAH in several ways, most prominently that they liked boys' toys and outdoor play and were not eager to get married and have babies (Ehrhardt & Baker, 1974; Money & Ehrhardt, 1972). The main problem with these studies was that the data were obtained from interviews with the girls and their parents, usually by people who knew whether the participant had CAH or not. This means that there was considerable subjectivity; that is, the researchers might have inadvertently led the interview and interpreted interviewee responses in ways that were consistent with their expectations.

Modern studies of girls with CAH
As research methods got more sophisticated, researchers began to study the topic in ways that reduced some of the biases that were present in the early studies, particularly using measures that were less prone to the experimenters' expectations. One such series of studies examining children's preferences for boys' and girls' toys included several important methodological improvements (Berenbaum & Hines, 1992; Berenbaum & Snyder, 1995). In these studies, girls with CAH were compared to their sisters without CAH to control for factors that might be important for behavior and that would differ across families, including aspects of the family environment (such as how gender-typed the parents were) and general genetic background; behavioral measures were standardized across subjects, making it difficult for the experimenter to lead the girl to behave according to expectations; behavior was observed, recorded on videotape, and scored by someone who had had no contact with the girl and did not know if she had CAH or not. The study also included boys with CAH and their brothers without CAH for two reasons: (a) to make sure that the measures showed sex differences, and (b) to make sure that any differences between girls with CAH and their sisters reflected effects of androgen and not just effects of having a disease. The procedure was for the child to be brought into a playroom containing toys typically preferred by boys (e.g., toy cars, trucks, and Lincoln logs), toys typically preferred by girls (e.g., dolls and kitchen toys), and neutral toys equally preferred by boys and girls (e.g., books and board games) and asked to play with the toys however he or she wanted. The child's play was videotaped for 10 minutes and then scored by two independent people for the number of seconds the child played with boys' toys, girls' toys, and neutral toys.

The results of one aspect of the study are shown in Figure 6.2. As you can see, there is the expected sex difference in toy play: boys with and without CAH play more with boys' toys and less with girls' toys than do girls without CAH. As noted on the figure, the differences (d values) are large. The large sex differences mean that the measure is a good one for examining effects of prenatal hormones. As you can also see, girls with CAH play more with boys' toys and less with girls' toys than do their sisters without CAH, and again the differences are large. These differences are also seen when interests are measured in

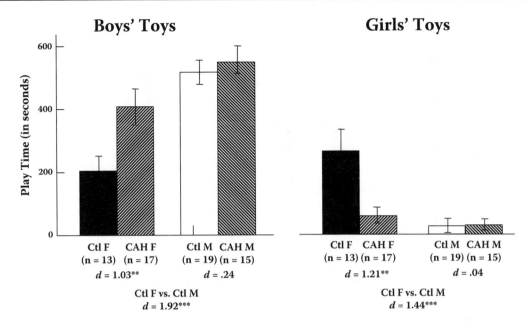

FIGURE 6.2   Time spent in play with boys' and girls' toys by children with CAH and their unaffected relatives during 10 minutes of play, averaged across two sessions. Bars represent group means; lines represent standard errors. Ctl: control (unaffected same-sex relatives); *d*: difference between group means/average standard deviation. Group differences were evaluated by one-tailed *t* test, **p < .01, ***p < .001. (From Berenbaum, S.A. & Snyder, E., *Developmental Psychology, 31*, 31–42, 1995.)

other ways: compared with their sisters, girls with CAH are more likely to pick a boys' toy (such as a toy airplane) when given a toy to keep, and report themselves and are reported by their parents to be more interested in boys' toys and activities and less interested in girls' toys and activities (Berenbaum & Snyder, 1995). When interests are measured in several ways like this, and the scores combined, the differences reflect not just averages but the entire group; the combined scores show very little overlap between girls with CAH and their sisters (Berenbaum & Snyder, 1995). It is characteristic of girls with CAH to play with boys' toys.

These findings have been replicated across laboratories and across countries, including the United States (Meyer-Bahlburg et al., 2004), the United Kingdom (Pasterski et al., 2005), and Sweden (Nordenström, Servin, Bohlin, Larsson, & Wedell, 2002). There is even some suggestive evidence from Japan: girls with CAH there drew pictures with masculine characteristics (e.g., moving objects, dark colors, and a bird's-eye perspective), as opposed to those with feminine characteristics (e.g., human figures, flowers, and light colors) (Iijima, Arisaka, Minamoto, & Arai, 2001). It is clear that girls with CAH like boys' toys and activities.

Females with CAH continue to be interested in male-typical activities into adolescence and adulthood, although published studies of older subjects have relied on self-reports and not on observations. Thus, compared with their sisters, teenage girls with CAH report greater interest in activities such as electronics, cars, and sports, and less interest in activities such as cheerleading, make-up, and fashion (Berenbaum, 1999). Again, as shown in Figure 6.3, there is little overlap between girls with CAH and their sisters. It is characteristic of teenage girls with CAH to be interested in male-typical activities. Adult women with CAH report that they are more interested than are their sisters in male-typical activities (Meyer-Bahlburg, Dolezal, Baker, Ehrhardt, & New, 2006). Across age (childhood, adolescence, and adulthood), females with CAH also express interest in male-typical careers such as being an engineer, a construction worker, and an airline pilot (Berenbaum, 1999; Meyer-Bahlburg et al., 2006; Nordenström et al., 2002). An interesting question is how these interests ultimately manifest themselves in actual career choice.

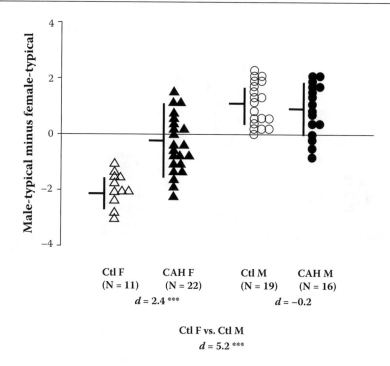

FIGURE 6.3   Sex-typed activity and interest preferences of teenage boys and girls with CAH and their unaffected sisters and brothers, represented as the difference between composites of male-typical and female-typical interests. Horizontal lines represent group means. Ctl: control (unaffected same-sex relatives). Circles represent individual boys; triangles represent individual girls. Open symbols are control children; black symbols are children with CAH. *d* = difference between group means/average standard deviation. Group differences were evaluated by one-tailed *t* test, ***p < .001. (From Berenbaum, S.A., *Hormones and Behavior, 35*, 102–110, 1999. With permission.)

Limitations of studies in girls with CAH

It is tempting to use these data to state unequivocally that sex differences in childhood toy play and adolescent activity interests result directly from the effects of excess androgens on the developing brain in utero. But, as we discussed above, CAH is not a perfect experiment—we have not actually manipulated hormones leaving everything else constant so we need to rule out other possible explanations, especially the effects of social responses to the girls' genitals and factors related to the CAH itself.

There are several pieces of evidence that suggest that masculinized toy play in girls with CAH results directly from prenatal androgen excess rather than from social responses. Parents report that they do not treat girls with CAH differently than they treat their unaffected daughters, but, of course, parents' reports may not necessarily reflect their behavior (Berenbaum & Hines, 1992; Ehrhardt & Baker, 1974). They also say that they wish that their daughters with CAH were less masculine than they are, and, interestingly, that their daughters without CAH were more masculine than they are (Servin, Nordenström, Larsson, & Bohlin, 2003).

The most compelling data about the issue are provided by two observational studies of play in girls with CAH, in which parent behavior was also studied. In the first study, girls with CAH and control girls were observed playing with sex-typed toys alone and with a parent (Nordenström et al., 2002; Servin et al., 2003). As expected, when alone, girls with CAH played more with boys' toys than did control girls. When the girls played with a parent, the difference between girls with CAH and control girls was not increased—and was, in fact, slightly reduced—suggesting that parents actually discourage rather than encourage sex-atypical play in their daughters with CAH. The second study provided converging support for this by observing parents' reactions to their daughters' toy play. Parents provided more positive feedback to girls with CAH than to their unaffected sisters for playing with girls' toys (Pasterski et al., 2005). Consistent with the evidence from girls with CAH, mothers' behavior does not appear to account for masculinized behavior in monkeys who were exposed to androgen (Goy et al., 1988). Female offspring who were exposed to androgens late in gestation had normal external genitals but were behaviorally masculinized in several ways, including rough play. Mothers' behavior, particularly inspection of offspring genitalia, was not associated with either the amount or kind of offspring masculine behavior.

Furthermore, behavior in females with CAH has been found to relate in a linear way to markers of the amount of androgen to which they were exposed when they were in the uterus. These markers include the type of genetic mutation they have and how severe their illness is. Thus, girls with CAH with the most severe genetic defect and exposure to the highest prenatal levels of androgen play the most with boys' toys (Berenbaum, Duck, & Bryk, 2000; Nordenström et al., 2002). In adult women, gender-typed hobbies and career interests are associated with disease severity and thus presumed degree of prenatal androgen exposure (Meyer-Bahlburg et al., 2006). In Figure 6.3, the girls with CAH whose scores overlap with those of control girls are those with the mildest form of the illness.

It is also unlikely that other abnormalities in CAH are responsible for the behavioral differences. For example, the other hormones that are abnormal, progesterone and corticosteroids, have smaller and less consistent behavioral effects than androgen and may actually prevent masculinization (Hull, Franz, Snyder, & Nishita, 1980). It also seems unlikely that the observed differences can be explained by the effects of merely having a chronic illness because boys with CAH are behaviorally similar to boys without CAH, and chronic illness per se is unlikely to only affect sex-typed behavior.

Convergence of evidence

Data from other sources confirm the findings in CAH and strengthen the case for androgen effects on toy play. We noted above the studies examining hormones in the blood of pregnant women and relating these levels to the offspring's behavior later on. One study looked at behavior in adults (Udry, 1994; Udry et al., 1995) and the other at behavior in preschool children (Hines et al., 2002). Both studies found evidence for androgen's effects on behavior such that indices of high testosterone in mothers were associated with masculinized gender-role behavior in their female offspring.

We focus on the study in children because the results are clear and relevant to the topic of this book (Hines et al., 2002). Sex-typed activity preferences were studied when the children were 3.5 years old, and were examined in relation to testosterone in mothers' blood during pregnancy. The results confirm the findings described above. When the researchers compared girls who had masculine toy and activity preferences at 3.5 years of age with girls who had feminine toy and activity preferences, they found that their mothers had differed in their testosterone levels during pregnancy: the testosterone levels were higher in women who were pregnant with daughters who eventually were rated to have masculine toy and activity preferences compared with those whose daughters had feminine preferences.

Converging data for androgen effects come from children with a Y chromosome who were reared as girls because of cloacal exstrophy, ablatio penis, or ambiguous genitalia because of lower-than-typical male prenatal androgen levels (as described in chapter 3 and discussed in more detail below in relation to gender identity). Reports from two cases of ablatio penis and a small series of boys with cloacal exstrophy who were reared as girls indicate that they are interested in male-typical activities and occupations (Bradley et al., 1998; Colapinto, 2000; Diamond & Sigmundson, 1997; Reiner & Gearhart, 2004). In a more systematic assessment of children with XY karyotype but a disorder of sex development resulting in low (for boys) prenatal androgen exposure, gendered play was directly related to degree of prenatal androgen exposure (Jürgensen, Hiort, Holterhus, & Thyen, 2007). For example, in a structured play task similar to that used in studies of girls with CAH, children without any androgen exposure (e.g., because of complete AIS) spent 21% of the time playing with boys' toys, whereas children with intermediate androgen exposure (e.g., because of partial AIS) spent about 66% of their time playing with boys' toys. It is especially intriguing that the time spent playing with boys' toys did not depend on whether the children with intermediate androgen exposure were reared as boys or as girls.

Not all data are consistent

Some studies using other methods do not confirm the data described above. Two studies of twins failed to find differences in gendered toy play between children with same- versus opposite-sex co-twins (Henderson & Berenbaum, 1997; Rodgers, Fagot, & Winebarger, 1998). Studies examining hormones in amniotic fluid failed to find a relation between testosterone in utero and parent-reported spatial play preferences in 7-year-old girls (Grimshaw, Sitarenios, & Finegan, 1995) or play activities in 4- to 6-year-old children (Knickmeyer et al., 2005). The problem is that it is hard to interpret these negative findings. There are several reasons for failures to find effects. With respect to the study of opposite-sex twins, perhaps testosterone from the male twin is not transferred to the female twin; that is, perhaps IUP does not have an effect in people as it does in other species. Alternatively, IUP effects might result from positioning between two members of the opposite sex, a very rare occurrence in human pregnancies. With respect to the study of amniotic hormones, perhaps the hormone measures were imperfect (a single sample may not be a reliable indicator of hormone levels, hormones may not have been obtained during the appropriate sensitive period for the development of brain regions involved in play preferences) or there were other issues (e.g., not enough variability in testosterone, small samples, problems with the behavioral measures). However, these failures might mean that androgens are important for producing differences between the sexes but not for producing variations within the sexes. The only way to resolve this issue is to conduct more studies.

How would androgens affect interests?

It is difficult for some people, especially die-hard social constructionists, to accept the findings that androgens affect interests. After all, toy trucks, computer games, make-up, and the like are all products of our society. As you will see in chapter 7, parents and other adults reward children for playing with toys considered appropriate for their sex. As you will see in chapter 9, children use gendered labels in deciding whether they like specific toys. But, from the data reviewed above, it is not far-fetched to suggest that society develops toys and labels partly to accommodate the different interests of boys and girls.

One way to test this idea is to look at the interests of monkeys who are not influenced by these social factors. The results of two studies indicate that monkeys show sex differences in response to children's sex-typed toys. In the first study, six toys were placed in monkeys' cages and the amount of time they came in contact with each was recorded (Alexander & Hines, 2002). There were two girls' toys (pot and doll), two boys' toys (car and ball), and two neutral toys (picture book and stuffed dog). The sex-typed (but not neutral) toys were differently appealing to the male and female monkeys: females contacted the girls' toys more than the males did, whereas males contacted the boys' toys more than females did. This was not a perfect experiment for several reasons: the toys were presented to groups of monkeys consisting of adults and their offspring, the toys were presented one a time, and the toys used might not be the best (e.g., a pot is not a toy, a doll may look like an infant). But similar results were found in another study: Juvenile rhesus monkeys given a choice between plush doll-like (girls') toys and wheeled vehicle (boys') toys played with same-sex toys more than opposite-sex toys (Hassett, Siebert, & Wallen, 2004). The results from monkeys are very intriguing and are consistent with the data described above in suggesting a biological basis for sex-typed interests.

It is interesting to speculate on the mechanisms underlying the biological basis for interests. What is it that causes someone who has been exposed to high levels of androgens during prenatal life to like toy cars or the remote control? There are many characteristics that differentiate boys' toys and girls' toys, such as the use of motion, color, texture, and shape. If you have any doubt about this, just walk down the aisle of your local toy mega-store. You will know whether you are in the aisle for girls' toys or boys' toys by how much pink and purple versus black, red, and green you see; by how many soft edges versus angles you see; and by how much noise the toys make and how much they move. It is interesting to note that these characteristics parallel sex differences found in other domains. When infants look at visual stimuli, boys prefer movement and girls prefer form and color (Serbin, Poulin-Dubois, Colbourne, Sen, & Eichstedt, 2001). In childhood activities, boys use motion more than girls do (Benenson, Liroff, Pascal, & Cioppa, 1997). In drawings, boys tend to draw mechanical and moving objects, use dark and cold colors, and have a bird's-eye perspective, whereas girls draw human figures, flowers, and butterflies, use light and warm colors, and array items in a row on the ground. As noted above, evidence that this reflects biological preferences and not social labels comes from data showing girls with CAH to draw pictures with masculine characteristics (Iijima et al., 2001).

Androgen Effects on Childhood Playmate Preferences

One of the largest and most pervasive sex differences concerns children's tendencies to segregate by sex (see chapter 11). Beginning early in childhood (age 2.5–3), children prefer to play with same-sex others, and this has consequences for later behavior, as discussed in chapter 11. There is considerable study of the causes of this phenomenon, and it is natural to ask whether biological predispositions contribute to it.

Girls with CAH are, in fact, masculinized with respect to playmate preferences, but not nearly to the extent that they are masculinized in toy play (or other behaviors, as described below). Thus, girls with CAH do have a slightly increased tendency to prefer boys as playmates (Berenbaum & Snyder, 1995; Hines & Kaufman, 1994; Servin et al., 2003). But, unlike the difference in toy play and activities, this difference is attributable to few girls, with most girls with CAH preferring girls as playmates, just like their sisters and most other girls.

Androgen Effects on Cognitive Abilities

There is moderate support for the notion that prenatal androgens influence later spatial ability. This evidence comes from multiple sources.

Girls and women with CAH

Females with CAH have higher spatial ability than their sisters in childhood, adolescence, and adulthood (Hampson, Rovet, & Altmann, 1998; Hines, Fane, Pasterski, Mathews, Conway, & Brook, 2003; Resnick, Berenbaum, Gottesman, & Bouchard, 1986). Although some studies have not shown a difference in spatial ability between CAH and control females, those studies generally used tests that did not show sex differences or had samples that were too small to detect the differences (for review, see Berenbaum, 2001). On the other end of androgen levels, males with low early androgen levels because of IHH have lower spatial ability than controls (Hier & Crowley, 1982). Importantly, the external genitals of males with IHH appear typical, suggesting that enhanced spatial ability in females with CAH is not due to social responses to their genitals.

Typical samples

Confirmation of the evidence from these experiments of nature comes from opposite-sex twins and studies of amniotic hormones. Females with a male co-twin have higher spatial ability than females with a female co-twin (Cole-Harding, Morstad, & Wilson, 1988). Seven-year-old girls who had high levels of testosterone in utero (amniotic fluid levels at 14–16 weeks of gestation) had faster mental rotation (an aspect of spatial ability) than girls who had low levels of prenatal testosterone (Grimshaw et al., 1995). It is important to note, however, that neither of these findings has been replicated.

Other cognitive abilities

We do not yet know about prenatal hormonal effects on other cognitive abilities, especially those that show a female advantage, such as memory, perceptual speed, and verbal fluency. These abilities show smaller sex differences than do spatial abilities, so we need large samples to see if performance is related to prenatal androgen exposure. Given the relatively low incidence of CAH, these studies are difficult to do, so no one has yet done a study with a large enough sample to answer this question adequately.

Gendered Social Behavior

Prenatal hormones also appear to affect some aspects of gender-related social behavior, although this is an area that is not as well studied as activities and interests or spatial ability. Again, most studies involve females with CAH and find them to differ from females without CAH.

Aggression

One of the most discussed social sex differences concerns aggression, and females with CAH do appear to be more aggressive than their sisters (Berenbaum & Resnick, 1997; Pasterski et al., 2007). There is also evidence from another condition to suggest that aggression is increased after exposure to early masculinizing hormones. In this second condition, females were exposed in utero to hormones called progestins, which have properties like androgen, with the exposure resulting from their mothers taking the hormones during pregnancy to prevent miscarriage (as mentioned above, this was before people were aware of the potential negative effects of taking hormones during pregnancy). The girls and their unexposed sisters were studied in childhood (ages 6–17 years). Results showed that the girls who were exposed to progestins were more likely than their unexposed sisters to report that they would use aggression in a conflict situation (Reinisch, 1981). There is also suggestive evidence from a study of opposite-sex twins: Girls with a boy co-twin reported more verbal (but not physical) aggression than girls with a girl co-twin. But, as we will discuss further below, biological influences on aggression are quite complex, and there is much that remains unknown.

Interest in babies

Females with CAH are less interested in babies and in motherhood than are their sisters (Dittmann et al., 1990; Ehrhardt & Baker, 1974; Leveroni & Berenbaum, 1998). Because females with CAH are somewhat less fertile than females without CAH, their reduced interest in babies might reflect a realization that they are less able to bear children. But this seems unlikely, because their reduced interest in babies is expressed in childhood, before they are likely to be aware of their fertility. Furthermore, women with TS, who are almost always infertile, do not show reduced interest in babies (Money & Ehrhardt, 1972), nor do males with CAH who also have reduced fertility (Leveroni & Berenbaum, 1998).

Other personal-social attributes

Females with CAH have been found to score lower than controls on personality measures on which females typically score higher than males. This includes a detachment scale, which measures empathy, intimacy, need for social relations, and maternal/nurturant behavior (Helleday, Edman, Ritzén, & Siwers, 1993); the Succorance scale of the Personality Research Form (PRF), which measures how an individual responds to another's need for help or comfort (Resnick, 1982); and a measure of social skills assessing both desire for social interaction and decoding of social cues (Knickmeyer et al., 2006).

Females with a male co-twin have also been found to be more masculine than females with a female co-twin on a trait not yet studied in CAH but that shows sex differences: sensation-seeking, which is interest in seeking physical and social adventures (Resnick, Gottesman, & McGue, 1993). But, other studies of opposite-sex twins have failed to replicate the difference in sensation-seeking and failed to find differences in other personality traits (Cohen-Bendahan, Buitelaar, van Goozen, Orlebeke, & Cohen-Kettenis, 2004; Loehlin & Martin, 2000; Rose et al., 2002).

Sexual Orientation

There is considerable interest in the origins of sexual orientation. What factors cause some of us to be heterosexual and others of us to be homosexual or bisexual?

CAH

Again, most evidence about androgen's effects on sexual orientation comes from studies of women with CAH. Because there are social constraints on expressing homosexual behavior (there are not many people interested in having sex with individuals of the same sex, and there is considerable societal disapproval of homosexuality), it is important to study arousal and not just experiences, and to use appropriate comparison groups. A major methodologically rigorous study of sexual orientation in women with CAH (Zucker et al., 1996) showed them to have less heterosexual experience, but not more homosexual experience, than their unaffected sisters. In interpreting this result, it is important to consider the potential effects for women of having genitals that look different and that function (either from the disease itself or from the surgery that was performed to make the genitals look normal). Therefore, it is particularly noteworthy that there were also differences between women with CAH and their sisters in sexual arousal and fantasy, such that women with CAH expressed more sexual interest in women and less sexual interest in men than did their sisters. This finding suggests that differences in sexual experience did not result from poor body image, reduced sexual sensitivity, or discomfort with intercourse because of genital surgery.

But, like the data on childhood playmate preferences (and unlike the data on toy preferences), the increased arousal to women reflects a few women with CAH, not most of them. Most women with CAH had heterosexual interests, and the others had bisexual, not exclusively homosexual, interests. Among the 30 women with CAH, 8 reported that they had sexual fantasies about both men and women (bisexuality), 2 reported no sexual fantasies, and 20 (two thirds) reported fantasies that were exclusively heterosexual. All 15 control women reported exclusively heterosexual fantasies.

These results have been confirmed in a separate sample of women with CAH (Hines, Brook, & Conway, 2004). Taken together, these two methodologically rigorous studies on women with CAH suggest that sexual attraction to women is somewhat influenced by exposure to prenatal androgen. It is possible, however, that the effects have been underestimated. Because of the social norms against homosexuality, women with homosexual interests might be less likely to participate or to reveal those interests than would women with heterosexual interests, so it is important to continue to study this issue and to work hard to make sure that the samples include everyone. There are no systematic data on sexual orientation in individuals with other DSDs, although case reports suggest that exposure to androgen increases sexual arousal to women, at least at high levels. For example, two individuals with ablatio penis reported sexual interest in women, despite the fact that one had male gender identity and the other female identity (Bradley et al., 1998; Colapinto, 2000).

Convergence of evidence

It is especially difficult to study sexual orientation in individuals with DSDs, because neither DSDs nor homosexuality is common, and thus the intersection of the two is very unlikely. Therefore, some scientists have studied this issue in an indirect way, by looking to see whether a variety of **biological markers** differentiate homosexual men and women from same-sex heterosexual comparisons. These markers are thought (not shown) to reflect prenatal androgen effects, so that people who differ from the norm in these markers are assumed to have been exposed to atypical levels of androgens in early development. Two of these markers—**otoacoustic emissions** and **2D:4D ratio**—were discussed in chapter 3. In these studies, gay men are hypothesized to be demasculinized and feminized, that is, to be less male-typical and more female-typical than heterosexual men, whereas lesbians are hypothesized to be masculinized and defeminized—that is, more male-typical and less female-typical than heterosexual women.

Some evidence is consistent with the hypothesis, but the picture is far from compelling (Cohen-Bendahan, van de Beek, & Berenbaum, 2005; Mustanski, Bailey, & Kaspar, 2002). For example, lesbians, but not gay males, have been found to be intermediate to heterosexual males and females on an aspect of auditory function (otoacoustic emissions) that shows a sex difference (McFadden & Pasanen, 1998), and on the relative length of the second and fourth fingers (2D:4D ratio) (Williams et al., 2000); the latter has been also found to differentiate females with CAH from controls in one study (Brown, Hines, Fane, & Breedlove, 2002) but not another (Buck, Williams, Hughes, & Acerini, 2003). Homosexual men have been reported to have a pattern of fingerprint asymmetry (differences between the left and right hands) that is more similar to heterosexual women than to heterosexual men (Hall & Kimura, 1994), but this has not been found consistently (Forastieri et al., 2002; Mustanski et al., 2002). Homosexual people are also more likely than same-sex heterosexual people to show sex-atypical interests, which were measured directly in adulthood and retrospectively in childhood (Bailey & Oberschneider, 1997; Bailey & Zucker, 1995; Lippa, 2002).

As an aside, we note that biomarkers have been studied in relation to other sex-related behavior, such as cognitive abilities. The results are complex and, at this point in the scientific story, not particularly enlightening, so we will not discuss them here. If you are interested in learning more about this field, see papers by Cohen-Bendahan et al., 2005; Kimura, 1999; McFadden, 1998; Putz, Gaulin, Sporter, & McBurney, 2004.

Gender Identity

In contrast to the strong effects of androgen on activity interests and spatial ability, androgen does not appear to have a large effect on gender identity, especially when androgen is only moderately elevated (as happens in people with DSDs). This is probably the most controversial topic in studies of hormonal influences on behavior. These studies concern a person's sense of self as a boy/man or girl/woman, and the extent to which the person is happy living as that sex.

CAH

The evidence from females with CAH is relatively straightforward and consistent across studies. The overwhelming majority of females with CAH identify as female throughout life and the very small minority of females with CAH who are unhappy as females or live as males are not necessarily those who have the most masculinized genitals or had the most prenatal androgen excess (Berenbaum & Bailey, 2003; Dessens, Slijper, & Drop, 2005; Meyer-Bahlburg et al., 2004; Meyer-Bahlburg et al., 1996; Zucker et al., 1996). Interestingly, the amount of gender dysphoria is about the same in the few who are reared as boys (Dessens et al., 2005).

Other DSDs

The rest of the evidence is not as clear as that from CAH, in part because the data come from conditions that are very rare, so the samples studied are small, and because assessment of gender identity is not always systematic. Some of the earliest evidence about androgen effects on gender identity came from males with **5α-reductase deficiency** (5α-RD) (Imperato-McGinley, Peterson, Gautier, & Sturla, 1979). Remember we said that males with 5α-RD are born with genitals that are feminized or ambiguous and usually are reared as females, but they virilize at puberty. In the initial study of gender identity in 5α-RD, 38 individuals with the condition were identified, but complete data were available only on 33 individuals, 18 of whom were reared as girls. At puberty, 17 of 18 changed to a male gender identity and 16 of 18 to a male gender role (mostly reflected here by sexual orientation, dress, and work situation). The large number of individuals who changed gender was interpreted to reflect the prominence of hormones over social rearing in the determination of gender identity (Imperato-McGinley et al., 1979).

The results are quite surprising in many ways—imagine changing your gender identity at puberty! (We note, though, that it did happen over the course of several years.) But the results are also subject to alternative explanations. First, note that the gender-identity change accompanied a bodily change. It might be easier to change gender identity than live with a body that does not match your identity (although some people do, as described below, and as happens with transsexual individuals). Second, the condition was known in the community because it occurred relatively frequently there, so the individuals (especially the younger ones) might have been recognized and reared with the expectation that they would eventually develop a male body. Most individuals with 5α-RD in this community are now reared as boys (which accounts for the fact that not all 33 people in the study were reared as girls). Third, males had considerably more freedom and status in the community than did females, so there might be considerable motivation to identify with the valued sex.

A recent review of the world's literature on individuals with of 5α-RD (Cohen-Kettenis, 2005) shows that there is considerable variation in outcome, with about 60% of those reared as girls changing gender. But the ones who changed gender were not necessarily those with the most masculinized genitalia, consistent with the data from girls with CAH.

Other small studies and recent reviews of the world's literature on gender identity in people with other DSDs (such as partial androgen insensitivity and micropenis) show that there is much variation. This variation in gender identity is not simply related either to androgen exposure or to sex of rearing, and, if anything, gender identity is more predictable from rearing than from prenatal androgen exposure (Mazur,

2005; Zucker, 1999). Males with micropenis can develop male gender identity and experience normal heterosexual activities, especially with testosterone treatment to increase penile size (Bin-Abbas, Conte, Grumbach, & Kaplan, 1999; Reilly & Woodhouse, 1989).

Given the evidence that males with micropenis do quite well when reared as males, and that rearing as males requires no surgery but surgery to rear as females does (further reducing the size of the penis to become a clitoris and making a vagina), most children with micropenis are now reared as males. It will be very interesting to study other aspects of their behavior to see if, for example, they have lower spatial ability or more interest in babies than do typical males.

Data from individuals with other DSDs are consistent with the notion that gender identity is not very strongly affected by exposure to moderate levels of prenatal androgen (e.g., Jürgensen et al., 2007). But, what about gender identity in people who are exposed to very high levels? This question is particularly important for treating boys with sex-typical androgen exposure whose penis is not normal, either because it was damaged in an accident or because of a disorder such as cloacal exstrophy. As mentioned in chapter 3 and above, these children have traditionally been reared as girls, because individuals were considered to be psychosexually neutral at birth and because it is easier to perform surgery to make a vagina than to make a penis (Money et al., 1955). As noted in chapter 3, there have been several strong challenges to this practice (Chase, 1998; Colapinto, 2000; Diamond & Sigmundson, 1997). Despite the attention to these unusual cases, there is unfortunately not very much systematic evidence about their gender identity.

The most well-known case is a normal boy whose penis was burned severely during circumcision and who was subsequently reassigned as a girl (Colapinto, 2000; Diamond & Sigmundson, 1997). Early reports indicated that the child adapted well as a female, but subsequent reports indicated that the child had never been happy as a girl. In fact, as an adolescent, the child requested surgery to be a boy. This person lived happily and successfully as a man for many years, marrying and acting as stepfather to his wife's children from her first marriage. Sadly, though, he committed suicide in 2004. It is not possible to know whether his depression and suicide resulted from the tragic accident and rearing as a girl or from other factors, including his family history of depression (his mother had a long history of depression and his twin brother committed suicide a few years before he did) (Colapinto, 2004).

This case has been widely publicized as support for the primacy of biology in the development of gender identity (e.g., Diamond & Sigmundson, 1997). Because this individual was a normal genetic male with a Y chromosome, testes, and exposure to normal male-typical hormones, especially high prenatal levels of testosterone—but reared as a female—his outcome suggested to some that gender identity is determined by early hormones acting on the developing brain and not by the social environment (Diamond & Sigmundson, 1997). But, the story is not so simple. The child was reared as a boy at least until the circumcision accident, which happened at 9 months of age. There was also considerable uncertainty about rearing for about a year after that and the surgery to create a vagina was not done until the child was 21 months of age. There is also some suggestion that the parents had reservations about the wisdom of the reassignment and therefore might not have been entirely consistent in rearing the child as a female. Furthermore, a similar case had a very different outcome. After a circumcision accident at the age of 2 months, this second child was reassigned as a female, and has reportedly adapted well, developing a female gender identity (Bradley et al., 1998).

A report (Reiner & Gearhart, 2004) from an ongoing study of boys with cloacal exstrophy reared as girls indicates that about half of these children identify as boys, and this has been interpreted to mean that gender identity is determined by prenatal androgen exposure and not by rearing. Nevertheless, there are several very important issues that require considerable clarification before we can accept this conclusion. First, the methods do not meet the criteria we usually set up for studies such as this. It is typical in studies such as this one to have some check on bias in the interviews by using interviewers who are unfamiliar with the hypotheses of the study, having the interviews scored by two independent raters, and having a comparison group so that interviewers and raters are blind to the participant's status (person with DSD or not). It appears that all of the interviews were done by one person who developed the study's hypotheses and who knew that all subjects had cloacal exstrophy; it is unclear whether there was independent rating of the interviews. It is also unclear how the interviews were used to generate the data that were provided.

The instruments used did produce summary scores that can be analyzed with traditional statistical procedures, but this information was not presented. This makes it hard for readers to see the results that support the conclusions and to draw their own inferences from the data.

Second, the conclusions in the paper rely on data collected from the parents rather than the children themselves. Given that gender identity is an internal sense of oneself as male or female, it is difficult to assess from others' reports. This means that some of the data reported actually represent gender role rather than gender identity. For example, parents appear to have judged that the child identified as a boy on the basis of the child's male-typical play. As we described above, data show that girls may have male-typical play and interests in the presence of female-typical gender identity; in fact, this is characteristic of girls with CAH, who were exposed to excess prenatal androgens. Furthermore, data from typical children show the independence of gender identity and gender-typed interests (Ruble, Martin, & Berenbaum, 2006).

Third, we need to consider the data in the context of normal gender development. For example, the authors state that most study participants stated the wish to be a boy, but this also occurs in typical children and girls with CAH without evidence of male gender identity (Ruble et al., 2006). This may reflect the advantages that boys and men have in most cultures.

Fourth, even in those children who did reassign themselves to male, it is not clear that androgen alone is responsible for the gender change. The social environment of these children is probably complicated. It is conceivable that the girls' boy-typical play made parents question the initial decision about female rearing, and this questioning was conveyed to the children. In the small number of females with CAH who changed gender, the change appeared to be associated with aspects of the social environment rather thandegree of prenatal androgen exposure (Meyer-Bahlburg et al., 1996).

Fifth, we are not told if gender identity is associated with overall psychological health. For example, are children with male identity happier and better-functioning than those with female identity?

Finally, not all of the children are reported to identify as boys, and other case reports of cloacal exstrophy indicate variations in gender identity with no clear indication of the percentage that identify as males or are unhappy as females (Schober, Carmichael, Hines, & Ransley, 2002; Zucker, 1999). In fact, the authors themselves state that, in this sample of XY individuals with cloacal exstrophy reared as females, ultimate identity was "unpredictable" (Reiner & Gearhart, 2004).

Going beyond these individual studies, a review of research from across the world indicates that most XY individuals with abnormal or absent penis (including, but not limited to ablatio penis and cloacal exstrophy) who are reared as girls grow up to identify as girls and women and to be happy with their assigned sex (Meyer-Bahlburg, 2005a). That conclusion highlights the limits of individual studies of small samples, and should make us all cautious about overgeneralizing from such data, however powerful and compelling they appear to be.

Thus, the evidence clearly shows that gender identity is not simply associated with prenatal androgen exposure, in contrast to several other gendered characteristics. Moderate levels of androgen present during prenatal development are not sufficient to masculinize gender identity. The other biological and social factors that modify androgen effects on gender identity are as yet unknown.

Summary: Early Organizational Hormones and Gender Development

The available evidence strongly supports the idea that prenatal androgens have an effect on a variety of behaviors that show sex differences. Most of the evidence comes from females with CAH, but there have been some confirmations from other experiments of nature and from individuals with typical variations in hormones. In particular, prenatal androgens appear to have a strong effect on activities and interests in childhood, adolescence, and adulthood, and on spatial ability, at least a moderate effect on other aspects of social behavior (aggression, interest in babies), and a smaller effect on partner preferences (playmates and sexual partner). Although androgens may affect gender identity, they appear to do so in a complicated

TABLE 6.1   Behavioral Differences Between Females with CAH and Control Females Compared to Sex Differences[a]

	SEX DIFFERENCE	CAH VS. CONTROL FEMALES
Childhood play and activities	3.3	1.5
Adolescent activities	2.4	1.3
Playmate preference	3.6	0.8
Sexual orientation	5.9	0.8
Interest in babies	1.0	0.7
Aggression	1.4	1.1
Spatial ability	1.0	0.7

Source: From Berenbaum, S.A., in *Developmental endocrinology: From research to clinical practice,* E.A. Eugster & O.H. Pescovitz, eds. (pp. 293–311). Totowa, NJ: Humana, 2002.
[a] Differences are expressed in standard deviation units (*d*).

way, with qualification by the social environment, and we need more data on this very important and very controversial topic.

Remember that the methods used to study behavioral effects of androgens are not perfect, and there are specific concerns about CAH. But it is important to put these limitations in perspective. Although some individual findings might be explained by factors other than androgens (e.g., social responses to the genitals of girls with CAH), they cannot account for all findings. The simplest explanation of the data involves the organizing action of prenatal androgen on the developing brain. This is underscored by several considerations: the convergence of evidence across methods (other experiments of nature, opposite-sex twins, normal variations in prenatal hormones), the consistency of the findings with theoretical expectations and with evidence from studies in other species in which hormones have been directly manipulated (described above), and the fact that androgen effects are found only on measures that show sex differences and thus would be reasonably expected to be sensitive to effects of early hormones.

An important point about the gender-atypicality of females with CAH is that the size of the effect (the difference between females with CAH and typical females) depends on the behavior examined. To give you an idea of this, Table 6.1 shows, for some behaviors, the differences (using *d*) between CAH and typical females compared with the differences between typical males and females. We use the latter (the regular sex difference) as a baseline because we are looking to see if hormones account for the sex difference and to control for measurement (if a behavior is not measured very well, none of the differences will be very big, so comparing the difference between CAH and control females to the sex difference provides a crude adjustment for measurement). Figure 6.4 takes the information in Table 6.1 and puts it into proportions or percentages. These can be interpreted as the proportion (or percentage) of the sex difference that is due to the effect of prenatal androgen. This analysis suggests that moderate androgens characteristic of females with CAH have larger effects on aspects of gender-role behavior and cognition than on sex of partners (as playmates and as targets of sexual arousal).

HORMONES AT ADOLESCENCE AND BEYOND

It has been traditional to think about the psychological effects of hormones later in life as temporary or transient, so that the effects occur only as long as the hormones are present. This is in contrast to the effects of hormones early in life; as we have just discussed, hormones that are present during prenatal development have a permanent effect on behavior, so that high levels of androgen during prenatal life produce permanent changes to the brain that result in masculinized behavior throughout life, even when

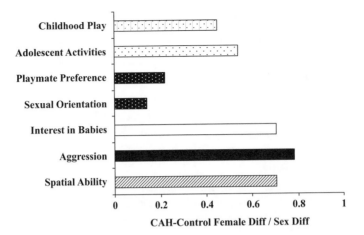

FIGURE 6.4   Proportion of the sex difference that is due to androgen (difference between CAH and control females divided by sex difference). (From Berenbaum, S.A., in *Developmental endocrinology: From research to clinical practice*, E.A. Eugster & O.H. Pescovitz, eds. (pp. 293–311). Totowa, NJ: Humana, 2002.)

androgen levels are not high. Some recent work, however, has suggested that hormones later in life might also have permanent organizational effects on the brain and behavior, a point to which we will return after we review the evidence about links between hormones and behavior in adolescence and adulthood.

Adolescent and Adult Hormone Effects in Nonhuman Mammals

Not surprisingly, studies of activational hormones have been guided by a substantial and systematic literature in nonhuman species. And, as with the evidence about effects of early hormones in other species, much of the evidence about effects of later hormones comes from studies in which the hormone levels of animals are directly manipulated, but there are also some studies of naturally occurring variations. The latter include changes in hormones similar to those occurring in people: increases in hormones at puberty, decreases in hormones in middle age, and variations associated with the female's estrus cycle. When hormones are manipulated, the animal's gonads (ovaries or testes) are also usually removed, so there is precise control of hormone levels without interference from the animal's own internally produced (endogenous) hormones. Unlike with early hormones, studies of later hormones usually involve injecting animals with hormones that are typical for their own sex (estrogen and progesterone for females, testosterone for males) because the goal here is to understand what these hormones usually do. Sometimes, manipulations involve injections of chemicals that counteract the effects of these hormones. Of course, all of these studies also include controls, with some animals receiving a fake manipulation (equivalent to a placebo), to ensure that behavioral changes are directly caused by the manipulation. In such studies, behavior—and often the brain—of the animal are studied shortly after the manipulation, because the questions concern immediate effects of the hormones. Studies include a variety of behaviors that show sex differences, both sexual and nonsexual behaviors.

Evidence for Activational Hormone Effects on Nonhuman Sex-Related Behavior

There is considerable evidence from other species that a variety of sex-related behaviors are influenced by hormones that circulate throughout the body after the animal achieves reproductive maturity, and that the effects occur through temporary (transient) changes in specific regions of the brain (for reviews see Becker et al., 2002; Hampson, 2007). For example, in both rodents and primates, estrogen facilitates aspects of learning and memory (reviewed in Williams, 2002). These cognitive changes may occur because of estrogen-induced changes to the structure of nerve cells in the hippocampus (an area of the brain known to be important in memory and learning); estrogen appears to increase the formation of spines on dendrites of neurons, facilitating transmission of information among neurons (reviewed in Woolley, 1998).

Hormones at Adolescence and Beyond in People

Sex hormones—this time, both androgens and estrogens—that are present during adolescence and adulthood change a variety of behaviors in rodents and monkeys. Similar effects are found in people, although the evidence is not as compelling as in other species or as compelling as the evidence regarding organizational effects. This reflects the difficulty involved in studying the issue in people in part because activational hormones are themselves influenced by several environmental events that are more common in human beings than in other species; such environmental events do not have as much effect on organizational hormones.

Methods for Studying Behavioral Effects of Later Hormones

It is logistically easier to study, in an experimental fashion, the human behavioral effects of later than early hormones; that is, it is easier to manipulate hormones in human adolescents and adults than in human fetuses. But, of course, it is still unethical to do these manipulations, so we rely on experiments of nature as well as studies of natural variations in levels of hormones.

Experiments of nature include people who receive hormone treatments, for example, because they have not started puberty on their own or they are changing sex (transsexuals). As always, such experiments are not perfect; for example, people with delayed puberty or desire to change sex may be different in other ways from people who do not receive hormone treatment.

Natural variations in hormones come in two types: natural differences in hormones among or between people and differences in hormones within a given individual. In terms of differences among people, there is considerable variation among people in their typical levels of sex hormones. This can be seen in Table 3.2 in chapter 3, which shows that there is a range of sex hormone levels in adults. We can take advantage of this variation, to see whether psychological characteristics differ among people with high versus low levels of estrogen or testosterone. There is also variation in hormone levels within a person across the day or other longer periods. Such differences within persons include changes in estrogen that occur in women across the menstrual cycle or at menopause, changes in testosterone that occur in men across the day or the year or at andropause (the decline in testosterone that occurs in middle age), and changes in hormones at puberty. We can take advantage of this within-person variation to study whether a person's psychological characteristics change when estrogen or testosterone levels change. These within-person variations can be difficult to study, requiring that people be followed across time, so they are often actually studied as between-person variations; for example, comparing a group of women at the midpoint of the menstrual cycle with a group of women during menses, or comparing two groups of boys who are at different points in pubertal development. In studies examining associations between hormones and behavior, hormone levels are measured from a person's blood or saliva, and these levels are considered to reflect the levels that are available in the brain and thus available to affect psychological functions.

The Evidence: Later Hormones Affect Adolescent and Adult Human Gender-Related Behavior

In general, the evidence suggests that both androgen and estrogen are differentially associated with cognition, affect, and social behavior, but that the links are complex and they do not flow in one direction.

That is, hormones not only affect behavior, but behavior may affect hormones. Because of our focus on gender development, we start with hormonal changes in adolescence, and bring in evidence from adults as it is relevant.

Do the changes in sex hormones and physical appearance at adolescence contribute to gender development? Research on pubertal change has focused on possible relations with two general categories of behavior. Emotion-related characteristics (negative affect, anxiety, self-esteem, aggression) are studied in part because some sex differences in distress and psychopathology emerge at puberty, as discussed in chapter 5, and because adolescence has a reputation as a time of fluctuating moods. Cognitive abilities are studied also because some sex differences emerge at puberty (although, as noted in chapter 4, some sex differences emerge earlier) and because variations in abilities have been associated with variations in circulating hormones in adults.

Hormonal Variations and Affect
(Emotion, Aggression, and Problem Behavior)

Hormonal increases at pubertal onset generally do not appear to increase negative affect or moodiness within the normal range (Buchanan, Eccles, & Becker, 1992), but they do appear to be partly responsible for girls' increased risk for serious depression at puberty, especially in those with genetic vulnerability (Angold, Costello, Erkanli, & Worthman, 1999). The increase in estrogen at puberty has also been shown to trigger the expression of genes involved in eating disorders (Klump, Perkins, Burt, McGue, & Iacono, 2007).

Some studies have focused on associations between hormones and affect across the entire pubertal transition. Results of those studies are not always consistent, but they do not provide support for the idea that psychological states can be easily explained by hormones (reviewed by Brooks-Gunn, Petersen, & Compas, 1995; Buchanan et al., 1992). For example, in one study of negative affect in girls aged 10–14, hormones accounted for 4% of the variance, social factors 8–18%, and the interaction of negative life events and pubertal factors 9–15% (Brooks-Gunn & Warren, 1989). Although most studies have focused on absolute levels of hormones, it is probably important to look at changes in levels; for example, how much hormones fluctuate within an adolescent across the day or the week (Buchanan et al., 1992).

There is some evidence that hormones are associated with aggression and behavior problems, particularly in boys (Buchanan et al., 1992; Susman et al., 1987). Some of the most intriguing evidence comes from a (rare) experimental study, in which children with delayed puberty were treated with hormones (testosterone for boys and estrogen for girls) to initiate pubertal development (Finkelstein et al., 1997). Treatment increased self-reported aggression in both boys and girls. Theory and previous data (especially from animals) explain the effect of testosterone on aggression in boys, but the effect of estrogen on aggression in girls is a bit puzzling.

There are numerous studies in adolescents and adults examining the association between aggression and the amount of testosterone that is circulating in the body. Meta-analysis of those studies shows that there is an association, but not a strong one: The correlation averages of .14, is similar in males and females, and is larger in adolescents than in adults (perhaps because there is more variability in both testosterone and aggression in the former than in the latter (Book, Starzyk, & Quinsey, 2001). But it turns out that the causal link between testosterone and aggression is not straightforward because psychological characteristics or states can actually change hormones. For example, testosterone levels increase in adult sports players who win, and in their fans (e.g., Bernhardt, Dabbs, Fielden, & Lutter, 1998; Booth, Shelley, Mazur, Tharp, & Kittok, 1989), and mood may be responsible for the effect of winning on testosterone levels (e.g., McCaul, Gladue, & Joppa, 1992). Furthermore, testosterone may not affect aggression per se, but rather social dominance (e.g., Mazur & Booth, 1998; Rowe, Maughan, Worthman, Costello, & Angold, 2004). To complicate matters even more, the effects of testosterone on behavior also depend on social context. In a longitudinal study of psychopathology, testosterone was related to nonaggressive symptoms of conduct disorder in boys with deviant peers and to leadership in boys with nondeviant peers (Rowe et al., 2004).

Other studies have examined affective changes in relation to hormonal changes across the life span; for example, associated with the menstrual cycle or menopause. In general, these studies find little association between hormones and mood (for review of menstrual cycle effects see Klebanov & Ruble, 1994), although hormones may trigger depression (including premenstrual distress) in vulnerable individuals (Rubinow & Schmidt, 2006; Steiner, Dunn, & Born, 2003).

Hormonal Variations and Cognition

Circulating sex hormones relate more strongly to patterns of cognitive abilities than to emotion. Most of this evidence comes from observational (nonexperimental) studies, for example, studies of cognition in women at different points in the menstrual cycle, and studies examining associations between people's natural hormone levels and their abilities; some confirmation comes from studies in which hormone treatment is given (Berenbaum et al., 2003; Hampson, 2002; Liben et al., 2002). High levels of estrogens appear to enhance verbal fluency and memory, starting at least in adolescence. Testosterone has a complex association with spatial ability: the best performance is associated with moderate levels of androgen in adults; that is, the highest scores are found in women with high normal (female) levels and in men with low normal (male) levels.

It is important to note that not all studies find these associations, probably because of methodological issues, especially low statistical power associated with relatively small sample sizes. We illustrate this issue with two studies in adolescents with different designs and different results.

The first study is the experimental study mentioned above, in which sex hormones were administered to adolescents with delayed puberty. A major advantage of this study is that adolescents' spatial ability was examined in association with hormones that were being experimentally manipulated in a double-blind study. In other words, sometimes youth received actual hormones (estrogen for girls, testosterone for boys) and sometimes they received placebos, and neither the teens nor the people administering the behavioral tests knew which treatment was received. This design allows us to know whether changes in hormones cause changes in cognition when other factors are held constant. Although the treatment produced changes in aggression (as noted above), it did not produce the expected changes in spatial ability (Liben et al., 2002). But, it is important to remember that failure to find effects in a single sample does not mean that there are no effects in the population to which the study is meant to generalize. In this case, potential limitations that were identified and discussed by the authors include the relatively small sample sizes (it is very difficult to do these studies, and their sample was larger than many but still not large enough to guarantee the necessary statistical power), the heterogeneous nature of the sample (there were varying reasons for delayed puberty, and at least some adolescents also had atypical hormone exposure as a result of other conditions such as Turner syndrome that might be expected to affect behavior). It is also possible that a different spatial test, specifically, a measure of three-dimensional mental rotation ability, might have been more likely to produce effects, but two of the three spatial tasks used show reliable, moderate sex differences.

The second study in adolescents was not experimental, but it involved a longitudinal design so that adolescents' spatial ability was examined in association with hormones that changed naturally, allowing us to know whether natural changes in hormones are associated with changes in cognition (Davison & Susman, 2001). Results showed that testosterone was linearly and positively associated with spatial ability (higher testosterone, higher spatial ability) in both sexes, but the results were more consistent for boys than for girls. But, we need to invoke some caution before concluding that testosterone is good for spatial ability for several reasons. The spatial measures used in this study were ones that do not show large sex differences (block design and two-dimensional rotation) and thus would not be expected to be strongly associated with testosterone. In contrast to findings in adults showing that men with the highest spatial ability have the lowest testosterone, these findings in teens showed that boys with the highest spatial ability have the highest testosterone; this may reflect the fact that adolescent boys' testosterone levels are lower than those of adult men. Although longitudinal designs are much better than cross-sectional ones, they still do not allow us to say definitively whether changes in hormones cause changes in cognition, because other factors might be responsible for producing changes in both.

Pubertal Timing

Hormones may have effects on behavior in another interesting way: through their effects on the timing and tempo of puberty—that is, when children start pubertal development and how long it takes them to complete the process. As we noted in chapter 3, children vary considerably in pubertal timing and tempo.

There is a considerable amount of literature showing that pubertal timing has important consequences for people when they are going through puberty and continuing into adulthood (reviewed by Mendle, Turkheimer, & Emery, 2007; Steinberg & Morris, 2001; Susman & Rogol, 2004; Weichold, Silbereisen, & Schmitt-Rodermund, 2003). As we noted in chapter 3, there is discussion about the best way to measure pubertal development, including the initial onset of puberty; for example, what is the best indicator of puberty and should it be measured by ratings of physical appearance or by change in hormone levels? (Dorn, Dahl, Woodward, & Biro, 2006). Most of the work in the area relies on reports of the adolescents' physical development (e.g., breast size in girls or penis size in boys, underarm hair), from the teenagers themselves or from their parents. Although this is not as good as having physical development evaluated by health professionals, it is a reasonably good approximation, especially if the interest is in whether the teen is on-time, early, or late (rather than in nailing down a specific age for specific physical changes).

Girls who mature at a younger age than their peers (**early maturing girls**) have more emotional distress and problem behavior (e.g., delinquency, substance use, early sexuality) than on-time peers, with some—but not all—evidence suggesting that the effects persist into adulthood. Among boys, late maturers have low self-esteem compared with on-time peers, whereas early maturers are more popular and have better self-image and achievement but are more likely to engage in delinquent, antisocial, and sexual behaviors and substance use. The psychological effect of pubertal timing appears stronger and more pervasive for girls than for boys, but the topic has not been studied much in boys because it is not as easy to mark puberty for them as it is for girls. This issue is also discussed in chapter 11 when we talk about peer influences.

A key question concerns the mechanisms that are responsible for the observed associations between pubertal timing and psychological function. It is unclear how much they reflect direct effects of hormones acting on the brain versus responses by the teenager and others in her environment to the psychological (including cognitive) and physical changes induced by the hormones; most likely, they reflect complex combinations of biology and social experiences. We know that some of the psychological effects of pubertal timing play out through the social environment. For example, girls who mature early associate with older and male peers who expose them to risky substances and activities (Weichold et al., 2003), and early maturers' higher rate of externalizing behavior has been linked to parents' use of harsh-inconsistent discipline (Ge, Brody, Conger, Simons, & Murry, 2002). These effects also depend on the social context in which children are embedded, so they are increased or decreased by the places in which children are found. For example, early maturing children living in disadvantaged neighborhoods were significantly more likely to affiliate with deviant peers (Ge et al., 2002). Adverse consequences of early maturation were found only for girls who attended coeducational schools and not for those who attended all-girls' schools (Caspi, Lynam, Moffitt, & Silva, 1993).

Adrenarche

Most work on the psychological effects of pubertal timing concerns gonadarche and increased production of hormones from the gonads, particularly testosterone and estradiol. But, as we noted in chapter 3, **gonadarche** is preceded by **adrenarche**, and there are some intriguing suggestions about the psychological role of androgens produced by the adrenal glands in this early stage of puberty: The onset of sexual attractions coincides with adrenarche, occurring at about age 10 in both boys and girls (McClintock & Herdt, 1996). Having early adrenarche may place girls at risk for psychological problems (Dorn, Hitt, & Rotenstein, 1999).

Puberty as an Organizational Period?

Work in rodents suggests that the hormonal changes that occur at puberty may serve to change the brain permanently, and thus act as another organizational period (e.g., Sisk & Zehr, 2005). Variations in pubertal timing will then produce variations in brain organization that have permanent psychological effects. It is possible that some of the effects described above might actually reflect these permanent changes to the brain induced by hormones, such as the consequences of variations in pubertal timing. At this point, however, the evidence does not allow firm conclusions. Because this hypothesis has generated many interesting ideas that are currently being tested in people, some exciting findings are likely to appear in the near future.

Summary: Adolescent/Adult Hormones and Gender Development

The consequences for gender development of sex hormones in adolescence and adulthood are not as clear as those of early sex hormones, but some patterns do emerge. Hormones that circulate in the body during adolescence and adulthood appear to relate to some characteristics, such as aggression and aspects of cognition, but not others, such as normal mood. Changes in hormone levels at puberty appear to affect gender development. Increases in estrogen increase the likelihood of depression in some (but not most) girls, and increases in testosterone increase the likelihood of aggression and behavior problems in boys. Hormonal changes at puberty also have indirect effects on behavior. For example, girls who start puberty early are at risk for a variety of behavioral problems in adolescence, with effects likely to persist into adulthood, but whether these problems emerge also depends on the girl's social situation. Overall, hormone-behavior links are complex, played out through and modified by social and psychological factors. Returning to the quote with which we opened the chapter, this means that it is unlikely that an estrogen bomb—or estrogen injections to individuals—will have significant behavioral effects, although estrogen does appear to facilitate memory to a small extent.

BRAIN PERSPECTIVES ON GENDER DEVELOPMENT

It is very tempting to look to the brain for explanations of gender development, specifically to think that innate differences between males and females in one or another part of the brain account for sex differences in behavior. After all, behavior is subserved by the brain, and the behavioral effects of sex hormones described above must be mediated by the brain. Furthermore, the brain is a physical structure, just like the genitalia, so it must be influenced by the same factors that affect the body, that is, genes and hormones. But, the path from genes to hormones to brain to behavior does not flow in only one direction. Both the brain and hormones are affected by our experiences. As we discussed in chapter 3, there is not an absolute relation between genotype and phenotype; whether and how genes are expressed depends on other genes and the environment. Thus, it is not surprising that we cannot find simple answers to questions about sex-related behavior by looking for sex differences in the brain. But, the interesting questions rarely have simple answers. Nevertheless, given that the brain is the place where biology and culture come together, it is important to examine the brain more carefully.

Behavior is subserved by the brain, but that does not mean that behavior is rigidly determined by brain structure. Although the main outline of brain structure is determined early in development, aspects of brain structure change throughout life. Consider some ways in which this happens. The myelin sheath that surrounds axons (and facilitates transmission of information) continues to develop into puberty. Receptors increase and decrease in number and response to levels of specific neurotransmitters, and these might change as a result of our behavior. Synaptic connections between neurons change with learning. Genes do not result in fixed and unchanging phenotypes, but get turned on and off in response to other genes and environmental events. All of this is important because it means that it can be hard to know whether sex differences in the brain cause sex differences in behavior or result from them. It is important to remember this when we consider links between the brain and psychological sex differences.

Historical Perspectives: The Basis for Current Work

The simplest theories about neural underpinnings of gender development focus on explaining sex differences in psychological characteristics by sex differences in the size of the brain. An early version of this theory, prominent for many centuries, focused on the fact that men's brains are larger than women's brains by about 10% on average. This was used to justify women's subordinate position in society: Men's high social status was attributed to their large brains (and, of course, women's low status to their small brains) (Shields, 1975). Not surprisingly, much—but not all—of the sex difference in brain size can be attributed to the sex difference in body size (Halpern, 2000). But, even if men have a relatively larger brain than women after correcting for body size, it does not mean that size is what accounts for cognitive or emotional differences unless such an association is shown directly; that is, through a direct correlation between brain size and cognition or emotion within sex. After all, men are taller than women, but it is silly to suggest that height differences account for cognitive or emotional differences. But the argument would be a little less silly if it turned out that height was related to cognition or emotion within sex; for example, if tall women are smarter than short women and tall men are smarter than short men. Although some studies do suggest that there is a small association between brain size and intelligence (McDaniel, 2005), studies of overall brain size are not that interesting for understanding behavioral sex differences because the latter are specific (remember, there is no sex difference in general intelligence) and more likely to reflect specific aspects of brain organization and not simply brain size.

Therefore, most contemporary research focuses less on overall brain size than on specific aspects of brain structure and specific brain regions and tries to address the question of whether any observed sex differences in the brain actually underlie psychological differences (e.g., by determining whether variations within sex relate to emotion or abilities). Such work has been substantially facilitated by the availability of brain imaging techniques including structural and functional **magnetic resonance imaging** (MRI). This field has exploded in the past few years, but much of the work is very technical, so it is not practical to provide an exhaustive review here. Furthermore, most of the work is conducted on adults and is not particularly relevant to our understanding of gender development in childhood and adolescence. Therefore, we provide a brief summary of the work and discuss what it tells us—or could tell us—about brain underpinnings of gender development. For those of you interested in knowing more, there are papers that describe this work in detail (e.g., Goldstein et al., 2001; Hamann & Canli, 2004; Lenroot et al., 2007; Resnick, 2006).

Sex Differences in Cerebral Hemispheric Specialization (Lateralization)

As we discussed in chapter 3, the cerebral cortex is divided into two hemispheres that have different roles in psychological processes, known as **hemispheric specialization** or **lateralization** (for reviews, see Banich, 2004; Bryden, 1982; Springer & Deutsch, 1998). The left hemisphere plays a key role in language, sequencing, and analytic thought, whereas the right hemisphere has its major role in synthesis and in simultaneous processing (including spatial skills). The hemispheres are connected by the **corpus callosum**, which facilitates transmission of information across hemispheres. Most people demonstrate the classic pattern of lateralization; that is, left-hemisphere specialization for language and sequential processing, right hemisphere specialization for synthetic processing. But, some left-handers have right-hemisphere specialization for language. But, even among people who show the classic pattern, there are individual differences in the extent to which specialization occurs; that is, some people have more specialized or lateralized hemispheres than others. In particular, there are sex differences in hemispheric specialization/lateralization, with women showing somewhat less lateralization than men, on average.

Some Evidence for Sex Differences in Lateralization

Sex differences in lateralization were first discussed in the 1980s and the initial evidence about those differences came from studies of people with brain damage and from perceptual asymmetries in typical people (McGlone, 1980; Voyer, 1996). For example, after damage to the left hemisphere, women are less likely than men to develop language problems. Women have less perceptual asymmetry than do men, so that, for example, women are more likely than men to use both hemispheres to process language tasks.

Recent brain imaging studies confirm the sex differences in lateralization. These studies use **functional magnetic resonance imaging** (fMRI), a technology that produces images of the brain while participants solve specific tasks. fMRI studies demonstrate that men and women make different use of the two hemispheres when they process information. One of the first such studies involved observations of the brain while participants solved a rhyming task (Shaywitz et al., 1995). This task activated parts of the frontal lobe, indicating that these parts of the brain are important for processing this type of task. There was a sex difference in the extent to which the left and right frontal regions were involved: men used the left only, whereas women used both the left and right hemispheres. What is particularly compelling about this study is that the sex difference was large and, in fact, there was little overlap between men and women.

Sex differences in lateralization are accompanied by sex differences in anatomical asymmetry. When the structure of the brain is examined with MRI, men show bigger left-right differences than do women in several ways, such as the volume of the cerebral hemispheres, the gyri and sulci (the patterning of the folds and grooves in the cortex), the size of regions of the temporal lobe known to be involved in language-related areas (Shapleske, Rossell, Woodruff, & David, 1999), and the distribution of gray matter (Good et al., 2001; Kovalev, Kruggel, & von Cramon, 2003; Yücel et al., 2001).

The Psychological Significance of Sex Differences in Lateralization

Sex differences in lateralization are important because they might represent the brain underpinnings of sex differences in cognition and behavior (Harris, 1978; Levy, 1974). For example, it has been hypothesized that women's better language and poorer spatial skills (compared with men's skills) result from the fact that women have language represented in both hemispheres. Lateralization is thought to influence cognition for two reasons. First, more of the brain is thought to be devoted to language in women than in men, as evidenced by their reduced perceptual asymmetries and better ability to retain language after damage to the left hemisphere. Second, because the neural circuitry necessary for language abilities is different from that necessary for spatial abilities (which may be what caused lateralization to evolve in the first place), the early development of language skills in the right (atypical) hemisphere hindered the development of the neural circuits subserving spatial ability. As fascinating as this hypothesis is, there is unfortunately little direct evidence to show that the reduced lateralization in women compared with men is directly associated with enhanced verbal and diminished spatial skills. For example, in the rhyming study described above (Shaywitz et al., 1995), the large sex differences in lateralization of brain activation difference was not associated with a performance difference; that is, women's activation of both hemispheres was not associated with better rhyming scores than men's activation of only the left hemisphere. This could be because the task was easy, so there was not a lot of variability. Thus, as intriguing as this study is, it also shows us some of the difficulties involved in making inferences about sex differences in cognition from sex differences in brain function. Furthermore, the sex difference in lateralization appears to be considerably smaller than the sex differences in cognition, meaning that lateralization cannot be the sole reason for the cognitive differences.

Sex Differences in Gray and White Matter

Sex differences are found in fine-grained aspects of brain structure that relate to function. Several researchers have looked at the relative amounts of gray and white matter, which contain cell bodies and fiber tracts, respectively. Some, but not all, studies suggest that females have more cortical gray matter (e.g., Good et al., 2001; Rabinowicz, Dean, Petetot, & de Courten-Myers, 1999; Witelson, Glezer, & Kigar, 1995), whereas males have more white matter (e.g., De Bellis et al., 2001; Giedd et al., 1999). Variations in gray matter might have implications for how well a task can be performed, whereas variations in white matter might have implications for processes that involve coordination among multiple brain areas. Women also appear to have their nerve cells packed more tightly than do men, at least in one section of the temporal lobe, as measured by neuronal density (number of neurons per unit volume) (Witelson et al., 1995).

Sex Differences in Regional Brain Structure

Sex differences in the size of specific brain regions are suggested to underlie cognitive and emotional sex differences. The premise of studies on this topic is that if a particular region subserves a particular psychological function, then variations in the size of that region might produce variations in that function. Consider two examples. Given sex differences in emotion, and the role of the **orbital frontal cortex** and **amygdala** in emotion, researchers have asked whether there are sex differences in the size of these regions. Given sex differences in cognition, researchers have asked whether there are sex differences in regions of the temporal lobe that relate to language or in regions of the parietal lobe that relate to spatial ability.

Preoptic Area of the Hypothalamus

There is one region of the brain that received particular attention, especially when researchers first started to study brain sex differences with modern techniques. This region is the **preoptic area of the anterior hypothalamus**. It is of interest for two reasons. First, it has a high density of hormone receptors. As discussed in chapter 3, hormones differ dramatically in males and females, and, as discussed earlier in this chapter, these hormones affect behavior. Second, it was one of the first regions found to differ between male and female rats. The region was given the name **sexually dimorphic nucleus of the preoptic area of the hypothalamus**, abbreviated as SDN-POA. The SDN-POA of male rats is about 7 times larger than that of female rats (Gorski, Gordon, Shryne, & Southam, 1978). Since the SDN-POA was first described, there have been many reports of similar sex differences in a variety of nonhuman species (Wallen & Baum, 2002). Importantly, there are parallel structures in human beings, and one of four nuclei of the human anterior hypothalamus (INAH-3) appears to be smaller in women than in men (Allen, Hines, Shryne, & Gorski, 1989; LeVay, 1993), and perhaps also in homosexual than in heterosexual men (LeVay, 1993).

Corpus Callosum

There has also been much interest in the corpus callosum (CC), the bundle of fibers that connects the left and right cerebral hemispheres and allows transfer of information between them. A report on autopsied brains showed that certain portions of the CC, especially the **splenium**, are more bulbous and larger in women than in men (de Lacoste-Utamsing & Holloway, 1982). Subsequent studies and meta-analyses, most using MRI in normal individuals, are inconsistent, with some suggesting that women do have a larger CC after adjustment for brain size (Driesen & Raz, 1995), and others concluding that they do not (Bishop & Wahlsten, 1997). Sex differences in CC are potentially important because women's reduced lateralization would result in more need for communication between the hemispheres. An intriguing study actually relating CC size to cognition (Davatzikos & Resnick, 1998) found that the size of the splenium was positively correlated with cognitive performance in women but not in men.

Sex Differences in Cortical Brain Structure

There is now a considerable number of studies comparing specific brain regions in men and women. Unfortunately, they do not produce a consistent pattern of findings (for summaries and details, see

Goldstein et al., 2001; Nopoulos, Flaum, O'Leary, & Andreasen, 2000; Raz et al., 2004; Resnick, 2006). This may reflect differences across studies in methodology, high statistical errors because of small sample size and the many regions that are examined, and the large number of associated statistical tests performed.

Developmental Sex Differences in Brain Structure

Developmental changes in the structure of the brain, including sex differences, are only beginning to be understood (Durston et al., 2001; Giedd, 2004; Giedd et al., 1999; Gogtay et al., 2004; Lenroot et al., 2007). There are some limited data on early brain sex differences (Durston et al., 2001). Boys have a larger average brain than girls do. This parallels the sex difference found in adults, but the difference in children is difficult to attribute to a difference in body size, because boys and girls differ only slightly in size before puberty (as discussed in chapter 3). When the sex difference in overall brain size is considered (and statistically controlled), there are sex differences in just a few regions. Compared with girls, boys are seen to have a larger amygdala (important in processing emotion) and a smaller **caudate** (known primarily for its role in regulating voluntary movement), and perhaps a smaller hippocampus (important for learning and memory). Speculations about the clinical implications of these size differences (Durston et al., 2001) concern the roles of these regions in psychological disorders that show sex differences. For example, the caudate is implicated in attention deficit hyperactivity disorder and Tourette syndrome, so the smaller caudate in boys might be related to their higher incidence of these conditions. It is important to note, however, that these findings have not been replicated, and, as noted above, findings in adults often fail to hold up across studies. Furthermore, as discussed below, direct links between sex differences in brain and behavior have yet to be established.

Some of the most exciting work has come from a long-term longitudinal study tracking brain development in individual children, and the ways in which this development differs for boys and girls (Lenroot et al., 2007). This work, using MRI, has shown the subtleties of sex differences in brain development. The brains of both sexes show development across time, but girls appear to reach the peak earlier in development than boys. In the cerebral cortex, the volume appears to peak at age 10.5 in girls and age 14.5 in boys. Gray matter increases and then decreases in both sexes, with the peak occurring 1–2 years earlier in girls than in boys. White matter increases in both sexes throughout ages 3–27, but boys have a steeper rate of increase during adolescence. This study shows the importance of longitudinal data and the need to compare the sexes not just at a single point in time, but also across development.

The Significance of Sex Differences in Regional Brain Structure

There are few strong and consistent findings regarding sex differences in regional brain structure. It is unclear what significance should be attached to sex differences in the size of specific areas (Lenroot & Giedd, 2006; Paus, 2005). Size has generally not been associated with function, and brain structure can—and does—change in response to experience. For example, variations in taxi-driving experience are associated with variations in the size of the hippocampus (Maguire et al., 2003). Thus, even if reliable sex differences in brain structure emerge, it will be difficult to determine whether they are the cause or the consequences of sex differences in behavior.

Sex Differences in Regional Brain Function

Paralleling structural MRI studies on sex differences in the size of specific brain regions are fMRI studies examining sex differences in the activation of specific regions in response to psychologically relevant stimuli or tasks. fMRI reflects changes in blood volume and the use of oxygen. There are also other methods that have been used to study the brain at work, including electrophysiological recordings and measures of blood flow and of glucose metabolism. There are now a considerable number of studies describing sex differences in brain function using fMRI, but most of them concern adults and are thus not as relevant for gender development as we might like. Therefore we provide just a sample of these studies, focusing on a few studies of brain regions that might underlie sex differences in cognition or emotion (for additional information, see Resnick, 2006).

Sex Differences in Brain Processing of Cognition

When we discussed sex differences in lateralization, we discussed a study of language processing (Shaywitz et al., 1995) that showed men and women to make different use of the left and right hemispheres in deciding if nonsense words rhymed. This study provides specific information about a region within the cortex that differs in men and women, in particular the **inferior frontal gyrus**. Women used both the left and right inferior frontal gyri as they solved the task, whereas men used only the left gyrus. There was little overlap between the sexes in patterns of brain activation, but the activation difference did not translate into a performance difference, perhaps because the task was easy.

Another interesting study concerns brain activation for navigation, an important spatial ability that shows sex differences, both in performance level (men better than women) and in strategy (men preferring to use geometry and women to use landmarks), as discussed in chapter 4. Researchers used fMRI to study if men and women activated different regions as they went through a three-dimensional virtual-reality maze. Results showed that men performed the task more quickly than women and that there were sex differences in brain activation corresponding to strategy differences. Men were more likely to use the left hippocampus and women the right parietal and prefrontal regions, and this was suggested to reflect men's use of geometric cues versus women's use of landmarks (Grön, Wunderlich, Spitzer, Tomczak, & Riepe, 2000). This study is particularly intriguing because it parallels a study in rats discussed above showing that females preferentially use landmarks and males use geometric cues in solving a spatial task, and that these sex differences are produced by early sex hormones (Williams & Meck, 1991).

Sex Differences in Brain Processing of Emotion

The amygdala is a brain region that has received a lot of attention in general because of its role in processing emotion and in particular because of sex differences in emotion and mental illness (Hamann & Canli, 2004). Meta-analysis of studies of sex differences in amygdala response to the presentation of emotional stimuli (Wager, Phan, Liberzon, & Taylor, 2003) suggests that there is not a sex difference in overall activation to emotional stimuli, but that there is a sex difference in lateralization of activation, with men showing greater lateralization, consistent with their generally increased hemispheric asymmetry. This means that sex differences in lateralization are not confined to the cortex.

It has been proposed that the amygdala mediates sex differences in aspects of emotional processing (Hamann, 2005; Hamann & Canli, 2004) and in sexual arousal (Hamann, Herman, Nolan, & Wallen, 2004). For example, consider the study on sexual arousal (Hamann et al., 2004). The researchers asked if there are sex differences in the brain that parallel sex differences in response to visual sexually arousing stimuli; men show greater interest in and responsiveness to these stimuli than do women. Brain activity was recorded with fMRI while participants viewed sexual stimuli. Results did reveal sex differences in brain responses to sexual stimuli, with the amygdala and hypothalamus more strongly activated in men than in women. The effect was not a reflection of sex differences in arousal, because the sex differences in brain activation were observed even when women reported greater arousal. The researchers suggested that "the amygdala mediates sex differences in responsiveness to appetitive and biologically salient stimuli...and may also mediate the reportedly greater role of visual stimuli in male sexual behavior, paralleling prior animal findings."

Hormones and the Brain

Can we tie together the studies of hormonal influences on behavior and studies of brain sex differences? Hormonal effects on behavior most likely occur through effects on the brain, although, as we noted above in describing IUP effects, hormones might also affect behavior through effects on the body, such as on musculature. Thus, we consider whether brain structure or function has been directly associated with prenatal (organizational) and circulating (activational) hormones in people, as they have been in other species (e.g., Isgor & Sengelaub, 2003; Juraska, 1991; Roof & Havens, 1992; Williams & Meck, 1991).

Early Hormones and the Brain

There are two intriguing imaging studies in females with CAH. One study of brain structure showed both boys and girls with CAH to have smaller amygdala volume than sex- and age-matched controls, but no other differences in brain structure (Merke et al., 2003). A subsequent study of brain function with some of the same participants showed amygdala activation to negative facial emotions to be greater in females with CAH than in typical females (Ernst et al., 2007). These results are not simple to explain, because it is unclear how the amygdala relates to the psychological characteristics that most differentiate females with CAH from typical females, and because some changes in the amygdala may reflect effects of cortisol rather than androgen (recall that individuals with CAH have a deficiency in cortisol, and sometimes cortisol replacement treatment actually causes them to have too much cortisol, which might affect the brain). The possibility of cortisol effects is made more likely by findings of differences in boys as well as girls with CAH.

Future work in individuals with CAH might focus on task-specific brain activation related to characteristics demonstrated to differ in females with CAH compared to unaffected females, such as activity interests and spatial ability. For example, it will be interesting to see whether women with CAH are more like men or women in their brain response to navigation tasks.

Circulating Hormones and the Brain

There is some evidence that estrogen affects gender-related cognition through effects on brain activity (Maki & Resnick, 2001). For example, there are changes across the menstrual cycle in women's brain activity during the solution of mental rotation tasks, and postmenopausal women receiving estrogen therapy show changes in brain activation during the performance of memory tasks.

Interesting questions concern the ways in which changes in sex hormones at puberty affect behavior through effects on the brain. For example, it is important to know how estrogen affects the brain to increase the likelihood of depression in teenage girls but not boys, and how testosterone affects the brain to increase the display of aggression in teenage boys much more than in girls. Furthermore, in light of suggestions from animal work that variations in pubertal timing affect behavior through changes to the organization of the brain (Sisk & Zehr, 2005), it will be interesting to study whether early maturing girls' increased risk of psychological problems is associated with specific brain changes, particularly in regions that are known to mature at puberty.

Summary: Brain Sex Differences and Gender Development

We have only presented a small sample of studies that have examined sex differences in the brain and invoked these differences to explain many of the psychological differences we described in the previous two chapters. It is extremely likely that there will be more such work in the next few years, as part of the burgeoning interest in understanding the neural substrates of a variety of psychological characteristics—from response to stress to musical and spatial abilities to economic choices to response to sexual stimuli. We want to make you good consumers of those studies, so we leave you with a final word on their value and limitations.

It is hard to deny the value of knowing more about the brain and the amazing variability among people in the ways that the brain is configured and functions. But, it is important to remember that the differences that are observed (e.g., between men and women) represent the accumulation of their genes and experiences, the melding of their biological and social histories. The brain is (fortunately) not a static organ; it changes in response to experience. So it is difficult to know whether sex differences in the brain produce sex differences in behavior or result from differences in the experiences of men and women.

Furthermore, it is essential that researchers show how brain sex differences are directly tied to psychological sex differences; that is, that they show that the brain difference accounts for the psychological difference. We also want to ensure that the association is causal; that is, that the brain produces those differences. We cannot manipulate the brain and examine corresponding changes in the characteristics of interest, but we can examine if naturally occurring changes in the brain (e.g., those associated with age, brain damage, drugs, or a genetic condition) are associated with corresponding changes in the psychological characteristic. That would get us closer to understanding how the brain actually influences gender development.

CHAPTER SUMMARY

Behavior is influenced in some ways by the same factors that cause the body to differentiate as female or male. Biological theories of gender development focus on both distal and proximal explanations. Evolutionary theories invoke sexual selection as a mechanism leading to sex differences in behavior. Some evidence is consistent with these theories, but work remains to be done to demonstrate that contemporary gender roles arose through selection.

Nevertheless, there is very good evidence that biological factors play a role in shaping gendered behavior, most prominently sex hormones that are present during prenatal development. Studies from several different methods converge to indicate that prenatal androgens masculinize behavior, especially activity and interest preferences, spatial ability, and some aspects of social behavior. There is suggestive evidence that genes on the X chromosome might also contribute to sex-typed behavior, especially spatial ability. Although there is currently no evidence for the behavioral importance of the Y chromosome, this topic bears watching in light of suggestive evidence in other species. The biological determinants of gender identity are yet to be established. Biological factors, especially sex hormones, continue to be important for gender development during adolescence and adulthood. There are sex differences in aspects of brain structure and function, but these have generally not been directly tied to psychological sex differences. Both biological and social contributors to gendered (and nongendered) behavior have their effects in the brain, although there is much yet to be learned about sex differences in the brain and the specific ways in which these differences affect and are affected by behavior.

Social Approaches to Gender Development

7

There is an interesting contrast between the behavior of the two sexes....When a little boy first catches sight of a girl's genital region, he begins by showing irresolution and lack of interest....It is not until later, when some threat of castration has obtained a hold upon him, that the observation becomes important to him: if he then recollects or repeats it, it arouses a terrible storm of emotion in him and forces him to believe in the reality of the threat which he has hitherto laughed at....The little girl behaves differently. She makes her judgment and her decision in a flash. She has seen it and knows that she is without it and wants to have it. (Freud, 1927, p. 137)

In this chapter we will consider five social and cultural theories of children's gender development. In general, these theories can be said to emphasize the role that children's experience in their environment plays in shaping or influencing their gender roles. First, we will return briefly to Freud's psychoanalytic theory as well as a contemporary, feminist psychoanalytic theory. We will follow this with an examination of learning theory and social learning theory, a view that emphasizes the importance of mechanisms such as reinforcement, punishment, and especially observational learning in shaping behavior. The third theory we will examine in some detail is social role theory, which was developed by social psychologist Alice Eagly and her colleagues to show how sex differences in the behaviors and roles of adults may be related to social processes such as stereotyping and expectancy confirmation. The fourth theory we will examine is Urie Bronfenbrenner's Ecological Theory of Development, which considers children's development in a series of nested contexts. The final theoretical model we will examine in this chapter is social constructionism, a postmodern theory that argues that gender roles and behaviors are socially constructed.

PSYCHOANALYTIC THEORY

In chapter 2 we discussed psychoanalytic theory from a historical perspective. We saw that Freud emphasized knowledge of genitals as a key aspect of children's gender development, and identification with same-sex parents as the basis for children's formation of gender identities and roles. As we learned in chapter 2, when researchers studied identification during the 1960s, they eventually concluded that there was little evidence that identification with same-sex parents was the basis for children's gender development (Hill, 1960; Sears, Rau, & Alpert, 1965).

The Role of Knowledge About Genitals

What about knowledge of genital organs being critical for young children's gender development? Freud's own evidence consisted of clinical case histories interpreted to emphasize the role of the genitals. Others have often used anecdotes to support the concept. The psychoanalytic clinician Drew Westen told the following story: "prior to my entering psychology a coworker told me that her 6-year-old daughter had cried the night before in the bathtub because her younger brother, with whom she was bathing, had 'one of those things' and she did not" (Westen, 1990, p. 25). On the other hand, there are probably just as many anecdotes suggesting the reverse reaction. Tavris and Wade, also reporting on a bath time event, recalled the story of a little girl who, after seeing her young cousin's penis, remarked: "Mommy, isn't it a blessing he doesn't have it on his face" (Tavris & Wade, 1984, p. 202). These stories are fascinating, and they certainly do demonstrate that children's understanding of events is often different from adults'. However, they are not especially helpful as evidence in support of the theory. What about research on the topic? We will discuss children's use of their knowledge of genitals in categorizing males and females when we discuss cognitive aspects of gender development in chapter 9. For now, what is most relevant is that research indicates that conscious knowledge of genitals occurs somewhat later than Freud believed, and that many aspects of gender development (e.g., toy, activity, and peer preferences) take place prior to knowledge of genitals (Bem, 1989; McConaghy, 1979).

Nancy Chodorow: A Contemporary, Feminist, Psychoanalytic Theorist of Gender Development

Nancy Chodorow is a psychoanalytic feminist sociologist. Consistent with the general psychoanalytic view, Chodorow thinks that differences in boys and girls' development arise out of their experiences of early life in the family, and that gender identity and gender roles develop through identification with parents (Chodorow, 1978, 1989, 1994, 1995). Chodorow argues that the central event in children's early experiences is being cared for predominantly by their mothers. She thinks that there are many consequences of maternal caregiving for boys' and girls' senses of identity, for their attitudes and relationships with the other sex, and for the position of each gender in society as a whole, specifically for the devaluation of women.

Object Relations

Chodorow's model is based on **object relations theory**, a psychoanalytic model that focuses on infants' and young children's relationships with significant others in their lives, usually their parents, and especially their mothers (Chodorow, 1989; Westen, 1990). These significant people are the objects to whom the children relate. Chodorow argues that the early months and years of children's lives are focused on separation and individuation—the formation of a separate identity from their primary caretaker, their mother. In her view, girls are reared by a caretaker who is like them, and who is available to them regularly, day after day. Following infancy, most of the other caretakers that girls experience during childhood are also female. This then results in them having a sense of connectedness with their caretakers, who in turn have a sense of connectedness with them because all are female. In the long run, this leads to a greater sense of connection with other people in general, and a greater difficulty with separation and the formation of the girl's own identity. Chodorow argues that a major disadvantage for girls and women is that, because of the importance of connectedness and relationships, they can easily be exploited within these relationships, and they have more difficulty with the formation of strong identities as individuals.

Boys, on the other hand, are reared by a caretaker who is different from them, and from whom they must separate to form a masculine identity, particularly during the Oedipal period. Rather than form an identity as a result of a relationship with a caregiver, a boy forms his identity through his understanding of the male role. As we saw in chapter 2, several theorists (Emmerich, 1959; Heilbrun, 1965; Lynn, 1962) who used the psychoanalytic concept of identification also concluded that boys had more difficulty identifying in relationships because of the distance of their fathers from their daily lives, so Chodorow's ideas about this are not unique. As did these early identification theorists, Chodorow thinks that boys are not able to develop a masculine identity in a relationship with a caretaker who is like them, but nonetheless they need to form one. Chodorow believes that there are at least two major consequences to this kind of identification for boys. One is that in achieving their masculine identity boys need to deny the feminine, as well as their initial identification with their mothers. Because the masculine is not so readily available to them in their daily lives, and the feminine is, what becomes masculine is whatever is not feminine.

Therefore boys are likely to become misogynous—despising and denigrating anything feminine, including women themselves. Another result is that boys are more likely to become socially isolated and have difficulties forming close relationships because they have no close relationship with a male caretaker.

The importance of the sex of caretakers

In Chodorow's view, the major reason for this set of circumstances is that women are the caretakers of children, and the solution is for caretaking of young children to be equally shared by men and women. Should that be the case, both boys and girls could develop identities in relationship with caregivers of both sexes. This would have positive results for both male and female children, with both being able to develop identities that allow for separation and connectedness. There would also be benefits for society as a whole, particularly in creating a climate in which men and women were equally respected and valued.

There is, in fact, evidence that in societies in which fathers are the regular caretakers of infants such as among the Aka pygmies in Africa, gender roles and relations are more egalitarian, boys learn their roles from interacting with their fathers, and women are held in higher esteem (Hewlett, 2000). However, although this research is consistent with Chodorow's premise, it is difficult to know the direction of cause and effect: Are gender roles egalitarian because men take care of infants, or do men take care of infants because gender roles are egalitarian for some other set of reasons?

Evaluation of Psychoanalytic Theory

Ironically, despite the fact that Freud's theory has had a huge impact on the culture, its position within scientific psychology has always been problematic (Leahey, 1994). As we saw in chapter 2, experimental psychology was developing during the same time period when Freud was elaborating his theories and doing his writing, but most experimental psychologists simply ignored his work. The major reason was that most psychologists did not find his methods and theorizing consistent with the scientific questions they were pursuing. Freud himself was convinced that psychoanalytic theory was scientific, and he believed that the data he collected by interpreting a very small number of clinical case histories was adequate for the scientific endeavor. However, many psychologists and philosophers of science have disagreed, and have concluded that Freud's theory has failed to meet the test of being a scientific theory (Cioffi, 1998; Leahey, 1994). Similar points have been made about other psychoanalytic theories, including Chodorow's (Bussey & Bandura, 1999; Rossi, 1981). However, psychoanalytic theory has certainly served as a way to organize thinking about gender development, so has clearly been useful to psychologists and others. In that sense it fits well with Overton's (1998) ideas about the theorist being like the architect who provides structure and meaning to the knowledge-building process.

You may recall from the discussion in chapter 2 that psychoanalytic theory did serve as an important impetus to generate research about children's gender development during the 1950s and 1960s (Bronfenbrenner, 1960; Kagan, 1958; Sears, 1957; Sears et al., 1965). Researchers did everything they could to find evidence that boys identified with their fathers and girls with their mothers, but they often failed to find support for this very basic set of predictions derived from psychoanalytic theory. Not surprisingly then, other theoretical models came to replace psychoanalytic theory. For these reasons, psychoanalytic theory no longer plays much of a role in organizing or explaining scientific research on the topic of children's gender development.

If psychoanalytic theory is no longer a viable scientific theory, what is it? As Leahey has pointed out, psychoanalytic theory faces a dilemma: "Either psychoanalysis cannot be tested—in which case it is a pseudoscience—or it can be tested—in which case, it is at best a very poor science" (Leahey, 1994, p. 68). Several scholars have concluded that psychoanalysis is better suited to fields in the humanities such as **hermeneutics** or **literary criticism** (Leahey, 1994; Westen, 1990). Hermeneutics was originally the interpretation of the bible, but has developed into a philosophical field involving interpretation of human experience, whereas literary criticism involves interpreting the meaning of literary texts. In those areas psychoanalytic theory is still playing a major role today.

LEARNING THEORIES

Learning theories in one form or another have played a very important role in generating and organizing research in psychology throughout most of the 20th century. The behaviorist school of psychology, with its emphasis on learning, began with John Watson's famous paper in 1913 (Watson, 1913). Watson urged psychologists to abandon the mentalistic concepts of the structuralists and functionalists, and to focus on the study of objectively observable behavior. For the next 50 years psychology was dominated by learning theories. Learning theorists, including Tolman, Guthrie, Hull, and Skinner (Schultz & Schultz, 1992), all emphasized various aspects of the learning process, although there were clear differences among them. For example, Hull was committed to a rigorous mathematical theory of learning, whereas Skinner was opposed to such theories, and argued for a strict focus on the observation and empirical study of the conditions under which behaviors were affected by the principles of learning. Despite their differences, the early learning theorists studied behavior of animals in the laboratory, and looked for the effects of **reinforcements**, **punishments**, and other learning mechanisms on the behavior of these animals.

A traditional learning theory approach to gender development would definitely consider reinforcements and punishments as playing a role in boys' and girls' development. For example, in a study by Fagot (1985), preschool teachers' responses to the communicative behaviors of toddlers were observed over the period of 1 year. Early in the study, the behavior of the boys and girls was similar, but 1 year later, boys were more aggressive and more likely to whine, cry, and scream than girls were, and girls were more likely to simply talk to the teacher. Strikingly, the researchers found that this was quite predictable from the teachers' responses to the children over the year of the study. Teachers responded pleasantly to the gentle communication attempts of girls, and simply ignored them when they whined or acted aggressively. Boys' whining and aggression led to loud scoldings or other forms of attention, whereas their gentle attempts at communication were often ignored. Learning theory would call responding to behavior **reinforcement,** and ignoring behavior **extinction**. Reinforcement increases the frequency of behavior and extinction reduces its frequency. Attention, even in the form of scolding, often functions as a reinforcer, and acts to increase the frequency of behavior.

As we consider the impact of parents, peers, teachers and other agents of socialization later in the book, there will be many examples of how some behaviors are reinforced, punished, or extinguished more often in one sex than the other.

Social Learning Theory

The applicability of learning theories to the study of social behaviors in human beings, and hence gender development, changed dramatically with the advent of **social learning theory** (Bandura, 1977; Bandura, Ross, & Ross, 1961; Bandura & Walters, 1963) in the 1960s. Social learning theory included a role for reinforcement, extinction, and punishment in the learning of social behaviors, but from its beginning it also emphasized the role of **imitation and modeling** on complex human social behaviors, rather than focusing on simple behaviors in laboratory animals as learning theorists had typically done in the past. As we saw in chapter 2, Mischel (1966; 1970) was the first to present a social learning view of children's gender development. Since that time social learning theory has always played a significant role in organizing and generating some research about children's gender development.

The Role of Imitation and Modeling

One of the particularly important contributions of social learning theory was its emphasis on imitation and modeling. It is important to point out that modeling is not simply imitating a particular behavior; it also involves the learning of rules that one can use to create new behaviors that have not specifically been observed, but are similar to the ones that the child has seen others do.

Much information about gender is available for children to observe and imitate. Boys and girls are given different names, clothing, toys, and room decorations. Children can easily observe that children of their own sex receive similar items and treatment, whereas children of the other sex get different items than they do. Children can observe the behavior and activities of their parents, grandparents, neighbors and teachers, as well as information provided by the media. From the moment they are born, children are immersed in a sea of information about what boys and girls and men and women do. However, children are not exposed only to the information associated with their own sex. Boys see what their mothers do, and what their sisters wear, and what toys are advertised to girls, just as they see what their fathers do, and what clothing and toys are given to them and other boys. If observational learning is to play a major role as an explanation of children's gender development, two things must be demonstrated. First, the research must show that boys are more likely to imitate the behavior of other boys and men, and the reverse for girls. Secondly, to support this theoretical position, it would be desirable to show that certain kinds of behaviors or models of one sex or the other are more available to either boys or girls for them to observe. Both of these phenomena have been supported by the research.

Do boys imitate other males and girls other females?

A boy cannot choose to imitate other boys or men unless he knows that he is male and the people he is imitating are also male, and unless he attaches significance to maleness. For example, a blue-eyed child could notice that another person also has blue eyes, but unless he thinks that is an important characteristic of both himself and the other person, it is not likely that he will be more inclined to imitate blue-eyed models as opposed to others. Part of the answer lies in social interactions with others, perhaps especially adults. There is research showing that when adults attach significance to certain physical characteristics, children also come to think such characteristics are important to attend to (e.g., see the discussions in chapters 8, 9, and 13 about peer relationships and intergroup theory and research).

As we consider children's imitation of others who are the same sex as they are, we need also to at least ask why gender is so significant. To some extent, the answer to that question lies in its extraordinary pervasiveness in social life. Almost every aspect of children's lives as they grow up attaches meaning to gender. Think of other characteristics that children might have, such as religion, ethnic background, or social class. Certainly these characteristics are relevant to children's experiences and development, but none is as pervasive in organizing the social world of children as is gender. Of course gender is not an arbitrary characteristic. Being male or female has biological as well as social implications, so it is understandable that it is so pervasive in social life.

Are boys more likely to imitate other males, and girls to imitate other females? The simple answer to that question is yes, but the more complex answer is under some conditions, but not always. Social learning theorists have designed experimental studies to examine the role that imitation and modeling play in gender development. In a very creative study, Bussey and Bandura (1984) showed 2- to 5-year-old children videotapes of adults playing the game "Find the Surprise." The video began with six models, three of each sex, sitting on chairs beside a woman who invited them to play the game. She told them that they would have a chance to find a sticker hidden in one of two boxes. All of the men behaved one way, and all of the women behaved another. In one version of the videotape all of the men wore a green Mickey Mouse cap with Mickey's picture facing the front, and all of the women wore a blue Mickey Mouse cap with the picture facing towards the back. When a woman went to look for the sticker, she began to march slowly towards Box A, saying "forward march," followed by "march, march, march." Once she came to the box she picked up a koala bear and made it jump from the lid of the box, saying "jump, jump." When she opened the box, she said "bingo," and took the sticker to a paper hanging on the wall behind the boxes, and stuck it in the top right corner, saying "lickit-stickit," and "up there." A man, on the other hand, said "get, set, go," when he got up, and "left-right, left-right" as he walked stiffly towards Box B. He made the koala bear fly from the lid of the box, saying "fly, fly." When he opened the box, he said "a stickeroo," and took it and stuck it on the lower left corner of the paper saying "weto-smacko," and "down there." When children had an opportunity to play the game themselves, girls were more likely to imitate the women, and boys were more likely to imitate the men. After measuring the children's spontaneous imitation of the models, Bussey and Bandura measured their knowledge of what the male and female models did, and found no difference between boys' and girls' knowledge of the behaviors demonstrated by either men or women. This illustrates a very important point: children learn about the behavior of both males and females, and yet they choose to imitate the behavior done by others of their sex.

In a second experiment reported in the same paper, Bussey and Bandura (1984) manipulated the amount of power videotaped child models had in controlling the resources of a game. They demonstrated that children were still inclined to imitate others of their sex, but they also showed substantial imitation of models of the other sex when those models were shown as having a great deal of power. Boys in particular were unlikely to imitate female models unless they had power.

In the everyday world, it is usually the case that children will see many males and females behaving differently from each other. For example, a child could observe that many girls play with Barbie dolls, many women cook, and many girls and women wear dresses and jewelry. Experimental research has shown that when there are several models of the same sex modeling the same behavior, children are more likely to imitate it (Bussey & Perry, 1982; Perry & Bussey, 1979; Ruble, Balaban, & Cooper, 1981).

For example, in a study by Perry and Bussey (1979) 8- and 9-year-old children were shown videos of eight adult models (four men and four women) who indicated their preferred choice for one of two items on 16 pairs of gender-neutral items (e.g., did they prefer a banana vs. an apple, or a plastic toy horse vs. a toy cow). In one experimental condition all four men chose the same item on all 16 pairs, and all four of the women chose the other item in each pair. In the next experimental condition, three of the four men and one of the women chose the same item (and vice versa), and in the last experimental condition, half the men and half the women made the same choices. The children were then tested on their own preferences for these items. There was also a control condition in which the children did not see any models making the choices, but were simply tested on their own preferences.

When their preferences were tested, the children were more likely to choose the items chosen by the models of their sex, especially when all of the same-sex models had made the same choice. As can be seen in Figure 7.1, when half the models of their sex chose particular items, the children chose those items

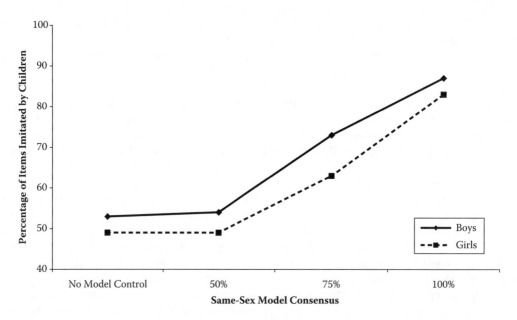

FIGURE 7.1   Children are more likely to imitate same-sex models when there is greater consensus among them. (Data from Perry, D.G. & Bussey, K., *Journal of Personality and Social Psychology*, 37, 1699–1712, 1979.)

about half the time, but when all of the models of their sex did so, children chose those items 80–90% of the time. In a second study, 8-year-old children saw a man or a woman consistently make choices that were different from three other models of their sex. That is, three men always made the same choice, and one man, always the same man, consistently differed from the other three. Similarly, one woman model made different choices than three other women. In a later modeling situation, the children were given the opportunity to imitate the behavior of one man (or one woman), who had earlier been shown as consistently behaving differently than other men (or women), or similarly. The children, especially boys, were much more likely to imitate the behavior of the same-sex models who had a history of behaving similarly to the same-sex majority.

It seems to be the case that children determine that certain behaviors are for one sex or the other when they see them being done mostly by one or the other. The primary role of models seems to be to provide information about what most males and females do, not that children simply imitate a model that is male or female. In fact, as we have seen from the research above, if a particular male or female model does something different from what most males or females do, children are not very likely to imitate that behavior.

It is also the case that, when children take part in psychologists' studies, they have observed much gendered behavior outside of the laboratory. In the laboratory children are generally disinclined to imitate a model behaving in a gender-inappropriate way (Frey & Ruble, 1992). In other words, the gender-appropriateness of the behavior is more powerful than the sex of the model if there's a discrepancy. Interestingly, several studies have also shown that boys are more inclined to imitate male models, and to avoid imitating the behavior of females, than girls are to imitate females or to avoid imitating males (Bussey & Perry, 1982; Luecke-Aleksa, Anderson, Collins, & Schmitt, 1995; Slaby & Frey, 1975). As we discuss in more detail in chapter 9, researchers have also found boys to be more inclined to imitate masculine tasks and to avoid imitating feminine tasks, regardless of the sex of the model (Bauer, 1993). So it is fair to say that boys are especially resistant to imitating gender-atypical behavior.

Exposure to same-sex models

As a second central issue with respect to the role of modeling in children's gender development, Bussey and Bandura (1999) have suggested that it is important to show that boys and girls have more exposure to models of their own sex. Of course in much of the social world children see people of both sexes. Nonetheless, there are some situations in which it has been shown that boys have more exposure to the behavior of other males, whereas girls have more exposure to the behavior of other females. For example, Hoffman and Teyber (1985) made more than 1,500 observations of children and adults in public places, and although they found that children in general were more often with women than with men, boys were with men more than girls were, and girls were with women more than boys were. On an anecdotal level, parents could probably report that the adults who supervise the gender-segregated recreational activities of school-aged children (e.g., sports, dancing) are very often the same sex as the children they are supervising. For example, one of us had two sons who played Little League baseball for several years, and neither ever had a female coach. However, most children interact with female and male adults quite frequently, and the major differential exposure to models of the same sex is not really associated with adult models, but with other children. Peer interactions are highly segregated, especially during the elementary school years, providing children with overwhelming exposure to the social behaviors of other children of the same sex. Later we will discuss what kinds of behaviors children do in these gendered peer groups.

Imitating gender-atypical behavior

Because it is clear that children are very resistant to imitating gender-atypical behavior, it is very difficult to modify children's gender-related behavior. With the advent of the women's movement, attitudes in society changed about the desirability of gender roles, and these attitude changes affected developmental psychology as well. Gender development researchers began to note the disadvantages of rigid gender norms and roles, and hence developed studies to modify children's gender role behaviors and beliefs (for a review of intervention research see Bigler, 1999). Some of this research has focused on changing children's attitudes and beliefs about gender norms, and some has focused on changing children's behavior, although as Bigler has pointed out, changing behavior may be more controversial.

In one very interesting study (Katz & Walsh, 1991) children observed videotapes of other children engaging in behavior usually associated with the other gender, and who were either reinforced for doing so or received no reinforcement. That is, after the videotaped child model played with a cross-gender toy, or aspired to a cross-gender occupation, either another child or an adult came over to the model and made positive comments like "Those things you did look like fun." When the child models were reinforced, children were more likely to imitate the behavior of the models. However, the study found a powerful effect of the sex of the experimenter who interacted with the children (not the model). Children of both genders, but especially boys, imitated more cross-gender behavior when a male experimenter interacted with them than when a female experimenter did so. The researchers suggested that children see male adults as "the custodians of gender norms" (Katz & Walsh, 1991, p. 349). Hence, they argued that adult males are probably more likely to influence children to become more flexible in their gendered behavior than are adult females.

Despite the fact that some research has shown short-term imitation such as that seen in the study by Katz and Walsh (1991), much of this research has found it very difficult to make any substantial or long-term changes in either attitudes or behavior, especially in boys (Bigler, 1999; Katz, 1986; Liben & Bigler, 1987). We can think about two issues regarding that research. First, most of the experimenters who have been present in this modification research have been female (see the discussion in Katz & Walsh, 1991), and secondly, any intervention is likely countered by much more gender-stereotyped behavior in the rest of the child's experiences than the short exposure to nontraditional behavior in the experiment in which the child participated.

However, gender norms have changed in the past 40 years (e.g., Barnett & Hyde, 2001). Children are exposed to many models, and not all behave alike. As some models, either figures in the media or in children's own lives, change their gender role behaviors, children can see these new norms, and choose which behaviors to imitate. It is also the case that some people (e.g., some parents) may reward traditional gender roles, whereas others may reward nontraditional roles, and different children may be exposed to more or less traditional influences.

The Transition to Social Cognitive Theory

As social learning theory evolved, Bandura came to emphasize more cognitive factors in addition to basic learning mechanisms (Bandura, 1986, 1992, 1999, 2001), and the theory has become known as **social cognitive theory**. Because of its emphasis on cognition, we will save our discussion of social cognitive theory for the next chapter.

Evaluation of Social Learning Theory

Social learning theory grew out of scientific research on behavior and has certainly served as a guide to research in many areas of psychology, including children's gender development. The changes from learning theory to social learning theory to social cognitive theory also reflect the kinds of changes that epitomize a scientific approach: the theory is supposed to change when research findings cannot be accounted for by the current version of the theory. The major question of evaluation then, is to what extent research confirms or contradicts the theory's predictions. Is there evidence that reinforcement, punishment, observational learning, and direct teaching influence children's gender development? Because we have not yet discussed the research on parents' and teachers' treatment of children, the modeling of gender norms in books, television and other media, nor have we looked at children's peer groups, this question is difficult to answer convincingly at this point. We will see later that there is certainly evidence in support of a learning approach, but also some in contradiction.

One of the criticisms that has often been directed towards learning theories is that they have seen the child as a passive recipient of influence. For example, children often distort information provided to them in modeling studies, particularly if the information is counter stereotypic (Bigler, 1999; Liben & Bigler, 1987). That suggests that children actively form their own ideas about gender, and are not simply passive recipients of influence from the environment. This is one of the major reasons why social learning theory moved in the direction of a more cognitive approach.

A more serious criticism concerns learning theory's lack of attention to children's underlying cognitive development. It is the case that several modeling studies have found that the level of children's cognitive development influences their tendency to attend to same-sex models, to recall the models' behavior correctly, and to imitate them. In the next chapter we will discuss the cognitive theories of gender development. One important theory, Kohlberg's (1966) cognitive developmental theory, proposed that children's understanding of gender, particularly gender constancy, affects the extent to which children imitate same-sex models. Several studies (Bussey & Bandura, 1984; Frey & Ruble, 1992; Luecke-Aleksa et al., 1995; Ruble et al., 1981; Slaby & Frey, 1975) have shown that children, especially boys, with a greater understanding of the constancy or permanence of gender are more likely to imitate same-sex models. Findings such as these are difficult to explain without incorporating the constructs of the cognitive theories; that is, without focusing on children's level of cognitive development as a part of the equation. Up to this point, learning theories have not focused on the question of developmental change to the degree that is necessary to guide developmental research (Grusec, 1994; Martin, Ruble, & Szkrybalo, 2002).

One final criticism of learning theory and social cognitive theory concerns the limited attention given by the theory to biological or evolutionary influences on gender development. Throughout its history, learning theory has tended to emphasize environmental influences on behavior without incorporating a well-developed role for biological processes. It is not possible to fully account for gender development without incorporating a biological approach – in particular, a biosocial perspective (Maccoby, 2000; Wood & Eagly, 2002).

SOCIAL ROLE THEORY

Social psychologist Alice Eagly (1987) has proposed **social role theory** of sex differences and similarities, recently updated in collaboration with colleagues Wendy Wood and Amanda Diekman (Eagly, Wood, & Diekman, 2000; Wood & Eagly, 2002). Social role theory was proposed as a result of the findings of research using **meta-analysis** to examine sex differences in social behaviors and personality characteristics. The meta-analytic research had discovered consistent differences between the sexes in a variety of behaviors. Although some of the differences were not especially large, Eagly and her colleagues argued that they had significant cumulative impact, and hence it was important to understand the roots of these differences.

In addition to the research on sex differences, there was also much ongoing research on gender stereotypes—what people think about how males and females are different. That research also found the people held rather consistent and predictable views about such differences. Importantly, the researchers found there was some degree of similarity between the sex differences that meta-analyses were uncovering, and the stereotypes that people had about males and females. That is, the stereotypes could be described as reasonably accurate.

The consistency between the sex differences and gender stereotypes research raised questions about how they might be related. For example, if people think that young girls are delicate and in need of assistance, or that boys are rowdy and disobedient, does that have an impact on how boys and girls are treated? Then, does the treatment continue to influence the expected behavior? Do boys then become more rowdy and disobedient because of the way they are treated? For some time social psychologists have shown how powerful social expectancies are in shaping behavior. Eagly and her colleagues proposed that behavioral differences between males and females are affected by the stereotypes that people hold. Another important question is where the stereotypes come from in the first place. They proposed that the stereotypes that people hold about males and females are affected by the roles that men and women play. Roles lead to stereotypes, stereotypes lead to expectancies, expectancies lead to treatment, and treatment leads to behavior, and the whole process continues in a never-ending cycle.

Gender Roles

At the center of social role theory is a focus on gender roles, especially the roles of homemaker and economic provider. The fact that men and women have these roles is obviously not a historical accident; they are related to the biological capacities of each, and to the production needs of societies. Certain tasks could be accomplished more easily and efficiently by one sex or the other. Men's greater physical strength was needed for certain occupations and activities, especially in preindustrial societies. Women, on the other hand, become pregnant, give birth, and nurse infants, and hence it is not arbitrary that childcare responsibilities have shaped their lives throughout human history.

Personality Characteristics Associated With Gender Roles

The role of homemaker is seen as having **communal or expressive characteristics**, and the role of economic provider is seen as having **instrumental or agentic characteristics**. That is, homemakers are seen as kind, considerate, helpful, nurturant and caring, and economic providers are seen as competent, independent, assertive, and having leadership qualities. In fact, it seems to be the role that influences people to think that others have such characteristics. Research has shown that people in the domestic role, whether they are male or female, are seen as having communal traits, and similarly, people of either sex who are in the employee role are seen as having agentic traits (Eagly & Chrvala, 1986; Eagly & Steffen, 1984, 1986; Steffen & Eagly, 1985). Eagly and her colleagues thus argue that the characteristics that are attributed to men and women are very heavily influenced by the roles of homemaker and provider.

It is also the case that people approve of these characteristics in men and women, and believe that men and women ought to differ in these ways. For example, the communal characteristics of women are highly valued. That women are kind and concerned about the needs of others, especially the needs of children and family members, is seen as very positive. Eagly (2000) suggests that these very traits are the ones that are then seen as qualifying women for domestic roles, and female-dominated occupations like nurse and teacher. On the other hand men's agentic characteristics are also valued, and seen as qualifying them for the world of work, especially for positions of power.

Gender Roles and Power

Social role theory also takes the position that gender roles are intricately tied to status and power (Eagly et al., 2000). Although the nurturant aspects of it are admired, the homemaker role has lower status than the provider role. Although most women today are employed during some part of their adult life, they are typically in lower-status occupations than men are and are often in occupations in which communal characteristics are valued. Women are also found much less often in high levels of corporations than are men. Put simply, men usually have higher status and more public power than women do.

Personality Characteristics, Power, and the Link to Social Behaviors

Eagly and her colleagues argue that the differences in beliefs about men and women, and in the degree of social power available to each sex, lead to differences in the social behaviors each is able to perform. They contend that people know the stereotypes, and hold stereotypic expectancies about the characteristics and behaviors of others on the basis of their sex. People also know that these stereotypical characteristics are valued for each sex, that others have these expectations for them, and will reward them for displaying the characteristics valued for their sex. This leads to a situation in which stereotypes are confirmed as people act out these expectancies in social interaction. Women are deferential and nurturant because they lack power, and because they know that others will respond positively to these characteristics, and because others do respond positively. Men are assertive and independent because they have power, and because others respond positively to them when they behave this way. Eagly and her colleagues call these processes **expectancy confirmation** and **self-regulation**.

Much research in social psychology with adults demonstrates the roles that expectancy confirmation and self-regulation play in social behavior. The process is often called a **self-fulfilling prophecy** (Eagly et al., 2000). People communicate their expectations to others both verbally and nonverbally, and then respond positively when a person behaves in line with these expectations. Additionally, people have expectations for their own behavior, and are affected by the expectations of others. These processes operate at a very subtle level, however. People are not necessarily aware that they are engaging in this kind of process.

In a very striking demonstration of expectancy confirmation, Skrypnek and Snyder (1982) had pairs of undergraduates negotiate a division of labor on a series of tasks that were gender stereotyped to a greater or lesser degree, or were gender neutral. For example, they had to choose which one of them would attach bait to a fishing hook or decorate a birthday cake. The partners were in different rooms and could not see or hear each other, and interacted via a signaling system. In all cases one member of each pair was male and the other was female. However, the male members of the pair were either told their female partner was female, or were told she was male, or were given no information about her. The female member of the pair knew nothing about her partner. When men believed their partner was female, they gave her more feminine stereotyped tasks, and were less willing to respond to her preferences when she expressed them. Even more strikingly, these women began to choose more feminine tasks for themselves. Keep in mind that these women did not know what information their partners had been given, nor did they know what sex their partners were, so they were simply responding to expectancies that their partners were communicating to them.

Changing Social Roles

One important prediction of social role theory is that, as social roles have changed for men and women, people's attitudes about their characteristics ought to change (Eagly et al., 2000). Related is the prediction that as attitudes change, so do the characteristics of men and women, in response to the general processes of self-regulation and expectancy confirmation in line with the new roles and attitudes. These are important predictions, because they suggest the possibility of relatively rapid change in gender norms and roles. In a set of meta-analyses, Twenge (1997a; 1997b; 2001) has indeed shown that attitudes about the characteristics of women have changed over the past 30 years, and their characteristics have also changed. People's attitudes about gender norms have become more flexible, women's characteristics are now seen as being more similar to men's, and women have become more assertive. Note however, all of these changes have been in the direction of women becoming more like men, not the reverse.

Children's Development and Social Roles

Social role theory focuses predominantly on adults. What about children's social roles? Eagly and her colleagues (Eagly et al., 2000) discuss research on childhood socialization primarily as it relates to the development of competencies and skills in adults. In their view, there is clear research evidence demonstrating that parents, especially fathers, and especially regarding sons, steer their children in the direction of gender-typed activities and interests such as clothing, chores, toys, and other interests. They argue that this socialization influences children's developing skills, as well as helping them learn that gender is an important social dimension. Although Eagly and her colleagues note these socialization differences, they do not think they are the only factors in creating gender differences in behavior (Eagly, 1997). They also emphasize the ongoing processes, throughout life, of expectancy confirmation and self-regulation.

Evaluation of Social Role Theory

Despite its very prominent role in theorizing about gender among social psychologists, little research on children's gender development is currently being conducted from the perspective of social role theory. It is not really a theory of gender development, although it certainly has implications for developmental processes. The most plausible link between the tenets of social role theory and children's gender socialization focuses on socializing boys for instrumental or agentic roles, and socializing girls for expressive ones. There is, in fact, evidence that this does happen. One of the most obvious things that children can learn from observing their parents is that women have the major responsibility for looking after children (Leaper, 2002). In terms of direct treatment, there is evidence that parents are more likely to tolerate and encourage greater expression of emotion in girls, that they encourage a greater focus on affiliation in girls, that they are more likely to foster self-confidence in math and science for boys, that they assign gender-typed chores, and that they foster gender-appropriate activities and interests (Leaper, 2002). So, although little of the research on children's gender socialization has been generated by social role theory, much is consistent with it.

Additionally, the question of expectancy confirmation has implications for children's development. In chapter 1 we discussed a study of infants' abilities to crawl down a slope and their mothers' judgments about those capabilities (Mondschein, Adolph, & Tamis-LeMonda, 2000). You may recall that, despite the lack of differences between boys and girls, mothers underestimated girls' capabilities and overestimated boys'. When we discuss parents' and teachers' interactions with boys and girls we will see this pattern again. This pattern of findings certainly has relevance for a theory that portrays gender differences as being influenced by stereotypes, expectancy confirmation, and self-regulation.

BRONFENBRENNER'S ECOLOGICAL THEORY

In the 1970s, developmental psychologist Urie Bronfenbrenner proposed an ecological theory of children's development (Bronfenbrenner, 1979; Bronfenbrenner & Morris, 1998). In developmental psychology this has been a very important viewpoint about children's social development, although it was not developed specifically with gender development in mind. Bronfenbrenner conceptualized children's development as being influenced by a series of processes involving the child and the environment. Bronfenbrenner considered the environment as a set of nested systems or layers (see Figure 7.2), with the child at the center. Bronfenbrenner refers to the child's actual environment as the **microsystem**. The microsystem consists of the actual interactions the child experiences. These experiences may be in the family, or with other children in the neighborhood or at school, with teachers, or with coaches and others. A child has a set of characteristics (e.g., temperament, age) some of which are influenced by the child's biology. The child's characteristics influence how people in the environment interact with and treat that child, and this treatment continues to affect the child's development. Gender certainly is one of a child's important characteristics.

Here we can consider a single example of several facets of the microsystem related to the expression of emotion. We already know that, from a very early age, boys come to avoid expressing emotions that signal vulnerability, but that there is little evidence that the physiological basis of emotion differs between boys and girls. There are probably several processes in the microsystem that might influence this aspect of gender development. Parents put more pressure on boys to control certain emotions, especially sadness or fearfulness (Eisenberg, Cumberland, & Spinrad, 1998), and they are less likely to talk about emotions that signal vulnerability with boys (Fivush & Buckner, 2000). In addition, they respond differently to emotional behavior in boys and girls, attending more to sadness and fearfulness in girls and to anger in boys—giving the emotional behavior of boys and girls a different payoff or reward (Chaplin, Cole, & Zahn-Waxler, 2005). Peers also are part of the microsystem. In their peer groups, even as preschoolers,

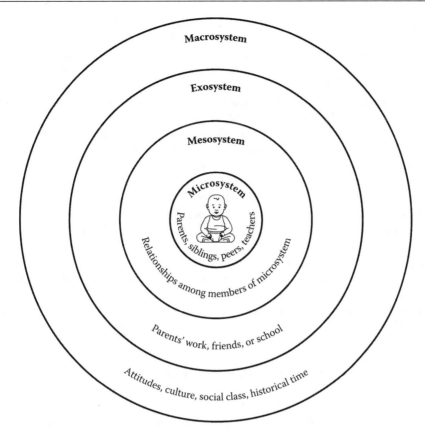

FIGURE 7.2 Bronfenbrenner's Ecological Model consisting of nested systems of influence on development. (Adapted from Bronfenbrenner, U., *The ecology of human development.* Cambridge, MA: Harvard University Press, 1979.)

boys are ridiculed by other boys for expressing vulnerable emotions such as fear (Kyratzis, 2001). Finally, children's books, television, movies, and computer games rarely show images of fear and sadness in male characters.

After the microsystem, the next layer in Bronfenbrenner's ecological system is the **mesosystem**. This refers to the interactions or connections among the various parts of the environment that affect the child. For example, a child's parents may socialize with other parents in a neighborhood, or may volunteer at the child's school or daycare center. Parents select neighborhoods, schools and religious institutions that can impact on children's development. In terms of children's social development in general, Bronfenbrenner held that children were likely to develop best when there were strong, consistent, and supportive relationships among the significant parts of the child's environment. If parents, parents of peers, teachers, and members of religious organizations worked together to support the child's development, and shared similar values (e.g., about the importance of schoolwork), this was likely to be beneficial to children, he thought. There is in fact evidence that many aspects of children's lives outside the family do impact their development in significant ways (e.g., Rose et al., 2003), and it makes sense that it would benefit children to have peers, teachers, and parents who are consistent in their influence. For gender development, it would be fascinating to examine the attitudes or gendered behaviors of children with consistent or inconsistent influences from significant individuals and institutions in their lives. As with the microsystem, we can again use emotion as an example. If parents interact with significant people in the child's life to reinforce a message related to emotional expression, that would be an example of the mesosystem at work. Consider the possibility of a father having a conversation with a coach encouraging the coach to support the son's control of his feelings of sadness or fear.

Bronfenbrenner's next layer is the **exosystem**. This refers to experiences that the child does not take part in directly, but that may impact on the child indirectly. A good example of the exosystem consists of experiences that parents have outside the family that may affect the parents' interactions with their children. Parents' influences at work or school (e.g., if they return to or continue in school after their children are born) may influence how they treat their children. The social support they receive from friends and coworkers may assist them in their roles as parents. For example, a mother may hear a coworker's views about the inappropriateness of emotional vulnerability in a particular boy or man, and take that message to heart, later interacting with her son to further influence him to avoid such emotional expression.

The next layer in Bronfenbrenner's system is the **macrosystem**. This refers to the general cultural context of development. This could be as narrow as social class in a particular country, or the entire culture of a group, a nation or even the world. Clearly, for gender development the significant changes in gender attitudes and gender roles that have taken place over the past several decades is potentially important. There is certainly evidence that attitudes about gender and family roles have changed over the past several decades (Thornton & Young-DeMarco, 2001) would be a significant part of the impact of the macrosystem on children's gender development.

The final part of Bronfenbrenner's system is the **chronosystem**. This refers to chronological change, either in the child or the environment. The cultural context may change, the child's family moves or has another child, the mother gets a job outside the home—all of these events change the ecology of the child's development. One particularly important part of the chronosystem is the child's age. Certainly children have different experiences and are treated differently as they grow older.

Ecological Theory and Gender Development

Applying Bronfenbrenner's ecological theory to children's gender development makes a great deal of sense, although it has not specifically generated a great deal of research on topics related to gender development. One group of researchers who have argued for and examined an ecological context of gender development in the family is Susan McHale and Ann Crouter and their colleagues (e.g., Bumpus, Crouter, & McHale, 2001; Crouter, Head, Bumpus, & McHale, 2001; Crouter, Manke, & McHale, 1995; McHale, Crouter, & Whiteman, 2003; McHale, Updegraff, Helms-Erikson, & Crouter, 2001). We will discuss some of their research in detail in our chapter on the impact of the family on children's gender development. For now, though, we can say that their research shows that parent work roles, parent gender attitudes, the presence of siblings, and the gender composition of siblings in the family all impact on how boys versus girls are treated in the family. Children, especially girls, are more likely to be encouraged to have traditional gender roles when their parents have traditional gendered attitudes, their mothers are not employed outside the home, and when there are children of both sexes in the family. Boys are less likely to be assigned to do household chores, but that is most likely to be the case when they have sisters and traditional parents.

Evaluation of Bronfenbrenner's Ecological Theory

As we said earlier, more than any other theorist of children's social development, Bronfenbrenner has urged us to put children's development in context, to study it in children's natural environments, and to understand how complex the processes of human development truly are. His theoretical view has been very compelling to developmental psychologists—it just makes so much sense. With respect to it having generated research on the many processes involved in children's gender development, it is perhaps fair to say that there is much to learn about the ecological context of children's gender development, but it is certainly the case that we expect the ecological context to make a difference. In chapter 10, when we learn about the role of the family in gender development, we will see that family ecology impacts gender development in very interesting ways.

SOCIAL CONSTRUCTION THEORIES OF GENDER

To discuss **social construction** theories of gender development we need to return to the discussion of feminism that we began in chapter 1. There are many kinds of feminism, and many places where a feminist perspective can be found in the study of children's gender development. Feminists can be found in every tradition in the study of children's gender development. However, as we pointed out previously, there's a difference between feminism as a philosophy of life, and feminism as a theoretical basis for scholarship. The view that gender is socially constructed is the most explicitly feminist theory of all views of children's gender development. It is also the view that departs the most from the empirical tradition of psychology.

A Postmodern Perspective

Social constructionism is a **postmodern** perspective (K. J. Gergen, 1985; 2001; M. Gergen, 2001). **Modernism** came about as the world moved from the Dark Ages to the Enlightenment, when modern science came into being (K. J. Gergen, 2001). Psychology as a science grew out of the modernist perspective, at the heart of which is the assumption that there is an objective world which can be discovered. Every theoretical tradition that we have discussed to this point takes that assumption as its starting point. Modern scientists, psychologists included, generally believe without question that it is possible to use the methods of science to come to understand the nature of the world. In contrast, the postmodern perspective assumes that such objective knowledge is never truly possible.

A key element of the postmodern view is that knowledge is not objective. Rather, it is socially constructed, affected by time, place, culture, and the social experience of the knower (K. J. Gergen, 2001). People who share time, place, and culture can share in the socially constructed knowledge, but there is no objective reality that humans can know which can be removed from these constraints. Postmodern theorists do not argue that there is no objective reality—just that human knowledge of reality is inextricably linked to social time and place. A very key part of this perspective is that one's values are always part of the research process, and that there is no such thing as value-neutral research (Russell & Bohan, 1999).

Postmodernism and the Social Construction of Gender

There are at least two implications of this view for the study of gender. One is to question the extent that we can learn objective information about gender development that is independent of social time and place, or of the values of the person collecting the knowledge. However, that implication of postmodernism is no different for the study of gender development than for anything else that psychologists study. The second issue, however, is more central, and that concerns the social construction of gender itself.

A very basic example of the social construction of gender is the view that there are two genders (Beall, 1993). As we discussed in chapter 1, there are some cultures that allow for a third gender category. Social constructionists also contend that beliefs about the nature of males and females, masculinity and femininity, and male and female roles are socially constructed. For example, anthropologist Barry Hewlett (Hewlett, 1989, 1992; 2000) has studied parenting behavior among the Aka pygmy culture in Africa. In this foraging society, both mothers and fathers spend much of their days together foraging for food and looking after their children. Fathers do almost as much childcare as mothers do. Children's constructions of male and female adult roles, then, could be expected to differ from ideas that North American or European children might construct, and they do. For example, Aka children do not believe that food preparation and childcare are feminine activities.

Social constructionists contend that cultural beliefs about gender differences exist because they are functional (Beall, 1993), or at least they have been in the past. Gender roles provide for a division of labor between men and women that served a function for childrearing and production tasks and they serve to create interdependence between men and women. If there is a division of labor between men and women, then each will need the other to form a family unit. As was the case for Eagly's social role theory, most contemporary social constructionist theorists suggest that the functions served by gender roles are less and less important today in modern industrialized cultures than they were in the past.

Power, again

Social constructionists also emphasize the role of power and status in gender relations (Leaper, 2000b; Lorber, 1991, 1994; Yelland & Grieshaber, 1998). They point to the lower social status of women as a central facet of gender, and they want to know how children's socialization continues to foster these kinds of inequities. For example, in peer groups boys often show evidence that they know they are a higher status group than girls are (Leaper, 2000b). Social constructionists want to know why boys come to believe that. It is also the case that feminist social constructionists often prefer to de-emphasize the role of biological factors in creating differences between males and females, at least in creating differences in their opportunities and position in society.

Having gender versus doing gender

Social constructionists also emphasize that rather than "having gender," people "do gender" (Lorber, 1991, 1994; Messner, 2000; Yelland & Grieshaber, 1998). That is, people act in ways to confirm their gender, and to make gender a salient category of social life. In their study of children's gender development, social constructionists are likely to study three things in particular. First, they study cultural systems of gender, including relationships between gender, race, and class (Leaper, 2000b). Second, they study cross-cultural and historical differences in gender roles as a way of illustrating the social construction of gender, as in the example of the Aka culture, above. Third, they are likely to examine how the socialization of children, in the family and in the culture as a whole, inculcates gender roles and the structure of gender relations.

Social Constructionists' Methods

Social constructionists often choose research methods that are different from the usual quantitative studies common in developmental psychology. Among these methods are **focus groups, collaborative research with the participants, discourse analysis, ethnography**, and the use of **narratives** (Gergen, Chrisler, & LoCicero, 1999; Wilkinson, 1999). Most of this research is qualitative rather than quantitative, and often originates from disciplines other than psychology. Social constructionists also address questions about whether particular research has value, in terms of whether it can be used for the good of humankind (K. J. Gergen, 2001; Russell & Bohan, 1999).

An example of constructionist research

To examine a model of social constructionist research we can return to Messner's (2000) study of his 5-year-old son's first year playing soccer that we discussed in chapter 1. You may recall the interaction between the Barbie Girls and the Sea Monsters. In his article, Messner analyzes his and his son's gendered experience in the soccer league at three different levels: the **interactional level, the structural level,** and the **cultural level**. The interactional level is well illustrated by the story in chapter 1 when the boys began to yell "No Barbie" at the girls who were singing and circling around the Barbie doll in the wagon. When the girls ignored their chants, some boys began to invade the girls' space and yell menacingly at them. Some girls looked puzzled, whereas others chased the boys away. Parents eventually broke up the altercation.

Messner argues that, in their dance around the large Barbie doll, the girls were performing gender, and in attacking them the boys were also. However, the boys' performance of masculinity was specifically in opposition to femininity, particularly in their expression of masculine dominance. Messner says that the parents saw their children's behavior as a natural unfolding of inherent differences between the boys and girls, rather than as a gendered performance. He argues that, unless one engages in a structural and cultural analysis of such behavior, it is easy to be misled into seeing the children's behavior as the parents do. He emphasizes that despite the fact that the children's behavior was overwhelmingly similar as they played in the soccer league, because of the gendered social structure it is almost impossible to see the similarity.

At the structural level the soccer league had a clear division of labor for adult males and females. Each team had a coach, the vast majority of whom were male; each team also had a manager who was responsible for organizing snacks, making reminder calls, and the end-of-the-year party. Most team managers were women, and were often called the "team mom." Messner argues that this structure reinforces a gendered division of labor and power relations between men and women because coaches were of higher status than team moms. As another structural aspect of the league, children's teams were divided by gender. He noted that such had not always been the case in this soccer league; younger children had been in coed teams in previous years, but it was decided to make them segregated because of the children's tendency to get into same gender groups on their own during half time and practices. Messner notes that no one would choose to segregate a children's sports league if children self-segregated informally on the basis of race, but they were quite comfortable doing so on the basis of gender.

Messner distinguishes between the structural and cultural level of analysis and gives several examples of cultural symbols of gender that reinforce the gender differentiation in the league. These symbols included such things as uniform colors (e.g., no boys' teams were issued pink), team names chosen by the children and their coaches, and messages from toys (like Barbies). Messner concludes that, by taking an event from daily life such as this, and submitting it to a structural and cultural analysis, one can see that it is more important to ask not how boys and girls are different, but rather under what conditions and in what circumstances gender is more or less significant in organizing social relations.

Messner is a sociologist, and examining structural and cultural aspects of gender is a more central aspect of that discipline than of developmental psychology, as are the qualitative methods discussed above (Jordan & Cowan, 1995; McGuffey & Rich, 1999; Messner, 1990). These kinds of general cultural processes are often called the **macrosystem**, a term we have already seen in Bronfenbrenner's model. Processes that operate at an individual level can be called **microsystem** processes (Leaper, 2000b). Developmental psychologists are typically more concerned with the microsystem—with the factors that influence an individual's development. So, do developmental psychologists do social constructionist research on children's gender development? At this point not very often—this is not a mainstream perspective in developmental psychology, but there are psychologists doing this kind of research, especially in Australia and England (e.g., Epstein, Kehily, Mac an Ghaill, & Redman, 2001; Hay, Castle, Stimson, & Davies, 1995; Kelly, 1993; Yelland, 1998).

Developmental psychologists look at the social construction of gender

Using a feminist postmodern analysis, Grieshaber (1998) studied twenty Australian couples who were about to have their first child, to examine how they went about thinking about and planning for their babies. Grieshaber asked whether the couples wanted to know about the sex of their baby ahead of the birth, and why or why not. Of those who asked for the knowledge following ultrasound during the pregnancy (about half of them), the main reasons were to prepare themselves as to how to think about the child, to plan for a name, and to purchase gender-appropriate items and colors. Grieshaber refers to this as constructing their child as a gendered being.

Grieshaber also examined the parents' stated preferences for a child of one gender or the other. Many parents expressed no preference, but of those who did, more preferred sons. This was especially so of fathers, and many mothers who preferred to have a son said it was because it was important to their husbands. The reasons for wanting a boy were often tied to the fact that this was their first child. They suggested that an older boy would be more dominant, or be able to look after younger siblings, especially younger sisters. Parents, especially fathers, expressed the view that the world was more dangerous for girls. Another of the concerns expressed in their wish for sons was to carry on the family name. Grieshaber points out that these reasons are social constructions; the one implying that girls need to be protected, and the other being something that girls cannot do under the social system in which these families lived. The parents (mostly mothers) who professed a desire for daughters, said they wanted girls to dress up, or to be like them, or to be like younger sisters they never had. One mother said she did not like adolescent boys, and hence would prefer daughters. Again, these can be said to be social constructions.

Grieshaber also asked the expectant couples to imagine interacting with their infants. Many of the fathers imagined interacting with their children (boys or girls) beyond the stage of infancy, especially in the context of sports or camping. The majority did not discuss infants or caretaking. Grieshaber points out that their original constructions of fatherhood were not of nurturance, and were highly gendered. Mothers, in contrast, did talk about looking after their infants. Several also discussed their expectations that the fathers would also be involved in these activities. To conclude, Grieshaber saw her research as an exploration the way that expectant parents constructed a gendered infant, as well as a gendered self in the role of a parent.

In another social constructionist analysis, Blaise (2005) observed children performing gender in their kindergarten classroom. She discussed the children's clothing: boys only wore shirts and pants or shorts, whereas girls had many options. One such option was the "girly girl" style. The girly girls wore frilly outfits with matching barrettes and other accessories, many of which were pink. She reports that Holly, a girly girl, informed Madison not to play in the glue table: "That center was gooey and messy. Don't go there, especially if you want your clothes to stay pretty" (Blaise, 2005, p. 93). Of course, when girls wear clothes of this sort, and when they are reluctant to get dirty or messy, then that limits the experiences that they are willing to take part in. Another group of girls were the "cool girls." These girls wore clothing that Blaise suggested belonged more in a nightclub than a kindergarten classroom. They included sophisticated and sexy outfits including low cut tops and boots. Blaise makes the point that in making such clothing choices, children are doing or performing gender.

Girls often talked about makeup, appearance and beauty, and getting boyfriends (recall that these children were in kindergarten!). Their pretend play focused a great deal on these kinds of themes. Blaise's analysis of boys' gender performance centered on their denigration of beauty, fashion, anything associated with girls or femininity, and in their imaginary play as powerful superheroes.

There are also examples of developmental psychologists using the quantitative methods most common to our discipline, yet organizing the findings in a social constructionist framework. Robyn Fivush and her colleagues (Adams, Kuebli, Boyle, & Fivush, 1995; Buckner & Fivush, 2000; Fivush, 1989, 2000; Fivush, Brotman, Buckner, & Goodman, 2000; Kuebli, Butler, & Fivush, 1995; Kuebli & Fivush, 1992; Reese & Fivush, 1993; Reese, Haden, & Fivush, 1996) have studied children's interactions with their parents as they talk about past events, especially events involving emotion. Fivush and her colleagues have found differences in how mothers and fathers talk with their children, how boys and girls talk with their parents, and how parents and children of both sexes talk to each other, as well as effects of the particular context. Even when parents and children discuss the same event, they discuss it differently depending on the gender of both the parent and the child. As Fivush puts it, "reminiscing is a gendered activity" (Fivush, 2000, p. 99). Fathers tend to talk less to their children than mothers do, although both talk more with daughters than sons. Parents of both sexes also discuss more aspects of emotional experiences with daughters, especially negative emotional experiences like sadness. However, although sadness is discussed more with daughters, anger is discussed more with sons. By the age of 3 or 4 girls are able to recollect more details of emotional experiences than boys do, and they are more likely to identify sadness as feminine and anger as masculine, which is not terribly surprising given experiences like these.

In one study (Fivush et al., 2000) parents and their 3-year-old children discussed past events in which the child had been happy, sad, angry, and afraid. Parents took part in an interview alone with the child at their home. They were given index cards with the words "happy," "sad," "angry," and "scared" on them, shuffled into random order, and asked to sit with the child and converse naturally about a past event in which the child experienced that emotion. Conversations were tape-recorded, transcribed, and coded. The researchers were interested in three issues: how long was the conversation about each emotion, how many and what kinds of statements were made about the emotional aspects of the experience, and how many emotion words were used. Compared to fathers, mothers had longer conversations with their children, talked more about emotion, used more emotion words, and talked more about the causes of the children's emotions. Both parents talked much more about sadness with daughters, even though boys and girls themselves did not differ in how much they talked about it.

Evaluation of the Social Constructionist Approach

One of the clear strengths of this approach is its emphasis on the extent to which people focus on and emphasize gender in all kinds of circumstances in which it is not the least bit necessary, as in Messner's (2000) example of 4- and 5-year-olds playing soccer. There is really no reason why gender needs to be an issue for young children as they play soccer. The physical skills necessary to play the game are very similar for children in this age range. The behaviors involved in playing the game are the same for both sexes. Team colors, names, coaches and the like do not need to be organized around gender lines. Yet, parents, coaches, and children themselves constructed a gendered experience. More than any other theoretical perspective, the social construction approach focuses our attention on the extent to which this happens. Social constructionists remind us of how frequently gender is socially constructed when there is no compelling reason for it to be.

However, one key criticism that has been leveled against social constructionism as a model of children's gender development is related to its lack of incorporation of biological and evolutionary processes as well as cultural universals. For example, as we have already seen, historically and cross-culturally women do the majority of childcare (Geary, 2000; Kenrick & Luce, 2000). Across a large number of cultures children play in same-gender groups, boys are more aggressive and dominance-oriented in these groups, engage in more rough and tumble play, and girls are more communal and intimate (Best & Williams, 1997; Geary, 1999; Geary & Bjorklund, 2000). Sociologist Richard Udry (2000) has argued that there are biological limits on what can be socially constructed by the genders. He argues for a biosocial model, a model that incorporates biological, socialization, and cultural influences on gender differences. He is particularly convinced that prenatal hormone exposure is the most critical biological factor in putting limits on the social construction of gendered behavior. Eleanor Maccoby (2000), in a recent article summarizing theoretical perspectives on children's gender development, made exactly the same point—that evolutionary and biological approaches must be incorporated in any model of gender development. However, Maccoby also pointed out that there have been huge changes in gender roles in the last century, and these changes are too rapid to be accounted for by biological or genetic factors. Hence, there is a need to also incorporate social and cognitive approaches. Nonetheless, the fact remains that social constructionists often appear to imply that boys and girls are born as equivalent blank slates, only to be constructed into masculine and feminine beings by the culture. That belief is inconsistent with research showing the impact of biological factors on gender development.

Probably the central issue for the evaluation of postmodern and social constructionist approaches is that the philosophical position that all knowledge is socially constructed, even scientific knowledge, puts this approach into conflict with the basic assumptions of modern science (K. J. Gergen, 2001). This issue is not necessarily related to the study of children's development or to the study of gender. In fact, there have been angry and contentious disagreements between scientists and postmodern theorists in several scientific fields (e.g., Gross & Levitt, 1994; Kuznar, 1997; Sokal & Bricmont, 1999). These are not questions that can be resolved with research—they are questions of people's basic belief systems. Do you think that the methods of science can be used to understand the processes of human development? Is there an objective reality that can be discovered, or is all human knowledge socially constructed? Related to these questions is the role of qualitative versus quantitative research. Those scientists who accept the premise that rigorous scientific research can lead to objective information about human behavior and development, often see qualitative research as methodologically less rigorous, rather like interesting pilot studies that one can use to generate ideas that need to be systematically studied quantitatively. At this point, a reasonable conclusion is that social constructionist approaches have generated very little research on children's gender development in mainstream developmental psychology, but of course they may in the future.

CHAPTER SUMMARY

In this chapter we have examined five social and cultural theoretical approaches to the study of children's gender development: psychoanalytic theory, learning and social learning theory, social role theory, ecological theory, and social constructionist theory. Psychoanalytic theory, in its original Freudian version, proposed that children develop masculine and feminine traits and roles by identifying with their parent of the same sex. Chodorow's modern, feminist version of psychoanalytic theory proposes that children's gender development is affected by being cared for primarily by their mothers, hence girls learn to connect with their caretaker and boys learn to distance themselves from her. Although there is some support for the notion that when fathers are involved in caring for young children, there are more equal relations between the sexes, and less devaluation of women, there are multiple factors that influence both father care and relations between males and females. In general, empirical research has not been very supportive of either of these versions of psychoanalytic theory, and neither is a very influential contemporary model of children's gender development within developmental psychology.

Social learning theory, and later social cognitive theory, is an explanation of complex human social behaviors using the principles of learning, such as reinforcement and punishment. In particular, modeling and imitation are thought to be among the most important processes influencing the development of these kinds of behaviors. Because of the emphasis on cognitive processes in the current version of social learning theory, social cognitive theory, we have left our primary discussion of this theory for the following chapter.

Social role theory proposes that gender differences arise primarily because men and women play different social roles, these roles lead to stereotypes, and the stereotypes are expressed in behavior though processes of expectancy confirmation and self-regulation. Much research in social psychology supports the basic ideas of social role theory. Social role theorists propose that children's socialization is linked to these stereotypes and adult roles, and that children also come to be affected by the expectancies of others and to regulate their own behavior to be consistent with gendered expectations. There is developmental research that can be used to support these propositions, however little developmental research has actually been generated by this theoretical approach. The major critiques of social role theory come from evolutionary psychologists, who argue that many sex and gender differences arise from evolutionary pressures to mate and reproduce successfully.

Urie Bronfenbrenner's Ecological Theory holds that children's social development should be seen in context. Children have personal characteristics (including gender), they grow up in families, neighborhoods, schools, and other social institutions, and their development takes place in a cultural and historical context. All of these factors should be taken into account when examining the influences on children's development. This view seems like a very sensible way to look at social development in general, and gender development in particular, but has yet to generate a significant amount of research in this area.

The final theoretical model we discussed was social constructionism and postmodernism. This view takes the position that all knowledge is socially constructed, and that gendered behaviors come about through social construction. People do not have gender, they do gender. One important strength of this approach is that it focuses attention on the extent to which gender is socially constructed. However, little research in developmental psychology has been done within a social constructionist framework. The major criticisms of a social constructionist approach concern the issue of biological limits on social construction. Social constructionists often do not seem to incorporate a place for biological influences. The perspective that is most consistent with the majority of research on children's gender development is a biosocial perspective—one that incorporates many different interacting causal forces affecting the development of boys and girls into masculine and feminine beings.

Cognitive Approaches to Gender Development[1]

8

Yes, I think all girls like dolls. But boys don't. And that's just the way it should be. Because they're girls' things, you see. The police say so. If girls doesn't play with girls' things, her would just go to jail. (Brent, age 4, from Bailey, 1993, p. 46)

So far, we have described theoretical approaches to gender development that focus on causal factors from either biology (chapter 6) or the external social environment (chapter 7). The final chapter in this part of the book describes approaches that focus on causal factors that reside in the child's own cognitive characteristics. As with most divisions in psychology and elsewhere, the boundaries dividing theories into these three chapters are not sharp ones. In particular, there are theories discussed in the current chapter that still give the environment a very heavy role, and thus they could legitimately have been covered in the prior chapter. Still, all the theories we cover here are theories in which cognitive characteristics of children—their interests, their knowledge, their beliefs, their abilities to reason logically, and so on—hold a particularly important role in the way that gender development is said to progress.

TYPES AND QUALITIES OF THEORIES

Cognitive-Environmental Theories

We will cover two major kinds of approaches. We have labeled the first one **cognitive-environmental**. This approach is one that—like the theories discussed in chapter 7—puts a heavy emphasis on the role of the environment. What distinguishes it from the approaches discussed earlier, though, is that it simultaneously assigns great weight to the characteristics of the person who is *in* that environment. The best exemplar of this approach and the one that we discuss in detail here is **social cognitive theory**, which comes out of both traditional **learning theory** and **social learning theory**. As explained in chapter 7, learning theory is an approach in which core learning processes like reinforcement and punishment are hypothesized to apply to all organisms in all contexts. Thus, these processes apply to a rat learning to press a bar in its cage to receive food pellets as well as to an athlete learning how to refine his arm movements on the pitcher's mound to throw a strike. In early work, child psychologists used these learning processes to explain age-linked changes in children's behavior across a wide range of domains (Bijou & Baer, 1961) or to inform interventions (Horowitz & Paden, 1973). Others refined theoretical and empirical work in this tradition and applied it to children's gender development in particular (Bandura, 1977; Bandura & Walters, 1963; Mischel, 1966; 1970).

---

[1] Lynn Liben was the primary author of Chapter 8.

Although early learning theorists held that what was happening in the environment could explain children's behaviors, their later modifications awarded greater theoretical roles to qualities of the children themselves. It is for this reason that we have included their theories in the current chapter. Because the emphasis has been on children's cognitive qualities (rather than, for example, their personalities or emotions), this family of theories has come to be known as social cognitive theory (Bandura, 1986, 1992, 1999, 2001).

Developmental-Constructivist Theories

We have labeled the second set of theories we cover in this chapter as **developmental-constructivist**. Like cognitive environmental theories, these give an important role to individuals' cognitions. But in these theories, the cognitions are of a particular kind—those that are constructed (or created) by individuals themselves. They thus fall under the umbrella of general **constructivist theories** holding that individuals create their own knowledge. The clearest illustration of a constructivist approach is Piagetian theory. Piaget's basic premise was that children create or construct their own knowledge via their interactions with the physical and social world (Piaget, 1970). When the developmental constructive process is focused on gender, the approach is labeled **gender constructivism** (Liben & Bigler, 2002).

Within the section on the developmental-constructivist approach, we will cover theories of three types: cognitive stage theories, schema theories, and intergroup theories. The first of these emphasizes the importance of underlying qualitative changes in cognition. These are changes in logical reasoning processes that affect children's understanding of the physical world, how they think about time and space, about their social worlds, and so on. Among the domains to which these processes are applied is gender. The best-known and most fully articulated theory in this tradition, and the one discussed in this chapter, is Kohlberg's (1966). Within the literature on gender development, it is commonly referred to as **cognitive developmental theory** (the term we will use as well), although this terminology is somewhat confusing because Piaget's general theory of cognitive development is also commonly called cognitive-developmental theory.

The second developmental-constructivist theories we cover—schema theories—are those for which the major construct is (not surprisingly) the schema. The term **schema** is used to refer to some internal set of ideas that people have about a domain that organizes the way that they understand, think about, and remember domain-related information. **Gender schema theories** (GSTs) thus concern the ways in which children build and then apply gender schemas to the way they interact with, and then use gender-related material in the environment. We will discuss two schema theories, including, first, the original description of gender schema theory and its extensions (Martin & Halverson, 1981; Martin, Ruble, & Szkrybalo, 2002), and second, a variant on this model that we refer to here as dual-pathway gender schema theory (Liben & Bigler, 2002).

The third developmental-constructivist position we cover is the **intergroup approach**. This approach is also highly constructive insofar as it rests on the premise in social psychology that individuals are active in their attempt to understand the world of human groups and are driven to develop and maintain positive views of themselves (Tajfel & Turner, 1986). Although intergroup theories described within social psychology largely ignored issues of development, some concepts from intergroup theory have long played a role in developmental work. Illustrative is the "in-group versus out-group" distinction that—as discussed later—is central to gender schema theory (Martin & Halverson, 1981). Recent developmental work has drawn on intergroup theory to focus more explicitly on the formation of groups, particularly with respect to the evolution of social stereotypes and prejudices (Bigler & Liben, 2006, 2007) and on the consequences of such groups for children's beliefs and behaviors (Killen & McKown, 2005; Levy & Killen, 2008; Rutland, 1999; Rutland, Cameron, Milne, & McGeorge, 2005). In this chapter we will cover an exemplar of the former, known as **developmental intergroup theory** (DIT). This theory, like all intergroup theories, is domain general (i.e., designed to explain all forms of group bias), but gender is one of the domains to which it has been applied (see Arthur, Bigler, Liben, Gelman, & Ruble, 2008).

Distinguishing Constructivism and Constructionism

Before leaving our introductory comments about the developmental-constructive theories we will cover, it is important to point out that there are two very similar terms that should not be confused: developmental constructivism and social constructionism. As explained in chapter 7, social constructionism sees the social environment (of a particular era, a particular culture, a particular place) as defining and even creating constructs or ideas such as gender or race. In this view, knowledge, beliefs, and behaviors about gender can be understood only within a given time and place. As we discussed in chapter 7, of particular interest to developmental social constructionists are the ways in which the surrounding social context (family and culture more generally) account for children's gender constructs, roles, and behaviors.

Thus, what both social constructionism and developmental constructivism share is the notion that there is not a singular, unchanging external reality. In both, outcomes in the individual (knowledge, beliefs, and so on) are seen as the consequence of active and changing processes. Where they differ is in the locus of the change and action. For social constructionists, the primary locus is the ever-changing society. So, for example, social constructionists argue that children's beliefs about women directly reflect the images of women that are portrayed in the media; if those images are different in different eras, children's beliefs will be different. In contrast, for developmental constructivists, the locus is the changing (developing) child. Thus, developmental constructivists look to the developing *child's* emerging cognitive processes to explain why beliefs about women change: differences in children's abilities to form and manipulate logical categories could account for differences in beliefs about women. (We should add that although we have used the terms distinctively in this book, others sometimes use the term social constructivism to refer to social constructionism, and thus if you read other sources, you should be careful to determine which meaning is intended.)

Theoretical Versus Empirical Foci

Our final introductory comment for this chapter concerns our coverage of theoretical ideas versus empirical research. The current chapter is designed primarily to introduce you to the major theories of gender development in which children's cognitions have a central role. For the most part, we postpone until chapter 9 our discussion of empirical research on gender cognitions. However, on occasion we include brief descriptions of empirical findings to clarify the theoretical arguments. These empirical examples are given only for the developmental-constructivist approaches because empirical illustrations of the theoretical constructs relevant to the cognitive-environmental approach (e.g., reinforcement, imitation, modeling) were already provided in chapter 7.

THE COGNITIVE ENVIRONMENTAL APPROACH

The Foundations of Learning Theory

Learning theory had a powerful role in psychology for many years. In part, its appeal was the idea that a group of mechanisms (like **reinforcement** and **punishment**) could be used to explain how learning occurs across settings as varied as schools and volleyball courts, across behaviors as varied as reading and hunting for food, and across organisms as varied as rats and humans. Social cognitive theory, as explained earlier, is rooted in learning theory and thus makes heavy theoretical use of basic learning mechanisms. Crucial is the notion that learning and behavioral change occur because of what is encountered in the environment.

Rewards and Punishments

When this approach is applied to the domain of gender, the argument is that boys and girls come to behave differently because the consequences of given behaviors differ for boys and girls. If, for example, a girl and boy each shows their parents or friends their newly polished fingernails, one child is likely to be greeted with smiles and admiration (reward) and the other with dismay and disapproval (punishment). Thus, the mechanisms of reinforcement and punishment are said to play a major role in what behaviors boys and girls acquire (Mischel, 1966), just as they play a major role in what behaviors laboratory animals acquire.

Observational Learning

Learning also occurs through **imitation and modeling**. Undoubtedly the best-known studies of observational learning are those conducted by Albert Bandura and his colleagues using a large, inflatable "Bobo" doll (Bandura, Ross, & Ross, 1961). In these studies, children watched models perform novel actions on the Bobo doll, and were then observed to see whether they would repeat those same novel actions later. In subsequent work using this imitation paradigm ("paradigm" simply refers to a kind of methodology; thus this could also be called an imitation method), researchers manipulated variables such as the model's apparent power, whether the gender of the child and the model matched, and whether the model was performing gender-typical or gender-atypical behaviors. We described some research using this paradigm in chapter 7, and in chapter 9 we will describe some of the implications of the findings for gender development. For now, though, we simply want to discuss the importance of observational learning from the perspective of theory.

What makes observational learning so interesting theoretically is that it can be thought about in two ways. One way to conceptualize observational learning is to emphasize the primary role of the environment. Under this view, the environment is responsible for what is available in the environment for the child to imitate. That is, the environment provides some kinds of models rather than others. For example, the environment exposes children to female models who perform actions associated with preparing dinner and male models who perform actions associated with fixing car motors. If those actions were reversed, boys and girls would end up imitating different behaviors. In addition, one can think about the child's tendency to imitate in the first place as a consequence of environmental contingencies. In this interpretation, the child is assumed to have had earlier experiences of being rewarded for imitating appropriate models, and punished (or ignored) for imitating inappropriate models. These prior experiences not only lead the child to learn particular behaviors that were modeled; they also lead to the more general lesson of the reward value of imitating in general. When applied to gender, this means that eventually girls learn that imitating female models is rewarded. Thus, girls would come to imitate behaviors displayed by female models, even in the absence of specific environmental contingencies rewarding a particular imitative behavior.

A second way to think about observational learning is one that gives a greater role to the individual. Under this interpretation, there is greater focus on the cognitive foundations on which modeling can be based. Consider a case in which a child observes a film of a model pummeling a Bobo doll in a particular way, and then later enacts that same pummeling. The child must have stored a representation of the event, have generalized the imitative function (without needing to experience specific environmental contingencies for the child's ongoing actions), must have deduced the analogy between the model's limbs and movements and the child's own, and so on. Over the years, social learning theory has increasingly come to recognize the role of cognitive factors like these, thus explaining why in its current form it is known as **social cognitive theory** (Bandura, 1986; Bandura, 1992, 1999, 2001).

Influences on Gender Development

Social cognitive theory proposes three major influences on behavior, with interactions among the three. Bandura calls this interaction **triadic reciprocal determinism** (Bandura, 1992, p. 2). A scheme

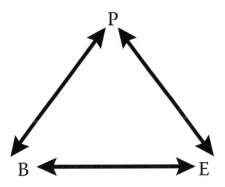

FIGURE 8.1 Schematization of triadic reciprocal determinism. B signifies behavior; P signifies the cognitive, biological, and other internal events that can affect perceptions and actions; and E signifies the external environment. (From Bandura, A., in *Six theories of child development: Revised formulations and current issues*, R. Vasta, ed. (pp. 1–60). Bristol, PA: Jessica Kingsley. With permission. Copyright © 1989 by JAI Press Inc.)

representing this triadic influence is shown in Figure 8.1. The three factors in Bandura's (1992) social cognitive theory are behavior (B), personal cognitions and perceptions (P) (and the factors that influence these perceptions including biological factors), and the external environment (E). Bandura believes that these factors always influence one other, although not always in the same way for every situation or for every behavior. Nor are they always necessarily the same strength, but all three factors are always involved.

Bandura extended his cognitive theoretical model to the study of children's gender development (e.g., Bandura, 1992), giving gender development extensive coverage in collaborative work with Kay Bussey (Bussey & Bandura, 1999). An example from one of Michael Messner's sons illustrates how these three factors might work:

> When he was about three, following a fun day of play with the five-year-old girl next door, he enthusiastically asked me to buy him a Barbie like hers. He was gleeful when I took him to the store and bought him one. When we arrived home his feet had barely hit the pavement getting out of the car before an eight-year-old neighbor boy laughed at him and ridiculed him: "*A Barbie*? Don't you know Barbie is a *girl's toy*?" No amount of parental intervention could counter this devastating peer-induced injunction against boys' playing with Barbie. My son's pleasurable desire for Barbie appeared almost overnight to transform itself into shame and rejection. The doll ended up at the bottom of a heap of toys in the closet. (Messner, 2000, p. 777)

In social cognitive theory, the little boy's behavior (B) could be thought about as consisting of several elements: his original play with dolls at the neighbor girl's house, his request for a doll, his trip to the store to get one, and his eventual rejection of the toy. His personal cognitions (P) include his interest in the toy because he had fun playing with it, his belief that it was a reasonable thing to request, and his ultimate belief that this was not a toy he should be interested in. The environment (E) responded in several ways. First, the little girl provided the toy in the first place, second, his father took him to purchase one, and finally the older boy ridiculed his interest in the toy (who ultimately seemed to wield the most influence). This is an excellent example of how these three factors might interact and influence each other, and it should be easy to see how one of the factors can override others depending on the particular circumstances.

Bussey and Bandura (1999) suggest that there are three main ways that gender development is learned: first, imitation and modeling of gendered behavior; second, experiencing the consequences of the child's own gender-linked behavior; and third, direct teaching of gender roles. For example, children may observe television commercials for toys that are being marketed very differently for boys and girls. Children's own toy choices and even how they play with the toys may be influenced by these commercials, just as children's behavior with a Bobo doll is influenced by the behaviors they had seen being modeled in the videotape. As for consequences for a child's behavior, a young girl may find that she gets a great deal of attention from adults when she is wearing a frilly dress and has her hair done (e.g., "Oh how pretty you look today!"), much more than she gets when she is wearing a practical set of overalls and a ponytail. An example of direct teaching comes from an exchange one of us heard while watching a Little League game. A young boy, about a year and a half old, fell off the bleachers and started to cry. In response, his mother said, albeit quite soothingly, "Stop crying. Big boys don't cry." The impact of experiences like these depends on a variety of factors including the age of the child. Very young children can observe and imitate others, but need language skills to understand explicit instructions or comments about the appropriateness of their behavior.

Types of Environments

Bussey and Bandura (1999) also suggest that there are three kinds of environmental inputs: the **imposed environment**, the **selected environment**, and the **constructed environment**. The imposed environment is that part of the environment that the child cannot choose. For example, children must attend school, and many other aspects of the environment are chosen for children by their parents or others. Some parents send their children to daycare, or to religious training, or to visit their grandparents; they often choose the books, television, toys, and video games that the children have in their homes. The selected environment, on the other hand, is the one that children choose for themselves. Children may pick their own clothing, toys, activities, and playmates, and these aspects of the environment also influence their behavior. For example, if a young girl insists on wearing dresses, it may influence what activities she can engage in on the playground or what motor skills she can learn. If a boy signs up for a class in the martial arts, he is unlikely to develop nurturing skills in that context. The older children become, the more they choose their own activities and interests, and the greater the potential for these choices to further influence their developing interests and skills. Finally, the constructed environment involves what children construct for themselves with respect to what they choose to think about or how they use something in the environment. For example, in a study of children's use of highly stereotyped toys, O'Brien, Huston, and Risley (1983) noted that when boys chose to play with a dollhouse, they incorporated tools into their play (e.g., hammering the doll house roof) about 80% of the time. Thus, although the dollhouse might appear to provide an object that supports traditionally feminine, home-related roles, in actuality, the boys use the dollhouse in a way that supports traditionally masculine, tool-using roles.

Aspects of Gender Development

Bussey and Bandura (1999) argue that the mechanisms of learning and social influence affect four aspects of gender development. The first concerns knowledge and competencies, including behaviors such as how well a child learns to cook, throw a baseball, read a map, feed a baby, or change a flat tire. The second aspect covers the expectations about gendered behavior and roles; for example, one ought to wear makeup or nail polish, spit on a baseball field, or remain out of the work force to care for one's young children. The third aspect of gender development consists of standards to evaluate one's own behavior, for example, thoughts about whether one's own behavior conforms to gendered standards as in wondering if one had been too domineering or competitive, or perhaps too weak.

The fourth aspect of gendered behavior that Bussey and Bandura consider is **self-efficacy beliefs**. Self-efficacy has been a critical aspect of Bandura's recent theorizing (e.g., Bandura, 1999, 2001), and refers to the extent to which people believe that they have control over the events that happen to them, or that they are competent and capable. People might, for example, have varying feelings about their ability to control outcomes in the jobs they get, the power they have over deciding how to spend their day, or their influence over whether they are selected for a sports team or an award. Feelings of self-efficacy interact with gender development in complex ways. As a general rule, girls and women may come to feel more competent in feminine domains and boys and men in masculine domains.

Overall, though, Bussey and Bandura argue that girls feel less control over important outcomes in their lives.

Comparing Social Cognitive Theory to Other Approaches

In summary, social cognitive theory rests on the foundation of learning theory in which the external environment is thought to play the major role in accounting for behavioral outcomes, including those associated with gender development. We have seen that as social learning theory has evolved into social-cognitive learning theory, there is an increasingly greater role assigned to factors that are internal to the individual.

At first glance, it might seem as though adding internal factors like these into learning theory accounts of gender development might completely wash away the boundary between environmentally motivated approaches to gender development and constructive approaches to gender development. To some degree that may be true. That is, even those who emphasize environmental mechanisms to account for gender development—labeled **gender environmentalists** by Liben and Bigler (2002)—recognize that what any given individual brings to the environment plays a role in how that individual is affected by the environment. However, for the most part, the origins of the internal factors are themselves understood as environmentally determined. For example, girls' greater propensity to imitate female rather than male models can itself be traced back to earlier environmental contingencies—that is, to differential rewards and punishments for imitating females' versus males' behaviors. Children are said to develop inner **self-sanctions** (Bussey & Bandura, 1999) but these, too, are explained as internalizations of sanctions that had previously been experienced in the external world. Likewise, their notions of self-efficacy are also sex-linked because of a history of sex-differentiated external supports and encouragement for gender-linked behaviors. Eventually children come to believe that they are more competent in domains that are defined by others as "appropriate" for their sex.

Thus, social-cognitive approaches to gender development are really on the border between gender environmentalism and gender constructivism. Although social cognitive theory assigns an important role to internal factors, the origins of these internal factors are external. The theories we discuss next—under the umbrella of constructivism—also assign an important role to internal factors. However, in these theories the internal mechanisms do not owe their primary origins to the external world, but are instead the product of self-driven, constructive developmental processes.

THE DEVELOPMENTAL CONSTRUCTIVIST APPROACH

Overview

As explained in our introductory comments to this chapter, the theories we discuss in this section are those that have a constructivist foundation. Theories within the category of gender constructivism are those that "emphasize individuals' own constructive processes in the creation and use of gender concepts and behaviors" (Liben & Bigler, 2002, p. 7). These cognitive approaches emphasize "the motivational consequences of gender concepts; the active, self-initiated view of development; and focus on developmental patterns" (Martin et al., 2002, p. 903). As was true for the environmental theories discussed earlier in this chapter, "emphasis" is different from "exclusivity." That is, even theorists who emphasize self-driven, constructive mechanisms by no means deny that the environment plays an important role in gender development. Thus, although the role of self-construction is evident in the theories we cover in this section of the chapter, the environment is not irrelevant. We will cover three major approaches that fit under this umbrella heading, described in the order in which they emerged: cognitive-developmental stage theory, gender schema theory, and finally, intergroup theory.

Kohlberg's Cognitive-Developmental Stage Theory of Gender

Historical Beginnings and Theoretical Contrasts

The groundbreaking volume entitled *The Development of Sex Differences* edited by Eleanor Maccoby (1966; see chapter 2) contained not only the chapter by Mischel on social learning theory described earlier, but also one by Lawrence Kohlberg that described his cognitive-developmental analysis of what he labeled sex-role concepts and attitudes. Early in his chapter, Kohlberg notes that "Oddly enough, our approach to the problems of sexual development starts directly with neither biology nor culture, but with cognition" (Kohlberg, 1966, p. 82). This statement is as interesting for what it denies (biology and culture) as it is for what it offers (cognition) because it reflects Kohlberg's felt need to reject the prevailing notion that the origins of gender outcomes can be attributed to the "interaction between biological givens and cultural values" (p. 82). For Kohlberg—as for Piaget from whom Kohlberg drew his fundamental theoretical premises—the self actively selects from, organizes, and transforms the "aliment" (the metaphorical food or material) that is available in both the physical and social worlds. Again, this position does not deny that both biology and culture have important roles in gender development. But it places the child's own cognitive processes in the driver's seat for determining how gender development progresses.

Thus, Kohlberg's theory, like Bandura's social cognitive theory, stresses the role of cognition. There are, however, two ways in which the treatment of "cognition" differs dramatically between them. The first concerns the origins of cognitions, and the second concerns the mechanisms by which those cognitions evolve.

With respect to origins, for Bandura, cognitions are primarily internal consequences of prior experiences. For example, cognitions might be stored symbolic representations of previously witnessed events (such as how a same-sex model acted with a Bobo doll), or might be rules that have been internalized from prior reinforcements and punishments (e.g., internalized "self-sanctions" developed from how others rewarded or punished the child's gender "appropriate" vs. "inappropriate" behavior). In contrast, for Kohlberg (1966), cognitions are the product of self-driven processes: "In regard to sex-role, these **schemata** that bind events together include concepts of the body, the physical and social world, and general categories of relationship (causality, substantiality, quantity, time, space, logical identity, and inclusion)" (p. 83). In Kohlberg's view, then, children develop gender-related beliefs and behaviors as the result of using their own basic conceptions about the world (including those concerning their own and others' bodies). "Learning is cognitive in the sense that it is selective and internally organized by relational schemata rather than directly reflecting associations of events in the outer world" (Kohlberg, 1966, p. 83).

The two theories also differ with respect to change, that is, with respect to what behaviors or concepts evolve over the life course. Social cognitive theory, like learning theory on which it is founded, begins from the position that there is stability or a steady state, and that change occurs as the result of newly encountered experiences or events that are imposed from the outside. Positions like these fall into the category of **mechanistic theories** (Overton, 1984). These are theories in which machines serve as the metaphor for human development: machines change only as a consequence of the application of an external force. In contrast, cognitive-developmental theory takes movement or change as a given, that is, as something that is entailed in the very nature of the individual. Positions like these fall into the category of **organismic theories** (Overton, 1984). These are theories in which living, biological organisms are the metaphor for human development: living organisms are inherently active. Without activity and change in an organism, there is death. Thus, in this model or metaphor, activity and growth are given; they are premises, not consequences that need to be explained.

Applying an organismic theoretical approach to gender development in particular, Kohlberg (1966) thus posited that there are developmental changes, saying: "sex-role …attitudes change radically with age development. These age changes do not seem to be the result of age-graded sex-role socialization, but rather to be 'natural' changes resulting from general trends of cognitive-social development." He added: "because children's sex-role concepts are essentially defined in universal physical, or body, terms, these concepts, too, undergo universal developmental changes" (p. 83). In short, Kohlberg saw the fundamental developmental changes that take place in a variety of arenas (e.g., physical changes, understanding of causality, logical relations) as playing the most important causal role in the development of gender concepts and attitudes.

The Developmental Course of Gender Constancy

Particularly central to Kohlberg's theory are three cognitive achievements: gender identity, gender stability, and full gender constancy (or gender consistency). Kohlberg (1966) used the term **gender identity** to refer to children's abilities to identify themselves as boys or girls. Today, we would be more inclined to use the term "self-labeling" for this idea and reserve the term "gender identity" to refer to the degree to which individuals feel fully identified and comfortable with their biological sex. (The latter is how the term "gender identity" is used by Egan & Perry, 2001, as mentioned briefly in chapter 1; we will return to this version of gender identity in chapter 9). Being able to identify one's own sex is a critical first step in the cognitive-developmental theory of gender development, and according to Kohlberg, it is accomplished when children are as young as only 2 or 3 years old. Having recognized their own sex, children then seek to do same-sex things, in turn finding that doing them is rewarding. Thus, the theory assumes that sex-typed behavior and attitudes emerge as children recognize their own sex. Using a boy to illustrate the sequence, Kohlberg (1966) summarized the sequence as: "I am a boy, therefore I want to do boy things, therefore the opportunity to do boy things (and to gain approval for doing them) is rewarding" (p. 89).

Kohlberg explicitly contrasted the sequence he suggested to the sequence that had been proposed in Mischel's social learning theory. In the latter, social rewards are viewed as the driving force: "I want rewards, I am rewarded for doing boy things, therefore I want to be a boy" (p. 89). What is centrally different about these two approaches is that in Kohlberg's theory, categorizing oneself as a boy is the critical first step. In the social learning theory approach, the boy need not have even an inkling about his gender categorization. He need only experience a particular set of environmental contingencies (e.g., being punished rather than praised for using nail polish or for crying) to learn to enact boy-like behaviors. Having come to enact boy-like behaviors, he then views himself as a boy. In short, for cognitive-developmental theory, gender identity (i.e., self-categorization as a boy or girl) is viewed as a *cause* for gender-role learning; for social learning theorists, gender identity (correctly seeing oneself as a boy or girl) is a *product* of environmentally controlled gender-role learning.

Even once children know that they are boys or girls, Kohlberg (1966) proposed that it takes another couple of years before they demonstrate mastery of **gender stability**, which refers to understanding the lasting nature of gender. Until children have mastered gender stability—typically somewhere around 4 or 5 years of age—they show confusions about the continuous nature of going from boy to man or girl to woman. That stability is not obvious to very young children is evident from the following anecdote Kohlberg (1966, p. 95) recorded between Jimmy who was just turning 4 and his friend Johnny who was 4.5 years old:

> Johnny: I'm going to be an airplane builder when I grow up.
> Jimmy: When I grow up, I'll be a Mommy.
> Johnny: No, you can't be a Mommy. You have to be a Daddy.
> Jimmy: No, I'm going to be a Mommy.
> Johnny: No, you're not a girl, you can't be a Mommy.
> Jimmy: Yes, I can.

Kohlberg suggests that there is nothing special about this problem. Rather, it simply reflects the child's cognitive limitations more generally: "the cognitive-developmental view holds that the child's difficulties in establishing gender definition closely parallel his difficulties in establishing stable definitions of physical concepts in general and that the former are resolved as the latter are" (Kohlberg, 1966, p. 94).

Finally, the third cognitive achievement is the child's understanding that an individual's gender is fixed, and thus that it remains constant even in the face of various superficial changes in appearance. As discussed in greater detail in chapter 9, the terminology for this last achievement has differed somewhat across sources and investigators. In recent years, the convention is to refer to this final component of understanding as **gender consistency**. Sometimes, however, the term **gender constancy** is used to mean mastery of this highest level of understanding in particular; sometimes the term gender constancy is used to refer to the global construct (encompassing all three levels of understanding). Irrespective of how it is labeled, this third phase of understanding is studied by asking children about gender-category membership of a particular person or doll in the face of changing paraphernalia associated with the other sex. For example, having identified another child as a boy, a participant child might be asked about that other child's sex after a series of transformations such as adding long hair, a skirt, and so on. Kohlberg reported that it was not until the age of about 6 or 7 years that children routinely understood that people of one sex were not changed to the other sex simply as a result of these superficial transformations.

Once again, Kohlberg (1966) attributes children's initial difficulty, and later their understanding of full gender constancy (i.e., gender consistency), to general cognitive development that allows an increasing understanding of transformations in the physical world. Particularly relevant is a growing understanding of **conservation**, commonly illustrated in Piaget's work by reference to liquid quantity (e.g., Piaget, 1970). In a prototypical demonstration, two identical beakers contain identical amounts of liquid, and the child easily judges that they contain the same amount to drink. While the child watches, the liquid from one beaker is then poured into a beaker of a different shape; for example, one that is much thinner and taller than the first. The child is asked whether the two beakers now contain the same amount of liquid or if one or the other has more. Before the age of about 6 or 7, "preoperational" children typically respond that there is more in the thinner beaker on the basis that the liquid level comes up so much higher. After the age of about 7, "concrete operational" children reason that there is still the same amount. They understand that although the liquid level is higher, the beaker is narrower. They understand, too, that there must be the same amount to drink because nothing has been added or removed. The cognitive growth that lets children understand that the liquid quantity remains unchanged despite the superficial transformation (pouring it into a new container) also allows the child to understand that the person's sex remains unchanged despite superficial transformations (e.g., donning a skirt or wig).

Summarizing Kohlberg's Approach

In short, the foundation on which Kohlberg's approach rests is cognitive-developmental theory. He theorizes that children's developing ability to understand deep-level consistency in the face of superficial transformations is a general progression. This progression enables children to understand conservation of gender (i.e., full gender constancy or gender consistency) just as it enables them to understand conservation of liquid quantity. For Kohlberg, the starting point in the process of gender development is children's recognition that they are either boys or girls. Simply identifying one's own gender is enough to begin to motivate the child to learn about and behave in a way that is consistent with that gender. But as children develop gender stability and full gender constancy, the motivation becomes even stronger for children to actively seek out, process, and apply the information about gender that is available in their environments (Martin et al., 2002; Ruble, Martin, & Berenbaum, 2006). The idea of an active information processor is also at the heart of gender schema theory, discussed next.

Schema Theories of Gender Development

Conceptual and Historical Foundations of Schema Theories

In gender schema theories—as in all theories falling under the umbrella of constructivist approaches—the child's own qualities are thought to play an active role in gender outcomes. As we have just seen, in

Kohlberg's cognitive-developmental approach, the primary focus is on how basic cognitive developmental progressions (e.g., coming to understand conservation in general) influence children's information-seeking and resulting knowledge and self-qualities. In gender schematic approaches, the primary focus is on how children's basic understanding of gender and their **gender schemata**—their own attitudes and knowledge about gender—affect their interactions with, and processing of objects, people, or events in the world. Because gender schemata affect the child's cognitive processes like perceiving, interpreting, or remembering gender-related material (i.e., gender-schematic processing), they have profound effects on developmental outcomes more generally. If, for example, gender-schematic processing leads a young girl to believe that all auto mechanics are men, she would then be unlikely, say, to engage in tool-related toy play or mechanical hobbies, unlikely to hang out with people in a workshop, unlikely to take certain courses in school. Ultimately she would not only have little chance of becoming an auto mechanic, but also of pursuing other educational and career opportunities that rely on tool use, mechanics, graphic diagrams, and so on. Thus, even though gender schemata themselves may seem to address relatively limited aspects of human behavior, their effects can be extremely far-reaching.

Gender schema theory is part of a long tradition of constructive approaches to human behavior that have appeared not only in developmental psychology (e.g., Piagetian theory) but also in both social and cognitive psychology. In 1932, for example, Bartlett showed adults social stimuli (drawings of people or stories) and asked them repeatedly to draw or tell what they remembered after minutes, hours, weeks, and even months. When the drawings or stories depicted people and cultures that were strikingly unfamiliar to the participants, over successive attempts, the reproductions became less and less like the originals and more and more like people and stories that would normally be found in their own culture. These changes were thought to be due to the way in which new information is filtered through cognitive schemas. Bartlett showed that people had difficulty remembering materials that were culturally foreign, and that if they were able to remember the material at all, they were likely to distort the material so that it eventually became consistent with their own cultural knowledge and attitudes.

During the 1970s, many cognitive psychologists demonstrated that participants' memories for material could be dramatically altered by manipulating the context in which that material was embedded. A classic study was one in which college students were given a verbal passage and were later asked to reproduce it (Sulin & Dooling, 1974). Some students were told that the passage was about Helen Keller and other students were told that it was about Carol Harris, who was an unknown (fictitious) person. When given memory tests after short (5 minute) or long (week) intervals, students who had been told that the passage was about Helen Keller falsely recognized sentences from the passage that were not actually there, but that made sense for a story about Helen Keller. Similar memory intrusions were not evident in the students who had been given the Carol Harris context. Taken together, these kinds of studies were powerful in demonstrating that people do not just passively absorb material that they encounter. Instead, people actively process that material, transforming it in various ways depending upon their general attitudes and knowledge.

Early research on schematic processing in children followed the same general paradigm, although within developmental psychology a major interest was in how children's progressing concepts would affect their memories. To explore this issue, investigators favored memory stimuli that were related to concepts known to undergo age-linked change. Illustrative are studies in which the stimuli were related to children's growing spatial concepts. For example, young children find it difficult to understand that something can be straight up and down (vertical) when the base is not flat (horizontal), a confusion commonly seen when young children draw tilted chimneys on slanted roof tops, or tilted trees on a hillside. In one study of the power of schematic processing, children were shown an upright flag on a hillside and asked to reproduce it from memory (Liben, 1975). As anticipated, young children commonly reproduced the flagpole as tilted, even though they had just seen the correct vertical picture moments earlier. Their underlying cognitive spatial schemas did not support processing and recall of this seemingly simple perceptual stimulus. Interestingly, if they were asked to reproduce the same stimulus months later, children sometimes produced reproductions that were actually more like the original stimulus than were the drawings they had produced immediately, a change presumed to reflect progression in their underlying spatial concepts (Liben, 1977).

Beginning in the 1970s and 1980s, developmental investigators began to show that children's beliefs about gender affect information processing similarly. Specifically, and as we explain in more detail in chapter 9, investigators found that children have a more difficult time remembering pictures or stories that contradict prevailing gender stereotypes than they do in remembering material that is traditional. For example, children who saw a film portraying doctors and nurses of both sexes were more likely to remember the male nurses as doctors than the reverse (Cordua, McGraw, & Drabman, 1979). Children who saw drawings of men and women engaged in either gender-stereotyped occupations (e.g., a male construction worker) or in counterstereotyped occupations (e.g., a male secretary) were able to recognize or reproduce significantly more of the former than the latter, and were more likely to distort the sex of the character or activity in counterstereotyped pictures (Liben & Signorella, 1980; Martin & Halverson, 1983; Signorella & Liben, 1984). Even when children remembered counterstereotyped pictures they reported being less confident in their own memories (Martin & Halverson, 1983). Studies like these established the power of gender-schematic processing for memory in children.

Gender Schema Theory

The basic model

At the same time that theoretical and empirical work was demonstrating the power of conceptual schemas for children's understanding and remembering material in cognitive domains such as spatial cognition (Liben, 1975) and social domains such as gender (Liben & Signorella, 1980), Martin and Halverson (1981) were developing a "a schematic processing model of sex typing and stereotyping in children" now simply referred to as gender schema theory (GST). Their model is reproduced in Figure 8.2.

This figure presents the illustrative case of a girl encountering a doll. Martin and Halverson (1981) posit that the girl "will decide first that dolls are self-relevant; second, that dolls are 'for girls' and 'I am a girl,' which means that 'dolls are for me'" (p. 1120). Given this evaluation, the girl will then approach the doll and interact with it in various ways, and thereby come to learn more about it, how it may be used, and so on. In this manner, she becomes far more knowledgeable about dolls and thus acquires detailed information about them. In contrast, because she views trucks as for boys and thus not "for me," when she encounters a truck, she avoids it, and thus fails to develop more detailed knowledge about trucks, how they might be played with, operate, and so on.

The roles and definitions of schemas

As might be guessed from the label "gender schema theory" as well as from the focus on the concept of "schema" in the preceding paragraphs, the key construct in Martin and Halverson's (1981) model is the schema. They define schemas as "naïve theories that guide information processing by structuring experiences, regulating behavior, and providing bases for making inferences and interpretations" (p. 1120). Gender schemas are presumed to arise from individuals' tendencies to categorize information, combined with the fact that gender categories are physically salient and are functionally used in the surrounding environment. We will return to the importance of the environmental context in more detail later in the chapter when we discuss intergroup theories.

Martin and Halverson (1981) included two types of gender-related schemas in their model. They called the first an **in-group/out-group schema**, said to consist of the information that "children need to categorize objects, behaviors, traits, and roles as being either for males or for females" (p. 1121). Essentially these schemas contain information about what the culture defines as being appropriate for, or linked to males versus females. We should point out that although Martin and Halverson refer to these as "in-group" and "out-group" schemas, we think that an easier way to think about these would be as "masculine" and "feminine" schemas. One reason for preferring the latter terms here is that their theory is specifically concerned with gender, and thus gender is the dimension along which in-group and out-group is defined. As discussed later when we cover intergroup theories, children may identify themselves as members of in-groups using dimensions that have nothing to do with gender (e.g., as members of groups defined by race, ethnicity, or fans of a given sports team). And although many of the same processes apply as children

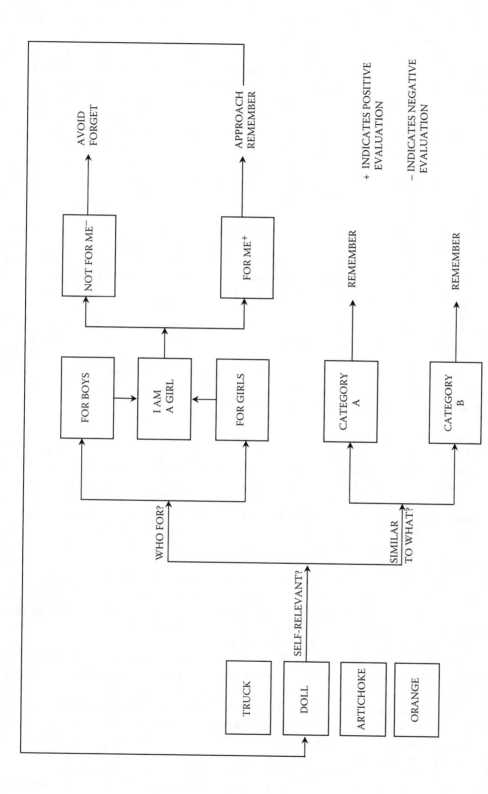

FIGURE 8.2   The schematic-processing model of sex role stereotyping proposed by Martin and Halverson. The figure depicts the processes as they might be expected to function for a girl. (From Martin, C.L. & Halverson, C.F., *Child Development*, 52, 1119–1134, 1981. With permission.)

learn about other kinds of groups, labeling the schemas here as masculine and feminine helps to remind us that we are focusing on gender in particular. In GST, knowing which group one belongs to (e.g., which sex you are) is of central importance for various theoretically important issues (e.g., whether you are likely to engage with or ignore something you encounter in the environment), but even if you are completely outside the dimension entirely, you can still build schemas about masculine and feminine categories.

To make this point, imagine that a creature from Mars (a planet that we are presuming has no gender distinctions!) came to the United States and observed humans' appearance and behaviors. Assuming that the Martian were a good social scientist, it could, with reasonably high accuracy, figure out what the culture defines as appropriate for, or linked to males versus females. For example, the Martian could link some observable physical features of humans to which restaurant bathrooms are used, which type of human uses makeup, plays football, wears high-heeled shoes, and so on. (In the later section of this chapter on intergroup theories it will become clear why Martians would be able to figure out these links, but for now we will simply assert that in our current society it would be possible.) Thus, Martians would be able to develop these masculine versus feminine schemas even though they find themselves completely outside the humanoid groups entirely, and thus, for them, the in-group versus out-group distinction is meaningless (i.e., they belong to neither gender group.) Irrespective of what labels one assigns, however, the key idea is that these schemas in Martin and Halverson's model refer to the child's knowledge about what is for males and what is for females. Thus, the overall schema allows children to make inferences and to form expectations about males and females, in turn influencing social judgments and interactions.

The second type of schema included in Martin and Halverson's (1981) model is the **own-sex schema**, which they describe as "a narrower, more detailed and specific version of the first [i.e., in-group and out-group schema], consisting of the information children have about the objects, behavior, traits, and roles that characterize their own sex" (p. 1121). This schema is explicitly tied to the gender of the child who has it. Martin and Halverson proposed that children develop particularly detailed knowledge in their own-sex schema and far less knowledge about their **other-sex schema**.

Schema-based processing and consequences

To illustrate how both kinds of schemas work together, let us return to the auto mechanic example. The overall in-group/out-group (or masculine/feminine) schema contains the information that fixing cars is an action that is "for males." If the child is a boy and encounters something that is related to fixing a car (for example, his family has stopped at the local station to get a flat tire fixed), he would probably conceptualize what is going on as relevant for him (it would be relevant for his own-sex schema). He would therefore be motivated to pay attention to the drill used to loosen the lug nuts, to how the mechanic removes the tire, gets the soapy water, sprays it on the tire to look for signs of escaping air, patches the nail hole, re-mounts the tire, and so on. Through events like these, the boy would develop more differentiated, richer information about car repair in his own-sex schema. If the same flat-tire scenario had involved a girl rather than a boy, she would also have processed the service station scene as "for boys." But she would have judged the scene to be irrelevant for her. Thus, she would not have been motivated to pay attention to, and thereby add to her knowledge about, repairing tires. As a result, her own-sex schema would not become as detailed and differentiated in the arena of auto repair as would a boy's.

The theoretical construct of the schema—whether drawn from a domain related to cognitive development (e.g., Landis, 1982; Liben, 1975) or gender development (e.g., Liben & Signorella, 1980; Martin & Halverson, 1981)—is hypothesized to affect a range of behaviors and cognitions. For example, in their original presentation of gender schema theory, Martin and Halverson (1981) drew on their theoretical arguments and on a broad range of empirical research to suggest that gender schemas serve to regulate behavior, lead people to organize and attend selectively to information, and facilitate schema-based inferences and interpretations of newly encountered information. They likewise noted that schema-based processing entails some liabilities such as leading to distortions in interpreting or remembering information that is inconsistent with the schema, and to increasing the person's susceptibility to **illusory correlation**; that is, thinking that two things are associated more strongly than they actually are. In chapter 9 we will return to these issues by describing some specific empirical studies that illustrate the powerful effects that gender schema can have on information processing in just these ways.

Cognitive foundations of gender-schematic processing

So far, our discussion of gender schema theory has focused primarily on how the two kinds of schema (i.e., in- and out-group schemas; own- and other-sex schemas) work together to lead children to develop and enact increasingly detailed information about activities, objects, and behaviors that are related to their own sex. As Martin and Halverson (1981) note, however, these processes take as a given that the child tends to (and is able to) group information into categories. For the processes described above to work, children must be able to recognize their own sex, they must also be able to identify others as male or female, and they must be able to systematically sort activities, objects, and behaviors into male and female categories. None of these individual components is easy or automatic.

The first classification challenge concerns children's ability to categorize themselves as male or female. This component of the process is, of course, the focus of Kohlberg's (1966) theorizing about gender constancy reviewed earlier. As already discussed, Kohlberg suggested that children must not only know their gender label (identity), but also know that gender remains the same over time (stability) and despite changes in appearance (consistency or full constancy). Martin and Halverson (1981) focus primarily on the first of these, suggesting that children need only identify themselves as boys or girls (gender identity) to motivate the processes described above. In chapter 9, we will return in more detail to the issues of different levels of gender understanding (i.e., identity, stability, and full constancy); how these levels are most appropriately assessed (i.e., with what measures), and what the empirical evidence has shown about the importance of these different levels of understanding for gender development.

The second classification challenge concerns children's abilities to identify others as members of the male or female categories. Again, we will discuss research relevant to this achievement in some detail in chapter 9. Although under some circumstances even infants seem able to make these distinctions early and accurately, under other circumstances, even older children may find it difficult.

Finally, the third classification issue concerns children's abilities to systematically link things like toys, activities, occupations, clothes, and so on to males and females. Under some circumstances, categorizing may require an understanding of **multiple classification**—the ability to classify objects along two dimensions simultaneously. Multiple classification can be illustrated by considering a scrambled pile of red and blue chips and red and blue balls. Simple classification would involve dividing the pile along a single dimension, as in putting all the red things in one box and all the blue things in another (or as in putting all the chips in one box and all the balls in another). Multiple classification would involve sorting the objects along both color and shape dimensions simultaneously. So, for example, given a box evenly divided into four quadrants, all red objects would be in the top row and all blue objects would be in the bottom row, while, simultaneously, all chips would be in the left column and all balls would be in the right column. Multiple classification is relevant to gender because it allows the child to appreciate simultaneous membership in two categories; for example, that a female fire fighter is simultaneously a member of the category of women and the category of fire fighters. Indeed, correlational data have linked children's immature multiple classification skills to their difficulty remembering gender nontraditional stories; experimental research has shown that when children's multiple classification skills are enhanced through intervention, those children are better able to remember gender nontraditional stories (Bigler & Liben, 1992).

Summarizing and extending early gender schema theory

In summary, in the gender schema theory originally proposed by Martin and Halverson (1981), children are said to come to understand to which gender group they belong, and develop categories that link objects, behaviors, activities, and traits to males or females. Then, when they encounter something in the environment (e.g., an object such as a worm or ribbon, or an action such as throwing a football or knitting), they evaluate whether or not it is or is not relevant to their own gender. If it is, they approach it and develop increasingly differentiated knowledge or skills. If it is not, they avoid it, thereby further distinguishing themselves from members of the other sex.

What should be apparent from the discussion of Martin and Halverson's model is that it is in some ways similar to the one proposed by Kohlberg (1966). The core idea in Kohlberg's theory—the importance of the child's knowledge of being a boy or a girl—is likewise an essential foundation of the model proposed by Martin and Halverson. Furthermore, both the approaches reviewed so far are highly constructive insofar as they view children's new knowledge and behaviors as dependent on what the children themselves do, rather than on what they happen to encounter in the surrounding environment. Both theories explicitly reject the idea that children's knowledge structures, behaviors, skills, and so on are determined directly by the external environment. They differ in their focus with respect to gender understanding, with Kohlberg focusing on the child's sophisticated or complete understanding of gender constancy and Martin and Halverson focusing on children's early identification of their own gender ("I am a girl so I want to be like other girls").

The original formulation described in Martin and Halverson (1981) has been foundational for contemporary work on gender schema theory by Carol Martin, Diane Ruble, and their colleagues. In recent papers summarizing and extending this approach, they (e.g., Martin et al., 2002; Martin & Ruble, 2004) reiterate and refine many of the core ideas of cognitive-developmental approaches already discussed (e.g., the important motivational role of self-identification as a boy or a girl; the active, self-driven nature of gender development, the ways in which children's gender schemas affect how new incoming material is interpreted and remembered), and offer additional empirical evidence for these processes. In addition, they have proposed and begun to investigate empirically a three-phase model of changing gender stereotypes as a function of age. They argue that phase one involves toddlers' and preschoolers' initial learning of gender-related characteristics. In phase two, spanning roughly the ages of 5 to 7 years, children consolidate their stereotypes and thus tend to hold very rigid views about gender. In the final and third phase, which extends beyond middle childhood, children enter a stage of flexibility. As was true in the original presentation of gender schema theory, Martin and Ruble (2004) connect these phases to more general development of cognitive functioning, particularly to children's developing classification skills. It is clear from this and other contemporary research that the ideas generated by Kohlberg in 1966 and by Martin and Halverson in 1981 are continuing to motivate empirical and theoretical work.

Dual Pathway Gender Schema Theory

Basic features of the dual pathway approach

The second gender schema theory we discuss, labeled **dual-pathway gender schema theory**, is in the same general tradition of the gender schema theory described by Martin and Halverson (1981) and developed in later work (Martin et al., 2002). It was first described in a monograph entitled *The Developmental Course of Gender Differentiation* (Liben & Bigler, 2002). Pathway models share core attributes with earlier schema approaches, including: (a) conceptualizing the child as an active participant in determining outcomes rather than a passive recipient of what is in the external environment, (b) assigning a central role to constructive schemas that filter and transform environmental material, and (c) positing a motivational role for the child's gender identity (in the sense of being able to identify one's gender).

Developmental pathways described in Liben and Bigler (2002) extend earlier constructivist approaches in two ways. First, the pathway models make the role of individual differences more explicit than they had been in earlier developmental schema models. Second, they describe in more detail two pathways towards gender differentiation. One is an attitudinal pathway (similar to the gender schema theory of Martin & Halverson), which posits that gender attitudes play a major role in guiding the child's decision about engaging in some behavior (e.g., believing that dolls are "for girls" is likely to lead a girl to play with, and a boy to avoid, a doll). The other is a personal pathway that posits that a child's engagement in some activity will affect the child's attitudes about that activity (e.g., a boy who becomes engaged in ballet will then come to believe that both boys and girls, not only girls, should participate in ballet). Each of these two models is described in more detail below.

The attitudinal pathway model

The key constructs and processes involved in the attitudinal pathway model are shown in Figure 8.3. As noted above, the theoretical approach depicted in this pathway is the one closest to the gender schema theory proposed by Martin and Halverson (1981). The flow of the process of gender differentiation showed here places children's *attitudes* in the key causal position. That is, as in the original Martin and Halverson model, it is the content of the child's gender schemas (containing information about what is appropriate for males and females) that influences whether or not the child engages with something in the environment.

Two **individual difference** constructs are highlighted in the model, shown as "filters" depicted in ovals in Figure 8.3. The first is a gender salience filter that concerns whether or not the child has, activates (that is, calls upon), and uses gender schemas. The reason for including this filter is to model explicitly that children differ in the strength or salience of their gender schemas. It is probably easiest to understand this factor by thinking about people you know as adults. Some people are likely to see almost every interaction and situation through gendered lenses, whereas others seem more or less oblivious to gender—they just do not seem to notice it. As gender researchers, our own gender salience filters are probably particularly strongly developed. When we go to a meeting, we are likely to notice if all or virtually all of the presentations are being given by men. Someone with a less active gender salience filter might well go to the meeting and not even notice the gender distribution of the speakers.

The same kinds of variations are also apparent in children. If you keep yourself attuned to children's behaviors, you may well encounter incidents suggesting children's vigilance to gender. For example, while on a recent camping trip one of us was in the campground bathroom when a mother and her preschool son entered. The boy saw a small sink next to the adult sinks, and he asked if it was for boys. His mother explained, "No this is the girls' bathroom, but you're a little boy, so it's okay." Not satisfied, he said, "No, is *this* for boys?" The mother tried again to explain that it was the girls' bathroom, but increasingly insistent, her son asked "No, no. Is the sink for boys?" Then, she looked at the little sink, and seemed to sort of give up, and said, "Yes, this is a boy sink." This anecdote provides a nice illustration of how some people seem particularly motivated to characterize things, people, and actions they encounter along gendered lines (and perhaps along age-linked lines as well!). In the words of the attitudinal pathway model, this little boy might be said to have a strong gender salience filter. Later in this chapter (when we discuss DIT) we will talk about what kinds of qualities of environments and what kinds of cognitive characteristics of children may differentially encourage dividing the world along gendered lines, but for now, the main point is simply to note that children vary in the degree to which they are attuned to gender categories and thus the degree to which they try to fit what they encounter into those categories.

At the extremes, the distinction among individuals with respect to the propensity to approach the world through gendered lenses is captured well by the concepts of **gender schematic** versus **gender aschematic** individuals proposed by Bem (1981). In her terminology, people who are gender schematic approach the world through gendered lenses. People who are gender aschematic do not. Note that the construct that is being discussed here is about the individual rather than the context. That is, there are also *situations* that are differentially conducive to noticing gender. For example, a woman is more likely to notice gender if she finds herself in a meeting with 25 men and no other women than she would if she finds herself in a meeting in which there are roughly equal numbers of men and women. But some people are generally more or less focused on gender regardless of the situation.

Irrespective of how children end up with differentially strong gender salience filters, once these filters are in place, they are thought to have a profound effect on children's later experiences. As shown in Figure 8.3, when children are deciding whether to engage with some object, person, or event (hereafter abbreviated as OPE) in the environment, those who are gender schematic apply their attitudes about whether that OPE is appropriate for someone of their own sex. Note that the individual-difference construct in this model refers to children's attitudes towards or endorsement of cultural stereotypes rather than to children's knowledge of those cultural stereotypes. As will be discussed in more detail in chapter 9, knowledge comes very early and virtually universally; almost all children come to learn the cultural gender stereotypes, but their attitudes about them vary.

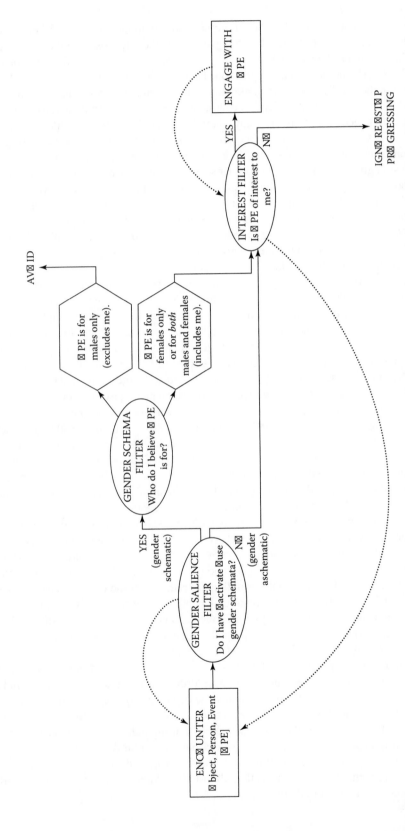

FIGURE 8.3 The attitudinal pathway model illustrated for a female. Constructs in rectangles represent behaviors, those in ellipses represent decision filters, and those in hexagons represent gender schematic cognitions/beliefs. (From Liben, L.S. & Bigler, R.S., *Monographs of the Society for Research in Child Development*, 67, 2, 2002. With permission.)

To continue examining the flow chart shown in Figure 8.3, a child who is gender-schematic thus judges whether a particular OPE is appropriate for someone of his or her sex. If it is not, the child simply avoids the OPE, and that is the end of the environmental engagement. If the OPE is judged to be appropriate for someone of the child's sex, or if the child was gender-aschematic and thus simply bypasses the gender schema filter entirely, the next individual-difference construct comes into play. This is the **interest filter.** The inclusion of this filter in the model highlights that any particular child will find some OPEs more appealing than others, completely apart from anything to do with gender schemas. A given child's idiosyncratic combination of interests would presumably be accounted for by past experiences and the child's particular profile of abilities, personal qualities, and so on. For example, a child might find a tool set interesting to use for building something, not simply in relation to whether the child views the tools as stereotypically male, but also in relation to the child's fine motor skills, spatial skills, attention span, past experiences in woodworking shops, and similar factors.

There are several other noteworthy features of the model shown in Figure 8.3. One is that there are reciprocal associations among constructs shown in the figure as feedback arrows (the dotted lines). For example, the feedback arrow that goes from engagement back to the interest filter implies that the very act of engaging with an OPE will in turn affect interest in it. So, for example, if a child does end up participating in some activity—such as using tools to build something out of wood—the experience is likely to build relevant skills, sense of accomplishment, confidence, and thereby make that child even more likely to engage in the next woodworking opportunity that is available in the environment.

The feedback arrow that goes from the two filters (gender and interest) back to the initial encounter symbolizes that how (or even whether) an OPE is encountered depends on the child's own qualities. That is, OPEs do not simply impose themselves on children who happen to be there. Instead, children selectively engage with different aspects of what is available in the environment. In short, the "environment" is not a fixed entity that is the same for every individual but is instead always something constructed in interaction with the individual. This theoretical orientation would thus reject Bussey and Bandura's (1999) idea that there is an "imposed" environment. That is, in this view, no environment could ever be completely imposed because in this view children are always presumed to be actively selecting and constructing their experiences.

In summary, in the attitudinal pathway model, the child's gender schemas play a powerful role, although these schemata are thought to be differentially operative and differentially strong in different children. There are feedback loops that allow experiences to alter the child's tendency to seek out additional encounters in the environment, and that allow engagement experiences to modify the interest filter. What this model does not, however, provide is a route for affecting the gender schemas themselves. The second model described by Liben and Bigler (2002) provides such a pathway.

The personal pathway model

The second model, called the *personal pathway model,* is shown in Figure 8.4. As you can see from comparing Figures 8.3 and 8.4, the same major constructs appear in both models. The primary differences between the two models concern which factors are given the most central position, and how the various components and mechanisms interact with one another. Whereas in the attitudinal pathway model what is viewed as the most powerful force is the content of child's gender schemata about others, in the personal pathway model what plays the primary role is the profile of the child's own interests and qualities (represented by the interest filter in Figure 8.4). In this model, decisions about whether to approach an object, person, or event offered in the environment are guided first and foremost by the child's own interests. If a particular set of interests lead the child to engage with the OPE, gender may or may not be relevant, depending on whether the child has or activates a gender schema. For children who are gender-aschematic (i.e., those who do not wear gendered lenses and would not, for example, take note that a toy of interest was being played with only by children of the other sex), the child's interest in interacting with the OPE would have no effect on that child's gender schema. The child's interest filter would be changed by the encounter only to the extent that engagement with that OPE had increased or decreased his or her interest in that OPE. (e.g., learning to use a new tool

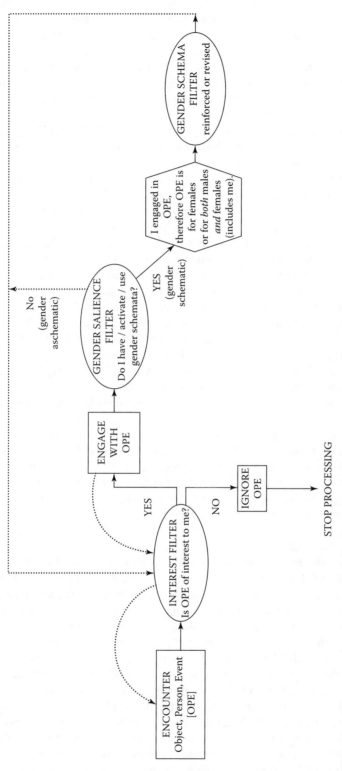

FIGURE 8.4 The personal pathway model illustrated for a female. Constructs in rectangles represent behaviors, those in ellipses represent decision filters, and those in hexagons represent gender schematic cognitions/beliefs. (From Liben, L.S. & Bigler, R.S., *Monographs of the Society for Research in Child Development, 67*, 2, 2002. With permission.)

might open up even more opportunities for engine repair and thus increase interest in auto mechanics even more.)

For children who have active gender schemata, however, their own engagement would also feed into the child's gender schema. That is, the child's own engagement in some OPE would affect beliefs about whether the OPE is for boys or girls in general. It is as though the child reasons: "I did activity X. I know I am a boy. Therefore activity X must be for boys (or for both boys and girls)." Indeed, there is evidence from earlier research that once children find a particular toy appealing, they are likely to assume that others of their own sex will as well (Martin, Eisenbud, & Rose, 1995). In short, an important contribution of the personal pathway model is that it highlights the idea that children's own personal qualities—wherever they may have originated (e.g., in genetic endowment, in earlier experiences)—may ultimately affect their beliefs about others. Liben and Bigler (2002) thus refer to this as the "self-to-other" pathway. The contrast is to the more usual "other-to-self" pathway (as in the attitudinal pathway model) in which the child applies beliefs about others to the self.

As an illustration of how the personal pathway model might work, Liben and Bigler (2002) suggested the case of a boy who during the Christmas season is taken to a performance of the ballet, *The Nutcracker Suite*. Because of his particular qualities (perhaps his own gracefulness, a love of music, pleasure from performing), he finds it appealing, and asks to (and is allowed to) begin ballet classes. If gender is at least somewhat salient for this boy, having participated in ballet and identifying himself as a boy, he would then go on to believe that ballet is "for boys." Even if the boy had initially entered the ballet class with the view that ballet is "for girls only," this experience of personal engagement would be expected to lead to a revision in his gender schema such that he would come to believe that ballet is for *both* boys and girls. Indeed, this is essentially the plot line of the movie *Billy Elliot*, in which a young British boy takes up ballet much to the consternation of his father and older brother. The idea that children's sense of masculinity or femininity can persist unscathed even through the force of nontraditional behaviors or interests is also a position taken by Spence (1984, 1993). In the pathway model, the expectation is not only that the child maintains his or her own sense of masculinity or femininity, but also that the experience may be expected to lead the child to evolve towards having more flexible attitudes about the given OPE.

Liben and Bigler (2002) reported empirical longitudinal data that are consistent with this proposed personal pathway effect. Sixth-grade children were given measures designed to assess their gender attitudes about what men and women "should" do as well as measures designed to assess the degree to which the child's own personal qualities or interests were gender traditional. Both measures drew items from the domains of occupations, activities, and traits (as explained in more detail in chapter 9). For example, using an item drawn from the occupational domain, a question aimed at assessing the child's attitudes would be: "Who should be a plumber? Only men, only women, or both men and women?" and a question aimed at assessing the child's own interests would be: "How much would you want to be a plumber? Not at all, not much, some, or very much?" These same children were given these attitudinal and self measures 4 times over a 2-year period. The data from the boys showed a pattern consistent with the self-to-other pathway specified in the personal pathway model. That is, although there was no initial link between boys' responses on the attitude measure (their gender stereotypes) and their responses on the personal measure (their own interests), there was a longitudinal effect. Specifically, boys who early in sixth grade endorsed greater numbers of traditionally feminine traits as self-descriptive went on to evidence more flexible gender attitudes towards others by the end of seventh grade.

In summary, the pathway models are compatible with the qualities of other constructivist gender theories in general, and with the gender schema theory of Martin and Halverson (1981) in particular. What they make more salient than earlier theories are the roles of individual differences among children, and the routes by which children's own personal interests, behaviors, and qualities may affect gender attitudes. The attitudinal and personal pathways are not conceptualized as mutually exclusive alternatives, but rather as co-occurring processes that collectively and simultaneously contribute to gender development.

Interestingly, there is a core (and critical) assumption in both groups of developmental-constructive theories discussed so far that often goes unnoticed. This assumption is that gender is a salient dimension for categorizing behaviors of others and self in the first place. But one may step back and ask why gender categories assume so much importance. The final developmental-constructive approach to gender development we discuss—intergroup theory—addresses the ways that children's constructive processes interact with environmental conditions to make gender so important.

Intergroup Theories

The Origins of Intergroup Theory

The final approach we cover in this chapter is under the umbrella of intergroup theories. These theories originated with the work of a European psychologist, Henri Tajfel. World War II drew researchers' attention to group conflict. Many researchers were interested in the question of how stereotypes and prejudices could develop so strongly as to fuel the kind of hatred that resulted in the Holocaust. Although most researchers of the era focused on the role of emotion, Tajfel hypothesized that cognitive factors played a role in intergroup biases. He and his colleagues (Tajfel, Billig, Bundy, & Flament, 1971) conducted a series of studies in the late 1960s and 1970s demonstrating that the categorization of individuals into groups—even groups that were created in random or meaningless ways—was sufficient to produce bias. For example, people were given a task in which they were asked to estimate the number of dots on a page. After a few chances to estimate dots, some people were informed that they were over-estimators and others were informed that they were under-estimators. In actuality, labeling someone as an over- or underestimator was determined randomly by the researcher. Participants were then given an opportunity to distribute money or rewards to others for doing the estimation task. When participants allocated the rewards, they did it in a way that systematically favored their own group. This was true even when the people making the allocations did not, themselves, benefit directly. Thus, their behavior could not be explained by simple selfishness. The research methodology that Tajfel and his colleagues developed—creating novel groups by experimental assignment—and the theories they generated to explain the data, dominated the study of stereotyping and prejudice in social psychology for decades.

At the core of intergroup theory is the belief that characteristics that are internal to individuals—particularly the inherent need for positive self-regard—lead individuals to perceive groups to which they belong (in-groups) as superior to groups to which they do not belong (out-groups). Such a view is constructivist because it holds that these beliefs are internally generated, not explained by the environmental information supporting the beliefs. The theory simultaneously posited that the environment provided an important trigger of bias by influencing the process of categorization. A particular person might be valued in one situation because in that context the person is categorized as an in-group member (e.g., as a fellow American soldier on the battlefield) and yet discriminated against in another situation because that same person is categorized as an out-group member (e.g., as a sole representative of a minority racial/ethnic group attending a social function).

Several decades of research have generated a great deal of knowledge about the conditions that lead to intergroup biases among adolescents and adults. Early research established that competition between novel groups promotes biases (as in the well-known "Robber's Cave" study by Sherif, Harvey, White, Hood, & Sherif, 1954/1961 discussed in chapter 11). Intergroup theories have generally been applied to understanding the formation and consequences of groups typically thought of as social in origin (such as Democrats and Republicans) rather than to understanding groups often thought of as natural in origin (such as gender). In addition, intergroup theories formulated within social psychology have largely ignored issues of development. Both these limitations have meant that historically, intergroup theorists have rarely addressed gender development.

Increasingly, however, concepts from intergroup theory have been incorporated by developmental psychologists into the way that they approach gender development. As noted earlier, for example, the in-group versus out-group distinction has a central role in gender schema theory (Martin & Halverson, 1981). Still more recently, intergroup theory has been used to guide experimental research on the way that children acquire a sense of identity as members of a particular group and distance themselves from those who are outside their group (Bigler, Jones, & Lobliner, 1997, see chapter 11). Intergroup theory has also informed correlational research on the existence and consequences of children's groups based on dimensions such as race, nationality, and team loyalty (Abrams, Rutland, & Cameron, 2003; Killen & McKown, 2005; Levy & Killen, 2008) in addition to those based on gender (Arthur et al., 2008; Powlishta, 1995). Below we discuss one developmental theory in the intergroup tradition, describing its key tenets and its relevance for gender development.

Developmental Intergroup Theory

The foundations and goals of developmental intergroup theory
In this section we describe DIT (Bigler & Liben, 2006, 2007). As in other intergroup approaches rooted in social psychology, DIT begins with the observation that social categories play an important role in how people think about themselves as well as how they think about and interact with others. Indeed, social group categories are important from virtually all theoretical perspectives. They provide the very foundation for constructs like in-group, out-group, own-sex schemas, and gender stereotypes that are central to the constructivist theories discussed already. They are also implicitly involved in the social cognitive view of gender development because social categories lie beneath whether someone identifies someone else in the environment as being matched to, or not matched to, oneself, and thus as being someone who should be imitated or ignored.

When approached from a developmental perspective, though, an important question is why particular groups take on importance in the first place. That is, why do some kinds of human qualities (e.g., skin color, biological sex, religious group, political party) get selected as qualities that define social groups that, in turn, affect people's self-definitions, behaviors, attitudes, prejudices, and social interactions? It is important to interject here that although intergroup theory (and its developmental version) is directed primarily to understanding stereotypes and prejudices in particular, the consequences of stereotypes and prejudices are broad. We made this point earlier when discussing gender-schematic processing using the example of the young girl who avoids playing with toy tools because of gender stereotypes. We noted that through a series of intermediary steps (e.g., less experience in later life with real tools, avoidance of certain educational experiences, dismissing certain kinds of careers, and so on), the consequences of even seemingly narrow gender stereotypes can be huge.

The same is true for the kinds of stereotypes and prejudices studied by intergroup theorists. That is, stereotypes and prejudices are important not simply because people carry around attitudes that affect the way they think about various social groups, but also because they result in people having very different experiences and life goals. One particularly dramatic illustration of the far-reaching nature of stereotypes and prejudices may be found in the phenomenon known as **stereotype threat**, discussed in chapter 4. When people feel threatened by the knowledge that others hold expectations or prejudices about them, they evidence changes in their own behavior (e.g., Steele & Aronson, 1995). Furthermore, prejudices often prevent people from having certain kinds of experiences and opportunities, as when girls were officially excluded from shop courses, and boys were officially excluded from home economics courses. Thus, although these theories focus on a highly defined topic, they are relevant to a wide array of phenomena.

DIT proposes that there are two broad kinds of factors that have an impact on the emergence of stereotypes and prejudices. One is linked to the environmental conditions the child experiences; the other is linked to the constructive processes associated with the child's developing cognitive skills. Insofar as DIT identifies the environmental context as important, it is reminiscent of social-cognitive theory. Insofar as DIT identifies self-motivated, active mechanisms of developmental cognition as important, it is reminiscent of cognitive-developmental and gender schema theories.

DIT was designed to be domain-general rather than domain specific. Within the sub-discipline of developmental psychology (albeit not within the sub-discipline of social psychology), this generality is unusual. That is, much work in developmental psychology focuses on developmental outcomes in a single kind of social category (e.g., race or gender), often suggesting theoretical mechanisms relevant to only a particular group, for example, groups defined by gender, race, obesity, sexual orientation, nationality, and so on. The literatures they tend to draw from are thus often specialized, and sometimes the kinds of explanations they propose can sensibly apply to only the particular group studied. For example, some have suggested that prejudice towards African Americans and blackness may be linked to fear of darkness and night (Williams & Morland, 1976) or that the propensity to categorize others by sex or body type is fueled by an evolutionary drive towards finding healthy reproductive partners (Buss, 1994). Mechanisms like these are not broadly applicable across different social groups or prejudices. Although not denying that group-specific mechanisms may exist, the focus of DIT is on identifying general conditions that foster stereotypes and prejudice irrespective of the basis of the particular group.

In summary, the goal of DIT is to outline the processes by which children come to form social stereotypes and prejudices. It is designed to be domain general (i.e., addressing the formation of stereotypes and prejudices across different kinds of social groups); it suggests the importance of interactions between environments and individuals; and it addresses the ways in which developmental changes in those individuals have a profound impact on how these processes operate. Although DIT was developed and initially described as a domain general approach (Bigler & Liben, 2006, 2007), it can also be applied to specific groups in particular, including the one relevant to this book—groups defined by gender (Arthur et al., 2008). Thus, in the remainder of this section, we will discuss the general mechanisms proposed in DIT drawing our examples of how DIT operates primarily from the realm of gender. Examples of how intergroup mechanisms work in other arenas (e.g., race, nationalities) may be found in the original description of DIT (Bigler & Liben, 2006) as well as in other research in the intergroup tradition (e.g., Killen, Lee-Kim, McGlothlin, & Stangor, 2002; Killen & McKown, 2005; Levy & Killen, 2008; Rutland, 1999; Rutland et al., 2005).

The environmental conditions that make social groups salient

The DIT model concerns both the formation of social stereotypes and prejudices (see Figure 8.5) and the maintenance or modification of social stereotypes and prejudice (see Figure 8.6).

The first step is establishing the psychological salience of particular person attributes. The very existence of this construct conveys the core premise of DIT, namely that attributes of people—qualities such as skin color, hair color, sex, or body build—do not *automatically* or *inherently* carry psychological salience (that is, they are not necessarily particularly noticeable or noteworthy to others). Instead, they must become salient in some way.

One factor relevant to which person-qualities become psychologically salient is the degree to which the qualities are perceptually discriminable, or easy to see. So, for example, skin color is more likely to be a psychologically salient basis for grouping than religion because the former is visually more obvious. How perceptually discriminable is gender? As we will discuss in chapter 9 and as reported in other reviews (Martin et al., 2002), research has shown that even infants can distinguish men and women, but it is not yet clear whether this is accomplished by seeing biologically given perceptual cues or by distinct cultural markers. Irrespective of whether the data eventually lead to the conclusion that even very young children are sensitive to perceptual cues that mark biological sex, it is undoubtedly true that cultures routinely exaggerate visible differences by paraphernalia such as different clothing, hairstyles, make up, and ornaments (Arthur et al., 2008). In light of these markers, DIT would argue that gender is particularly well poised to become a psychologically salient basis for categorization.

A second factor is proportional group size, which suggests that a person-quality marked by numerical imbalance is likely to be psychologically salient. Given that the proportion of males and females in the population at large is roughly equal, this factor might seem unlikely to render gender salient for creating social stereotypes and prejudice. However, for many important aspects of their lives, children are in gender-imbalanced contexts. For example, school facilities (especially those for younger children such as daycare centers) are staffed largely by women, and activities (e.g., ballet classes, scouting, and sports teams) tend to be highly gender segregated. These contexts are thus also conducive to enhancing the psychological salience of gender.

A third factor is explicit labeling and use. When others in the environment label or explicitly use a quality to organize the environment in some way, its psychological salience increases. It is particularly easy to see the operation of this mechanism in the case of gender. For example, many languages

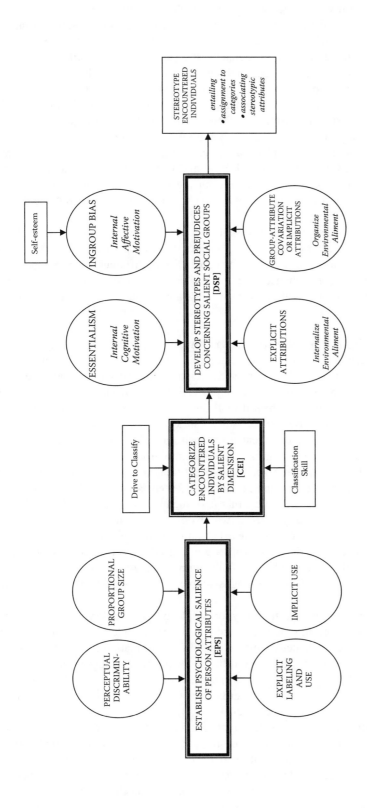

FIGURE 8.5 The processes involved in the formation of social stereotypes and prejudice as described by DIT. (From Bigler, R.S. & Liben, L.S., in *Advances in child development and behavior*, Vol. 34, R.V. Kail, ed., pp. 39–89, San Diego, CA: Elsevier, 2006. With permission.)

are filled with gender-based divisions. Even English, which is relatively less gender-marked than, say, French or Spanish, requires distinguishing male and female referents in pronouns. Many specific words likewise include gender markers as in the words "actor" and "actress" or "salesman" and "sales-woman." Even young children are aware of the gender restrictions of gender-marked job titles (Liben, Bigler, & Krogh, 2002). Some languages, like Hebrew, have masculine and feminine forms for all job titles (Shechner, Liben, & Bigler, 2006). Additionally, people often specify gender in passing. In a study of parent-child storybook discussion, for example, Gelman, Taylor, and Nguyen (2004) found that even when there are generic alternatives available (e.g., "You are such a good child!"), parents use gender-specific terminology (e.g., "You are such a good girl!") over half the time. It is not only language but also the functional use of gender that increases the salience of gender. For example, the salience of gender is increased when teachers ask boys and girls to line up separately for recess or alternate explicitly between boys and girls in asking for the week's classroom helper. DIT predicts that both gendered language and functional use of gender will increase the psychological salience of gender as a basis for social grouping.

The fourth factor is implicit use, referring to situations in which there is, on the face of it, sorting along a particular person-quality, but there is neither explicit labeling nor explanation for that sorting. For example, environments in which Black and White people live in different neighborhoods and attend different schools set up conditions to enhance the psychological salience of skin color. Similarly, in the domain of gender, having almost all female daycare workers and all male U.S. presidents enhances the psychological salience of gender.

The role of child qualities in forming social groups and attaching meaning to them

So far, our discussion has been focused on environmental conditions that affect the psychological salience of particular human qualities. But as would be expected given that DIT is discussed under the umbrella of developmental-constructivist theories, children also play an active role in the formation of stereotypes and prejudices. Indeed, children are assumed to be self-motivated learners. They are motivated to categorize the world around them, and thus they use their classification skills to sort individuals into groups, using the qualities that the environment has made salient as the basis for their categorizations.

What moves the child from simply categorizing people into groups to attaching meaning to those groups in the form of beliefs (that is, stereotypes) and affect (that is, prejudice)? One process contributing to children's developing stereotypes and prejudices is **essentialism**. As defined and studied by Gelman (2003), essentialism involves the beliefs that first, members of categories are alike in important ways, including ways that may not yet be known or observable, and second, that there is some underlying causal source for those shared qualities. The latter is the "essence" of being a member of the category, hence the term "essentialism." In chapter 9 we will discuss research showing that young children hold essentialist beliefs about gender. The quote with which we began this chapter is an excellent example of essentialist thinking. The reasoning is simple: girls have particular tastes in toys; girls are just like that.

A second process is **in-group bias**, the tendency for people to favor their own group or in-group. We illustrated this process earlier when introducing intergroup theory: people assigned more rewards and thought more highly of over- versus under-estimators (on the dot estimation task) depending on which group they thought was "theirs." It appears to be difficult for people to believe that other groups are superior to, or even equal to, their own. This process underlies both formal research findings and endless anecdotes about the fierce favoritism that boys and girls, men and women, show to their own sex. Again, we will discuss this process in more detail in chapters 9 and 11.

Also relevant are constructive processes that store or infer generalities from material about social groups that is encountered in the environment. The simplest of these concerns **explicit attributions.** This refers to the process by which children internalize stereotypes that they hear expressed directly by others (parents, media, and peers). This process is closest to direct teaching as described in social learning or social cognitive theory. Again, the opening quotation of the chapter provides an example of explicit statements about boys versus girls that one peer might hear another express, and then internalize.

Observational studies of children's own behavior has indeed documented that children make many explicit verbal statements about gender, virtually all of them reflecting cultural stereotypes (Kowalski & Kanitkar, 2002). Although explicit gender-stereotyped comments by parents appear only very infrequently in laboratory settings (Gelman et al., 2004), this may reflect parents' monitoring their behavior when being observed. Each of us has personally observed parents providing explicit gender-stereotyped lessons to their children. One example mentioned earlier was the mother at the Little League game who said "Stop crying. Big boys don't cry." Another of us recently heard a mother at a family gathering admonishing her son to "Stop crying like a girl." It is clear that children continue to be exposed to explicit and strongly stated gender attributions (e.g., the ones above that convey the message that it is girls, not boys, who cry).

There may be more subtle explicit attributions as well. For example, both adults and peers often use generic noun phrases that characterize social groups as a whole, rather than commenting on a particular individual (Arthur et al., 2008; Gelman et al., 2004). For example, a comment such as "Girls are good at sewing" may lead children to generalize about the link between sex (female) and a characteristic (good at sewing) more readily than a would a more specific comment such as "This girl is good at sewing." Some evidence showing the importance of this kind of language is discussed in chapter 9.

A fourth and final constructive process represented in DIT concerns how children make sense of **group-attribute covariation** or **implicit attributions**. Covariation refers to some attribute (such as an action, trait, or skill) being systematically linked to some group category (here gender). We earlier made the point that DIT posits that covariations will enhance the *salience* of particular qualities for forming social groups. But in addition, DIT proposes that a child exposed to covariations will try to make sense of them, inferring that there must be some reason for the covariations they see. For example, as mentioned earlier, children may notice the perfect covariation between gender and the U.S. presidency. In the absence of teaching children anything explicit about discriminatory laws, opportunities, and practices, they are left to make implicit attributions about the reasons for the observed covariation. In this case children might infer that there must be differences between men and women in intelligence, skills, drive, or other qualities presumed to be relevant to the presidency. Consistent with this expectation, Arthur, Hughes, Patterson, and Bigler (2006) found that young children expressed the belief that the reason there were no female presidents is because women have weaker leadership skills than do men. Many additional illustrations of the avenues by which children are exposed to covariations (e.g., via media, children's books, observing division of labor in their own homes) and the way in which they may interpret these are provided by Arthur et al. (2008).

Maintaining or modifying stereotypes and prejudices

Having formed social stereotypes and prejudices as outlined in Figure 8.5, children then apply these stereotypes and prejudices to each newly encountered individual. Additional processes come into play to maintain or modify these stereotypes and prejudices on the basis of these encounters as shown in Figure 8.6. As should be relatively clear from this figure, when a child encounters someone who is consistent with existing beliefs (e.g., a female nurse or male construction worker), the encounter simply strengthens the prior schema or existing set of stereotypes or prejudices. When, however, a child encounters someone who is inconsistent with stereotypes, the outcome is different. If the encountered person is not stereotypic and the child's existing stereotypes are applied to that encounter, one possibility is that the encountered individual will either be forgotten altogether, or will be distorted in memory. If distorted to become stereotype consistent, the encounter functions as if it had been stereotype consistent, and thus it, too, strengthens the existing stereotype. The alternative is that the child is able to use more advanced multiple classification skills and thereby encode the seemingly incompatible pieces of information. To revisit an example given earlier, illustrative would be a case in which a child could understand that the person encountered was both a woman and a fire fighter. These expectations are, of course, fully consistent with predictions and data derived from earlier gender schema theory approaches (e.g., Liben & Signorella, 1980; Martin & Halverson, 1981, 1993).

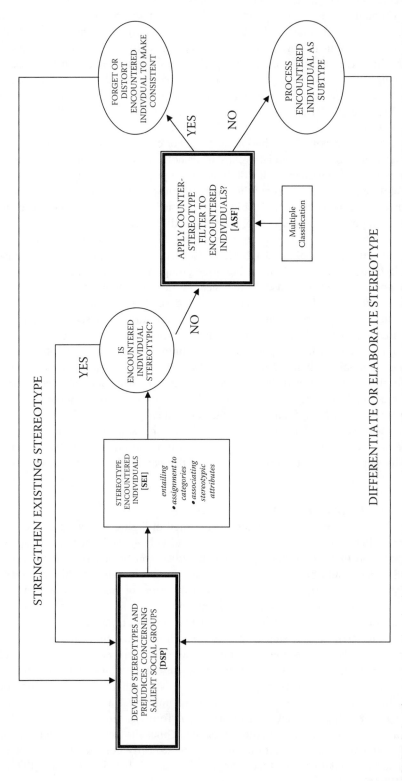

FIGURE 8.6 The processes involved in the maintenance and revision of social stereotypes and prejudice as described by DIT. (From Bigler, R.S. & Liben, L.S., in *Advances in child development and behavior*, Vol. 34, R.V. Kail, ed., pp. 39–89, San Diego, CA: Elsevier, 2006. With permission.)

Concluding Comments About Developmental-Constructivist Theories

As a group, the theories we have covered in this section all conceptualize children as active agents in their own gender development. Social cognitive learning theory, too, recognizes that the child's own qualities will have an effect on the impact of the environment (e.g., acknowledging that the child's own gender will affect the likelihood of imitating a male vs. a female model provided by the environment). In this view, child qualities are important primarily because they set conditions (prerequisites) for environmental input. The role of the child's qualities in constructive theories is more dynamic. Children's gender schemas control not only whether environmental stimuli are attended to, but also the way in which they are processed. Cognitive schemas can distort external information so that the environment "as understood" or the environment "as remembered" is very different from the environment "as is." The child's own cognitive processes and attitudinal schemas are contributors to the way that gender is conceptualized and thus to the way that the child ultimately behaves.

CHAPTER SUMMARY

In this chapter we have reviewed theories in which children's own cognitive characteristics are thought to play a major role in the way that gender development proceeds. These theories do not deny the importance of biological influences or the role of environmental factors. But compared to theories reviewed earlier in this book, they do place more emphasis on children themselves in determining gender outcomes.

Within this chapter, the broadest level division we made was between the cognitive-environmental approach and the developmental-constructivist approach. The former is an approach that bridges between the learning theories covered in chapter 7 and the child-driven constructivist approaches discussed in the second part of the current chapter. It posits a strong role for environmental experiences (as in learning theory) but it simultaneously recognizes that the impact of that environment will be influenced by the cognitive qualities of the person experiencing that environment. The best representative of this approach is the work of Bussey and Bandura (1999). They identified three major routes by which children develop their gendered behaviors, interests, and beliefs: first, by imitating behaviors of same-sex models; second, by experiencing consequences that come from their enacting behaviors that are differentially associated with their own or the other gender in our society; and third, by learning from direct instruction from adults or peers about what is and is not appropriate for their sex. Findings from research studies evaluating this approach are described in both earlier and later chapters, and provide considerable support for the mechanisms identified by Bandura and Bussey.

The theories discussed under the term "developmental-constructivist" assign an even greater role to the child in gender development. We began by reviewing the stage theory approach developed by Kohlberg almost half a century ago. What are probably the most noteworthy aspects of Kohlberg's (1966) theory are first, that he placed in such a central theoretical position children's cognitions or understanding about gender (most importantly, the idea of gender constancy); and second, that he approached children's developing concepts of gender as a reflection of more general cognitive development. In other words, he suggested that the child's gender development could be understood as a particular case of cognitive development (e.g., developing understanding of classification or categorization; developing understanding of conservation).

The second group of developmental-constructivist theories we discussed were gender schema theories. After describing some of the early research in social and cognitive psychology that established the role that individuals' schemas have for the way that experiences are understood and remembered, we turned to discussions of schematic processes in children's gender development. First, we reviewed the gender schema theory initially proposed by Martin and Halverson (1981). They suggested that children develop knowledge about what is for boys versus girls and, having identified themselves as members of the category of boys or girls, pay greater attention to information that is related to their own sex than to the other sex. As in schema theories that have been proposed to underlie processing of other kinds of cognitive and social information, GST holds that these gender schemas likewise support better memory for own-sex information, thereby further expanding the richness and repertoire of own-sex schemata.

Next we described dual-pathway models (Liben & Bigler, 2002), which are consistent with GST, but make two features of the constructive process more salient. First, the dual-pathway models explicitly identify the role of individual differences in the model. Second, and as implied by the dual label and by the presentation of two flowcharts, they make two pathways of gender development explicit. The attitudinal pathway is similar to that modeled by Martin and Halverson (1981). Children are thought to combine their knowledge of what is culturally defined as for girls versus for boys with knowledge of their own gender to decide how to act (i.e., whether to pursue boy things or girl things). This is labeled the other-to-self direction because it proposes that knowledge about how others behave influences the child's own behaviors. The personal pathway model posits the reverse route. Here, the child is assumed to act in certain ways or pursue certain interests because of some idiosyncratic talents or experiences, and then to use those actions or interests to develop attitudes about what is associated with boys or girls more generally.

The last theoretical approach, intergroup theory, was rooted in work by social psychologists Tajfel and Sherif, who showed how prejudices could be generated by establishing groups. Researchers began using key concepts from an intergroup perspective as part of their theories of gender development quite early (Martin & Halverson, 1981), with more recent work continuing to blend approaches from social psychology and developmental psychology more fully (e.g., Bigler & Liben, 2006, 2007; Levy & Killen, 2008). We reviewed both environmental and cognitive-developmental factors that have been hypothesized to contribute to the generation and maintenance of stereotypes and prejudices.

The theories we have covered in this chapter have many qualities in common. They all attribute some important part of gender development to qualities of children themselves. At the same time, they all recognize that children are not growing up in a vacuum, and that the surrounding context also plays a powerful role on gender outcomes. In a sense, all approaches discussed in this chapter acknowledge what any contemporary developmental psychologist acknowledges, which is that developmental outcomes are the result of a complex interplay among biology, experience, and self-directed processes.

Although the theoretical approaches we have described in this chapter share a commitment to the importance of multiple factors, they emphasize somewhat different processes. Furthermore, the way they interpret the same factor differs. For example, both the cognitive-environmental approach and the developmental-constructive approach identify the role of children's own cognitions as an important factor. In the former, however, these cognitions are conceptualized as largely environmentally determined on the basis of past experiential histories. In the latter, these cognitions are conceptualized as emerging from highly active, self-directive processes. Because the different theories emphasize different critical mechanisms, they tend to design somewhat different kinds of empirical tests, as will be evident in the next chapter, in which we discuss research on the ways that children's gender cognitions affect their own gender development.

The Cognitive Self as an Agent of Gender Development[1]

9

A father and son were in a terrible car accident. The father was killed at the scene of the accident. The boy sustained a serious head injury and was taken by ambulance to the hospital. As he was being wheeled into emergency surgery, the neurosurgeon looked at the stretcher and said "Oh my God! That's my son."

Does this story make logical sense? If you were not caught by the trap of reflexively assuming that neurosurgeons are men, presumably you had no difficulty interpreting the vignette. But even if you avoided this trap, you can be confident that many fellow readers—even in the 21st century—will be puzzled by the story. Just a decade or two ago, it would have been the exception, not the rule, to have concluded immediately and effortlessly that the neurosurgeon was the boy's mother. It was within this time frame that one of us told this story at a family gathering. With a single exception (someone who had received her medical degree in 1939), everyone was stumped. They guessed that perhaps the doctor was the sperm donor, a stepfather, and offered several other completely illogical possibilities.

We begin this chapter with this personal story for two reasons. First, it shows the powerful effect that the broader cultural context can have, even when there is contradictory personal experience. The family members described above had, after all, been living with a female doctor in their midst for decades, and yet they fell into the trap of having the cultural stereotype that doctors are men overshadow their ability to draw a logical conclusion. Second, it provides an excellent example of the ways in which the information and events available in any particular environment do not simply get absorbed and used by all people in some single, fixed way. Instead, environmental information and events are interpreted and used differently depending on the cognitive qualities and past experiences of the individuals encountering them. In this case, the same stimulus (a brief story) was interpreted correctly by one person and incorrectly by everyone else, even though all may be presumed to have had the general cognitive capacity needed to understand it.

The purpose of this chapter is to review empirical research on children's gender-relevant cognitive qualities, and to show how these cognitions have an impact on children's own further gender development. Note that in this chapter, we are not asking what accounts for children's gender-relevant cognitive qualities. Some of those qualities are themselves the product of the gender-development mechanisms that we discussed earlier in the book or the product of mechanisms that we will discuss in later chapters. Instead, in this chapter we are asking how a particular child's gender-related knowledge, beliefs, or general cognitive qualities influence what that child takes from further experiences that are encountered in life. This is what we mean by referring to the cognitive self as an "agent" of gender development.

We should note that there are other ways that one might approach the question of how individuals, themselves, contribute to their own development. For example, one might ask how biological qualities of the child (e.g., the child's genetic endowment, levels of prenatal exposure to testosterone, physiological changes associated with puberty) affect gender outcomes. Or, one might ask how qualities or behaviors of the child serve as agents of other children's gender development. Research relevant to the former is

---

[1] Lynn Liben was the primary author of chapter 9.

discussed in chapter 6; research relevant to the latter is discussed in chapter 11. Here, though, we are focusing on how self-related cognitions affect further gender development.

Before turning to the topic itself, we would like to explain why we have placed the "self" agent at the beginning of Part IV of the book, which covers several agents of gender development. We did so because we believe that children's cognitive qualities affect the impact of the other agents covered in subsequent chapters—family, peers, schools, and media. Of course, the very qualities of any particular child are themselves, in part, a product of past exposure to those other external agents. Thus, we could just as reasonably have placed the self chapter last. This dilemma is really just another demonstration of a general point we have made and will continue to make in this book, namely that the various processes we discuss are reciprocal and interactive ones, not linear and independent ones. But, because we have to begin somewhere, we have chosen to begin with the self who—at least from the perspective of developmental psychology—is at the center of our attention (e.g., see Bronfenbrenner's model shown in Figure 7.2), and is always present even as other agents (family, peers, media, school) come and go.

In the next three sections of the chapter we discuss the emergence and development of three major kinds of gender cognitions. Specifically, we first discuss evidence concerning children's gender categories—their abilities or tendencies to divide people into distinct male and female groups. Second, we discuss children's gender concepts; that is, how children think about gender. Third, we discuss children's developing knowledge and beliefs about gender correlates; that is, what children believe is related to being male versus female. In the final two sections of the chapter, we discuss research on the consequences of gender cognitions. Within these sections, we first discuss ways that components of information processing—attention, encoding, and memory—are affected by a range of gender cognitions. Finally, we discuss ways that one gender cognition in particular—gender constancy—has been linked to other aspects of development.

GENDER CATEGORIES

Introduction

There is an implicit assumption underlying much of what is discussed in this entire book that it is easy and common to categorize individuals as being male or female. If, for example, adults did not see an individual child as being either a boy or girl, how would they know whether to respond with delight or horror at a particular child's polished nails? If a child did not somehow carry knowledge that he was a boy or she was a girl, how would that child gravitate towards children of the same sex as playmates or attend in greater intensity to own-sex rather than other-sex behaviors? As should be clear from earlier parts of the book, there are competing theories about how these differentiations are made, including whether they are somehow hard-wired into our biological systems or learned as a result of exposure to the functional use that is made of gender in the surrounding environment. But at the level of description (i.e., entirely apart from theoretical explanation), is there evidence that young children can distinguish males from females, and if so, how early can it be accomplished and what cues are used? In the following section we discuss research addressed to these questions.

Empirical Study of Gender Categorization

Exploring Gender Categorization in Infants

Researchers have long been intrigued by whether infants categorize human beings into two gender groups. Because infants cannot be asked directly to do something such as sort pictures of people into two piles, investigators have had to develop nonverbal methods to test infants' tendencies to organize objects and people into categories. In this section, we describe the methods and findings from research on infant gender categorization.

Habituation methodology

A common methodology for testing infants' abilities or tendencies to categorize is the **habituation** method, introduced in chapter 5. This method is based on the fact that individuals—including babies—get bored when they see the same thing over and over again. Thus, when shown the same stimulus (picture, object, or event) repeatedly, infants gradually show less and less interest in it. In other words, they habituate to the stimulus. Habituation can be assessed by changes in physiology (e.g., a change in heart rate) or more simply, by changes in looking.

For example, if one were to show an infant a series of photographs of cats, the infant might look at the first one for some amount of time (e.g., 10 seconds), perhaps about as long to the next novel cat picture, but as each successive new cat picture appeared on the screen, the infant would look at it for a shorter and shorter time. Eventually when a new cat picture appeared, the infant—now completely bored by cats— would look away almost immediately. This infant would be said to have habituated to cats.

What is conceptually important is the idea that in order for the infant to have become bored or habituated in this example, the infant is assumed to have some kind of cat category. Otherwise, each new cat would have been just as interesting as the one before. Once the infant has reached some preset habituation criterion (e.g., looking half as long at the new stimulus than the infant had looked at the first stimulus), a test stimulus (e.g., a dog picture) is shown. The key question is whether the infant's attention recovers; that is, whether the infant looks at the new stimulus rather than looking away. If there is renewed interest (referred to as **dishabituation**), the inference is made that the infant treated the test stimulus as from a different category than the one from which the habituation stimuli had been drawn. By cataloging which categories do and do not lead to the recovery of interest, researchers can determine what kinds of category distinctions infants make (e.g., perhaps distinguishing cats from dogs, but perhaps not hamsters from chipmunks).

Preferred-looking methodology

In a similar method called the **preferred-looking** paradigm, the infant is first familiarized to a particular category by showing a fixed number of examples of that category (e.g., 10 trials with pictures of different cats) and then shown two novel stimuli, presented side by side (Quinn, 2005). One stimulus is drawn from the same category as the familiarization stimuli (in our example, a novel cat) and the other is drawn from a different category (e.g., a dog). Of interest is whether the infant will systematically prefer (look longer at) the stimulus from the new category. If the infant does so, it implies that the infant has differentiated new-category exemplars (here dogs) from familiar-category exemplars (here, cats).

Empirical findings on infant gender categorization

The methods just described have been used to study whether infants divide people into male and female categories. In one early study, Cornell (1974) reported that when 6-month-old infants (but not 5-month-old infants) were familiarized to faces of one gender, they did prefer looking at a face from the other-gender category more than at a new face from the same-gender category. This shows that at least by 6 months, babies do seem to make a gender distinction.

Having found that infants make a distinction between males and females, investigators have then tried to discover the basis on which they make it. To address this question, Leinbach and Fagot (1993) first habituated 5-, 7-, 9-, and 12-month old infants to either male or female faces. They then showed the babies a picture of a face of the other sex (i.e., for infants habituated to males, the new picture would show a female; for infants habituated to females, the new picture would show a male). The results were that the two oldest age groups dishabituated to a face of the other sex, thus showing that infants at these ages do indeed divide male and female faces into different groups.

To learn what basis infants were using to distinguish between male and female faces, Leinbach and Fagot modified their stimuli for a second study. This time they tested only 12-month-old infants, but using three new conditions. In one condition they removed differentiating hair length cues from the stimulus faces, in the second they covered differentiating clothing cues, and in the third they removed both hair and clothing cues. The response patterns were quite different from those observed in the initial study. Specifically, now the 12-month-old infants no longer dishabituated to pictures of the other sex. These data suggest that most infants who distinguished between males and females in the first study probably did so on the basis of characteristics that are culturally linked to sex (like hair length and clothing) rather than on the basis of physical characteristics that are biologically determined (such as relative sizes of nose and face).

Evidence on when gender categories are formed

Another important question in the categorization literature concerns whether infants arrive at the experimental sessions with gender categories, or if instead gender categories are built up as a result of participating in the research session itself. To address this question, Younger and Fearing (1999) began by habituating 7- and 10-month-old infants to a series of interspersed male and female adults' faces. Infants then experienced three test trials. One trial showed a face that was unambiguously male or female (face qualities had been judged earlier by independent adult raters). A second showed a face that was ambiguous with respect to gender. The third showed an entirely different stimulus—a teddy bear. The bear was used just to make sure that the infants had not simply become so bored with the entire procedure that they would not respond to anything new. Infants did show renewed interest to the teddy bear, demonstrating that they had remained sufficiently alert to make the remaining results on gender valid. This finding means that it is justified to look at the findings from the other two cases, which we do next.

During the course of the habituation trials, if the infants had been using just a general category of human faces (i.e., not dividing them into separate male and female categories), then both the typical and ambiguous test faces should have fit within that general "people" category. In this hypothetical scenario, neither test face should have led to recovery of interest (dishabituation). If, however, infants had been fitting each face exemplar into two separate pre-existing male and female categories, in this hypothetical scenario, the new gender-ambiguous face would be novel (thus eliciting dishabituation), whereas the new gender-typical face would be seen as just another face (thus eliciting no recovery of interest). The actual data that were obtained showed a different pattern in the two groups tested. The 10-month-old infants dishabituated to the gender-ambiguous face, but the 7-month-old infants did not. This data pattern shows that older—but not younger—infants had entered the study with pre-existing male and female categories.

Spontaneous use of categories: evidence from sequential touching

Another question that investigators have explored is whether infants spontaneously apply gender categories that they may have. One method used to address this question is **sequential touching**, in which objects from different categories are placed randomly within the infant's reach. Of interest is whether infants touch or grasp the objects in any systematic pattern. For example, if a scrambled collection of cows and dogs are placed on the highchair table, and the infant touches all the dogs before touching any cows, the investigator may infer that the infant differentiated dogs from cows.

In applying the sequential touching paradigm to study 18-month-old infants' gender categories, Johnston, Bittinger, Smith, and Madole (2001) randomly placed eight male and female dolls (distinguished by hair length and clothing) on a tray, and asked 18-month-olds "What can you do with these?" In other trials, Johnston et al. (2001) presented toy animals and vehicles. These objects were included because prior researchers (Mandler & Bauer, 1988) had shown that infants of this age did touch vehicles and animals in patterns that indicated categorization. Infants' responses to the vehicle versus animal stimulus set could thus be used as a yardstick against which to measure infants' responses to the gender stimulus set.

Infants' behaviors were recorded for 2 minutes. The data showed clear evidence that infants differentiated the vehicle versus animal toys, but not the male versus female dolls. Johnston et al. (2001)

wondered whether perhaps the different categorization behaviors for the two kinds of stimuli stemmed from two different kinds of category contrasts in their stimuli. That is, perhaps the vehicle-animal distinction was relatively easy because it drew the contrasting categories from two different "levels" of categorization (inanimate vs. animate objects are at two different global levels of categorization), whereas the male-female distinction was relatively difficult because it drew the contrasting categories from within a single level (men and women are from the same global category of people). Thus, in the third study, Johnston et al. (2001) compared sequential touching in the case of males and females (both members of the category of people) to sequential touching in the case of cows and horses (both members of the category of animals). As before, 18-month-olds showed no evidence of the spontaneous application of male versus female categories. However, this time they behaved similarly on the comparison stimuli (cows vs. horses). It was not until 22 months that babies showed evidence of within-level categorization, and it appeared in both gender and animal domains. These data imply that the male versus female distinction is probably not a unique one, but rather is part of children's developing ability to make increasingly finer distinctions within any given category.

The research described in this section examined evidence of children's infants' gender categorization using nonverbal looking and touching methods in the laboratory. In the next section we turn to evidence of gender categorization in older children whose behaviors can offer other kinds of evidence of categorization.

Evidence of Gender Categorization in Language and Sorting Tasks

Once infants and toddlers transition from being preverbal beings to verbal ones, another kind of data can reveal their understanding of gender categories: their use of gender-specific labels for themselves and others. Obviously children master this division by the early elementary school years, by which point virtually all children label themselves boys or girls correctly (the exceptions being the rare children who are said to have a gender identity disorder, see chapter 1). Children at this age are also almost universally perfect in using terms like boy, girl, man, woman and in using gender-based pronouns (he vs. she) and possessives (his vs. hers). What is in question is when these labels emerge.

Naturalistic evidence from production and comprehension of language

One approach to determining when children are able to label themselves and others correctly as boys or girls, men or women, is to monitor children's production and comprehension of language. Illustrative is a large project by Fenson, Dale, Reznick, Bates, Thal, and Pethick (1994) that was designed to determine language-development norms as assessed by the MacArthur-Bates Communicative Development Inventories (CDI). The investigators reported that some gender-specific words were among the first produced by infants and toddlers. For example, over the 8- to 30-month age ranged covered by the CDI, parents reported (via check lists) that the word "boy" was produced by 58% of the children; "girl" was produced by 51%, "man" by 51%, and "lady" by 74%. These four words, respectively, emerged on average, at 20, 22, 22, and 26 months. On reports of comprehension (rather than production), words referring to people were included on the list of words that were most widely known early. Not surprisingly, heading the list were the words "mommy" and "daddy," reported as understood, respectively, by 90 and 86% of 8-month-old children. Of course, whether these words are used to discriminate between adults of two different sexes versus to label the child's two particular parents (much as proper names might be used) is not clear from naturalistic parent reports of children's spontaneous language production and comprehension.

Another naturalistic study was specifically addressed to 13- to 36-month-olds' production and comprehension of gendered language (Stennes, Burch, Sen, & Bauer, 2005). For the parent checklist, these investigators included items drawn from the CDI as well as additional vocabulary items that had been independently rated as being either masculine or feminine. The data from this investigation, consistent with those from Fenson et al. (1994), showed that gender words like boy, girl, man, and lady are produced and understood early in life.

Evidence of categorization from labeling and sorting tasks

In addition to monitoring spontaneous vocabulary development, researchers have tested young children's mastery of gender distinctions by asking children to interpret or apply gender labels to themselves and others. Prototypical methods include asking children to apply labels such as "boy," "girl," "man," or "woman" to drawings or photographs of various people, or to sort photographs into labeled boxes (e.g., "put the boys in here"). Photographs have depicted other children, adults, or the participant children themselves.

One of the early studies of this kind was by Thompson (1975) who tested 24-, 30-, and 36-month-old children and included measures designed to test labeling of self and others. Among several other measures, Thompson included a "self-sort" test. First, two photographs were taken of the child (one a head shot, and one a full-length view), and these photographs were interspersed with six photographs of long-haired girls in dresses and six photographs of short-haired boys in long or short pants. Children were first asked to sort paper dolls (again, long-haired figures in dresses and short-haired figures in pants) into either a box for boys or a box for girls, and they were then asked to sort the photographs. The dependent variable for the self-sort task was simply whether the child placed his or her own two photographs into the correct box.

Thompson reported that performance was only just above chance at 24 months, and it was not until 36 months that virtually all children were correct (percentages correct for the three age groups, respectively, were 55, 75, and 95%). More recent investigators, however, have reported higher levels of success in early gender self-labeling. For example, Campbell, Shirley, and Caygill (2002) reported that 67% of children 24–28 months were correct in self-labeling their gender. It is unknown whether the differences are due to differences in methods, samples, or the era in which data were collected, but even this higher level of performance shows that at least some very young children have not mastered the vocabulary to label themselves.

The study by Thompson (1975) described above also included measures designed to study children's ability to label others. In a "gender label identification test," the same 24-, 30-, and 36-month-old children were shown pictures of "generally stereotypic" males and females, and were asked to point to which showed each of the following: boy-girl; man-woman, father-mother, mommy-daddy, brother-sister, he-she, him-her, his-her. Similar to the data reported for self-labeling, Thompson reported that the percentages correct for this task for the three ages were, respectively, 50, 75, and 88%, again showing only chance performance at the youngest age. Somewhat better performance has been reported in later work. For example, in a study by Weinraub, Clemens, Sockloff, Ethridge, Gracely, and Myers (1984), 26-, 31-, and 36-month-old children were shown pictures of males and females (both adults and children) and were asked "Who is this? What kind of person is this?" Any generic sex-related response (e.g., lady, boy) was scored as correct. Collapsing over participant sex, correct responses were given significantly more often than chance by 74, 88, and 86% of children in the three age groups, respectively.

A slightly later study by Leinbach and Fagot (1986) built on both prior studies to develop a psychometrically strong measure of children's ability to succeed on labeling tasks. In their procedure, children were given a male and female face (either two adults or two children), side by side, and asked to point to which showed a given label (e.g., "mommy"). The criterion for passing was 10 correct of 12 (a criterion that makes it highly unlikely for a child to be credited with a pass on the basis of chance responding). On the task with children's faces, under 8% of the children below the median age of their sample (26 months) passed compared to 50% of the children above the median age. For the task with adults' faces, the parallel data were 55 and 97%. As discussed by Leinbach and Fagot (1993), the earlier success with adult items might reflect the greater importance and familiarity of adults for young children, the more highly discriminable features of adult faces (e.g., due to clothing, hairstyles, more distinct facial features), or some combination of factors.

Evidence from sorting tasks with artificial stimuli

More recently, investigators have been able to manipulate stimuli to study the importance of biologically determined physical differences between males and females (e.g., the relative size of the nose; the structure of the jaw) versus culturally determined differences (e.g., hair style, cosmetics, clothing). In one study of this kind (Wild, Barrett, Spence, O'Toole, Cheng, & Brooke, 2000), hairstyle and clothing cues were digitally eliminated from faces from children (ages 7- to 10-years) and adults. For the child participants (7- and 9-years of age), the resulting pictures were printed in color, and children were asked to use stickers to mark each face as either a boy or girl (for photographs of children) or as a man or woman (for photographs of adults). For the adult participants, the faces appeared one at a time on a computer screen, and participants were asked to respond by pressing an appropriately labeled key on the keyboard. In all groups, faces were given in blocks by age, counterbalanced for order (i.e., all child and then all adult faces, or the reverse).

The data showed that on the adult faces, categorization success differed significantly (and dramatically) across the ages tested. The 7-year-olds were only just above chance, the 9-year-olds were solidly above chance, and all adults categorized the faces perfectly. All participant groups had a harder time categorizing children's faces. In fact, the 7-year-olds' performance was no better than chance. These data suggest, again, that the cultural markers of sex play a powerful role in gender categorization, even at ages far beyond infancy.

Summary

The research on categorization described in this section of the chapter shows that, quite early, children do distinguish between males and females and understand and apply gender-related labels successfully, a conclusion similar to that reached in other reviews of early categorization literature (Martin, Ruble, & Szkrybalo, 2002). This division is made easier in our culture than it might be because many salient cues (e.g., hair length, makeup, clothes) are statistically correlated with biological features (e.g., facial structure). Thus, children may distinguish people on the basis of biological features, cultural features, or both kinds of features. The data currently available suggest that gender categorization is probably not present at birth, and that children spend at least much of their first year experiencing others not as "males" and "females" but rather as "people" more generally. They do, however, begin dividing people into gender groups during late infancy. Much is left to be learned about the processes by which children come to categorize by gender during the second year of life, what accounts for the substantial variability among children in how early and readily they categorize by gender, and what consequences emanate from the these categorizations.

GENDER CONCEPTS

Introduction

The prior section addressed children's abilities or tendencies to distinguish males from females and to understand or produce gender specific language correctly. But there is more to conceptual knowledge of gender than merely sorting individual human beings into one or the other dichotomous gender category. In this section we discuss research addressing children's developing **meta-cognition** about gender—that is, their thinking about gender.

Interestingly, there has been surprisingly little research asking children directly about the way they think about gender, even in the face of research on children's thoughts about the causes of differences between males and females (e.g., Smith & Russell, 1984; Ullian, 1976). In writing this book, we were startled to realize that we know of no research in developmental psychology in which children are asked seemingly obvious and direct questions such as "what is gender?" or "what does it mean to be a boy or a girl?" Of course, as probably became evident during the first few pages of chapter 1, the answers to these definitional questions about gender are not obvious to adults, even to adults whose scholarly work is focused on gender!

Most of the research described in the prior section (e.g., the work by Leinbach & Fagot, 1986; Thompson, 1975; Weinraub et al., 1984) assumes that there are two categories—male and female—and that any given individual can be placed into one of those two categories on the basis of observable physical features. How else could we even ask children to sort photographs into the "boy box" and the "girl box" or to label individual children or photographs as boys, girls, men or women? As researchers, we usually provide no information about the to-be-sorted people other than physical appearance (typically clothed people). If we were not using a physically based dichotomy ourselves, how else could we score children's responses as correct or incorrect?

We can, of course, infer from various research and even everyday occurrences the bases that are used to categorize people into the two groups. The studies described earlier (e.g., studies that manipulate depicted hair length or clothing of the to-be-sorted or categorized items) tell us something about the criteria that children rely on, but we do not know if children have conscious, meta-cognitive access to these criteria (i.e., whether children can explicitly name the dimension they use to sort individuals), or whether they would defend them as appropriate criteria if explicitly asked to think about them.

There are anecdotes that suggest that at least some children use the same specific criterion that most adults would use as the key definitional factor, namely genitalia. A particularly famous anecdote relevant to this issue is one that was described by psychologist Sandra Bem. One day, her four-year-old son, Jeremy, decided to wear barrettes in his hair to nursery school. Bem described the incident in her book, *An Unconventional Family,* as follows:

> Several times that day, another little boy had asserted that Jeremy must be a girl, not a boy, because "only girls wear barrettes." After repeatedly insisting that "Wearing barrettes doesn't matter; I have a penis and testicles," Jeremy finally pulled down his pants to make his point more convincingly. The other boy was not impressed. He simply said, "Everybody has a penis; only girls wear barrettes." (Bem, 1998, p. 109).

It is pretty clear from this incident that for Jeremy, the defining criterion for being a boy is having penis and testicles, but having them is independent of the presence or absence of barrettes. In contrast, for his classmate, wearing barrettes is a defining criterion for being a girl, although wearing them implies nothing about having a penis and testicles (because both boys and girls are asserted to have them). The two children therefore differ with respect to what they believe to be a sex-defining criterion (penis vs. barrettes), but they are similar insofar as neither believes that an individual's membership in the boy or girl category carries an implication about the other characteristic (barrettes vs. penis, respectively). Beliefs about the implications of category membership comprise another important aspect of gender cognitions, as discussed next.

Gender Essentialism

The Concept of Essentialism

The conversation of Jeremy and his classmate demonstrates the possibility of believing that identifying someone as a boy or girl (whatever the basis for determining group membership) is not necessarily informative about all other physical or behavioral qualities. At the other extreme is the belief that knowing whether someone is a boy or girl is completely informative about their other qualities. Study of children's cognitions about what gender-category membership implies is the focus of work on **gender essentialism**, itself a subtopic within the broader topic of **essentialism** introduced in chapter 8. Essentialism has been defined as "the belief (often erroneous) that members of a category share an inherent, non-obvious property (essence) that confers identity and causes other category-typical properties to emerge" (Gelman, Taylor, & Nguyen, 2004, p. 1).

Gelman et al. (2004) have argued that very young (preschool) children in particular tend to hold essentialist views of social groups such that once children know if someone is a member of some group (such as a racial or gender group), they believe that they can infer many other properties about that person. Importantly, a gender-essentialist stance is not simply an appreciation of some statistical association between a person's sex and other properties. It is a belief that there is something inherent in being a male versus female that carries with it different properties.

As discussed briefly in chapter 8, two ideas are at the core of psychological essentialism (Gelman, 2003). One is that members of a given category are presumed to be similar to one another in ways that go beyond the surface similarities that one can see, even without empirical evidence about such similarities. For example, someone who believes in gender essentialism would believe that women are alike not only insofar as they share certain observable features (e.g., have well-developed breasts) but also share invisible, underlying features (e.g., care a great deal about interpersonal relationships). The second idea is that the explanation for these similarities is presumed to rest in something about the very nature, foundation, or "essence" of the group, here, something that might be referred to as "womanness" or perhaps "femininity." The precise form that the essence is assumed to take might be different at different ages, in different cultures, and with different experiences.

Empirical Research on Essentialism

Developmental work on gender essentialism has addressed children's beliefs about the pervasiveness of differences between males and females and about the degree to which differences in their different appearance, internal qualities, and behaviors are inborn and impervious to environmental influence.

In one study designed to evaluate children's beliefs about the innate nature of gender differences, Taylor (1996) told 4- to 10-year-old children and college students about infants of one sex who were raised either on an island on which all adults were of the infant's own sex (labeled the "same sex environment" by Taylor, abbreviated SSE) or on an island on which all adults were of the other sex (labeled the "opposite sex environment" by Taylor, but referred to here as "other sex environment" here, abbreviated OSE). Participants were asked how those infants would ultimately develop with respect to twelve qualities Taylor classified as *stereotyped* (e.g., "wants to be a ballet dancer" and "gets into fights a lot") and four that she classified as *biological* (e.g., "has a body like a girl's/boy's"). An additional four questions were *control* questions that asked about the environment (e.g., "Does Chris go to school with girls/boys on the island?") which were aimed at making sure that the child remembered the facts about the environment in which the infant was raised. (As an aside, it is interesting to note that Taylor, herself, is revealing her own beliefs about which qualities are and are not rooted in biology vs. culture. For example, she might have placed "gets into fights a lot" into the biological category on the basis of the kinds of biological data on aggression reviewed in chapter 6.)

The results showed that across all age groups, participants predicted that the physical qualities of the target child (those queried by the four "biological" questions) would reflect the target infant's described biological sex. So, for example, participants in all age groups expected that a boy infant would grow up to have a body like a boy irrespective of whether that infant had been raised in a same- or other-sex environment. Predictions for the stereotyped properties, however, differed with participants' ages. In the three youngest age groups (4-, 5-, and 8-year-olds), participants believed that boy infants would grow up to have male stereotyped qualities and girl infants would grow up to have female stereotyped qualities irrespective of what kinds of adults inhabited the island (i.e., children at these ages answered no differently under the SSE and OSE conditions). However, among the three oldest age groups (9- and 10-year-olds and adults), answers differed significantly for the OSE and SSE conditions. In these three groups, participants expected that infants raised in the other-sex environment would be far less likely to display qualities typically associated with their biological sex. These data suggest that children's belief in gender essentialism is initially very strong, but decreases across age.

In short, there is considerable evidence that children tend to assume that gender category membership carries many implications about gender distinctions in a range of behaviors and physical qualities, and that this assumption diminishes with age. As discussed in the context of the description of developmental intergroup theory in chapter 8, one foundation for these age-linked gender phenomena probably rests in the progression of children's general logical reasoning skills. That is, young children are driven to try to make sense of the world around them, and thus they strive to categorize when possible. Early on (in pre-school and in early elementary school years) they can categorize on only one basis at a time. As a result, they are likely to hone in on a single association and generalize it. This tendency is illustrated by an anecdote reported in Bjorklund (2000) in which a child saw two men order pizza and one woman order lasagna and then concluded that men but not women eat pizza! Research by Gelman et al. (2004) has documented that children are exposed to high levels of gender labeling and implicit essentialist language (e.g., "boys are trouble makers" rather than the less generic "Tom is a trouble maker") even from parents who explicitly espouse highly flexible gender attitudes. It is thus perhaps not surprising that children develop these essentialist beliefs about the meaning and origins of gender.

Gender Constancy

Foundations of the Concept of Gender Constancy

Kohlberg's formulation of gender constancy

A second gender concept that plays a major role in gender development is the concept of gender constancy. As discussed briefly in chapter 1 and in more detail in chapter 8, the concept of gender constancy was introduced by Kohlberg (1966) as a core component of his cognitive-developmental approach to gender development. Most importantly, he argued that children's growing understanding of gender constancy plays the key (causal) role in leading children to acquire knowledge and enact behaviors that are culturally associated with their own sex.

Specifically, he argued that the first relevant cognition is the child's early identification of his or her own gender, referred to by Kohlberg as an understanding of gender identity, and said to occur "sometime late in the second year of life" (Kohlberg, 1966, p. 93). Kohlberg (1966) acknowledged that even successful self-identification as a boy or a girl does not imply that the child can correctly categorize others. Indeed, he suggested that it may be another couple of years before children "learn to label others correctly according to conventional cues" (p. 94). But Kohlberg added that: "Obviously there is more to the development of a stable gender identity than this" (p. 94). One part of the "more" is understanding that gender remains the same over the life course, referred to as gender stability (illustrated in chapter 8 by the conversation between Johnny and Jimmy about growing up to be a mommy or a daddy).

Even after being able to link being a boy with becoming a man or daddy (and being a girl with becoming a woman or mommy), children must still come to understand the immutable nature of each gender category: "The child's gender identity can provide a stable organizer of the child's psychosexual attitudes only when he [or she] is categorically certain of its unchangeablilty" (p. 95). For Kohlberg, the test of this certainty is the child's ability to maintain the constancy of gender categories even in the face of appearances (physical or behavioral) to the contrary. Thus, to be credited with full understanding of constancy, the child must be able to affirm that gender remains unchanged even when appearances have changed. For example, the child must demonstrate knowledge that a boy remains a boy even if he wears a skirt, a wig, or lipstick, and even if he plays with dolls.

Challenges of terminology

Unfortunately, Kohlberg's original presentation of these ideas did not always make clear to which of the three levels of understanding he was referring when he talked about gender constancy. Equally problematic, the field has come to use the term "gender constancy" in many ways, including to refer to: (a) full cognitive understanding of all components described above (b) specific understanding of the highest component of understanding (i.e., recognition of unchanged gender despite changed appearance) and (c) cognitions concerning any of the three components.

We join others (e.g., Ruble & Martin, 1998) in believing that many of the apparent discrepancies in the theoretical and empirical literatures related to gender constancy stems from confusion about how the term "gender constancy" is used. In addition, we believe that the specific labels for the three components are not as informative as it might be. Given that there are already established theoretical and research literatures on these topics, it would be hopeless to try to switch to new terminology here. Thus, our discussions will make use of conventional terminology which labels the three progressive components described above as, respectively, gender identity, gender stability, and gender consistency (Martin et al., 2002; Slaby & Frey, 1975; see also chapter 8). However, it may be helpful to think about the first as gender labeling, the second as gender continuity, and the third as gender immutability, leaving the term "gender constancy" to refer to the global, overarching concept formulated by Kohlberg.

Below we discuss research addressed to the developmental progression of all aspects gender constancy; we postpone until the final section of the chapter (*Consequences of Gender Cognitions*) discussion of research concerning the impact that gender constancy has on other aspects of children's development.

The concept of gender constancy in a contemporary context

Before turning to research on children's developing understanding of gender constancy, it is important to point out that theories and empirical work in this area have not yet addressed **transgender.** Transgender refers to living (to varying degrees) as a member of the "other" sex—that is, as a member of the sex that is "opposite" one's biological birth sex. There has been increased publicity (e.g., see Brown, 2006) and professional attention (APA Task Force on Gender Identity Gender Variance and Intersex Conditions, 2006) to people who elect to change their own gender through self-identification (e.g., filling out forms by checking the category of the other sex), behaviors (e.g., changing one's name from Carol to Carl or the reverse, and wearing clothes traditionally associated with the other sex), and perhaps medical interventions (e.g., taking hormones and undergoing surgery to acquire physical characteristics of the other sex). However, we know of no research on children's knowledge and understanding of this particular challenge to the traditionally assumed "fact" of gender constancy, and thus our discussion focuses on children's developing understanding of traditional gender constancy that assumes that birth sex is permanent and immutable.

Empirical Research on Gender Constancy

Early empirical research was aimed primarily at testing whether there would be empirical support for the existence of the phenomenon of gender constancy, whether there would be distinct phases of understanding, and, if so, whether these would be found to emerge in the sequence suggested by Kohlberg (and linked, as hypothesized, to Piagetian stages of cognitive development). Also of interest was identifying the ages at which these cognitions emerged and solidified.

The role of children's justifications

Among the early studies designed to study gender constancy was one by Emmerich, Goldman, Kirsh, and Sharabany (1977). Their major focus on whether children's understanding of gender constancy would show—longitudinally—increasingly sophisticated levels of reasoning identified in Piagetian theory. Thus, as in other Piagetian research, Emmerich et al. (1977) studied not only the correctness of children's answers but also the kinds of justifications children offered for their responses.

Specifically, these investigators showed children a series of drawings, explicitly identifying the depicted child's gender (e.g., "This is Janie; Janie is a girl"). Then they made some perceptually visible change (e.g., changing the depicted child's hair style or clothing) and then asked the child questions such as "If Janie has her hair cut short like this, what would she be? Would she be a girl or would she be a boy?" First, they recorded whether the child gave the correct constancy (consistency) response (e.g., "Janie would still be a girl"). In addition, they coded whether children's justifications (a) relied on a clear statement or implication of gender invariance, called operational consistency (e.g., "She can't change because she was born a girl"); (b) referred to some attribute of the person, called "stimulus description" (e.g., "She would still be a girl because she is wearing high heels"); or (c) provided no consistency justification at all (e.g., "I don't want him to be a girl" or more simply "I don't know"). These and other measures (e.g., of intellectual functioning) were given to over 300 children from a Headstart program beginning when they were about 4 years old. Children were given the tasks again in each of the next three years, allowing Emmerich et al. (1977) to look for patterns of stability or change within children over time.

The findings on children's accuracy confirmed Kohlberg's observation that young children have difficulty in understanding the permanent nature of gender. The findings from the explanation data supported the expectation that there would be a transitional level of understanding in which children could correctly assert the permanence of gender but would be unable to justify it with operational reasoning. Interestingly, however, even by the final assessment (when children were roughly 7 years old), many had still not achieved operational consistency. Furthermore, some children who had achieved it at an earlier testing session fell back to a lower level of performance at a later test session. These findings show that the concepts are not completely stable (or that the measures are not completely reliable).

The investigators suggested that a possible explanation for the unexpectedly late mastery of gender constancy might lie in the nature of the Headstart sample for which the two-dimensional pictorial stimuli might have been particularly hard to process (Sigel & Cocking, 1977). As evident in the research discussed next, subsequent investigators designed their work to evaluate the possibility that the type of stimulus affects children's performance on gender constancy tasks.

The role of stimulus and target variables

In keeping with the general interest in Piagetian theory at the time, investigators (e.g., DeVries, 1974) continued to study the connection between the gender concepts identified by Kohlberg and cognitive stages identified by Piaget. In addition, they also began to study the importance of stimulus and task variables in assessing gender constancy. Illustrative is work by Marcus and Overton (1978) who compared children's understanding of gender constancy when children were asked to answer questions related to themselves versus questions about other children, and when they were asked to answer questions about representational (drawn) children versus questions about real (live) children.

Specifically, kindergarten, first-, and second-grade children were given four gender constancy tasks, two to assess constancy about self, and two to assess constancy about others. Each of these was given in a "pictorial" and "live" format. In the pictorial format, children were given a booklet in which the first page depicted either a long-haired girl dressed in a skirt or a short-haired boy dressed in pants. On the second page appeared a depiction of a child of the other sex. The first page was cut in half horizontally so that half the page at a time could be turned. Thus, depending on whether none, one, or both halves of the first page were turned, the picture showed a picture of a child of the original sex (always matched to the participant child's sex), a picture with the original sex on one half (top or bottom) but of the other sex on the other half, or showed a picture of a child entirely of the other sex. For the "self" version of the pictorial task, the face was the participant's own, inserted from a Polaroid photograph of the child. For the "other" version of the task, a schematic image of a boy or girl was used. The live format followed essentially the same procedure, except that the pictures were enlarged into two carnival-like, life-size cardboard figures with head-size openings. For the self version, the child put his or her own head into the opening. The carnival figures faced a mirror so that the participant child could see the entire cut out when it was the child's own head that filled the opening. For the "other" version of the task, a classmate put his or her head into the opening while the child looked from the front.

In all cases, standard gender constancy (consistency) questions were asked, testing whether the participant child judged that the depicted child would remain a girl (boy) through transformations of just hairstyle, just clothing, or both. Children were also asked whether the depicted child (self or other) would remain the same sex if play interests changed, or if the depicted child really wanted to become a member of the other sex. Any given participant child received one pictorial task and one live task, and received one self- and one other-version in each mode (thus resulting in two tasks each).

Although the results were complex in detail, of particular relevance here were several key findings. First, children generally displayed understanding of gender constancy for themselves earlier than they did for other children. Second, and contrary to the investigators' initial expectations, children overall gave more advanced gender constancy responses on the pictorial than the live format. The authors suggested that perhaps the life-size transformation changes (e.g., in hair style) appeared more realistic than small pictorial ones and were thus harder to counteract by mental processes. Interestingly, this modality effect was moderated by age. Specifically, it was the children in the two younger groups who were affected by modality. They found it significantly harder in the live format to retain the concept of gender as permanent in the face of life-sized transformations that made the other child look so much like a child of the other sex. By second grade there was no modality effect, suggesting that once gender constancy is better established, children are less susceptible to variations in the way that the concept is probed.

Findings from the Marcus and Overton (1978) study and other similar studies (e.g., Wehren & De Lisi, 1983) led to the general conclusion that it was not until the age of about 6 or 7 years that children master full gender constancy, a conclusion consistent with the original description of the development of gender constancy given by Kohlberg (1966) and reviewed earlier in chapter 8. This conclusion has not, however, gone unchallenged. Some investigators have argued that the kinds of measures used by researchers steeped in the cognitive-developmental tradition of Kohlberg have grossly underestimated children's understanding of gender constancy by using what amount to trick questions, or by using confusing stimulus materials.

Evidence of early mastery of gender constancy

One of the best-known challenges was mounted by Bem (1989). She argued that even very young children (as young as 3 years) know about gender constancy but have difficulty on the classic measures because researchers hide from the child the criterion that really matters—genital evidence of the target child's biological sex. She criticized the classic Emmerich stimuli for being artificial, and for leaving open the possibility that the child was answering the gender constancy question in relation to the drawing rather than in relation to the child depicted in the drawing. That is, if one creates a drawing that initially looks like a boy, but then modifies it by adding, say, long hair and a dress, even adults might well agree that what was initially a drawing of a boy had become a drawing of a girl. That is, a drawing does not in and of itself have a reality as male or female; its meaning is determined by the person making the representation. Thus, a change in the drawing could be viewed as affecting a change in the depicted character's sex, and perhaps this is the change to which children were referring in their responses. Thus Bem argued that the traditional tests grossly underestimated young children's understanding of gender constancy.

In her own work, Bem (1989) thus used different stimuli to explore children's understanding of gender constancy. These stimuli are reproduced in Figure 9.1. Bem first showed participant children (aged 3 to 5 years) a photograph of a nude toddler (referred to as a "baby" to the children and in the text below). In the study, Bem referred to the boy baby as "Gaw" and the girl baby as "Khwan" which are Thai names that were presumed to be entirely gender neutral for children living in the United States. When participant children were initially shown the nude photograph, they were asked whether the pictured baby was a boy or girl, and then asked to explain how they knew. When children did not explicitly name the genitals, they were asked probe questions designed to elicit this information if the child knew it. For example, the child was asked if there is "anything about Gaw's body that makes Gaw a boy?" (or girl, if the participant child had said Gaw was a girl).

The photograph was then placed in a folder so that the baby's genitals were no longer visible. The participant was then shown a new photograph of the same baby (e.g., Gaw) pictured with clothing and hairstyles that were mis-matched to the toddler's genitals. For example, Gaw (whose penis had shown in the first photograph) now appeared fully clothed in a pink frilly dress in the second photograph. After making sure that the child knew that the photograph was "still the same baby" the child was asked: "What does Gaw look like—a boy or a girl?" followed by "What is Gaw really—a boy or a girl?" and finally, "What makes Gaw really a boy/girl?" A third photograph showed the same baby in a gender consistent outfit; for example, Gaw dressed in polo shirt, football in hand. Again, children were asked to

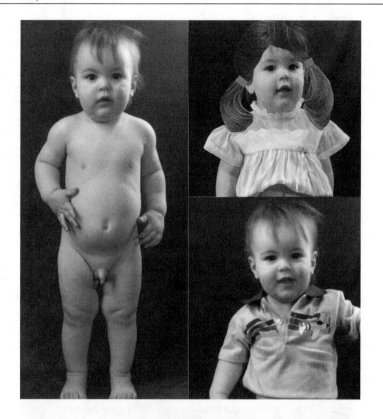

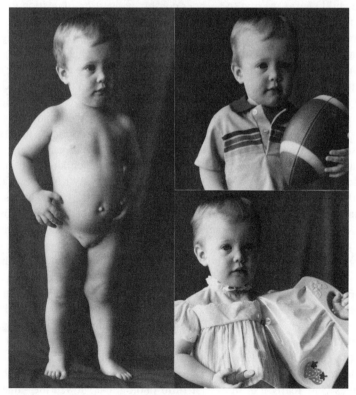

FIGURE 9.1   The photographs used by Bem, (1989) to measure gender constancy. (From Bem, S.L., *Child Development*, *60*, 649–662, 1989. With permission, and with appreciation to Sandra Bem for providing the original photographs.)

confirm that it was still Gaw, and then to answer the same set of questions as in the gender-inconsistent case.

The key result Bem stressed from this work was her finding that fully 40% of 3-, 4-, and young 5-year-old children were able to give constancy answers, with success rates dramatically higher than those typically reported on traditional gender constancy tasks, in which almost all children this young incorrectly name the sex matched to the clothing in which the child has been dressed. Importantly, Bem found that it was not just some chance subset of the children who showed gender constancy. Instead, the children who answered the constancy questions successfully were those who—irrespective of their chronological age—had explicitly distinguished males from females on the basis of genitals. These children knew that for determining gender, it is genitals that matter, even when they are currently hidden from sight, and even when they are contradicted by visible cultural gender cues (e.g., such as a baby with a penis wearing a frilly pink dress and lipstick).

Continuing Issues in the Study of Gender Constancy

Perhaps not surprisingly, the study by Bem (1989) did not settle the question once and for all. Scholars continue to find that some basic issues plague the gender constancy literature (Ruble & Martin, 1998; Martin et al., 2002). One set of issues is definitional. Investigators often fail to specify adequately which aspect of gender constancy is under discussion. Are the researchers in a particular study attempting to investigate the appearance (or consequences) of what have been called gender identity (labeling), gender stability (persistence), or gender consistency (immutability)? If the construct itself is not carefully specified, there can be little hope for agreement about how best to measure it, or, in turn, for what the data reveal about what children understand.

The second set of issues concerns measurement. Should children's understanding be assessed on the basis of their yes/no responses to questions (e.g., "Is Jamie still a girl?") or on the basis of the justifications they give for their responses? Unless children are asked to explain the reason for a given response, a seemingly correct answer (i.e., an answer that appears to show an understanding of gender constancy) may in actuality be demonstrating only **pseudoconstancy** (Emmerich et al., 1977; Martin et al., 2002). Should any defining feature of the child be considered an inadequate basis on which to justify a gender-constant response? For example, in Bem's research, would the justification that "Gaw is still a boy because he has a penis" be a justification that Emmerich et al. would classify as a "stimulus description" equivalent to the justification that "Jamie would still be a girl because she is wearing high heels"? Must children be resistant to appearance changes irrespective of the modality in which they are shown? For example, should they resist the notion of changed gender when the change is shown in a drawing? A photograph? A digital character of one sex being morphed into a character of the other sex? Questions like these have no easy answers, particularly in light of the issue of transgender mentioned earlier in this chapter.

To resolve some of these methodological issues, it will be important to conduct research that compares, directly, the patterns of findings that are evident when different measures and different scoring criteria are used. Studies like these have recently begun to appear. Illustrative is a study by Ruble, Taylor, Cyphers, Greulich, Lurye, and Shrout (2007) who gave children both forced-choice measures and open-ended measures that required children to justify their answers. Consistent with the hypothesized importance of methodology, conclusions about developmental patterns of change in gender constancy appear to be somewhat different depending on which precise measure of constancy is employed.

Conclusions

The research on gender constancy reviewed in this section demonstrates that the original concepts identified by Kohlberg (1966) do, indeed, emerge gradually during early childhood. There remains some uncertainty, however, about how early the various components of gender constancy appear, and about how soon full gender constancy (consistency) is mastered. Taken together, this research literature demonstrates the importance of distinguishing conceptually among the various subcomponents of gender constancy described in chapter 8 (identity, stability, and consistency) and of selecting methodologies targeted to each carefully. In the final section of the chapter, *Consequences of Gender Cognitions,* we will return to gender constancy by addressing how these cognitions may affect children's further gender development.

Multidimensional Gender Identity

We end this section by discussing multidimensional gender identity as conceptualized by Egan and Perry (2001). This work really spans the current section (on the way children conceptualize gender) with the next section (cognitions about the correlates of gender) because—as will become clear below—Egan and Perry's conception of gender identity involves not only children's knowledge and beliefs about their own gender (similar to the gender identity concept of Kohlberg) but also about gender norms (i.e., about what is associated with being male or female). Thus, Egan and Perry's (2001) use of the term not only encompasses, but extends beyond Kohlberg's original meaning so that it refers to the way that individuals know, understand, and accept their own sense of gender.

More specifically, Egan and Perry (2001) proposed five components of gender identity: **membership knowledge**—the individual's knowledge of his or her own gender; **gender typicality**—the degree to which the individual perceives his or her own qualities as similar to the qualities of others in the same gender group; **gender contentedness**—the degree to which the individual is satisfied with his or her own gender, ranging from complete contentedness to extreme dissatisfaction (called gender dysphoria, Bradley & Zucker, 1990, see chapter 1); **felt pressure**—the degree to which the individual feels demands either from oneself or from others to conform to one's own gender group norms; and finally, **intergroup bias**—the belief that one's same-sex group is superior to the other sex group (consonant with intergroup theories discussed in chapter 8).

The description Egan and Perry (2001) give of gender identity suggests that in part they view it as a cognitive, reflective, self-conscious construct, although in large part it is also a highly affective, emotion-laded construct.

> It seems likely that most people devote at least some time to reflecting on questions like these: How well do I fit with my gender category? Must I adhere to the stereotypes for my sex or am I free to explore cross-sex options? Is my sex superior or inferior to the other? We believe that beginning in childhood, people do ask these questions of themselves (p. 451).

They assess gender identity by asking children to make "integrated, summary judgments about gender and self that transcend perceptions of functioning within specific domains of sex typing (p. 452)." For example, for gender typicality, girls [boys] are asked to rate themselves with respect to whether "they are a good example of being a girl [boy]"; for gender contentedness, whether they "feel cheated that there are some things they're not supposed to do just because they're a girl [boy]"; for felt pressure, whether they "think their parents would be upset if they wanted to learn how to fish or hunt [to knit or sew]"; and for intergroup bias whether they "think that boys [girls] are more annoying than girls [boys]." They gave these measures to children in fourth through eighth grades, and found the measures to be reliable and reasonably stable.

Findings were consistent with their hypothesis that gender identity is multidimensional insofar as the different measures elicited different patterns of responses. Perry and colleagues have offered some speculations about developmental emergence and change over a broad age range (preschool through early adolescence, see Carver, Yunger, & Perry, 2003), although they have not yet tested these developmental speculations empirically. To date, though, they have demonstrated that various components of gender identity are related to individuals' adjustment outcomes (Yunger, Carver, & Perry, 2004). Given the heavy affective (rather than cognitive) emphasis of research on this concept to date, we will not discuss this program of research in further detail in the current chapter. We do, however, anticipate that there will be increasing attention to the integration of the affective and cognitive components of this approach in the near future.

Summary

In the earlier section of this chapter on categorization, we reviewed the development of children's growing distinctions between males and females, but without considering how children consciously think about gender categories. The current section on gender concepts has focused on ways in which children explicitly think about gender. We have seen that young children may vary with respect to what they view as defining criteria, but irrespective of which criteria they favor, they appear ready to articulate and even defend them quite strongly. Good illustrations of this point are Jeremy Bem's insistence that a penis and testicles are the defining feature of boys, and his classmate's insistence that barrettes are the defining feature of girls. In addition, many young children endorse essentialist beliefs about gender, believing that the essence of being male or female pervades other qualities and is rooted in biology. At the same time that children are developing more differentiated understanding of both biological and cultural factors, they are developing an understanding of gender constancy and are developing more detailed ideas about where they personally fit within the gendered society in which they live. In the next section, we turn to children's growing knowledge and attitudes about that gendered society.

GENDER CORRELATES

Introduction

At the beginning of our earlier discussion of gender categorization, we pointed out that underlying much of the work discussed in this book is the implicit assumption that people can, in fact, be categorized into two groups, one male and the other female. There is a parallel implicit assumption about the sex-linked nature of many behaviors and characteristics of human beings (i.e., characteristics that are not directly used to divide people into male vs. female categories, but that are differentially linked to males vs. females). To return to our earlier example, just as we pointed out that an adult's differential reactions of delight versus horror to a girl versus a boy wearing nail polish would require that the adult had differentiated which child is a boy and which child is a girl, so, too, it would require that the adult knew (and endorsed the belief) that nail polish is for girls rather than for boys. In this section of the chapter we examine evidence that children have knowledge and opinions about the links between sex and a wide array of human behaviors and characteristics.

Gender Correlations and Gender Stereotypes

Without needing to take a position on why there are gender-linked connections, it is easy to demonstrate that some exist. For example, it is a matter of fact that women have disproportionate representation in jobs in that involve childcare or cleaning hotel rooms, that men have a disproportionate representation in being presidents of Fortune 500 companies and of the United States, and that men are more likely to play football whereas women are more likely to wear nail polish. We refer to these as **gender correlations** because they refer to qualities (e.g., occupations, leisure activities, grooming habits) that are statistically associated with gender.

Statistical correlations may provide a foundation for **stereotypes**, which have been defined as cognitive structures that contain "the perceiver's knowledge, beliefs, and expectancies about some human group" (Hamilton & Trolier, 1986, p. 133). Although some gender stereotypes may thus be based on gender correlations and hence contain what has been referred to as a "kernel of truth" (e.g., see Brigham, 1971; Martin, 1987), stereotypes may also arise in other ways; for example, from hearing someone make what are arguably completely unfounded categorical statements about a social group (see discussion of intergroup theory in chapter 8). Even when there is some statistical kernel of truth, a stereotype may exaggerate an association between gender and some quality far beyond any veridical statistical correlation. For example, to return to the opening anecdote of this chapter, it is statistically true that male neurosurgeons outnumber female neurosurgeons (a gender correlation), but that does not imply that only men can, should, or are inherently better suited to be neurosurgeons (a gender stereotype that we would soundly reject!).

Gender Correlates

In practice, it is often difficult to distinguish between knowledge that reflects some "truth" about differences between males and females (gender correlations) and knowledge that reflects some "conventional wisdom" about differences between males and females (gender stereotypes). Where one ends and the other begins is open to debate even among scientists (as many of the discussions in this book demonstrate). Thus, in the material that follows, we have combined both gender correlations and gender stereotypes under the umbrella term **gender correlates**. We use this broader term to refer to cognitions about gender-linked qualities irrespective of whether they are founded on a statistical association or are founded on the conventional wisdom of the surrounding culture.

Overview

We have organized our discussion into three subsections. In the first subsection we discuss research that examines knowledge of gender correlates in infants and toddlers who must be studied with nonverbal methodologies. In the second subsection we discuss research that examines knowledge of gender correlates in older children who can be asked directly about what qualities, behaviors, or objects they believe are associated with males versus females. To foreshadow the findings from the work we review in those first two subsections, the research provides strong evidence that even very young children are knowledgeable about many gender correlates, and virtually all children have acquired vast knowledge of them by the early elementary school years. Where children show more differences among themselves is in their attitudes about (or endorsement of) gender correlates. In the third subsection we thus discuss conceptual, methodological, and empirical distinctions between knowledge and attitudes. Ultimately, both knowledge and attitudes are contained in children's **gender schemata**; that is, the "interrelated networks of mental associations representing information about the sexes" (Ruble et al., 2006, p. 908). These schemata, in turn, affect a wide variety of outcomes, some of which we consider in the final sections of the chapter.

Knowledge of Gender Correlates in Preverbal Children

Just as researchers have long been interested in knowing how early in life children can and do differentiate between male and female people (see the first section of this chapter on gender categories), they have been long interested in knowing how early in life children know what is associated with being male or female. As was the case in investigating questions about gender categorization in very young children, researchers have designed methods that can enable them to learn about very young children's knowledge of gender correlates. Below we review illustrations of such research using looking-time methods and research using imitation methods.

Looking-Time Studies

In the earlier section on *Gender Categorization*, we reviewed evidence from looking-time research bearing on children's ability and tendency to divide people into two separate categories of males and females. We saw reasonably strong evidence that children can discriminate between males and females even during infancy, although there is still uncertainty about the qualities on which infants base their responses (e.g., physical features? hair length? cosmetics?) and the causal factors that led them to categorize (e.g., inborn predispositions? a history of differential experiences with male vs. female adults? formation of categories during the experiment itself?). In this section of the chapter we will describe research from looking-time methodologies that address a slightly different question: Given that the infant can distinguish males from females (for whatever reason, and on whatever basis), what does the infant associate with those categories?

Looking-time data on linking voices to males versus females

In one study addressed to explore the information infants may have linked to gender, Poulin-Dubois, Serbin, Kenyon, and Derbyshire (1994) tested whether infants systematically associate men's and women's voices with male and female faces. Prior research had already shown that babies this young can distinguish the two kinds of voices perceptually. The new question was whether infants had linked (correlated) different kinds of voices to men versus women prior to entering the research study itself.

Poulin-Dubois et al. (1994) tested 9- and 12-month old infants with a preferred-looking paradigm described earlier. They assembled photographs of faces that adults had judged to be stereotypically male or female. Similarly, they selected recordings saying "Hi baby! Look at me! Here I am. Look at me!" that had also been judged by adults to sound stereotypically male or female. On a given trial, a pair of photographs was shown, one of a man and one of a woman. Then one of the audio recordings was played. Of interest was whether the infants would systematically look at the male face for a male voice and the female face for a female voice.

The data from this study showed evidence that young female (but not male) infants' associated female voices with female faces. Specifically, female infants (especially those in the older, 12-month-old group) looked longer to the female face when the voice was female. There was no evidence at either age that infants associated the male voice with the male face.

Poulin-Dubois et al. (1994) then conducted a second study in which they tested only 9-month-old infants and used only the most highly gender stereotypic faces and the most highly stereotypic voices from the first study. With these more compelling stimuli, this time the pattern was similar for both male and female infants, with both male and female 9-month-old infants linking female voices to female faces. Again, there was no comparable effect with the male voice-face pairings.

Looking-time data on linking gendered toys to males versus females

Using a similar paradigm, Serbin, Poulin-Dubois, Colburne, Sen, and Eichstedt (2001) studied whether infants would differentially link male and female faces to objects that are differentially associated with the two genders in our culture. In the first study, they tested 12-, 18-, and 23-month-olds. In half the test trials, the child first saw an image of the face of either a prototypical boy or a girl. Next they saw an image of a pair of toys, one drawn from the masculine category of vehicles (tractors, cars, or trains) and the other from the feminine category of dolls (clothed baby or rag dolls). They then heard a boy's or girl's voice (matched to the gender of the child in the photograph) saying "Where's my toy? Find my toy!" Of interest for these test trials was whether children would look at the toy that "matched" the gender of the depicted child's face and voice. If so, it would provide evidence that these infants already knew the cultural links between boys and vehicles and between girls and dolls.

In the remaining half of the trials, the pair of toys appeared without having been preceded by a child's photograph and voice. Of interest from these trials was whether infants—in the absence of information about another child's gender—would show a systematic preference for looking at the toy that "matched" their own gender. In other words, would male infants show preferential looking to the vehicle and female infants show preferential looking to the doll?

The data on children's looking preferences for themselves (i.e., in the absence of seeing another child's picture or hearing another child's) were clear. At both 18 and 23 months (although not yet at 12 months), children showed clear looking preferences along traditional gender lines. That is, males looked significantly longer at vehicles, whereas females looked significantly longer at dolls. The data from this first study gave no evidence that infants had parallel knowledge about other children's gender-linked interests. That is, there was no evidence of a systematic tendency for infants to look longer at the toy that "matched" the gender of the child in the photograph.

The investigators were, however, hesitant about concluding that children under two years do not associate vehicles with boys and dolls with girls because they noted a possible problem in the way the infants had responded to their method. Specifically, the investigators noticed that the infants in their study appeared to be extremely interested in the toys shown in the pictures, sometimes exclaiming and naming the toys with great excitement (e.g., "Look! Truck! Truck! *My* truck"). The investigators reasoned that this interest and excitement may well have interfered with infants' abilities to retain the information about the gender of the child in the photograph that had been shown prior to the photographs of the toys.

To address this issue, Serbin et al. (2001) conducted a second study with 18- and 24-month-old infants in which the presentation order of the two types of images was reversed. This time, the infant first saw a screen with only a single toy (a doll or a vehicle), and then saw a screen showing both a boy's and a girl's face. The question now was whether infants would show preferential looking to the child whose gender "matched" the gender of the toy.

The results showed that female infants (at both 18- and 24-months) matched boys' faces to vehicles and girls' faces to dolls. The male infants, however, did not show the same tendency to link gender of the pictured children with the culturally stereotypical toy. Additional research is needed to determine whether this difference between male and female infants reflects different rates of cognitive development, differential exposure to gender-linked events, differential attention to people-related experiences, or any one of several other potential explanations.

Looking-time data on linking gendered activities to males versus females

Several similar studies have been conducted to examine young children's knowledge of the association between children's or adults' gender and activities that are classified as masculine or feminine in our culture. For example, Serbin, Poulin-Dubois, and Eichstedt (2002) used a preferential looking paradigm with 24-month-old infants, showing them both men and women engaged in prototypically feminine activities (putting on makeup, feeding a baby, ironing), prototypically masculine activities (hammering, taking out garbage, fixing a toy) or culturally neutral activities (e.g., turning on a light). Reasoning that surprising events will garner more attention, the investigators expected that toddlers—if they had already established beliefs about the activity-correlates of gender—would look longer at cross-gender actions (e.g., a man putting on lipstick; a woman hammering) than at traditional actions (e.g., a woman putting on lipstick; a man hammering).

Consistent with predictions was the finding that toddlers looked longer at men seen performing culturally feminine activities. However, contrary to expectations, the parallel effect did not occur for the reverse "violation" of women performing culturally masculine activities. The researchers hypothesized that one possible explanation for the different level of effect might be that children had experienced different levels of exposure to traditionally masculine versus traditionally feminine activities in their homes. To explore this possibility, they examined parents' responses to a survey about whether their children observed the various actions used in the study (e.g., hammering), and if so, whether the activities were typically performed by mother, father, or by both.

The results from the survey showed that the feminine activities chosen for the study were indeed more likely to be encountered, and were more consistently seen being done by the child's mother than the parallel case for masculine activities. (For example, toddlers often saw their mothers—and only their mothers—putting on makeup whereas they relatively infrequently saw anyone fixing a toy, and when they did, it was roughly equally likely to have been by the child's mother or father).

These data underscore the relevance of the personal, idiosyncratic experiences of a particular child as well as exposure to broadly available cultural gender stereotypes (e.g., through books, television, and experiences outside the home). Again, we are reminded here of Bronfenbrenner's discussion of the relevance of micro-, meso-, and macrosystems in children's development (see chapter 7 and Figure 7.2).

Imitation Studies

Another method that has been used to explore preverbal children's knowledge of the relation between gender and various activities or qualities is imitation. In this research approach, the child sees an action being performed, and the critical data concern whether the child imitates the demonstrated action in a way that provides evidence of the child's knowledge of gender correlates.

Illustrative of this approach is research by Poulin-Dubois, Serbin, Eichstedt, Sen, and Beissel (2002). In their first study, they tested 24-month-old toddlers by demonstrating nine activities, divided equally among masculine (e.g., shaving), feminine (e.g., rocking a baby), and neutral (e.g., sleeping). Each activity was first modeled with a gender-neutral toy (a monkey). For example, to model shaving, a plastic shaver was held in the monkey's hand, and the blade was moved on the monkey's face while the interviewer said "Swish, swish."

During the first (familiarization) stage of the study, the child was introduced to the props (e.g., the razor) and to two gendered dolls, verbally labeled as "mommy" and "daddy" dolls by the interviewer. After allowing the child to play with the various props during familiarization, the experimenter repeatedly demonstrated the use of each of the props with the gender-neutral monkey. The monkey was then put away, and the child was given the prop and the two gendered dolls, and was told "Now it's your turn. Can you show me [vocalization associated with the demonstrated action, e.g., "Swish, swish"]?"

The findings differed for girls and boys. Among the girls, there was strong evidence of knowledge of the link between activities and gender. That is, girls enacted culturally feminine activities significantly more often with the female (mommy) doll and enacted masculine activities significantly more often with the male (daddy) doll. This pattern held across all activities with the exception of one masculine activity (rough and tumble play). Among the boys, however, there was no parallel finding. That is, although boys made use of both dolls in their play, they showed no systematic pattern in selecting the male versus female dolls to enact traditionally masculine versus feminine behaviors.

As in the preferred-looking study by Serbin et al. (2002) already described, these investigators examined parents' reports of toddlers' experiences with the target activities (e.g., shaving) in the child's own homes to try to determine if differential exposure could explain the observed sex difference in infants' behaviors. Although there were some minor differences in reports of what boys and girls experienced (e.g., girls were significantly more likely to see their mothers put on makeup than were boys), the overall the level of experienced gender divisions in the home showed no significant differences between girls and boys.

Serbin et al. (2001) considered the possibility that boys might simply take longer to acquire knowledge of the gendered nature of the behaviors studied. They thus conducted a second study with slightly older boys (31 months). Data from this older group did provide evidence of boys' knowledge of the gendered nature of actions. However, the effect was limited to the masculine activities. That is, boys were significantly more likely to select the daddy doll than the mommy doll for the masculine actions, but they were not significantly more likely to select the mommy doll for the feminine actions. Survey data were again examined. These data were consistent with the expectation that children were exposed in their own homes to traditional gendered divisions of the target activities.

Summary of Findings Concerning Preverbal Children

Overall, then, the data from these studies show that even preverbal infants and toddlers have begun to pick up gender correlates, although they also show variations in relation to both infant and stimulus characteristics that are not yet well understood. There have been a few studies in which girls show earlier or broader knowledge of gender correlates than boys, but additional research and meta-analyses will be needed before it will be possible to judge whether this is a reliable finding.

Knowledge of Gender Correlates in Verbal Children

Once children develop more verbal facility, their knowledge and beliefs about the gendered nature of various qualities and activities may be studied more directly by simply asking them to assign items to males or females. This is much like explicit gender categorization tasks, except now rather than asking children explicitly to sort people into male and female groups, children are asked to assign qualities and behaviors to one or the other of the two sexes.

Sorting Studies

An early investigation using this method was conducted by Kuhn, Nash, and Brucken (1978). They studied 2- and 3-year-old children's knowledge of male and female attributes by using two paper dolls, one named Lisa, and the other named Michael. The interviewer told the children some things that one doll said, and the child was asked to identify which doll had spoken. To introduce children to the task, children were first asked to pick out that doll said: "My name is Lisa," "My name is Michael," "I'm a boy," and "I'm a girl." All children responded correctly.

For the test trials, the experimenter explained that she would show "pictures of things nursery school children like you do and play ... and tell you what someone said." For each item, the child was then asked to indicate which of the two dolls, Lisa or Michael, said it, and was asked to put the selected doll into the picture. For example, the child was shown a picture with roads, cars, and related objects, and was asked to identify which doll said "I like to play with cars" and then to place the selected paper doll on the picture. Children were given several additional tasks assessing other constructs (e.g., gender constancy) but for the purposes of this discussion, what is relevant were the data on children's tendency to assign traditionally masculine items to Michael and traditionally feminine items to Lisa.

The findings are difficult to describe in detail because (a) children assigned some items to the traditional gender but others were assigned randomly or systematically to the doll of their own sex; (b) on some items, both 2- and 3-year-olds demonstrated gender knowledge whereas on others, only older children did so; and (c) on some items both boys and girls made traditional gender assignments but on other items the two sexes responded differently. There was no obvious explanation for why some items were responded to one way whereas others were responded to in a different way. However, despite this unevenness in the item-specific data, the overall pattern of findings did show clearly that on average, even by 2 years, children were more likely to assign traditionally masculine items to Michael and traditionally feminine items to Lisa. Thus, children demonstrated that they already knew many of the correlates between gender and the kinds of items Kuhn et al. had queried (household chores, children's toys and games, expected occupations, behaviors, and psychological traits).

In another early study, Weinraub et al. (1984) also asked young children (26-, 31-, and 36-month-olds) to complete a variety of gender-related tasks among which was a sorting task. The materials for this task included three 8-card picture sets, one set depicting adult tasks or jobs (e.g., a picture of a fire engine, hydrant, and burning building), one depicting adult possessions (e.g., a picture of a makeup mirror, eye shadow, and lipstick), and the third depicting children's toys (e.g., a dump truck). All items included in the task had been rated earlier by adults as being strongly masculine or feminine. Children were shown two boxes, one with a picture of a man and boy; the other a woman and girl and were told "This is the box for men and boys [ladies and girls]. All the pictures for men and boys [ladies and girls] go in this box." Children were then given picture cards and asked them to put each "into the box where it belongs."

The data showed that children as young as 26 months reliably assigned items to male versus female boxes in a way that was, overall, consistent with adults' divisions, and that by 36 months, the majority of children were aware of these divisions. Interestingly, however, the bulk of the gender divisions were found for items depicting adults' possessions and tasks rather than items depicting children's toys.

A third early study by Reis and Wright (1982) examined children's knowledge of the gender correlates of traits such as "weak," and "gets into fights." A particularly interesting feature of this study was that it included both cross-sectional data (children were drawn from four age groups, each spanning a

6-month period beginning at 3 years and ending at 5 years) and longitudinal data (children were retested six months after the initial assessment). For each item, children were asked to point to a silhouette of a male or female figure to respond to short descriptions such as: "One of these people cries when something good happens and when everything goes wrong. Which person cries a lot?" The investigators concluded from their findings that first, there was considerable early gender knowledge (even at the youngest age, children assigned traits to the culturally "correct" sex more than would be expected by chance), second, that both cross-sectional and longitudinal data showed that children's knowledge of gender correlates increased with age.

Leinbach, Hort, and Fagot (1997) conducted a more recent investigation using a similar methodology with children age 4, 5, and 7 years. What makes this study different from those conducted earlier is not only that the research covered older ages, but also that it encompassed a broader scope of items. Specifically, in addition to asking children to sort occupational and activity items such as those used in the studies described above (e.g., hammer, broom, firefighter hat, dress, ribbon, truck), children were also asked to sort metaphorical items that have been linked to gender in adults (Bem, 1981).

The metaphoric items used for this study were obtained by first asking a group of adults to generate masculine and feminine objects or qualities, and then selecting those that could be depicted graphically for further testing. In addition, to capture the suggestion made by Bem (1981) that roundedness is viewed as feminine and angularity as masculine, three pairs of items were added by the investigators: square/round, angular/curved, and fir tree/maple tree. The 75 items that resulted from this process were then given to a new group of adults to rate on a 7-point scale ranging from "extremely masculine" at one end to "extremely feminine" at the other. On the basis of these ratings, 38 highly gendered metaphoric items were selected for the actual study. Examples of metaphoric items included, for masculine: bear, fire, rough (burlap) and grasshopper; for feminine: heart, butterfly, soft (cotton), and feather. Also included were 10 metaphoric items that had received neutral ratings and 10 gendered items like those used in earlier studies.

Children were interviewed individually and, as in other studies, were asked to respond by putting each item card into one of two boxes, one of which was marked by pictures of a boy and man and the other by pictures of a girl and woman. Specifically, children were told that the cards would have "pictures of things people could look at, or play with, or use to work with. Some of these things are more for girls and women, and some things are more for boys and men. If you think [a card] is mostly a girl kind of thing, put it in this box, and if you think it is a boy kind of thing, put it in this one" (p. 114). When the item was a quality, it was named, and if the quality was a texture, the child was invited to feel it; for example, "It's rough, isn't it? Just something rough."

As in the other studies reviewed above, the detailed findings were complex, but overall, the data from the study lead to the general conclusion that children assigned items at above-chance levels to the "appropriate" masculine or feminine box. Adding to the credibility of this result was the finding that children assigned items rated as neutral by adults in roughly equal proportions to the masculine and feminine boxes. Children also assigned metaphorically masculine items (square, fir tree, angular) to the masculine response box (although a comparable pattern was not found for the metaphorically feminine items of round, maple tree, and curved). Again, these data showed that the incidence of "appropriate" assignments (both conventional and metaphorical) increased with age.

Summarizing Data From Sorting Studies

The data from the four sorting studies just discussed consistently demonstrate the early emergence of children's knowledge about the link between gender and various qualities and activities. However, they simultaneously show that early emergence does not imply early mastery. For example, as mentioned earlier, Kuhn et al. (1978) found inconsistencies across the particular items they included in their study, across the ages tested, and between boys versus girls. Weinraub et al. (1984) found that children's knowledge of the gendered nature of children's toys took longer to emerge than their knowledge of the gendered nature of adults' roles and possessions, and that there was still variability among children within the age span tested. Similarly, although Reis and Wright (1982) showed that children assigned traits to the "appropriate" male versus female options significantly more often than would have been expected by chance (i.e., 12.5 of 25 items or 50%), the absolute numbers of "correct" answers were not high (collapsing across ages, they were 54% at time 1 and 59% at time 2, and even among the oldest children at time 2 they were only at 60% which is still far from ceiling). And finally, as just discussed, Leinbach et al. (1997) found that although overall children assigned items to the "appropriate" gender at a rate that was above chance, they failed to do so for a considerable number of individual items—both conventional (e.g., dishes) and metaphorical (e.g., circular).

Many more sorting studies have been conducted during the last few decades. Findings from this work have been summarized both in narrative reviews (Arthur, Bigler, Liben, Gelman, & Ruble, 2008; Ruble et al., 2006; Signorella, 1987; Signorella & Liben, 1985) and meta-analytic reviews (Signorella, Bigler, & Liben, 1993). Taken together, this body of work shows that children's knowledge of gender correlates is already evident even during the preschool years. That is, although there remains some uncertainty about exactly when (or even the order) at which children become knowledgeable about various gendered domains (e.g., adult possessions and occupations; children's toys and games; adults' and children's personality traits), even young preschoolers show some knowledge about cultural gender stereotypes early, and this knowledge continues to grow rapidly during the early elementary school years. This conclusion does not, however, mean that there are neither developmental nor individual differences beyond preschool in the domain of gender correlates, as will become evident in the next section of the chapter.

Attitudes About Gender Correlates

As just reviewed, there is compelling evidence that even by preschool, children are knowledgeable about a wide range of gender correlates, and that their knowledge advances quickly to become almost universally strong by middle childhood. This developmental pattern with respect to the early emergence and stability in knowledge of gender correlates does not, however, necessarily imply that children's *endorsement* of these gender correlates follows an identical pattern. In this section of the chapter we discuss conceptual, methodological, and empirical work on knowledge and attitudes about gender correlates.

Conceptual Distinctions Between Knowledge and Attitudes

The distinction between one's knowledge of gender correlates and one's attitudes about or endorsements of gender correlates probably seems obvious once we pose a pair of questions like the following: "Who usually bakes cookies? Mostly men, mostly women, or equal numbers of men and women?" versus "Who should [or can] bake cookies? Only men, only women, or both men and women?" Questions like the former tap individuals' beliefs about the distribution of some activity, behavior, or quality. These beliefs might have been built up by storing actual experiences (e.g., monitoring the numbers of men and women they have seen baking cookies). Or, these beliefs might have been built up by acquiring knowledge of the cultural stereotype about the gendered nature of baking, perhaps on the basis of having seen differential proportions of men and women portrayed baking in picture books or television programs; perhaps learned from having heard family members always asking mom, rather than dad, to bake cookies; or perhaps even having heard specific stereotyped remarks such as "Women bake the best cookies. Men are so helpless in the kitchen!"

An individual who knows either a factual gender difference (gender correlation) or a cultural belief (gender stereotype) about a gender difference need not, however, personally endorse the belief that males and females should differ in that way. In other words, it is perfectly possible for someone to be aware of an actual or stereotypic difference without necessarily believing either that there is something inherently different about men and women with respect to some behavior like cookie-baking that inevitably places them on the path towards differential skill and involvement in the baking process, or that prior experiences have rendered men incapable of baking cookies such that, going forward, women should do more of the cooking-baking than men. In short, individuals who uniformly know that it is mostly women who bake cookies or even that it is women who bake the best cookies may still hold different opinions about whether only (or mostly) women should or can bake cookies.

Theoretical Arguments for Distinct Concepts and Developmental Trajectories

Roughly a quarter-century ago, Signorella and Liben (1985) made explicit the distinction between children's knowledge versus attitudes about gender stereotypes and argued that the two constructs must be measured differently. In that article, gender stereotype knowledge was defined as "children's understanding of which activities and behaviors most people in our culture assign to either women or men" and gender stereotype attitudes were defined as "the degree to which children agree with [endorse] the gender stereotypes that exist in our culture" (pp. 1–2).

On the basis of what is known about cognitive development in general, Signorella and Liben (1985) also argued that the two aspects of stereotyping should be expected to follow different developmental trajectories. First, given that as children get older they may be expected to accumulate more and more knowledge about the physical and social worlds they inhabit, Signorella and Liben hypothesized that the knowledge component of gender stereotypes would be expected to increase as children progress from the early preschool years to the early and middle elementary school years. Thus, if children were tested with a measure that tapped children's knowledge of cultural gender stereotypes, children would be expected to show age-linked increases in stereotyping scores over that period. After that, scores would be expected to level out as virtually all children would have already learned the gender stereotypes of their culture.

Second, given that as children get older they become better able to reason hypothetically and to consider alternative hypotheses, Signorella and Liben (1985) also hypothesized that the attitudinal component of gender stereotypes would be expected to decrease in rigidity as reasoning skills advanced. Thus, they hypothesized that if children were tested with a measure that tapped children's endorsement of cultural gender stereotypes, children—starting in middle to late elementary school when children's hypothetical-deductive reasoning skills are increasing—would show age-linked declines in stereotyping scores (i.e., show increasing flexibility).

Signorella and Liben (1975) argued further that findings on the developmental course of gender stereotyping in earlier research that appeared to be inconsistent might actually be the result of using different kinds of measures in different studies. Consistent with this possibility, they noted that most studies that found age-linked increases in stereotyping had used knowledge measures (e.g., Edelbrock & Sugawara, 1978 [sex-role discrimination measure]; Thompson, 1975; Williams, Bennett, & Best, 1975), whereas most studies that found age-linked decreases in stereotyping had used attitude measures (e.g., Garrett, Ein, & Tremaine, 1977; Urberg, 1982).

Distinguishing Knowledge Versus Attitudes in Measures and Empirical Data

Designing an attitude measure

Given this analysis, Signorella and Liben (1985) identified four major task qualities that should be considered when designing knowledge versus attitude measures. One quality concerns the inclusion of a nonstereotyped response option, viewed as a necessity for an attitude measure. If children are given only male and female response options, the child cannot offer anything other than a gender-specific response, no matter what the child may believe. If forced to assign an item (e.g., baking cookies) to either men or women, children would be likely to fall back on their knowledge of the cultural stereotype and assign the item to women, even if they, personally, do not hold the attitude that only women should bake cookies.

A second quality concerns the type of question that is asked. If the goal is to measure attitudes rather than knowledge, it is important to use questions in a form such as "Who can/should do/be ____?" rather than in a form such as "Who usually does/is ___?" The former question probes opinion whereas the latter question probes information about a factual condition that may, indeed, be gender biased. A third quality concerns the number of response options. Citing past research (e.g., Garrett et al., 1977) reporting young children's confusions when they are faced with more than three response choices, Signorella and Liben (1985) suggested that the number of choices be limited to three when testing preschool children. The fourth quality they addressed is the content of the specific items. In particular, they note the importance of ensuring that children across the age ranges tested are familiar with the cultural gender stereotypes of the individual items. If they are not, the child's endorsement of items cannot reveal anything about the child's gender attitudes.

On the basis of the analysis just outlined, Signorella and Liben (1985) thus developed a Gender Attitude Scale for Children (**GASC**) that used the "should/can" question about items drawn from a range of domains (e.g., leisure, household, and occupational activities). Individual items on which an initial sample of children had made "errors" (assigning a masculine item to only girls/women or a feminine item to only boys/men) were dropped from the final version of the measure. Children were offered a neutral response option ("both men and women") in addition to the two gender-specific choices, thus limiting response options to three.

Empirical data relevant to the knowledge versus attitude distinction

Empirical data from the GASC reported by Signorella and Liben (1985) showed that as predicted, children became more flexible with age (i.e., older children were more likely than younger children to answer that "both men and women" could do various activities rather than answering that "only men" or "only women" could do something). Even stronger empirical support for the distinction between methods that tap knowledge versus attitudes about gender stereotypes comes from a meta-analysis by Signorella et al. (1993). Prior studies of children's gender stereotypes were entered into the meta-analysis, coding for both child variables and task variables. Major child variables included the child's own sex and age. Major task variables included the type of question ("can/should" vs. "usually" questions) and the type of response options (contrasting studies using only two, forced-choice options vs. three options that included the flexible "both" option in addition to the two gender-specific options).

An additional distinction specified by Signorella et al. (1993) concerned the target of the stereotype. Specifically, they argued that there was often inadequate clarity with respect to whether what was being examined in a particular research study was something about the child's view of others or, instead, something about the child's view of self. This lack of clarity becomes particularly important in theoretical or empirical work that concerns the sequence in which various components of gender evolve (e.g., see the discussions in chapter 8 concerning the gender schema model proposed by Martin & Halverson, 1981, or the attitudinal and personal pathway models proposed by Liben & Bigler, 2002). Thus, Signorella et al. (1993) also categorized studies with respect to whether the targets that children were asked to rate were others or themselves, and then, to make the scope of the meta-analysis manageable, included only the former category of studies in their meta-analysis.

For the present discussion, the most important conclusion from this meta-analysis was that the data confirmed the importance of both the form of the question and the range of response choices. That is, results were as predicted by the conceptual analysis of what would be expected developmentally for a measure of knowledge versus a measure of attitudes. Studies that employed the "usually/is" type of question and that offered children only two choices (i.e., provided the "men/boys" and "women/girls" options but not the "both" option) indeed showed an increase in stereotyped responding as children got older. This is precisely the pattern of findings that would be expected for a measure of children's knowledge. In contrast, studies that employed the "should/can" type of question and allowed children to assign items to "both" as well as to the two gender-specific options, showed a decrease in stereotyped responding with age. This is precisely the pattern of findings that would be expected for a measure of children's attitudes, which could be expected to become increasingly flexible with age.

Extending measures for developmental research

The GASC measure just described has proven useful for assessing elementary school children's attitudes about others and has provided empirical data relevant for testing several theoretically derived predictions. For example, some memory studies discussed later in the chapter examined children's abilities to remember gender nontraditional pictures in relation to their gender attitudes as measured on the GASC. However, the GASC was designed for a relatively narrow range of ages, and had a restricted range of items. Thus, subsequent investigators (Liben & Bigler, 2002) designed another suite of measures that extended the GASC in several ways. Specifically, the new measure sampled items from three domains— occupations, activities, and traits (hence referred to as the **OAT** scales)—and were designed to assess gender attitudes towards others (attitude measures, or AM) and sex typing of self (personal measures, or PM). Parallel forms have been developed for young adults (OAT; Liben & Bigler, 2002), children (COAT, Liben & Bigler, 2002), preschoolers (POAT, Liben, Bigler, Shechner, & Arthur, 2006), and are currently being extended to mature adults (MOAT).

The OAT scales have been used as dependent measures to test various kinds of research questions, but what is relevant for the current discussion is simply the observation that the data emerging from these scales are consistent with the points made in discussing the development of the GASC measure (Signorella & Liben, 1985) and in the meta-analysis by Signorella et al. (1993): patterns of developmental findings differ depending on targets (self vs. other) and on the psychological construct being tapped (knowledge vs. attitudes).

Summary

Without doubt, research demonstrates that children are knowledgeable about many of the correlates of gender. By early childhood, children are able to assign various kinds of items (e.g., toys, jobs, traits) differentially to males and females in ways that largely match adult divisions. Children are even able to differentiate between some masculine and feminine metaphors. At the same time that data reveal considerable knowledge, however, they also reveal many limitations. For example, as discussed in detail above, there is considerable variety across ages, items, individual children, and sometimes participant sex with respect to participants' success in linking items to the culturally "appropriate" or "correct" gender. Research that has attempted to examine the emergence of this knowledge within infancy has also suggested that the process of learning gender correlates is an extended and uneven one, perhaps highly dependent on what a given child has experienced in his or her own immediate environment. Children are also extremely knowledgeable about the stereotypes about gender in their culture, irrespective of whether they themselves personally endorse those stereotypes. Research has only recently provided the assessment tools that allow lifespan study of stereotype knowledge and stereotype endorsement across a range of domains. At the risk of sounding repetitive, we must end this summary as we did earlier ones by acknowledging that there remain many unanswered questions, even as the field has provided ever better tools for addressing them.

THE EFFECTS OF GENDER COGNITIONS ON INFORMATION PROCESSING

Introduction

In the prior three sections of this chapter we discussed evidence showing that children develop a range of cognitions related to gender. Even infants, and certainly young children, routinely distinguish between males and females and know a great deal about what is associated differentially with each. They master both receptive and productive gendered language. They develop an understanding of various concepts concerning their own and others' genders, as well as learning what qualities and activities are statistically or stereotypically associated with each. In the two final sections of this chapter we review research that has addressed the consequences of these various cognitions.

There is an organizational challenge to describing consequences of gender-related cognitions. The most obvious organizational approach would be to take each of the three kinds of cognitions covered above—gender categorization, gender concepts, and genders correlates—and discuss, sequentially, how each has consequences for other developmental outcomes. The problem with this seemingly obvious organization is that the three kinds of cognitions are themselves highly interrelated, and virtually any research that addresses the influence of one also addresses the influence of the others. Thus, the topics cannot really be covered in distinct sections. The most obvious alternative is to organize the discussion on consequences by kinds of outcomes (e.g., toy play, peer selection, educational decisions, occupational aspirations and roles) and ask how each is affected by the three types of gender cognitions. The problem with this potential organizational strategy is that the list of outcomes is virtually endless. Ideally one would want to develop a full matrix of cognitions and outcomes and show the complex, overlapping, and reciprocal relations among them.

Recognizing that it would be impossible to fulfill this ideal in a single chapter, what we have done instead is to select two bodies of work that illustrate the associations between gender cognitions and outcomes, and discuss each of them, respectively, in the two final sections. In the current section we address how a single outcome – information processing—is influenced by gender cognitions. **Information processing** may be defined as how individuals attend to, encode, and remember environmental stimuli such as events, pictures, or stories. We have selected this as our illustrative outcome because it is a basic process that underlies many more specialized outcomes we might have selected (e.g., career aspirations). In addition, it is an area that offers decades of relevant research with many well-established findings. In the next and final section of the chapter, we select one particular component of the many gender cognitions we discussed earlier—gender constancy—and describe a small sample of research that addresses how it has been linked to various outcomes.

Conceptualizing Information Processing

As we saw in chapter 8, individuals' own qualities profoundly affect the way that they process information. For example, in introducing gender schema theory, we mentioned Bartlett's (1932) early demonstration that when people are asked to reproduce stories drawn from a foreign culture, their reproductions become successively more like those of their own cultural traditions. It is possible to see reconstructive processes operating in the realm of gender as well. Illustrative is a story that appeared several years ago in one of our local community newspapers. The article began by reporting that the National Science Foundation had just named a new group of "Presidential Young Investigators." The second paragraph of the story began by identifying one of the awardees as "Susan Brantley, assistant professor of geosciences." Two paragraphs later the story continued: "A native of Rochester, NY, Brantley earned his bachelor of arts, master of arts, and doctorate from Princeton University." One might hypothesize that the reporter's gender schema did not permit him to process the information that a woman (as implied by the name "Susan") was an award-winning geoscientist. A similar story a few years later reported "Ellen DiCarlo of Monroeville has been appointed instructor in engineering. He comes to the campus possessing bachelor of science and master of science degrees from the University of Connecticut."

At what point might gender cognitions affect information processing? First, gender cognitions might affect what children pay attention to or engage with in the environment. Second, gender cognitions might affect **encoding**; that is, the way that children assign meaning to or organize what they have just experienced. Third, gender cognitions might affect what then happens to that information over time, perhaps affecting whether the child remembers the information accurately, or even whether the child remembers it at all. In the following section we sample work relevant to these three components of information processing.

Attention or Engagement

If we had sensitive enough instruments, we could theoretically measure and describe any given veridical (real) environment in all its detail; for example, recording who is present and what they are doing, what objects are present and how they are arranged, sounds, smells, temperature, lighting, and so on. But the **functional environment**—the way that the environment is experienced by a particular person—will differ for individuals depending on how they direct their attention and depending on with which aspects of the environment they actively engage. Our goal here is to ask whether attention and engagement are affected by children's gender cognitions. A particular focus of research in this arena has been to ask whether children pay attention to models and their behaviors in a gender-differentiated manner.

Differential Imitation of Gendered Models and Actions

One relevant research literature that demonstrates gender-differentiated attention to what the environment offers is the work on imitation conducted by Bandura and by other social learning theorists reviewed in chapter 7. As discussed there, children who watched models performing novel behaviors were later more likely to imitate the novel behaviors performed by the model of their own sex than by the model of the other sex (e.g., Bandura, Ross, & Ross, 1961; Grusec & Brinker, 1972; Wolf, 1973). The greater tendency to imitate same-sex rather than other-sex models is particularly strong when there are several models of each sex and actions are consistently distinguished by model sex (Bussey & Perry, 1982). A significantly greater tendency for a child to imitate a same-sex model depends on the child being able to categorize self and others as being male versus female and to note the match or mismatch between self and other. It is noteworthy that in this group of studies, the behaviors exhibited by male and female models were novel and counterbalanced across children. This means that a differential tendency for boys to imitate what they have observed men doing (or girls to imitate what they have observed women doing) cannot be explained by a match between what boys and men (girls and women) inherently find interesting.

Imitation may be affected not only by the fact that children group themselves and others into male and female categories; it may also be affected by children's knowledge about the different actions that are associated with being male versus female (i.e., by their knowledge of what we earlier labeled gender correlates). Indeed, in addition to a greater propensity to imitate a model of the same sex than a model of the other sex, research has shown that children also have a greater propensity to imitate actions culturally associated with their own sex. For example, Bauer (1993) demonstrated very young children's tendencies to differentially enact masculine versus feminine behaviors by sex. Boys and girls, 25-months old, watched a sequence of culturally masculine or culturally feminine actions. In an illustrative masculine item—building a house—the experimenter modeled putting a roof on a house, inserting a nail into a hole, hammering the nail, and then painting the house. In an illustrative feminine item—making breakfast—the experimenter modeled cracking an egg, stirring it, pouring the egg into a pan, and then tasting the result.

The data from boys (but not girls) were consistent with the notion that children are differentially attentive to actions culturally linked to their own sex. That is, boys were significantly more likely to reproduce the male-stereotyped sequences, although girls did not imitate differentially. More research is needed to determine whether the difference in patterns for boys and girls reflects a sex difference in the tendency to imitate same-sex actions, something about children's familiarity with the particular activities selected or perhaps their inherent attractiveness, or whether it reflects the fact that the experimenter was a woman (so that girls' tendency to imitate actions of females may have overshadowed their tendency to avoid imitating "masculine" actions).

Differential Engagement With Gendered Objects and Activities

The studies just discussed asked whether children are more likely to imitate a model who is of the same sex or who is performing actions culturally associated with the child's own gender. Another research approach has been to ask whether boys and girls seek out and attend to different objects or activities (apart from what a model is doing) in ways that appear to reflect their gender cognitions about categories and correlates. Given how large a role toy play has in children's lives, the domain that has probably attracted the most research of this kind has concerned toy play. Paralleling the findings from imitation studies just discussed, there is evidence that children's cognitions about their own gender lead them to favor engaging with toys that are gender "matched" or gender "appropriate." That is, toys that are categorized as "for girls" are more likely to attract interest from girls, and the reverse holds for boys.

Of particular interest in the current context is whether these preferences reflect children's self-gender cognitions—that is, their knowledge of their own gender category. As discussed in some detail in chapter 8, cognitive-developmental and gender schema theorists (e.g., Kohlberg, 1966; Martin & Halverson, 1981) believe that children's recognition of their own gender leads them to seek out same-gender objects or activities. To support this hypothesis, it would not be enough to find that girls tend to play more with what are traditionally considered to be feminine toys whereas boys play more with what are traditionally considered to be masculine toys. A tendency for girls to play with feminine and boys to play with masculine toys could conceivably just reflect systematic differences between girls' versus boys' toys coupled with systematic (but noncognitive) differences between boys and girls.

For example, researchers have noted that boys prefer to play with toy vehicles more than with dolls, and girls have the reverse preference. One hypothetical but noncognitive explanation for the observed difference might be that boys are inherently more attracted to objects with moving parts and girls are inherently more attracted to objects that are soft and cuddly. Such a difference might be understood in evolutionary terms by suggesting that toy preferences reflect differential selection for behaviors associated with action, exploration, and travel (males) versus behaviors associated with more local domestic functions such as caring for children (females). There is some evidence of biologically driven gender differentiated toy preferences. For example, and as discussed earlier in chapter 6, female and male vervet monkeys show gender differentiated toy choices much like those of human boys and girls (Alexander & Hines, 2002), and girls with CAH who have higher than normal prenatal androgen exposure show greater interest in male-typical over female-typical toys (Berenbaum & Snyder, 1995). Furthermore, there have been findings that boys are attracted to boys' rather than girls' toys even earlier than they can show the ability to answer questions about which toys are for which sex (Blakemore, LaRue, & Olejnik, 1979; Perry, White & Perry, 1984). Thus, even without gender cognitions, a boy might be drawn to cars and a girl to dolls.

How might one test the idea that children's gender cognitions may contribute to attracting boys and girls to engage more with culturally "gender appropriate" toys even apart from biological or noncognitive learning explanations? One approach would be to test whether boys and girls differentially prefer toys that are actually identical, but are described to children as being boys' versus girls' toys. Such a condition can be achieved in experimental research in which the identical (novel) toy is identified as a boys' toy to some children, and as a girls' toy to other children. If under these circumstances boys and girls are attracted differentially to these toys, it would provide strong evidence that just knowing that a toy is for boys or for girls is enough to elicit different interest from boys and girls even in the complete absence of actual differences in the toys' qualities.

A study of this kind was conducted by Bradbard and Endsley (1983). They assembled a group of gadgets (e.g., a pizza cutter and burglar alarm) that were generally unknown to preschool children. The interviewer then talked individually with preschool children, introducing them to the name of each gadget and identifying each as something that either boys, girls, or both boys and girls like to use. Consistent with the idea that children are affected by knowing that an object is "for boys" versus "for girls," the data showed that when given a chance to play with the gadgets, children explored the "own sex" objects significantly more than either the "both sex" or "other sex" objects, and they explored the "both sex" objects more than the "other sex" objects. Additional studies have reported similarly enhanced exploration of "own-sex" objects that in actuality were not associated in any way with gender (i.e., they were novel objects varyingly labeled as "for boys," "for girls," or "for both boys and girls") even when there was an incentive to play with the objects labeled for children of the other sex (Bradbard, Martin, Endsley, & Halverson, 1986), and even if the own-sex toy was considerably less attractive than the other-sex toy (Martin, Eisenbud, & Rose, 1995).

Taken together, the findings discussed in this section support the idea that children's cognitions—both about their own gender group membership (gender identity in the sense used by Kohlberg) and about what is "for boys" versus "for girls" (what we earlier referred to as gender correlates)—affect children's decisions about what to engage with in the environment.

Encoding

Assuming that the child has attended to and in some way engaged with something in the environment, there is still room for the individual's cognitions to influence the way that the encountered information is interpreted or encoded. Several investigators have recognized that children's gender cognitions may lead them to have difficulty in actually interpreting what they see or hear.

Encoding Errors

A good example of a gender-schema based encoding problem comes from a study in which 6- to 12-year-old children were taught explicitly that it was interests and training—not gender—that determines who can do different jobs (Bigler & Liben, 1990). For example, children were taught that to be a construction worker it did not matter whether someone was a man or a woman, but rather what matters is liking to build things and learning to use machines. After learning these rules, children practiced applying them. For example, during a lesson, children were told: "Ann loves to build things. Ann knows how to drive a bulldozer" and they were then asked: "Could Ann be a construction worker? How do you know?" Some responses suggested that children had difficulty encoding the information that was presented when it was inconsistent with their gender cognitions. For example, one child said "Yes [Ann could be a construction worker] because he followed the rules." Like the newspaper reporter who seemed to have difficulty connecting a person named Susan with a geoscientist, this child seemed to have difficulty understanding that a bulldozer operator named Ann called for the pronoun "she."

As an example from everyday life rather than from research, a feminist colleague of ours, attempting to raise her children in a nonsexist manner, reported reading a story to her children. The main character in the story is a turtle named Franklin, and in this episode, Franklin visits the doctor for a cracked shell. The doctor, introduced as "Dr. Bear" is shown in the book dressed in a lab coat, high heels, and pearls. Our colleague asked her listening daughters, roughly 4 and 8 years old, whether Dr. Bear was a man or a woman. Both responded without hesitation that Dr. Bear was a man!

There have also been more formal descriptions of encoding difficulties reported in the research literature. In a study by Martin and Halverson (1983) that will be described in more detail later, 5- and 6-year-old children were initially asked to identify the sex of the actors shown in activity pictures as they were presented. Of those errors that occurred, 84% were cases in which the actor was performing an activity associated with the other sex (e.g., a boy holding a doll), leaving only 16% occurring with pictures showing a stereotypic link between activity and sex. Similarly, in a more natural picture-reading context, Gelman et al. (2004) reported that 2.5-year-old children referred to a pictured woman as a man or pictured man as a woman three times more often if the depicted characters appeared in gender nontraditional activities (as in a woman driving a truck or a man performing ballet) than if the depicted characters appeared in traditional activities.

Encoding Organization

Encoding concerns not only the accuracy with which incoming information is interpreted, but also the way that incoming information is organized. Research using different kinds of learning tasks has revealed the effects of gender cognitions on encoding organization.

Evidence from the phenomenon of proactive inhibition

A classic demonstration of the role of gender categories and correlates on the organization used to encode incoming information comes from early research by Kail and Levine (1976). They made use of the well-established finding that if participants are given successive lists of related words to learn, performance falls off when trying to remember later lists in the series. Similar items stored in memory from earlier lists interfere with learning conceptually related new items on the later lists. This phenomenon—in which new learning is diminished by prior learning of related material—is referred to as **proactive inhibition (PI)**. After a decrement occurs, if the next list contains items drawn from a category that the participant encodes in a separate category from that used for items in the prior lists, performance recovers, a phenomenon known as **release from PI**.

Kail and Levine used a release from PI paradigm to test whether 7- and 10-year-old children organized items by their masculinity and femininity. On the first four trials, words to be remembered were those with either masculine or feminine associations, leading to proactive inhibition. On the critical fifth trial, items were drawn from the other category (i.e., feminine if trials 1-4 had been masculine; masculine if trials 1-4 had been feminine). With the category shift, boys showed a release from PI as did girls who had shown themselves to be relatively more feminine in a sex-role preference task administered separately from the memory task. These findings suggest that the masculinity-femininity dimension of the words was encoded by these three groups of children (i.e., boys who had given masculine responses on the preference task, boys who had given feminine responses, and girls who had given feminine responses).

Evidence from discrimination learning

In another investigation of the role of gender cognitions for encoding, Carter and Levy (1991) tested 3- to 6-year-old children using a discrimination-learning task. In such tasks, participants are shown two stimuli at a time (e.g., a red square on the left and a blue circle on the right), and are asked to pick one. After each answer the child receives feedback about whether the choice was correct or incorrect. By answering a series of such pairs, the child eventually figures out which of the possible dimensions is the one that defines correct answers (in this example, color, shape, or left-right position). For example, the child might learn that the red one is always correct, and neither shape nor left-right position matters. Researchers are interested not only in how long it takes participants to figure out the correct dimension; they are also interested in how easily participants can switch gears if the experimenter makes a change in the critical dimension. For example, after giving 10 trials in which the red one is always the correct choice, the researcher might change the rules so that now it is always the circle that is correct. How readily the child can make the shift to the new dimension is affected by whether or not the child had been paying attention to that newly correct dimension in the first place.

Carter and Levy (1991) applied this paradigm to gender by having sex-type as one dimension of the stimuli (e.g., a baby doll vs. a toy truck) and size as another dimension. They also gave children a measure of their own sensitivity to gender, identifying children as being either **gender schematic** (i.e., as explained in chapter 8, children who tend to view the world in terms of gender) or **gender aschematic** (children who do not tend to view the world in terms of gender).

They found that—in comparison to the gender aschematic children—the gender schematic children took significantly more trials to switch from the sex-type dimension to the size dimension, and significantly fewer trials to switch from the size dimension to the sex-type dimension. In other words, the sex-type of the stimuli seemed to be readily available to the gender schematic children. For these children, tasks that require them to pay attention to gender are relatively easy whereas tasks that require them to ignore gender are relatively hard. Children who were gender aschematic were not affected one way or another by which dimension was used to define correct responses. Taken together, these results are consistent with the idea that some children (those who are gender schematic) routinely encode the world around them in terms of gender as they process information.

Memory

The findings covered in the prior sections concerned situations in which children had attended to something in the environment (attention) and then initially interpreted or organized the encountered material (encoding). In this section we turn to the next step in the process—how information is remembered over time. Without question, it is this next step in the flow of information processing—memory—that has attracted the greatest attention in the gender development literature. Under the rubric of memory research, investigators have focused on whether gender cognitions affect whether children remember information at all, and if so, whether they remember the information accurately or instead distort it in some way. The effects of two major kinds of cognitions on memory have received the most attention. The first concerns the degree to which children's cognitions about themselves (e.g., their knowledge of their own gender; the greater detail of their own-sex schema) lead them to remember material relevant to their own gender better than they remember material relevant to the other gender. The second concerns the degree to which children's cognitions about males and females in general (i.e., their knowledge or endorsement of cultural gender stereotypes) lead them to remember schema-consistent material better than schema inconsistent material. In the following section we sample research from each of these two major approaches in turn.

Differential Memory for Own-Gender Versus Other-Gender Material

Theoretical expectations
The cognitive theories discussed in chapter 8 lead to the expectation that children will remember material related to their own sex better than material related to the other sex, an expectation that has been supported by a range of research, some of which is sampled below.

Illustrative research on differential memory for own-gender versus other-gender material
One study relevant to this prediction of differential memory is the one by Bradbard and Endsley (1983) discussed earlier in which children were exposed to novel objects that were described as either for boys or for girls. As already reported, the data showed that children explored "own-sex" objects more fully than "other-sex" objects. In addition, and relevant to the current focus on memory, children also recalled the names of own-sex objects better than those of other-sex objects. A similar finding of a memory advantage for own-sex items was reported in a later study (Bradbard et al., 1986), even among some groups of children who had not shown greater exploration of the toys labeled as for their sex. The advantage in memory of own-sex material is consistent with the general phenomenon identified in social-cognitive psychology as the **self-reference effect**, a term used to refer to greater attention and memory for self-relevant material (Kuiper & Rogers, 1979; Rogers, Kuiper, & Kirker, 1977; see also a meta-analysis by Symons & Johnson, 1997). The findings are also consistent with Martin and Halverson's (1981) predication that children will develop their own-sex (in-group) schemas in far more detail than they will develop other-sex (out-group) schemas.

Not every individual study has shown support for this own-sex memory bias, however, and early reviews summarizing empirical work relevant to differential own- versus other-sex memories were inconclusive. Some (e.g., Ruble & Stangor, 1986) concluded that the data provided evidence for an own-sex memory bias, whereas others (e.g., Schau & Scott, 1984) argued that the data did not allow this conclusion.

Meta-analysis of research on differential memory for own-gender versus other-gender material
To move beyond conclusions that can be reached from narrative reviews, a meta-analysis was conducted to summarize the empirical data on differential memory for masculine and feminine material depending on the child's own sex (Signorella, Bigler, & Liben, 1997). In order for a research study to be entered into the meta-analysis, it had to include both male and female characters in the to-be-remembered materials, and both boys and girls had to be given both masculine and feminine materials. An additional criterion

for inclusion of studies in the meta-analysis was that the study had to avoid confounding (i.e., always link-ing) sex of the character shown with the stereotyped gender of the activity. An example demonstrates the reason for this criterion. Suppose a study showed all children a picture of a man fixing a car (male shown in a stereotypically masculine job of auto mechanic) and a woman standing in front of an elementary school class (female in a stereotypically feminine job of teacher). If boys showed better memory for the auto mechanic than the teacher, it could be either because boys have better memory for male characters than female characters or because boys are more likely to remember culturally masculine jobs. It would be possible to separate out the effects of sex of character from cultural stereotype of activity only if both boys and girls saw male and female characters engaged in both masculine and feminine activities. Thus, only studies that gave the full range of items to both boys and girls were included in the meta-analysis.

Studies entered into the meta-analysis varied with respect to the difficulty of the memory task. One dimension on which difficulty varied was by the type of memory task: **recognition** versus **free recall**. In recognition tasks, children are asked to select the original material from several choices, or to look at items and say whether they had been seen earlier. For example, children might be asked to pick which of 5 pictures was the one shown earlier, or they might be shown one picture at a time and asked, for each, whether it was "old" or "new." In free recall tasks, children are asked to reproduce the material in some way (e.g., describe or draw the original stimulus). Recognition tasks are generally easier than recall tasks because they provide something that might look familiar and trigger memory. (This difference is well known to college students in the difference between multiple choice vs. essay tests.) Another dimension on which difficulty varied was the **retention interval**; that is, the time between when children were initially exposed to the material and when they were asked to recognize or recall it. Longer delays are expected to be more difficult. Both these variables were of interest because it was hypothesized that a same-sex memory advantage might be more likely to occur with more difficult memory tasks.

Of greatest interest for our present discussion were the conclusions reached through this meta-analysis concerning memory for own- versus other-sex characters. Consistent with the notion that chil-dren remember materials better if they are relevant to their own sex, when the character in the story or picture was male, boys tended to remember more; when the character in the story or picture was female, girls tended to remember more. These findings were not affected by task difficulty. That is, this result held for both easier recognition tasks and harder recall tasks, and it held for both short and long delay intervals.

There was a parallel (and quantitatively even stronger) effect for the cultural sex typing of the to-be-remembered materials: boys showed stronger memories for culturally masculine items and girls showed stronger memories for culturally feminine items. These effects were even greater with more difficult memory tasks (i.e., with recall rather than recognition tasks and with longer rather than shorter delays). Thus, these findings are similar to those from the work on imitation described earlier: children have a greater tendency to imitate and remember same- than other-sex characters, and an even stronger tendency to imitate and remember activities traditionally associated with their own sex (irrespective of the sex of the person engaging in that activity).

Differential Memory for Traditional Versus Nontraditional Material

Theoretical expectations: group-level and individual-level predictions

The cognitive theories discussed in chapter 8 also lead to the expectation that children will remem-ber material more easily if it is consistent with the content of their gender schemas. Many studies have addressed the question of whether children, in general, are better able to recall stereotype-consistent (gender traditional) material than stereotype-inconsistent (gender nontraditional) material. Of interest in this work are both the quantity of recall (e.g., does the child recall more traditional than nontraditional pictures?) and the accuracy of recall (e.g., does the child recall the nontraditional material as it was shown, or does the child distort it in some way?). Most studies address these questions at the group level by asking whether children—overall—show better memory for gender traditional material. Some studies, though, ask the finer-grained question of whether variations among children with respect to gender cognitions are related to variations in memory (e.g., do children who hold particularly strong gender stereotypes have a particularly difficult time remembering nontraditional material?)

Illustrative research with a group-level approach

In one of the early studies investigating the question of memory for stereotype consistent versus inconsistent material, Koblinsky, Cruse, and Sugawara (1978) read stories to fifth-grade children. Embedded in each story were male and female characters who displayed traits and actions that were either consistent or inconsistent with gender stereotypes that they had shown were held by children of the same age. A story about a children's circus is illustrative.

> While Bill sewed the clown costume, Mary looked for rags and soft things to stuff his stomach...Bill was messy and there were lots of clothes lying around the clubhouse. When the clown suit was finished, the children began to look for their old bicycle....Mary sat down to fix the broken bike seat. Bill sat on the floor and played roughly with Tabby, pretending to be a great animal trainer. (Koblinsky, Cruse, & Sugawara, 1978, p. 455)

Soon after they heard the stories, children were asked which character had performed each of several actions (e.g., fixed the bike seat) or had displayed a particular trait (e.g., was rough). As predicted, and consistent with the hypothesis that children's gender stereotypes would affect the way that children process and remember new information, children showed significantly better memories for stereotype-consistent actions and traits (e.g., "Bill was messy") than those that were stereotype-inconsistent (e.g., "Bill sewed the clown costume"). Children had particular difficulty remembering male characters that had performed or displayed feminine behaviors and traits.

Combining both group-level and individual-level approaches

A later investigation by Liben and Signorella (1980) also tested the prediction that children in general would show better memories for material consistent with cultural gender stereotypes (traditional) than they would for material inconsistent with those stereotypes (nontraditional). In addition, however, they also addressed the finer-grained within-child questions. To do so, they tested individual children's own levels of endorsement of gender stereotypes (using the GASC measure described earlier). They predicted that it would be the highly stereotyped children who would show differential memory for traditional versus nontraditional material.

Children (6–9 years) were shown drawings of men and women engaged in jobs and activities that were either gender traditional (e.g., a man dentist; a woman secretary), nontraditional (e.g., a woman construction worker; a man librarian), or neutral (e.g., a man reading a book; a woman riding a bicycle). After viewing a deck of cards with 60 such pictures and following a 5-minute delay, children were given a second deck of cards and asked to make old/new judgments for each picture. Half the pictures were indeed old, identical to those shown originally, but in the rest, the sex of character had been changed (e.g., a female dentist shown originally was replaced by a male dentist in an otherwise identical scene). There were two major predictions.

First, children—especially those with strong gender stereotypes—were expected to be better at recognizing "old" pictures that had originally been traditional than at recognizing "old" pictures that had originally been nontraditional. Indeed, as expected, highly stereotyped children correctly recognized more old traditional pictures than old nontraditional drawings, whereas less stereotyped children did not show this differential memory effect. Second, children—again, especially those with strong gender stereotypes—were expected to falsely recognize certain kinds pictures. At the level of group analysis, as predicted, children were more likely to (incorrectly) think they had seen a picture that appeared traditional in the recognition test when it had originally been nontraditional than the reverse. For example, children were more likely to say "yes" to a picture of a male construction worker (when they had actually seen a picture of a female construction worker) than they were to say "yes" to a male secretary (when they had actually seen a picture of a female secretary). At the level of within-child analysis, however, the prediction did not hold. That is, the distortions were comparable in both highly and less stereotyped children.

One possible reason that the data did not support the within-child prediction could be that the recognition task was too easy. Children have been shown to have remarkably good abilities to distinguish old from new pictures. Thus, in later studies, other types of memory tasks were used. One approach has been to use free recall tasks described earlier. Free recall tasks are particularly good for studying potential distortions because they do not constrain the child's answers in any way. But there are disadvantages as well. Free recall tasks are difficult, particularly for young children, and thus there may be few data points to interpret. If young children cannot remember anything at all, it would be impossible to find better memory for gender traditional material or to see any distortions! Furthermore, because responses are free to vary in any way, they are challenging to code reliably. A few studies have, though, employed free recall tasks, and have provided data relevant to distortions.

Research with recall tasks: group- and individual-level data

One study by Signorella and Liben (1984) used a free recall task with the traditional, nontraditional, and neutral pictures like those used in the earlier recognition study described above. Children (in kindergarten, second, and third grades) were shown a series of pictures (e.g., a female dentist), and then, after a 5-minute delay, asked to "name as many of the pictures as you can. What pictures did you see?" This paradigm offered children the chance to distort the original nontraditional material by reversing the sex of the character (e.g., remembering a male dentist) or by distorting the depicted activity (e.g., remembering her as a dental hygienist rather than as a dentist). To test the more specific prediction that distortions would be more common among more highly gender stereotyped children, an individual measure of gender stereotyping (the GASC, described earlier) was also administered to each child.

Among the various findings, what is most relevant here is that as predicted, highly stereotyped children—across the three ages—recalled more traditional than nontraditional pictures, whereas less stereotyped children did not show this difference. In addition, more reconstructions were produced by children who were highly stereotyped than by those who were less stereotyped, and almost all of these reconstructions transformed nontraditional items into traditional ones, rather than the reverse. For example, the picture of the male secretary was recalled by one child as a "typewriter repairman," and the picture of the woman judge was recalled by another child as a "cafeteria worker."

Research with free and probed recall tasks: group- and individual-level data

Another memory task that combines the advantages of recognition and free recall is the cued or **probed recall** task. In these tasks, the child is given some cue about the original stimulus and is then asked to fill in some additional information about the original stimulus. Illustrative of this approach was a study by Martin and Halverson (1983). Among the tasks they used (not all of which are described here), 5- and 6-year-old children were shown 16 pictures of people performing either stereotype consistent or inconsistent activities (e.g., a girl playing with a doll vs. a girl sawing wood). As in the recognition and free recall studies just described (Liben & Signorella, 1980; Signorella & Liben, 1984), the goal was to determine if gender schemas about the sexes were powerful enough to cause children to distort their memories of whether they saw males or females in the pictures.

In this study, the pictures were presented in a way that was likely to enhance children's attention and processing: children were asked to examine the pictures to identify the sex and age of each actor, and then to rate how similar they were to the person in the picture. Without being warned that there would be a memory task, a week later, children were asked to remember any of the pictures they could (free recall). They were then given two probed recall tasks. In an activity probed recall task, they were shown 16 old and 8 (interspersed) new pictures of activities, and for each were asked if they remembered seeing someone doing that activity. In a sex of actor probed recall task, each of original activities was named, and children were asked (verbally) if they had seen a girl, boy, man, or woman performance performing it. A week or two after memory testing, children were given the Sex Role Learning Inventory (**SERLI**, Edelbrock & Sugawara, 1978), which is a measure that assesses children's preferences for traditionally masculine or feminine activities (sex role preference scale or SRP) and knowledge of cultural sex roles (sex role discrimination scale or SRD).

Particularly relevant to our present discussion are the findings concerning memory distortions. First, although the free recall task elicited recall of only a small number of items, it did provide evidence of distortion that was consistent with gender stereotypes. Children more commonly reversed the sex of actors when the original depictions were stereotype inconsistent than when they were stereotype consistent. Data from the sex of actor probed recall tasks were similar in that when asked specifically about the sex of the actor who had been shown performing a particular activity, children were more likely to answer incorrectly if the original picture had been counterstereotyped. Interestingly, the data from the activity probed recall measure were more complex. Consistent with the notion of better memory for schema-consistent information, children tended to remember female actors who were performing traditionally feminine activities better than female actors performing traditionally masculine activities. However, the reverse held for male actors. It was the male actors performing traditionally feminine activities who were remembered best. Martin and Halverson (1983) suggested that probably these counterstereotyped depictions fell so far outside the norm that they were even more memorable than schema consistent material.

The other aspect of Martin and Halverson's findings relevant to the present discussion concerns the data on individual differences in children's own gender schemas. As in other research that has examined individual differences in stereotyping in relation to memory, the expectation was that schema-based distortions should be more prevalent among children who hold stronger gender stereotypes than among those who are less stereotyped. The data did not, however, support this prediction. As suggested by Martin and Halverson (1983), one explanation of the failure to find an association might lie in the **restricted range** in stereotyping scores: most of the SERLI scores among children were very similar. When scores on a measure are all clustered together, it is virtually impossible to find an association between the scores on that measure and anything else. This restricted range is itself likely to reflect some of the limitations of the SERLI that have been identified elsewhere (Liben & Bigler, 2002; Ruble et al., 2006; Signorella & Liben, 1985); for example, the chore-like nature of the feminine items, and the use of forced choice response options on the sex-role discrimination (SRD) questions used in SERLI.

To address these issues, Martin and Halverson (1983) designed some additional ways to look at their data, devising alternative systems for scoring children's responses on the SERLI as well as alternative ways for scoring children's memory. Using these systems, they did find some evidence for variations across children that linked patterns of stereotyping and patterns of memory, although these were not identical to those of earlier studies.

Using an experimental design to study the link between gender schemas and memory

In general, then, there has been considerable (although not perfect) support for the prediction that children who are more highly gender schematic will show stronger schema-consistent memory distortions (e.g., Carter & Levy, 1988; Levy, 1989; Martin & Halverson, 1993; Signorella & Liben, 1984). The investigations discussed so far that have included assessments of gender schemas in individual children have thus provided correlational evidence for the relation between gender schemata and memory.

As always, though, correlational data leave open the possibility that two variables are associated not because one influences the other, but rather because both are linked to a third variable. For example, both lower stereotyping and better memory might each independently stem from higher levels of general intelligence. One way to examine whether children's stereotypes have a causal effect on memory is to intervene in some way to change children's stereotypes, and then to see whether children who experimentally acquired more flexible attitudes then show better memory for nontraditional material. This approach was used in a study by Bigler and Liben (1990) with 6- to 12-year-old children.

Children were first given a measure of their level of stereotyping (the GASC), and then they were assigned to either to either an experimental or control group so that initial stereotyping scores would be matched in the two groups. Children in both groups then received classroom lessons about 10 occupations. Children in the experimental group were taught the rule that it is skills and interests, not gender, that determines whether someone can hold particular occupational roles. They then practiced applying the rules to 10 specific occupations (e.g., the example of Ann, the construction worker, described earlier). Children in the control group were taught lessons about the same 10 occupations using information about these jobs typically given to children of this age. For example, the control class discussed questions such as "What does a construction worker do for your neighborhood?" Following the lessons, children were again given the GASC as a measure of stereotyping. In addition, the GASC question format ("Who can be a(n) _____ [job name]? Only men, only women, or both men and women?") was used with the 10 jobs that had been taught in the occupation lessons.

The data showed that on both the GASC and the taught jobs, children who had been categorized as highly gender stereotyped at the beginning of the study were no longer highly stereotyped if they had been assigned to the experimental lessons. If they had received the control lessons, however, they still gave highly stereotyped responses to the GASC and taught jobs.

Given that the intervention succeeded in reducing gender stereotypes in the experimental group, the critical question to address for the present purpose is what happened to these children's memory for stereotype-inconsistent material. To examine this question, children heard 12 stories (one per day) in which a child character interacts with an adult character who is depicted in either a gender traditional (e.g., a male astronaut) or nontraditional (e.g., a female dentist) role other than those explicitly taught in the lessons. Children were then interviewed individually and asked five questions about each story. The first two questions were unrelated to occupations or gender and answers served to test whether children had been paying attention. The third tested the child's memory for the gender of the child, which served to test memory for gender when stereotypes were irrelevant. The final questions were the critical ones for this study because both concerned the person in the occupation. Specifically, the fourth required the child to respond with information about the occupation and the fifth was phrased to lead the child to use a pronoun, thereby indicating how the child remembered the portrayed person's gender.

The finding most relevant for the present discussion concerns memory performance by children who were in the experimental versus the control groups. The data showed that the two groups performed comparably on the first three types of questions that were completely unrelated to gender. They also performed comparably on the last two gender-related questions when they were questions about traditional stories. These data suggest that the two groups were well matched with respect to general memory ability, attentiveness, and so on. Where they differed, however, was in their performance on the last two gender-related questions when they were questions about the nontraditional stories. On these, the children who had been in the experimental group showed significantly better memory. This pattern of results thus provides experimental support for the suggestion derived from the earlier correlational studies: It does indeed appear that the strength of gender stereotypes in individual children affects memory for gender-related material.

Illusory correlations as an index of stronger schema-consistent memory

Thus far, in discussing research addressed to the role of gender schemas on memory, we have covered studies in which the dependent measure concerns either the quantity of information remembered (e.g., the number of traditional vs. nontraditional items recalled) or the quality of information remembered (e.g., distortions in memory of the gender of the person in a picture). We close this section by describing another kind of impact of gender schemas that had been predicted in both social psychology (Hamilton & Rose, 1980) and developmental psychology (Martin & Halverson, 1981)—**illusory correlation.** This phenomenon is mistakenly thinking that one has seen stereotype-consistent material more often (or stereotype-inconsistent material less often) than one actually has.

In one of the few empirical studies examining this process in children, Meehan and Janik (1990) showed first- and second-grade children 36 different pictures of men and women engaged in culturally stereotyped, counterstereotyped, and neutral activities. Within each of the 6 picture types, half (3) of the pictures were shown three times each. Two minutes after having seen the 72 acquisition pictures, children were shown 54 recognition pictures and for each they were asked to say whether the drawing had been shown never, once, or three times before. Consistent with the concept of illusory correlation, children less commonly remembered nontraditional than traditional pictures that had been seen three times before. Thus this more quantitative aspect of memory is also affected by underlying gender cognitions.

Summary

Taken together, the findings discussed in this section support the conclusion that what children remember about gender-relevant material is strongly influenced by their knowledge about gender correlates as well as by individual differences in the degree to which individual children endorse cultural gender stereotypes. With respect to the former, there is evidence from a wide range of memory tasks that, with few exceptions (e.g., particularly strong violations of male gender norms), children remember schema-consistent information better than schema-inconsistent information. Furthermore, there is considerable evidence that children distort memories of schema inconsistent material in ways that transform them into schema consistent material. The data bearing on effects of individual differences are also generally supportive of the prediction that it is highly gender stereotyped children who will be especially likely to show better memory for traditional than nontraditional material and will be more likely to distort nontraditional material when they do to recall it. These individual differences are more likely to be observed with more rather than less sensitive measures of the individuals' gender stereotypes, and with more rather than less difficult memory tasks. Evidence from studies on illusory correlation is also consistent with the general prediction that memory processes are affected in ways that enhance or exaggerate memories for stories, pictures, and events that are consistent with traditional cultural stereotypes.

Summary

As is probably obvious from the variety of topics covered in this section, information processing is relevant to virtually every aspect of human behavior and thought. It affects which aspects of the environment are even noticed, the form and structure that information takes as it is incorporated into the human mind, and the way in which (if at all) the information is retained for later use.

The findings reviewed in the section on attention support the general notion that children attend with greater intensity to things they encounter (be they people, objects, or events) if they are somehow linked to their own sex rather than to the other sex. The findings reviewed in the section on encoding demonstrate that a given stimulus is not understood and interpreted in the same way by each person. Even when two people are focusing their attention on the same aspect of the environment, they can interpret it very differently depending on their own prior cognitive structures or schemata. For example, a particular person in a white lab jacket in a dental office may be interpreted or encoded as a dentist by one person and by a dental hygienist by another simply because each observer has entered that office with more versus less traditional gender schemas. Finally, the findings reviewed in the section on memory show that gender cognitions have an even greater impact on processing with the passage of time. Gender stereotypes affect the absolute amount of information that is recalled as well as the accuracy of what is recalled. Individuals who hold stronger gender stereotypes find it particularly difficult to remember nontraditional information, and they are particularly likely to distort it, especially as their memory systems are taxed by more difficult memory tasks or by longer retention intervals.

THE IMPACT OF GENDER CONSTANCY

Overview

In the immediately preceding section, we selected an illustrative outcome—information processing—and reviewed evidence that demonstrates that various components of information processing are affected in powerful ways by a range of gender cognitions. In the current and final section of this chapter we take the reverse the approach and select an illustrative cognitive input—gender constancy—and discuss research that addresses its impact on other aspects of gender development.

The study of gender constancy, like information processing, is a vibrant and long-standing research area. One branch of research on gender constancy has been on the construct itself. This work has focused on defining and verifying the existence of its component developmental milestones, designing reliable and valid measures of each component, studying the concurrent association between understanding of gender constancy and understanding of theoretically related cognitive achievements (e.g., understanding conservation of liquid quantity), and establishing the ages at which the various components of gender constancy emerge and how these timetables may be affected by factors such as culture, socioeconomic status, and exposure to relatively more versus less gendered environments. We have already included extensive discussions of many of these issues, some in chapter 8 when we described the theoretical origins of the construct within Kohlberg's (1966) cognitive-developmental approach to gender, and some earlier in the current chapter when we were describing children's developing gender concepts.

A second branch of research on gender constancy has been addressed to the role that achieving gender constancy may have for other dimensions of gender development. It was, of course, an interest in the consequences of gender constancy that was at the heart of Kohlberg's (1966) initial formulation of the concept. That is, as discussed in considerable detail in chapter 8, Kohlberg (1966) hypothesized that it is children's knowledge of being either a boy or a girl that motivates them to acquire boy-like or girl-like qualities and behaviors. In a phrase, Kohlberg viewed the process (illustrated for boys) as "I am a boy, therefore I want to do boy things" (p. 89). This identification of oneself as either a boy or girl (referred to as gender identity in Kohlberg's terminology) constitutes only the first phase of a more protracted process of reaching a mature concept of gender constancy. As reviewed earlier, children next come to understand that gender remains the same over the life course (referred to as gender stability), and then, finally, to understanding that gender remains unchanged, even despite changed appearance (referred to as gender consistency).

There is, though, some confusion about precisely which of the three phases of gender constancy Kohlberg believed motivated children's gender development. In some places he seemed to suggest that only the most basic gender labeling (identity) is needed, whereas in others, he seemed to suggest that full constancy (including gender consistency) is needed. Even apart from Kohlberg's initial theoretical formulation, later theorists have offered alternative hypotheses about the impact that different phases of constancy might have on children's gender development (e.g., Huston, 1983; Martin et al., 2002; Ruble et al., 2007).

Many studies have been conducted to examine whether the mastery of gender constancy seems to affect a wide variety of outcomes such as greater participation in own-sex (i.e., as culturally defined) activities, peer groups, interests, and dressing habits. Rather than attempt to review the breadth of this work, instead we describe three specific studies in some detail as a means of illustrating this research literature. We close this section by offering some generalizations about the broader range of findings.

Early Research on the Impact of Gender Constancy

An early and by now classic study in this area is one by Slaby and Frey (1975). Preschool children (ranging in age from 26 to 68 months) were first given gender constancy measures that assessed labeling, stability, and consistency components of gender constancy. They were then shown a 5.5-minute film in which a man and woman were performing everyday activities such as popping corn, playing musical instruments, and drinking juice. The two figures appeared on different sides of the screen so that it would be easy to tell which character the child was watching. Consistent with the hypothesized importance of gender constancy for children's selective attention to same-sex models, the data showed that children's relative preference for watching the same-sex model over the other-sex model in the film increased successively with each advancing level of gender constancy. Furthermore, the link between gender constancy level and selective attention held even when chronological age was statistically controlled, thus suggesting that it was something more than the general experience that comes with living longer that mattered.

In another early study, Ruble, Balaban, and Cooper (1981) explored the potential link between gender constancy and children's responses to gendered, televised toy commercials. The experimenter first escorted children (ranging from 44 to 77 months) to a room where the child was asked to watch a cartoon. When the experimenter left to make a phone call, children watched the cartoon which, for most children, was accompanied by a one minute toy commercial for a gender neutral toy (a movie viewer). The commercial was filmed in either a masculine or feminine version by showing the toy being played with either by two boys or by two girls. The gender of the narrator of the commercial matched that of the children in the film. Children in the control group saw no commercial at all.

Children's watching times were observed through a one-way mirror. The experimenter then reappeared briefly, explaining that the child was now free to play with toys in the room. Among them was the movie viewer shown in the commercial as well as three additional gender neutral toys. Children's toy play was then observed for 5 minutes. Following the play session, children were asked several other questions about the toys (e.g., how much they liked each one; whether they would give each to a boy or a girl) and about the commercials (e.g., which toy had been shown in the commercial and whether girls or boys had been playing with it). Finally, children were given the gender constancy interview designed by Slaby and Frey (1975), although the responses were scored with a modified scoring system that differentiated more finely within children's understanding of gender consistency. Using this measure, children were categorized as having relatively more- or less-advanced understanding of gender constancy (called the high and low gender constancy groups, respectively).

Given the variety of measures, not surprisingly, there were several complex findings. What is particularly relevant here, though, are the findings that demonstrated a connection between children's responses on the gender constancy measures and what they took from the gendered toy commercial. Most importantly, only children in the high gender constancy group were strongly affected by the gendered nature of the commercial. These children tended to avoid the toy if they had seen it being played with by children of the other sex. Children in the low gender constancy group did not show this gendered effect. The pattern of responses to the question about whether the toy was appropriate for boys or girls paralleled the behavioral toy play data. That is, only children in the high gender constancy group responded in a gendered manner; for example, saying that a toy that had been played with by boys in the commercial was appropriate for boys but not for girls. Overall, the findings from this study support the notion that once children achieve an advanced understanding of gender constancy, they are more attentive to, and more likely to apply and extend whatever gender-linked information they see (or think they see) in the environment.

Although this study was published over a quarter century ago, it raised many of the most important conceptual and methodological issues that have been at the forefront of contemporary work. One important issue raised concerns the contrasting patterns of associations among gender constancy, age, disproportionate attention to same-sex models, and knowledge of cultural gender stereotypes. Level of gender constancy—but not age—predicted to differential attention to same-sex models and to more gendered assignment of the toys. Gender constancy did not, however, predict to children's knowledge of the cultural stereotypes of toys found in the everyday environment—age did. This contrast foreshadows contemporary arguments about the importance of using measures that distinguish between knowledge versus endorsement of gender stereotypes, a topic covered at some length in the earlier section of the chapter.

A second issue emerging from the Ruble et al. (1981) study concerns the importance of studying distinctions within the overall construct of gender constancy. The importance of measuring specific constructs within gender constancy rather than measuring some overall, global construct has continued to be a focus of contemporary work on the impact of gender constancy on other outcomes.

Contemporary Research on Gender Constancy

A third illustrative study by Ruble et al. (2007) continues in a similar tradition. However, rather than examining outcome variables related to differential attention and recall of own- versus other-sex models, the outcome examined was children's endorsement of gender norms or stereotypes. In this study, children

(3–7 years) were first given a gender constancy measure, again modified from Slaby and Frey (1975). Care was taken in selecting, combining, and scoring items to allow for separate assessments of the components of gender constancy. Furthermore, in keeping with a methodological point they noted had been made decades earlier (e.g., Emmerich et al., 1977; Wehren & De Lisi, 1983) but not always heeded, they required children to explain their reasoning to avoid having "pseudoconstancy" mistakenly be interpreted as true constancy.

Children were also given measures of their attitudes about violations of gender norms. Again, the investigators designed measures to discriminate among different aspects of these beliefs, specifically including questions about knowledge (e.g., "Who usually wears nail polish, boys or girls?"), rule-based rigidity ("Is it wrong for boys to wear nail polish?"), self-rigidity ("Would you like to be friends with a boy who wears nail polish?"), and fear of changing sex (e.g., "Are you afraid you would become a girl if you wore nail polish?). Also assessed was how central gender was to the child, and the child's beliefs about how their parents and peers would respond if they were to be seen playing with something traditionally associated with the other sex.

Again, the complexity of the design precludes describing findings fully, but what is particularly important here are some general conclusions about the association between various aspects of gender constancy and various outcomes related to children's gender-related beliefs. As expected, the data showed several such associations. First, in general, children who had reached more advanced levels of understanding gender constancy tended to have more flexible beliefs. Once children reached the stage of understanding gender stability, they showed decreased levels of rigidity for many of the variables. This pattern of findings is consistent with the hypothesis offered by Huston (1983) that perhaps once children become confident that superficial behaviors cannot change someone's actual sex, they become more relaxed about breaking gender norms.

A second general conclusion supported by the data is that some of the observed relations between gender constancy and gender beliefs were mediated by a middle-level achievement of gender constancy—gender stability—rather than by the most advanced achievement of gender constancy—gender consistency. This conclusion is interesting not only because of its bearing on theoretically derived hypotheses, but also because of its bearing on the methodological issues that have been raised throughout this chapter (and indeed, throughout the entire book) The precise way in which a construct is measured plays a critical role in patterns of data that emerge.

As noted initially, the three studies just described serve only as illustrations of research in this area. They neither individually nor collectively permit generalizations about the association between gender constancy and the wide range of outcomes that have been studied and the even wider range of outcomes that could be studied. Thus, in our closing section, we provide some more general comments about research in this area.

Summary

One theme that runs through the work reviewed above is the importance of methodology in assessing gender constancy. In particular, it is important to recognize that gender constancy is not some global, monolithic achievement that children either have or do not have. To borrow a phrase coined by Michael Chandler (1988) in discussing another aspect of cognitive development, it is critical to avoid a "one miracle view" of gender constancy. It is not a switch that turns from off to on at some point in early childhood. Instead, it undergoes a series of progressions in component concepts. In addition to assessing multiple components of gender constancy separately, it is important to find ways to assess the reasoning that lies behind a given response to a given question. As Ruble et al. (2006, p. 862) noted, "Care must be taken because the "errors" of older children may not reflect a lack of understanding and because high level responding among 3- to 4-year-olds may not reflect a true understanding of constancy." Methods must differentiate between two kinds of seemingly "wrong" or "right" answers, perhaps by designing more sensitive questions, or perhaps by requiring children to explain their reasoning (as in the study by Ruble et al., 2007 discussed above).

Second, there is by now quite a large body of research that has been addressed to the link between gender constancy and a variety of outcomes. In addition to the outcomes addressed in the illustrative studies reviewed earlier (selective attention, same-sex modeling, gender beliefs), components of gender constancy (specifically, gender identity and stability) have been shown to be related to greater same-sex activity choice, clothes, peer preferences, and affective responses to gender (see Martin et al., 2002). However, not all studies find the predicted associations. To mention only a few examples, studies have failed to find an association between gender constancy and performance on a gender-based sorting task (Levy & Carter, 1989; Serbin & Sprafkin, 1986) and to performance on a toy choice task (e.g., Bussey & Bandura, 1992; Lobel & Menashri, 1993). Thus, it is not yet possible to say with certainty how much impact gender constancy actually has on other domains or behaviors.

Third, even within the group of studies finding support for the theoretically predicted link between gender constancy and some outcome, there is variability with respect to which component of gender constancy seems to be critical. Significant associations are sometimes restricted to the highest stage of gender consistency, but sometimes they relate to the less advanced stage of gender stability or even to the least advanced stage of gender identity. In a recent narrative review, Ruble et al. (2006) suggested that when gender constancy does relate to some outcome, it most commonly relates to earlier stages of understanding (i.e., gender stability or gender identity) rather than the most advanced one (i.e., gender consistency).

It seems possible to conclude definitively only that gender constancy plays an important role in children's acquisition of gendered behaviors and attitudes. It is not yet possible to reach firm conclusions about how the mechanisms work in detail. This research area appears to us to be a particularly strong candidate for a meta-analysis. It also appears to be a strong candidate for research using experimental methods such as those that have been successful in other arenas. For example, one could provide an intervention designed to enhance some children's understanding of gender constancy and then test to see whether these children behaved differently from control children on some theoretically linked behavior (e.g., imitation of same-sex models). Although to our knowledge no studies of this kind have yet been published, at least one is underway (Arthur, Bigler, & Ruble, 2004). Perhaps by the time the next edition of this book is written, there will be both meta-analytic and experimental data on which to base more definitive conclusions about the consequences of different aspects of gender constancy.

CHAPTER SUMMARY

This chapter began with a vignette illustrating the way that gender cognitions can affect the way that people process information they encounter in everyday life. In the three sections that followed, we reviewed empirical research that documents children's developing gender-related categories, concepts, and correlates. Even during infancy, children begin to divide the world into male and female categories. With development, they become increasingly knowledgeable about the meaning of those gender divisions and concepts. They likewise become knowledgeable about how a whole range of domains are linked to gender. Children vary considerably in the rates at which they develop these categories, concepts, and knowledge, and show even more dramatic variations in the degree to which they endorse societal stereotypes about gender.

In the final two sections we reviewed a range of research on consequences of gender cognitions. The review of research on information processing showed well-documented influences of gender cognitions on the way that environmental information is attended to, encoded, and remembered. The review of research on the effects of gender constancy demonstrated a range of associations between cognitions and outcomes. Although many individual studies have found empirical support for hypothesized links, the research literature is far from consistent. One clear lesson from research is the importance of developing strong methods for assessing specific constructs. Additional research is needed both to provide better ways of summarizing the data already in hand (e.g., through meta-analyses) and to extend the database in new directions (e.g., through experimental and correlational designs).

Collectively, the material reviewed in this chapter has documented a rich set of ways in which children's cognitive selves affect the way they then interact with the people, objects, and events that surround them, thus supporting the general thesis of this chapter that children are important agents of their own further development. Of course, children are only one of the many agents that play an important role. In the chapters that follow, we consider some of the other powerful agents in process of gender development.

The Family as an Agent of Gender Development

10

"Stop crying, Ranny," said Battle shortly. "Bluet can cry her eyes out if she wants to, because she's a girl, but you can't, or I'll take the switch to you promptly." (Welty, 1982, p. 91.)

In the next several chapters we will be considering the impact of various socialization influences on the process of gender development. We will consider the impact of peers, school, and the media on various aspects of children's gender-related behaviors and cognitions. In this chapter, we will consider the impact of the family. That obviously will include the impact of parents, but also of siblings. We will consider family attitudes about gender, and various types of families (e.g., traditional, feminist, single parents, and gay and lesbian families). Although there is not much research on the topic, we will also examine the impact of grandparents on children's gender development.

PARENTAL PREFERENCE FOR CHILD SEX

If gender were unimportant, parents would never wish for a child of one sex or the other—but of course they sometimes do. Consider the story told by Carmen bin Laden, sister-in-law of the infamous terrorist, Osama bin Laden (bin Laden, 2004). Carmen, a young woman of Swiss and Iranian descent who was raised in Switzerland, married one of Osama's many half-brothers from the wealthy Saudi Arabian family. After marriage, Carmen and her husband both attended the University of Southern California, where her first daughter was born. She tells how her husband simply walked out of the room after her daughter's birth—clearly an extreme example of a father strongly preferring to have a son.

Strong preference for sons is not unique to the Middle East. In many developing countries in Africa and Asia parents continue to prefer male children (e.g., Ataca & Sunar, 1999; de Silva, 1993; Hortacsu, Bastug, & Muhammetberdiev, 2001; Khanna, 1997; Kiriti & Tisdell, 2005; Wen, 1993; Winkvist & Akhtar, 2000). In some countries, China and India in particular, selective abortion—in which unwanted females are aborted—has produced a situation in which there are many more males growing into maturity than females. Female Chinese infants have also been available for adoption by westerners at a much higher rate than male infants. This, of course, leaves these young men with few young women to marry.

In the Western world, the strong preference for male children seems to be disappearing, especially among women. Through the 1970s (Williamson, 1976) both men and women preferred boy children if they could have a child or children of only one sex, or they preferred boys as firstborns. Also, many families would keep trying to have another child if they had not yet had a boy. This may no longer be the case. Recent research with North American, Australian, and European parents (Andersson, Hank, & Rønsen, 2006; Brockmann, 2001; Grieshaber, 1998; Hammer & McFerran, 1988; Marleau & Saucier, 2002; McDougall, DeWit, & Ebanks, 1999; Pollard & Morgan, 2002; Pooler, 1991; Steinbacher & Gilroy,

1990; Swetkis, Gilroy, & Steinbacher, 2002) finds that the most common preference is to have one child of each sex or to have no preference one way or the other. There may be a small tendency for men to still want to have sons, especially as firstborns, but women are much less likely to express a preference for either sex, and some prefer to have daughters.

Even so, there are other indications that a subtle preference for sons may remain. Some researchers have reported that when there is a son in the family the parents are less likely to divorce (Katzev, Warner, & Acock, 1994). Moreover, when parents are unmarried when their child is born, they are somewhat more likely to marry quickly after the child's birth when their child is a boy (Lundberg & Rose, 2003). Finally, fathers seem to be more involved with the family when at least some of the children are boys (Harris & Morgan, 1991), and earn more money once they have a son as compared to a daughter (Lundberg & Rose, 2002).

Even though there does not seem to be much of a preference for children of one sex or the other in modern industrial societies, there is some evidence that when parents do have such a preference, the child's development may be affected. In one longitudinal study in Sweden (Stattin & Klackenberg-Larsson, 1991) parents' preferences for a child of one sex or the other were measured before the child was born (in the mid 1950s). The children and their parents were then followed through age 18, with one follow-up in the children's early twenties. The researchers found that the parents spent more time with children of the preferred sex, thought they had fewer problems, and had a better relationship with them in adolescence. These effects were relatively small overall, but they were most notable in the relationships between fathers and daughters.

TYPES AND MECHANISMS OF PARENTAL INFLUENCE

We can consider parental influence on gender development as being of four main types. First, parents create a gendered world for their children. They give them gender-related names; they purchase clothing, toys, and other items that are associated with one gender or the other; and they choose gendered activities or opportunities (think karate and dancing) for their young children and assign particular types of chores to older children. We can call this kind of action **"channeling or shaping"** children in gendered ways (Eisenberg, Wolchik, Hernandez, & Pasternack, 1985).

Second, parents may interact differently with their sons and daughters. They may be more willing to physically punish their sons than their daughters. They may avoid talking about emotional topics that signal vulnerability with their sons. They may play more roughly with sons, tossing them up in the air as toddlers, or roughhousing with elementary-aged boys in a manner that they don't do so with girls. Perhaps they talk about relationships more often with their daughters. This second type of parental influence can be called **"differential treatment"** of boys and girls.

Third, parents may provide **direct instruction** for their children (Parke & Buriel, 1998). Some of the instruction concerns the parent's views about appropriate social behavior. A father may tell a son that he shouldn't cry, or a mother may insist that a daughter wear dressy feminine clothes to a social occasion. In other cases, the instruction may be for certain skills or tasks. For generations mothers taught daughters household skills like quilting or cooking, and fathers taught their sons farming or other skills such as blacksmithing. Today's children may be instructed in sports, household tasks, or other gendered skills by one parent or the other.

Finally, parents serve as **models** for their children to imitate. If mothers and fathers behave differently, especially if the parents' actions are consistent with the actions of other men and women whom the child observes, children may come to imitate such gender-related actions and behaviors. If one parent has more power to make decisions in the home (e.g., the mother), but the other parent controls the money and has more power in the world outside the home (e.g., the father), then children may learn about power relations between men and women, or what to expect in relationships between the sexes, or what roles men and women play in the world. In other words, parents are among the gendered models available for children to imitate.

Channeling or Shaping: Parents Create a Gendered World

We've all heard stories of the father who went out and purchased a baseball and glove immediately after his infant son's birth. Today, when parents often know their child's sex months before the baby is even born, the process may begin sooner. Parents purchase toys, clothing, furniture, room decorations, and other items for their children on the basis of gender. One study demonstrated that infant boys and girls are dressed so differently that it is almost impossible not to tell the sex of an infant, even when they have no hair to be styled or cut in a boy's or girl's style (Shakin, Shakin, & Sternglanz, 1985). Girl babies have ruffles, puffy sleeves, and pink or yellow outfits, whereas boys' clothing is blue or red and is more likely to be decorated with sports' motifs. People have even been known to tape bows on the bald heads of baby girls (Fagot, 1995). Clearly, clothing, hairstyles, and hair ornaments (if there is hair) are the major ways in which gender is publicly identified in infants and young children.

As they grow older, boys and girls have different clothing, toys, objects and decorations in their bedrooms (Pomerleau, Bolduc, Malcuit, & Cossette, 1990; Rheingold & Cook, 1975). Girls are more likely to have dolls and stuffed animals, and boys to have vehicles and sports equipment. In chapter 12 we will consider the characteristics of boys' and girls' toys, and what kind of impact toys may have on children's development. For now, it is worth remembering that children's toys are very much linked to gender, that toys are among the aspects of gender role socialization provided by parents, and that play with certain kinds of toys may develop particular skills and attitudes and not others. Parents also choose different room decorations for boys and girls. It would not be surprising to see the bedspread and curtains in a boy's room to have a football or baseball design, and for a girl's room decorations to have flowers and ruffles. It is also the case that the colors of boys' and girls' clothing and room decorations differ—even the color of their pacifiers.

Boys' and Girls' Names

Almost the first thing that parents do is name their child, and names are quite obviously based on gender. But there are differences between boys' and girls' names other than the fact that some names are for boys and some are for girls. Boys are more likely to be given more traditional or "standard" names, and the range of possible names for boys is smaller (Barry & Harper, 1995; Lieberson & Bell, 1992). Girls' names vary more over time, but the popularity of boys' names is much less likely to fluctuate. The names that girls are commonly given today are often quite different from the names given to girls some years ago (e.g., Mildred vs. Madison), whereas boys are more likely to be given names that have existed for a long time—sometimes for centuries (e.g., David or Jacob). Parents are also more likely to make up new names for their daughters, and some of those names are rather frivolous (e.g., "Sunny"). Boys are also much more likely than are girls to be named after a parent or other relative (McAndrew, King, & Honoroff, 2002).

Interestingly, names that were used for boys and are later adopted for girls usually become girls' names over time (Barry & Harper, 1982). For example, in the past, names like Beverly and Evelyn were men's names. Once parents start to use names for girls, the names first become gender neutral, but eventually the names become used for girls only. Similarly, names used for both sexes (sometimes with different spellings) gradually also become names for girls (e.g., Leslie/Lesley; Marion/Marian; Francis/Frances; Tracy/Tracey). Today, traditional boys' names like Taylor and Madison are being used for girls, and soon we might expect that no one will choose these names for boys. All of these findings seem to suggest that parents see their sons in a more traditional manner right from the start, and that they are uncomfortable with an unusual name for a boy, especially a potentially feminine-sounding one.

Activities

Parents also choose activities for their children. For example, parents may take their young daughters to ballet lessons and their sons to karate. Although it is changing in Western cultures, one activity that has often had much more significance for boys than for girls is sports. We have already noted that boys have more sports' equipment and more sports' themes in their rooms. Parents believe that their sons have more athletic talent than their daughters, and that sports are more important for boys (Fredricks & Eccles, 2002). Parental encouragement of athletic activities for boys is among the reasons for boys' own greater interest in sports (Jacobs & Eccles, 1992). There is also evidence that when girls' parents (especially their fathers) are interested in their daughters' athletic involvement, their daughters are more involved in sports (Jodl, Michael, Malanchuk, Eccles, & Sameroff, 2001). Of course we need to emphasize that the child's actual talent in a domain like sports certainly influences interest in and involvement in that domain, and that practice and motivation to improve play very important roles in skill development. No one becomes a skilled musician or athlete without spending hours and hours of practice improving those skills, but it is clear that parents are one of the influences on the motivation to actually practice.

Differential encouragement of gendered activities for boys versus girls

In some of the findings discussed above, there was an indication that parents are especially likely to encourage sons to adopt gendered behavior and interests (Lytton & Romney, 1991). In particular, parents seem to be especially likely to encourage their sons to avoid feminine characteristics and interests, perhaps even more than encouraging them to adopt masculine ones. In one recent study (Kane, 2006), parents of preschoolers were interviewed about their sons' and daughters' gendered interests and characteristics, and especially about gender nonconformity in their children. Parents of daughters were often positive about their daughters' masculine activities and interests (e.g., "she does a lot of things that a boy would do, and we encourage that," and "I never wanted a girl who was a little princess, who was so fragile.... I want her to take on more masculine characteristics.", Kane, 2006, p. 157).

Some parents of sons were positive about certain feminine characteristics or interests in their sons, primarily those associated with nurturance, empathy, and the development of domestic skills. However, the most common response of parents of sons was to be very negative about femininity in sons, especially when it was associated stereotypic feminine appearance (e.g., frilly clothes, dresses, makeup), or toys linked to these aspects of femininity (e.g., Barbie dolls). Parents reported directly steering their sons away from such interests (e.g.,"He's asked about wearing girl clothes before, and I said no.... He likes pink, and I try not to encourage him to like pink just because, you know, he's not a girl.... There's not many toys I wouldn't get him, except Barbie.", Kane, 2006, p. 160). These parents also discouraged emotionality, crying, and "sissy" behavior in sons. Some fathers even reported calling their sons "babies" or "girls" when their sons cried in response to minor injuries.

Results like these suggest that, although parents encourage gendered activities and interests in both boys and girls, that they do so much more in sons. Some of the discouragement of femininity in sons appears to be directly linked to recognizing the greater value given to masculinity, some to concern that others would treat their sons negatively if they had feminine characteristics, and some to a fear in parents' minds that such interests are linked to male homosexuality. Fears that masculinity in girls would lead to rejection or predict homosexuality were much less common amongst the parents studied by Kane.

Academic Subjects

Another area of parental encouragement is for various academic subjects, particularly mathematics, science, reading and language arts, but also in fields like fine arts and music (e.g., Andre, Whigham, Hendrickson, & Chambers, 1999; Lynch, 2002). Parents hold gender-stereotyped beliefs about children's competence in such academic domains, and these stereotypes shape how parents think about their own children's abilities in stereotyped domains. That is, parents tend to underestimate their own child's ability if the stereotype favors the other sex, and overestimate their child's ability when the stereotype favors their child's sex (Jacobs & Eccles, 1992; Tenenbaum & Leaper, 2003).

When parents hold gender-stereotyped beliefs about academic domains, the parents' beliefs come to shape the children's perceptions about their competence. In fact, children's perceptions about their own ability (especially for girls in math) has been shown to be influenced more by their parents' perceptions about the children than by the children's own grades (Fredricks & Eccles, 2002; Herbert & Stipek, 2005; Jodl et al., 2001). This is a startling finding. Put in concrete terms, a girl with excellent grades in math may come to think she isn't very good in math at least partly because her parents have been subtly communicating gender stereotyped beliefs about girls' in competence in math. This is important because children's perceptions of their own ability influence what courses they take in high school, and what future career plans they make. If subtle gendered expectations that do not accurately reflect the children's actual or potential abilities are communicated to children, then children's future career choices are surely impacted.

Chores

Parents also assign different chores to boys and girls. If you are female, you may recall doing your own laundry or helping with the dishes when your brother didn't have to. Or, if you are male, you may recall being required to cut the grass or shovel snow while your sister watched television. One meta-analysis of differential treatment of sons and daughters by parents found that the encouragement of gender-typed activities and chores was the most consistent type of gender socialization by parents (Lytton & Romney, 1991) with an effect size of about a third to a half of a standard deviation ($d = 0.33$–0.50). Boys were especially likely to be given gender-typed chores.

But the assignment of household chores is actually a bit more complicated. Many more household tasks are defined as feminine than as masculine, and whether boys or girls are asked to do them often depends on the sibling composition of the family, the parents' gender role attitudes, and whether the mother is employed outside the home (Crouter, Head, Bumpus, & McHale, 2001; McHale, Crouter, & Whiteman, 2003). Typically, firstborns do more household chores, and in general, girls do more household chores than boys do, especially once they reach adolescence. Sons are even less likely to be asked to do feminine chores when parents have traditional attitudes about gender. For example, in a family with traditional attitudes (especially on the part of fathers), assuming she is old enough to do them, a younger sister may be more likely to be expected to do more chores than her older brother, whereas in other families, the firstborn of either gender is more likely to be doing them (McHale, Crouter, & Tucker, 1999). However, children of both sexes are more likely to help with household tasks when their mothers are employed and when they are in single-parent households. Also, when a family has only sons, the sons are more likely to be assigned "feminine" chores (e.g., kitchen, laundry, or childcare chores) as compared to families in which daughters are available to do them. So this is clearly a complicated issue. Unlike toy or activity choices, the necessity of getting the work done may well override gender-related concerns.

Channeling or Shaping: Conclusions

In this section, then, we have examined the extent to which parents create a gendered world for their children. We have seen that parents sometimes have preferences for children of one sex, especially for boys. Children are given names, clothing, toys, room decorations, and other items that are gender-related. Parents choose different activities for sons and daughters, and they encourage them to have different interests and to excel in different academic and occupational arenas. They seem to think that sons are more capable, competent, and perhaps smarter than their daughters. Parents, especially fathers, put more pressure on sons to avoid feminine interests and characteristics than they do daughters to avoid masculine ones. Indeed, some are even proud of daughters with masculine attributes.

To conclude, parents treat boys and girls differently with respect to many core aspects of gender-typed behavior. In one meta-analysis of this type of socialization, effect sizes (d) were on the order of 0.3–0.5 (Lytton & Romney, 1991). Boys are especially likely to be socialized in line with gender norms.

Parents' Interaction With Sons and Daughters

In the same meta-analysis just mentioned (Lytton & Romney, 1991), the authors concluded that, except for the encouragement of gender-typed behavior and a few other domains, parents treat boys and girls very similarly overall. However, some researchers have disputed Lytton and Romney's conclusions, or at least suggested that they underestimated the extent to which boys and girls are treated differently by parents. We will begin by looking at infants, and we will consider research on several different ways in which parents seem to act somewhat differently with boys and girls as they grow and develop.

Infancy

Parents' initial expectations about infants

About 30 years ago a group of researchers (Rubin, Provenzano, & Luria, 1974) undertook an ingenious study. They interviewed 30 pairs of parents whose first infant (half boys and half girls; all full-term and healthy) had just been born. They asked both mothers and fathers to use 18 adjective pairs to rate their babies. The adjective pairs were on opposite ends of a continuum (e.g., strong-weak; big-little, relaxed-nervous; active-inactive). The male and female babies' physical characteristics were also measured and found not to be different—the boys and girls were of equal length, weight, and physical health.

Both mothers and fathers rated daughters as softer, finer-featured, littler, and more inattentive. Although the basic trends were similar for mothers and fathers, fathers were especially likely to say that sons were firmer, larger featured, better coordinated, more alert, stronger, and hardier, and that daughters were at the opposite ends of those scales (e.g., less alert, weaker, more delicate). One striking thing about the findings of this study was that there were very few differences in the infants' actual characteristics, but still the parents saw their infants in gender-stereotyped terms from the moment they were born.

Recent research suggests that these processes continue today. Although parents don't seem to perceive large differences between boy and girl infants, they do continue to see boys as larger, stronger, more athletic, and less emotional (Karraker, Vogel, & Lake, 1995; Teichner, Ames, & Kerig, 1997), as well as more competent or capable. You may recall a study we discussed in chapter 1 (Mondschein, Adolph, & Tamis-LeMonda, 2000), in which mothers of 11-month-old infants were asked to estimate their babies' abilities to crawl down an inclined ramp. Mothers of the boy infants estimated that their babies could crawl steeper slopes and thought their sons would be more willing to attempt to crawl down more difficult slopes than did mothers of girls. In reality, however, the baby boys and girls were equally good crawlers, and attempted to crawl down ramps of equivalent slope. These mothers had no idea that their gendered expectations were influencing their beliefs about their own children's capabilities.

So, parents have gendered expectations about infants right from the beginning. These perceptions of infants' characteristics are important, although they are not the only or even the most powerful factor in influencing how parents behave with their infants. The infant's own characteristics, temperament, and behavior are very important factors in influencing how parents treat them (Leaper, 2002). It is also possible that boys and girls behave somewhat differently and that such differences affect how parents act. For example, infant boys are somewhat less developmentally mature or irritable; therefore, parents may have to work harder to soothe them and thus end up treating boys and girls differently on average, but not simply because of any gendered expectations.

Meeting infants' basic physical needs

Infants are highly dependent on their caretakers. Caretakers must be able to interpret the infant's signals (e.g., crying, fussing, turning away, smiling) and respond appropriately to meet the infant's needs. Parents must feed and look after the infant, or the infant will die. In Western countries it is easy for us to assume that parents are as likely to look after male as female infants, but in other parts of the world such is not necessarily the case. There are some reports that in countries with strong son preferences, when resources are scarce, girls are less likely to be breastfed for an extended period and are therefore more likely to suffer from malnutrition (Faisel & Ahmed, 1996; Government of India, 1990), although when supplemental resources are provided the government, girls benefit (Holmes, 2006). Girls in such countries may also be less likely to receive medical care when injured. A recent study in Egypt (Yount, 2004) found that mothers were more likely to take sons for medical treatment (especially more expensive private medical care), and that this tendency was found even for well-educated mothers. Women who lived with their husband's family were especially less inclined to get medical care for their daughters. There is reason to believe that such practices contribute to a greater survival rate for males in early childhood (Yount, 2001). However, other reports in developing countries have not found these kinds of differences between boys and girls (UNICEF, 2004), and some have found that in some polygynous societies girls receive better nutrition and physical care (Gillett-Netting & Perry, 2005), so it isn't clear how widespread such practices are, even in the developing world.

Even when parents do provide equivalent physical care to boys and girls, they may expend family resources somewhat differently. One study of family expenditure patterns compared American families with one or two sons to families with one or two daughters (Lundberg & Rose, 2004). They found some subtle spending differences suggesting that families were making slightly greater investments in sons in some spending categories, and in daughters in others, although the effects were more notable when there was only one child in the family than when there were two. More money was spent on clothing when there were only daughters, and more money on housing when there were only sons in the family. The authors concluded that housing can be seen as more of a long-term investment, and clothing can be seen as short-term consumption. Indeed, housing is the most important investment that most families make, and is important to the kind of neighborhood and school a child may have access to. Of course, wealthier families are likely to have access to more advantaged neighborhoods and schools whether they have sons or daughters, but this study suggested that, when they have the income and opportunity to make such housing choices, the parents of sons shift more of their spending towards this kind of long-term investment. But because we already know that there is more emphasis on appearance and clothing for girls, it may be that parents are expending the resources that they think are most important for the long term benefit of boys and of girls, but that this long term benefit differs—appearance for girls and academic success for boys.

Attachment

One of the most central early developmental processes is the attachment of infants to their caregivers. The relationship between caregiver behavior and the infant's subsequent quality of attachment is a very important one. Whether infants develop secure or insecure attachments to their caregivers involves a complex interaction among infant and caregiver behaviors and traits, as well as characteristics of the environment. However, most researchers in this area would agree that among the most critical determinants of a secure attachment is the responsiveness of the caregiver to the infant's signals and needs (Ainsworth, 1993; Belsky, 1999). There is very little reason to think that this kind of sensitive caretaking is affected by the infant's sex in a simple manner. There are reports that infants of one sex are more often securely attached, sometimes boys (e.g., Williams & Blunk, 2003) and sometimes girls (Barnett, Kidwell, & Leung, 1998). At times, there have been complicated interactions between the child's and the parent's sex, the child's temperament, and other aspects of family life as they relate to the child's attachment classification. For example, boys have been found to have less secure attachments to their fathers in families when the mothers are employed outside the home and when marital strain also exists (Braungart-Rieker, Courtney, & Garwood, 1999). However, the predominant picture is that infant sex is not a major factor in attachment.

Interactions involving toys

Earlier we pointed out that parents provide different toys and other gendered items for boys and girls. Parents also interact differently with boys and girls in the presence of such toys and objects. When parents have been observed with their infant boys or girls in playrooms in which masculine and feminine toys were available from which to choose, they (especially fathers) are more likely to choose traditional boys' toys for their infant sons and girls' toys for their infant daughters, and more likely to respond positively to sons when they play with boys' toys and to daughters when they play with girls' toys (Caldera, Huston, & O'Brien, 1989; Fagot & Hagan, 1991; Jacklin, DiPietro, & Maccoby, 1984; Snow, Jacklin, & Maccoby, 1983). Parents aren't likely to be punitive to a baby boy who chooses a feminine toy. For example, it is not very likely that parents yell loudly at a 6-month-old baby boy to drop that doll he just picked up. Rather, they seem unlikely to offer him such a toy, and more likely to smile at him or touch him gently when he picks up a truck or blocks instead. Because this is such a subtle process, parents may not even be aware that they are acting in this way.

The Socialization of Emotion

Look back at the quote at the beginning of this chapter. The father in Eudora Welty's story insisted that his son was not permitted to cry. This, of course, is a classic example of the type of gender socialization that people think of when they consider how parents treat boys and girls differently. Indeed, emotional expression is a central facet of gender roles in many cultures. The stereotypes of the emotional female (e.g., fearful as well as loving and tender-hearted), and the stoic, although sometimes angry male, are certainly very common. In chapter 5 we discussed how, by a very early age, boys come to avoid express-ing emotions related to fear, sadness, and vulnerability. Now we will look at how early interactions in the family contribute to these differences in children's emotional behaviors.

From infancy onwards, children engage in a variety of emotional behaviors—some positive and some negative. Children laugh, cry, and express anger. How do parents respond to these behaviors? There are certainly differences among parents, across cultures, and in response to different emotions. As suggested by Nancy Eisenberg and her colleagues:

> Different parents have different goals with regard to the socialization of emotion. For example, some parents believe that emotions, especially negative emotions, are bad and should be controlled and not expressed. These parents are likely to try to teach their children to minimize, ignore, deny, or prevent the experience and expression of negative emotion. Other parents feel it is desirable to be in touch with one's emotions and to express them in socially acceptable ways; these parents are likely to be supportive of chil-dren's expression of emotion (Gottman, Katz, & Hooven, 1996). Moreover, parental goals are likely to vary across emotions. For example, in some families (or cultures) it may be quite acceptable to express sadness but not anger. (Eisenberg, Cumberland, & Spinrad, 1998, p. 242)

Although Eisenberg and her colleagues were not specifically addressing the gender socialization of emo-tion, it is easy to see how their ideas would apply to differential responses to emotions expressed by boys and girls. Parents may be more comfortable with emotional expression in girls in general, especially in the case of emotions like fear or sadness. On the other hand, they may tolerate the expression of emotions like anger in sons, but not to the same degree in daughters.

Parents' responses to children's emotional behavior

Even in infancy, when parents have been observed interacting with their infants, there is evidence that they respond to boys' emotions by acting to lessen the intensity of the emotional response (Brody, 1999). We already know that there are some differences between male and female infants that may affect how parents respond to their babies' emotions. Boys have a higher activity level, are some-what more developmentally immature, and as a group may be more slightly more irritable or hard to soothe (Eaton & Enns, 1986; Weinberg, Tronick, Cohn, & Olson, 1999). Infant girls are somewhat more responsive to social interaction (Brody, 1999), and are better able to "read" facial expressions of emotion (McClure, 2000). These differences in the babies' own characteristics could certainly contribute to differences in how parents interact with them, but gendered expectations could also have an effect.

As an example of how mothers communicate emotions to infants, we can look at a study of **social referencing** of emotional messages (Rosen, Adamson, & Bakeman, 1992). In this study, mothers and their 12-month-old infants were brought to a laboratory and given the opportunity for the mothers to communicate emotional messages to the babies about a novel, animated toy (e.g., a monkey suspended on a chain that made noises as its tail curled and uncurled, or a cow that mooed, wagged its tail, and moved its legs). The toys were thought to be unusual and interesting, but likely to produce uncertain responses in the infants, who probably hadn't likely seen similar objects in the past. This is also an age in which infants are increasingly mobile, and might often encounter unfamiliar objects as they explore their surroundings.

At first, the mothers and infants were seated on a blanket and given the opportunity to play together with simple toys for infants. Then the mother put the baby at one corner of the blanket with toys in front of him or her, and seated herself on a chair at the other corner of the blanket. When the novel animated toy was introduced, the mothers were instructed to communicate to the infant from a distance either a happy message that the toy was pleasant and safe, or a message indicating that the toy might be dangerous, and the infant ought to be afraid. In one set of trials the mothers were simply asked to produce such messages, and in other set of trials the mothers were trained in how to show fear or happiness through their facial expressions. The study found that infants commonly looked to their mothers as a source of information about the emotional meaning of such novel events, and also that they responded to the messages produced by their mothers. Interestingly, female infants were more responsive to their mothers' messages, especially in the "fear" condition. Both male and female infants stayed closer to the toy than to their mothers in the "happy" condition, but only female infants stayed closer to their mothers than to the toy in the "fear" condition. Mothers' messages to the babies also differed. In the "happy" condition, messages to boys and girls were similar. But in the "fear" condition, although few of the messages were judged to be really fearful, the mothers' messages to boys were judged to be more fear-invoking than their messages to girls. That is, they exposed their daughters to milder messages about fear. However, their daughters were more responsive to these milder messages, and stayed further away from the toys. The researchers predicted that the mothers would act more fearful around their daughters, but they clearly didn't. This study demonstrates how complex these early messages about emotion must be.

There are other studies showing emotion-related differences in parents' interactions with infant sons and daughters. As we discussed earlier, boys may have more difficulty regulating their emotions in infancy, and parents may feel the need to "work harder" to help boys come to regulate emotions. It is also reasonable to assume that they think it is more important that boys eventually come to be able to do so (Leaper, 2002). Hence, it may not be surprising that parents have been found to behave more responsively to the emotional displays of male infants (Malatesta & Haviland, 1982; Weinberg et al., 1999), and to be more consistent and harmonious in their emotional responses to their sons over the months of infancy (Biringen et al., 1999). Parents have also expressed a wider range of emotions in their interactions with daughters, suggesting that mothers are more comfortable with their baby daughters expressing many different kinds of emotional behavior.

As children grow older, parents continue to respond differently to the emotional behaviors of boys and girls. Questionnaire and interview studies, in which parents are asked how they respond to their children's emotional behavior, have sometimes found that parents of preschoolers report that they don't treat their sons' and daughters' emotional behavior differently (Eisenberg & Fabes, 1994; Roberts, 1999), and have sometimes found that they do. When a difference is found (e.g., Birnbaum & Croll, 1984), it is often along the lines of parents saying they would tolerate more anger from sons and more fearfulness in girls.

With elementary-aged children, there is more consistency in the findings. Parents typically report that they are more punitive towards the emotional behavior of boys (Eisenberg, Fabes, & Murphy, 1996), and that they put more pressure on boys to control their emotions, especially to suppress crying and expressions of sadness and fear (Casey & Fuller, 1994; Eisenberg et al., 1998).

Children are aware of such pressure. From early elementary school and continuing through the high school years, girls say that their parents think it is more acceptable for them to cry or to express sadness or pain than it is for boys (Shipman, Zeman, Nesin, & Fitzgerald, 2003; Zeman & Shipman, 1997), and boys report that their parents are more tolerant of expressions of anger and aggression from them than girls report (Perry, Perry, & Weiss, 1989).

In addition to questionnaires or interviews, there are also some direct observations of parents' responses to their children's emotional behaviors, and again the finding is that parents are more likely to attend to girls' expressions of sadness and vulnerability, and to boys' expressions of anger (Fabes et al., 1994). In fact, boys' angry behavior is more likely to have a payoff – angry boys are about twice as likely to get what they want from their mothers than are angry girls (Chaplin, Cole, & Zahn-Waxler, 2005; Radke-Yarrow & Kochanska, 1990). In an interesting example, one set of researchers examined naturally occurring toddlers' squabbles over toys or other objects—a very common occurrence with young children (Ross, Tesla, Kenyon, & Lollis, 1990). The mothers in this study were primarily interested in restoring harmony between their own child and the playmate when the squabbles occurred. As a rule they were more likely to focus on the other child's wishes, usually trying to persuade their own child to give up the object. However, mothers of boys were more likely to let their sons "have their own way" than were mothers of girls. This is certainly consistent with a social learning explanation of boys' anger being **reinforced**, and girls' being **extinguished**.

In another study of emotional expression in preschoolers (Chaplin et al., 2005), and again in the same children in elementary school two years later, parents (in this case, especially fathers) gave in to expression of anger more often in boys and expressions of emotional vulnerability in girls. These behaviors increased over the two-year period under study in response to the attention they received. Clearly then, these studies demonstrate that parental attention is one kind of reinforcer that increases expressions of sadness and anxiety in girls and anger in boys.

Parent-child emotion talk

Researchers have been very interested in examining the kinds of conversations that parents and their children have about emotional issues. Robyn Fivush and her colleagues (Fivush, 1998; Fivush, Brotman, Buckner, & Goodman, 2000; Reese, Haden, & Fivush, 1996) have done several longitudinal studies in which the conversations of mothers and fathers with daughters and sons in their own homes were recorded and examined. In general, the parents were asked to converse with their children about events from the past. The parents typically chose to talk about happy and interesting events, such as going to the zoo or other entertaining places and to family events like weddings. In one such study Fivush (1998) asked the parents and their children to sit together quietly and discuss special events that they had shared in the past. Parents could select any events they wished and talk about them freely. There were two observations, one when the child was about 3 years old, and another 2 years later when the child was about 5. Fivush found that mothers and fathers did not differ from each other, but that both parents used more emotion words with daughters than with sons. Also, although the 3-year-old boys and girls used similar numbers of emotion words, by 5, the girls were using more emotion words than the boys, especially with their mothers. Fivush also noted that parents were especially likely to talk more about sadness and negative emotions with daughters.

Although it is unlikely that this would be parents' intentions, Fivush and her colleagues (e.g., Fivush & Buckner, 2000) emphasize that it is possible that the emphasis on sadness in the family socialization of daughters may be contribute to the greater rates of depression in adolescent girls and adult women. For example, consider these two narratives between mothers and their 3-year-old children. The first child is a girl.

M: You were very sad, and what happened? Why did you feel sad?
C: Because Malaika, Malaika she was having [unintelligible word].
M: Yes.
C: And then she stood up on my bed and it was my bedroom. She's not allowed to sleep in there.
M: Is that why you were sad?
C: Yeah. Now it makes me happy. I also [unintelligible word]. It makes me sad but Malaika just left ... and then I cried.

M: And you cried because...
C: Malaika left.
M: Because Malaika left, and did that make you sad?
C: And then I cried [makes crying sounds] like that. I cried and cried and cried and cried.
M: I know. I thought you were sad because Malaika left, but I didn't know you were sad because Malaika slept in your bed. (Fivush & Buckner, 2000, p. 246)

Now consider a similar exchange about sadness between a mother and her son:

M: Do you remember when we were at Debbie's house yesterday, and it was time to go home?
C: Yeah.
M: When I came in the door and you cried? Do you remember? Why did you cry?
C: Because I wanted to.
M: Why did you cry when you saw me?
C: Because um the movie was over and you and I had to go and I wanted more grape juice.
M: You knew that it was time to go and the movie was over and you wanted more grape juice?
C: Uhhuh.
M: Why didn't you want to come home?
C: Because I didn't want to.
M: Did that feel good or bad?
C: Bad! (Fivush & Buckner, 2000, p. 246)

Fivush and Buckner point out how much richer the conversation is between the mother and daughter, but also how the sadness in the daughter's case is much more focused on interpersonal relationships. Fivush and her colleagues have done several studies over the years on this topic (e.g., Buckner & Fivush, 2000; Fivush et al., 2000; Kuebli, Butler, & Fivush, 1995; Reese et al., 1996). They have consistently shown that both mothers and fathers are more likely to talk about emotions with daughters, and that the emotion talk between parents and daughters is much more likely to focus on vulnerability, sadness, and relations with others, and that over time daughters come to be much more likely to focus on such issues themselves.

Other researchers (e.g., Chance & Fiese, 1999) also find that parents are more likely to discuss emotions with daughters. In one interesting study, conversations about emotions between older siblings and mothers with younger siblings (Dunn, Bretherton, & Munn, 1987) were observed. In this study, the younger siblings were barely out of infancy (18 to 24 months of age), but both mothers and older siblings talked more about emotions with younger daughters as compared to younger sons. As has been seen repeatedly in Fivush's research, this study found that by the time they were two years old, girls themselves were more likely to engage in conversations about emotion than were boys.

Prosocial Behavior

As you may recall from chapter 5, there is some evidence that girls may be somewhat more likely to be kind, considerate, and helpful to others (Eisenberg & Fabes, 1998). There are a few studies looking at parents' socialization of this kind of prosocial behavior (e.g., Hastings, Rubin, & DeRose, 2005; Spinrad et al., 1999). The research shows that parents' socialization practices impact the prosocial behavior of both boys and girls. Parents who are more authoritative (impose rules, but are flexible and democratic), believe that prosocial behavior is in their child's nature (rather than a function of the situation), and who discuss prosocial behavior with their young children are more likely to have both sons and daughters who behave prosocially (Hastings, McShane, Parker, & Ladha, 2007). Interestingly, this research shows that mothers have a more powerful impact on children's prosocial behavior than fathers' do. There is not much evidence that mothers use these strategies more with children of one sex than the other. Nonetheless, boys with such mothers may show their prosocial behavior in particularly masculine ways (e.g., taking turns), whereas girls with such mothers may show more feminine forms of prosocial behavior (e.g., being considerate or giving in to other children), thus showing complex interactions between socialization and gendered behavior.

Despite their lesser influence, fathers have been found (Hastings et al., 2007) to be more likely to respond positively (e.g., with affection or praise) to daughters' prosocial behaviors than to sons'. Nonetheless, fathers who talk to their sons about prosocial acts are likely to have sons who behave more prosocially.

Parents' Use of Language With Sons and Daughters

We have seen that parents talk differently to sons and daughters about emotion. Of course parents and their children talk about many things, and there are several gender-related differences in their conversations. In one meta-analysis of the research on parents talking to their children (Leaper, Anderson, & Sanders, 1998), the authors examined differences in how mothers (there weren't enough studies to look at fathers) talked to their sons versus their daughters. They found that mothers talked more to daughters ($d = -0.29$), and were more supportive in their speech to daughters ($d = -0.22$). These differences, especially in amount of talking, were noticeably larger in toddlers ($d = -0.64$) as compared to older children. That is, mothers talked more to daughters particularly when they were very young. More recent research with infants and toddlers finds this same pattern—mothers talk more to daughters (Clearfield & Nelson, 2006). We already know that early language skills are stronger in girls than boys (Bornstein, Hahn, & Haynes, 2004), and this enriched input from mothers could certainly be one of the reasons for their higher level of skill, although it might also be a response to more skillful daughters.

Mothers were also more likely to use directive speech (e.g., telling the children what to do), with daughters than with sons, but only with school-aged children ($d = -0.18$), not with toddlers, preschoolers, or adolescents (Leaper et al., 1998). Finally, the authors noted that observations in the children's homes and other natural settings generally found larger differences in how parents talked to their children than studies that took place in the laboratory.

Several studies by Dorothy Flannagan and her colleagues examined one particular kind of conversation (Flannagan, 1996; Flannagan, Baker-Ward, & Graham, 1995; Flannagan & Perese, 1998). Mothers often ask young children about events that took place during the day (e.g., "What did you do at school today?"). Although there is a great deal of similarity between mothers' conversations with sons and daughters about school, there are some intriguing differences as well. Flannagan has reported that mothers of boys are more likely to focus on learning-related tasks and mothers of girls are more likely to focus on the girls' relationships with others and on emotional themes. This fits well the expressive/instrumental distinction that is at the core of gender roles, and suggests that mothers are actively socializing children into these roles via their conversations with them.

Responses to Children's Risky Behaviors

We have already learned that boys are more likely to take risks than girls are, and that some of this risk taking may be advantageous (e.g., being willing to guess on the SATs), but that other risk taking may lead to an increased likelihood of injury or death (Byrnes, Miller, & Schafer, 1999). In fact, accidents and related injuries are a leading cause of childhood death, and boys are more likely to die of such causes. Morrongiello and Dawber and their colleagues have done several studies of parents' behavior towards sons and daughters in risky situations (Morrongiello & Dawber, 1998, 1999, 2000; Morrongiello & Hogg, 2004). They have done experimental studies such as the one we reported on in an earlier chapter, in which toddlers were observed with potential risks such as hot coffee or poisonous household cleaners (none of the items were actually harmful); observational studies on playgrounds and in the home; and questionnaire studies of parents. Overall, this research has demonstrated that, beginning in their toddler years, boys are inclined to take more risks and to be less obedient when parents (especially mothers) ask them to refrain from doing something risky. However, the research also shows that parents are more concerned about possible injury to their daughters and to intervene more quickly to provide assistance to prevent such injury. Mothers also seem to believe that sons' risky behaviors can't be modified, but daughters' can (Morrongiello & Hogg, 2004). Such beliefs could subtly influence mothers to be more forceful or confident in intervening with daughters because they apparently think they can do more about the risky behaviors of their daughters. In addition to tolerating more risky behavior in sons, parents also actively encourage certain kinds of risk-taking in boys, but less so in girls. These kinds of risky behaviors are related to the development of competence (e.g., sliding down a "firehouse" pole). So, overall, sons take more risks, and parents both tolerate more risk taking, and even subtly encourage it in some instances.

Discipline

Parents of young children are concerned about their children's safety and want them to follow everyday rules (e.g., picking up toys, saying 'please' and 'thank you,' eating with utensils, sharing with others) in addition to wanting their children to try new activities and delay gratification (Gralinski & Kopp, 1993). With older children, they are likely to want their children to continue to follow appropriate social rules, and to get along with others, as well as to do their schoolwork and chores around the home. There is little reason to think such goals vary a great deal for boys and girls. However, there is good evidence that parents' disciplinary efforts are somewhat harsher with sons than with daughters, and that sons are more likely to receive physical punishment (Day, Peterson, & McCracken, 1998; Lytton & Romney, 1991; Newson & Newson, 1987; Straus & Stewart, 1999), especially by mothers.

Part of the reason that boys receive stricter discipline is that they are more likely to be temperamentally difficult—to be irritable, prone to anger, and to refuse to comply with parental requests. Of course, there are wide individual differences in these characteristics; many boys have easy temperaments and there are certainly girls who do not. In general, when children are difficult to handle, parents often react by increasing their disciplinary efforts, becoming stricter, and using more physical punishment. Unfortunately, such efforts often backfire, and act to make the child even more difficult and noncompliant.

This process seems to happen with boys more than with girls (McFadyen-Ketchum, Bates, Dodge, & Pettit, 1996). In one 10-year longitudinal study of approximately 1000 children between the ages of 1 year and 20 years (at Time 1 children ranged in age from 1–10; they were interviewed again 8 and 10 years later), the researchers (Bezirganian & Cohen, 1992) examined the children's temperaments, their relationships with parents, and the parents' disciplinary practices. They found little difference in temperament between the youngest boys and girls. This is important because it was not the case that parents were harsher with boys because they were more difficult to start with. However, boys became more difficult by middle childhood.

As expected, parents used more forceful discipline with difficult children. Girls did not respond to this discipline by becoming more noncompliant and difficult, but boys did, and they did so particularly in response to punishment and discipline given by their mothers. The authors suggest that boys are particularly sensitive to "aggression" by females, and that they interpret punishment and discipline delivered by their mothers as female aggression. The authors argue that boys respond to this female aggression by becoming more temperamentally difficult, and even more resistant to their mothers' control. As we will see when we discuss children's specific relationships with fathers and mothers later in this chapter, these findings fit in with others that show that boys' and girls' relationships with mothers and fathers are affected by gendered behaviors and expectations.

In conclusion, then, much research suggests that boys are more likely to receive harsh discipline and physical punishment more than girls do. However, this may result at least partly from boys' resistance to being controlled by their mothers, who are, after all, typically the ones who are responsible for the majority of their everyday care and socialization.

Responses to Children's Aggression

As we already know, boys are more aggressive physically and verbally than girls are and girls are somewhat more likely to show social or relational aggression. We also know that boys are more approving of physical and verbal aggressive behavior—they think it is more acceptable (Huesmann, Guerra, Zelli, & Miller, 1992). Perhaps parents' reactions to aggression contribute to these differences between boys and girls.

Most of the research on parental reactions to aggression concerns physical aggression. In a study which examined elementary school children's beliefs about their parents' responses to their aggression against other children (Perry et al., 1989), boys expected less parental disapproval for behaving aggressively than girls did. It was also the case that children of both sexes expected less disapproval for responding aggressively when someone else attacked them, and less disapproval for behaving aggressively towards boys than towards girls. Indeed, boys apparently felt encouraged by their parents to stand up for themselves in the face of other boys attacking them.

The study above measured children's beliefs about how parents might respond to their aggression. It is obviously important to study what parents actually do. When Maccoby and Jacklin (1974) examined the research done before the early 1970s, they were unable to find any evidence that parents were more tolerant of aggressive behavior in sons than daughters. In general, parents didn't seem to approve of it much in anyone. Since that time, there have been few direct observations of differential responses to aggression in very young children, and the findings are not consistent. Some researchers have reported parents treating the aggression of infant or toddler boys and girls similarly (e.g., Fagot, 1978), but others have found that it is discouraged more in girls (Power & Parke, 1986). Once children are somewhat older, by elementary school age, there is more consistent evidence that parents disapprove of aggression more in daughters than they do in sons, that they act more consistently to diminish it in daughters, and that they tolerate it more in sons (Martin & Ross, 2005; Mills & Rubin, 1992; Rubin & Mills, 1990).

Serious aggression and conduct disorder

It is important to distinguish between lower levels of "everyday" or milder aggression, and more serious, persistent, and antisocial aggression. It is not unusual for young toddlers to throw tantrums and hit, kick, or bite others, even their parents. Physical aggression typically declines as children grow older, and there are only a few children who remain seriously aggressive once they enter elementary school. Although there are girls who behave very aggressively, seriously aggressive children are much more likely to be boys. There are several excellent longitudinal studies in several different countries (Eron, 1992; Moffitt, Caspi, Rutter, & Silva, 2001; NICHD Early Child Care Research Network, 2004) following such children. These studies report that children who remain seriously aggressive often experience multiple family risks (e.g., poverty, maternal depression, parental insensitivity, parental substance abuse). Of course, many of these risks would be experienced equally by both boys and girls, but there is evidence that this kind of family risk is especially likely to increase hostility and serious aggression in boys (Kerr, Lopez, Olson, & Sameroff, 2004).

When parents use physical punishment, are angry and rejecting, and fail to provide any reasons for why aggressive behavior is inappropriate, their children are more likely to continue to show aggression and other troubled behavior of this type as they grow older. This happens more often to boys, especially punishment for the child's own aggression (Eron, 1992). Girls are punished less for their aggression, but when they are punished, they are more likely to receive psychological punishment (e.g., disapproval). Of course, the punishment boys receive is probably intended to reduce their aggression, but we know that even punishment is a form of attention, and that it has the potential of actually increasing this behavior, rather than decreasing it. Physical punishment also increases anger and hostility, and serves as a model for aggressive behavior. Thus boys are more likely than girls to receive the kind of parental treatment that would increase serious aggression.

Less is known about the development of serious aggression or conduct disorder in girls (Zahn-Waxler & Polanichka, 2004). Many of the risk factors are similar for boys and girls, but girls with conduct disorder are especially likely to have had disordered relationships and to have suffered from sexual abuse (Ehrensaft, 2005).

So, although this picture is complicated, what appears to be the case is that parents do not like their daughters to behave aggressively, and that they put increasing pressure on girls to refrain from such behavior as they grow older. With boys, there is a difference between serious and mild aggression, with mild aggression being ignored or tolerated ("boys will be boys"), and serious aggression or antisocial behavior being associated with family and social risks, and with receiving physical punishment of a sort that may result in an eventual increase in the behavior, rather than the desired decrease. Girls who engage in serious aggression and antisocial behavior have many similar risk factors in childhood, but seem to be even more likely to have experienced especially disordered relationships and sexual abuse.

Encouragement of Autonomy Versus Dependence

Parents generally find they need to strike a balance between controlling, monitoring, and disciplining their children, and permitting their children to be independent and make decisions for themselves. Naturally, this is very likely to change as children grow older, as parents typically permit and encourage greater independence in older children. From a gender development perspective we would want to know if the balance between control and autonomy granting differs in parents' interactions with boys and girls. It appears that it does; boys seem to be granted more **autonomy**.

With very young children, parents are more likely to provide assistance to toddler girls when they ask for help and to ignore similar help-seeking in boys (Fagot, 1978). Over time, this leads girls to ask for help more often. Parents also are more intrusive with young daughters, providing assistance even when such assistance is not requested or needed (Martin, Maccoby, & Jacklin, 1981). Finally, there is also evidence that mothers (but probably not fathers) tolerate somewhat more disobedience from sons, leading sons to become more likely to question their mothers' authority and refuse to comply with their requests (Maccoby, Snow, & Jacklin, 1984).

During the elementary school years, there continues to be evidence that parents are more directive with girls and give them less autonomy or independence than they do boys. For example, in one study of children between the ages of 6 and 11 (Pomerantz & Ruble, 1998), the authors examined mothers' control and autonomy-granting in five areas of their relationship with their children: helping (e.g., with schoolwork); monitoring (e.g., making sure chores are done "correctly"); decision-making (e.g., telling a child what decision to make vs. letting her make it on her own); praising (e.g., using controlling praise such as giving money vs. more low-key praise); and discipline (e.g., punishment, reprimands, or simple discussions).

The study found that mothers were more controlling and less autonomy-granting with school-aged daughters in all areas except discipline. For example, mothers were more likely to closely monitor their daughters and to tell them what to do as opposed to allowing them to do it themselves. The researchers also found that children who were granted autonomy were less likely to blame themselves for failure. So the socialization pattern associated with girls was also more likely to make them feel less competent and more at fault for their failures.

Another important kind of autonomy-granting concerns children's freedom to explore their neighborhoods and to spend time in their own pursuits or with friends without a great deal of parental monitoring. In early childhood, during the toddler years, children are not likely to do much exploring of the neighborhood, but there is evidence that parents encourage their toddler-aged daughters to remain physically closer to them, whereas they permit boys to explore their surroundings further from the parents, as well as permitting them to play by themselves in the home for a time (Fagot, 1978; Lindahl & Heimann, 1997, 2002).

Once children reach school age parents continue to grant girls less freedom and autonomy, and they are more concerned about their girls' safety outside the home. One longitudinal study in urban England (Newson & Newson, 1976, 1987) found that parents were more likely to closely monitor girls' whereabouts once they reached school age, picking them up at school and requiring them to inform parents where they are going. The Newsons even reported that a few of the 7-year-old boys (but none of the girls) were often gone from home for hours at a time, and their whereabouts were not known by their parents.

Similar findings exist for adolescents. Some research has reported that parents are particularly likely to give daughters messages about being careful not to walk alone at night, and to let their parents know where they are (Hill & Lynch, 1983). However, some of the research on school-aged children and adolescents was done quite a few years ago, and it has been difficult to verify that this phenomenon still exists, at least in North America. It would be hard to imagine today's North American parents permitting 7-year-olds (even boys) to be gone for hours at a time without knowing their whereabouts. Although some researchers have continued to find greater monitoring of daughters, especially in adolescence (Dishion & McMahon, 1998), others have not been able to find supporting evidence (Bumpus, Crouter, & McHale, 2001; Crouter, Helms-Erickson, Updegraff, & McHale, 1999; Crouter, Manke, & McHale, 1995). Rather, they have found parents to be more or less restrictive of sons and daughters depending on the children's birth order (younger children are supervised more), the sibling composition of the family, the particular children, the mothers' work hours, and the gender role attitudes of parents. Apparently, some modern parents monitor boys more than girls because they fear that boys are more prone to "getting into trouble." Also, once children show evidence of a tendency to misbehave, parents often step up their degree of monitoring. Thus it is not always a simple matter of parents monitoring girls more than boys in later childhood and adolescence.

Parents' Play With Sons and Daughters

We have pointed out that parents select different toys for their sons and daughters, and that they respond differently to male and female infants' toy play. Parents continue to play with toys with their children as their children grow older. With older children there is an even greater tendency on the part of parents, again especially fathers, to actually be punitive towards cross-gender toy play, especially in boys (Langlois & Downs, 1980), and they may indeed be well aware of what they are doing.

Different kinds of toys elicit different behaviors from the parents and children as they play with them together. Some research (Caldera et al., 1989; Leaper & Gleason, 1996) has found that when young children play with dolls and other social pretend play (e.g., playing house or store) together with their parents, parents use more complex language, ask more questions, and name more objects. The least likely toy context for expansive language use by parents involves play with vehicles, although play with vehicles is more likely than play with other toys to lead to imaginative, but non-language sounds (e.g., vrooom, vroom). It is also the case that social pretend play with objects (e.g., playing store) is associated with more collaborative play with parents (Leaper, 2000a; Leaper & Gleason, 1996). When boys and girls are provided with different experiences as they play with toys together with their parents, they gain different amounts of practice with particular social and cognitive skills. It should be obvious, then, that parent-child play in gendered contexts has a potential for impacting several aspects of children's behavior such as collaboration and language development.

Parents also play with their children in other ways. One of the most often noticed of these differences involves **rough-and-tumble** play. This type of play includes such things as tossing children up in the air, tickling, chasing, and roughhousing. We already know that boys are more likely than girls to engage in this kind of play, and in fact, young girls are sometimes wary of other children who play in this rough manner.

Parents are more likely to engage in rough-and-tumble or physical play with sons than with daughters. We have probably all seen family interactions in which fathers and sons chase each other and pretend to fight by doing things like dropping ice cubes down each other's shirts or tickling each other, from the time the children are toddlers until well into the children's teenage years. The important point we want to make here is that parents (both mothers and fathers, but especially fathers) are more likely to play physically with sons (Haight, Parke, & Black, 1997; Lindsey & Mize, 2000, 2001). Therefore, sons experience more of this kind of play in the family, and fathers also appear to serve as a model for this type of play. Longitudinal research has found that one of the most important precursors to playing this way by early elementary school age is having had a father play in this fashion when the child is a toddler and preschooler (McBride-Chang & Jacklin, 1993).

Another kind of play that parents and children do together has been called **pretense play** or sometimes just "pretend play." This is play using objects and articles to pretend or assume roles (e.g., playing house, school, or storekeeper-customer). Like rough and tumble play, this is a kind of play that children can do amongst themselves, and we have already seen that girls are more likely to play in this manner with other girls. Both mothers and fathers do more pretense play with daughters than with sons, and children of both sexes do more of it with mothers than they do with fathers (Lindsey & Mize, 2000, 2001), again leading to the conclusion that mothers may serve as a model for this kind of play.

Interactions Related to Boys' and Girls' Capabilities and Competence

A little earlier in this chapter, we showed that parents seem to think infant daughters are less competent than infant sons. This continues as children grow older. Parents think that sons are somewhat smarter than daughters, despite the fact that girls typically do better in school (Furnham, Reeves, & Budhani, 2002; Furnham & Thomas, 2004). Parents especially think that their sons' mathematical and spatial skills are better than their daughters'.

Parental stereotypes about boys and girls are one of the influences on children's beliefs about their own competence. Jacquelynne Eccles and Alan Wigfield and their colleagues (e.g., Wigfield, Battle, Keller, & Eccles, 2002) have done several studies on the effects of parents' interactions on children's developing competencies in several domains, mathematics, science, and sports in particular. They have suggested at least four possible mechanisms of parental influence on the development of children's skills and competencies.

First, parents may make different kinds of **attributions** about their children's academic or athletic performance. Making different attributions means that parents assume different reasons for boys' and girls' performance, and hence may give boys and girls different messages about the reasons for their good or poor performance. For example, consider mathematics. Parents may imply to sons that their excellent performance in mathematics is due to inherent ability, and to daughters that their good performance is due to cooperative behavior and neat and tidy work. One context in which parents make these attributions is when they help with homework—many parents apparently take over and do the work for their daughters or tell them how to do it, which then can undermine the daughters' beliefs in their own abilities (Bhanot & Jovanovic, 2005; Pomerantz & Eaton, 2000).

These kinds of attributions have been shown to influence motivation to succeed, especially when one finds the work difficult. When they first encounter difficulty or failure, sons may be led to believe that they need to work harder because, after all, anyone with inherent ability can succeed if they just work hard enough. Daughters, on the other hand, may be more likely to think that this failure means that they just do not have what it takes to do well in math.

Eccles and Wigfield think that academic performance in certain domains is affected by three other kinds of behavior from parents. Parents encourage children to take up various activities or to enroll in certain classes that support the development of skills that they think are more natural or more important for one sex or the other. For example, they may sign a son up for computer classes or a daughter for dancing. Parents also provide toys and other items like computers more often to one sex, and these items can influence skill development in certain areas but not others.

Finally, parents talk differently with sons and daughters about certain academic subjects and careers, particularly those related to math and science. For example, both mothers and fathers are more likely to use scientific vocabulary with sons with respect to many different scientific fields, but especially in physics (Tenenbaum & Leaper, 2003; Tenenbaum, Snow, Roach, & Kurland, 2005). In one interesting study observing children and parents in a science museum, parents were much more likely to give scientific explanations to their sons than their daughters when viewing the exhibits (Crowley, Callanan, Tenenbaum, & Allen, 2001). All of these kinds of actions are likely to increase sons' competence and interest in such domains as math and science, or similarly, in sports.

Conclusions About the Differential Treatment of Sons and Daughters

We have examined many different ways in which parents might treat sons and daughters differently. We have noted that, in many ways, contemporary parents treat boys and girls very similarly overall, and that they are likely to treat particular children differently than others depending on factors such as their age, birth order, or temperament. However, there are some ways in which parents seem to consistently treat boys and girls differently.

We began by showing that parents created a gendered world for children by naming them with particular boys' and girls' names, by purchasing toys, clothing, and other materials that are defined as appropriate for one sex or the other, and by encouraging their participation in various activities. Parents also reinforce gender-related behavior by attending to boys and girls who are playing with gender-appropriate toys, and they play in different ways with boys' and girls' toys, enhancing the development of different skills in boys and girls.

Parents assign different household chores to their sons and daughters, and tend to assign more chores to daughters overall, although this tendency is affected by the family's configuration. Parents also seem to hold subtle beliefs about their children's competence in various domains such as science, mathematics, and athletics, and to treat their sons and daughters differently because of those beliefs. There is also evidence that parents' beliefs come to affect their children's own beliefs about their competence, and in turn to affect their performance.

Parents hold different expectations about infant boys and girls, and seem to think that infant and toddler girls are less capable than boys. Even when older, girls are thought to be slightly less intelligent and competent overall by their parents, especially as compared to firstborn boys. In non-Western countries parents sometimes seem to provide poorer physical care for female children. In the West, physical care differences are not apparent, but there is evidence that parents of sons may shift more resources into long term investments such as better housing.

One of the clearest ways in which parents treat boys and girls differently is in the domain of emotion. Parents work harder to get sons to control their emotions at an early age, and are more tolerant of vulnerable emotions like sadness and fear in daughters than sons. On the other hand, they permit more anger from sons, and are more likely to reinforce this anger by giving in to the demands of their angry sons. Parents' conversations about emotion are also different with boys and girls. Parents talk more about emotions like fear and sadness with daughters, and they focus those conversations on interpersonal relationships and the feelings of others.

In general, parents talk more to daughters than sons, and they have more supportive conversations with them. When children arrive home after school, parents talk more to sons about their academic work, and more to daughters about their friends and social relationships.

When young children take risks, parents are more likely to intervene to prevent harm when the child is a girl, and they believe that there is little they can do about sons' risk taking. There is also evidence that parents use stricter disciplinary efforts and more physical punishment with misbehaving sons than daughters, but they also tolerate more "ordinary" aggression from boys. However, when children are seriously aggressive, they punish such behavior harshly in their sons. Over time this parental behavior appears to make difficult sons even more difficult, whereas difficult daughters may be more likely to improve over time.

Parents appear to give sons more autonomy and permit greater independence than they do for daughters. Finally, parents are more likely to engage in physical and rough-and-tumble play with sons, and in quieter play that focuses on pretend role-playing with daughters.

To conclude, although some research has concluded that parents treat boys and girls similarly overall, there are also some consistent differences in the family-related socialization of boys and girls, although some are quite subtle. Nonetheless, most of these differences are clearly related to gendered role expectations for the two sexes.

Direct Instruction About Gender

When we began this chapter we outlined four ways in which parents might socialize gender in their children: choosing gender-related activities, toys, and clothing (channeling or shaping), interacting differently with boys and girls, giving direct instruction about gender, and finally, mothers and fathers modeling different gender-related behavior. It is to direct instruction that we now turn.

It is difficult to summarize research findings on the topic of direct instruction about gender, as much of it is imbedded in the work which has studied differential treatment of boys and girls, and which we have already discussed. For example, parents may provide both direct and indirect messages about the appropriateness of various activities, academic subjects, emotional displays and similar topics to boys and girls.

One way we can examine this topic, however, is by looking at research on the topic of conversations about gender itself. Gender development researcher Carol Martin (2000) once told a story about her 4-year-old niece, Erin. Erin was drawing pictures of stick-people, some of whom had eyelashes, and some did not. When asked, Erin reported that only girls have eyelashes, and that boys do not have them. In a similar example, one of us had a student in a gender development class who reported that the preschool aged daughter of his roommate assigned gender to various animals. She stated that birds, horses, bunnies, cats, puppies, giraffes, chipmunks, and tigers were girls' animals, but lions, sharks, wolves, dinosaurs, snakes, eagles, alligators, and monkeys were boys' animals. Furthermore, hippos, zebras, and cows were for both girls and boys.

There is more than anecdotal evidence that children form such beliefs about gender. In an interesting series of studies, Leinbach, Hort, and Fagot (1997) demonstrated that, by the age of 4, children identified items as masculine or feminine on the basis of metaphorical cues such as color and softness or roughness. For example, a butterfly, something soft, a heart, and the color pink were assigned to females, whereas a bear, the emotion of anger, a sharp, angular line, and the color blue were assigned to males.

These kinds of ideas can be called **gender essentialism**. Essentialist beliefs are those take the position that differences between the sexes exist to be discovered, are generally biologically based and unchangeable, and are categories rather than overlapping distributions. In an extensive longitudinal study Gelman, Taylor and Nguyen (2004) examined how parent-child conversations about gender might contribute to children's essentialist beliefs. The researchers observed mothers and their 2- to 6-year-old children engaged in conversations about gender in response to a picture book. The picture book contained both gender-stereotypical and counter-stereotypical examples of behavior in both children and adults (e.g., a man ballet dancer, a boy playing football, a woman chopping wood, a girl cheerleader). On each page a person was pictured engaging in some activity, accompanied by the statement: "Who can [do the activity]?" For example, a picture of a woman chopping wood had the phase "Who can chop wood?"

The researchers measured several aspects of children's knowledge and attitudes about gender stereotypes and norms (see chapter 9 for some of the details about these findings). However, our main focus here is on how the mothers and children talked about gender. Gelman and her colleagues found that both children and mothers referred to gender more than 90% of the time when they talked about the pictured characters. Mothers and children both used generic references to gender a great deal of the time (e.g., "girls can sew"), implying that one gender in particular is likely to do that particular behavior. Even if neither mother nor child was discussing stereotypes when referring to the character's gender, mentioning gender this often would have the effect of emphasizing its importance. For example, mothers mentioned gender much more than other characteristics such as age or ethnicity of the characters.

The authors concluded that gender appears to be a very significant feature of how people are referred to in everyday conversation between mothers and children. You can think of how often a parent might simply call a child a boy or a girl (e.g., "oh, what a good boy you are being today") to get a sense of how frequently gender categories are used in children's everyday conversations with others.

The mothers and children affirmed (e.g., "that's for girls, not for boys") stereotypes as well as denying them (e.g., "anyone can do it"). Children were more likely to affirm stereotypes than to deny them, but only at the ages of 4 and 6; 2-year-olds showed little tendency to do one more than the other. Children's insistence that stereotypes be followed were often quite emphatic (e.g., "girls can't play football"). Both boys and girls indicated that stereotypes be followed in a positive sense (e.g., "Dad can catch frogs"), but boys were especially emphatic about insisting that stereotypes be followed in the negative sense (e.g., "Men can't knit.").

Although children were inclined to support gender stereotypes, mothers affirmed stereotypes as often as denying them, and often asked neutral questions about the counter-stereotyped activities portrayed (e.g., "Who can play with dolls?"). However, when the authors looked only as the stereotype-consistent pictures in the book, they found that mothers were much more likely to affirm stereotypes than to deny them. That suggests that it may have been the stereotype-inconsistent pictures in the books that were drawing this expression of gender neutrality from the mothers. In fact, there were very noticeable differences in how the mothers talked about the stereotype-inconsistent pictures than the consistent ones. For example, the counter-stereotyped pictures (e.g., a man knitting) generated more statements in opposition to the stereotype, and more indication that gender equality was to be expected or valued.

Assuming that most of the images depicted in children's everyday experience are consistent with gender stereotypes, it might be expected that stereotypes would be affirmed in conversations between parents and children more often than not (because that is how the mothers behaved with the stereotype-consistent pictures). Also, as we will see in the next chapter, there is a great deal of stereotypic information in the media available for children to see, and for them to discuss with their parents. Therefore, it is reasonable to expect that children experience a great deal of emphasis on gender as an important characteristic of people and on gender stereotypes in their everyday conversations.

Mothers and Fathers: The Modeling of Gender-Related Behavior

Another concern of gender socialization is how mothers and fathers themselves behave differently. From a social learning theory perspective, this is a modeling or imitation effect: children learn how males and females act by watching their mothers and fathers interact with the children themselves, with each other, and with others. In this section of the chapter we will consider several important aspects of the different types of behavior typically shown by mothers and fathers, remembering of course that not all fathers and mothers behave in these general ways.

Time Spent by Mothers and Fathers With Children

Two-parent families in Western cultures

One of the clearest differences between mothers and fathers is that mothers spend more time caring for and interacting with children (Geary, 2000; Sandberg & Hofferth, 2001). One study of time spent by parents (Gauthier, Smeeding, & Furstenberg, 2004) on various activities with their children in 16 industrialized countries between 1961 and 2000 found that both mothers and fathers had increased the amount of time spent with children over that period. Even though fathers had clearly increased in the amount of time spent with children over that period, mothers still spent substantially more time with their children than did fathers. That was so whether the mothers were employed outside the home or not. To put this in context, in 2000, full-time employed mothers of at least one child under 5 years of age spent 2.2 hours per day on direct childcare (on average across the 16 countries), homemaker mothers spent 3.4, and fathers spent 1.2. Many of the countries only had data available concerning time spent on childcare, but the researchers had extensive data on many different kinds of activities (e.g., reading, playing) that parents did with their children from Canada in 1998. In every type of activity except play, mothers (whether they were employed or not) spent more time with children than men did.

Much other research in a variety of cultures, social classes, and families confirms this general principle: mothers spend more time with children. For example, research on African American parents of infants, including families from a variety of social classes, marital statuses, and employment statuses, consistently shows that mothers devote more time to childcare and other household chores than fathers do (Hossain & Roopnarine, 1993; Roopnarine, Fouts, Lamb, & Lewis-Elligan, 2005).

Mothers are also typically more likely to be the primary parent in charge of children's lives—to play the "managerial" role with respect to the children (Parke, 2002). They are more likely to choose pediatricians and babysitters, and to determine the kind of food the child eats, and even to manage their access to peers, at least in early childhood. So overall, it is clear that mothers are more involved with their children than are fathers.

There are a variety of reasons why fathers spend less time and play less of a management role with children than mothers do. One concerns their earning potential. Men make more money than women do in the workplace (U.S. Department of Labor, 2006), and when children arrive families usually need additional income. It makes little practical sense for men to reduce time in the workplace to spend with children, if one result would be that the family's income would be decreased to a greater extent than if the children's mother reduced her work time. In fact, men's role as fathers in Western societies since the Industrial Revolution has been defined as economic provider, suggesting that direct interaction with children is not necessarily seen as an integral part of being a father (Mintz, 1998), and that income provision is central. Of course, in contemporary society that definition of fatherhood is changing, but the provider role is certainly still a key part of it.

Another reason is men's socialization in their own families and in the culture as a whole. Childcare responsibilities are clearly thought to belong to women, and men have rarely grown up thinking that they would spend much time with their own children (McBride & Darragh, 1995). Women often have a network of family members and friends to whom they can turn for support in their roles as mothers, and men typically do not.

A third reason for men's lesser role with children, perhaps a surprising one, has been labeled "gate-keeping" (Kazura, 2000). Many mothers see themselves as the parent predominantly responsible for children, and they actively or perhaps in a more subtle manner act to keep fathers less involved with their children than they are themselves. In fact, when fathers are highly involved with their children, it is often because their wives influence them to be (McBride & Darragh, 1995).

Single-parent families

So far we have been considering families in which two parents are available. When only one parent is present in the home because of divorce, parental death, or single parenthood, from the time of the child's birth, mothers are much more likely to be custodial parents than are fathers. Therefore, fathers in these families are often considerably less likely to interact with their children. This has been called "the two faces of fatherhood" (Furstenberg, 1988). Fathers in two-parent families in industrialized countries have been increasing the amount of time they have spent with their children in the past several decades, and some fathers in these families spend a great deal of time with their children (Pleck, 1997; Yeung, Sandberg, Davis-Kean, & Hofferth, 2001). However, as single-parent families have become increasingly common over this same time period, divorced and single fathers have been much less available to their children.

A culture of involved fathers: the Aka pygmies

Anthropologist Barry Hewlett has spent many years studying the Aka pygmies in Africa (Hewlett, 1991, 2000). These fathers spend a great deal of time interacting with their infants, holding them, interacting with them, and caring for them nearly as much as mothers do. Although the mothers spend somewhat more time with their infants, the fathers spend a great deal of time, more than anyone else (e.g., siblings). The Aka obtain much of their food from a collaborative net hunt, in which all the adults must cooperate, men and women included. Hewlett has concluded that men spend so much time with infants because of the essential equality of men and women in the food-providing role and the need to cooperate to get food, and because husbands, wives, and their young children spend a great deal of time together. Because men spend so much time around their young children, fathers and infants become attached to each other, and the infants then come to seek out their fathers, who enjoy interacting with them, further driving the degree of interaction.

However, in most cultures in the world, our own included, it is clear that mothers spend more time with and are more involved with children than fathers. When considering the issue from a gender development perspective, it should be obvious that children can learn powerful messages about the roles of men and women when their mothers have more responsibility for their well being than do their fathers.

Mothers' and Fathers' Interactions With Children

We know that fathers spend less time than mothers with their children, but most fathers spend some time, and some fathers spend a great deal of time with their children. And when they spend that time they may do many of the same tasks that mothers do. After all, many of children's needs are unrelated to gender, and if only one adult is present, he or she capable of doing the necessary caretaking. However, there are some notable differences in how fathers and mothers typically interact with their children. We would remind you, though, that these are average differences, and that they are not necessarily large, nor do they apply to everyone. Even so, these differences can serve as models for children to learn about what mothers and fathers, and men and women in general, do with children.

Mothers are caretakers and fathers are playmates

Especially with young children, fathers tend to be playmates and mothers to be caretakers. This is especially true when the kind of play is rough, physical play—tossing toddlers in the air, tickling them, and roughhousing. One of us once did a study observing two-parent families with an infant and a preschooler in their own homes (Blakemore, 1990). During one observation a father and the preschool child were watching television while the infant crawled around the room, largely ignored by the father and older sibling. The mother was busy with household tasks but interacted with the infant regularly. During a commercial on television, the father picked up the baby, tickled and bounced him, while the infant laughed enthusiastically. Once the program resumed, the father placed the infant back on the floor, and returned to watching the television.

This has been one of the most consistent differences that researchers have reported between fathers and mothers—fathers play and mothers caretake (Kazura, 2000; Lewis & Lamb, 2003; Paquette, 2004). As noted already, fathers' play style tends to be very physically active; when mothers play, their play tends to be quieter and more verbal (Carson, Burks, & Parke, 1993; Yogman, 1981). This kind of play is not limited to very young children. Fathers continue to be more playful as children grow older, especially with their sons. It is not unusual to see a father chasing or tickling or wrestling with an older child in a way that is much less likely for mothers.

This difference in play style is found in several different cultures but not all. Fathers in North America and parts of Europe have regularly been found to have this characteristic play style (Lewis & Lamb, 2003), but not fathers in Sweden, India, or Taiwan (Lamb, Frodi, Frodj, & Hwang, 1982; Roopnarine, Ahmeduzzaman, Hossain, & Riegraf, 1992; Sun & Roopnarine, 1996). Also, the Aka fathers discussed earlier do not play in this physically active style with their infants and toddlers (Hewlett, 1991). In North America, there are some families in which parents share caretaking roles, and physical play is not as likely to characterize these fathers' interactions (Roggman, 2004).

Involvement in and knowledge about their children's lives

During the school years both mothers and fathers are involved with the school and activity-related tasks of their older children (e.g., monitoring and helping with homework; attending athletic, musical, and other such activities in which their children are involved), but mothers continue to spend more time with their children and to do more caretaking (Lewis & Lamb, 2003). As children become adolescents, mothers and children have more varied topics in their conversations than do fathers and children, who focus predominantly on school, sports, and issues like handling money (Collins & Russell, 1991). Mothers also know more details about their children and adolescents' lives and relationships outside the family (Updegraff, McHale, Crouter, & Kupanoff, 2001). In sum, mothers have more extensive interactions with their children.

Styles of interaction

Parents' interaction styles also differ. Mothers are somewhat more responsive and comforting to children than fathers are from infancy onward. In general, fathers tend to be more authoritarian, show less flexibility or give-and-take in their interactions with their children (Kazura, 2000; Kochanska & Aksan, 2004), and are more directive in their speech (Leaper et al., 1998). Put bluntly, fathers are more likely to tell children what to do, and less likely to listen to their input.

Mothers are also more likely to focus on the needs of others when talking with their children – to focus on how their behavior impacts other people. For example, in an observational study of parents' responses to children's misbehavior towards their siblings, fathers were more likely to emphasize that the behavior was not fair or right, whereas mothers were more likely to focus on whether it was kind or considerate and to emphasize the feelings and needs of the siblings (Lollis, Ross, & Leroux, 1996).

Given these differences, it stands to reason that both boys and girls, but especially girls, consistently report that they feel closer to their mothers than to their fathers, at least in North America and Europe (Claes, 1998; Collins & Russell, 1991; Paterson, Field, & Pryor, 1994). The kind of interactions that children and adolescents have with mothers have may be something of a double-edged sword, perhaps especially for the mothers themselves. Mothers and children have a more responsive and flexible pattern of interactions—mothers spend more time with their children and they talk about more issues, so it is understandable that children seek out their mothers to confide in, and that they develop a closer relationship with them.

Probably because they have somewhat more intimate relationships with their mothers, as well as more experience with their mothers giving in to them, children have more disagreements with mothers than with fathers, are less likely to comply with their mothers' requests or obey their commands, and are more likely to treat fathers respectfully or deferentially. It may also be the case that as children become aware of the higher status of men in general, it influences them to be less respectful towards their mothers. Certainly, this is a point of frustration for many mothers. It can also be a stressor to some mothers to carry the personal concerns of their children in a manner not often done by fathers.

Because fathers have been found to be somewhat more demanding and distant, one might expect that fathers would be more likely to physically punish children. This would fit with the stereotypical notion of mothers threatening children with their fathers' punishment (e.g., "wait until your father gets home"). However, in recent years research has generally found either that mothers punish more (largely because they spend more time with children), or that the degree of physical punishment of mothers and fathers is similar (Nobes & Smith, 2000).

To conclude, mothers spend more time with their children, know more about them, their interests, and their friends, and interact with them in a greater variety of ways. They are also more flexible and responsive to their children's input. Hence, children are closer to their mothers, turn more often to them with their concerns, but are also less likely to obey them without question, and sometimes push them harder than they do their fathers.

Parent and child gender

Some have also wondered whether the particular combinations of parent-child pairs as a function of gender differ in unique ways. For example, perhaps mother-daughter relationships are closer than father-daughter or father-son relationships. Maybe father-daughter relationships are the most distant of all. However, one review of the research on this topic found few unique patterns in the four dyads across most families (Russell & Saebel, 1997).

Most of these comparisons, though, involve examining families with sons to families with daughters. The families who seem to be most likely to develop such differential relationships are those in which sons and daughters are both present in the same family. Birth order and family attitudes about gender also matter. The family configuration which has been shown most likely to show such differential mother-daughter versus father-son relationships are those in which parents (especially fathers) have traditional attitudes about gender, when there are children of both sexes in the family, and when the siblings include an older brother and a younger sister (McHale et al., 1999). Much more research examining the impact of the family configuration on within-family gender socialization is needed before these effects can be disentangled.

THE IMPACT OF DIFFERENT KINDS OF FAMILIES

Not all families are the same, of course, and not all families have the same attitudes about gender-related behavior in their children. Some families simply adopt without question the prevailing gender-related attitudes and expectations in their culture, whereas others engage in a concerted effort to reject the cultural constraints of gender. Psychologist Sandra Bem has written about the efforts that she and her husband Daryl took to socialize their two children, Jeremy and Emily, without traditional gender roles (Bem, 1983). The Bems made every effort not to model gendered behaviors themselves, nor to have different expectations for their son or their daughter. After the children reached early adulthood Bem wrote a book about their experiences (Bem, 1998). In a final section of the book, the children added their own reflections on their gender-neutral upbringing. Both noted that their vocational pursuits were conventional for males and females (Jeremy with math and physics, and Emily with music and theater), but that otherwise many aspects of their behavior were completely unconventional. Jeremy discussed his interest in intense discussions of the emotional lives of others, his occasional wearing of skirts, and his close friendships with girls. Emily discussed her reluctance to shave her rather hairy legs, yet her wish to be a sexy and attractive woman in the face of cultural standards for women to have hairless legs and underarms. Both were very resistant to organizing the world in terms of heterosexuals and homosexuals.

There are many other families who make every attempt to reduce the impact of gender on their sons and daughters as they grow to adulthood. In addition to personal stories such as Bem's, there are empirical studies of the impact of such different kinds of families on children's development. We will consider three kinds of research: comparisons of gender-liberal and traditional families; single-parent families; and families in which the parents are gay and lesbian, particularly the latter.

Traditional and Nontraditional Families

Parents Committed to Equality of Parenting and (Sometimes) Feminism

When we discussed the amount of time fathers spend with their children, we noted that some fathers spend a great deal of time with their children. Not all of these fathers are members of families like the Bems who are trying to reduce the impact of cultural norms about gender, but some certainly are. In one recent study, several families who were committed to equal parenting were interviewed by Deutsch (1999). These were often highly educated, professionally employed parents who were committed to sharing the roles of both provider and parent equally. For example, one mother of a 2-year-old said:

> We both take very active roles. From the beginning, there's no reason for us not to do exactly the same thing in terms of childcare. My husband and I do the same job; we work in the same department at the same college with the same teaching schedule. We do everything the same, so it seems completely irrational that one of us would have to do more with the baby....We both believe that pretty strongly and we divide things equally. (Deutsch, 1999, p. 16)

There were also parents with modest incomes who worked on different shifts so that one parent was always present with the children. These parents often had rather traditional attitudes about gender roles despite the fact that the fathers were sharing parenting equally. They often continued to see the mother as the primary parent in a way that the other group of parents did not. Their major reason for sharing parenting equally was to avoid non-family childcare for their children in the face of their financial need for two incomes. In addition to concerns about the expense of non-family care, these parents often expressed negative attitudes about it (e.g., that it was unsafe, or of low quality, or that they wanted to raise their own children and not have others doing it).

Other researchers have found parents committed to shared parenting and to reducing the impact of gender on their children. In one study of African American families (Hill, 2002), the majority of families continued to follow traditional gender norms, particularly for sons. Some were committed to equal opportunity for daughters in the workplace once they reached adulthood, but still expected "ladylike" behavior from them, especially in their relations with men, and in their gendered roles in the home. For example, one mother said about whether she would encourage her daughter to believe that men and women should have equality: "I will in one sense, but not in another. In terms of the family, I'm teaching her that a man is supposed to take care of her...but in the workplace, I'm teaching her that they are equal" (Hill, 2002, p. 499).

But some of these African American parents were committed to equality across the board. They did not conform to gender roles as parents in their own home lives, they shared parenting and household tasks, and they wanted full equality for both their sons and their daughters. These parents were more likely to be well educated, more likely to have had educated parents themselves, less likely to adhere to conservative religious views, and less concerned about homosexuality, especially in sons.

What percentage of couples are living their lives sharing parenting equally, and are committed to reducing the impact of gender in their children's lives? At this point we really do not know, but it is certainly a relatively small percentage of couples (Deutsch, 2001). Research on such couples illustrates how very difficult it is for parents to construct truly egalitarian family and parenting roles for many reasons: financial, cultural, and individual (Knudson-Martin & Mahoney, 2005).

From a gender development perspective, our question concerns the impact of both shared parenting and a commitment on the part of parents to minimizing the role of gender in their children's lives. These are clearly different issues. There is some research on the general question of the impact of shared parenting on children's development. Some of this research examines children's cognitive and social development, issues that are generally beyond the scope of this book. Suffice it to say that there is good evidence that children benefit both intellectually and socially when their fathers are involved with them (Rohner & Veneziano, 2001). It is a clear advantage to children to have two highly committed and interactive parents.

Our major concern in this book is gender development. When children have actively involved fathers, and when parents are committed to gender equality, what is the impact on the children's gender-related knowledge and behaviors? Beverly Fagot and her colleagues have studied this question longitudinally with very young children. They looked at parents' behavior with young toddlers, and then followed the children's gender-related knowledge and behavior a year or so later. They found that parents with more liberal gender-related attitudes, and with highly involved and liberal fathers, were less likely to reinforce stereotyped toy play, and their children were slower to learn gender labels and stereotypes and to play with gender stereotyped toys (Fagot & Leinbach, 1995; Fagot, Leinbach, & O' Boyle, 1992). Other research finds that children in such families have less stereotyped interests and more flexible attitudes about adult roles in the family and the workplace (Deutsch, Servis, & Payne, 2001; Kulik, 2002; McHale et al., 1999; Risman & Myers, 1997; Weisner & Wilson-Mitchell, 1990). One study found that girls from these families do not show a decline in math performance during middle to high school, a decline that is often found in girls' traditional homes (Updegraff, McHale, & Crouter, 1996).

One observational study examined differential parental treatment of several gender-related behaviors: assertiveness, aggression and anger, noncompliance, large motor movements, compliance, crying, dependency, self-reflection, and withdrawal (Hsu, 2005). They found that some parents responded more positively to sons' masculine behavior (aggression, noncompliance, motor movements, etc.) and to daughters' feminine behavior (crying, dependency, withdrawal, etc.) but others did not. Boys whose parents responded more positively to the masculine behavior and less positively to the feminine behavior, themselves showed more masculine and less feminine behavior. Similarly, girls whose parents responded more positively to the feminine behavior and less positively to the masculine, showed more feminine and less masculine behavior. Children whose parents were less likely to respond in gender-specific ways, were less likely to show such gender-related behavior. That is, there was clear evidence of a role for differential parental reinforcement in influencing gender-related behavior in their children.

However, children with nontraditional parents are not without any gendered behavior. Although they may have flexible attitudes about adult roles, children in these families have been shown to have stereotyped attitudes about children's behavior, to think that boys and girls are different in interests and behavior, and they indicate that they themselves prefer gendered interests and activities (Deutsch et al., 2001; Risman & Myers, 1997). Interestingly, there is some evidence that boys whose fathers who are very nurturing are more interested in feminine activities than other boys are (Deutsch et al., 2001).

So, we can conclude that the children of parents who are very committed to reducing the role of gender in shaping their children's lives have some success in doing so, but that their children are also affected by gendered messages in the culture at large.

Single-Parent Families

Most single-parent families are headed by mothers, although there are some father-headed families. There is a considerable amount of research on the impact of single parents on many aspects of children's development (e.g., see Weinraub, Horvath, & Gringlas, 2002), but our major concern is the impact of living in a single-parent home on gender development.

Single parents do not necessarily have less traditional attitudes about gender norms, but their behavior is often less traditional. If there is only one parent in the household, that parent must do all the tasks that need to be done until the children are old enough to help their parent. For example, a single-parent mother must do the cooking, cleaning, shopping, and laundry, but also the grass-cutting, snow-shoveling, and car maintenance that may fall to fathers in two-parent homes. The single-parent father must also do all of these tasks. Therefore, children in single-parent homes have the model of a parent whose day-to-day behavior does not necessarily conform to gender norms. As we discussed in chapter 2, in the heyday of psychoanalytic theory, researchers were concerned about the impact of "father absence" on children's gender development (e.g., Leichty, 1960). Because children were thought to learn gender roles from their parents, boys especially were said to need a father with whom to identify. In recent years, however, the question of the impact of single parents on gender development has concerned modeling and imitation, rather than any proposed psychodynamic impact.

Some research has found children from single-parent families to be less gender stereotyped, and to have more flexible attitudes about gender roles, especially about women's roles (Leve & Fagot, 1997; Mandara, Murray, & Joyner, 2005). However, other studies find gender role interests and behaviors of children from single-parent homes, including those who have virtually no contact with their fathers (Stevens, Golombok, Beveridge, & Alspac Study Team, 2002), to be comparable to those of other children. Thus, although there is some support for a conclusion that the children of single parents have less stereotyped gender development, the findings are not consistent.

Gay and Lesbian Parents

Children live with gay and lesbian parents for many reasons. Some gay men and lesbians have been members of heterosexual couples who bore their own biological children. When the parents separate and one or the other enters a homosexual relationship and has custody of the children, the children become members of the new family along with their parent. Sometimes gays and lesbians adopt children, and lesbians, in particular, often conceive children through donor insemination (sometimes called "the lesbian baby boom," Patterson, 1998). In the case of adoption and donor insemination, the children may live in a family with gay or lesbian parents for their entire lives. When lesbians use donor insemination to conceive a child, the families vary in the extent to which they maintain a relationship with the children's biological fathers—some are very involved, whereas others are completely anonymous.

It should be noted that far more families consist of lesbians with children than gay men with children. Although about 25% of gay men are fathers, few have regular custody of their children, partly because mothers have custody more often in general, and partly because of particular discrimination against gay men. Also, it is much more difficult for gay men to choose to become fathers than it is for lesbian women (i.e., via donor insemination). It is also the case that the gay male "culture" is said to be less focused on children and family than is that of lesbians (Bigner, 1999). Consequently, much of the research we have on the impact of having gay and lesbian parents involves children living in lesbian families, and some of those children were conceived in heterosexual marriages or other relationships that subsequently ended.

From a developmental process perspective, it is important to note the difference between simply living in a family with lesbian parents and being more likely to experience certain kinds of interactions because one has lesbian parents. Lesbian mothers may behave differently as parents than heterosexual mothers typically do, and they may also provide different gender-related modeling.

When researchers compare lesbian couples with heterosexual couples as parents, they generally find that lesbians are more likely to equally share the caretaker, homemaker, and breadwinner roles, as compared to heterosexual couples who are more likely to specialize—women spending more of their efforts on caretaking, and men on working outside the home and earning income (Chan, Brooks, Raboy, & Patterson, 1998; Patterson, Sutfin, & Fulcher, 2004; Solomon, Rothblum, & Balsam, 2005; Stacey & Biblarz, 2001). Some research has also found that lesbian mothers are less likely to use physical punishment and more likely to engage in imaginary play (Golombok et al., 2003), but overall the parenting behaviors of lesbian and heterosexual mothers are similar. Because mothers tend to possess more knowledge about parenting than do fathers, having two mothers seems to result in having somewhat more knowledgeable parents overall (Flaks, Ficher, Masterpasqua, & Joseph, 1995).

Over the past few decades there have been many studies of the development of children from gay and lesbian homes. Again, general social and emotional development is beyond the scope of this book, but suffice it to say that the cognitive, social, and emotional development of such children has been repeatedly found to be similar to that of other children (e.g., Allen & Burrell, 2002; Anderssen, Amlie, & Ytteroy, 2002; Chan, Raboy, & Patterson, 1998; Golombok et al., 2003). Relationships with parents are more important to children's outcomes than is their parents' sexual orientation, and the self-esteem and adjustment of children with lesbian parents is at least as good as that of other children, if not better (Stacey & Biblarz, 2001). There are two areas in which children from gay and lesbian homes may differ from children in more traditional households. Probably not surprisingly, they are more likely to find it necessary to keep their family arrangements secret from others until they are certain of acceptance. Some experience teasing or rejection from other children because of their mothers, and such teasing can be unpleasant and painful (Tasker & Golombok, 1997). Nonetheless, peer relationships in adolescence are comparable to those of children from homes with heterosexual parents (Wainright & Patterson, 2008).

The second area in which children of lesbian mothers may differ from other children is in their gender-related attitudes and behavior. Some studies have suggested that, at least in early childhood, these children's gender-related behaviors and attitudes are indistinguishable from those of other children (Golombok et al., 2003; Patterson, 1992). This may be especially so of boys. Indeed lesbian mothers report a sense of pressure to make sure that their sons conform to stereotypical gender norms, as though the mothers are under particular public scrutiny about their possible influence on their sons' masculinity (Kane, 2006). However, other studies find a greater tendency for these children to reject some stereotypical gender-related behaviors. Daughters of lesbians are reported by some as particularly likely to do so (Stacey & Biblarz, 2001).

This may differ for younger and older children. Once they reach older childhood and adolescence, there is quite good evidence that children of lesbian mothers have more liberal and flexible attitudes about gender, are less likely to be constrained by societal gender norms, are more accepting of homosexuality, and are more likely to explore homosexual relationships themselves. Compared to other children, they are much less likely to assume that heterosexuality is "normal" and homosexuality is not (Gabb, 2004; Stacey & Biblarz, 2001). However, the majority have a heterosexual sexual orientation once they reach adolescence and adulthood (Bailey, Bobrow, Wolfe, & Mikach, 1995; Golombok & Tasker, 1996).

In conclusion, we can see that there are some modest influences of nontraditional families on children's gender development. When parents specifically undertake an effort to reduce the impact of gender socialization on their children, or when they live relatively untraditional lives with respect to gender roles, they have some impact on their children, especially once the children are older.

THE IMPACT OF SIBLINGS

Children are not only influenced by their parents. The sibling configuration of a family is one of the most central features of a child's experience growing up. The presence of sisters might guarantee a boy's exposure to certain toys and games and to interactions with girls on a regular basis. This is particularly so in light of the fact that children's peer relationships outside the family are so dominated by children of the same sex. Birth order might also be a consideration. A girl with an older brother might have different gender-related experiences than a girl with a younger brother.

Sibling Configuration

We have already discussed the finding that the sibling configuration of families affects what chores are assigned to children. We know also that, as children grow older, mothers spend somewhat more time with daughters and fathers with sons (Tucker, McHale, & Crouter, 2003), so having siblings of the other sex is likely to affect a child's interactions with parents. A mother who has no daughters may treat her sons quite differently than a mother who has daughters. But what about the impact of brothers and sisters themselves on children's gender development?

One summary of the research (Wagner, Schubert, & Schubert, 1993) found that girls with brothers, especially older brothers, had more masculine interests. Boys with sisters, on the other hand, had more feminine interests when they were young, but were even more masculine than boys without sisters as they grew older. In the academic domain, having a brother seemed to improve math performance of both boys and girls, whereas having a sister improved the verbal performance of boys. It is well known that firstborns achieve at a higher level than later-born children. Wagner's review found this to be especially the case for girls, with younger sisters of older brothers being notably disadvantaged in this area.

One recent study examined more than 5,000 children born over a nearly 2-year period in an area of southwest England (Rust et al., 2000). The authors studied all children at age 3 with at least one older sibling younger than age 12 and compared them to children with no siblings. To measure gender development, the authors used a standardized instrument, the Preschool Activities Inventory (PSAI), which assesses children's characteristics, activities, and preferred toys. The findings were clear: boys with older brothers were more masculine than boys with older sisters, and boys without siblings had masculinity scores in between the other groups. The findings for girls were parallel. Some of these results were fairly large (e.g., $d > 0.50$). Thus, an older sibling influenced a younger sibling's gender development in the direction of the older sibling's. This finding is presented in Figure 10.1.

There were some additional findings of interest. Older brothers influenced younger siblings (both boys and girls) to have more masculine and fewer feminine interests. Older sisters, on the other hand, influenced younger brothers to have more feminine interests, but the brothers' masculine interests were not reduced compared with those of other boys. Older sisters influenced younger sisters to have fewer masculine interests than other girls, but not to have more feminine ones. The authors concluded that this pattern of results was likely related to the higher value accorded to masculine activities, making it easier for older brothers to influence their siblings' interests than for older sisters to do so. They also noted in peer relationships that boys are especially resistant to being influenced by girls and suggested that similar dynamics may play out in sibling relationships.

There is also evidence that the least gender-typed activities in which children take part are those they do with their siblings (McHale, Kim, Whiteman, & Crouter, 2004), especially opposite-sex siblings. Also, children who engage in more cross-gender activities often become somewhat less gender stereotyped over time in both their characteristics and their interests, so having a sibling with whom a child can experience the activities of the other gender is a potentially very important influence on gender development.

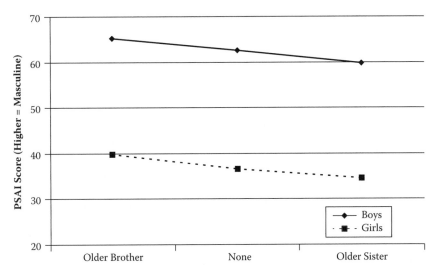

FIGURE 10.1   Gender role of younger siblings. (Data From Rust, P.C., *Journal of Social Issues, 56,* 205–221, 2000.)

The impact of siblings is not limited to having a brother versus a sister. Some siblings are more or less traditional in their gender attitudes and behaviors, and children in general become somewhat less traditional as they move into adolescence. One study found that gender-related attitudes on the part of older siblings had a greater impact on younger siblings' gender-stereotyped interests and attitudes than parents' attitudes did (McHale, Updegraff, Helms-Erikson, & Crouter, 2001). Parents' attitudes did not have a great deal of effect on children's gender-related characteristics, but when they did, parents were more likely to affect firstborns than later borns. Thus, it is clear that family configuration, parents, and siblings do not affect gender development in a simple, straightforward manner.

The Special Case of Fraternal Twins

Another way that the impact of sibling sex on gender development has been studied is to look at **fraternal twins**. Some fraternal twin pairs are same sex, and other twin pairs consist of one boy and one girl. These twins share the same home environment, but they also shared the same prenatal environment. As you recall, there is animal research showing that female fetuses are masculinized by hormone exposure that results from developing next to males in utero (Clark, Vonk, & Galef, 1998; Ryan & Vandenbergh, 2002). What about human children?

As you may recall, there is some research showing that brain organization is affected to some degree in female fraternal twins (Cohen-Bendahan, Buitelaar, van Goozen, & Cohen-Kettenis, 2004). The behavioral research has produced a mixed pattern of findings. Girls with twin brothers appear to be somewhat more aggressive and sensation-seeking than other girls (Cohen-Bendahan, Buitelaar, van Goozen, Orlebeke, & Cohen-Kettenis, 2005; Resnick, Gottesman, & McGue, 1993). On the other hand, girls with twin brothers have been found to have about the same degree of interest in feminine toys and activities as other girls (Rodgers, Fagot, & Winebarger, 1998). Indeed, one study of twins included a comparison group of girls with older brothers (Henderson & Berenbaum, 1997). They found little effect on girls' toy play when the girls had a twin brother, but girls with an older brother showed somewhat more play with boys' toys, and less play with girls' toys than the other girls.

One set of researchers followed a very large sample of twins longitudinally. Almost all twin pairs born in Finland between 1983 through 1987 (more than 5000 twins) have been followed by this research group (Rose et al., 2002). When the twins were 16, the girls' interest in feminine activities, occupations, and the like were assessed by a questionnaire. There was no evidence that the girls with twin brothers were more interested in masculine activities or occupations than were girls with twin sisters. So, overall, some aspects of gender-related behavior in girls seem affected by having a twin brother (e.g., sensation-seeking and aggression), but most do not.

Gender and the Nature of Sibling Relationships

One set of researchers interviewed children about their sibling relationships (Edwards, Mauthner, & Hadfield, 2005). They reported that sisters often spend much time talking together. For example, one 11-year-old said of her older sister: "A sister is someone to help you, to help you with your homework, someone to talk to, someone to look after you and be kind to you..." (Edwards et al., 2005, p. 505). Brothers, on the other hand, were more likely to report activities that they did together. When sisters talked of their brothers, they were more likely to describe shared activities than shared talking, as they might have done with sisters. Hence, the focus on activities that characterized brothers also seemed to characterize brother-sister pairs. There were exceptions to this general trend, in which some brothers focused on the communicative aspects of their relationships and some sisters on shared activities.

There are both pleasurable and unpleasant aspects of both dimensions of the siblings' relationships. It is fun to talk with your brother and fun to play games with him. However, overall relationships involving two sisters are closer, and involve less conflict and less aggression than those in which at least one partner is a boy (Dunn, Slomkowski, & Beardsall, 1994; Hoffman & Edwards, 2004; Martin & Ross, 2005). Interestingly, by adolescence, girls' relationships with siblings often have the same emotional tone as their relationships with parents, but boys' relationships with siblings and parents are more independent of each other (Oliva & Arranz, 2005). However, the spacing of siblings (close vs. far apart in age) as well as the characteristics of the particular individuals involved are also factors in the sibling relationship. It is quite clear that both brothers and sisters can be kind and supportive or hostile and aggressive to one another (Goodwin & Roscoe, 1990).

Siblings Affect Peer Relationships

Peer relationships are also affected by having siblings (Updegraff, McHale, & Crouter, 2000). Both boys' and girls' friendships with others outside the family are affected by whether they have a brother or a sister, and whether that sibling is older or younger than they are. For example, girls with brothers, especially older brothers, appear more tolerant of friends who are controlling. Perhaps they get used to such tactics because they have brothers. Boys with older sisters seem to seek out especially masculine friends, and girls with older brothers to seek out particularly intimate relationships with their friends. Perhaps children seek in their friends relationships that compensate for what is missing in sibling relationships. In addition, adolescent girls with older brothers seem to be more likely to adhere to conservative standards for their own sexual behavior (Kornreich, Hearn, Rodriguez, & O'Sullivan, 2003). Thus, it appears to be the case that the impact of siblings on gender development is not a simple matter.

Sexual Orientation

Another aspect of gender development that has been linked to siblings is sexual orientation. There is fairly consistent evidence that boys with older brothers are more likely to be homosexual than boys with no older siblings or with only older sisters (Blanchard, 1997; Bogaert, 2005b; Cantor, Blanchard, Paterson, & Bogaert, 2002). The more older brothers a boy has, the greater the probability that he will be gay. For example, Blanchard (2001) has estimated that a boy with four older brothers would be 3 times as likely to be gay as a boy with no older brothers. Overall, this is not a large effect—the d is about 0.25. One recent report, however, suggests that the finding only applies to very feminine gay men, but not to other gay men (Bogaert, 2005a). Interestingly, there is no similar relationship between birth order and sexual orientation for girls, only for boys.

Of course, we might wonder why such a phenomenon would come about. There is some evidence that at least some men who are homosexual show more feminine interests in childhood (Bailey & Zucker, 1995). Therefore, it might seem more plausible that boys with older sisters might be more likely to be gay. But this pattern has no evidence at all in support of it. At this point, the phenomenon is not very well understood, but most of the explanations focus on biological changes in the mother's reproductive system as a result of previously bearing male fetuses (Blanchard, 2001).

Siblings and Gender: Conclusions

To conclude, there is some research on the impact of siblings on children's gender development. Older brothers seem to influence their younger siblings of both sexes to have somewhat more masculine interests, and to a somewhat lesser degree, older sisters influence their younger siblings to have more feminine interests. Girls with twin brothers may be more impulsive and aggressive than other girls, but any impact on other gender-related interests and activities has been difficult to document. Interestingly, having an older brother seems to have a greater impact on a girl's masculine interests than having a twin brother.

Peer relationships, especially in adolescence, also seem to be affected by the sex of one's siblings. Girls with older brothers appear to be more tolerant of domineering friends, and boys with sisters appear to be attracted to friends with especially masculine interests. Finally, boys who have older brothers are more likely to be homosexual.

OTHER FAMILY RELATIONSHIPS

For most of us, our families include individuals other than our parents and siblings. We have grandparents, aunts and uncles, and cousins. These family members play very significant roles in some children's lives and are much more distant for others. Some children's cousins may play with them daily, and those relationships may have very similar effects to those siblings. We really know very little about the impact of these other family relationships on gender development, although a little is known about the role of grandparents.

Grandparents and Gender Development

Some children's grandparents raise them in their own homes. Others, although they are not playing parental roles, live with or very close by to the children and their parents during many years of the children's developmental years. Still others see their grandchildren only occasionally. We do know that for many children, grandparents are very important. Grandparents may provide a link to family history, serve as a buffer between parent and child, and provide important sources of support and caretaking when parents are undergoing their own crises or disruptions (Brown & Roodin, 2003).

Our concern is with gender development. Gender can affect the grandparent-grandchild relationship at three different levels: the sex of the child, of the parent, and of the grandparent. For example, it is very consistently found that grandmothers have closer relationships with grandchildren than do grandfathers (Mills, Wakeman, & Fea, 2001; Smith & Drew, 2002; Uhlenberg & Hammill, 1998). As is the case with mothers, grandmothers interact more with their grandchildren than grandfathers do, and maintain greater emotional closeness. Of course some grandfathers have very close relationships with their grandchildren, and it is interesting to note that some grandfathers behave more nurturantly with their grandchildren than they did with their own children (Drew, Richard, & Smith, 1998).

The interaction between gender and the behavior of grandparents to their grandchildren has not often been studied. But when it has, gender has played a role. In one study of the interaction between grandparents and their adolescent grandchildren, the grandparents were shown to behave in a more authoritarian manner towards granddaughters than grandsons (Mueller, Wilhelm, & Elder, 2002). This, of course, fits with the same pattern of granting less autonomy to daughters that we reported earlier for parents.

Maternal and Paternal Grandparents

Whether the grandparents are the child's mother's parents or the child's father's parents is also a factor. **Maternal grandparents** typically have greater access to and closer relationships with grandchildren than **paternal grandparents** do (Dubas, 2001; Mills et al., 2001). This is not always found, because one of the important influences on relationships between grandparents and grandchildren is the closeness of the relationship between the child's parents and grandparents. When grandparents have a close relationship with their own adult children and their children's spouses, then this tends to strengthen the grandparents' relationships with their grandchildren (Fingerman, 2004). That can happen with sons and daughters-in-law as it can with daughters and sons-in-law. However, because women typically maintain family relationships (e.g., mothers and their adult daughters) throughout adulthood, children's relationships with their maternal grandparents are often closer.

Grandsons Versus Granddaughters

Most reports find that boys and girls have equally close relationships with their grandparents—both typically having closer relationships with grandmothers (Eisenberg, 1988), although not always (e.g., Block, 2000). As grandchildren reach young adulthood some researchers find granddaughters are closer to grandmothers and grandsons to grandfathers (Dubas, 2001), so the closeness of the relationship may not be simple, nor is it necessarily the same at all ages (of both the grandparent and grandchild).

From the grandparent's perspective the grandchild's sex is not critical; grandmothers and grandfathers usually report no difference in their degree of closeness to their grandsons or granddaughters (Block, 2000). More important is the sex of their own children; they report greater closeness to the children of their daughters than to the children of their sons (Fingerman, 2004).

The Impact of Parental Divorce

The divorce of a child's parents (or the death of a parent) is one factor that can certainly impact a child's relationship with grandparents. One study found that, in single-parent families, grandparents were more likely to help single-parent fathers than single-parent mothers with certain activities (e.g., caring for the grandchild overnight), possibly because single-parent fathers were thought by their own parents to need more help with caretaking (Hilton & Macari, 1997). However, in general, the study found that it was the custodial parent's parents who were the most involved as grandparents. Because mothers are more likely to have custody of children following divorce, again it is their parents who tend to have greater access to and closer relationships with grandchildren.

Grandparents: Conclusions

Although there is not very much research on the topic of the impact of grandparents on gender development, what there is shows a great deal of similarity with that of parents. Mothers and grandmothers spend more time, and have closer relationships with children. The mothers of the children's mothers are especially likely to do so. The small amount of research that does exist on the grandparents' actual behavior towards grandchildren is consistent with that of parents. However, grandparents clearly play a different role for most children than the role played by parents. Much about how this role relates to gender development is unknown.

CHAPTER SUMMARY

There are four mechanisms of gender socialization by parents: parents interact with boys and girls differently, they channel their interests into different domains, they tell them to behave differently, and they model different behaviors for them to emulate.

In the past, and in many places in the world today, parents would rather have sons, but that preference is not often found in the industrialized West today. There is some evidence that fathers are especially committed to their families when they have sons, and that certain kinds of economic resources may be spent to enhance the long-term educational prospects of sons.

Perhaps the clearest kind of differential socialization of boys and girls concerns gender roles themselves. Boys and girls are given different names, clothing, toys, and room decorations, and are encouraged in different activities. Girls are likely to be assigned to do more household chores. One very important, and possibly less obvious form of gendered treatment concerns academic subjects. In domains such as mathematics, parents' stereotyped beliefs and subsequent differential treatment of sons and daughters become powerful influences on children's eventual competence. Indeed, many parents appear to have subtle attitudes that girls are less competent, capable, and intelligent than are boys.

There are many studies supporting a conclusion that parents interact differently with sons and daughters. In most of the contemporary world, boys' and girls' early needs, both physical and emotional, appear to be met equally well, but other kinds of interactions do show differences. Parents respond more positively when their children choose gender "appropriate" toys, and when children play with those toys, they develop different skills. Parents' play with boys and girls differently, with boys experiencing more physical and rough-and-tumble play, and girls experiencing more pretend play involving language and social roles. When parents and children play in imaginary settings playing pretend social roles or with dolls, language use is amongst the most sophisticated, and when they play with vehicles, the least. The first type of play is more likely with daughters, and the second with sons.

A very important kind of parental socialization concerns emotion. Beginning in infancy and continuing through childhood, parents work harder to get boys to control their emotions, especially emotions that signal vulnerability such as sadness and fear and emotional behaviors such as crying. On the other hand, parents permit and give in more to anger in sons. Therefore, sons come to learn that their anger leads to a payoff. Parents talk more about emotion with girls, especially when emotion concerns vulnerability and is centered on interpersonal relations.

Parents talk differently to boys and girls. They talk more to girls, and are more likely to tell girls what to do. With girls they talk more about social relationships, and with boys, they talk more about their academic work. Parents and children also talk a great deal about gender itself.

Parents tolerate and encourage greater risk taking and "everyday aggression" in their sons, but, in general, their discipline is stricter. Boys receive more physical punishment, and are more likely to be responded to with frustration and anger. Such parental behavior may backfire and produce even more aggression and anger.

Parents are more likely to encourage independence in sons, and to grant them autonomy to do things for themselves. They are more controlling of daughters, more likely to restrict their activities in the interest of their safety, and more likely to provide help to them, even when the help is not needed.

Mothers and fathers also behave differently. Mothers spend much more time with their children, have more extensive relationships with them, know them better, and are closer to them. Mothers are usually the executive decision-makers for children. Whereas mothers do more caretaking, in many cultures fathers spend more time in active play. Mothers are more responsive and flexible with their children, and hence they typically experience more conflict with them. Fathers are more likely to forcefully tell children what to do, and children are more likely to do it. Nontraditional families are less likely to treat children in gendered ways, and their children are more likely to have more flexible attitudes about gender roles, although many aspects of their behavior and interests differ little from the behavior and interests of other boys and girls.

Whether a child has siblings, the sex and birth position of those siblings impacts gender development. When a child has an older brother, that child's behavior is more likely to be stereotypically masculine, and when a child has an older sister, the reverse has been shown. Children's relationships with siblings are the least gendered relationships that they have with others, so this appears to be an area in which the impact of gender is less than in other social relationships. Relationships that involve sisters are typically more intimate and less conflicted than relationships that involve brothers, or those of a brother and a sister.

Children's relationships with their grandparents are also affected by gender. Like mothers, grandmothers spend more time with and are closer to their grandchildren than are grandfathers. Children typically spend more time with and are closer to their mothers' parents than their fathers'.

In conclusion, many of children's experiences in the family are affected by gender. However, it should be noted that there are few meta-analyses of this research, and we know very little about the effect sizes of any differential treatment. It is reasonable to expect that when such meta-analyses are completed the effect sizes will vary greatly.

The Peer Group as an Agent of Gender Development

11

Just as there are separate doors for boys and girls, there are also separate parts of the schoolyard. At the front, outside the teachers' entrance, is a dirt field covered with cinders, the boys' playing field. At the side of the school, facing away from the street, is a hill, with wooden steps going up it.... By custom, this is reserved for the girls, and the older ones stand around up there in groups of three or four, their heads bent inward, whispering, although boys sometimes make charges up the hill, yelling, and waving their arms. (Atwood, 1988, p. 51)

Think back to your own childhood. Who were your friends, and what did you do with them? Did it matter whether you were at home in your own neighborhood versus whether you were at school? If you were like most children, the majority of the friends you recall from childhood are likely to be children who were the same sex as you, at least if they were available. This phenomenon is richly recounted by novelist Margaret Atwood in her book *Cat's Eye*, a story about the tormented relationships of a group of girls. In the story Atwood describes the young protagonist's relationship with her own brother at school:

Lining up is the only time I see my brother at school. At home we've rigged up a walkie-talkie with two tin cans and a piece of string, which runs between our two bedroom windows and doesn't work very well. We push messages under each other's doors, written in the cryptic language of the aliens...
But in the daytime I lose sight of him as soon as we go out the door. He's up ahead throwing snowballs, and on the bus he's at the back, in a noisy whirlpool of older boys. After school, after he's gone through the fights that are required of any new boy at any school, he's off helping to wage war on the boys from the Catholic school nearby...
I know better than to speak to my brother during these times, or to call his or any boy's attention to me. Boys get teased for having younger sisters, or sisters of any kind...If he's teased about me, he will have to fight some more. For me to contact him, or even to call him by name, would be disloyal. I understand these things, and do my best. (Atwood, 1988, p. 51–52)

In this chapter we will consider the impact of peer relationships on children's gender development. It is one of the most basic aspects of social relationships in childhood that children play in same-sex peer groups, a phenomenon known as **gender segregation**. As we have noted earlier in this book, playing primarily in same-sex groups and having friends who are predominantly the same sex as oneself is one of the most robust differences between boys and girls across most if not all cultures in the world (Geary & Bjorklund, 2000).

In this chapter we will consider the following topics. First, we will examine the developmental progression of gender segregation—when it takes place and how it changes as children grow older. Second, we will examine the characteristics of the interactions that take place in the groups—what some have called the "two cultures" of childhood. We will follow that with a consideration of the various factors that seem to influence children's tendencies to prefer friends and playmates of the same sex. We will also consider the nature of popularity in boys' and girls' peer groups, children's friendships, and the special circumstance of boys and girls in youth gangs. We will consider romantic and dating relationships as children move into adolescence. Finally, we will consider the impact of peer group interaction on children's gendered behaviors and the implications for adult behavior. It will be a central message of this chapter that children contribute to their own gender socialization.

THE DEVELOPMENTAL PROGRESSION
OF GENDER SEGREGATION

If you asked the average person when boys and girls start to play in same-sex peer groups, the answer might be by the start of elementary school, but it is actually much earlier. There is not much evidence for same-sex peer preferences during infancy or the second year of life (Campbell, Shirley, Heywood, & Crook, 2000; Shirley & Campbell, 2000). By the age of 2, however, the situation changes. There are several studies showing that between the ages of 2 and 3, children start choosing more same-sex peers for play partners and friends (Howes, 1988; LaFreniere, Strayer, & Gauthier, 1984). Girls are the first to show this preference, around 24–27 months, but boys soon follow and eventually have stronger same-sex peer preferences than girls do. The preference for same-sex friends increases rather dramatically between the ages of two and six. For example, one longitudinal study found that 4-year-olds were spending about 3 times as much time with children of the same sex (as compared to spending time with at least some children of the other sex present), but by the age of 6 they were spending more than 10 times as much of their playtime with same-sex children (Maccoby & Jacklin, 1987). From 80 to 90% of older preschoolers show a marked preference for same-sex peer relationships, many never playing with a child of the other sex (Martin & Fabes, 2001). Although some preschool children play with boys and girls to a fairly equal degree, it is very rare for young children to play more frequently with other sex than same-sex children.

Once children reach elementary school, they continue to spend much of their free playtime with children only or mostly of the same sex. It is hard to put a number to how frequently they do so, because it varies by culture, even by the type of school that children attend (Aydt & Corsaro, 2003), but it is reasonable to assume that it happens much more than half the time, possibly as much as 80% of the time (Maccoby, 1998; Thorne, 1993). Most of the rest of elementary children's play is in mixed-sex groups; again, very little play takes place with children predominantly or only of the other sex.

During the elementary school years children spend more time in gender-segregated groups when adults are not present, particularly when they are on the school playground. Classrooms are not as likely to consist of primarily same-sex interaction in the same way that playgrounds are (Thorne, 1993), because the presence of teachers seems to reduce gender segregation. Outside of school, children's friendship groups at home and in their neighborhoods are primarily same-sex also, if such friends are available. Some children may not live in neighborhoods with many same-sex children, and such children tend to play with whatever children are available. But as soon as there is a choice and a group of children available for them to play with, most children choose to play mostly with other children of their own sex.

Adolescents also prefer friends of the same sex, and gender segregation continues to be found as children enter middle and high school (Pellegrini & Long, 2003; Richards, Crowe, Larson, & Swarr, 1998). As adolescents grow older, however, friendships of the other sex become more common (Strough & Marie Covatto, 2002); adolescents certainly express more positive views about interactions with the other sex than younger children do. And of course, heterosexual dating relationships may begin by early to mid-adolescence (Pellegrini & Long, 2003). So gender segregation continues, but it tends to lessen once children become adolescents.

THE "TWO CULTURES" OF CHILDHOOD

It is often said that boys and girls grow up in two different cultures (Maccoby, 1998; Tannen, 1994a; Thorne & Luria, 1986). The idea is that, despite being raised in the same basic culture, and the same homes, and going to the same schools, the peer group experiences of boys and girls are so different that they amount to different cultural experiences for children. There are certainly debates about whether the "two cultures" notion is an appropriate way to look at peer group experiences (Thorne, 1993; Zarbatany, McDougall, & Hymel, 2000), because after all, boys and girls do interact with each other and share many common experiences in their families, schools, and cultures. Also, boys' and girls' interactions are often quite similar, probably more similar than they are different, although people sometimes seem to ignore that similarity (Leaper, 1991).

Differences in the Characteristics of Boys' and Girls' Peer Groups

Despite their similarities, boys' and girls' groups have been found to differ in the following basic ways: group size, degree of interconnectedness, themes in pretend play, play styles, activities, competition, aggression, conflict, dominance hierarchies, separation from adults, and use of language (Maccoby, 1998). By the late preschool period, boys' groups tend to be larger (Benenson, Apostoleris, & Parnass, 1998; Thorne & Luria, 1986). There is also research showing that, when given a choice, boys prefer larger groups than girls do (Benenson, 1993; Markovits, Benenson, & Dolenszky, 2001). In fact, the preferred group of girls seems to be a **dyad** (two people), or at most a **triad**. In an interesting study of young adolescents at summer camp, boys' cabins (five boys) were said by the counselors to form a coherent unit, whereas girls tended to form two- or three-person groups, or to form relationships with girls from other cabins (Savin-Williams, 1979). In another study, groups of six same-sex 5- and 6-year-olds (described in Benenson, Apostoleris, & Parnass, 1998) were given the opportunity to play together. The boys were much more likely to interact as whole group, spending 74% of their time doing so, whereas the girls quickly divided up into two- and three-person groups, and only spent 16% of their time as a whole group. So it seems to be the case that boys prefer and play in larger groups than girls do across much of childhood.

The peer group seems to be especially important to boys. Boys' peer groups are more interconnected. That is, most of a boy's friends are likely to be in the same group of boys, whereas girls are more likely to have individual friends who are not part of the same group. Girls seem to be less interested in having extensive peer relationships and report less enjoyment from peer relationships (Benenson, Morganstein, & Roy, 1998). Related to this tendency to particularly value their peer relationships, boys may spend much time attending to other boys in the classroom as opposed to paying attention to the teacher. Also, even as preschoolers, but definitely during the school years, boys are also more likely to play farther away from adults (Maccoby, 1998).

Boys and girls also play different kinds of games and activities. In a classic study of children's games, Janet Lever (1976) found that boys' and girls' games differed in the following ways: (a) boys were more likely to play outdoors, in larger groups, and in more age-heterogeneous groups; and (b) boys were more likely to play competitive or formal games and sports. Lever also reported that boys' games and activities lasted longer, and that girls were more likely to play boys' games than boys were to play girls' games. Other research supports the finding that organized games and sports are especially characteristics of boys' groups (Bradley, McMurray, Harrell, & Deng, 2000; Vilhjalmsson & Kristjansdottir, 2003), and of course, many sports require larger groups.

Play Styles With Peers

Boys and girls also have characteristic play styles. Preschool boys in groups are likely to take part in high-energy, boisterous play, and to engage in loud yelling and play fights (Pellegrini & Smith, 1998). Indeed, boys appear to have a great deal of fun engaging in this kind of physical play. Pitcher and Schultz (1983), who observed preschool boys and girls at play, noted that the boys enthusiastically wrestled, made machine-gun sounds, chased one another with guns, pretended to shoot each other and play dead, put clay in each other's hair, and otherwise engaged in high-spirited physical play. In a similar vein, one group of researchers observed preschool boys ramming bicycles into other children, but girls rode carefully, avoiding hitting others (Dunn & Morgan, 1987). Several researchers have noted that young boys' play often borders on aggression, a theme we will find is the case with older boys as well.

Whereas boys may be more likely to play in a boisterous and active style, preschool girls are more likely to take turns and cooperate with each other (Maccoby, 1998). Their pretend play often involves domestic activities (e.g., toy kitchens), family interactions, and familiar settings (e.g., playing mommy or daddy, school, or store). In addition to nurturant play with dolls, girls also play with dolls that involve appearance, clothing, and hairstyles—the ever-present Barbie dolls. In their observations of preschoolers, Pitcher and Schultz also reported that girls were often "the guardians of propriety, order, and superior know-how" (Pitcher & Schultz, 1983, p. 11).

Boys and girls may also use the same toys in different ways. For example, Pitcher and Schultz reported that girls cuddled, fed, and diapered dolls, whereas boys probed the dolls' hair and leg motions and removed their clothing. Boys used tinker toys to make guns, and girls used them as chopsticks to eat Chinese food. They also noted that children used the same physical spaces for different activities. Consider the following example in which a group of boys and then girls used a toy kitchen in different ways:

> Three boys came to the area, manipulated the dishes, and said they were going to cook. Each put a dish in the stove, then sat at the table. One went to the stove to retrieve his dish. "Hey, we're cooking fire!" he shouted. The others grabbed their dishes, pretended to eat the "fire," and laughed loudly, as over and over again, they engaged in pretend fire eating and falling down dead. Shortly thereafter, two girls came to the same place. They stirred the pots and pans, named the pretend ingredients—sugar, flour, and cinnamon. Refrigerator and stove doors were opened and shut, dishes were "washed." The girls assembled and prepared a "meal" that was put on the table. They then sat down at the table, and each pretended to drink a cup of coffee. (Pitcher & Schultz, 1983, p. 16)

The styles shown by preschool children continue into the elementary school years. Elementary-aged boys are often said to dominate the playground space, leaving the periphery for the girls (Dunn & Morgan, 1987). Aggression and rough and tumble play continues to be characteristic of boys' groups (Reed & Brown, 2001), and boys seem to experience games in which they attack and chase one another as great fun. Girls also continue to be more likely to play in smaller groups, and to focus more often on relationships.

Dominance

Boys' groups are more organized around dominance

One important phenomenon in peer groups is the establishing of a **dominance hierarchy**. This consists of a hierarchy from the most dominant child down to the child most dominated by other children. Dominance hierarchies are generally more characteristic of boys' groups and are more stable in boys' groups than in girls' groups (Savin-Williams, 1979). When a group of boys come together for the first time, such hierarchies are established rather quickly (Pettit, Bakshi, Dodge, & Coie, 1990). In fact, some boys use rough and tumble play and aggression to establish dominance, and some research finds that once there is a stable dominance hierarchy in a group of boys, aggression may be less frequent (Pellegrini, 1995). However, by adolescence some boys high in the dominance hierarchy seem to use rough and tumble play as well as forms of real aggression in a mean and hurtful, rather than a playful, way (Pellegrini, 2003).

Boys' groups engage in longer episodes of conflict than girls' groups do (Putallaz, Hellstern, Sheppard, Grimes, & Glodis, 1995), and high-status boys often engage in extended conflict as part of establishing their dominance in the group. These boys dominate the social interaction in general, and are typically the leaders of the group. It is also common in late childhood or early adolescence for boys who are higher in status to torment rejected or isolated boys, and to call them names like "sissy" or "fag" (Thorne & Luria, 1986).

Is this dominance related to violence and physical aggression?

In one thoughtful analysis of this characteristic of boys' peer relationships, sociologists Michael Kimmel and Matthew Mahler (2003) examined the relationship between such experiences and school violence such as that at Columbine High School in Colorado. They note that boys overwhelmingly perpetrate this kind of school violence. They found that several of the boys who engaged in school violence at various high schools across the country, shooting and killing their classmates at random, had been harassed and tormented by their more popular peers. In particular, these skinny, awkward, or "geeky" boys had been repeatedly labeled as "sissies" or "faggots." Of course, cruelty from peers rarely causes teens to behave violently; neither should violence be considered an acceptable response to peer torment. However, Kimmel and Mahler argue that this aspect of adolescent male peers groups is highly gendered, and that questioning the masculinity of less popular and socially skilled boys by their peers is one of the cruelest aspects of teen social life.

Girls' Groups Are More Egalitarian

Girls' groups are more egalitarian and more likely to be supporting and encouraging of one another (Zarbatany & Pepper, 1996). They are more likely to take turns in speech, to agree with another speaker, to respond to what someone else has said, and to give another person a chance to speak (Maccoby, 1990; Thompson & Moore, 2000). They are also more likely to talk about emotions, especially emotions like fear and vulnerability (Kyratzis, 2001). Girls are more focused on intimate relationships themselves, more likely to self-disclose, as well as to touch one another, stroke one another's hair, and comment on each other's appearance (Thorne & Luria, 1986; Underwood, 2003). In the elementary and middle school years girls speak amongst each other about who is "nice" or "mean," and they are very much preoccupied with who is whose friend.

We already know that boys value assertiveness and dominance, but there is also evidence that girls specifically devalue these traits. In one study of preschoolers (Sebanc, Pierce, Cheatham, & Gunnar, 2003) children were observed in same-sex groups of four engaging in a movie viewer task. This task permitted only one of the four children to watch the movie, whereas two others were needed to operate the viewer (one turned a crank out of reach of the child viewing, while another pushed a button to turn on a light). Clearly the child who was able to watch the movie needed to secure the cooperation of two other children. In their groups, some children were able to watch more than others, essentially by dominating the interaction so that other children would help them watch. The children were ranked from the most to least dominant as a function of how much viewing time they were able to secure. In the boys' groups, dominance was linked to peer acceptance—other boys liked the dominant and assertive boys. However, in the girls' groups, the dominant and assertive girls were not liked by other girls. In fact, the most cooperative girls (the ones who got to see the movie least) were liked the most. Other research with elementary school children (Hibbard & Buhrmester, 1998; Putallaz et al., 1995) supports the general conclusion that girls do not like other girls who are assertive or dominant.

We should not think that girls' groups are only intimate and kind; girls can also torment one another; recall our discussion of social and relational aggression from chapter 5. Girls' aggression seems to focus on manipulating the very relationships they so value. They are particularly known for saying spiteful and mean things about other girls behind their backs, or purposefully excluding them from participating (Goodwin, 2002; Underwood, 2003), as in "You can't be my friend if you are going to play with her." Girls certainly report that these experiences are very painful to them (Owens, Slee, & Shute, 2000), and it is fair to say that neither boys nor girls have a monopoly on either kindness or meanness to other children. Rather, they seem to manifest both their mutual support and their cruelty in somewhat different ways.

Social Speech

We pointed out already that boys' language often includes profanity and insults toward other boys. There are other elements that are more likely to characterize the social speech of boys. Preschool boys have been observed to be more likely to make non-word emphatic sounds (e.g., car noises) than girls (Farris, 1992). Boys are also more inclined to interrupt one another and to try to tell a better story than the last person's—for example, "If you think that's something, listen to what I did . . . ." Boys often talk to one another in very direct ways, giving commands and telling one another what to do. For example, in two studies, one with White and one with African American children, Campbell Leaper (Leaper, 1991;

Leaper, Tenenbaum, Shaffer, 1999) studied pairs of boys and girls between 5 and 7 years of age who played together with a puppet. Sometimes the children were in same-sex pairs, and sometimes boy-girl pairs. Although the speech of the boys and girls was more similar than different, boys were more likely to attempt to dominate one another, and to issue direct commands to one another, saying things like "Do this!" or "Kick your chair!" Leaper observed that girls were more likely to speak in cooperative or collaborative ways (e.g., "I'll do a choo-choo train with you," or "You go first."). Interestingly, Leaper and his colleagues also reported that both boys and girls were more likely to speak coercively when their play partner was a boy than when they played with a girl.

In an extensive observation of inner city African American boys and girls, Goodwin (1990) noted that boys were quite comfortable making comparisons among one another that reinforced their rank in the hierarchy—at indicating who is better at something. Girls, on the other hand, actively resisted such comparisons, and monitored other girls who tried to seem better than others. Whereas the boys she observed were comfortable with other boys bragging about their skills or possessions, girls considered such activities selfish or conceited. For example, in discussing a girl named Annette, one girl implied that Annette was "showing off" for wearing a particular blouse, and another suggested that it was impossible to be friends with someone who tried to be different or better than others. Other researchers (Best, 1983; Eder, 1985) have noted similar issues in girls' groups—it seems to be breaking some kind of subtle rule to say good things about oneself or to achieve status in girls' groups, but not so in boys'.

Conflicts in Boys' and Girls' Groups

Boys are also more likely to engage in conflict. Beginning in the preschool period, boys are more likely to disagree, and to argue and fight than girls do in their peer groups (Howes, 1988; Pitcher & Schultz, 1983). Sometimes such conflicts turn into actual physical assaults. We would not want to assume that boys fight and disagree with each other most of the time; they do not. As we have already seen, boys have a lot of fun interacting with each other. But conflicts and aggression are notably more characteristic of boys groups, and some boys simply refuse to comply with other boys' requests, or are very insistent in getting their own way. For example, in a series of observations of preschoolers in England, Dunn and Morgan (1987) reported that bicycles were the most popular playground toy. They observed some boys intimidating others to give them a bicycle by holding on to the bike and shouting at the child who had it until the other child gave it up. Girls only got bikes by picking up ones that were not in use, or by asking a teacher to intervene.

Young girls certainly also engage in conflicts, but they seem to be more likely to mitigate those conflicts in a style sometimes referred to as "yes, but ..." (Kyratzis & Guo, 2001). This is a style in which a girl may imply that she is agreeing with another girl, but then go on to list reasons why she is refusing to comply. Linguist Amy Sheldon has used the term **double-voice discourse** (Sheldon, 1992, 1997) to describe assertive girls who attempt to resolve conflicts by "saying it with a smile," or "being nice" while pursuing their own desires. For example, Sheldon (1997) observed three 4- and 5-year-old girls who had been playing with some vehicles and dinosaurs, and who each had a toy person. One of the girls, Eva, wanted to direct the play into a pretend marriage scenario, however she only wanted to include one of the other girls (Kelly) but not the other (Tulla). Tulla asks how she or her character will be included. In time Eva tells Tulla that her toy character has to be the little brother, and informs her that he is not born yet, so she will have to wait to take part. Tulla does not much like this turn of events, and keeps trying to be included, eventually leading to an angry outburst, although it takes a long time to get to that point.

As children grow through the school years they become more socially skilled, but differences in the styles in boys and girls persist, although at a somewhat more sophisticated level. Both boys and girls come to value conflict resolution and to devalue aggression as they grow older. However, girls continue to be more likely to mitigate conflict, to use rationales to argue for their positions, and to be less likely to use direct physical or verbal aggression (Crick & Ladd, 1990; Hartup, French, Laursen, Johnston, & Ogawa, 1993).

Rule Breaking in Boys' Groups

Boys are also more likely to break adults' rules when they are with groups of other boys. Barrie Thorne and Zella Luria (1986) observed fourth and fifth grade children at three schools—one in California, one in Michigan, and one in Massachusetts. They reported that boys loved to use profanity, often yelling "shit" or "you fucked up." This is remarkably like the study of preschoolers (Pitcher & Schultz, 1983) discussed earlier. The little boys in that study engaged in a kind of precursor to profanity by using words like "piss" and "ka-ka." Boys in other cultures have also been observed using similar words (Farris, 1992). Boys seem to enjoy the "naughty" aspect of using words like this. In Thorne and Luria's observations, when a teacher told the boys to stop using such language, they soon resumed it once the teacher was out of sight. Indeed, it seems to be an enjoyable risk for boys to break rules together. In addition to the use of profanity, rule breaking in general is a more common phenomenon amongst groups of boys. Thorne and Luria found in their observations that teachers were usually reluctant to punish groups of boys who broke rules, and that this reluctance confers a kind of power for groups of boys that simply does not happen for groups of girls.

Cross-Cultural Considerations

So far, it may sound like boys and girls develop these styles simply because they are boys and girls, an explanation that is often labeled **essentialism**. As previously discussed in chapters 8, 9, and 10, an essentialist explanation generally holds that boys' and girls' behavior is inherent in the child, rather than a result of social processes. Some researchers have found, though, that these styles vary somewhat across cultures or groups within a single culture. Among American children, both African American and Latina girls use the direct conflict strategies that are more often said to be associated with boys (Goodwin, 1990, 1995), although they still retain other aspects of conversational styles that are like those of White girls.

In a study of 4- and 5-year-old children from the United States and mainland China (Kyratzis & Guo, 2001), the researchers compared groups of children interacting with each other. In both countries, groups of three boys and three girls were the focus of study, including two Asian-American children in the U.S. sample. The American girls used the double-voiced strategy that we have already discussed. The Chinese girls, on the other hand, behaved quite differently, and according to Kyratzis and Guo, similar to the more direct styles of African American and Latina girls in the United States.

As you might expect, the American boys in Kyratzis and Guo's study certainly used the direct commands and "heavy-handed" conflict strategies that we have discussed already that are characteristic of them. What about the Chinese boys? Like the American boys and Chinese girls, they did use direct commands, but followed them with attempts to soften or mitigate the conflict, similar to the styles often seen in American girls.

So what can be made of the finding that the styles that are so often described as almost inherently characteristic of boys and girls peer groups are not always found in other cultural settings? Kyratzis and Guo argue that assertiveness is a more valued characteristic for middle class Chinese girls than for middle class American girls, and at the same time, assertiveness is somewhat less valued for Chinese boys than for American boys, and that the cultural expectations influence the styles found in the children's interactions. They also suggest that children's styles fluctuate depending on the particular settings. Neither Chinese nor American girls or boys are always assertive or always conciliatory, but rather they may change depending on the circumstances.

Characteristics of Boys' and Girls' Peer Groups: Conclusions

We have seen that there are some differences in the styles of interactions found in boys' and girls' peer groups. Boys' groups tend to be larger, focused on activities (especially sports), more hierarchical, and more likely to involve domination and conflict. Boys fight more, and sometimes ridicule and torment less popular or skilled boys. However, they also have a great deal of fun in their groups as they engage in lively physical activities. They are also more likely to engage in rule-breaking, again sometimes apparently in a spirit of fun.

Girls, on the other hand, are more likely to play in smaller groups, one-on-one being especially appealing to girls. They play more quietly, often engaging in pretend play focused on domestic themes. Outright conflict is less likely for girls, who often mitigate disagreements while at the same time pursuing their own ends. Of course, girls may purposefully exclude others using social or relational aggression, but that aggression is focused squarely on relationships themselves. Campbell Leaper (1994a) has described the differences between girls' and boys' groups as being concerned generally with affiliation or interpersonal closeness versus assertion or independence. He argues that boys tend to stress independence and self-assertion over affiliation, but girls are more likely to coordinate a desire to affiliate with other children with their own wish to assert themselves. We have also seen that these characteristics vary somewhat in different cultural settings.

WHY DO CHILDREN PLAY IN GENDER-SEGREGATED GROUPS?

Despite the fact that some aspects of play styles or language use may vary depending on culture or circumstances, the fact remains that boys generally play with other boys and girls generally play with other girls, and we need to ask why that is the case. Several explanations have been proposed, and we will examine some of the most widely supported ones here.

Compatible Play Styles

Recall that boys have a lot of fun with rough and tumble play, and that they are often concerned with issues of dominance. Because girls are the first to avoid boys, around the age of 2 years, some researchers have hypothesized that girls find boys' rough and tumble play and their focus on dominance aversive—that they are wary of it, and do not like it. For example, one of us once observed a preschool girl and her slightly older brother playing in the home of another boy. The boys were jumping off some chairs, and over an up-side-down child's table, yelling, and generally having great fun. The little girl was scrunching her fists in a ball, and saying to the boys "Stop it! Stop it!" This was clearly not a fun activity for her! Although some girls clearly do enjoy this kind of high-spirited play, the research finds that many do not, and that this may be one of the reasons that girls first begin to avoid boys—that they simply do not want to play with anyone who plays like this. Boys, on the other hand, seem to be attracted to this kind of play, finding it fun and exciting.

In a study of very young children (26–40 months) in their first year of preschool (Moller & Serbin, 1996; Serbin, Moller, Gulko, Powlishta, & Colburne, 1994), the researchers found that much social interaction at this young age was in mixed-sex groups. When looking at dyads, about 60% of the time the two children playing together were same sex, and about 40% of the time a boy and girl played with each other. In larger groups, only 22% of the time did these groups consist only of children of the same sex. Playing with a child of the same sex was more common for girls than for boys, consistent with the earlier emergence in girls that we have already discussed. In fact, Serbin and her colleagues found that 62% of the girls, as compared to 21% of the boys, played with same-sex peers above chance levels. What is key for the notion of behavioral compatibility, though, is that the boys who were the most active and disruptive were more likely to play with other boys, and the girls who were the most socially sensitive were more likely to play with other girls. This suggests that the process of gender segregation at very young ages begins at least partly because girls (especially socially sensitive ones) avoid other children who play roughly, and boys (especially active and disruptive one) seek out children who play this way, and most children who play this way happen to be boys.

What about older children? A study of sixth and seventh graders found that boys who particularly liked physical activity and rough play especially liked to play with other boys and to avoid girls, whereas girls who expressed liking for these activities more than most girls were more likely to choose boys among their friends (Bukowski, Gauze, Hoza, & Newcomb, 1993). In addition to physical play styles, there is also evidence that elementary school girls do not like the dominance and competition that are characteristic of boys' groups. Even competition amongst other girls makes many girls uncomfortable (Benenson et al., 2002).

Occasionally researchers have examined whether play styles or gender itself is the more critical factor in determining which peers children prefer to play with. When they are contrasted (e.g., would a boy prefer to play with another boy whose play style is not masculine, or with a girl with a masculine play style?) researchers have reported that boys between 4 and 8 years of age prefer girls with masculine play styles to boys with feminine ones (Alexander & Hines, 1994). Girls' preferences depend on age, with younger girls preferring girls as playmates regardless of their play style, and older girls preferring boys with a feminine style to girls with a masculine one. Overall, then, the research findings support the notion that differences in play styles are at least part of the reason that young children choose others of their sex as friends and avoid children of the other sex, and that this process continues to operate throughout the school years.

Ability to Influence the Other Sex

Some research has found that, as they go through the preschool years, girls are increasingly unable to influence boys. In a study of children between the ages of 3 and 5 years (Serbin, Sprafkin, Elman, & Doyle, 1984), boys were more likely to try to influence other children (especially other boys), and as they grew older, were especially likely to do so by using direct requests or demands (e.g., "Give me that truck"). They were also more successful in having their requests granted. Girls, on the other hand, increased in the use of indirect and polite requests (e.g., "I need the truck," "May I have the truck?") as a way to influence other children. Of course, polite requests are exactly what parents and teachers would like their children to do when expressing their desires. Unfortunately for the girls, although this form of influence was effective with other girls, it did not work well with boys. Boys' influence attempts were just as likely to be as effective with girls as with boys. Other researchers (Charlesworth & LaFreniere, 1983; Fagot & Hagan, 1985; Jacklin & Maccoby, 1978) have confirmed that girls are not able to influence boys as well as they can influence the behavior of other girls, but that boys are able to influence other children of both sexes.

One study of 4- and 5-year-olds in boy-girl pairs (Powlishta & Maccoby, 1990) gave children the opportunity to view a cartoon in a movie viewer that permitted only one child at a time to see the movie, and required the assistance of the other child to continuously push a button so that the movie would play. In another condition the movie simply played continuously—no one had to push the button. When cooperation was required, the boys were able to watch the movie more often—essentially by occupying the movie viewing window and influencing their female play partner to push the button for them. But this only happened when no adult was present in the room. When an adult was present, boys and girls watched the movie an approximately equal amount of time. Apparently boys can modify their dominating behaviors when they know an adult is monitoring the situation. In an observational study of playground behavior of preschoolers in England (Dunn & Morgan, 1987), a similar phenomenon was observed. Boys monopolized the most attractive outdoor toys unless girls were able to get the teacher to intervene on their behalf.

In another study of 4- to 7-year-old children (Maccoby & Jacklin, 1987), one group of girls was especially likely to avoid boys and to spend their playtime almost exclusively in the company of other girls. It may seem contradictory, but the girls who were the most active and outgoing compared to other girls (called "feistier" by Maccoby and Jacklin) were somewhat more likely than other girls to avoid boys.

Now one might expect that these tomboy-like girls would be the ones who would like to play with both boys and girls, but they were not. Maccoby and Jacklin suggested that these girls were perhaps the least likely to tolerate the dominance attempts of boys, and hence especially motivated to avoid them.

What do these findings imply for the underpinnings of gender segregation? For girls, at least, it makes sense to avoid boys. Why play with someone who monopolizes the toys and will not do what you ask him to do? This does not provide boys with a reason to avoid girls, however.

Knowledge of Gender

Do boys and girls begin to choose to play with children of their own sex once they know that they are boys or girls (gender identity)? For example, once a little boy knows he is a boy, is that the time he starts to find boys appealing as play partners? This kind of knowledge occurs at a very young age (around age 2 to 2.5), and by the time that the majority of children are consistently playing with same-sex peers in the late preschool period, they would clearly know that they are boys or girls. So, to answer this question, we need to look at very young children—children who are just beginning to acquire gender identity. Some research in fact finds that children less than 2 years of age who are able to accurately label gender are indeed more likely to play with same-sex peers (Fagot, 1985b; Fagot, Leinbach, & Hagan, 1986). However, since by about 2.5 years of age virtually all children do know whether they are boys or girls, this kind of knowledge is no longer much of an influence in predicting which children are especially likely to play with same-sex others, and which are not (Moller & Serbin, 1996; Serbin et al., 1994). However, that does not necessarily mean that children do not continue to use information about gender in their choice of playmates, it just means we can no longer use it to look at which children do so more frequently than others.

Knowing and Preferring Gender-Stereotyped Activities

Do Gender Stereotypes Influence Peer Choices?

What about other kinds of gender-related knowledge, or preferences for playing with gender-stereotyped toys or engaging in other gendered actions? Are children who are stereotyped in other ways (e.g., who know that toys are gender stereotyped, or who especially prefer to play with same-gender toys) also the most likely to play with same-sex peers? Put concretely, do little girls end up with other little girls because they are all playing in the toy kitchen, and do little boys play with other boys because they all enjoy playing with trucks and cars? This would seem to make some sense, and of course all of these things increase with age over the early years of childhood. Knowledge of gender stereotypes seems to develop in pretty much all children through the years of early childhood, whereas the extent to which children display preferences for playing with gendered toys or engaging in other gendered activities varies (Signorella, Bigler, & Liben, 1993). However, even though both knowledge and preferences are increasing during early childhood, the research findings offer little support for the notion of a direct relationship between stereotyped knowledge or preferences (Maccoby & Jacklin, 1987; Moller & Serbin, 1996) and choosing to play with same-sex peers. That is, the children who have more stereotyped toy or activity preferences are not necessarily the same children who spend more time with same-sex peers. It is also worth pointing out that boys appear to develop gendered toy preferences before girls do (Blakemore, LaRue, & Olejnik, 1979), but girls develop peer preferences before boys do.

Same-Sex Playmates Influence Gender Stereotypes

Although there is not much evidence that gender-stereotyped toy and behavior preferences lead children to choose to play with same-sex peers, there is some evidence that the reverse happens. In a short-term longitudinal study of 3- to 5-year-old children, Martin and Fabes (2001) found that children who spent more time in same-sex groups in the fall increased in their gender-stereotyped behavior by the spring of the same school year. In other words, playing in same-sex groups seems to contribute to learning gender-stereotyped behavior. We will return to this issue when we later consider the impact of peers on gender development.

Children also develop beliefs about peer groups themselves. Children believe that other children prefer to play in same-sex groups, and they also believe that other children approve of play with others of the same sex as compared to play with other-sex children (Martin, Fabes, Evans, & Wyman, 1999). Children also believe that other children of their sex like them better, and they expect more rejection from other-sex children (Bellmore & Cillessen, 2003). These kinds of beliefs increase with age from the preschool to early elementary period, and the more strongly children hold such beliefs, the more likely they are to play with same-sex peers (Martin et al., 1999). In other words, children appear to use their beliefs about the appropriateness of same-sex play partners to guide their choices of friends.

Cooties, Boy Germs, Romances, and Borderwork

It is not especially likely that very young children, 2- and 3-year-olds for example, are paying much attention to the phenomenon of gender segregation. However, by the late preschool period girls and boys do seem to be much more aware that boys and girls "belong" in different groups, and they begin to torment one another by entering into each other's play areas (Pitcher & Schultz, 1983). In their observations of preschoolers, Pitcher and Schultz noted that by the age of 4 or 5 boys were beginning to treat girls as though they were inferior, whereas girls resorted to insulting boys and asking for help from the teacher to allow them to have access to toys or play areas. This is of course similar to the research showing that girls have a hard time influencing boys.

Once children are in school, and especially by mid- to late elementary school, boys and girls interact with each other's groups. Thorne (1993) coined the term "borderwork " to describe the teasing and chasing that takes place between groups of boys and girls. Although boys and girls may chase each other in same-sex groups, boy-girl chasing has a special character about it. Thorne and Luria (1986) describe such rituals in some detail. The chases may have names like "boys chase the girls," "chase and kiss," or "kiss and kill." Boys may run into a group of girls and poke or tease them. Girls may threaten to chase and kiss boys, and hence contaminate them with "germs," "cooties," or "girl stain." Unpopular girls, those who are social outcasts, poor, or overweight are sometimes known as "cootie queens"—their touch would be especially contaminating to boys. Boys could also contaminate girls, but it apparently was not as common in Thorne and Luria's observations and there were no "cootie kings."

It is clear from these descriptions that there is an element of budding heterosexuality about these chase rituals. By mid-to-late elementary school, girls spend much time engaged in conversation about who "likes" whom, and who is "going together." Girls also talk about which boys they like, and which ones are "cute." They sometimes plot amongst each other to get particular pairs together. Just as they are focused on who is whose friend in their same-sex groups, they also focus on who is whose "boyfriend" or "girlfriend." Of course, these relationships are mostly imagined rather than real at this age. Boys, on the other hand, hardly ever talk about such issues among themselves.

Especially when children of both sexes are present, it is common for children to tease one another about being a boyfriend or girlfriend of someone, or of "liking" a particular child of the other sex (Thorne, 1993; Thorne & Luria, 1986), and this is usually seen as embarrassing. So, although girls may enjoy talking about boyfriends and girlfriends amongst themselves, both boys and girls are often mortified if they are teased in public about such relationships.

Here is a possible mechanism, then, for the maintenance of gender segregation during the school years. Children clearly sexualize boy-girl relationships and mercilessly tease any children who show undue interest in someone of the other sex. Such treatment is generally painful enough to keep most children far away from relationships with the other sex, at least in public.

In-Group Favoritism

One of the most well established characteristics of human social life is that people tend to prefer and value their own group (the in-group) more than another group defined as different from them in some important way (the out-group). As discussed in some detail in chapter 8, this has been studied in some depth by social psychologists known as social identity theorists (Tajfel & Turner, 1986) and is known as **in-group favoritism**. As a counterpoint to in-group favoritism, people often show **out-group hostility** and reject others who are not part of their group. Often these groups are based on such factors as religion or national origin, but sometimes all it takes to develop this dynamic is for people to be in any group and for there to be another group to oppose (think about sports fans of one team vs. another). It is certainly the case that boys and girls (and, for that matter, men and women) constitute such in- and out-groups.

The classic study (Sherif, Harvey, White, Hood, & Sherif, 1954/1961) of this phenomenon in children is known as the "Robber's Cave" experiment, because it took place at Robber's Cave State Park in Oklahoma. In the study, 22 11-year-old boys who were camping in the park under adult supervision were assigned to two roughly equivalent groups. At first the two groups did not know about each other, and were permitted to develop their own leaders, rules, and activities in the park. In the second phase of the study, they became aware of the other group and were given the opportunity to take part in competitive games against each other. There was a strong division and hostility between the two groups—a clear "us" versus "them" situation. This is, of course, exactly the nature of in-group/out-group relationships.

In another interesting study (Bigler, Jones, & Lobliner, 1997) elementary school children between the ages of 6 and 9 at a summer educational program were assigned to wear either yellow or blue t-shirts. The children were then placed in one of two kinds of classrooms: classrooms in which the teachers essentially ignored the t-shirt colors, and classrooms in which the teachers specifically organized the children into groups (e.g., children with blue shirts line up in one line, yellow in the other) or gave them the opportunity to do certain activities on the basis of their t-shirt colors. These teachers made reference to shirt color six or seven times every 20 minutes, although they did not favor one group over the other. After 4 weeks of being in the summer program the children whose teachers emphasized the group differences were found to treat their fellow group members as having many more positive characteristics than children in the other group. That is, children with the same color shirt as each other had become an "in group." When you think about these findings, consider how frequently parents, teachers, and the media emphasize the importance of gender group membership to children.

You will probably recall from chapter 8 that one of the important theories developed to understand the process of gender development is **developmental intergroup theory** (DIT). This theoretical view emphasizes the importance of intergroup processes to gender development, most especially the tendency to think in terms of one's own sex as the in-group, and the other sex as the out-group. Here we are arguing that intergroup processes are among the factors that act to increase gender segregation in peer groups.

In an interesting series of experimental studies, Underwood and Hurley and their colleagues (Underwood, Hurley, Johanson, & Mosley, 1999; Underwood, Schockner, & Hurley, 2001) trained elementary aged child "actors" to behave rather obnoxiously in a video game with peers. They found that the children playing the game with the actors were much less likely to try to get along with obnoxious child actors of the other sex. That is, they seemed to be much more motivated to tolerate obnoxiousness in children of their own sex. All of these findings, then, suggest that one of the factors that influences children to play with others of their own sex is the general human tendency to associate with and value others who are similar to them in some significant way, and to avoid and devalue those who are different.

Status and the In-Group: Do Boys Have Higher Status?

So far we have seen that, at least in early childhood, both boys and girls think that their own sex is the better one. However, sometimes children attribute certain characteristics only to one sex. Powlishta (1995) found that 8- to 10-year-old boys and girls both attributed certain traits only to males or females; the ones they attributed to males were very much linked to power (crude, loud, fights), whereas those attributed to girls were related to helplessness (shy, dependent, sorry for self). This pattern suggests that children are aware of greater male power, at least by elementary school. Despite the fact that children tend to think that being loud and fighting is not very socially desirable (Serbin, Powlishta, & Gulko, 1993), these views of boys and girls are consistent with the general idea that, although girls may be nicer, boys are more powerful and competent (Lutz & Ruble, 1994).

Although girls are the first to avoid the other sex, by the late preschool period, and certainly in elementary school, boys are much stronger enforcers of gender boundaries. Boys are much less likely to permit girls to enter their groups than girls are to permit boys to enter theirs, and boys are much more punitive to other boys who cross such gender boundaries than girls are toward tomboys (Leaper, 1994a; Thorne & Luria, 1986). Even preschool boys try to avoid seeming feminine (Kyratzis, 2001). Of course, the critical question is why boys are more likely to do this. Campbell Leaper (1994a; 2000b) has suggested that the reason that boys maintain stronger gender boundaries is that they know they have higher status than girls do—that it is worse for a boy to be like a girl than vice versa. Leaper points out that these things are exactly what members of higher status groups do in general. Members of a higher status group are more likely to maintain boundaries between the groups, and are less likely to take on characteristics of the high-status group than the reverse. As another point in support of this contention, the direct requests we discussed earlier (Serbin et al., 1984) are more characteristic of high status groups, whereas indirect or polite requests are more often associated with lower status groups. As we know already, all of these factors are associated with boys' and girls' groups, thus it is logical to conclude that, even in childhood, boys are aware that they are members of a higher status group.

Adult Influence

Here we ask if it is adults who are shaping children into playing with others of the same sex. In families, parents are likely to want their young children to play well with siblings or neighborhood children regardless of those children's sex. They are also likely to invite relatives and friends to bring their children of both sexes to play with their own children. The small amount of research examining the relationship between parents' gender role socialization efforts and their children's same-sex peer preferences finds little evidence that parents are acting directly to increase children's preferences for playing with same-sex peers. Maccoby and Jacklin (1987) examined the relationship between mothers' and fathers' gender role socialization efforts and the peer preferences of their sons and daughters. For daughters there were no relationships with either parent, and for sons there was a relationship only with fathers, but it was in the opposite direction to what might be expected. Fathers who put *more* pressure on their sons to adopt masculine gender roles had sons who were *less* likely to prefer boys as playmates at age 4 and again 2 years later. Maccoby and Jacklin suggest that perhaps the fathers might have thought that their sons were not masculine enough, and were trying to counteract those characteristics. Regardless, this study certainly does not provide evidence that parents were increasing gender segregation.

As for the influence of teachers, we have already seen that at school children are more likely to play predominantly with children of their own sex in the absence of adults, and that teachers actually act to increase interactions among children of both sexes (Thorne, 1993). Indeed, children are reported to especially dislike teachers who work hard to get them to interact with children of the other sex (Maccoby & Jacklin, 1987).

Although there is little evidence that adults are actively working to increase gender segregation, they may have more subtle influences on it. Children have many opportunities to observe parents' and other adults' own friendships. If adult behavior serves as a model for children to observe, they can clearly notice that men tend to have other men as friends, and women tend to have other women as theirs. It is also the case that teachers often bring gender to the attention of children in the classroom (e.g., "the boys should line up here and the girls over here"). As adults take part in the gendered nature of social life, they can certainly influence children's views that gender should something one attends to, so in that way, they may certainly have an influence on children's gender segregation.

Why Do Children Play in Gender-Segregated Groups? Conclusions

So what can we conclude about the reasons that boys and girls choose to play in segregated groups? It seems clear that not one single factor is at the root of this phenomenon. One factor that may be involved is play styles. The research we have examined suggests that the rough and tumble play style of boys, and their focus on dominance, is aversive to some number of girls. Many boys, on the other hand, may find this play style appealing and are attracted to others who play like this. Play styles continue to be different as children grow older, and these different play styles seem to be at least part of the reason why children play with others of their own sex.

Very young children who know whether they are boys or girls are somewhat more likely to choose to play with others of their sex. As children grow older, and their cognitive skills increase, they are likely to be influenced by the general human tendency to be attracted to others who are similar to them in some important way. Therefore, another of the reasons for why girls play with girls and boys play with boys is that gender is a socially significant characteristic, and people generally associate with others who are similar to them, and are somewhat hostile toward people who are different. Also, even in childhood, gender seems to be infused with heterosexual implications, and the sense of the two sexes as "opposites." This can be seen in the chasing and teasing, which takes place between boys and girls in the elementary school years.

We have also noted that boys maintain gender boundaries more strongly than girls do, and that young girls are less able to influence boys than vice versa. Apparently, both boys and girls come to know that boys and masculinity have higher status than girls and femininity, and for boys in particular, this is a reason to maintain gender boundaries.

POPULAR BOYS AND POPULAR GIRLS

What makes a popular child or adolescent, and is it different for boys and girls? One of our students recounted this story to us recently: Two elementary schools girls were together on the school playground. One was apparently playing in some dirt under playground equipment. The other girl, on observing her, stated: "Get out of the dirt Alison. Popular girls don't play in the dirt." Clearly she had an opinion on the subject!

Two Ways of Measuring Popularity

Sociometry

Researchers have conceptualized popularity in two rather different ways (Parkhurst & Hopmeyer, 1998; Rodkin, Farmer, Pearl, & Van Acker, 2000). One group of researchers has used **sociometry**, in which they ask children which other children they like (or would like to play with), and which ones they do not like. This procedure can be used to calculate both **social preference** (the number of times a child is named as "liked" minus the times named as "disliked") and **social impact** (visibility, or the number of times named as both liked and disliked). It is then used to create several different categories of children on the basis of the intersection of social preference and social impact (Newcomb, Bukowski, & Pattee, 1993; Rubin, Bukowski, & Parker, 1998). Popular children are high in both preference (being liked), and because they are consistently named as liked, they are also high on impact. Other categories included rejected (frequently named as disliked; low in preference, high in impact), neglected (few nominations in either liked or disliked; low in preference and impact), average (average on both impact and preference), and controversial (both liked and disliked by several children; high on impact, but average on preference). Here we will be concerned primarily with popular children.

Using the sociometric technique, popular or well-liked children are generally found to be friendly and responsive. They show leadership, they play in socially appropriate ways, have good social skills for their age, possess other valued abilities, and are often physically attractive (Rubin et al., 1998). Many of these traits are not related to gender; children like both boys and girls who are like this. Interestingly, well-liked popular children of elementary school age, especially boys, are also found to be more likely to maintain gender boundaries in their peer interactions than are other children (Sroufe, Bennett, Englund, Urban, & Shulman, 1993). Apparently, maintaining one's distance from children of the other sex is associated with being socially competent in the eyes of other children at this age.

The Sociological Measure of Popularity

There is a second way that popularity is studied in elementary aged children and especially in adolescents. The researchers study the children or adolescents who are at the top of the social hierarchy at their school, and who often engage in certain activities considered to be prestigious in that setting (e.g., sports or cheerleading). Participants may simply be asked who the popular kids are, and researchers tabulate the number of times that certain individuals are mentioned. Other researchers have done observations of children's or adolescents' peer groups to determine which children are seen by others as popular (Adler & Adler, 1995, 1998). This research method is sometimes referred to as the **sociological** approach because it is often used by sociologists.

What is most interesting about these two ways of studying popularity is that they do not always overlap. Children and adolescents who are popular in the sociometric way (socially skilled, kind, and well liked) are not always the "popular kids" in their school, and the popular kids are not always well liked. They are sometimes seen as exclusionary, conceited, dominant, aggressive, and just not very nice (Adler & Adler, 1995; Parkhurst & Hopmeyer, 1998). There is, in fact, evidence that by late elementary school popular children specifically exclude and torment others in order to consolidate their own popular status. Consider these examples:

> Me and my friends would be mean to the people outside of our clique. Like, Eleanor Dawson, she would always try to be friends with us, and we would be like, "Get away, ugly." (Adler & Adler, 1995, p. 153)

> Robert: One time he [a popular boy] went up to this kid Hunter Farr, who nobody liked, and said, "Come on Farr, you want to talk about it?" and started kicking him, and then everyone else started doing it ... [When the researcher asked "Robert" why Hunter Farr was picked on, he replied:] Cause he couldn't do anything about it, 'cause he was a nerd. (Adler & Adler, 1995, p. 154)

It is also the case that leaders in popular cliques use similar forms of domination with insiders who are lower in the group's hierarchy. High status insiders may coerce lower status insiders to play pranks or torment others who are outside the popular group. In other words, in popular cliques there is often a dynamic that includes cruelty to lower status children both inside and outside the group. The dominance and cruelty seem to help to reinforce the social standing of those at the top. This phenomenon seems to operate in both boys' and girls' groups, although physical aggression is more likely among boys, whereas social and relational aggression seems to happen in both sexes (Adler & Adler, 1995; Cillessen & Mayeux, 2004). This is probably one of the reasons that some people recall their middle and high school years with less than happy memories.

Some researchers have examined this "antisocial" aspect of the behavior of children and adolescents who are high in social status—the popular kids. Although most of the research done on this question has been with older children and adolescents, one recent study (Nelson, Robinson, & Hart, 2005) found that some preschool girls who were high in social standing, but "controversial" in sociometric status, were more relationally aggressive with their peers. So it appears that this tendency may begin at a young age, although it certainly may become more frequent as children grow older.

Research conducted on the behavior of popular girls (e.g., cheerleaders) as they move into junior high school (Adler & Adler, 1998; Eder & Kinney, 1995) has found that such girls do in fact become more exclusionary over time as they consolidate their own status in an elite peer group.

In fact, some popular children of both sexes become more relationally aggressive and cruel to those of lower social standing as they grow older and enter high school (Cillessen & Mayeux, 2004; Rose, Swenson, & Waller, 2004), but girls especially are judged harshly by other children for these exclusionary tendencies. Boys seem more able to consolidate their popularity and still be seen as likeable, despite the fact that popular boys are often aggressive and exclusionary to those lower in the social hierarchy.

Comparing the Sociometric and Sociological Approaches

Using both the sociometric and sociological methods together in the same study can lead to the identification of three types of popular children (Lease, Kennedy, & Axelrod, 2002; Parkhurst & Hopmeyer, 1998), as well as a fourth group of children who are not popular by either measure. The three popular groups are (a) high in popular status and well liked, (b) high in popular status but not well liked, and (c) well liked but not high in popular status. You can probably think back to your own high school experience and think of someone from each of these three groups. For example, one of us attended a small rural high school where there were certainly some conceited and exclusionary popular kids, but one well-liked cheerleader who went out of her way to be kind and considerate to everyone.

What is of special relevance to us is the gendered aspects of both of these kinds of popularity. We have already seen that boys who are dominant and assertive or even aggressive are more likely to be liked by their peers than are girls who have these characteristics. We have also seen that girls who engage in conflict with other girls often do so in a less direct fashion—trying to be nice as they assert their own wishes. These issues are primarily related to likeability. Even by early elementary school, well-liked girls are less likely to engage in conflict (Putallaz et al., 1995), and when disagreements arise, such girls are more likely to provide explanations to back their positions than are other children.

One study of particular relevance for our discussion of the gendered aspects of popularity examined fourth through sixth grade boys and girls using both the sociometric and perceived popularity measures (Lease et al., 2002). In addition to the measures of social prominence and likeability, the researchers also measured the children's ability to dominate other children and several other personal and behavioral characteristics (e.g., smart, athletic, snobby, cool, bully, disruptive, physically aggressive, relationally aggressive) as rated by other children. Finally, they had teachers report on the children's economic background and possessions, as well as the children's physical attractiveness.

First, for both boys and girls, being liked was strongly associated with being seen as popular, so there was clearly overlap between these two kinds of measures. Factors associated with both among both boys and girls included being prosocial, bright, well off financially, and physically attractive. Similar to the findings of other research (e.g., Adler & Adler, 1998), physical attractiveness and family wealth (partly related to the clothing and possessions it provided) were especially important for girls, whereas athletic skill was especially important for boys. However, some socially prominent children (i.e., popular kids) of both sexes were often seen as exclusionary and socially aggressive, and when popular children were not well liked by the group as a whole, it was usually related to this tendency to bully and exclude others.

In general then, the research leads to a picture of a popular and well-liked boy as being nice looking, considerate and socially skilled, and probably good at sports. A boy who is liked but not necessarily popular (in the sense of being socially prominent) may have less in the way of athletic skills or physical attractiveness, but otherwise have similar characteristics. On the other hand, a popular but not necessarily well-liked boy is likely to be athletically skilled and dominant, as well as sometimes unruly, disruptive, or bullying (Rodkin et al., 2000). He may torment and exclude others who are lower in social status than he is. Like similar boys, a popular and well-liked girl is also likely to be considerate and socially skilled. She is also likely to be physically attractive and well off financially. When a popular girl is not well liked, it is probably due to her being socially exclusionary or relationally aggressive—a snob. A girl who is well liked, but not necessarily socially prominent, may be less likely to be physically attractive or wealthy, but certainly likely to be considerate and socially skilled.

Popularity and Academic Success: Different for Boys and Girls

Researchers have observed an interesting set of findings with respect to academic performance and popularity that is different for boys and girls. Being very poor at schoolwork in elementary school is likely to be associated with social ostracism for both sexes. For boys, good academic work is generally associated with social acceptance through elementary school, but by late elementary school boys sometimes come to hide or downplay strong academic ability in the interest of maintaining social standing (Adler, Kless, & Adler, 1992). African American boys in particular have sometimes been found to devalue academic success in other boys (Graham, Taylor, & Hudley, 1998) and in general are less likely to devalue even very poor academic performance than are other boys. However, even disadvantaged African American children, both boys and girls, associate academic success with popularity more often than not (Xie, Li, Boucher, Hutchins, & Cairns, 2006). Boys who have very strong academic performance in the absence of athletic skill, physical attractiveness, or social dominance, are often labeled as "brains" or "nerds" and regularly experience social rejection.

Girls, on the other hand, do not suffer social stigma if they do well at school as long as they possess the other attributes associated with popularity. Indeed, academic success is often highly valued by both White and African American girls (Graham et al., 1998; Kennedy, 1995), although it does not seem to be related to popularity in terms of social status in a simple way. That is, some popular girls are excellent students, although others are not. Girls tend to associate with other girls who are similar in academic performance to themselves, but both poor students and good students can be popular, especially if they are economically well off and pretty (Adler et al., 1992). The fact that today some girls who are excellent students are also popular may be a change from previous times when girls feared being "too smart" for boys to like them (Eder, 1985).

Other than the finding that African American boys do not lose social standing for poor academic performance, there is not a great deal of research examining the correlates of popularity in different ethnic groups in North America, or in other countries across the world. In the United States, one study of White, African American, and Latino children (LaFontana & Cillessen, 2002) found that the characteristics of both liking and social status were similar in all three groups, except for small differences in the perception of the importance of academic ability for popularity (Latino children thought it more important than did the other groups). In other words, all three groups thought that physical appearance and social skills were important for popularity, and that athletic skills were especially important for boys.

As a final comment on popularity, there is some evidence that popularity among same-sex peers has some similarities with popularity among other-sex peers. In one 2-year longitudinal study of middle students' beginning dating relationships (Pellegrini & Long, 2003), the researchers found that boys who were dominant were more likely to begin dating, and that as they started to date, their degree of dominance actually increased. Other than dominance, another consistently reported factor associated with boys' early popularity with girls is being an athlete in a high-profile school sport like basketball or football (Adler & Adler, 1998; Eder & Kinney, 1995).

To conclude, there are two ways of measuring popularity, and they lead to somewhat different patterns of findings. Popular and well-liked children of both sexes are generally socially skilled, are leaders, and typically do reasonably well in school. Boys who are high in social status are often dominant and have good athletic skills. If such boys are not well liked, it may be because they are aggressive or cruel to others lower in the social hierarchy. Popular girls are typically physically attractive and financially well off. Those who are not well liked are often seen as conceited and exclusionary.

BOYS' AND GIRLS' FRIENDSHIPS

So far we have spent most of this chapter discussing peer relationships in the group as a whole. Many important peer relationships take place between two children who are friends—at the level of a dyad. As we already know, girls especially focus on small groups of two or three friends, but of course boys have close friendships too.

Children begin to establish friendships in the preschool years (Gottman, 1983; Howes, 1996). Even children less than 2 years old can be identified as friends. Consider the following example:

> Anna and Suzanne are not yet 2 years old. Their mothers became acquainted during their pregnancies and from their earliest weeks of life the little girls have visited each other's houses. When the girls were 6 months old they were enrolled in the same child care center. They now are frequent play partners, and sometimes insist that their naptime cots be placed side by side. Their greetings and play are often marked by shared smiles. Anna and Suzanne's parents and teachers identify them as friends. (Howes, 1996, p. 66)

Children who are friends spend time and have fun with each other, have shared interests, and provide each other with affection and social support (Howes, 1996; Newcomb & Bagwell, 1995; Zarbatany, Ghesquiere, & Mohr, 1992). These characteristics of friendship can be found from the toddler period through adolescence and adulthood, although the character of older children's friendships is naturally different from that of toddlers'. Having mutual friends is beneficial for children's development—for both their cognitive and their social development (Newcomb & Bagwell, 1995; Rubin et al., 1998). Children who are rejected by peers clearly show poorer adjustment than children who have friends. Indeed, it is much more important to adjustment to have some close friends than it is to be popular.

Although many aspects of friendships are the same for boys and girls, there are some notable differences. We already know that girls tend to have fewer friends and that they are more likely to have friends who do not know one another, whereas boys' friends are more likely to all be part of the same group. In addition to these features, one of the most consistently noted differences in the nature of boys' and girls' friendships is that girls' friendships are more intimate (Buhrmester, 1996; Gottman, 1986; Jones & Costin, 1995). Girls talk more about themselves, especially about their feelings and personally relevant events and relationships. Girls' friends are often rated as being more likely to be said to care about them, support them, and accept them. Boys' friendships, in turn, are more likely to center on games and activities, especially those with high levels of physical activity. The difference in the degree of intimacy and sharing of emotion can be found from early childhood, but it becomes especially relevant by early adolescence (Buhrmester, 1996; Zarbatany et al., 2000).

Possibly for both these reasons (greater intimacy and more isolation from peer networks) there is some evidence that girls' close friendships are more fragile and less stable than boys' are—they do not last as long (Benenson & Alavi, 2004). In one recent study (Benenson & Christakos, 2003) children in fifth, seventh, and ninth grades were asked about their three closest friends. They were asked about how long they had been friends, how frequently they interacted, how much the child would be affected if the friendship ended, and whether the friend had ever done anything to damage the friendship. The children were also asked similar questions about previous friendships that had ended.

When Benenson and Christakos averaged the children's responses across their three best friends, boys and girls responded similarly. However, when they examined responses about the children's "best friend," they found that, in all grades, girls' current closest friendships had begun more recently. Also, compared with boys, more of girls' previous best friendships had ended. Although the reported emotional responses of both sexes were actually similar when relationships had ended, girls were more likely to report that their lives had been disrupted when a close friendship ended. Finally, even though their current best friendships were shorter, girls reported that their friends had already done more things to damage the friendship. Benenson and Christakos speculated about why girls' best friendships are more unstable. Perhaps girls' friendships are more intense, therefore making inevitable conflicts more difficult to handle when they arise. Also, the fact that these friendships are more likely to exist in isolation from peer networks may contribute to their vulnerability.

Girls' intimate friendships may have some other drawbacks. Sometimes girls spend time dwelling on their problems with their friends. One term for dwelling on one's personal problems is **rumination**. Rumination is "focusing inward on feelings of distress and personal concerns rather than taking action to relieve their distress" (Nolen-Hoeksema, 2001, p. 175). You can think of it something like: "This is upsetting. In need to think about why I am upset. I need to talk to others about why I am upset. I need to dwell on it. By dwelling on it, maybe I can solve it." Although it may seem as though thinking and talking about a distressing situation may be useful, doing too much of it to the exclusion of other strategies actually seems to make the distress worse, and has been implicated in increasing the risk of depression. It turns out that girls often do this together, an activity that has been called **co-rumination** (Rose, Carlson, & Waller, 2007). Although this may bring girls closer together and enrich their friendships, it also seems to increase depression and anxiety. For boys, co-rumination has been found to increase support from their friends, but not to have the added drawback of increasing depression or anxiety (Rose et al., 2007).

Cross-Sex Friendships

Although most close friendships are between same-sex pairs, children do have friendships with children of the other sex, especially during the preschool years. Gottman (1986) reports on an observation of young children in which more than one third of 3- and 4-year-olds had a cross-sex best friend, but by the age of 8, no one did. Interestingly, even though such friendships are uncommon, especially among elementary-aged children, researchers have reported that children who have friends of the other sex have better social skills, and that such friendships are often very rewarding and stable (Gottman, 1986; Howes & Phillipsen, 1992; Zarbatany et al., 1992). Also, young adolescents who have more friends of the other sex are more likely to transition more smoothly into dating relationships, and more likely to sustain such relationships over time (Feiring, 1999).

By early adolescence there is an increasing tendency for both boys and girls to have friends of both sexes and interactions that involve both—in other words, gender segregation decreases (Connolly, Craig, Goldberg, & Pepler, 2004; Feiring, 1999). Young adolescent boys and girls often engage in group activities in which both sexes are present. Many of these interactions are not romantic in nature, but such group interactions often serve as an introduction to dating and heterosexual romantic relationships for many adolescents.

Both friends and dating relationships arise out of the peer network, but even young adolescents recognize the difference between friendship and romance, attributing both passion and commitment to the latter but not the former (Connolly, Craig, Goldberg, & Pepler, 1999). Nonetheless, one of the most important characteristics that older adolescents and adults attribute to their romantic partners is that they are friends, often best friends (Furman, 1999). So it is reasonable to assume that peer relationships in childhood and adolescence serve as a foundation for later romantic relationships.

DATING AND ROMANTIC RELATIONSHIPS

As adolescents enter puberty, the probability of romantic relationships, both heterosexual and homosexual, increases (Collins, 2003). Between the ages of 12 and 18, the percentage of young people who say that they have had a romantic relationship in the past year increases from about 25% to about 70%, with girls reporting slightly more than boys at younger ages (Carver, Joyner, & Udry, 2003). Many of these relationships, especially during early adolescence, are relatively short-lived, the average duration being about 4–8 months (Zimmer-Gembeck, 2002).

Sexual Orientation and Sexual Identity

Sexual orientation is often seen in terms of categories (e.g., heterosexual or homosexual); however, there are good reasons to think of sexual attraction in terms of a continuum from strong and consistent attraction to people of the same sex to strong and consistent attraction to people of the other sex. One widely used scheme is known as the Kinsey scale (Sell, 1997), which is a seven-point scale ranging from entirely heterosexual (K0), through entirely homosexual (K6), with the midpoint (K3) being equally heterosexual and homosexual. A person would be said to fall somewhere on the scale. For example, a man with attraction only to other men, and whose sexual behavior had been only with other men would be rated K6 on the scale. Ratings on the Kinsey scale take into account both fantasy and behavior, and do not depend on an individual's self-defined **sexual identity** as heterosexual, homosexual, bisexual, or none of these. These are important distinctions, because many individuals experience attractions to others of the same sex or they have periodic same-sex sexual experiences, but they never identify themselves as gay or lesbian. Also, some individuals adopt one identity for periods of their lives and another identity later (Diamond, 2008). Others are not willing to adopt any identity at all.

Research findings show that children typically experience their first erotic attractions and feelings around the age of 10, probably as sex hormones are being produced by the maturing adrenal glands (McClintock & Herdt, 1996), and many individuals recall their first crushes and sexual attractions around this age. However, it is during adolescence that individuals usually begin to adopt their sexual identities and establish significant romantic and sexual relationships. For sexual minority youth, this can be more challenging as most cultures identify heterosexuality as normative, and cultural institutions provide much more support for the development of heterosexual relationships. However, in recent years more people in Western cultures have developed greater acceptance for gay and lesbian relationships. Nonetheless, sexual minority youth still experience more obstacles as they establish significant romantic relationships (Diamond, 2003a). Also, although understanding and acceptance of homosexuality has increased, acceptance of bisexuality and shifting sexual identities has been slower to come (Diamond, 2008).

Heterosexual Relationships

When adolescents begin heterosexual dating, the number of same-sex friends and the time spent with them often decreases, especially if those friends do not also begin to date (Zimmer-Gembeck, 2002). Sometimes conflicts and jealousies erupt as young people spend less time with same-sex friends and more time with boyfriends or girlfriends, and the friends left behind become resentful. Girls are especially likely to place a relationship with a boyfriend above their same-sex friendships (Feiring, 1999), and they spend more time than boys do thinking about dating relationships (Richards et al., 1998). Also, girls who begin to date early have been found to be more relationally aggressive (e.g., girls who try to keep others out of their group, or who ignore or stop talking to friends), further contributing to difficulties among girls as some begin to date (Pellegrini & Long, 2003). However, girls who begin to date early seem to spend more time in same-sex peer groups than other girls do, possibly to seek social support at this time of transition.

Sex Differences in the Transition to Heterosexual Relationships

Early and more extensive involvement in heterosexual dating has sometimes been found to be associated with poorer psychological adjustment, more experience of abuse, more involvement in antisocial activity such as drug use, and not surprisingly, more sexual activity (Brendgen, Vitaro, Doyle, Markiewicz, & Bukowski, 2002; Cauffman & Steinberg, 1996; Compian, Gowen, & Hayward, 2004; Zimmer-Gembeck, Siebenbruner, & Collins, 2001), especially for girls. These patterns are also associated with academic difficulties and lower educational aspirations, again especially for girls. However, those who are already at risk for problem behaviors begin to date sooner, so the cause-effect relationship may go both ways (Pawlby, Mills, & Quinton, 1997).

There are other ways in which it seems that girls are more likely than boys to find the transition to heterosexual romantic relationships difficult. Researchers have reported that boys increase in power as they begin to date, whereas girls decrease in power, and that boys receive more support from their dating partners than girls do (Furman & Buhrmester, 1992). Girls who "go steady" extensively in early adolescence have also been found to have lower self-esteem than other girls (McDonald & McKinney, 1994). Interestingly, McDonald and McKinney reported that girls who went steady in the past in early adolescence, but were no longer going steady, had higher self-esteem, suggesting that terminating such early steady dating relationships is associated with higher self-esteem for girls. Of course, again we could not know the cause and effect of this relationship.

The characteristics of other-sex partners that boys and girls are first interested in also differ. Girls are more interested in "nice" personality characteristics in their boyfriends, and boys in girls' appearance and the probability that they will be sexual (Compian & Hayward, 2003; Feiring, 1999). Girls' early popularity with boys is associated with physical attractiveness (including being thin), clothing and material possessions, and taking part in high-status activities like cheerleading (Adler et al., 1992; Eder & Kinney, 1995; Halpern, Udry, Campbell, & Suchindran, 1999). Not surprisingly, then, adolescent girls believe that they will be more likely to date if they are more attractive and thin. Consequently adolescent girls who date are more likely to diet and to have disordered eating behaviors (Cauffman & Steinberg, 1996).

The importance of weight and appearance for girls as dating begins

One 2-year longitudinal study examined the relationship between weight, dieting, eating disorders, dating, and sexual behavior in African American and White girls (Halpern et al., 1999). In general, girls thought that both physical attractiveness and having a boyfriend were important. Several were concerned about their weight and appearance, especially when they were overweight, and this concern was much higher in White girls. About one third of the African American and half of the White girls were dieting at any given time. In African American girls, dieting and being overweight were related and were found at about the same frequency. In White girls, however, dieting was about 5 times more frequent than was being overweight; that is, they were much more likely to diet when they were not overweight. On the other hand, the African American girls in this study were more likely to be overweight. So, although they were not as "obsessed" with thinness as the White girls were, they were more likely to actually be overweight.

The girls also expressed concern that their appearance and their weight were likely to affect boys' interest in them and their probability of going on a date. As it turned out, this was a realistic concern, particularly for White girls and for Black girls whose mothers had college degrees; that is, whose social class was higher. The probability of girls in these various groups not having a date over the 2-year period of the study can be seen in Figure 11.1. It is clear that these two groups of girls are less and less likely to have a date the more they weigh. Put more strikingly, even girls of average weight are less likely to go on dates than are underweight girls. The authors estimated that a White girl of average height for this age group (about 5 ft. 3 in.), who weighed 125 pounds would be twice as likely to have no dates as a girl weighing 110 pounds, and one who weighed 140 pounds would be 3 times as likely to have no dates as one who weighed 110 pounds. They suggested that when adolescent girls, even those of normal weight, express concerns about their weight and diet to try to reduce it, they are in fact responding to a social reality.

What boys and girls want in their partners

There are also differences in boys' and girls' expectations about the nature of peer relationships. Girls' history of interactions in their peer groups tends to support close, intimate relationships, and boys' interactions are more likely to have focused on excitement and fun, but less on closeness and the expression of feelings. Hence, boys and girls have had a different history of close relationships as they begin to date (Gottman & Carrère, 1994). The skills and motivation to establish an intimate, heterosexual relationship is more likely to be associated with girls' peer histories than with boys'. There is some evidence that boys feel more awkward about communication with their partners than girls do, and also that girls are able to have more influence on their partners than boys are, so it appears that girls may have significant power in contemporary adolescent dating relationships (Giordano, Manning, & Longmore, 2006).

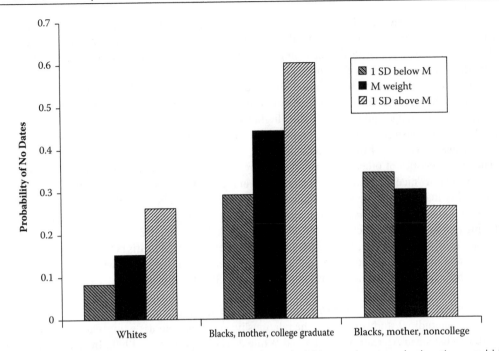

FIGURE 11.1 The probability that girls of various weights, ethnicities, and maternal education would have no dates in early adolescence. (Adapted from Halpern, C.T. et al., *Developmental Psychology, 35,* 721–736, 1999. With permission.)

Girls are more likely to be interested in love, romance, and the development of a close relationship (Feiring, 1999). If they engage in sex, it is typically in the context of such a relationship. Boys, on the other hand, are more interested in sex for its own sake and more accepting of casual sexual relationships (Carroll, Volk, & Hyde, 1985; Oliver & Hyde, 1993). Hence, boys and girls may come into conflict as boys pressure girls to increase the level of sexual involvement, and girls seek to delay it (Compian & Hayward, 2003). However, by late adolescence, boys are also interested in sustaining an intimate relationship, and they are more likely to self-disclose with their female partners and friends than with male friends (Feiring, 1999; Leaper, Carson, Baker, Holliday, & Myers, 1995). So, it is reasonable to assume that once the early stages of dating are past, heterosexual relationships have the potential to be mutually supportive for both sexes.

In fact, by late adolescence the nature of dating relationships appears to change and becomes generally more positive for both sexes. For many young adolescents, dating confers status in the peer group, but by college age that is a less significant function of dating. Also, over time, dating partners become less concerned with superficial aspects of the partner, such as appearance. Older adolescents and young adults become more concerned with the intimacy, care, commitment, and companionship that arise from romantic relationships (Zimmer-Gembeck, 2002), clearly an important part of the transition to adulthood. By later adolescence, intimate heterosexual relationships are related to lower levels of depression in girls, suggesting these more mature relationships become protective of mental health problems (Williams, Connolly, & Segal, 2001).

Gay, Lesbian, and Sexual Minority Relationships

We know much less about the normative development of gay and lesbian romantic relationships than of heterosexual relationships. In recent years, although researchers have studied the struggles of gay, lesbian, and bisexual adolescents, with concern towards supporting them psychologically and reducing the risk of depression, suicide, or victimization, less attention has been focused on the development of gay and lesbian romantic relationships themselves (Diamond, 2003a; Savin-Williams, 2003), although that is changing.

One widely held view of sexual identity formation is that gay and lesbian young people have a strong sense of homosexual orientation early on, are rarely attracted to the other sex, and with social support and acceptance can reach adulthood with a strong homosexual identity (Rust, 2003). Such a view is more consistent with the experiences of sexual minority boys than of girls, but it probably does not even apply to all boys (Diamond, 2006; Diamond & Savin-Williams, 2003). That is, the distinction between homosexual and heterosexual sexual identities is not always clear-cut, and many people do not adopt a single identity. Both attractions and identities seem to fluctuate to some degree, at least in some people. For this reason, the term **sexual minorities** has been adopted to reflect this reality. The term refers to individuals who have any sexual experiences that are not exclusively heterosexual, including attraction, fantasy, behavior, and/or a sexual identity that is not heterosexual.

Sexual minority adolescents often report experiencing attraction to both males and females, and many have relationships with other-sex partners in adolescence and young adulthood. This is especially true for girls. By adulthood, at least 80% of self-identified lesbians have had sex with men, whereas about 50–60% of self-identified gay men have had sex with women. Also, about 75% of lesbians have had a significant relationship with a man, as compared with about 45% of gay men having had a significant relationship with a woman (Baumeister, 2000).

On the other hand, young people who are members of sexual minorities are less likely than heterosexuals to have any significant relationships with partners during adolescence, partly because they find it difficult to find partners, and partly because they may fear making their sexual minority status known to others (Diamond, 2003b). They are also more likely to experience anxiety and depression in adolescence, have smaller peer networks and more fears about losing friends, and greater tendencies to drift away from friendships, as well as more worries about finding a satisfactory partner (Diamond & Lucas, 2004). However, it should be noted that there are many different patterns of romantic experience during adolescence for sexual minority youth. Some identify as gay and lesbian very early and have several sexual or romantic relationships before adulthood, some have a sense of this identity early on but do not act on it until adulthood, others adopt a sexual minority status during adolescence or young adulthood but fully identify as heterosexuals for the rest of their lives (i.e., gay until graduation), and still others adopt different identities at different points in their lives.

Milestones for Sexual Minority Youth

There are at least four important milestones for sexual minority youth: experiencing same-sex attractions, self-labeling as a member of a sexual minority, same-sex sexual experiences, and disclosure of one's minority status to significant others. As already noted, there is certainly variability in both the timing and experience of such milestones. Interestingly, from our perspective, these trajectories differ for males and females. Sexual minority boys typically experience all of these milestones at younger ages than do girls. Sexual minority boys often have a sense of being atypical for their gender, as well as having same-sex attractions at young ages (Bailey & Zucker, 1995; Diamond & Savin-Williams, 2003); such experiences are much less likely for girls.

Sexual minority boys

One recent study (Savin-Williams, 2004) interviewed 86 sexual minority men between the ages of 17 and 25 about their first sexual experiences. About half of the 86 participants reported sexual experiences with males and females, six had no sexual experience at all, two reported sexual experience with females only, and the remainder with males only. The majority (84%) of first sexual experiences were with other boys; the average age of first sex with a boy was about 14 years of age, and with a girl about 16 years of age. The majority of the first same-sex partners were close in age to the participant, and the majority (70%)

were friends with whom they regularly interacted. About 15% of the first same-sex partners were family members (typically cousins or brothers) and the remaining 15% were strangers. The young men reported that some of their partners went on to heterosexual relationships and marriage as they grew older; for some of the partners, then, these early homosexual relationships were not associated with a long-term sexual minority identity.

When sexual activity took place between friends, the partners usually remained friends, often continuing the sexual activity for some time—even years. When partners were strangers, the young men were usually older (e.g., mid- rather than early adolescence) when they had their first sexual encounters. Some of the strangers developed friendships after the sexual experience. Most of these young men thought that their motivations for the first sexual experiences were exploration, curiosity, or lust; neither love nor obligation to the partner were mentioned with any frequency as a motivation.

As they became older, these young men came to see their enjoyment in such activities as indicating that they were gay. When they began to have sexual relationships with partners who were not part of their network of friends, a sexual minority identity became more and more likely in their own minds. None of them thought that a same-sex sexual experience affected their identity (i.e., it did not "make them gay"). Rather, their orientation was there already, and the sexual experiences were a fulfillment of a homosexual identity.

Sexual minority girls

Sexual minority girls' early experiences are rarely so explicitly sexual. Rather, their focus is more likely on romance with someone they know well. It is not unusual for a girl to experience same-sex attractions only after developing a close emotional relationship with another girl. One characteristic experience of sexual minority adolescent girls is the **passionate friendship** (Diamond, 2000, 2002). These are emotionally intense friendships that include some features of romantic love such as intense feelings of passion, jealousy, and possessiveness, as well as physical contact such as holding hands or cuddling, but typically do not involve explicit sexual interactions. Such friendships are particularly characteristic of early adolescence. Young women who have been interviewed about such friendships are usually adamant that these friendships are not sexual. They typically see them as in between ordinary friendships and romantic relationships and different from each. For many sexual minority girls, the passionate friendship never becomes sexual. However, some of these friendships do become sexual over time, and experiencing such a friendship may begin the process of identifying as a lesbian for some young women. In general, lesbian relationships develop out of close friendships because the emotional component is critical to girls. It is important to note, however, that passionate friendships may not be unique to sexual minority girls. The existence of such friendships among boys or exclusively heterosexual girls has not been studied, so it is not clear whether they are a unique or more common experience of sexual minority girls.

As already noted, sexual and romantic relationships with men are characteristic of the majority of sexual minority women (Rust, 1993, 2000). An 10-year longitudinal study of young sexual minority girls and young women who were between the ages of 16 and 23 at the beginning of the study (Diamond, 2006, 2008), found that by the end of the study 100% of the women indicated that they had attractions to men at least some of the time (70% indicated such attractions at the beginning of the study). Many of these young women redefined their sexual identities over the period of study (e.g., from lesbian to bisexual, or from bisexual to heterosexual, etc.). Of those whose daily attractions were mostly to women, approximately one sixth changed their identities over the time of the study, whereas of those whose attractions were evenly split between men and women, about 75% changed their identities, so it was clear that attraction was related to identity. However, it was also the case that this questioning of identity was not a fixed process—the young women revisited the issue time and again. Some were unwilling to accept any label at all. The findings of this study are consistent with others in finding that, in women, sexual orientation and identity are often in flux, sometimes for years. This seems to be much less the case for boys and men (Diamond & Savin-Williams, 2003; Savin-Williams, 1998), although we do not have longitudinal studies examining such identity transformations in boys and young men. Interestingly, more than half of self-identified lesbians (and many heterosexual women) report that their sexual orientation is a choice, and far fewer men do (Baumeister, 2000; Rosenbluth, 1997).

Romantic and Sexual Relationships: Conclusions

In early adolescence peer relationships serve as the foundation for developing romantic and sexual relationships. It should be clear that gender has a significant impact on how these early relationships proceed, and that gender plays a larger role in how these relationships are experienced than does sexual orientation or sexual identity. Boys, whether they identify exclusively as heterosexual or are members of sexual minorities, are much more likely to begin such relationships with an explicit focus on sexuality. Girls are more likely to be focused on friendship and romance, which lead eventually to sexual behavior. Of course, in time both sexuality and a close relationship with a partner become important to both.

GENDER AND YOUTH GANGS

One significant type of peer relationship for young people takes place in youth gangs. Researchers who study youth gangs generally define a gang as a group of young people, usually ranging in age from about 14 to 25, having the following characteristics: a formal structure, a leader or leaders, a specific territory or turf, interaction among group members, and involvement in criminal or delinquent behavior (Flannery, Huff, & Manos, 1998; Klein, 1995). Many groups of young people have some of these characteristics, but it is engaging in criminal activity, often both violent and drug-related, that particularly defines a gang, even by gang members themselves (Bjerregaard, 2002).

Although gang members are usually teenagers, younger children often become associated with gangs, especially between the ages of 11 and 13, but sometimes as young as 8 (Klein, 1995). These children are sometimes called "wannabes," that is, kids who hang around wanting to be associated with the gang. Some gangs even recruit younger children to continue the gang into the future.

For our purposes, the critical aspect of youth gangs is their relationship to gender. For many years, most people assumed that gang members were primarily male. Reports often indicated that well over 90% of gang members were male, and it was common in the past to think that girl gang members were secondary to the real activity of the gang—that girls in gangs were mainly girlfriends or sisters of the male gang members. Perhaps girls have increased in gang membership in recent years, or perhaps girls in gangs were ignored by earlier researchers; either way it is clear that girls now make up somewhere between 20 and 45% of gang members. In most cases gangs have members of both sexes, although a small number of gangs have only boys in them, and an even smaller number have only girls. Among various ethnic groups, the only instances of all-female gangs appear to be among African Americans (Laidler & Hunt, 2001), although most African American girls who are in gangs are in mixed-gender gangs. By the time that adolescents are 18 or 19 years of age, there appear to be fewer girls than there are at younger ages, probably a maximum of 20% (Esbensen, Deschenes, & Winfree, 1999; Maxson & Whitlock, 2002; Miller, 2002). Therefore, one clear conclusion is that girls who join gangs typically leave them at younger ages than boys do.

Most young people who belong to gangs are poor, and many are from the inner city, although increasingly there are gangs in smaller communities (Klein, 1995). Gang members are usually from the same ethnic background; there are African American, Asian, Hispanic, and White gangs (Maxson & Klein, 1995). Young people who join gangs often live in crime-ridden, dangerous neighborhoods—environments characterized by drug use, abuse, and unstable families. Young people growing up in these settings often have little hope for the future, and little reason to assume that involvement in education is worthwhile. In these difficult environments, gang members often provide support to one another, sometimes more support than troubled parents are able to provide, and this cohesiveness makes it very difficult for the criminal justice system to eliminate gang activity (Klein, 1995).

Although boys and girls join gangs for similar reasons (e.g., for fun, for protection, because they knew someone already in a gang), boys appear to be somewhat more interested in joining a gang to get money, for excitement, and for protection, but girls are more likely to say that a sense of belonging and affection are particularly important reasons to be in a gang. Also, engaging in sexual activity at a younger age is somewhat more predictive of girls who join gangs than it is of boys. As compared with boys in gangs, girls who join gangs seem to be somewhat more likely to have especially troubled family lives, and to have siblings or other family members who are already in gangs. Despite these differences, the general conclusion is that boys and girls in gangs are more similar than they are different (Esbensen et al., 1999; Maxson & Whitlock, 2002; Miller, 2002).

It is clear that gangs include both boys and girls among their members, and that boys and girls join gangs for similar reasons, but are there differences in the activities of male and female gang members? Overall, as was the case with reasons for joining, many of the activities engaged in by male and female gang members are similar. However, several studies indicate that girls in gangs are less likely to engage in criminal activity than are boys in gangs, and less likely to be victimized by other gang members (Esbensen et al., 1999; Maxson & Whitlock, 2002; Miller, 2002). Even though they are less involved in crime than boys in gangs, girls in gangs are more delinquent than young people of both sexes from similar environments who do not belong to gangs. One systematic study of about 6,000 boys and girls from public schools in 11 cites across the United Stated reported the following:

> The gang boys are more delinquent than the girls, but the girls are far from innocent bystanders. Fewer gang girls admit to committing [various violent and criminal offenses] than do the gang boys, yet 39% of the girls report attacking someone with a weapon, 21% indicate that they have shot at someone because they were told to by someone else, 78% have been involved in gang fights, and 65% have carried hidden weapons. And it is not that they have engaged in these behaviors only once. The gang girls attacked someone an average of 2.48 times in the previous 12 months, participated in more than seven gang fights each, and hit someone with the intention of hurting him or her an average of more than eight times. On the whole, the girls report committing about half as many crimes as do the boys. (Esbensen et al., 1999, p. 41–42)

Some research has investigated how gang members see gender roles. Tough or violent behavior, even criminal activity, as well as involvement in sexuality at a young age are certainly more characteristic of masculine gender roles than of feminine. Is the same true within gangs? With respect to sexuality, the traditional double standard seems to be in evidence among gang members as well as elsewhere. Consider the response of this male gang member in New Zealand when asked why female gang members were called "hos," "bitches," or "rootbags."

> F--- what else are they? What else are they man—they're f------ bitches, f----- sakes. Can't exactly call them ladies....Cause if they were ladies they wouldn't be hanging out with hoods like us. (Eggleston, 1997, p. 107)

Female gang members also have rules about what behavior is feminine. One study of African American, Hispanic, and Asian gang members found that the girls agreed with the sentiments expressed above, believing that sexual promiscuity was not acceptable for girls, including for girls in gangs (Laidler & Hunt, 2001). The researchers reported that girls are also likely to say that they avoid or minimize alcohol and drug use because it increases the risk of engaging in sexuality or being victimized, and they look down on girls who become addicted to drugs and who engage in promiscuity. Girls in gangs certainly do use alcohol and drugs, but they may do so only in the presence of other girls, or if they do use them when boys are present they watch out for one another to reduce the risk.

So, what conclusions can we reach about boys and girls who join such gangs? These young people often come from poor and dangerous neighborhoods and troubled families. They join gangs because they know other gang members, for a sense of connection to others—to belong, for fun and excitement, to provide money, and to give themselves a sense of safety. While in the gangs, young people engage in significant criminal activity, including the use of violence. But, compared with boys, girls seem to especially depend on the gang to provide social support that they cannot find in their families, are less likely than gang boys to engage in criminality, and are considerably more likely to leave gang activity by mid-adolescence. There is clearly a double standard about both sexuality and excessive drug or alcohol use among gang members. Otherwise, boys and girls in gangs are generally quite similar.

THE IMPACT OF PEERS ON GENDER DEVELOPMENT

Up to this point in this chapter we have discussed the characteristics of boys' and girls' peer groups, and the gendered nature of popularity and of friendships. Although there may have been implicit in this discussion a notion that these experiences affect boys' and girls' gender development, in this section of the chapter we will deal explicitly with the research on the impact of peers on gender development. We will consider two issues in general—the tendency of peers to reinforce gendered behavior in other children, and the impact of the different interactional styles (the two cultures) on boys' and girls' behavior.

Responses to Gendered Behavior by Other Children

Children Imitate, Reinforce, and Punish Other Children's Gender-Related Behavior

Even very young children respond to the gendered nature of other children's behavior. In a series of studies, Beverly Fagot and her colleagues demonstrated that children as young as 18–20 months of age respond differently to children who are behaving in gender-appropriate ways in at least three different ways. First, both boys and girls receive more positive responses from other children when they are playing with same-sex peers than with other-sex peers (Fagot, 1985a; Fagot & Patterson, 1969). Second, play with gendered activities (e.g., playing with boys' or girls' toys or games) is responded to differently. Boys receive the clear message from other boys that they should avoid cross-gender activities, but girls' cross-gender behavior is more likely to be tolerated by other preschoolers (Fagot, 1985a). Third, play styles are also noticed and responded to by other children. Boys who play in an active or rough and tumble play style are responded to more positively by other boys; however, girls who play in this active way are not usually responded to negatively by other children, although they may be ignored (Fagot, 1984).

So we can see that having same-sex friends is expected of both sexes, but cross-gender behavior in boys receives more negative reactions from other children, especially from other boys. In one study, Fagot (1977) showed that 3- and 4-year-old boys who engaged in cross-gender play were so often rejected that they played alone at least 3 times as much as other children did, and boys who showed consistently feminine behavior and interests received extremely negative peer feedback. The same was not so of girls whose interests were masculine.

Not only do children respond to the gendered behavior of others, there is also evidence that children's behavior is affected by the actions of their peers. One clear example is toy play. When a boy plays with a particular toy, other boys are attracted to it, and similarly girls are attracted to toys that other girls are seen to be playing with (Shell & Eisenberg, 1990). The reverse also happens. Simply the presence of other children reduces the amount of time that preschoolers spend playing with toys associated with the other gender (Serbin, Connor, Burchardt, & Citron, 1979).

Boys are especially affected by their peers' responses. In one 2-year longitudinal study of preschoolers who were 18- to 24-months old at the beginning of the study (Fagot, 1981), boys' behavior and interests became more masculine and less feminine in response to their peers' responses to them. When girls demonstrated masculine behavior, their peers ignored them, and consequently tomboys remained relatively stable in this kind of behavior over the 2-year period. Although peers were not punitive toward high levels of physical activity in girls, teachers were, and that particular kind of masculine behavior did become less common over time in girls.

In two longitudinal studies (Fagot & Hagan, 1985; Fagot, Hagan, Leinbach, & Kronsberg, 1985), Fagot and her colleagues examined 1- to 3-year-old children's responses to the assertive and aggressive acts of others such as grabbing toys, hitting, or yelling at other children. Girls' aggressive and assertive behaviors were more likely to be ignored by others than such behaviors by boys were. Boys especially were likely to ignore girls' actions. Fagot and Hagan (1985) concluded that, over time, a response pattern like this would be more likely to convince boys that they can have an impact on others and convince girls that their assertive acts do not produce much in the way of results, especially with boys.

Fagot's research, which is among the most sophisticated and systematic that we have on this topic, dealt largely with preschoolers. There is some research with elementary-aged children, demonstrating that children who cross gender barriers are not well liked, and that they show less social competence in other ways as well (Sroufe et al., 1993). Also, it is quite clear from the research that we discussed earlier in this chapter that children of all ages have a strong expectation that children will play in gender-segregated groups, and that friendships will primarily be with others of the same sex.

With respect to toy choices, there is evidence that older boys are a little less rigid in these choices than are preschoolers. Elementary-aged boys are less affected by the presence of peers in deciding what toys they like, and less rigid in following gender stereotypes in general than are younger boys (Banerjee & Lintern, 2000). However, there are many studies demonstrating that elementary-aged children judge gender-atypical behavior, toy, and activity choices in their peers as undesirable (Blakemore, 2003; Levy, Taylor, & Gelman, 1995; Martin, 1989; Moller, Hymel, & Rubin, 1992; Zucker, Wilson-Smith, Kurita, & Stern, 1995), and that they are particularly likely to think that boys ought to conform to gender norms.

Children and Adolescents Feel Pressure to Adopt Gender Norms

As we noted previously in chapters 8 and 9, some researchers have examined children's and adolescents' own "felt pressure" from peers to conform to gender norms. When older children and adolescents believe that they are not very typical for their gender, and at the same time they feel pressure from peers to be so, adjustment difficulties such as depression or low self-esteem are more frequent (Yunger, Carver, & Perry, 2004). This seems to be a particular problem for gay and lesbian adolescents, because heterosexuality is certainly a key component of gender norms that becomes very salient in adolescence (Carver, Egan, & Perry, 2004). However, when adolescents who do not think they are very typical for their gender are accepted by peers, adjustment difficulties do not result to the same degree (Smith & Leaper, 2006). This illustrates the very important role that peers play in affecting the relationship between gender-typical behavior and adjustment.

Imitation, Reinforcement, and Punishment: Conclusions

Children clearly choose to play with toys and with other activities that are used by same-sex children. There is also evidence that peers respond to the gendered behavior of other children, and that they are especially negative towards boys who engage in feminine activities. Over time, children's interests in toys and other gendered activities change in response to the impact of peers toward them. Peers are unmistakable reinforcers and punishers of gender norms. In the case of older children and adolescents, this kind of peer pressure is associated with adjustment difficulties in young people who feel atypical for their gender.

The Influence of Peer-Group Play on Behaviors and Skills

Influence on Stereotyped Behavior

Some recent research conducted by Carol Martin, Richard Fabes, and their colleagues has examined the effect of spending time interacting with same-sex peers during the preschool years on several aspects of children's gendered behavior. In one study (Fabes, Martin, & Hanish, 2003), children's play styles were examined as a function of the composition of the peer group. As expected, boys played in larger groups and in a more active and forceful way. Children's behavior tended to change when they played in mixed-sex groups. For example, a girl who joined a group of boys was more likely to play in an active style than when she played with other girls, and likewise, a boy who joined a group of girls was less likely to play in an active and forceful way than when he played with other boys. However, this finding only applied to playing in groups of children of the other sex. Simply playing with one child of the other sex in a dyad had less influence on the styles of interaction children used. Both boys and girls were also less likely to play with gender-stereotyped toys or activities when playing in mixed-sex groups than when playing exclusively with children of their own sex. This pattern of results suggests that same-sex peer groups reduce the opportunity for both boys and girls to experience the play style associated with the other sex, and that playing with children of both sexes enhances the opportunity for children to develop a well-rounded set of social skills and abilities.

Time spent in the peer group matters

Additional research by Martin and Fabes has shown that children's social behaviors and academic skills are influenced by the extent of time they engage in same-sex versus other-sex play. In one longitudinal study lasting over the course of a school year (Martin & Fabes, 2001), children who spent more time in the exclusive company of same-sex peers were more likely to play in gender-stereotyped ways at the end of the year. For example, the more time that a boy spent playing only with boys, the more likely he was to play in a rough and active style, and the more he showed other gender-stereotyped behavior by the end of the school year (but not necessarily at the start of the year). Other research (Fabes, Martin, Hanish, Anders, & Madden-Derdich, 2003; Fabes, Shepard, Guthrie, & Martin, 1997) has found that gender interacts with the children's temperament in determining the impact of same-sex peer groups. Boys with arousable temperaments, or with poor ability to regulate emotion, seem to increase in problem behaviors and decrease in academic performance when they play more often with other boys. In contrast, girls with such difficult temperaments benefit from play with other girls. Clearly the specific styles of play in boys' and girls' groups had either positive (girls) or negative (boys) effects on children with poor abilities to regulate emotion. Across all of their studies on this issue, Martin and Fabes and their colleagues have interpreted their findings as **dosage-dependent** effects. That is, the more time children spent in the company of same-sex peers, the greater the effect on their gender-stereotyped play styles and interests or on their social and academic behavior.

Other research with older children also supports the general conclusion that the more time children spend with same-sex peers and in stereotyped activities, the more gender-stereotyped their attitudes, behaviors, and personality characteristics become (McHale, Kim, Whiteman, & Crouter, 2004). In this study, Susan McHale and her colleagues followed 10-year-olds for 2 years. They measured time spent with same- and other-sex peers, with parents, and with siblings, as well as the children's interests, activities, self-esteem, academic performance, and gender-related attitudes. They found that by age 12, children who had spent more time with same-sex peers and in gender-stereotyped activities were more traditional on a variety of measures of gender development. The findings were complex, and not all were consistent with this general conclusion; however, the general pattern was nonetheless clear. As an example, girls who took part in sports and who spent time with their fathers and with male peers when they were older were more likely to be interested in math in school and less likely to be interested in the language arts. Because this was a longitudinal study the researchers were able to examine the impact of the children's earlier interests and activities on their later characteristics.

Impact on Mental Health and Social Adjustment

In an intriguing theoretical model concerning the impact of boys' and girls' peer relationships on adjustment, Amanda Rose and Karen Rudolph (2006) have suggested that one of the most important aspects of peer relationships is that the different styles of boys' and girls' peer groups and peer interactions puts each sex at risk for certain mental health outcomes and is at the same time protective in other arenas. As we know already, girls are more likely to have emotionally supportive and close friendships, but those friendships are often more vulnerable to breaking up. We also know that girls are more likely to be exposed to psychological stress in their relationships, and to co-ruminate (discuss interpersonal difficulties and problems with each other) extensively when one or the other or both face personal problems. Girls are also more focused on empathic concern for their friends, and the impact of their behavior on others. Rose and Rudolph suggest their peer experiences put them at risk for developing internalizing disorders such as anxiety and depression, but at the same time make it less likely that they will engage in antisocial behavior.

In Rose and Rudolph's model, boys' risk factors are a mirror image of girls'. Boys are more likely to engage in rough and tumble, and physically exciting, fun play, which can serve as a distraction from interpersonal difficulties. Their peer relationships are more stable, they are exposed to fewer peer stressors, and experience less frequent discussion of interpersonal difficulties with peers. However, they experience more physical aggression and direct victimization by peers and are also more tuned in to maintaining status in a dominance hierarchy. Rudolph and Rose suggest that this kind of peer style can lead to a greater probability of engaging in troublesome and antisocial behavior, and at the same time can be protective against internalizing disorders.

Adult Romantic and Marital Relationships

One of the most significant issues that has been examined with respect to peer influences on gender development concerns the "different cultures" notion we discussed earlier in this chapter. Boys and girls are thought to engage in different styles of interactions in their peer groups, leading to somewhat different expectations about the nature of interactions with others, and to different social skills, strengths, and weaknesses. An important question concerning childhood peer interactions is related to the extent to which boys and girls have develop a limited range of relational skills in their childhood peer groups and if those relational skills have an influence on their adult relationships.

In consideration of the impact of childhood gender segregation on adults, Eleanor Maccoby (Maccoby, 1998) has outlined three outcomes. First, gender segregation continues, and people still expect to have a great deal of their social interaction with individuals of the same sex. Second, interaction styles continue to be different. Third, men have grown up being more concerned with issues of power and dominance and ignoring the influence attempts of girl peers, whereas women have grown up with more egalitarian peer relationships and have been as likely to have been influenced by one sex as the other. Maccoby believes that these three themes impact heterosexual relationships, the world of work, and parenting.

The impact of gender segregation on adult relationships

Gender segregation itself continues into adulthood; same-sex friendships are the norm throughout life. In their friendships, there is substantial similarity in the gendered styles that children use and those of adults. Like girls, women's interactional styles have been said to be more egalitarian, expressive, and polite, whereas the interactional styles of men (like those of boys) are said to be more competitive, direct, and hierarchical (Aries, 1998). Women are more likely to have close female friends with whom they share confidences and to take efforts to mitigate conflicts that may arise. Men, on the other hand, are more likely to share activities with their male friends (e.g., sports, poker), but less likely to spend time discussing personal feelings or relationships (Wright, 1998).

Although same-sex friendships are the norm, in the United States (and presumably other similar Western societies) young adults are becoming rather likely to have close friends of both sexes. Interestingly, both men and women report that their friendships with women are emotionally closer (Reeder, 2003). Additionally, some research has found that women are more emotionally responsive in interactions with both their male and female friends (Leaper et al., 1995). These findings suggest that it may indeed be the case that women reach adulthood better able to develop or sustain intimate relationships.

The impact on marital relationships, intimacy, and conflict

One domain of particular importance in adulthood is heterosexual romantic relationships and marriage. John Gottman, a researcher who has studied marital conflict for many years, has argued persuasively that, indeed, childhood peer relationships make the development of satisfactory marital relationships difficult. With colleague Sybil Carrère, Gottman suggests that boys' interactions in their peer groups facilitate high-energy, adventurous play, but play that avoids expression of emotion (Gottman & Carrère, 1994). They argue that boys learn that expression of emotion is disruptive to productive play, and they learn to handle their own negative emotions through pursuing the goal of exciting, competitive play. Girls' play, on the other hand, teaches them to confront their own fears and distress by expressing them directly, and by offering support and affection to their friends.

Therefore, when boys and girls reach adolescence and adulthood, they might be expected to approach heterosexual relationships differently. Gottman and Carrère argue that, as a result of their experiences in all-girl peer groups, girls have become experts in interpersonal relationships, and hence they are more likely to confront relationship difficulties rather than to avoid them. Girls, however, have also reached adulthood with less experience with dominance and power, especially in relationships with males. Boys, on the other hand, reach adulthood with more experience in dominance and in getting their own way, but much less experience in handling interpersonal conflict and difficult emotions. Males have also had considerable experience ignoring the influence attempts of female peers.

There is much research showing that women are more likely to be demanding, emotional, and confronting in marital relationships than men are (Gottman & Notarius, 2002). In fact, there is a type of marital conflict known as the "demand-withdraw" pattern, in which one partner demands that the other address issues of concern, whereas the other withdraws or "stonewalls" with silence in response to the demander (Eldridge & Christenson, 2002). It is probably not surprising that women are more likely to be the demanders and men the withdrawers. Gottman and others (e.g., Jacobson, 1989; Stanley, Markman, St. Peters, & Leber, 1995) have argued that these patterns are linked to childhood peer group socialization, as well as to differences in power between men and women. Gottman and Carrère conclude "one could not ask for a greater preparation for disaster in marriage than this sex segregation and differential socialization of the sexes" (Gottman & Carrère, 1994, p. 214).

The Impact of Childhood Gender Segregation on Workplace Relationships

Workplace segregation

Maccoby (1998) suggests that relationships between the sexes in the workplace are also likely to be affected by experiences in childhood peer groups. Gender segregation continues to be very common in the workplace (Boraas & Rodgers III, 2003), including in much of the industrialized world. Many jobs are exclusively or predominantly female (e.g., secretaries, childcare workers), whereas others are predominantly male (e.g., miners, plumbers). There is even evidence that women are more likely to learn about job openings from other women, and men to learn about them from other men (Hanson & Pratt, 1995).

In recent years, workplace segregation has decreased in some occupations, although generally only in previously male-dominated occupations requiring advanced education. There is much less change in traditionally female jobs (e.g., elementary teachers, nurses), and for either male or female jobs that require less education. The "blue collar" and "pink collar" jobs are still overwhelmingly done by individuals of only one sex. It is also the case that when women begin to enter a previously male-dominated occupation, they often work in lower paying specialties, or as part-time or temporary workers (Reskin, 1993). Therefore segregation continues even if it is less obvious.

Workplace interactions

A great deal of conversation in the workplace is social, and people certainly have gendered conversations at work. Female coworkers may be more likely to talk informally about fashion, shopping, or children, whereas men may be more likely to talk about sports or cars. There are also differences in styles of interaction with men being more hierarchical and direct, as well as being more likely to joke and tease, and women being more likely to be indirect. Sometimes these style differences can lead to miscommunication between men and women who work together (Tannen, 1994b).

One key aspect of the world of work is that "men's" jobs topically have higher status or prestige than "women's" jobs. It is partly the fact that they are associated with men that give these jobs higher status, and of course the pay in men's jobs is also higher than in jobs traditionally associated with women (Boraas & Rodgers III, 2003). In fact, as we have discussed already, children even think that pretend jobs said to be done by men have higher status than the same jobs said to be done by women (Liben, Bigler, & Krogh, 2001). Given that men have had and continue to have higher status occupations, interactions between men and women continue to be affected by these differences in status (Barnett & Hyde, 2001).

When women enter previously male-dominated occupations

Of particular interest is the interaction between men and women when women enter traditionally male-dominated occupations. There are several studies showing that women who are the first to enter a predominantly male field have difficulties adapting to the style of interactions of their coworkers, and are often treated dismissively. This has been especially true of women who enter blue-collar occupations (Yoder & Berendsen, 2001). The same is not reported of men who enter predominantly female jobs, who are actually welcomed by their female colleagues (Ott, 1989). It is interesting how this mirrors the patterns in childhood peer groups in which boys are very unwilling to permit girls to enter their groups, whereas girls are much more accepting of boys who wish to play with them. Recall also that this is a pattern associated with higher status people's treatment of those with lower status—a kind of gatekeeping to keep them out.

Men and Women as Parents

Mothers are the more involved parents

Peer group interactions in childhood are also likely to have an impact on adults' roles as parents (Maccoby, 1998). As we have stressed earlier in this book, one of the most well-established gender-differentiated behaviors is that girls and women do more childcare. Mothers have much more responsibility, both in caretaking and in simply monitoring and interacting with their children than do fathers (McHale, Crouter, & Whiteman, 2003). Even when men take on childcare responsibilities, it is rarely at the same level as that of women, and play as opposed to caretaking is often their way of interacting (McHale et al., 2003).

In addition to spending more time with their children, interacting with them more, and monitoring more of their activities and needs, mothers talk to their children differently than do fathers (Leaper, Anderson, & Sanders, 1998). Fathers are more directive and ask more questions of children. Mothers are generally more supportive (although also more negative), and children talk about a greater range of topics with their mothers. There is more give-and-take in the conversations of mothers and children, whereas fathers are more controlling (Maccoby, 1998).

Children's relationships with mothers and fathers are different

One of the implications of these styles is that children may develop different kinds of relationships with their parents. Perhaps because of their less directive style and the more mutual relationships that they have had with their mothers, children and adolescents have more disagreements with their mothers and are somewhat more respectful or deferential to fathers (McHale et al., 2003). Although there are exceptions to these general patterns, there is much support for the notion that children of both sexes, although especially daughters, develop closer relationships with their mothers (Claes, 1998; Collins & Russell, 1991; Freeman & Brown, 2001; Lieberman, Doyle, & Markiewicz, 1999). As children reach adolescence and young adulthood, it is primarily mothers to whom they turn to help solve their personal concerns.

It is easy to see a link between the interpersonal styles favored by girls and their roles as nurturing parents in adulthood. Women have developed an egalitarian and mutually responsive style that they continue to use with their children, especially with their daughters. Men, on the other hand, continue to use the more dominant styles of their peer groups, as well as a focus on physical play. It is also easy to see a link between the wild fun that young boys have in their groups and the way that fathers engage in high-spirited physical play with young children.

CHAPTER SUMMARY

In this chapter we have examined children's peer relationships. Beginning around the age of 2, children generally prefer to play with others of the same sex. During the elementary school years this tendency is very strong. In these same-sex groups, there are unique styles of interaction—styles that are sometimes referred to as different cultures. Boys engage in active, high-spirited, physical play, and tend to have very well-established dominance hierarchies. Boys are more likely to break social rules when they play in groups. Girls are more likely to play in dyads, to be egalitarian, and to focus their play on domestic themes. They are more likely to play near adults (especially when boys are around), and to follow adults' rules. Both boys and girls play in less stereotyped ways when they play with children of both sexes and there is evidence that having friends of both sexes is associated with developing better social skills.

There are many reasons for the phenomenon of gender segregation. There is evidence to indicate that, as soon as they know that they are boys or girls, young children are somewhat more likely to play with same-sex children. Choosing same-sex peers seems to develop sooner in girls, who appear to find the physically active play style of boys aversive and hence avoid it. Boys, on the other hand, find this style of play exciting and appealing and are attracted to others who play in this way. Preschool girls have a hard time influencing boys and therefore have good reason not to play with boys when boys are unwilling to listen to them. Playing in same-sex groups can also be seen as part of the general tendency to associate with others who are similar. Once they reach the late preschool period, and especially in the elementary years, boys are stronger enforcers of gender segregation than girls are. They become especially resistant to allowing girls access to their activities. This is probably due to them becoming aware that they are members of a higher status group.

One important dynamic in children's peer groups is borderwork. Boys and girls tease and chase each other at the edges of their peer groups. In these chase rituals they sometimes act as though children of the other sex can contaminate them. Although elementary aged girls spend much time discussing boyfriends and girlfriends amongst themselves, such relationships are more imagined than real. Both boys and girls are generally embarrassed by public attention to relationships with the other sex.

Popularity and social status differ for boys and girls to some degree. Children of both sexes who are socially skilled, considerate, reasonably good at school, and attractive are likely to be well liked by their peers. Athletic skill is an especially important attribute for boys' popularity, whereas physical appearance and economic advantage are especially important for girls. Both boys and girls who are high in social status may behave in an exclusionary, aggressive, or hostile way to children lower in the social hierarchy, although the particular forms of their cruelty may differ.

Friendships are important to both boys and girls, but girls have smaller social networks, and more fragile friendships. Boys' friends are more likely to center on activities, whereas girls' are more likely to be concerned with interpersonal intimacy and mutual support. When adolescence arrives, young people retain their same-sex friendships, but many young people today also have friends of the other sex. Dating relationships also enter the picture in adolescence, and sometimes friendships suffer as more time is given to dating partners. Boys seem to gain in power and interpersonal support in heterosexual relationships than girls do.

One special kind of peer relationship takes place in youth gangs. Gangs typically exist in poor and disadvantaged urban neighborhoods and attract members of both sexes for similar reasons, including social support, fun, excitement, protection, and money. Boys who join gangs may be especially interested in economic advantage, whereas girls seem to be particularly seeking social support. Gang girls engage in less criminal activity and leave gangs at a younger age than boys do.

Same-sex peer relationships have an impact on children's development. Children have been shown to reinforce gendered activities and interests in their peers and to reject children whose play and interests are not consistent with gender stereotypes. Social skills are also learned in gender-segregated peer groups. The more frequently that children play only or predominantly with others of their sex, the more stereotyped their play styles and interests become. The styles of interaction learned in childhood peer groups have implications for adult relationships, the world of work, and for parenthood. A reasonable conclusion is that children's skills, interests, and abilities can be enhanced if they have friends and play partners of both sexes.

The Media as an Agent of Gender Development

12

They all went off to discover the Pole,
Owl and Piglet and Rabbit and all;
It's a thing you discover, as I've been tole
by Owl and Piglet and Rabbit and all.
Eeyore, Christopher Robin and Pooh
And Rabbit's relations all went too-------
And where the Pole was none of them knew...
Sing Hey! for Owl and Rabbit and all. (Milne, 1974, p. 118)

The quote at the beginning of this chapter is from A. A. Milne's classic children's book, *Winnie-the-Pooh*. Many of us may remember having the book read to us as children, or reading it to our own children. The delightful stories of these characters are favorites of thousands if not millions of readers of children's books worldwide. But how many of us realized as we enjoyed these stories that all of the major characters, save Kanga, are male?

In this chapter we will examine the nature of children's literature, television, video games, and toys. Once we have described the content of each of these domains, we will discuss research on the impact of these socialization experiences on children, when such research is available. That is, once we know what books, television, video games, and toys are like, we will look at some research that examines how such characteristics and qualities of children's media and toys influence their development.

CHILDREN'S BOOKS

Reading to children is, of course, a desirable activity in which parents can stimulate children's vocabulary, develop their reading skills, and share enjoyable quiet time together (Weinberger, 1996). From a gender development perspective, however, we would want to know how the content of young children's books contributes to the socialization of gender roles. From books, children can learn what boys and girls and men and women are like, and what they do. They can use such information to make judgments about other people, and to help them form ideas about their own place in the world. For example, one of our children had a book, passed down from a relative, in which a mother needed to be rescued from a mouse by her young son. What sort of a message might young children receive if such stories were read to them on a regular basis? Would such a message make a difference in a boy's view of himself or in his attitudes about girls and women, or even about his mother?

Picture and Story Books for Young Children

More Male Characters and Gender Stereotypes

Two issues have been studied about young children's books: the percentage of characters that are male or female, and the stereotyped portrayals of males and females (both children and adults) in these books. Several studies in the 1970s (e.g., Hillman, 1974; Pyle, 1976; St. Peter, 1979; Weitzman, Eifler, Hokada, & Ross, 1972) looking at literature going back as far as the beginning of the 20th century, found that many more males appeared in the books—as main characters, as lesser characters, and in pictures. Although most of this research was done in North America, there were similar findings in Europe and Australia (e.g., Bereaud, 1975). One widely cited study (Weitzman et al., 1972) from this period examined **Caldecott and Newbery medal** award-winning and honor books, as well as Little Golden Books and other children's books from the 1940s through the 1960s. In the award-winning books they found 11 male human characters pictured for every female character, and an astonishing ratio of 95 male animal characters to every female animal character. Ratios of male to female characters in the other books were not as dramatic, but there were always more male characters in the stories, as well as in the titles and the pictures. Also, even when characters may be intended to be gender-neutral (often animal characters with no discernable gender) adults who read such books to children typically refer to the characters using masculine pronouns (DeLoache, Cassidy, & Carpenter, 1987). Even though it is sometimes assumed that masculine pronouns are gender neutral, there is in fact much evidence that both children and adults interpret "he" as referring to males (Hyde, 1984; Madson & Hessling, 1999). Therefore, children are still exposed to more male characters even when the characters are not specifically identified as male by the books' authors.

These studies also found very gender-stereotyped portrayals of both children and adults. For example, men were shown in many more occupational roles, and their occupations required more education and skill than the occupations in which women were shown. Adult women were rarely portrayed outside the home, and were shown as looking after and serving others, especially family members. Women also played magic roles such as fairy godmothers or witches. In childhood, boys were often portrayed outdoors, whereas girls were indoors; boys were active, engaged in exciting and heroic activities, and solved problems, whereas girls were passive and needed assistance; boys led and girls followed; and boys did things and girls watched. Weitzman and her colleagues (1972) described an example in which the only girl in one book sits quietly in a corner, and another in which a wife carried wood but never speaks. In one story a "fool" seeks to find a princess to marry. According to Weitzman and her colleagues:

> The princess is shown only twice: once peering out of the window of the castle, and the second time in the wedding scene in which the reader must strain to find her. She does not have anything to say during the adventure, and of course she is not consulted in the choice of her husband; on the last page, however, the narrator assures us that she soon "loved him to distraction." (Weitzman et al., 1972, pp. 1129–1130)

Changes Over Time

Another of these early studies examined books before (1903–1965) and after (1966–1975) the advent of the women's movement and found little change between the two periods (St. Peter, 1979). However, some recent research (Clark, Guilmain, Saucier, & Tavarez, 2003) has reported subtle changes in both the number of female characters and gender stereotyping across the decades of the 20th century between the 1930s and the 1960s, with both numbers and stereotyping increasing and decreasing as society's views about women's roles changed. This is important, because it makes it clear that children's books are an integral part of the gender socialization process.

Once publishers were made aware that people had concerns about sexism in children's literature, they attempted to provide more books about girls and to represent more flexible roles for both sexes (Paterson & Lach, 1990; Turner-Bowker, 1996). There have been several studies since the 1970s examining both of these issues in children's literature. Many have focused on award-winning books such as the Caldecott and Newbery books as well as other books recommended by associations of librarians. Because these books are considered the best of children's literature, children's libraries and schools can almost always be assured to purchase them. However, other studies have also examined the kinds of children's books that one could easily purchase in a supermarket, such as Little Golden books.

Research conducted from the 1980s though the beginning of the 21st century has found that efforts to decrease sexism in children's literature have had some impact. The number of books about girls has increased, and although there are still more male characters, the ratio of male to female characters has become less dramatic (e.g., Davis & McDaniel, 1999; Grauerholz & Pescosolido, 1989; Hamilton, Anderson, Broaddus, & Young, 2006; Kinman & Henderson, 1985; Kortenhaus & Demarest, 1993; Nilges & Spencer, 2002; Purcell & Stewart, 1990). The numbers have varied from study to study, but are generally on the order of at least 1.5–2 times as many male as female main characters. Still, this is clearly an improvement.

The nature of the portrayals of female characters has also changed over this period (Allen, Allen, & Sigler, 1993; Clark, Lennon, & Morris, 1993; Hamilton et al., 2006; Kortenhaus & Demarest, 1993). Girls are now more likely to be shown in active and instrumental roles, and women to have a variety of occupations in addition to domestic roles. Even downright counter-stereotypical roles are now much easier to find. However, stereotyped portrayals remain (Crabb & Bielawski, 1994; Turner-Bowker, 1996). For example, Turner-Bowker (1996) examined Caldecott Medal and Honor books through the mid-1990s and found that male characters were more active and powerful. However, female characters were seen as more positive than males, especially in terms of qualities like nurturance and goodness. This, of course, is consistent with the general finding that we have discussed previously, that girls and women are valued for these kinds of qualities.

Girls and women change but boys and men do not

Although portrayals of girls and women became less stereotyped over this period, the same cannot be said for portrayals of boys and men. Even today, boys are rarely shown doing activities that might be considered feminine, and men are rarely seen caring for children or doing housework (Diekman & Murnen, 2004; Evans & Davies, 2000). A recent examination of the portrayals of fathers in children's books concluded that men are portrayed as absent, uninvolved, and somewhat incompetent as parents (Anderson & Hamilton, 2005). The authors wondered if these kinds of portrayals contribute to the way in which boys grow up to see themselves as fathers as distant rather than actively involved parents.

Unbalanced portrayals and stereotypes still exist

We have seen that children's books have improved with respect to more balanced portrayals of the sexes in recent years; however, gendered portrayals still exist, especially of boys and men. It is also important to keep in mind that older books are still widely available. Little Golden Books and similar storybooks that are no different from those purchased for children in the 1950s or 1960s can still be purchased in supermarkets today. Parents keep their children's books and read them to their grandchildren, and people buy and sell books at garage sales. Libraries, daycare centers, and schools do not throw away old books until they fall apart, and it is easy to find a book written decades ago to read to children. Think back to the quote from *Winnie-the-Pooh* at the beginning of this chapter; so the fact that newer books are less gender stereotyped does not mean that older ones are not read to today's children.

Why More Male Characters?

One question that might be asked is why have there been fewer girls in children's stories? One traditional answer has been that girls will read books about boys, but boys will not read books about girls, and so a reasonable marketing decision for a publisher would be to balance books in favor of those about boys. This notion fits well with a phenomenon we have seen again and again in children's gender development: that boys maintain strong gender boundaries in opposition to anything associated with girls or femininity, whereas a similar degree of avoidance of boys and masculinity is not found in girls. For example, Elizabeth Dutro described the following observation of a little boy who entered a school library unaware that some books were "off limits" because of their gendered characteristics, and left the library "painfully aware" of that fact:

> One day, years ago, at the close of their weekly visit to the school library, I watched a class of kindergartners lined up at the door holding their reading choices. One 5-year-old boy clutched a book based on Walt Disney's *Beauty and the Beast*. The boy standing behind him spotted the book in his friend's hands and began making gagging noises. Other boys soon joined in with, "Oooh, you're going to read a girl's book?" and taunting, "Ha ha, he's a girl, he's a girl." The accused quickly slipped out of line, ran to a nearby shelf, and exchanged the book .... I also noticed that the book choices of the kindergarten girls in that same line did not appear to be influenced by gender. Girls clutched copies of *Lyle the Crocodile* (Waber, 1973), *Frog and Toad Are Friends* (Lobel, 1979), *Where the Wild Things Are* (Sendak, 1988), and *Pinocchio* without seeming to notice they were all about males. (Dutro, 2002, p. 376)

Touching on a similar issue, one group of researchers (Greever, Austin, & Welhousen, 2000) examined children's attitudes about a specifically non-gender-stereotyped book for children, *William's Doll* (Zolotow, 1972). This story, considered to be a landmark book for the time, tells of a young boy named William who wanted a doll as a toy. In the story his father buys him other toys (e.g., a basketball and a train), his brother ridicules him as a "sissy," but eventually his grandmother purchases a doll for him. Ellen Greever and her fellow researchers happened on a file folder containing some responses to the story from 26 elementary school children obtained in the 1970s by a former colleague who had since retired. They decided to present the story to another group of 24 children in the same school in1997. The children in both time periods had positive as well as negative responses to the idea of a boy having a doll. Among the positive responses from boys and girls in both time periods was a focus on learning to be a good father, a message that is explicit in the story itself. For example, one young boy stated:

> I think it was nice for the grandma to buy William a doll so he could know how it feels to be a father. Then when William would be a father he would be a good father and care for his children in the right way. (Greever et al., 2000, p. 327)

Interestingly, however, the number of responses from boys focusing on the need to learn how to care for children were much more common in the 1970s. Only one boy in 1997 (the one quoted above) indicated that to be a good father was a positive reason for a boy to have a doll, whereas seven did so in the earlier sample.

The negative responses to the idea of having a doll fell into a variety of categories (e.g., his friends would make fun of him or his father would not like it), but the most common one from both boys and girls was that boys do not play with dolls and should not want them. As stated by two young boys: "He was only interested in playing with his doll, which I think is kind of weird. I would have chosen a M16 K. A. 60 assult [*sic*] rifle" and "I really like the part where his brother and the boy next door called him a creep and a sissy" (Greever et al., 2000, p. 328). Obviously, one counterstereotyped story did not make much of an impression on some of these children! Interestingly, among the boys more of the responses were positive in the earlier than the later time period (boys' responses were 70% negative in 1997 versus 36% in the earlier group; girls' responses were about 30% negative in both time periods).

To conclude, there are many studies of the characteristics of picture books for young children. The older research demonstrated that many more males were portrayed in these books and that portrayals of both males and females were gender stereotyped. Recent books have somewhat more gender balance and fewer stereotyped portrayals, at least of female characters.

Books for Older Children and Young Adolescents

Boys and girls do have different preferences in their reading materials through the school years: boys are more likely to prefer nonfiction or adventures or books about sports, girls are more likely to prefer fiction and books about relationships, and both sexes to prefer books with gendered content (Cherland, 1994; Langerman, 1990). Some research suggests that older elementary and middle school girls read more than boys do, sometimes because they are encouraged by mothers to remain safe indoors doing something worthwhile (Lehr, 2001).

Many books for older children are marketed specifically to boys or girls, but there has been little quantitative examination of their characteristics. The few examinations of these books that have been published tend to be written by scholars in the humanities, or by educators and reading teachers, and are not likely to be extensive content analyses like the ones that examine picture books for young children. For example, consider this analysis of the Harry Potter books: "From ghosts to wizards, the subtext of Harry's novels is that boys have great adventures and girls are studious, weepy, or simpering" (Thompson, 2001, p. 43). Thompson points out that even the male ghosts have more fun than the female ghosts.

Research on books for older children and young teens (Armstrong, 2001; Lehr, 2001) has found that they portray dependence and "goodness" in girls, as well as their potential victimization in genres such as horror stories. Boys, on the other hand, are more likely to solve problems and to be assertive and independent, but are also more likely to be portrayed as violent. Many books marketed to girls focus on appearance and relationships, but there are also books for girls with female characters who have nontraditional roles and characteristics (surely we all remember Nancy Drew!). Children of these ages also read teen magazines and comic books, and these also provide highly gendered portrayals (Lehr, 2001; Worthy, Moorman, & Turner, 1999). Comics marketed to boys often include images of male superheroes as well as significant amounts of violence (Kirsch & Olczak, 2001; Pecora, 1992). Magazines marketed to teenage girls, on the other hand, clearly focus on appearance (clothing, makeup, hairstyles, and thinness), the importance of relationships with boys, and tend to show girls as dependent (Garner, Sterk, & Adams, 1998; Peirce, 1990; Willemsen, 1998). Interestingly, magazines for teen boys are usually focused on specific topics such as hobbies like guitars or skateboarding, although both boys' and girls' magazines have content about heterosexual relationships. One analysis of teen magazines for girls and boys in the Netherlands described the relationship articles in girls' magazines as being about "How can I catch him and keep him?" and in boys' magazines as being about "How can I dump her afterwards?" (Willemsen, 1998, p. 859).

Reading Practices of Older Children and Adolescents

There are a handful of ethnographic studies on the reading practices of elementary and middle school children, although more of them focus on girls than on boys. Dutro (2002) conducted a yearlong participant observation on the reading activities in a classroom of predominantly African American fifth grade boys and girls. These children had a literature-based school curriculum and took part in many group and individual discussions about books throughout the year. Dutro noted that boys were very reluctant to read any books designated specifically for girls, and that was especially so of the less popular boys, who were often teased by more popular or athletically talented boys (Dutro, 2002). When given opportunities to select books for themselves, the boys studiously and loudly avoided such books and chose books for themselves that were gender-neutral or about subjects such as sports. Although the girls also typically chose books specifically marketed to girls, some girls chose boys' books, and seemed to be taunting their male classmates with their choices:

> As names are called, most of the girls go straight to the American Girls book or the Babysitters Club book. Three girls in a row however, Neena, Sese, and Jade, walk deliberately to the front of the room and, throwing smug smiles at the boys at the front table, choose the basketball book. As the pile of basketball books shrinks the boys' anxiety levels rise. They start squirming in their seats and whispering to each other: "Oh man, I can't believe she took that book." (Dutro, 2002, p. 378)

When Dutro asked the children why certain books were "boys' books" or "girls' books" they named things like the subject matter (sports or babysitting), the pictures on the cover of girls or of boys, and the colors on the cover (specifically pink). They also mentioned comic books about superheroes and WWF (World Wrestling Federation) as being for boys. Dutro concluded that these children's reading of popular fiction was a highly gendered activity. However, despite the fact that the boys diligently monitored these gender boundaries in the classroom, they often told her in private that they would be glad to read a book about a girl.

Cherland (1994) conducted a yearlong ethnographic study of sixth-grade Canadian girls and noted that many books were shared among social networks of other girls. Although many of these books were series books (e.g., Babysitters' Club, Sweet Valley High), a variety of other books were also read and shared among the girls. Her examination of local bookstores found different books marketed to boys and girls, and a much greater selection of books available for girls. The children were also able to tell Cherland what they thought was the difference between boys' and girls' books. Boys' books were about animals and adventures and had mostly male characters. Girls' books, on the other hand, had both male and female characters, and were about relationships.

In another yearlong ethnographic study of seventh-grade midwestern American girls, Finders described the extent to which the girls used teen magazines (*Seventeen, Young Miss, Sassy,* and *Teen*) to learn "culturally specific ways of being a woman" (Finders, 1997, p. 59). The girls often read the magazines together, and took several with them to events like slumber parties. Status was achieved if one girl got the magazine before the others did. Girls who had bodies, clothes, or makeup most like those in the magazines were also awarded status in the other girls' eyes. Even though almost half of the space in these magazines is devoted to advertising (Evans, Rutberg, Sather, & Turner, 1991), the girls were seemingly unaware of that fact:

> I asked Tiffany to explain about the advertisements in the magazines. She insisted, "There aren't any ads." She proceeded to prove it to me. Pulling the latest issue of *Sassy* from her notebook, turning from ads to articles to full- and half-page ads, she argued, "This tells you about fingernail polish. This shows you about makeup. This is about zits and stuff. See?" (Finders, 1997, p. 64)

Although these girls were heavily invested in teen magazines, other research has shown that teen magazines are much more relevant to White girls like the ones Finders studied than to African American girls (Duke, 2002), who recognize that the lives pictured are not much like their own. Duke reported that older African American girls thought these magazines focused too much on appearance and relationships, and that Black girls were too sensible to focus so much on these issues.

Older Children's Books: Conclusions

To conclude, there are few studies about the characteristics of books and other reading materials for older children and about their reading practices. This research generally finds that reading materials for children of these ages are highly gendered, that boys and girls read different kinds of materials, and that girls may read more than boys, especially books.

TELEVISION

In the United States, less than 1% of homes do not have a television set (Kotler, Wright, & Huston, 2001), and the majority have more than one. Many children have a television set in their bedrooms. Children spend more time watching television, videotapes, and movies than they spend doing anything else except school or sleep (Comstock, 1993). As a point of comparison, between the ages of 2 and 18, children are estimated to spend about 3 hours a day watching television, another hour listening to music, another with the computer or video games, and less than an hour reading (Huston, Wright, Marquis, & Green, 1999).

Perhaps it is surprising, but children even begin to watch television as infants. Infants between 6 and 12 months of age are reported to watch television between 1 and 2 hours a day, increasing to 2–4 hours per day during the preschool period, to somewhat more during the school years, and then decreasing in adolescence (Paik, 2001).

Today there is a shift in school age children's use of electronic media slightly away from television towards video games and the use of the computer; however, television use is still the more frequent activity (Montgomery, 2000). It should also be pointed out that children spend much of their time watching programs intended for adults. Even by first grade about 40% of television time is spent watching programs for adults, by sixth grade this number is about 80% (Paik, 2001).

It is impossible to imagine that an activity so pervasive in children's lives would not affect their development. The important questions for those of us interested in gender development therefore concern what gender-related images are presented on television and how children's views of boys and girls and men and women might be influenced by what they see.

There are some differences between boys and girls in their television interests. Boys watch slightly more television overall, and are especially likely to watch more cartoons, action adventures, and sports. One notable difference is that boys in several different countries are particularly interested in watching programs containing violence (Knobloch, Callison, Chen, Fritzsche, & Zillmann, 2005). Girls often report not liking violence in cartoons or other programs (Lemish, 1998; Oliver & Green, 2001), and in general they watch more situation comedies and relationship or family dramas (Wright et al., 2001).

Gender and Television Programming

Children's Programs

There are several kinds of programming specifically intended for children: educational programs for young children, cartoons, and programs for older children, some of which have an educational component, whereas others are primarily entertainment.

Public television and educational programming

In the United States it is often said that educational programs on public television are among the best programs available for children, but even they have been found to have more male than female characters (Signorielli, 2001). Indeed, some years ago an analysis of educational television programs for young children *(Mister Rogers' Neighborhood, Sesame Street, The Electric Company,* and *Captain Kangaroo)* found a great deal of gender stereotyping being presented (Dohrmann, 1975). Of such programs, one of the most highly regarded is *Sesame Street.* Research has clearly demonstrated that children show cognitive and educational gains from watching it (Bickham, Wright, & Huston, 2001). But what about its images of gender? Early after it began, researchers reported that *Sesame Street* had many more male than female characters, especially among the cartoon and puppet characters that made up the bulk of the characters on the show. Hallingby (1987; 1993) found that 75% of the identifiable characters during the 1980s and early 1990s were male, and that more than 80% of the cartoon and Muppet characters were male. For example, there were no major female Muppet characters until Prairie Dawn appeared in the early 1990s (in case you're wondering, Miss Piggy was never on *Sesame Street*). In addition to the overwhelmingly male Muppets, Hallingby reported other sexist images:

> There was one on the number ten. The examples included a girl counting her ten toes followed by a male professor with ten triangles, a male bowler with ten pins, one boy with ten bells, another with ten toys, and a male baker with ten cakes. (Hallingby, 1987, p. 7)

In contrast to the Muppets, the human characters on *Sesame Street* are balanced between males and females, and include people of many ethnic backgrounds as well as people with disabilities. Although some stereotyped images of the human characters were found in the early years, those were soon gone, and *Sesame Street* today clearly attempts to present a variety of images for both male and female characteristics and roles. Also, in recent years two more female Muppets have been added to the lineup: Zoe and Rosita. Nonetheless, a quick glance at the cast of Muppet characters shows them to remain disproportionately male (Bert, Ernie, Big Bird, Grover, Cookie Monster, Oscar, the Count, Elmo, Telly, etc.), although their behavior is not necessarily stereotyped as masculine.

Other "educational" programming

Programming other than that on public television is also considered to meet the definition of children's educational television. In the United States, the Federal Communications Commission (FCC) mandates that, in order to be licensed, stations must provide programs that meet the educational needs of children (Kunkel, 1998). However, children's educational television is defined very broadly and includes such programs as *Saved by the Bell* and *Sweet Water High* (Barner, 1999). A content analysis of such programs found more male characters, no female central characters, males who were dominant and assertive and whose behavior led to consequences, and females who were nurturant and deferent and whose behavior was ignored much of the time (Barner, 1999).

Cartoons

More than half of all of children's television programs are found on cable channels such as Nickelodeon and the Turner Cartoon Network. A major programming staple of these channels is cartoons (Merskin, 2002), and children often watch them without adults. Beginning in the 1970s and continuing through the present (Merskin, 2002; Sternglanz & Serbin, 1974; Streicher, 1974; Thompson & Zerbinos, 1995, 1997) researchers have demonstrated that the world of children's cartoons is a disproportionately male world, and that children are aware that it is. The producers of children's programming, especially cartoons, apparently hold very strongly to the view that girls will watch programs about boys, but that boys will not watch programs about girls, and therefore a successful children's show must be predominantly about boys. Interestingly, in contrast with this view, there is research showing that boys will watch shows about interesting girl characters, at least if those characters do not have particularly feminine characteristics. In one recent study, Eliza Thornberry, a heroic female character in the cartoon *The Wild Thornberrys*, was popular with both boys and girls (Calvert, Kotler, Zehnder, & Shockey, 2003).

Not only are there more male characters in cartoons, but gendered images prevail. Female characters are more likely to be helpless, dependent, and complaining, as well as affectionate and nurturant. They are more likely to be found in domestic roles and in the home. Males are more likely to be shown as independent, assertive, competent, athletic, important, and brave. They are also more likely to be shown in leadership roles and in many different occupations, as well as being more likely to be shown as aggressive, violent, and dangerous. One content analysis of children's cartoons (Thompson & Zerbinos, 1995) examined 197 cartoons from the 1930s through the 1990s. They found that there were about 3 times as many male as female characters both in central and minor roles, and that male characters spent much more time doing virtually everything because there were so many more of them. They also found less stereotyping in the more recent cartoons, particularly for female characters, but as in the books that we discussed earlier, males were never shown looking after children. We should also keep in mind that, although the newer cartoons were less stereotyped, there are many older cartoons still readily available for children to watch. It is also the case that certain genres of cartoons provide more sexist and violent images than other genres. Adventure cartoons (e.g., *Batman*) have been found to be the most likely to have many more males and highly stereotyped images, whereas educational or family cartoons are the least likely to (Leaper, Breed, Hoffman, & Perlman, 2002).

Other children's programs

In addition to educational programs and cartoons, there are other entertainment programs for children. One example is the World Wrestling Federation (WWF), which is something of a cross between sports and entertainment and is clearly filled with violence. It often has images of good versus evil and highly stereotyped images of masculinity. In one study, elementary school children in Israel were interviewed about their viewing of WWF, as well as their attitudes about it (Lemish, 1998). School principals were also interviewed, and they often reported that children imitated WWF fights on the playground, some-times resulting in injury. Girls watched the program less than boys did (depending on the question, about 10% of girls compared with about 20-30% of boys). Boys expressed interest in particular characters, and could provide detailed descriptions of their favorite characters' appearance, characteristics, and fighting styles. Girls often reported that they thought the program was "gross," "disgusting," or "repulsive."

Television Intended for Adults

As we pointed out earlier, young children often watch entertainment programs that are meant for adults, and children who have older siblings in the home begin to watch adult programs sooner (Huston & Wright, 1996). In a recent review of several content analyses of adult television Signorielli (2001) demonstrated that there is a great deal of consistency in the gendered images presented on television, but that there have also been changes in recent years. Very consistently there are more male than female characters. The ear-liest research suggested the ratio at 3:1, and the newest research of both network and cable programs finds it ranging between 2:1 and 3:1, with women being more likely than men to be minor as opposed to central characters. The number of women is lowest during prime time, although in prime time programs women are more likely to be found in situation comedies than in other types of programs.

There are also differences in the characteristics of male and female characters (Signorielli, 2001). Women characters are younger than men, and more likely to have blonde or red hair. Most female char-acters are likely to be in their 20s and 30s, with few over 50. Although men over 60 are often seen having jobs, older women almost never are. Female characters, relative to males, are more likely to be very thin and attractive and to receive comments from others about their appearance (Lauzen & Dozier, 2002). Very few women on television are even slightly overweight. Whereas somewhat more men on television are overweight, there are negative references to overweight individuals of both sexes (Fouts & Vaughan, 2002). Nonetheless, it is not unusual in a television program for a somewhat unattractive or overweight man to be portrayed in a relationship with a much more attractive, younger, or thinner woman.

In older shows (many of which are still available in syndication, especially on cable TV) women rarely had occupations outside the home except as clerical workers, nurses, and teachers. In today's shows, women are much more likely to be portrayed in nontraditional occupations—both blue collar and pro-fessional; however, their personal lives and relationships with men are often portrayed in very gender-stereotyped ways. As is the case in other forms of media we have already discussed, portrayals of men have changed little over the years.

Another type of television that many older children and adolescents watch is music videos on chan-nels such as MTV. Content analyses of music videos have found many more males are shown (e.g., 80% of lead characters male); both sexes are shown in stereotyped occupations; males are more aggressive and dominant; females are more fearful, nurturant, sexual, and submissive; females wear more reveal-ing clothing; and females are more often the targets of sexual advances (Gow, 1996; Sommers-Flanagan, Sommers-Flanagan, & Davis, 1993).

Violence on Television

One issue that has been raised repeatedly is that television has many instances of violence. For example, film critic Michael Medved (as cited in Bushman & Huesmann, 2001) has pointed out that few of us have actually seen or known anyone who was murdered, and yet we can see murders on television every day. Medved suggests that more than 300 characters appear each night on prime time television programs, and each night about seven of them are murdered. By the time a child reaches adolescence, he or she has likely seen more than 8,000 murders and more than 100,000 other acts of violence on television (Bushman & Huesmann, 2001). Many more of the crimes depicted on television are violent crimes such as rape, assault, and murder, whereas in the real world most crimes are property crimes. In other words, television is much more violent than the world we live in. Analyses have shown that about 60% of television programs have violence in them, that violence is often engaged in by heroes or "good guys," rarely has negative consequences, is often shown as being funny, and does not show the realistic pain or suffering that would normally result from such acts (Bushman & Huesmann, 2001).

Children's Programs Are the Most Violent

It may be surprising to know that there is evidence that children's programming is actually more violent than programming designed for adults, although the type of violence is often different. A large and representative national study of violence in North American television, the National Television Violence Study (Wilson et al., 2002), compared programs designed for children under age 13 to those designed for older viewers. They reported that 69% of the children's programs contained violence compared with 57% of other programs. Children's programs also contained more episodes of violence per hour (6.5 as compared with 2.7). In children's programs many of the violent characters were not real human beings (cartoon characters, etc.), whereas in other programs almost all were real people. As compared with the adult programs, much of the violence in children's programs was "sanitized," in that it showed little "blood and gore," and was less likely to show real weapons such as guns. The violent characters in children's programs were somewhat more likely to be rewarded for their violence (about 30% of the time compared with 20%) and slightly less likely to be punished (about 20% as compared to 30%). In the children's programs most of the victims were not harmed by the violence, whereas in the adult programs harm was shown about half the time. Again, unlike that in adult programs, violence in children's programs was often clearly fantasy— something that could never actually happen, such as a character running off a cliff and hanging in midair for a few seconds before crashing to the ground. Finally, violence in children's programs was much more likely to be shown as being funny, largely because it was often shown in cartoons.

Certain kinds of children's programs were especially likely to be violent as compared with other kinds. Slapstick (e.g., *Road Runner, Tom and Jerry*) and superhero (e.g., *Power Rangers, Spiderman*) cartoons had multiple instances of violence in almost every episode, and adventure or mystery shows (e.g., *Scooby Doo, Beetlejuice*) had violence in about 90% of the shows; but social or relationship programs (e.g., *Care Bears, Flintstones*) had violence only about half the time, and magazine shows (e.g., *Sesame Street, Blue's Clues*) showed violent behavior less than 20% of the time (Wilson et al., 2002).

Televised violence is a gendered issue because almost all of the characters who engage in violence on television are male, in both children's and adults' programming. Also, as we already know, boys are more interested in and watch more of this type of programming. So, if televised violence has an impact on children's development, it is more likely to be boys who are affected.

Television Commercials

In addition to the kind of programs we have already discussed, commercial television is supported by advertisements for various products. There are several studies of commercials and advertising, including those that accompany both children's and adults' programming and are directed specifically at either children or adults. It is estimated that children are exposed to at least 20,000 commercials a year (Kunkel & Roberts, 1991). It may be surprising to know that young children cannot tell the difference between commercials and programming (Kunkel & Gantz, 1993), or at least are not aware that the intent of commercials is to sell products, and so there has often been special concern about the impact of commercials on children. It is often said that television has turned young children into consumers in a way they have never been before.

Commercials Directed to Adults

Many of the characteristics of commercials directed at adults (but that children see) are similar to those we have already discussed for programming: more males, young and attractive women, and gender-stereotyped characteristics (Signorielli, 2001). Although portrayals of women have become somewhat less stereotyped over the years, there is little evidence that portrayals of men have changed much (Allan & Coltrane, 1996). Similar to the findings with other media, men are rarely shown doing domestic work or caring for children (Kaufman, 1999). Research examining television commercials in North America, Europe, the Middle East, Australia, Africa, and Asia show remarkable similarities in the nature of this stereotyping over at least a 25-year period, but some differences as well (Arima, 2003; Furnham & Mak, 1999; Mwangi, 1996; Neto & Furnham, 2005; Skoric & Furnham, 2002; Uray & Burnaz, 2003). For example, Asian commercials appear to be the most stereotyped, but in Europe and North America some aspects of gender stereotyping have been decreasing, especially occupations for women and the depiction of equality in relationships (Bresnahan, Inoue, Liu, & Nishida, 2001). There are also differences between network channels and cable channels, at least in the degree and focus of the stereotyping. For example, on MTV (Signorielli, McLeod, & Healy, 1994), women do not appear as often as men do in the commercials, but when they are shown, they have very fit or beautiful bodies and skimpy or sexy clothing, The women are also typically much more attractive than the men, who in addition to their more ordinary physical appearance are also likely to wear more neutral clothing.

One notable characteristic of advertising is that over the years announcers or voice-overs in commercials have almost always been male (even for products used primarily by women), and although the percentage of male voices has decreased in the past few years, at least 70% of voice-overs are still male (Bartsch, Burnett, Diller, & Rankin-Williams, 2000). In fact, women are often shown using cleaning and household products as men inform the audience about them.

Commercials Directed to Children

Some commercials are directed specifically at children. About two thirds of these commercials are for toys, and the remainder mostly for snacks and cereal. The marketing of toys for children increased dramatically in the early 1980s and has had a large impact on which toys become the most popular for children, with children often requesting the toys that they see on television commercials (Pine & Nash, 2002). In countries like Sweden where toy commercials are banned, children request fewer toys than they do in countries like England and the United States, where such commercials are common. Furthermore, one study showed that when children's exposure to television was reduced, they asked for fewer toys (Robinson, Saphir, Kraemer, Varady, & Haydel, 2001). So it is quite clear that these commercials have an effect on children.

Like other media, commercials directed to children contain stereotyped images, more male characters, and are more often aimed at boys (Klinger, Hamilton, & Cantrell, 2001; Maher & Childs, 2003; Signorielli, 2001). Although there is not a great deal of cross-cultural research on the content of commercials for children's products, one study comparing American and Australian commercials (Browne, 1998) found that commercials in both countries had more male characters and showed stereotyped images, but the Australian commercials were significantly less stereotyped than the American ones.

Commercials directed at boys and girls are also physically different (Rovinelli & Whissell, 1998; Welch, Huston-Stein, Wright, & Plethal, 1979). Even if you did not know what the product was, you could probably tell the difference between commercials directed at boys and girls just by their physical qualities. Commercials for girls' products (mostly toys) have more slow transitions like fades and dissolves, softer background music, and quieter play, whereas commercials for boys' products are louder and more boisterous, have more aggression and more sound effects, show more active play, and have more cuts and abrupt transitions. Commercials directed to boys also use less repetition, shorter words, and are rated as more practical and less pleasant or emotional than commercials directed to girls. Some research has shown that by middle childhood children are aware of the physical features of commercials that are associated with boys' and girls' products and toys (Huston, Greer, Wright, Ross, & Ross, 1984).

In addition to being stereotyped, commercials are often violent, in fact even more so than the programs they sponsor (Shanahan, Hermans, & Hyman, 2003). Commercials directed at boys are especially notable for their demonstration of violence and aggression (Klinger et al., 2001; Larson, 2003). A study of toy commercials aired on network television stations in the United States in the 1990s (Sobieraj, 1998) found that 68% of the commercials for boys' toys showed an act of aggression, whereas not one of the commercials for girls' toys did so. Much of the aggression was in the context of ads for action figures and cars. In Sobieraj's words:

> This activity is especially common with action figures. Actors are shown manipulating action figures to shoot guns at one another, fight with knives, punch, and kick, and inflict harm in various other ways. One advertisement shows a boy using an action figure to launch a missile at another action figure. The victim is knocked into a wall that crumbles down on top of him. The boys in the commercials are also shown crashing cars .... In one of these commercials, the narrator encourages the viewer to play violently with the advertised car, saying: "Drive it like you hate it!" as the actor simultaneously crashes the car into a wall breaking it into several pieces. (Sobieraj, 1998, p. 22)

Sobieraj also found that in most cases when aggression was shown, it was shown with positive consequences for the actor using it (e.g., achieving victory, receiving smiles or "high fives" from someone else in the commercial). She found no one expressing concern or negative consequences for any of this aggression. In addition to aggression, domination was much more frequently shown in commercials for boys' toys (e.g., "you're in command," "take control"), whereas the girls in toy commercials talked about how much fun they were having or that they loved their toys. In the more than half of the commercials for girls' toys, there were references to physical attractiveness (e.g., gorgeous, beautiful, looking good), but there were no such references in boys' commercials. Girls were often shown sighing longingly over attractive clothing, looking in mirrors, combing their hair, and putting on cosmetics, whereas boys were never shown doing any of these kinds of activities.

Television: Conclusions

To conclude, there is much consistency in the research on gendered images presented to children on television. Regardless of whether the programming is for children or adults, and whether it is actual programs or commercials, more males are shown and stereotyped images are common. In recent years, female characters are somewhat less stereotyped in certain ways (e.g., more occupations) but not all (e.g., physical appearance and age). However, there is little evidence of much change in the portrayals of males. On commercial television, violence and aggression by males is very common.

VIDEO GAMES AND COMPUTERS

Video games and computers are also a significant part of the lives of children today. Preschoolers use computers or video games for only a few minutes a day, whereas by late elementary school children may spend more than an hour a day on such activities (Huston et al., 1999; Wright et al., 2001). When we discussed television and books earlier in this chapter, we found that there were somewhat different patterns in how boys and girls used these forms of media. That conclusion is even more striking for video games and computers. Boys play video games much more than girls do, and for boys especially these newer media may take the place of watching television (Huston et al., 1999; Willoughby, 2008). The average 8- to 13-year-old boy in the United States plays video games more than 7 hours a week, and some boys play more than 10 hours a week (Anderson & Bushman, 2001; Paik, 2001). Preschoolers play more educational games, whereas elementary-aged children are more likely to play sports and violent action games, and these latter kinds of video games are much more likely to be played by boys.

Gender-Related Content in Video Games

There is some research examining the gender-related content of video games for children (Gailey, 1996). One content analysis of the roles of girls and women in 33 popular Nintendo and Sega video games (Dietz, 1998) found that about 30% of the games had no human characters at all (e.g., *Tetris*). When there were characters, more than 40% of the games had no females. Although this study did not analyze male gender roles, it was clear from the titles of the games that virtually all of the games with characters had male characters (e.g., *X-Men, NFL Quarterback Club, MegaMan3*, etc.). When there were female characters, many were victims or "damsels in distress," sex symbols wearing skimpy clothing, evil obstacles to the game, spectators, or other support characters. Girls or women were heroes or action characters in about 15% of the games. Many of the games included violence or aggression, predominantly done by males. Nearly half of the games had violence against other characters, mostly fighting or shooting, and sometimes quite graphic. In fact, a study of E-rated (i.e., for anyone, similar to G-rated movies) video games found that violence was very common in these games, and that characters were often rewarded by advancing further in the game when they injured someone (Thompson & Haninger, 2001).

It is clear that many of the video games marketed for children are more appealing to boys than to girls, often because of the violence (Funk & Buchman, 1996; Funk, Buchman, & Germann, 2000). In fact, one researcher (Kafai, 1996, 1998) looked at what kinds of video games children would design themselves and found that boys were much more likely to include violence and adventure. Given that girls could make up half the market of video game purchasers, it is probably to be expected that video game producers would try to develop games that appeal especially to them, and they have begun to do so. One of the first was a game called *Barbie Fashion Designer* (Subrahmanyam & Greenfield, 1998), which has been quite popular. In the early 1990s a company named *Purple Moon* also began to develop video games for girls focusing on social relationships (Glos & Goldin, 1998). One of their well-known series, *Rockett's World*, involves such tasks as a girl negotiating her way around in a new school. Research finds that girls seem to prefer gender-neutral, nonviolent fantasy games like *Simlife*, in which children create social worlds; *Tamagotchi*, in which they keep artificial creatures alive as long as possible; or cards, skill, or strategy games like *Tetris* (Griffiths, 1997; Subrahmanyam, Kraut, Greenfield, & Gross, 2001).

Some video games are developed less for entertainment than for educational purposes, and that is especially true of games for preschoolers. Studies examining educational software for preschool and early elementary school children (Chappell, 1996; Drees & Phye, 2001; Sheldon, 2004) have found that it too has been dominated by male characters (especially in primary roles) and stereotyped images.

Computers and the Internet

Another media form used by children and adolescents today is computers and the Internet (Greenfield & Yan, 2006). Although some of the first research on Internet use found boys more likely to go online (Kafai & Sutton, 1999), and some differences in the patterns of use (e.g., boys play games more), the most recent conclusion is that boys and girls are very similar in their frequency of use of the Internet (Miller, Schweingruber, & Brandenburg, 2001). Both sexes use e-mail and instant messaging and both are coming to use these Internet activities as a regular part of their social lives. There is some research showing that gender influences social interaction in online chat rooms and forums. Adolescent boys are more likely to engage in explicitly sexual messages and girls are more likely to choose feminine or subtly sexualized names (Subrahmanyam, Smahel, & Greenfield, 2006). Girls also offer more apologies and "social niceties" (Cassell, Huffaker, Tversky, & Ferriman, 2006). Nevertheless, girls and boys are chosen as online leaders equally often, and many of the qualities that these leaders show are similar in the two sexes.

Finally, computers are often marketed to families as a way to improve their children's educational success. Content analyses of this marketing has demonstrated that it implies that computer use is more likely done by males, and that girls and women need help from men to use computers (Burlingame-Lee & Canetto, 2005).

TOYS

For centuries girls have received dolls as toys and boys are often given military toys. For example, toy soldiers have been found as far back as the 13th century (Varney, 2000), and they can easily be seen as the precursors of today's action figures. Although toys are not exactly a form of media, they do constitute an aspect of children's gender socialization and therefore we have chosen to comment on the characteristics of boys' and girls' toys in this chapter.

Some toys are gender-neutral; that is, they are not identified as being masculine or feminine. Here you may think of materials to draw, color, or paint; modeling clay; some board games; educational toys such as flash cards or materials to learn skills like counting (e.g., a cash register, a toy computer); as well as items for gross motor play like jungle gyms, swings, or slides. Nonetheless, it is obvious to any casual observer that toys are consistently identified with either boys or girls. There are many studies from the early part of the 20th century through the present demonstrating that boys and girls have different toys, that from about 12 to 18 months of age they play with different toys, and when asked say they prefer different toys (e.g., Benjamin, 1932; Delucia, 1963; Martin, Eisenbud, & Rose, 1995; Serbin, Poulin-Dubois, Colburne, Sen, & Eichstedt, 2001; Servin, Bohlin, & Berlin, 1999).

What Toys Do Boys and Girls Have?

More than 25 years ago Rheingold and Cook (1975) observed the toys and other objects present in 1- to 6-year-old boys' and girls' bedrooms. They found that these young boys and girls had the same number of books, musical items, and stuffed animals, and the same amount of furniture. Beyond those similarities, there were many differences in the kinds of toys and other objects that boys and girls had in their rooms. Boys also had a greater variety of different kinds of toys, and they tended to have more toys overall.

Boys had more vehicles of all kinds (e.g., toy cars and trucks, but also larger items like wagons), toys that they called "spatial-temporal" (e.g., shape-sorting toys, clocks, magnets, outer-space toys), sports equipment (e.g., balls, skates, kites), toy animals, garages or depots, machines, military toys, educational and art materials (despite the fact that these may be seen as gender-neutral), and more furnishings with animal themes. The category of vehicles was especially larger for boys. There were 375 vehicles in the boys' rooms and 17 in the girls'. Not one girl had a wagon, bus, boat, kiddie car, motorcycle, snowmobile, or trailer in her room.

Girls' rooms contained more dolls, dollhouses, domestic items (e.g., sinks, dishes, stoves), floral furnishings, and ruffles. As girls' rooms rarely had vehicles, boys' rooms rarely had domestic items. Although girls had more dolls, boys did have dolls. The researchers divided the dolls into three categories: male, female, and baby dolls. Girls had 6 times as many female dolls and 9 times as many baby dolls as boys did, whereas boys and girls had about the same amount of male dolls. In the boys' rooms, however, dolls were usually in such categories as cowboys and soldiers.

Another way that researchers have measured what toys boys and girls have is to examine children's toy requests (including their letters to Santa), or what toys are purchased for boys and girls. Such studies have consistently shown that girls ask for and receive more clothing and jewelry, dolls, and domestic and musical items, whereas boys ask for and receive more sports equipment, vehicles, military toys and guns, and more spatial and temporal items such as clocks (Almqvist, 1989; Bradbard, 1985; Richardson & Simpson, 1982). Interestingly, of the toys children receive, the ones they specifically ask for are more stereotyped than the ones parents spontaneously choose, which tend more often to be educational or artistic materials suitable for either boys or girls (Robinson & Morris, 1986). Nevertheless, it is clear that both parents and nonparents purchase gender-stereotyped toys for children, especially for boys (Fisher-Thompson, 1993; Fisher-Thompson, Sausa, & Wright, 1995). Some studies have also shown that salespeople steer customers in the direction of sex-appropriate toys for children (Reynolds, 1994; Ungar, 1982).

There is evidence of some change over the years in children's toy requests. A recent study of children's letters to Santa found that girls were as likely as boys to ask for real vehicles, sports equipment, and male dolls, whereas boys were as likely as girls to request clothing and educational or art toys (Marcon & Freeman, 1996). However, in the 21st century, girls continue to be more likely to ask for dolls and domestic items, and boys are more likely to ask for toy vehicles, military and outer space toys, action figures, and spatial toys. In a recent study in Sweden (Nelson, 2005), one of the most progressive countries in the world with respect to gender equality, very gender-stereotyped toys were still found in preschool children's collections.

Qualities and Characteristics of Boys' and Girls' Toys

Appearance and Violence

We have seen that boys more often have toys like spatial toys, military toys, and vehicles, whereas girls more often have dolls and domestic items. How else do boys' and girls' toys differ?

A few studies have examined the general characteristics of toys identified as boys', girls', and neutral (Blakemore & Centers, 2005; Miller, 1987). The attribute most strongly associated with girls' toys is a focus on appearance and attractiveness. You can think of Barbie dolls, of course, but one can also purchase such items as pretend makeup, perfume, jewelry, and plastic high-heeled shoes as toys for young girls. At the other end of the continuum, the characteristics most strongly associated with boys' toys are aggression and violence. Boys' toys include guns, swords, rockets, as well as bombs, hand grenades, and other military equipment—items that can be used to injure and kill others.

This can clearly be seen in the comparison between dolls or other human-like figures that are marketed to boys and girls—action figures and Barbie dolls especially. One examination of the characteristics of Barbie dolls versus action figures like G. I. Joe, and WWF figures (Klugman, 1999) described how boys' action figures differ from girls' dolls. Action figure play often involves bad guys fighting good guys. In fact, boys often hit or bang action figures together. Action figures often come with weapons and instructions about how to use them. Klugman pointed out that sometimes the weapons are part of the action figure's own body:

> Sometimes a part of the body itself might double as a weapon, as is the case with Robot Wolverine, who has "robotic arm weapons." "Squeeze Robot Wolverine's legs together and his arms fly off!" But The Tick (otherwise known as Human Bullets™) takes the cake for sacrificial body part: "Push the button on Human Bullets™ and see him shoot off his head. (Klugman, 1999, p. 172)

Klugman points out that the accessories for Barbie dolls and dolls of similar types are usually appearance-related items like combs and hair dryers that are used to act on the doll rather than for the doll to use. The accessories are often much too large for the doll herself and are clearly intended to be used instead by the little girl who plays with the doll. She also points out that boys' action figures are much more mobile and joined in several places, whereas Barbie dolls only have joints at the shoulder and the hip. In an intriguing analysis, she suggests that each action figure has a distinctive body shape, height, nationality, history, or allegiance, whereas the girls' dolls often appear to be no different from one another except in coloring, outfit, and name. The boxes containing such toys also differ. Action figures rarely have pictures of boys on the packages. Instead, the packages show the figures themselves, often more human-like than the actual doll, acting in various complex and highly colored illustrations. Language on the packages uses terms like "kill" and "destroy." The packages for girls' dolls use pastel colors, and show real girls playing with, holding, grooming, or gazing at the dolls.

Barbie dolls

Barbie dolls have been of particular interest. More than one writer has suggested that Barbie dolls are more than toys; they are a "cultural icon" (Norton, Olds, Olive, & Dank, 1996; Rogers, 1999). Translated into a human body, Barbie would be from 6 ft. 3 in. to 7 ft. 5 in. tall, with extremely slender and improbable body proportions (Pedersen & Markee, 1991). One estimate (Norton et al., 1996) calculated that, if they were life size, the probability that a woman would have Barbie's physical proportions was less 1 in 100,000, whereas the probability of a man having Ken's proportions were about 1 in 50. According to some estimates (see Rogers, 1999) almost all American girls have owned at least one Barbie doll, with the average young girl owning eight of them. Of course, Barbie dolls are not owned just by American girls; they are sold in more than 140 countries across the world (Rogers, 1999).

What is often pointed to about Barbie dolls is the emphasis on appearance, grooming, clothing, and hairstyles. In a study of young girls (Markee, Pedersen, Murray, & Stacey, 1994), the researchers found that the girls often mentioned the doll's physical features and appearance as the reasons for liking them (e.g., curly hair, being cute or pretty, shiny earrings, sparkly eyes, or particular clothes). They especially liked things that could be removed (e.g., clothes) or changed (e.g., hairstyles) while playing with them. Essentially, Barbie doll play consisted of dressing and grooming the dolls to make them more attractive, as well as fantasy play involving dressing up, going shopping, and especially getting married. As we mentioned already, in addition to Barbie dolls, their clothing, and other accessories, there are also numerous other appearance-related toys for girls.

American Girl

One popular set of toys for girls originally marketed in the United States, but now expanded to many other countries, is the American Girl (AG) doll collection. This set of dolls also includes books and other accessories, and also includes clubs of girls and their mothers organized around these dolls (Acosta-Alzuru & Kreshel, 2002). These dolls are larger than Barbie dolls, each character is historically based, and each has a clearly different identity. The dolls are based on particular periods in history (e.g., pioneer times, the Victorian period, pre-World War II) and include a variety of ethnic identities. Although the original dolls were based on American historical periods, new dolls in the Girls of Many Lands series have been developed based on many identities worldwide. As is the case with Barbie dolls, one can purchase many different items of clothing and accessories for AG dolls, including matching clothing for the girl who owns the doll.

Other Qualities of Boys' and Girls' Toys

There are other attributes associated with boys' and girls' toys, especially with moderately masculine and feminine toys. Boys' toys (e.g., balls and vehicles) are somewhat more associated with movement (Alexander, 2003; Alexander & Hines, 2002) and with spatial skill, construction, and science. Girls' toys are linked to the development of domestic skill (e.g., irons, stoves, dishes) and with nurturance (baby dolls). Boys' toys also seem to encourage fantasy play that is symbolic or removed from daily life, whereas girls' toys encourage fantasy play that centers on the domestic. Put bluntly, boys can use their toys to build something new or to imagine flying off to outer space, whereas girls can pretend to iron and do dishes, as well as to dress up and care for babies. One recent examination of a large number of attributes associated with boys' and girls' toys (Blakemore & Centers, 2005) also found that boys' toys were seen as more sustaining of attention, more exciting, more fun, more dangerous or risky, and more in need of adult supervision than were girls' toys.

Some years ago developmental psychologist Jeanne Block (1983) suggested that boys' toys may be more likely to provide feedback to children than girls' toys do; that is, the toy responds in some way to the child's behavior. As an example of a toy that provides feedback, you might think of slot car racers, radio-controlled cars, or electric trains, which respond to a child's manipulations of the controls. Video games are, of course, another excellent example. The research cited above (Blakemore & Centers, 2005) did find that this was indeed a characteristic of moderately masculine toys, but also of gender-neutral toys, and it was not especially associated with strongly masculine toys.

Strongly Stereotyped Toys Have Undesirable Qualities

One clear conclusion, however, from the most recent research on this topic is that strongly gender-stereotyped toys for both boys and girls have several undesirable attributes (e.g., excessive focus on appearance for girls, and on violence and aggression for boys), and that the most educational and enriching toys seem to be moderately masculine (e.g., scientific, construction, and spatial toys) and neutral (e.g., musical, artistic). It is also the case that some feminine toys are associated with learning other useful, albeit different, skills (e.g., nurturance, domestic skills).

Boys' and Girls' Toys: Conclusions

How can we summarize the nature of boys' and girls' toys? First, boys appear to have somewhat more toys than girls do, and they have more different kinds of toys; that is, a greater variety. Boys' toys appear to encourage imaginary play that is at least somewhat removed from everyday life (e.g., outer space toys). Boys' toys involve building things (e.g., Legos, construction toys) involve the use of visual and spatial skills, and may be more responsive to the actions of the child who plays with them (e.g., video games). Boys' toys also involve more violence and aggression than girls' toys do. Girls' toys, on the other hand, encourage imagination of everyday domestic life, focus on appearance and relationships, and involve nurturance to the young (e.g., baby dolls).

THE IMPACT OF TOYS AND THE MEDIA ON CHILDREN'S GENDER DEVELOPMENT

Up to this point in this chapter we have been discussing the gender-related characteristics of children's reading materials, television, video games, computers, and toys. We also want to know about the extent to which children's exposure to these materials influences their gender development. This is, of course, a much more difficult question to answer. Common sense might lead us to conclude that it would be impossible for these images not to have an effect. During their childhood years children spend thousands of hours playing with toys, reading or being read to, watching television and videotapes, and playing video games in which gendered images appear to be inescapable. It does not seem conceivable that a child could grow up and not be influenced by these images. However, there is a huge difference between what we might think seems likely on the basis of common sense, and what research has confirmed is indeed the case. As scientists, we must turn to the evidence of research.

Much of the research on the question of the influence of these materials on gender development has studied the impact of television, and to some extent video games as well, rather than that of books and toys. Possibly that is because the potential undesirable impact of television and video games on children's literacy skills and their aggressive behavior has simply generated more interest.

In this segment of the chapter we will examine the research on three issues. First, we will examine whether there is evidence that children's knowledge and attitudes about gender-related characteristics are affected by their experiences with books, television, video games, and toys. Second, we will examine whether boys' and girls' cognitive skills appear to be affected by the different kinds of play they engage in. Third, we will address the issue of the impact of the media on aggression. There is very extensive research on this last topic, and we could not hope to address all of the issues here. However, as we have pointed out already, the impact of the media on aggression is a gender-related issue, because it is primarily boys and men who display aggression in the media, and it is more likely to be boys who watch violence, who play with violent toys and video games, and who read stories and comic books with violent themes.

Gender-Stereotyped Knowledge and Attitudes

One possible impact of the gendered images that children read about in books and see on television and in their toys is that these images may lead children to believe that they ought to want particular toys, to have certain characteristics, behave in certain ways, and aspire to particular occupations. There is concern that such experiences may place limitations on children's development, or to encourage development of certain skills but not others. Consider the following quotes from adults recalling their childhoods:

> My parents bought me a nursing kit when I was about two, and this "toy" survived with me for a large part of my younger years. Even back then I felt like I might be able to heal the sick around me....As far back as I can remember, I always wanted to be a nurse.

> By playing with Meccano [a set of construction toys similar to erector sets], e.g., I may well have been developing problem-solving strategies and psycho-motor coordination.

> A solitary play toy of my earlier years had important socialization functions later on. I made a crystal radio set....The toy introduced me to other general areas of play and toys: electronic gadgetry...and communications technology. (All from Sutton-Smith, 1986, pp. 211–212)

Although these quotes concern toys, there is actually very little research about the impact of toys on children's gender-related attitudes or characteristics, although we will discuss some shortly. Much more research exists about television. Many studies have shown a relationship between watching more television and having more gender-stereotyped attitudes. In other words, the more frequently children watch television, the more they have gender-stereotyped and sexist attitudes, and the narrower the range of roles they find acceptable for men and women (Gerbner, Gross, Morgan, Signorielli, & Shanahan, 2002; Signorielli, 2001). Much of this research is correlational, so it is not always clear whether gender-stereotyped children might simply prefer to watch more television. However, one study used a naturalistic quasi-experiment and compellingly demonstrated that television might indeed be influencing children to develop more gender-stereotyped attitudes (Williams, 1985). This study was done in the mid-1980s on three Canadian communities. At the beginning of the study, one of the communities was relatively isolated and had no television available, the second had limited television, and the third had more extensive television. Shortly after the study began, some television was introduced to the community that had none, and the children were studied before television came to the community and again 2 years later. The children, especially girls, in the community with no TV had less stereotyped attitudes about gender than those who had TV available, and the attitudes of the children who had TV come to their community changed in a more stereotyped direction over the 2 years of the study (Kimball, 1985).

Another more recent study (Ward & Friedman, 2006) used both experimental and observational methods to study the impact of exposure to gender and sexual stereotypes on adolescents' acceptance of these stereotypes as well as on their own sexual behavior. Using observational measures, the researchers found that adolescents who watched more "sexy" television programs (e.g., *Sex and the City*) in their daily lives were more likely to endorse views of women as sex objects and men as sexually driven, and greater acceptance of recreational sexuality. Adolescents who watched more of these programs were also more likely to have experimented with sex themselves. Of course these associations could reflect adolescents selecting programs on the basis of their attitudes rather than their attitudes changing as a function of exposure to the programs. However, the researchers also found that experimental exposure in the laboratory to gender and sexual stereotypes increased acceptance of those stereotypes, suggesting that it was certainly possible that the real-life television exposure was, in fact, affecting the young people's attitudes.

Television appears to be especially likely to influence opinions about who ought to hold particular occupations, but it also has been shown to affect views about gender-related personality characteristics, chores, and activities, and attitudes such as "women are happiest when they are homemakers" or "men have more ambition" (Gerbner et al., 2002; Signorielli, 2001). Meta-analyses of the research on the impact of television on attitudes about gender (Herrett-Skjellum & Allen, 1996; Morgan & Shanahan, 1997) find the impact to be a rather small effect, with d on the order of 0.10. However, not all television is likely to have the same effect. There is some evidence, also from meta-analysis, that children who prefer to watch educational television rather than network or cable programming may, in fact, be less stereotyped (Signorella, Bigler, & Liben, 1993).

Experimental Studies Attempting to Reduce Stereotypes

There are also experimental studies in which children are exposed to nonstereotyped role models in either books or televised presentations, or to information counteracting gender stereotyping to see whether such interventions can change children's ideas about gender to become less stereotyped. Some of this research has shown at least short-term influence in reducing the extent to which children play with stereotyped toys or hold stereotyped views about activities or occupations, especially for girls and for children whose parents impose few limits on their television watching (Johnson & Ettema, 1982; Nathanson, Wilson, McGee, & Sebastian, 2002). However, summaries of the research have concluded that there are many more failures to show an impact of such counterstereotyped messages (Bigler, 1999; Liben & Bigler, 1987), particularly any impact that is more than very short term in its effects. One issue to keep in mind, discussed in more detail in chapter 9, is that children have been shown to distort or forget portrayals that are not consistent with gender stereotypes (Martin, Ruble, & Szkrybalo, 2002). If children do not actually attend to and remember gender-nontraditional information, they cannot be expected to use that information to modify their beliefs.

On the basis of this reasoning, some researchers have designed interventions that are aimed at trying to ensure that children actually encode the counterstereotypic information that is presented. For example, as described briefly in chapter 9, Bigler and Liben (1990), developed a classroom intervention on occupations in which children were specifically taught that whether or not someone could perform a given occupation depended on the person's skills and training, but not upon whether the person was a male or female. Children who participated in these lessons were better at remembering gender-nontraditional stories than were children who were given standard lessons on occupations. Of course, even the most successful short-term interventions are likely to have only limited effects because these experimental counterstereotyped portrayals or lessons are really only a drop in the sea of stereotyped messages to which children are regularly exposed.

Psychological Impact

There is also some research on the psychological impact of the gendered content of children's books. One interesting study exposing children to various stories over a 4-week period found that the self-esteem of both boys and girls increased when they heard more stories about same-sex characters (Ochman, 1996). Because we know there are more stories and television shows about male characters, this finding may be relevant to the developing self-esteem of girls, although recall from chapter 5 that there is little consistent evidence of a difference in the self-esteem of boys and girls before adolescence.

Appearance and Girls

There are a few studies of the impact of gender-stereotyped toys on children's gender stereotyping; however, the topic has not been systematically examined in the way that television has been. One particular concern for girls centers on the issue of images of very thin girls and women in the media and toys like Barbie dolls. For example these young girls appear to have internalized such concerns:

I want to look skinny like Elle MacPherson. (Gilbert, 1998, p. 66)

I don't like this story. I like the one where Cinderella is thinner and looks like Barbie. (Wason-Ellam, 1997, p. 435)

Is there evidence that concerns about weight or eating disorders are related to images of thin women in the media or of toys like Barbie dolls? Although it is important to recognize that many factors influence these conditions, and again to emphasize that most of this is correlational and not experimental research, there is evidence of a relationship between images of women on television and in fashion magazines and eating disorders and body dissatisfaction, even in elementary-aged girls (Clark & Tiggemann, 2006; Levine & Smolak, 1998). Pathological forms of dieting (e.g., using laxatives or diet pills, vomiting, skipping meals) or eating disorders in adolescent girls are more common in girls who read more of these materials (Thomsen, McCoy, & Williams, 2001; Thomsen, Weber, & Brown, 2002). One study followed elementary school-aged girls longitudinally and found that television watching and magazine exposure at one point in time was associated with a thinner ideal body image for adult women and more disordered eating a year later (Harrison & Hefner, 2006). One adolescent who had been anorexic since she was in junior high put it very clearly:

I would look at my body and then I would look at the bodies of people in the magazines, and they weren't the same. And I would always try to make my body the way I saw in the magazines. (Thomsen et al., 2001, p. 56)

The research discussed above is correlational, but there is also some experimental research examining women's feelings about their bodies (e.g., body image, physical attractiveness, weight satisfaction) after being exposed to media portrayals of thin women versus being exposed to images (pictures or videos) of more normal weight or even "plus-size" women. One meta-analysis of this research (Groesz, Levine, & Murnen, 2002) found that young women, especially those under age 19 and those with previous body image problems, did indeed develop more negative self images ($d = 0.30$) after viewing pictures of very thin women, at least in the short term.

One researcher followed adolescent girls over a 15-month period during which they were randomly assigned to receive a free subscription to a teen fashion magazine or to not receive such a subscription (Stice, Spangler, & Agras, 2001). The researchers also monitored the girls' reading of the magazine (which they clearly did). Overall, the girls in the magazine group did not increase in their dieting, negative emotions, body dissatisfaction, or rates of eating disorders; however, some of the girls did. Girls who started the study with higher rates of body dissatisfaction and a sense of pressure to be thin showed increases in depression and anxiety as a result of exposure to the magazine. When such girls reported low levels of social support from friends and family, they also increased in body dissatisfaction and symptoms of eating disorders over the course of the study. The authors concluded that, although general effects of reading the magazine were not found, vulnerable girls were clearly impacted negatively by the media messages.

There is also a quasi-experimental study examining the impact of television exposure on eating disorders in the Fiji islands (Becker, Burwell, Herzog, Hamburg, & Gilman, 2002). In this study, Western television was introduced to the islands, and the researchers followed the girls before and after they were regularly exposed to the kinds of programs that North American and European adolescents have been watching for decades. Eating disorders were rare before the television was available and increased dramatically in girls once they were watching it on a regular basis. For example, early in the study none of the adolescent girls had induced vomiting to control weight, but by 3 years later about 11% had done so. Dieting was rare before television, but once girls were watching regularly, more than 60% had dieted. When the girls were interviewed, more than 80% of them thought that they and their friends had been influenced by television and wanted to change their behavior or appearance to become more like the characters portrayed.

Finally, one recent experimental study in England presented girls between the ages of 5 and 8 with one of three types of picture books about "Mira," who was going shopping and getting ready to go to a birthday party (Dittmar, Halliwell, & Ive, 2006). In one experimental condition, the

Mira pictured was a Barbie doll. In the second condition, Mira was an Emme fashion doll. Emme is based on the "plus-size" model whose name is Emme, and presents a fuller-figured image to children than the Barbie doll does. In the third condition, the images were neutral and no dolls were pictured. The story was the same in all three conditions—just the pictures differed. After they read the stories, the girls' body esteem and body shape dissatisfaction were measured. The findings showed that the two youngest groups of girls (ages 5.5–7.5 years) had more body image dissatisfaction and more of a desire to have a very thin body after listening to the Barbie story, but not after the other two versions of the story. The oldest group of girls (ages 7.5–8.5 years) was more negatively affected by exposure to the Emme doll story—they had a larger discrepancy between their actual body size and their ideal adult body, although not their ideal child body, than the other groups—they wanted to be thinner as adults than they currently were as children. The authors assumed that these older girls had already been exposed to many images of very thin adult role models, including many images of Barbie herself, and had therefore already internalized that image, and that seeing Emme may have made them fear the possibility of a larger adult body.

Given that both observational research using data from the real world of children and adolescents' experiences, quasi-experimental research such as that done in Fiji, and experimental research manipulating such experiences all point to the same conclusion, it is certainly reasonable to conclude that these images of very thin girls and women do affect some girls' feelings about their bodies.

Cognitive Skills

The third issue that we examine is whether exposure to books, the media, computers, and toys influence children's cognitive skills. We have already briefly discussed the finding that educational television programs like *Sesame Street* produce educational and cognitive gains for young children. There is evidence of numerous positive influences on children's linguistic and academic skills from watching well-crafted educational, informational, and scientific television programs (Fisch, 2002). And of course, reading is of benefit to children's development of academic and literacy skills (Weinberger, 1996). Additionally, parents and teachers often think it is desirable for their children and adolescents to use computers and hope that they develop important academic and cognitive skills from using them, although preferably not just to play games (Subrahmanyam, Greenfield, Kraut, & Gross, 2001).

The major question related to gender development concerns whether particular books, toys, and media experiences affect boys' or girls' cognitive skills differentially. We do not really know if that is so for books or television. Whereas there has been much conjecture about how boys' toys might help them to develop better spatial skills, here again little research is available to help us answer that question definitively. Instead, much of this research has focused on computers, and particularly on the cognitive impact of video games.

Iconic Representation

One computer-related skill is iconic representation—the ability to "read" pictures and diagrams (Subrahmanyam, Greenfield et al., 2001). This skill is an important aspect of computer literacy because it is necessary to be able to quickly and accurately interpret the display on a computer monitor if one is to be skilled at computer use. Some research has shown that playing video games improves this ability, and that the iconic representation skill developed by playing video games can transfer to more scientific or educational uses of the computer (Greenfield, Camaioni, Ercolani, Weiss, Lauber, & Perucchini, 1996). Another cognitive skill that has been shown to improve when people play video games is the ability to pay visual attention to several different things at the same time (Green & Bavelier, 2003; Greenfield, deWinstanley, Kilpatrick, & Kaye, 1996). Because boys play computer games so much more than girls do, these findings have implications for the kind of computer-related skills boys and girls might develop that could influence their educational and occupational opportunities.

Spatial Skills

There are several studies of the impact of playing video games on spatial skills. From our discussion in chapter 4, you recall that spatial skills consist of several different kinds of abilities, and that one common distinction is among the skills of mental rotation, spatial visualization, and spatial perception (Linn & Petersen, 1985). Some research shows that spatial skills in children and adolescents of both sexes, especially spatial visualization and mental rotation, improve with practice playing video games (De Lisi & Cammarano, 1996; Okagaki & Frensch, 1994; Subrahmanyam & Greenfield, 1994). For example, one recent study gave 8- and 9-year-old boys and girls 11 or 12 half-hour sessions of playing *Tetris* (a spatial game) or *Where in the World is Carmen Sandiego* (a nonspatial game) over a 1-month period (De Lisi & Wolford, 2002) in a computer class at school. The children's two-dimensional mental rotation skills were measured before and after the video game experience. At the pretest, the boys' mental rotation skills were significantly better than the girls ($d = 0.94$). After a month of playing *Tetris* (but not *Carmen Sandiego*) on a regular basis, there was no sex difference in mental rotation skills. Both boys' and girls' spatial skills improved, but the girls' skills improved much more, thereby catching up to the boys'. Another video game training study with college students (Feng, Spence, & Pratt, 2007) showed dramatic improvements on spatial skills, again more for females, after only 10 hours of playing an action video game (*Medal of Honor: Pacific Assault*), although not after playing a puzzle game (*Ballance*). As the authors note "Non-video-game players in our study realized large gains after only 10 hours of training; we can only imagine the benefits that might be realized after weeks, months, or even years of action video-gaming experience" (Feng et al., 2007, p. 854).

Violence and Aggression

One of the most long-standing and extensively investigated questions about the impact of the media is that of aggression. As we pointed out already, this is an issue of relevance to gender development because it is much more likely to be boys who read aggressive books, play with violent toys and video games, and watch television programs and films that are filled with such images. We also know that boys enjoy such activities and that they enjoy play fighting, pretend aggression, and rough and tumble play in their social interactions (Pellegrini & Smith, 1998). Because boys enjoy these kinds of activities, toys, and media experiences, it is sometimes difficult to know whether exposure to violent media results in them becoming more aggressive above and beyond other influences on aggression.

Researchers who study the relationship between violence in the media (and toys) and aggressive behavior take care to emphasize that there is no reason to think that the media are the only or even the most important influence on aggressive behavior. Rather, it is more reasonable to see it as one of many potential influences (Bushman & Huesmann, 2001). That having been said, there is consistent evidence, gathered over the past four decades, that exposure to violence in the media does influence higher levels of aggression in children (Bushman & Anderson, 2001; Bushman & Huesmann, 2001).

There are hundreds of studies on the possible influence of violence on television over the past 40 years. Recent reviews have been emphatic in concluding that there is a link between watching televised violence and children's aggressive behavior, as well as with their aggressive or hostile thoughts and feelings (Bushman & Anderson, 2001; Bushman & Huesmann, 2001; Huesmann, Moise, & Podolski, 1997). A meta-analysis of the research on the effects of televised violence (Paik & Comstock, 1994) concluded that the effect size (correlation, not mean difference) of the relationship between watching violence and behaving aggressively was .40 for laboratory experiments, .30 for field experiments, and about .19 for naturalistic observations relating television watching to aggression in the real world. They also reported an effect size of .10 linking watching violence and engaging in criminal violence. As you recall from our discussions in chapters 4 and 5, these effect sizes range from small (.10) to moderate (.40). However Paik and Comstock concluded that an effect size of .10 is not necessarily trivial. In their words "10 viewers out of 100 being affected by televised violence, cannot be dismissed as an insignificant effect" (Paik & Comstock, 1994, p. 535).

Childhood Viewing and Adult Aggression

One important type of naturalistic study follows children longitudinally and examines the relationship between their television viewing in childhood and their aggressive or violent behavior in adolescence or adulthood. Rowell Huesmann and Leonard Eron have conducted much of this research, and they have consistently reported relationships between watching violent television in early childhood and aggressive behavior many years later (Eron, Huesmann, Lefkowitz, & Walder, 1972, 1996; Huesmann, Lagerspetz, & Eron, 1984; Huesmann & Miller, 1994). In one recent study (Huesmann, Moise-Titus, Podolski, & Eron, 2003) they demonstrated that regularly watching violent television between the ages of 6 and 9 was related to adult physical aggression in both sexes, and indirect (relational) aggression for women, and that the effect was independent of a variety of other factors known to be related to aggression such as social class and intelligence.

The research has also shown that effects of watching televised violence is largest for the youngest children—those under the age of 10 years, and especially those under 6 years. Older children, adolescents, and adults may be somewhat more protected from its effects because of their more sophisticated cognitive skill—they can better interpret the pretend nature of what they are observing. It is also interesting that the research often shows that both boys and girls are equally affected by this violence. Nonetheless, as we know already, boys watch more of televised violence, and they are also more likely to experience other influences that increase aggression.

Cartoon Violence Versus Realistic Violence

Earlier we discussed the difference in the content of violence in children's programs (largely cartoons) as compared to programs designed for adults. Because much of the violence on children's programs is clearly fantasy, rarely results in real harm to the victim, and does not show weapons like guns, why would it be of special concern for its impact on children? The answer is related to the kinds of effects that televised violence can have. In particular, one kind of effect that televised violence has been shown to have is a desensitization to the seriousness of aggression. That is, children may come to believe that aggression is not wrong, and they may become less emotionally aroused or upset by it (Bushman & Huesmann, 2001). Such feelings and beliefs can come to increase the probability that children will behave aggressively themselves and tolerate it in others. When aggression is as prevalent as it is in children's programs, when it is rewarded and not punished, when superheroes do it, when no one is really harmed by it, and when it is shown as being mostly funny or glamorous, the impact on desensitization is believed to be of great concern. There is also reason to believe that young children are most likely to become desensitized by funny or slapstick violence, and older children by seeing superheroes who are rewarded for using violence to save lives (Wilson et al., 2002).

Researchers Conclude That This Is a Real and Serious Issue

As an illustration of how seriously the research community views this issue, six professional societies, the American Academy of Pediatrics, the American Psychological Association, the American Academy of Child and Adolescent Psychiatry, the American Medical Association, the American Academy of Family Physicians, and the American Psychiatric Association recently released a strongly worded joint statement concluding that there is clear evidence of such a relationship:

> At this time, well over 1,000 studies—including reports from the Surgeon General's office, the National Institute of Mental Health, and numerous studies conducted by leading figures within our medical and public health organizations—our own members—point overwhelmingly to a causal connection between media violence and aggressive behavior in some children. The conclusion of the public health community, based on more than 30 years of research, is that viewing entertainment violence can lead to increases in aggressive attitudes, values and behavior, particularly in children. (American Academy of Pediatrics, 2000)

Video games too

There is also evidence of a link between playing violent video games and aggressive behavior. Two reviews, one narrative (Bensley & Van Eenwyk, 2001), and one meta-analysis (Anderson & Bushman, 2001) have both concluded that violence in video games influences children's aggression. As is the case with television, boys' and girls' behavior was affected similarly, but again we know that boys are much more likely to play these games. In the meta-analysis (Anderson & Bushman, 2001), the average effect size (again, correlation) between watching video games and aggressive behavior was .19, between these games and aggressive thoughts was .27, between the games and feelings of anger or hostility was .18, and between the games and measures of physiological arousal such as increased heart rate or blood pressure was .22. Some additional experimental research, conducted after these meta-analyses, has shown that when the characters in the game are rewarded for aggression, rather than punished for it, children's aggressive thoughts and behaviors are especially likely to be increased after playing the game (Anderson et al., 2004; Carnagey & Anderson, 2005). There is clearly much less research on the impact of video games than there is on the impact of television; however, the general view of developmental researchers appears to be moving toward seeing them as having similar effects on aggression.

Violent musical lyrics also seem to have an impact

Although we did not discuss the content of lyrics of the songs listened to by older children and adolescents, this is obviously another form of media to which children are exposed. Music is more complicated than television or video games because people are often doing other things while they listen to music, and the lyrics are sometimes difficult to understand. However, one group of researchers (Anderson, Carnagey, & Eubanks, 2003) reported on five studies of college students who increased in hostility and aggressive thoughts after listening to violent song lyrics. The researchers concluded that such short-term hostility produced by various forms of media exposure could lead to long-term effects by affecting social scripts and expectations about social relationships, and by gradually increasing hostile interactions with others. There is little research to inform us about the extent to which male and female adolescents prefer to (or actually do) listen to these kinds of lyrics. If song lyrics are anything like television and video games, violent ones are possibly more likely to be part of boys' lives than girls', but we do not know that for sure.

Violent toys may also impact aggression

In addition to television, movies, video games, and music, some toys are also violent. We have seen that boys' toys are more violent than girls' toys are, and that boys often enjoy playing with guns, military toys, and action figures. Probably because such toys have existed for centuries and because there are few clear studies about their effects, there is substantial debate about the potential impact of war toys, action figures, and guns on children's behavior (Goldstein, 1998; Smith, 1994). Some suggest that play with such toys is fun for boys, that they easily know the difference between play and real aggression, and that the toys simply fit in with styles of play that already exist (Sutton-Smith, 1988). The other side of the argument is that such toys promote aggression and violence as much as television and video games have been shown to (Varney, 2000).

What is the evidence? There are only a few studies examining the link between such toys and aggressive behavior. Two widely cited, but now somewhat dated, studies have often been used in support of the contention that war toys, guns, and similar toys increase children's tendencies to play aggressively (Potts, Huston, & Wright, 1986; Turner & Goldsmith, 1976). That is, when objects like guns were present, boys in particular played more aggressively. A review of about a dozen studies on this topic (Goldstein, 1995) concluded that play with war toys, guns, and similar toys increases aggressive play but does not increase real aggression—aggressively in other contexts. Of course, it makes good sense that aggressive play would increase in the presence of such toys. Surely children are more likely to show aggression when they play with guns or action figures because these toys clearly are intended to be played with in this way. However, Goldstein also concluded that the evidence about the effect of such toys on increasing aggressive play was limited to boys. That is, there was little evidence that these toys increased girls' aggressive play.

Many parents apparently believe that having toy guns increases children's tendencies to behave aggressively in general, and hence specifically choose not to provide them for their children (Cheng et al., 2003). There are a few studies on this question, but their findings are not consistent. In one such study (Watson & Peng, 1992) preschool children in the United States were observed engaging in either real aggression (e.g., fighting, kicking, biting) or pretend aggression (e.g., having action figures fight, making an object into a toy gun and pretending to shoot it) in free play in their daycare center. Children, especially boys, whose parents reported that they often played with toy guns at home (toy guns were not allowed at the daycare center) engaged in more real aggression, but not more play aggression, when observed at the daycare center. Of course, a study like this is correlational, and it is hard to know whether aggressive boys just do not like gun play more than other children do.

In another study, researchers in Holland (Hellendoorn & Harinck, 1997) observed kindergarten children at school engaging in either play aggression or real aggression. The children were observed in groups of three in a playroom containing both neutral toys and aggressive toys, including guns, swords and shields, fighter planes, space ships, and action figures. This kind of playroom with the presence of war toys at school was a rare event, but once they were reassured that they could play however they wanted in this special room, they did so. Although girls did play with the aggressive toys, boys were much more likely to do so. Real aggression (e.g., snatching toys away, physically assaulting other children) was very rare, and only boys did it.

The researchers examined the factors that related to the amount of play aggression the children showed in the playroom. In addition to the children's sex, there were several other predictors of play aggression, especially the presence of certain play partners. That is, play aggression arose in a social situation, and certain play partners were more likely than others to play in this way. However, there was little evidence in this study that having violent or war toys at home increased aggressive play in these children, and real aggression was too rare to study meaningfully.

So, except for some research that shows that the presence of aggressive toys increases aggressive play as compared with situations in which such toys are not present, there is not a great deal of convincing evidence that having and playing with these kinds of toys increases children's aggression in other situations. However, it is also clear that very little of this kind of research has been done compared with the amount of research that has been done on the impact of television.

One complexity here is that many violent toys available to today's children are linked to violent television programs, so one effect may influence the other. Sanson and Di Muccio (1993) examined this issue in a study. These researchers showed one of two cartoons (or no cartoon) to 60 Australian preschoolers. Neither cartoon had been shown on television in the area for more than a year. One cartoon called *Voltron* was about violent and aggressive outer-space robots, with many different kinds of weapons and themes of good versus evil. The other cartoon, *GummiBears*, was about animated magical bears that engaged in some adventures, chases, and teasing, but were not aggressive. The children were then provided with toy characters that matched those in the cartoons (e.g., Voltron action figures, or plastic and soft toy bears), and their play with the toys was observed. The highest amount of aggressive play was found in the children who watched the aggressive cartoon when they were observed with the action figures associated with that cartoon, so indeed the television exposure and the availability of the toys seemed to work together to increase aggressive play.

The Impact of Media on Gender Development: Conclusions

What then, can we conclude about the impact of children's toys, books, and the media on gender development? Largely because of the interest on the part of many researchers on the impact of television, we know much more about it than we know about toys or books. There is good evidence that children who watch more television have more gender-stereotyped attitudes. Also, young women who watch television and read fashion magazines are especially likely to hold to the ideal that girls and women are more valuable if they are pretty and thin, and there is some evidence of a contribution of these forms of media to eating disorders.

Although there has been much speculation about how children's toys might affect their cognitive skills, little systematic research has shown such a link. There are, however, a few studies suggesting that playing with video games increases children's general computer literacy, and if the games involved spatial manipulation they can increase the children's spatial skills, bringing girls' skills up to the level of boys'.

There are thousands of studies demonstrating the impact of televised violence on aggressive behavior, and on attitudes about the seriousness of aggression. There is even evidence of a small but consistent effect on the kind of aggression that is criminal in nature. Similar conclusions have been reached about the impact of video games. This effect of this type of media portrayal is of particular relevance to boys because they watch more of it, and the aggressive models are almost always male.

CHAPTER SUMMARY

In this chapter we have examined the characteristics of children's books, television, video games, and toys and the effects of these different forms of media on gender development. This research has painted a very consistent picture about the characteristics of the media that today's children are exposed to. Children see and hear more stories, television shows, cartoons, and video games about males. Many of these images are gender stereotyped in many different ways—physical appearance, age, personality characteristics, behaviors, and occupations. Female characters are nicer but also generally more passive and helpless, younger, and have more attention focused on their physical appearance. Male characters are more active and competent, more likely to be the spokespersons for products, and have more occupational roles but are the main participants in aggression and violence.

In recent years stereotyped images in books and television have changed to some degree, but generally only in portraits of girls and women. There are now more competent girls and women in books and on television, but few men are shown engaging in domestic or nurturant activities. It is also very important to point out that, despite these changes, older stereotyped books and television programs are readily available. Children see them all the time.

Children's toys are also gender-stereotyped. Boys are more likely to have vehicles and sports equipment, spatial and temporal toys, video games, and many different kinds of violent and aggressive toys. Boys also have more different kinds of toys and more toys overall. Boys' toys may also be more likely to respond to children's actions by providing feedback. Girls have more dolls, domestic items, and toys that focus on appearance.

Research on the impact of these forms of media has shown that when children see television more frequently they have more stereotyped views about gender. Girls who read fashion magazines are also more likely to have eating disorders or to feel that their appearance is not adequate. Also, there is some evidence that cognitive skills are affected in a positive way by experiences playing certain kinds of video games, especially those with a spatial component.

Finally, there is solid evidence that exposure to media violence, both television and video games, increases aggressive behavior and desensitizes children to the seriousness and potential harm of aggression.

The School as an Agent of Gender Development

13

> This year, the emerging characteristic of my class is that the boys have all the answers, and the girls (with a few exceptions) have none. This is most clear when we are having whole class activities or discussions. No matter how long we wait, the girls, unless compelled, are silent and offer no ideas. (Gallas, 1998, p. 111)

Children spend more time in school than they do anywhere else except at home, so it is certainly reasonable to assume that interactions that take place at school will have an impact on them. When you think of the influence of school on children's development, you probably first think of the academic impact—the curriculum of the school. At school children learn to read, write, and compute, and they learn about literature, history, geography, science, culture, and language. We can refer to this as the **formal curriculum** of the school—the academic subject matter that schools intend to teach to children. For the most part, at least in the industrialized world, the formal curriculum is very similar for children of both sexes. Even so, boys or girls may learn the formal curriculum differently, or they may be taught it differently, or they may be advised or choose to take different types of courses. If that is the case, even experiences with the formal curriculum can influence the process of gender development. But much more takes place in school than educating children in the formal curriculum. Researchers have identified at least three other types of curricula that are part of the school experience: the **informal curriculum**, the **null curriculum**, and the **hidden curriculum** (Koch, 2003). These three curricula are perhaps especially relevant to the process of gender development.

The informal curriculum consists of after-school activities like athletics, cheerleading, drama, student clubs, and student government. These activities take place at school, often at the end of the school day, but are not necessarily directly related to the goal of imparting knowledge of academic subject matter. The hidden curriculum consists of subtle gender-related practices that may take place in classrooms over the years (Koch, 2003). Such practices give children unstated messages about their place in the world of academic work. Students and teachers may not even be overtly aware of these practices, but over time they are likely to impact children's development. For example, if an elementary teacher has boys and girls line up in different lines, or if the teacher assigns them different tasks during classroom activities, or if more boys than girls take advanced placement (AP) classes in the physical sciences or computers, or if more girls take family life classes, these kinds of experiences would be part of the hidden curriculum. Finally, the null curriculum consists of material that is missing from the formal curriculum. From a gender perspective, this would include a focus on males or male experience in subject matter like history or social studies, and a lack of equivalent coverage about the experiences of females in history or in contemporary life (Koch, 2003).

As we consider the impact of school on children's gender development, we will be devoting greater consideration to the impact of the informal, hidden, and null curricula than to the formal curriculum. We will ask to what extent gendered lessons are learned at school and how they are learned.

We begin by considering boys' and girls' behavior and performance in school—their behavior in the classroom, their academic performance, their rates of dropping out of school, and the aspirations they develop for higher education and career choices in school. Following that discussion, we will consider teacher-student interaction in the classroom, one of the most important aspects of the school's hidden curriculum. As another part of the hidden curriculum, we will devote some coverage to the structure of the schools. For example, who are the teachers and does that change the higher one goes in the educational system? Who are the principals, administrators, and superintendents? Does this provide a message to children about the roles of men and women in the educational system? We will also consider the gendered aspects of certain academic subjects, and we will examine some research that has studied how children come to conclude that certain subjects are of more interest to one gender than the other. Finally, we will look at some recommendations for making the school experience equitable for both boys and girls. You may have heard that schools are more advantageous for one gender or the other. We will conclude that there are aspects of interactions that take place in schools that have some advantages and some disadvantages for both boys and girls.

ACADEMIC PERFORMANCE: HOW DO BOYS AND GIRLS PERFORM IN SCHOOL?

In most of the world's modern industrial democracies such as those in North America, Europe, and Australia, girls get better grades in school than boys do, beginning in early elementary school and continuing through university (Foster, Kimmel, & Skelton, 2001; Serbin, Zelkowitz, Doyle, Gold, & Wheaton, 1990; Sutherland, 1999; Younger & Warrington, 1996). The average difference in grades is not very large, and there are plenty of excellent male and not-so-good female students. Also, it is usually the case that the difference between the school performance of boys and girls is larger in elementary school than in high school and beyond (Gorard, Rees, & Salisbury, 1999). Nevertheless, it is clear that, on average, girls get somewhat better grades.

Related to their better academic performance, girls are also less likely to be required to repeat a grade (Koch, 2003), earn higher class ranks, and are now more likely to be awarded academic honors, at least through high school. In high school, girls are more likely to be enrolled in college preparatory programs. Although girls' academic performance is better overall, there are some differences by subject area. For example, boys are more likely to earn awards and honors in math and science, whereas girls are more likely to get overall honors and to earn awards in areas such as writing (Dwyer & Johnson, 1997).

Socioeconomic status is also linked to the relationship between gender and school performance. Although there are relatively small differences in academic performance between middle- and upper-class boys and girls, gender differences in academic performance are especially likely to be found among children of lower socioeconomic status. In general, economically disadvantaged children are more likely to perform poorly in school, but disadvantaged boys are particularly at risk for academic failure, school dropout, and becoming disengaged from academic endeavors (Arnold & Doctoroff, 2003). The difference between the grade-point averages (GPAs) of boys and girls is about 3 times as large among working-class children as among middle-class children (Dwyer & Johnson, 1997), and it gets progressively worse across the years of elementary school (Entwisle, Alexander, & Olson, 2007). In the United States it is especially large among disadvantaged African American children. Although working class or poor African American girls may perform more poorly in school than children from middle-class backgrounds, they do much better in school than working-class or poor African American boys do (Davis, 2001). This pattern of results suggests that teachers ought to be particularly aware of how they might act to improve the academic performance of such children (for some suggestions see Noguera, 2003).

In addition to their higher overall grades, girls are also more anxious about their academic performance, more distressed when they fail, and apparently more focused on pleasing their teachers (Pomerantz, Altermatt, & Saxon, 2002). Therefore their high grades seem to come at a personal cost. Of course there are different kinds of costs for children who are not as interested in doing well or in pleasing their teachers, and more of those children are likely to be boys, especially boys from disadvantaged backgrounds.

The situation is somewhat different when examining standardized tests, which do not always reflect the same relationships to gender that school grades do. You recall that in chapter 4 we discussed differences between boys' and girls' performance on standardized tests. We will not repeat that discussion here, but simply remind you that on average, even though their grades are poorer, boys do especially well in tests measuring mathematical and science performance, whereas girls are especially likely to do well in standardized measures of writing.

Learning Disabilities and Placement in Special Education

Boys are somewhat more likely to be mentally retarded and substantially more likely to be diagnosed with **attention deficit hyperactivity disorder** (ADHD), **conduct disorder**, **oppositional defiant disorder**, and **pervasive developmental disorders** such as **autism**. Children with all of these conditions are among those who are placed in special education programs. There are also special education programs for such conditions such as speech and language disorders, reading disabilities, **dyslexia**, or other learning disabilities. Boys are also more likely to be diagnosed with these conditions (Halpern, 1997; Miles, Haslum, & Wheeler, 1998; Rutter et al., 2004), typically at ratios of from 2:1 to 4:1. Overall, boys are about twice as likely as girls to be placed in special education programs in schools (Tschantz & Markowitz, 2003), and about 4 times as likely to be placed in programs for emotional and behavioral disturbance.

Recently, some researchers who study dyslexia and reading disabilities have come to the conclusion that, although boys are more likely to be diagnosed with and treated for these conditions, girls may be more likely to escape diagnosis (Osman, 2000). Boys who suffer from reading disabilities are more likely to have other conditions such as ADHD or emotional or behavior problems. These other conditions are more likely to bring boys to the attention of teachers who then refer them for assessment and special education services. Because girls with reading disabilities are less likely to act out in ways that are noticed by teachers, they tend to have more serious reading problems before they are referred for help.

COMPLETING HIGH SCHOOL AND CONTINUING ON TO POSTSECONDARY EDUCATION

Boys and Girls in Developed Countries

In recent years, in many developed countries such as those in Europe and North America, girls have been somewhat more likely than boys to complete high school (Sherman, Honegger, McGivern, & Lemke, 2003; Snyder, Dillow, & Hoffman, 2007). Average differences between boys and girls in high school graduation rates are very small and not always reported. Such differences become more noticeable, however, when socioeconomic status is taken into account. Boys and girls whose family background is of middle to upper socioeconomic class are equally likely to graduate from high school and continue on to higher education. It is in the lower socioeconomic classes that girls are more likely than boys to finish high school and continue their educations (Beattie, 2002; Entwisle et al., 2007). Because more girls and women from working class and poor backgrounds are continuing on to higher education than are boys and men from such backgrounds, it is now the case that there are somewhat more women enrolled in higher education overall than men, and that trend is expected to continue through the next decade (Gerald & Hussar, 2003; U.S. Department of Education, 2006). This, of course, is a reversal of previous trends, in which men were the ones who were the more likely to continue in education and to earn college and professional degrees (Snyder et al., 2007). Even though more young women are now entering higher education, the average level of education of women in the population is still lower than that of men when you consider adults across the lifespan. That is simply because in past decades more men earned college and graduate degrees, and of course these people are still members of the adult population.

Differences in College Major and Type of Degree

Although women are now somewhat more likely to pursue higher education, there are still differences as a function of college major and type of degree pursued. The higher the degree pursued (e.g., the Ph.D. compared to the bachelor's degree), the greater the proportion of men relative to women earning the degree. For example, in 2006 in the United States, 62% of the associate's, 57% of the bachelor's, 59% of the master's degrees, and 49% of the doctorates were earned by women (Snyder et al., 2007). As we discussed in chapter 4, men remain more likely to earn graduate degrees in mathematics, engineering, and the physical sciences, and in many of the professions. However, in 2003, for the first time in history, women outnumbered men as applicants to medical school in the United States (The Association of Medical Colleges, 2003). As women become more and more likely to earn college and graduate degrees, it is reasonable to assume that over time, the average educational attainment of women in the population in countries in some Western countries will become somewhat higher than that of men.

Boys and Girls in Developing Countries

Although girls in the developed world are at least as likely as boys to complete high school and are somewhat more likely to continue to postsecondary education, in developing countries the picture is quite different. In most of the developing world, girls and women have less access to education than boys and men do. About two thirds of the illiterate adults in the world are female (Slaughter-Defoe, Addae, & Bell, 2002). Girls and women in the developing world, especially those in rural areas, are often unable to get access to education. This is even the case at the elementary school level, a phenomenon that is essentially unheard of in the Western world because most developed countries have universal compulsory education. But in the developing world, especially in rural Asia and Africa, girls in particular may never receive any formal education or drop out of school at very young ages (Slaughter-Defoe et al., 2002). There is often little support for families that would like to receive educations for their daughters, as well as prevalent attitudes that an education will make a girl less marriageable. Indeed, many in the Western world were horrified when we learned that girls in Afghanistan under the Taliban were not permitted to go to school at all (Schulz & Schulz, 1999), and that adults who risked educating girls in private might be punished very severely if they were to be discovered. Although this situation was clearly extreme, Afghanistan is by no means the only place in the world where girls have difficulty achieving even a basic education.

The education of girls in the developing world is a very important issue, not just for gender equity. An increase in education for girls affects the entire society. Educated girls are more able to understand public health information, more likely to use contraception, to delay childbearing, and to treat their children in ways that enhance the children's health and development. In fact, research in the developing world suggests that the education of girls is one of the most important factors in reducing rates of poverty and child mortality world wide (LeVine, LeVine, & Schnell, 2001; Slaughter-Defoe et al., 2002).

Completing Education: Conclusions

To conclude, in the developed world, compulsory education is essentially universal, and both boys and girls have equal access to education. In such settings, girls have been found to perform somewhat better than boys, especially when the children come from less advantaged backgrounds. Today in North American and Europe, girls are somewhat more likely to graduate from high school and to continue into postsecondary education, although the differences are not very large and are highly related to social class.

In the developing world, the situation is quite different. There, many more girls than boys have difficulty having access to education, even in being able to gain the lowest levels of basic literacy.

BEHAVIOR AND ATTITUDES

Classroom Behavior

Karen Gallas, an elementary teacher, has written extensively about her experiences with boys' and girls' behavior in the classroom (Gallas, 1997, 1998). A quote from her work can be found at the beginning of this chapter. She refers to "bad boys" and "silent girls" as a description of a common set of gendered behaviors of children in the elementary classroom. Clearly not all children behave the same way at school, and that is true of both boys and girls. However, the two "types" do seem to resonate with many classroom teachers, and have certainly been reported by other researchers (Morgan & Dunn, 1988).

The "bad" boys Gallas describes are invariably seen as "cool." They are generally White, attractive, and socially skilled. Their "badness" comes from their constant attempts to be in power—the ones in charge of the classroom. They disrupt the ongoing activity, often by calling attention to themselves or by refusing to do as the teacher asks. Gallas says that their behavior is often disrespectful and offensive. She describes one of the bad boys, Tony:

> He refuses to participate in group discussions and harasses student teachers, music teachers, art teachers, gym teachers, and substitutes in a number of increasingly subtle ways. He sits in the back of the group, talking softly to his friend, ignoring requests to be quiet, turning his body away from a teacher when he is addressed. (Gallas, 1994, p. 58)

Gallas argues that these boys are always trying to maintain the upper hand—to be in charge of the social interaction. They behave disruptively and disrespectfully, and when they do they gain power and status, especially in the eyes of other boys. She thinks that such boys sense that, by her role, the teacher is of higher status than they are, and that they are always trying to diminish her status (Gallas, 1998). But, she argues, such behavior cuts these boys off from engagement in learning and thinking, and from a sense of community with the others in the classroom. This is a very interesting analysis, because it suggests that boys who achieve high status in their peer groups may carry their dominance-oriented behavior into the classroom, and that this behavior can lessen these boys' ability to profit from the educational environment.

Many researchers and classroom observers discuss the misbehavior of boys as being a common problem in schools. Some even report that girls are annoyed and distracted by such misbehavior, although one might assume that any serious student would find it annoying. Consider the remarks of this English schoolgirl:

> The boys are a nightmare at the moment. We don't get any work done in the lessons because the teachers barely get a chance to set the work before they're throwing people out of the classrooms and trying to make them shut up, putting them in detentions and sending them to the year office. Teachers tend to spend most of their time sorting out the disruptive ones rather than generally going round the classroom. It's better for learning if you've got the quieter class, I think. (Warrington & Younger, 2000, p. 500)

In another interesting analysis of classroom behavior, this time in a group of 7 year olds in a predominantly working class school in England, Reay (2001) discusses how the working class boys in the class had already started in the path of alienation from schoolwork, and focused much more on football and peer relationships. They frequently labeled girls as "stupid" or "dumb," partly in an attempt to gain status in the eyes of their male peers. In another illustration of the importance of social class, the two middle class boys in the classroom were much more likely to value academic work, although one of them was also very involved in sports. This latter boy was the most popular child in the classroom.

The girls, she found, fell into four different groups: "'the nice girls', the 'girlies,' the 'spice girls,' and the 'tomboys'" (Reay, 2001, p. 158). The nice girls were well behaved and worked hard in school, although they were more anxious and critical about their own behavior and schoolwork than were other children. The girlies observed by Reay were actively feminine girls who were especially concerned with hetero-sexual relationships. They spent their time discussing boyfriends and girlfriends, with writing love let-ters, and flirting with boys (recall that these are 7 year olds). The good girls and the girlies were frequent targets of harassment by boys, but the good girls avoided such harassment as much as possible by staying away from the boys who might be expected to torment them. The girls that Reay labeled spice girls were said to have attitude, and were sometimes seen by the classroom teacher as bad girls and not very nice. They were often quite assertive with boys. Her final group of girls was labeled tomboys. These were girls who were more interested in playing boys' games, and generally avoiding and denigrating the feminine.

One important point, served by this illustration, is that all girls and boys in classrooms are not alike. Certainly, there are individual differences in the behavior and interests of children of both sexes. However, we can still see the general trends of well-behaved girls who do well in school but who raise no waves, and boys who misbehave, who dislike schoolwork, and who seem to be drawn away from their work by peer groups and other interests.

Truancy and Misconduct

The bad boys that we have already discussed are not necessarily engaging in serious misconduct, but there are other children who do. It is not very likely a surprise when we tell you that the majority of these children are boys. As we have already discussed, boys are more likely to have conditions like oppositional defiant and conduct disorder, and more likely to engage in criminal and delinquent behavior. The behav-iors associated with these conditions certainly can manifest themselves in schools, and when they do, boys are more likely to engage in them. One special school-related delinquent behavior is truancy, and boys are disproportionately represented among the students who are truant from school in the United States, although the gender differential in truancy is not as large as it is for more serious delinquent offenses (Puzzanchera, Stahl, Finnegan, Tierney, & Snyder, 2003).

Not surprisingly, because they are more likely to misbehave, boys are also more likely to be punished, including receiving such sanctions as detentions or suspensions. This trend interacts with ethnicity and social class. Poorer children are more likely to be punished than children who come from more advan-taged backgrounds, boys are more likely to be punished than girls, and minority children are more likely to be punished than White children. These factors combine to produce the highest rate of punishments for children who have all three characteristics—in the United States, African American males, especially in urban school districts. These boys have been found to be suspended from school much more than other groups, even for fairly minor offenses such as disobedience. For example, in one study in Florida, almost 50% of the Black males in middle school had been suspended at least once, as compared to about 30% of the Black females, 25% of the White males, and 10% of the White females (Mendez & Knoff, 2003). There are similar findings for higher levels of misbehavior and punishment for boys, especially disadvan-taged and ethnic minority boys, in other Western democracies such as Australia and the United Kingdom (Foster et al., 2001; Meyenn & Parker, 2001).

Attitudes About School

Earlier in this chapter, we noted that girls are more likely to be anxious about performing poorly in school (Pomerantz et al., 2002). Girls have also been found to enjoy school and schoolwork more than boys do (Gentry, Gable, & Rizza, 2002), especially beyond the elementary years. Girls are also more likely than boys to think that school is fair, that teachers treat other children equitably, that they themselves are treated fairly at school, and that teachers are genuinely concerned about them (Nichols & Good, 1998). Looking at the issue from the other side, boys have been found to be more often alienated from school, not to like it, and to devalue educational endeavors (Trusty & Dooley-Dickey, 1993). This kind of alienation is not very common in elementary school, increases in the middle school years, and continues into high school. Such attitudes are of course related to poor academic performance, and predict the probability of dropping out of school. As we know already, boys are more likely to do very poorly in school and to eventually drop out.

The Role of Peers in Boys' Attitudes About School

There are some groups of boys whose peer interactions are an important source of this sense of alienation from school. Peer interactions among certain groups of boys (perhaps especially those from disadvantaged and from minority backgrounds, but others too) lead some boys away from being engaged in and committed to getting a good education. In fact, there is research that suggests that one important contribution to the low academic performance of boys from disadvantaged backgrounds is the general ecology of their environments, schools, neighborhoods, and peer relationships.

One recent study demonstrates how very important these factors are. These researchers (Leventhal & Brooks-Gunn, 2004) followed poor children and adolescents for three years to examine the impact of neighborhoods and schools on these children's academic performance. The children were part of a New York city project in which families either remained in their poverty-ridden neighborhoods, were given vouchers to move to other housing of their choice (usually also in poor neighborhoods), or were given vouchers that required them to move to neighborhoods that had few other poor families (low poverty housing). Boys in the third group improved their academic performance so that it was equal to that of girls in all three groups, and better than boys in the other two groups. The researchers investigated several potential influences on the boys' increased achievement in the low poverty neighborhoods, and found two factors in particular that were important: the boys spent more time doing homework than the boys in the other two groups, and their schools were safer. The researchers suggested that male adolescents, in particular, are probably especially vulnerable to the impact of physical threat at school. Clearly, neighborhood and school characteristics are a very important part of the peer environment that impacts on the academic performance of disadvantaged boys in particular.

To conclude, boys are much more likely than girls to misbehave in the classroom, and to engage in serious misconduct at school. Boys are also more likely to find the school environment unsupportive and to believe that teachers treat them unfairly. Girls, on the other hand, find their treatment at school to be fair, and are more likely than boys to enjoy school. In the classroom, they are more likely to behave in line with the teacher's desires for them, but also more likely to be silent and unnoticed, and to find aspects of school anxiety-invoking.

Boys' and Girls' Aspirations and Career Choices

The major purpose of going to school is to get an education so that a child can take his or her place in adult life. There is no doubt that, decades ago, boys and girls developed widely different career goals and plans for their futures as they were going through the educational system. Boys planned to be firefighters, police officers, plumbers, factory workers, attorneys, physicians, and engineers. Girls planned to become teachers, nurses, secretaries, hairdressers, and above all wives and mothers, as opposed to having a career or job outside the home at all. What about today?

In one fairly recent study (Bobo, Hildreth, & Durodoye, 1998) the researchers asked more than 1,500 elementary school children in Texas what they wanted to be when they grew up. The sample was ethnically diverse, and the researchers reported on the career choices of Anglo (White), African American, and Hispanic boys and girls from first through sixth grade. The children listed almost 100 different career choices, and about half the careers (45) were listed by children of both sexes (e.g., doctor, teacher, banker, singer, scientist). Boys listed 56 career choices that no girls mentioned (e.g., jockey, broker, CEO, truck driver, fireman), and girls listed 51 careers not chosen by any boys (e.g., mother, nurse, cosmetologist, writer, nun). So, clearly although there was a great deal of overlap in the careers chosen by both sexes, plenty of gender stereotypes remained. It should also be noted that girls were much more interested in adopting traditionally masculine career choices than boys were interested in adopting traditionally feminine career choices. Again we see that change in gender roles is much more likely for girls than for boys. The top career choices of children of the different ethnicities in various grades can be seen in Table 13.1.

TABLE 13.1 Top Career Choices of Children by Grade, Sex, and Ethnicity

1st grade boys			
Ethnicity	**Anglo**	**African American**	**Hispanic**
	Police officer	Athlete	Police officer
	Doctor	Police officer	Athlete
	Athlete	Teacher	Fireman
1st grade girls			
Ethnicity	**Anglo**	**African American**	**Hispanic**
	Teacher	Teacher	Teacher
	Doctor	Nurse	Singer
	Nurse	Dancer	Doctor
2nd grade boys			
Ethnicity	**Anglo**	**African American**	**Hispanic**
	Police officer	Athlete	Police officer
	Fireman	Police officer	Teacher
	Athlete	Doctor	Doctor
2nd grade girls			
Ethnicity	**Anglo**	**African American**	**Hispanic**
	Teacher	Teacher	Teacher
	Nurse	Nurse	Nurse
	Veterinarian	Doctor	Doctor
3rd grade boys			
Ethnicity	**Anglo**	**African American**	**Hispanic**
	Athlete	Athlete	Athlete
	Police officer	Police officer	Police officer
	Doctor	Doctor	Fireman
3rd grade girls			
Ethnicity	**Anglo**	**African American**	**Hispanic**
	Teacher	Teacher	Teacher
	Nurse	Nurse	Nurse
	Doctor	Doctor	Ice skater
4th grade boys			
Ethnicity	**Anglo**	**African American**	**Hispanic**
	Athlete	Athlete	Doctor
	Doctor	Police officer	Police officer
	Military	Doctor	Teacher
4th grade girls			
Ethnicity	**Anglo**	**African American**	**Hispanic**
	Teacher	Teacher	Teacher
	Veterinarian	Nurse	Doctor
	Lawyer	Singer	Nurse

(continued)

TABLE 13.1   *(Continued)*

5th grade boys

Ethnicity	Anglo	African American	Hispanic
	Athlete	Athlete	Athlete
	Doctor	Truck driver	Police officer
	Pilot	Doctor	

5th grade girls

Ethnicity	Anglo	African American	Hispanic
	Teacher	Doctor	Teacher
	Doctor	Teacher	Doctor
	Veterinarian	Lawyer	Fashion designer

6th grade boys

Ethnicity	Anglo	African American	Hispanic
	Athlete	Athlete	Athlete
	Doctor	Doctor	Police officer
	Military	Police officer	

6th grade girls

Ethnicity	Anglo	African American	Hispanic
	Teacher	Lawyer	Lawyer
	Lawyer	Nurse	Teacher
	Doctor	Doctor	Doctor

Source: Bobo, M. et al., *Professional School Counseling*, 1, 37–42, 1998. Adapted from Tables 1 and 2, pp. 39–40. With permission.

Other research confirms that children often make gendered career choices, and that they judge certain careers as more suitable for males than for females (Liben, Bigler, & Krogh, 2001). Certain jobs and careers (e.g., nursing, teaching and childcare, clerical work, and work in food services) remain female dominated, whereas others (e.g., fire fighting, construction, mechanics) remain predominantly male (Wooten, 1997), and children are aware of that fact. The physical sciences and engineering also remain male dominated. Although older girls become less stereotyped in their attitudes about career choices than are younger girls, and less stereotyped than boys are, they are still more concerned than are boys about working in fields that help people (Helwig, 2002), and in developing career choices that will be able to be combined with devoting time to children and family. In fact, overall, girls are more likely to consider many different kinds of adult roles than are boys, as they pursue their educational and career goals (Wigfield, Battle, Keller, & Eccles, 2002).

TREATMENT OF BOYS AND GIRLS BY TEACHERS

If you asked teachers if they treat their male and female students differently, they are likely to say that they do not, or at least that they try not to. Or, if they recognize that boys and girls often do receive different treatment, they might argue that it arises out of the children's behavior. For example, they may say that boys misbehave more, and hence receive more reprimands or punishments, but that it is not their intention to treat boys differently from girls. The research findings we will discuss suggest that the situation is more complex than this simple analysis suggests. Teachers are often unaware that they treat boys and girls differently. Also, some of the differential treatment comes months before the children begin to behave differently, suggesting that teachers' treatment contributes to the differences in children's behavior, rather than simply resulting from it.

Preschool Children

Let us look at one short-term longitudinal study done several years ago by Beverly Fagot and her colleagues (Fagot, Hagan, Leinbach, & Kronsberg, 1985). At the beginning of this study, the children were about 13 months old. Of course, this is well before the age that children even attend elementary school, but we can certainly see this study as relevant to children's experiences in preschool or daycare. In this study the children attended 2-hour group sessions twice a week for about a year, and were observed several times over the period. Each group of about 15 children was coordinated by three or four preschool teachers, about a quarter of whom were male.

The researchers observed the young children's attempts to communicate with the teachers, as well as their assertive and aggressive behaviors. They also observed the teachers' responses to the children's behavior. At the beginning of the study, the young children's behavior was similar—the boys and girls were similar in their degree of aggression, and in their frequency and types of communication with the teachers. A year later, there were differences in the boys' and girls' behavior. By age 2, the boys were more aggressive (e.g., grabbing, hitting, pushing, kicking), and were more likely to communicate with the teacher in negative ways (e.g., whining, crying, and screaming), whereas the 2-year-old girls were more likely to simply talk to the teacher than the boys were, as well as being less likely to behave aggressively.

The most striking aspect of this study was the teachers' differential responses to the boys' and girls' behavior early in the study, at the age when the children's behavior was essentially identical. Teachers were more likely to respond to girls when they talked to them, or when they made communicative gestures or touched the teachers softly. When the girls were responded to for these behaviors, it was typically positive in tone (e.g., talking, hugging, smiling, or praising). When the girls were assertive or aggressive, or when they whined, screamed, and cried, the teachers typically ignored them. For example, they responded to about 10% of the girls' assertive behaviors, as compared to about 40% of the boys' assertive behaviors. Boys, on the other hand, were more likely to be responded to when they were assertive or aggressive, and when they cried and whined; however, their gentle attempts at communication were more often ignored by the adults. When boys behaved aggressively or angrily the teachers often scolded them, or at least moved them to another part of the room to distract them.

So the pattern we see from this study is this: At a very early age, boys and girls were behaving similarly, but teachers responded differently to boys' and girls' identical behaviors. Girls were more likely to experience a teacher who was supportive and affectionate to them when they talked or gestured to her, but who ignored them when they acted up. Boys were more likely to experience a teacher who ignored their gentle attempts at communication, but who scolded them when they were aggressive or whiny. A year later, following this differential treatment, the 2-year-old boys and girls were behaving differently— the girls were more likely just to talk, and the boys to be aggressive and to cry and scream. We cannot necessarily assume that the change in the children's behavior over the course of the year of the study was due only to the teachers' responses to them, but it is certainly reasonable to assume that it contributed. It simply fits the general principles of learning that when behavior is responded to (even with scolding), it typically increases, and when it is ignored (or extinguished), it tends to go away. That is exactly what seemed to happen here.

Another early study examined preschool children who were a little older than those Fagot and her colleagues studied (Serbin, O'Leary, Kent, & Tonick, 1973). Serbin and her fellow researchers looked at the behavior of teachers of 3- to 5-year-old children in 15 different preschool classrooms. Like Fagot and her colleagues, they reported that teachers were more likely to respond to boys' aggression with loud reprimands, and to ignore such behavior in girls. For example, all of the teachers responded more frequently to aggression on the part of boys, on average three times as often. Again, consider that because boys' disruptive behavior gets teacher attention (even though the attention is in the form of a reprimand) this is a pattern that is likely to maintain or increase boys' disruptive behavior. Serbin and her colleagues also reported that boys were more likely to be responded to in general, but there was also a relationship between gender and how close the children were to the teacher. Girls received more teacher attention when they were close to the teacher as compared to when they were farther away from her, whereas the amount of attention boys received was not related to how close they were to the teacher.

Boys were also more likely to receive several different types of instruction from the teacher. They received brief direction (about 8 times per hour for boys, as compared to about 4 times an hour for girls), extended conversation (about 5 times per hour for boys; 2 times for girls), and extended direction about such topics as how to do things for themselves (about 2 times an hour for boys, and less than once per hour for girls) more frequently. When asked, the teachers were aware that they were reprimanding boys more loudly and more frequently, but they were not aware of the other differences.

The pattern in this study, then, suggested that boys were more likely to receive attention for disruptive behavior, and were more likely to receive instruction of a type that would help them learn to do things on their own. Girls, on the other hand, were more likely to be ignored unless they were close to a teacher (thus reinforcing their dependence on her), and less likely to receive any of several different types of instruction that would eventually promote their personal competence and independence.

Recent research looking at preschool children continues to find similar things. Boys receive more teacher attention overall, more instruction, and are more often given attention for behaving aggressively. Much of the attention given to young boys arises out of their greater tendency to misbehave, thus girls are more likely to experience interactions with teachers that are more positive or rewarding in tone (Dobbs, Arnold, & Doctoroff, 2004). One recent study of preschoolers also found that girls and boys were addressed differently (e.g., girls called "cutie," or "cuddle bug," and boys called "bud," or "little worm"), and provided with different toys and activities. Appearance was commented on more often for girls (e.g., "your hair looks very pretty") and strength and size for boys (Chick, Heilman-Houser, & Hunter, 2002).

Elementary and High School Students

Discipline, Feedback, and Instruction

Once they move on to elementary and high school, children continue to be treated differently by teachers. Some of this different treatment arises out of the fact that boys and girls behave differently, but not all of it does. If you have read stories in newspapers or magazines about the treatment of boys and girls in school, those reports probably referred to a couple of very influential reports. One was a report produced by the American Association of University Women (AAUW), titled: *How Schools Shortchange Girls* (American Association of University Women Educational Foundation, 1995), and the other is one of several reports about the research of Myra and David Sadker, which actually served as much of the basis for the AAUW report. The Sadkers have summarized the findings of their research in several articles (e.g., Sadker, 1999, 2000, 2002; Sadker, Sadker, Fox, & Salata, 1994), and in their book *Failing at Fairness: How America's Schools Shortchange Girls* (Sadker & Sadker, 1994).

The Sadkers have observed teachers' interactions with their students in more than a hundred different classrooms, usually in elementary schools. As a result of these observations, they reported several different ways that boys and girls are treated by teachers. The most noticeable difference that they report is that boys receive a great deal more of the teacher's attention than girls do. In the Sadkers' own words:

> The classroom consists of two worlds: one of boys in action, the other of girls' inaction. Male students control classroom conversation. They ask and answer more questions. They receive more praise for the intellectual quality of their ideas. They get criticized. They get help when they're confused. They are the heart and center of the interaction. (Sadker & Sadker, 1994, p. 42)

The Sadkers reported that boys squirm and wiggle in their seats and call out answers out of turn. Teachers often attempt to maintain a "raise your hand before you speak" rule, but boys apparently often break it, and shout replies to the teacher's questions. When girls call out answers out of turn, they are much more likely to be reprimanded for breaking the rule than when boys do the same thing.

For example, the Sadkers reported a scene in which four boys in a row were permitted to speak without first raising their hand, and when a girl did the same thing, she was told: "Okay, Kimberly. But you forgot the rule. You're supposed to raise your hand." (Sadker & Sadker, 1994, p. 43). They suggest that one such experience is not likely to have a major effect on Kimberly. They argue though, that this experience is much more likely to happen to girls repeatedly day-after-day, week-after-week, and year-after-year as they progress through the educational system. In their observations, boys called out about eight times as frequently as girls did, sometimes with responses that had little to do with the academic issue at hand. Nonetheless, teachers typically responded to the boys' comments. The Sadkers call this situation "an invitation to male dominance" in the classroom (Sadker & Sadker, 1994, p. 42).

The Sadkers also note that sometimes teachers take a long time before they respond to a student who is raising a hand politely in order to receive the teacher's attention. They describe situations in which boys raise their hands way up, wiggling and waving them in the air, and making noises like "Oooh, me, call on me," as compared to girls who raise their hands bent at the elbow in a tentative, and more uncertain gesture. Given these different styles, perhaps it is not terribly surprising that boys are likely to be grabbing the lion's share of the teacher's attention.

In addition to commanding the teacher's attention much more frequently, the Sadkers (1994, p. 54) also note that boys and girls receive different kinds of teacher feedback and instruction. They divide teacher responses into four types: praise, remediation (e.g., "check your addition"), criticism (e.g., "no, that's not correct") or even harsher criticism (e.g., "this is a terrible report"), and acceptance (e.g., a brief response such as "okay"). They report that both praise and criticism are rather uncommon, with praise happening about 10% of the time, and criticism about 5%. They find that many teachers never use either praise or criticism at all.

One of the most beneficial forms of teacher interaction, in their view, is remediation, which happens about one third of the time. Through remediation students can learn what they are doing wrong, and how to improve. The Sadkers reported that, although boys received more of all four categories of teacher interaction, they were especially more likely to receive "the most precise and valuable feedback" (Sadker & Sadker, 1994, p. 55). In their observations, they found that boys were more likely to be praised, corrected, helped, and criticized, whereas girls were more likely to be simply told "okay," a type of response that, in the Sadker's words "packs far less educational punch" (Sadker & Sadker, 1994, p. 55). Interestingly, teachers who observe videotapes of classroom interactions in which these patterns are made visible to them, often report that they do not want to criticize girls' work, in case the girls get upset by the criticism. In the words of one teacher "I let girls off the hook because they get so embarrassed when they're wrong" (Orenstein, 1995, p. 20). Male teachers in particular, seem not to want to hurt their female students' feelings, or to make them cry (Fennema, 1990).

So, we can see here an interesting pattern, in which boys get much more teacher attention, but the attention is not all negative. In other words, it is not just the case that this teacher attention is simply a desperate attempt to make boys behave themselves—it involves instruction as well. Have other researchers found similar things? Indeed they have.

One meta-analysis some years ago (Kelly, 1988) examined 81 different studies of gender differences in teacher-student interaction. Kelly looked at total interaction, praise for the quality of academic work, the appearance (e.g., neatness) of the work, and for behavior, as well as at criticism for those three categories. She also examined instruction given by the teacher to the children. In the meta-analysis, Kelly divided the children into various socioeconomic and ethnic groups, as well as in terms of their academic ability or performance. She included research from the United States, Canada, the United Kingdom, Australia, and Sweden.

Kelly reported consistently more interaction on the part of teachers with boys, but the difference was not very large—56% of interactions with boys, and 44% with girls. However, she argues that even this degree of difference could add up over the years of a child's schooling:

> But if this is worked out over the length of a child's school career, say 15,000 hours, it means that 1,800 more hours have been spent with boys than with girls....This is a considerable discrepancy, and one that deserves to be taken seriously by the teaching profession." (Kelly, 1988, p. 13)

Kelly also reported that girls were as likely to volunteer to participate, but that teachers were more likely to respond to boys, probably at least partly because of boys' greater tendency to demand such response.

In addition to finding that boys gained more attention period, Kelly also reported that boys received slightly more praise, more criticism for their behavior, and more academic criticism than girls did. Boys also received more instruction and more "high-level" questions. Kelly also reported that male teachers in particular were less likely to interact with female students, and virtually never criticized their academic work.

There are several other studies, in many different developed countries across the world in both elementary and secondary schools showing the same thing—that boys and girls are treated differently by teachers, with boys generally receiving more reprimands, more attention of all kinds, more feedback focused on their performance if they fail to do well (as opposed to their ability), and more feedback of a type that is likely to develop greater autonomy in academic tasks (Becker, 1981; Duffy, Warren, & Walsh, 2001; Lindroos, 1995; Okpala, 1996; Tsouroufli, 2002; Younger, Warrington, & Williams, 1999). It is also the case that certain kinds of disruptive or questioning behavior are consistently permitted or ignored in boys, but reprimanded in girls. Although these types of responses have been found in teachers of both sexes, some researchers have suggested that it is especially difficult for male teachers to tolerate girls who question the teacher's authority, and that such girls are routinely disliked by teachers in a way that similarly behaving boys are not (e.g., Robinson, 1992). Finally, several researchers have noted that girls receive more compliments from teachers about their appearance (e.g., hairstyles, jewelry, clothing) and messages about how pretty they are than do boys.

Some boys are punished more than others

We have already discussed the fact that minority boys, and boys who perform poorly in school often do not like school, and are more likely to think that they are unfairly treated there. Boys as a group clearly receive more of teachers' anger and punishments, and this is part of the reason for why children often think that school is a harsher environment for boys. Keep in mind, though, that some boys are more likely to receive this anger and punishment than other boys are. In the United States, African American boys have been found to have particularly difficult relationships with teachers in this regard (Davis, 2001). Boys who experience high levels of teacher punishment and school failure are the most likely group of any children to drop out of school, and clearly are at risk for failure in their adult lives as a result. As a group, girls like school better, and teachers appreciate girls' hard work and cooperativeness (Jussim & Eccles, 1995). Hence, many if not most of the interactions that girls have with teachers are pleasant and emotionally supportive.

Teachers' Interactions in Different Academic Subjects: Math in Particular

In addition to general treatment differences, some studies have found differences in teacher behavior dependent on academic subject matter. Mathematics instruction in particular has been found to be substantially more supportive, responsive, and autonomy-granting to male students. For example, in one series of observations in several advanced geometry classes (Becker, 1981), students were being taught to develop the ability to do their own proofs. One important type of teacher interaction in such a context stimulates students to keep trying until they are able to solve the problem on their own. Ten different teachers were being observed, and all of them gave more of this kind of encouragement to boys.

In particular, they were willing to keep trying and encouraging a boy until he could do it on his own. Becker observed that about 75% of these kinds of interactions went to male students and gave an extreme example of a teacher devoting 15 minutes of class time to a male student working through such a problem at the board with the teacher asking questions and giving him hints and clues while the rest of the class watched. Interestingly, the boys in these advanced math classes were not the sort who were likely to misbehave, so they were not getting attention for that reason. However, the teachers commented that they thought math was important to these boys' futures, and they needed to be encouraged to learn how to do it on their own. They seemed to think that girls do well because they turn in neat, well-done work, and that it is easy to ignore a well-behaved girl who sits quietly and does what is asked of her.

Not all teachers treat boys and girls differently of course. In one observation of several different high school mathematics classes, Koehler (1990) reports on an interesting contrast between two different honors math classes. Both were small classes with female teachers, with similar numbers of boys and girls in the class. Both teachers were good classroom managers, very effective teachers, and maintained high expectations for the students' performance. In one of the classes, the boys did better than the girls, whereas in the other class the girls' performance was similar to the boys', and equal to that of the boys in the first class. In other words, it was the girls who were more affected by the two different teachers. Koehler wondered why, so she examined more subtle differences between the classes.

In one of the classes (labeled Class B), the teacher provided more opportunity for the students to seek her help, and was very encouraging and helpful when they did so. In Class A, there was less in-class opportunity for help-seeking, and the teacher did not actively walk around the room and solicit questions when students were working on their problems. In other words, she was somewhat less approachable, and the students were more often forced to figure out how to do the work on their own.

Now of course, many of us might like the idea of a more helpful and approachable teacher, but it was in Teacher A's class that the girls did better. Koehler speculated that the reason was that because they were forced to work on their own, this was likely to help them to develop the ability to develop as autonomous or independent learners, especially in a subject like mathematics, which depends so much on the development of comprehension and specific skills. Students who are given too much help may not develop these skills for themselves. She argues that, in general, the kind of teacher treatment that girls typically receive leads to their being less likely to develop this kind of autonomy. This does, in fact, fit with the general pattern of results that we have already discussed.

Teacher Attitudes

There is also research that gives us something of an idea about why teachers seem to treat boys and girls differently. Teachers certainly express the view that boys are more difficult to control, and that they misbehave more frequently (Okpala, 1996). They even endorse different kinds of discipline for the same misbehavior in young boys and girls; preferring consequences or punishment for boys' misbehavior, and a more "contractual" process for girls' misbehavior, in which the child is given a role in deciding how to improve (Erden & Wolfgang, 2004).

We have already seen that teachers sometimes seem to think that boys have the capacity to do more original or high level work, if only they would just work harder (Shepardson & Pizzini, 1992; Warrington & Younger, 2000). Girls, on the other hand, are thought to get good grades at least partly because they do work hard and turn in neat, well-done assignments. Such attitudes about boys versus girls are found especially about mathematics (Fennema, 1990; Jussim & Eccles, 1992; McKown & Weinstein, 2002). In other words, teachers may find it more of a struggle to control boys' behavior, but they often express more positive attitudes about their inherent intellectual capacity, especially in math.

Teacher Treatment: Summary

How can we sum up the state of affairs for boys and girls in schools? It looks like there are benefits and problems for both sexes, but we need to keep in mind that all boys and all girls are not alike. Boys who struggle in school both academically and behaviorally, do seem to experience an especially negative environment at school. Girls who struggle academically are less likely to be at the very bottom of the academic heap, and also less likely to act out behaviorally. For them, school may not be the most supportive environment, but it clearly is not usually as unpleasant as it is for boys who perform poorly. Boys who excel academically and who have no behavior problems at school appear to have an especially supportive and nurturing environment in which to develop autonomous academic skills. Academically talented girls do not seem to have the same degree of support. If they are quiet and well behaved, they may be more likely to be ignored. When they struggle with demanding material, teachers may be more likely to provide assistance rather than insisting that they come to a solution on their own. If girls call out answers and are outgoing and questioning, teachers are more likely to stifle this kind of independence than they are with similarly behaving boys. One way to summarize this state of affairs is to conclude that school appears to be the least supportive of boys at the bottom and girls at the top of the academic ladder.

The Impact of Teachers' Treatment of Boys and Girls

What impact might teacher attitudes and behavior have on boys and girls? One obvious concern is that children who experience a harsh and punitive environment at school are not very likely ever to value academic work or to reach their academic potential. This issue is clearly one of gender, race, and social class, because this state of affairs is most likely to affect boys, particularly boys from disadvantaged ethnic minority backgrounds.

What about the impact of different kinds of teacher feedback on children's conceptions of their academic ability? Here we would like especially to examine the research of Carol Dweck and her colleagues. Dweck (2002a) has pointed out that very young children do not have well-developed conceptions of their abilities, that such conceptions take time to develop, and that they develop in a social context. Children come to construct ideas about the nature of ability and about their own strengths and weaknesses. Dweck also points out that the beliefs the child eventually constructs have implications for the child's motivation to work on certain tasks. For example, if a child comes to conclude that she does not have any ability in a particular domain, and that there is nothing she can do about her lack of ability, she is not likely to be very motivated to work hard or to excel in that field.

Mastery-Oriented and Helpless Children

Dweck and her colleagues have identified two motivational styles in children: a **mastery-oriented** style, and a **helpless** style (Burhans & Dweck, 1995; Dweck, 2002a). The difference between these styles is most critical when the children experience failure, and in what that failure implies to the child. When they fail, mastery-oriented children typically assume that they failed because they did not work hard enough. Failure means to them that they need to develop better strategies, to develop ways to understand the material better, go back to a lower level and relearn the material before proceeding, or to exert more effort. Helpless children assume that failure means that they lack ability and that nothing can be done to fix their lack of ability. Such a child may believe that ability or intelligence is fixed, and that one either has it or one does not. Dweck calls this an **entity theory of intelligence or ability**. Helpless children tend to believe that needing to work hard at something means that you must not have that ability—that having ability means that subject matter will come easily to you. Mastery-oriented children are more likely to believe that with hard work they can improve their ability in some area. Dweck calls this belief about ability the **incremental theory of ability**. Such children are also more likely to recognize that some domains require hard work no matter how much ability one has.

The beliefs that children develop have an impact on how they deal with academic failure. Helpless children are more likely to give up on an academic subject in the face of failure, whereas mastery-oriented children are more likely to be motivated to work even harder when they fail. Interestingly, these motivational patterns are not clearly tied to previous academic performance—some very good students believe that failure means that they lack ability, whereas some students whose previous performance has not been exceptional show mastery-oriented beliefs. It should be clear that the most serious implication of such beliefs is related to developing motivation to work even harder when one finds something difficult, or when one experiences failure, versus simply giving up at the first sign that this will not be an easy task.

Dweck and her colleagues have also identified two different kinds of achievement goals: **performance goals** and **learning goals**. Essentially, performance goals involve avoiding failure and "looking smart." Such children would probably be most interested in earning a good grade. Learning goals are less concerned with "looking smart," and more concerned with acquiring useful knowledge or skills. Naturally, most good students have some concern about their grades, and of course there are domains in which it is reasonable to think that people do have differing degrees of ability, so this is a matter of degree. But children with a learning goal would be more expected to be concerned about whether they learned something from the experience, and whether their skills improved. Dweck has also found that focusing on performance goals tends to be associated with a helpless orientation, partly because getting a good grade implies to the children that they are smart, as well as documenting it to others. Children who focus on learning goals are more likely to have a mastery orientation. To them, it is more important to actually acquire competence in the domain, as opposed to proving one's "smartness" to themselves or others by getting a good grade.

Research on the impact of teacher feedback on developing mastery or helpless orientations

Dweck has also done several studies to examine what kind of feedback from teachers and others is likely to contribute to children developing either mastery or helpless orientations. For example, Kamins and Dweck (1999) studied kindergarten children who played with a doll (representing themselves) who worked on a task and then made an error. In the first of two studies the doll was given one of three different kinds of negative feedback by the teacher. The first kind of feedback focused on the person (e.g., "I'm disappointed in you"). Another kind was concerned with the outcome of the task (e.g., "That's not the right way to do it"). The final kind of feedback concerned the process, and it was suggested to the child that there was another way to do the task (e.g., "Maybe you could think of another way to do it").

The authors (Kamins & Dweck, 1999) followed the first study with a second one. In the second study, children were given praise following a success experience, instead of receiving negative feedback after failure. There were six different kinds of praise used, three kinds of **person praise**, two kinds of **process praise**, and one kind of **outcome praise**. See Table 13.2 for examples of each kind. After their success experience, the children then experienced failure at another task.

The results showed that for both punishment and praise, when given a later failure experience, the children who were given the person feedback were more likely to think that failure made someone a bad person, and that "being bad" was a general attribute. They were also less likely to persist in the face of failure. The most effective type of feedback for helping the children to develop a mastery orientation was process feedback – feedback that suggested that they could do something about their failure. Other

TABLE 13.2   Examples of Person, Outcome, and Process Praise

Person Praise
Group 1: "I'm very proud of you"
Group 2: "You're a good girl"
Group 3: "You're really good at this"
Outcome Praise
Group 4: "That's the right way to do it"
Process Praise
Group 5: "You must have tried really hard"
Group 6: "You found a good way to do it, can you think of other ways that may also work?"

Source: Kamins, M.L. & Dweck, C.S., *Developmental Psychology, 35*, 835–847, 1999.

research done by Dweck and her colleagues (Mueller & Dweck, 1998) has corroborated that any kind of feedback that focuses on characteristics inherent in the person (e.g., intelligence), is more likely to produce helplessness, and feedback that focuses on processes related to the task (e.g., effort), is more likely to produce a mastery orientation.

How does this relate to children in the classroom? Some teachers are more inclined to hold entity theories of ability, whereas others are more likely to hold incremental views. For example, Carol Dweck herself once reported on her own sixth grade teacher's view about ability:

> When I was in sixth grade, my teacher seemed to equate our worth with our IQ scores. We were seated around the room in IQ order. If you did not have a high IQ, she would not let you clean the blackboard erasers, carry the flag in assembly, or carry a note to the principal. She let us know that in her mind, a high IQ reflected not only basic intelligence, but also character. The lower-IQ students felt terrible, and the higher IQ students lived in fear that they would take another IQ test and lose their status. It was not an atmosphere that fostered love of learning and challenge. (Dweck, 2002b, p. 55)

Almost anyone would recoil in horror at such a teacher, but teachers can hold entity beliefs in more subtle ways than this. In general, teachers who hold entity views are more likely to make quicker judgments about their students' abilities, and are less likely to modify their views in the face of new evidence (Butler, 2000). In time their feedback may come to affect their students' own judgments about themselves.

Now let us return to a consideration of gender. It should be obvious from our earlier discussion that teachers sometimes make different attributions about the success and failure of boys and girls. Boys, especially boys from middle class backgrounds, who fail in school are often thought to do so because they lack effort—that they are not working hard enough, or that they are careless or messy, or too interested in having a social life. Teacher feedback to such boys when they fail is likely to focus on the need for them to work harder—to put in more effort. When boys succeed, however, teachers are more likely to believe that they are doing so because they are smart. When they give feedback to academically successful boys, it is more likely to focus on the intellectual quality of their work. Girls, on the other hand, are more likely to receive a pattern of feedback that links their failures to lack of ability, and their successes to their responsible and cooperative behavior (Boggiano & Barrett, 1991; Tiedemann, 2000).

We might think then that boys would come to see themselves as failing because of a lack of effort and succeeding because of ability plus some reasonable effort, whereas girls might come to see themselves as succeeding primarily because of effort (or perhaps luck or an easy subject matter) and failing because of lack of ability. Does the research actually support these ideas? To some degree, yes, although not always. In one particularly extensive study (Stetsenko, Little, Gordeeva, Grasshof, & Oettingen, 2000) of children in Czechoslovakia, Germany, Japan, Russia, Switzerland, and the United States, both boys and girls blamed similar things (e.g., luck, hard work, ability) for their successes and failures. Both boys and girls were reasonable in their self-assessments; children who did better in school gave themselves credit for doing so. However, there was one consistent difference between the boys and the girls. When girls were doing very well in school, they were less likely than boys to credit themselves with having academic ability.

These kinds of findings do imply that the pattern of feedback that boys and girls receive is one contributing factor to girls being less inclined to credit themselves with high levels of ability when they perform well. Interestingly, in some of the countries that Stetsenko and her colleagues studied the gender differences were much more notable (e.g., in Russia, the United States, and Japan), than in others (e.g., in Switzerland), and they suggest that cultural context certainly seems to have an influence on how high-performing girls come to believe that they have high levels of ability.

It is important again to recognize that all boys and girls are not the same. Children of both sexes have different patterns of abilities and interests, and different experiences in school. However, it is reasonable to conclude that girls are somewhat more likely to develop a helpless orientation, and somewhat more likely to give up in the face of academic failure in challenging domains (Eccles, Wigfield, & Schiefele, 1998). Recall that we have already seen that girls are more likely to be anxious about their academic performance (Pomerantz et al., 2002), and anxiety is very likely to contribute to helplessness in the face of failure.

Teachers' Feedback to Boys and Girls: Conclusions

What can we conclude about the patterns of feedback that boys and girls experience in the classroom, and the effects they are likely to have? Again, let us emphasize caution in generalizing these findings to all children. There are many influences on children's academic performance, with children's home and family experience being especially important. Overall, social class and family background is a much more powerful factor in academic outcome than is gender.

Nevertheless, it is reasonable to conclude that gendered experiences in the classroom have some impact. As a group, boys are also likely to learn that they can dominate the social interaction of the classroom with impunity. However, some boys, especially those from disadvantaged backgrounds or those who have difficulty conforming to the social norms of school, experience the school environment as punitive and rejecting, and this experience is likely to contribute to their eventual academic failure. It is also the case that some boys' peer groups are often not very supportive of the kind of behavior that will lead to academic success, and this is disadvantageous for boys who are especially peer-oriented. Other boys, especially those who are reasonably well behaved and who perform well academically, tend to have experiences in school that are especially likely to support and enhance their development as autonomous learners. When these boys struggle with new material, teachers are more likely to demand that they continue to try until they succeed.

Girls whose academic performance is below the norm clearly do not have the kind of harsh school environment that similar boys do, but academically talented girls also do not have the kind of support from teachers that comparable boys do. They simply do not receive the kind of stimulating instruction that boys do. When they confront difficult material, teachers are more likely to help them with the task, at least partly to avert their potential emotional distress. There are also many quiet, well-behaved young girls, who may simply disappear into the background in school. Such girls may never experience the kind of simulation from their teachers that will move them to embrace a risky academic challenge. Those few girls who are inclined to try to question academic authority are likely to eventually learn that such behavior is not accepted from them in a way that it may be from their male peers.

TEXTBOOKS AND ACADEMIC SUBJECT MATTER

Textbooks are part of the formal curriculum of the schools, but they also have elements of the hidden (subtle gender-related practices) and null (material that is never covered—like women's history) curricula as well. When researchers started to examine storybooks in the 1970s and 1980s, they also looked at school textbooks and found similar things (Schau & Scott, 1984; Weitzman & Rizzo, 1975). As in storybooks, both male and female characters in textbooks were portrayed stereotypically. Female characters in textbooks had a smaller number of occupations depicted and were more likely to sit on the sidelines and watch males engaging in interesting activities. The small number of women discussed and pictured was particularly noticeable, especially in history and science. Of course, in history and science the majority of the significant contributions of the past were, in fact, made by men, so it is not likely that this will change any time soon. However, this tendency to focus on male-oriented topics is not limited to "the great men of science," or the past world leaders. For example, one early report found American history textbooks that gave more coverage to the "six shooter," than to the women's suffrage movement, which lasted almost a century (Trecker, 1971). The impact of the textbooks can be seen clearly when children are asked to report on famous people in history or science. Generally they can name an overwhelming majority of males and have a difficult time even thinking of any important female characters in these fields.

Recent research in several different countries demonstrates some improvement in the number of female characters, and a reduction in stereotyping, although generally only for females. As was the case in children's storybooks, males are still portrayed with a limited number of strongly masculine characteristics, and almost never engaging in stereotypically feminine activities or occupations (Allen & Ingulsrud, 1998; Deliyanni-Kouimtzi, 1992; Evans & Davies, 2000; Reese, 1994; Saminy & Liu, 1997; Whiteley, 1996; Witt, 1996). Despite the improvement, there is still a long way to go before textbooks present balanced gender portrayals to children.

It is also the case that college teacher education textbooks devote very little coverage to gender-related issues, and often themselves contribute to stereotyped messages about boy and girl students (Titus, 1993; Yanowitz & Weathers, 2004; Zittleman & Sadker, 2002). So although textbooks continue to provide stereotyped messages, and teachers continue to treat boys and girls differently in the classroom, little effort is devoted to informing future teachers about these issues. Unfortunately, research demonstrates that education students, our future teachers, know little about the kinds of gender-related practices that we have been discussing in this chapter (Pryor & Achilles, 1998).

STRUCTURE OF SCHOOLS

There are some additional structural aspects of the environment in schools that are gender related. Here we would like to consider three issues: who the teachers and principals are, teachers' use of gender as a category in the classroom, and extracurricular activities.

Where Are the Men and the Women in Schools?

It will not come as a surprise that the majority of schoolteachers are women. For example, in the United States almost 80% of the educators in elementary and secondary schools are female (Snyder et al., 2007). The younger children are, the greater the percentage of their teachers who are female. For example, almost all preschool teachers are female (Saluja, Early, & Clifford, 2002), more than 90% of elementary teachers are female, and about 65% of secondary teachers are female (Milloy, 2003). Male teachers of color are especially rare. This situation is the case in many countries in the world, not just in the United States (Cameron, 2001; Cushman, 2000), although there are some countries (e.g., Greece) where the teaching profession is more gender balanced (Hopf & Hatzichristou, 1999).

Looking at administrative and leadership positions in elementary and secondary education, again there are differences by gender. Overall, about 44% of school principals are women, but they are much more likely to be found at the elementary level (NCES, 2002). At the secondary level, more than 85% of principals are men (Holzman, 1992; Logan & Scollay, 1999). Considering the principalship as a training ground for becoming a superintendent, note that elementary principals almost never reach the highest levels of administration. Therefore, it is not surprising that fewer than 15% of the school superintendents in the United States are female (Glass, 2000).

Moving to postsecondary education, there are more male professors, and men are most likely to be found at the higher professorial ranks (Parsad & Glover, 2002). In 2002 in the United States, approximately half (49%) of the university instructors and lecturers were male, slightly more than half of the assistant professors (55%), even more of the associate professors (65%), and the large majority (80%) of the full professors were male (National Center for Education Statistics [NCES], 2002). Men are more likely to work at doctoral granting institutions, whereas women are more likely to work at 2-year community colleges (Tabs, 2002).

Consider what children and adolescents learn from this state of affairs. They learn, by observing, that the care and instruction of young children are the province of women. In charge of those women, (except generally at the preschool level) are male administrators—principals and superintendents. The higher one goes in the educational system, the more prestige and status associated with the position, and the more those positions are likely to be held by men. At the lowest levels of the educational hierarchy, women are an overwhelming presence, and at the highest levels, men are. Surely this is a lesson for children about the role that men and women play in the world, and the positions to which they might be expected to aspire.

Organizing the Educational Environment Around Gender

When you were in school did the teacher ask the boys to line up in one line, and the girls in another? Were there ever contests (e.g., spelling bees or the like) in which the girls were pitted against the boys? Did the teacher ever say "you boys be quiet," or "see how nicely the girls are behaving?" The issue that we are raising here concerns the extent to which teachers attend to children's gender to organize activities in the classroom.

In one dramatic demonstration of the potential impact of such practices, Rebecca Bigler (1995) assigned groups of 6- to 11-year-old children to a "gender" or "control" classrooms during a 6-week summer school enrichment program. With the cooperation of teachers who took part in the study, two classrooms were assigned as "gender" classrooms, two as "color" classrooms, and two as "control" classrooms. In the gender classrooms teachers referred to gender as much as possible. They used such things as bulletin boards for boys' and girls' pictures, boys' and girls' seats at opposite sides of the room, and very frequent mentions of gender in their speech (e.g., "all the boys should be sitting down," or "Amber, you can come up for the girls," Bigler, 1995, p. 1077). As much as possible the teachers did not use gender stereotypes in their comments, nor did they favor one group over the other. All they did is repeatedly bring gender to the children's attention.

In the color classrooms, the children were assigned to color groups (e.g., red vs. green group), and a similar process was used to enhance the children's noticing of the group color as a significant factor in the organization of the classroom (bulletin boards, repeated mentions of the groups, etc.). The teachers mentioned neither group color nor gender in the control classrooms.

When the teachers used the gender category frequently, even over such a short time (the manipulation lasted only 4 weeks of the 6-week class), the children increased in their gender stereotyping. In this study, the color condition did not have strong effects on the children's stereotyping of the two groups, or much impact on in-group preference. However, two subsequent studies by Bigler and her colleagues (Bigler, Jones, & Lobliner, 1997; Bigler, Spears Brown, & Markell, 2001) using a more powerful manipulation did find that placing children in arbitrary groups assigning t-shirts to mark their color group, as well as groups based on physical attributes (e.g., the light-haired children received light color t-shirts) did find that children perceived differences between the groups and rated their own color group more favorably than the other group. This was especially the case when one of the arbitrary groups was depicted as having higher status (e.g., posters showing that one color group being more likely to win various contests). When teachers in Bigler's studies did not use the gender or color categories, and made no mention of them, the children did not develop in-group preferences or stereotypes about their group or the out-group. Only when the teachers emphasized the group categories were the children's attitudes affected. This is consistent with developmental intergroup theory described in chapter 8.

There is also research showing that teachers can improve relationships between boys and girls by encouraging interactions among them. In one experimental study (Lockheed, 1986), involving about 50 teachers from two different school districts, a year-long intervention to decrease stereotyping and increase interactions among boys and girls was undertaken. Teachers in the experimental groups were educated about gender stereotyping in the classroom, and trained in methods designed to increase interactions between boys and girls. Control teachers simply continued to teach in their usual way. Children were given measures of attitudes and interests regarding gender at the beginning and the end of the academic year, and were observed in their classrooms for hundreds of hours during the year. In the experimental classrooms, boys and girls were much more likely to interact with each other. Although girls were equally interested in working with boys in both kinds of classrooms, boys in the experimental classrooms were more positive about working with girls than were boys in the control classrooms.

The implications of this research for the classroom are clear. When teachers are inclined to emphasize gender—to repeatedly organize the children into groups of boys and girls, or to mention the gender category on a regular basis—it is likely to heighten children's attention to the importance of gender, increase their tendency to use gender stereotypes, as well as increasing their inclination to value their own group and to devalue the other group. When teachers make specific attempts to decrease gender segregation, and to encourage interactions between the sexes, they can increase children's tendencies to interact with children of the other sex, as well as to develop positive attitudes about the other group.

Extracurricular Activities

Schools sponsor several extracurricular activities, and many of them may be unrelated to gender in any obvious way (e.g., French Club or Honor Society). Among the most gendered of extracurricular activities are sports and cheerleading, especially in high schools. Analyses of sports and cheerleading, at least in American high schools, have examined the kinds of behaviors encouraged by these two different activities. Athletes, especially in high profile male sports, are generally encouraged to be tough, to keep going despite discomfort or pain, to be competitive and to win, and to be part of a team or a group (Eder & Parker, 1987). There is generally a large difference in the status attributed to male and female athletes in these settings, with males having much more status. High status is more likely to come to girls who are cheerleaders rather than girls who are volleyball or basketball players. Compared to the expectations for athletes, especially male athletes, cheerleaders are encouraged to be pretty and cheerful, to focus on their appearance and weight, and to manage the display of any negative emotion. Cheerleaders are supposed to smile and convey enthusiasm and enjoyment. These kinds of gendered actions clearly become part of the atmosphere within secondary schools in particular.

Sexual Harassment in Schools

Apparently children commonly experience **sexual harassment** (unwanted sexual advances, teasing, jokes, etc.), even as early as elementary school (Murnen & Smolak, 2000). The AAUW did a follow-up study to their classroom interaction study that we discussed earlier in this chapter. In their second study of gender-related issues in schools, they examined the extent to which students are the recipients of sexual and other harassment by their peers in school (American Association of University Women Educational Foundation, 2001). In our chapter on peer interactions, we discussed issues of bullying and relational aggression that are often organized along gender lines. However, sexual harassment is a specific kind of peer interaction that also takes place in the school setting, most frequently in middle and high schools.

In their study of sexual harassment in schools (eighth through eleventh grades were studied), the AAUW reported that sexual harassment was very common. Their definition of sexual harassment can be seen in Table 13.3. Most students knew that these experiences were sexual harassment, especially when their schools had a sexual harassment policy, and when there was an attempt to educate the students about the issue. Both boys (79%) and girls (81%) reported experiencing these events frequently.

Certain of these experiences were more upsetting to students than others. Students were more upset if the harassment was physical, but some kinds of speech are also very distressing to students. In particular, the following events were particularly distressing: having sexual rumors spread about oneself, being called gay or lesbian, having sexual messages or graffiti written about oneself, having one's clothing pulled down; being spied on while showering or dressing, and being forced to do something sexual. Girls were somewhat more likely to say that sexual harassment was frequent (30 vs. 24% of boys). Except for being called gay or lesbian, which was equally upsetting to both sexes, girls were more affected by sexual harassment. Girls were more likely to say that it made them feel self-conscious (44 vs. 19% of boys), embarrassed (53 vs. 32% of boys), and more likely to say that they were afraid of it (44 vs. 20% of boys). Girls were also more likely to make changes in their behavior to avoid the person who had harassed them.

TABLE 13.3   Examples of Sexual Harassment in Schools

Made sexual comments, jokes, gestures, or looks
Showed, gave, or left you sexual pictures, photographs, illustrations, messages, or notes
Wrote sexual messages/graffiti about you on bathroom walls, in locker rooms, etc.
Spread sexual rumors about you
Said you were gay or lesbian
Spied on you as you dressed or showered at school
Flashed or "mooned" you
Touched, grabbed, or pinched you in a sexual way
Intentionally brushed up against you in a sexual way
Pulled at your clothing in a sexual way
Pulled off or down your clothing
Blocked your way or cornered you in a sexual way
Forced you to kiss him/her
Forced you to do something sexual other than kissing

Source: American Association of University Women Educational Foundation, *Hostile hallways.*
Washington, DC: AAUW, 2001.

Research on both elementary and high school students has supported the AAUW finding that girls are more distressed and affected by sexual harassment than boys (Murnen & Smolak, 2000). In one study of sexual harassment in a Canadian high school (Larkin, 1994), girls reported that they tried to avoid being alone while walking in the hall, or were careful about their clothing, limited their participation in certain activities (e.g., sports), and remained silent in class to avoid being harassed by other students, most often male students.

The Gendered Nature of Specific School Subjects

As they go through school, boys and girls come to conclude that certain subject domains are more associated with boys whereas others are more for girls. Children also express greater liking for the subject domains that are gender-related. In one recent study of high school students in the United States, Japan, and Taiwan, boys in all three countries expressed greater liking for math, science, and sports, whereas girls expressed greater liking for music, art, and language arts (Evans, Schweingruber, & Stevenson, 2002). These researchers also found that boys' scores on measures of general knowledge (mostly history, politics, current events, and science) and of mathematics were higher than girls' in all three countries, although they questioned whether, in their attempt to create a culture-fair test of general knowledge, they had created a gender-biased test. Nonetheless, the more that students were interested in a subject, the higher their score was on the items in the knowledge tests that measured those domains, suggesting that interest in a domain has an impact on students' academic achievement in that domain, and that gender may affect academic performance through its effect on interest in certain subjects.

Mathematics, computers, and science have been the focus of much research on the gendered nature of academic subjects. These subject areas are centrally important in many high-status and high-paying occupations, and if girls are less likely to achieve in these domains, their opportunities to have access to certain occupations are likely to be affected. Numerous studies in several countries have shown higher levels of anxiety and less confidence in their skills in mathematics, science, and computer use in girls (e.g., Baenninger & Newcombe, 1995; Dickhaeuser & Stiensmeier-Pelster, 2003; Dreves & Jovanovic, 1998; Freedman-Doan et al., 2000; Jones & Smart, 1995; Jones, Howe, & Rua, 2000; Roger & Duffield, 2000). Furthermore, there is evidence that teachers' behavior towards students contributes both to their interest in and their confidence in these domains (Carr, Jessup, & Fuller, 1999; Hatchell, 1998; Keller, 2001).

Whereas girls are less confident about math and science, the same thing may be said about the language arts and boys, although nowhere near as much study has been devoted to gender differences in these domains as there has been to math and science. As we already know, boys have more difficulty than do girls with both reading and writing, and they express less confidence and interest in both (Freedman-Doan et al., 2000; Wigfield & Eccles, 1994). Certainly the ability to express oneself in writing is centrally important to academic and career achievement in many areas of study, and performance in these areas is essential to getting a good education. Partly because it has not been researched to the same degree, there is less evidence that boys' beliefs about their lack of ability in reading and writing and their lack of interest in pursuing these domains can be specifically tied to teachers' treatment of them. However, although there is reason to be concerned about the low level of participation of girls in educational programs and careers in mathematics and the sciences, it is not very reasonable to conclude that there has been a shortage of men pursuing such fields as journalism and writing, either now or in the past.

THE MOVEMENT FOR GENDER EQUITY IN SCHOOLS

Since these issues began to be made public, many teachers and researchers have been concerned about changing the school environment to make it more gender fair. Up to this point, most (but not all) of those efforts have been devoted to improving the classroom environment for girls. For example, some research has found that girls prefer cooperative learning and working with other students, as opposed to working individually and competitively (Eccles et al., 1998). They value an emphasis on people and on applications of material to everyday life. It is certainly possible to incorporate such teaching methods and materials into disciplines that have not traditionally appealed to girls.

For teachers who are interested in suggestions for achieving gender equity in the classroom, there are reference guides for teachers that give suggestions about ways to change the classroom to make it more gender fair (e.g., Horgan, 1995; McNair, Kirova-Petrova, & Bhargava, 2001; Subrahmanyan & Bozonie, 1996). One important project, called *Gender Equity Right from the Start* (Sanders, Koch, & Urso, 1997a, 1997b), has developed many materials and exercises for how to include more information about women in math and the sciences, how to encourage girls in these fields, and how to modify feedback to boys and girls so that it is not as likely to perpetuate gender differences in the classroom.

Although less effort in the gender equity domain has been devoted to ways to improve the educational environment for underachieving boys, there have certainly been calls to do so (Kleinfeld, 1998; Noguera, 2003). For example, Pedro Noguero (2003) has written about the importance of strong and supportive relationships with teachers, an academically rigorous curriculum, high expectations, a safe and orderly school environment, and the involvement of parents in stimulating the academic performance of poor African American boys. Although there is good evidence that such factors work to enhance the academic achievement of all students, disadvantaged children, perhaps especially boys, often do not receive them.

Returning to the terminology that we used at the beginning of this chapter—the hidden, informal, and null curricula—by now you should be able to see how all of these aspects of the school environment operate. It may be difficult for individual teachers to change the informal curriculum (the clubs, the athletes, and the cheerleaders), but, for example, a school as a whole can make some changes in the way cheerleaders are chosen or how girls' sports are valued. The hidden curriculum consists of the ways that boys and girls are treated in classrooms, and the messages they receive about their behavior, their importance, and their roles in life as a result of this treatment. Here is a place where an individual teacher can make a difference. The Sadkers, for example, have conducted many workshops in which teachers observed videos demonstrating these different forms of treatment (Sadker & Sadker, 1993, 1994). Sometimes the videos were even of the teachers' own classes. Most teachers, when they become aware of these differences, are startled, because they genuinely believe that they do not treat boys and girls differently, and for the most part, they certainly do not want to. Many teachers who took part in their workshops made attempts to change these patterns in their own classrooms. There is also research demonstrating that teachers can and do make changes in their behavior and teaching methods, once they are aware that these issues exist (Lockheed, 1986). Children's performance is also affected by changes in the behavior of teachers designed to reduce gender stereotyping (Freeman, 1996; Matthews, 2004).

The null curriculum is the material about women and women's lives that is missing from the formal curriculum. This is also possible to change, both by school districts and by individual teachers. Information about women in science and history can be added into the curriculum, and as mentioned above, there are resources to help teachers make such changes.

WHAT ABOUT SINGLE-SEX SCHOOLS?

Because much of what takes place in school involves the differential treatment of boys and girls in the classroom, some have called for single-sex schools or classrooms. What does the research on single-sex schools show about these issues? Some research finds academic and or social benefits for both boys and girls in single-sex schools (Cairns, 1990; Woodward, Fergusson, & Horwood, 1999; Younger & Warrington, 2002), although more often researchers report that boys benefit from mixed-sex schools and girls benefit from single-sex schools (Heyward, 1995; Jimenez & Lockheed, 1989; Lee & Marks, 1990; Watson, Quatman, & Edler, 2002). Because male peer groups are one of the major factors that keep boys from succeeding at academic endeavors, it makes sense that the presence of girls in the classroom would improve the peer environment for boys. For girls, the classroom disadvantage is partly related to boys distracting them by acting up and by teachers giving more attention to high-achieving as well as misbehaving boys. It makes some sense also, then, that girls would benefit in schools by themselves. In fact, there is evidence that parents of girls are more interested in seeking out same-sex schools for their daughters than are parents of boys (Jackson & Bisset, 2005; Warrington & Younger, 2001) for exactly these reasons.

In North America, single-sex schools are usually private schools, which often are more selective (serve more economically advantaged children and have more involved parents), and have higher academic standards than public schools (Lee & Marks, 1992). Many also have a religious focus. These factors make it difficult to make meaningful comparisons between mixed-sex and same-sex schools. Even in England, publicly funded single-sex schools are disappearing, so parents who want to choose same-sex schools have to be able to afford private schooling (Jackson & Bisset, 2005).

One recent study compared high school girls in single- and mixed-sex public and private schools in the Canadian province of Québec (Vezeau, Bouffard, & Chouinard, 2000). In this study, Vezeau and her colleagues were able to find public and private schools of both types and to compare girls in both types of schools in both junior and senior high school. As expected, most of the private schools they studied were more academically demanding than the public schools. They found that in junior high school girls in private schools had better math performance and more positive attitudes about math than girls in public schools, and this was a more important factor than whether the schools were single or mixed sex. In senior high school, again private schools were associated with better performance and more positive attitudes than were public schools, but, for girls, being in a private all-girls school was associated with more positive attitudes and stronger performance than being in a private mixed-sex school. This was not found in public schools. The authors suggested that the boys in mixed-sex private schools are likely to be especially talented, and therefore their presence in the classroom may negatively impact girls in a manner less likely to be found in less academically demanding public schools; so the girls in a private same-sex school would benefit, but not girls in a public same-sex school. The complicated results of this study make it clear that many factors other than the gender composition of the student body have an impact on students' performance.

In Australia, the United States, and the United Kingdom, some school districts have recently begun to offer single-sex schools or to teach single-sex classrooms in mixed-sex schools as a response to the perceived academic difficulties of some children, especially boys (Warrington & Younger, 2001; Wills,

Kilpatrick, & Hutton, 2006; Younger & Warrington, 2002). The idea has been to provide a space for both sexes in the classroom. This trend reverses the general steady progression towards educating boys and girls in the same classrooms in all of these countries over the last several decades. In the United States these newer same-sex schools have been developed primarily to serve disadvantaged urban minority students (Salomone, 2006). Most of the examination of the impact of such classrooms consists of interviews and impressions in which people involved in such classrooms (parents, children, teachers) appear convinced that children benefit, but there is little solid evidence that children of either sex show academic benefits from these arrangements (e.g., see Wills et al., 2006).

One study in the United States examined the academic performance of disadvantaged fifth grade African American boys and girls in mixed- and single-sex classrooms in two inner-city public schools (Singh, Vaught, & Mitchell, 1998). There were four classrooms studied in this quasi-experiment: two mixed-sex classrooms, one classroom consisting only of boys, and one consisting only of girls. The four teachers were highly skilled and consisted of one male and three females; the man (who taught the all-boy class) and one of the women were African American—the other two were White. The authors measured achievement test scores and grades in several domains: reading, math, science, social studies, and attendance. The findings differed in the various domains (i.e., math, science, reading, etc.), and findings concerning grades differed from those of achievement tests. In general, girls had higher grades and higher achievement test scores regardless of their type of classroom, but girls in the single-sex classrooms scored particularly well in the mathematics achievement tests. There was no evidence that being in a single-sex classroom benefited boys' achievement test scores; indeed, except for reading (no difference) the boys in the single-sex classroom had consistently lower achievement test scores than all of the other groups. Grades, on the other hand, were generally higher in single-sex classrooms for both sexes, but especially for the girls. In other words, the girls' academic achievement (both grades and test scores) benefited from the single-sex classroom environment considerably more than the boys' did.

However, the boys in the single-sex classroom had better attendance records than boys in the mixed-sex classroom (5.77 days missed as compared to 13.39; comparable to girls' days missed of 5.13 and 5.57 in the two groups). The authors argued that this could be a very important benefit if it were to accumulate over several years (this study was only 1 year in duration). They thought that it was possible that being in a single-sex classroom (perhaps especially with a male African American teacher such as they had) had the potential to affect the motivation of these at-risk African American boys to do academic work, and that benefits might well accrue over time.

Another study has examined several single-sex and mixed-sex Catholic schools serving disadvantaged African American and Hispanic students (Riordan, 1994) and reported benefits for both boys and girls in single-sex schools. Single-sex schools had more students on academic tracks, more homework, and higher achievement test scores for both sexes. Riordan suggests that there are particular benefits for African American boys including more adult male role models (who often choose to work in such schools), more peer role models (because all of the top students will be the same sex and typically the same race), a more academically oriented peer culture, fewer discipline problems, and greater parental involvement in single-sex schools. This is striking considering that all of the schools he studied were Catholic schools, which are already known for an emphasis on classroom discipline and high levels of parental involvement.

Academic performance is not the only thing that might be affected by single-sex schools. Looking at social relationships in single-sex schools, one recent study took advantage of a natural experiment in which an American school district gave parents the opportunity to elect single-sex classrooms within a mixed-sex school for their fifth and sixth grade children. The researchers (Barton & Cohen, 2004) were able to follow the children from fourth (when they were in a mixed-sex classroom) through sixth grade, after they had spent 2 years in single-sex classrooms. They reported that boys in single-sex classrooms expanded their friendship networks with other boys—they had more friends than previously. Girls, on the other hand, increased in relational aggression, rejection, and victimization in fifth grade in the single-sex classrooms, although these negative outcomes declined by sixth grade. These researchers did not measure academic outcomes.

There is also evidence of greater gender polarization of academic subjects and extracurricular activities in mixed-sex schools (Stables, 1990). In other words, when girls are present, boys tend to think that subjects like music and drama are of less interest to them (i.e., are feminine), and girls are more likely to dislike subjects like physics, although the effect on boys is more pronounced. In single-sex schools, activities like choir, drama club, or debate teams are more open to the sex that is likely to avoid them in mixed-sex settings (Salomone, 2006). Once reaching adulthood, men who attended single-sex schools have more positive attitudes towards history, reading, and literature and are more likely to choose careers in the humanities (James & Richards, 2003). Such results suggest that academic subjects and activities are more likely to become associated with gender in children's minds when both sexes are present and may have an impact on limiting career choices from domains seen as appropriate for the other gender.

It is very clear that this is a complicated question, and that there are few, if any, truly experimental studies on this topic that follow children longitudinally. There are no easy answers to the question of whether single-sex schools or classrooms are likely to be better or worse than mixed-sex ones. However, there are some who are now arguing that single-sex schools or classrooms, as long as they maintain a commitment to educational equity for both sexes, are of equal rigor, expose boys and girls to the same curriculum, and have the potential to positively impact both boys and girls (Salomone, 2006), perhaps especially girls at the high end and boys at the low end of the achievement distribution. It is likely that we will see more on this topic over the next few years.

CHAPTER SUMMARY

In this chapter we looked at the impact of schools on gender development. We found that there are small differences in academic performance favoring girls. Girls tend to get better grades than boys, although by the later grades the differences are very small. Boys are also more likely to drop out of school and not to continue in higher education. These differences are highly related to social class. Relative to girls from similar backgrounds, it is mostly boys from working-class and disadvantaged families, and who are members of ethnic minority groups, who perform more poorly in school, who drop out, and who do not continue their education. Such boys also are more likely to get in trouble at school for misbehaving and are more likely to be punished, including being suspended from school. Although girls are more likely to earn good grades and to behave well in the classroom, they are more likely to be among the silent, hidden, and overanxious students.

The research on teacher interaction finds that teachers spend more time reprimanding boys for their misbehavior, but that they also provide more stimulating instruction to boys, especially to those boys who are at the top of the class academically. Girls are more likely to be ignored and to be provided with unneeded assistance, rather than being challenged to do the work on their own. These instructional differences are especially notable in science and math classrooms.

There are structural aspects of schools that differ along gender lines. Power and status is more likely to be in the hands of men (e.g., principals, superintendents), whereas the teachers at the lowest levels are most likely to be women. The farther one goes in the educational system, the greater the likelihood that it will be men who are doing the teaching.

Schools use gender to arrange classroom and extracurricular activities. Teachers may pit the boys against the girls in academic contests, and activities like sports and cheerleading are clearly organized around gender lines.

Sexual harassment of various kinds seems to be a regular occurrence in schools, although both boys and girls experience it. Girls, however, are more uncomfortable and afraid because of it and more likely to make adjustments to their lives to avoid it.

On a more optimistic note, many schools and teachers have made attempts to adopt more equitable instructional practices, and there is evidence that they can be successful at doing so. Among these efforts, some have suggested that single-sex schools may have benefits for the students most likely to lose out in the typical school environment: high achieving girls and low achieving boys.

Epilogue

> We see that whatever differential predispositions boys and girls may have, it is likely that the way they are enacted will depend greatly on the social conditions provided by the adults and peers with whom they interact. (Maccoby, 2000, p. 404)

We began this book by saying that gender is one of the fundamental ways in which human social life is organized and claimed that there are few factors that influence people's lives as much as sex or gender. One of the first things people want to know about a baby (these days, often early in a woman's pregnancy) is whether the child is a boy or a girl. Using this knowledge, parents and others choose names, room decorations, toys, and make other plans for the child's future. Yet, at least in the Western world of the 21st century, boys and girls have many of the same experiences and opportunities, and overall, the similarities between the sexes are as important as the differences. Nonetheless, sex and gender remain—and we think always will remain—central to the experience of life as a human being.

Now that we have neared the end of the book, we want to reflect briefly on the research and theory we have presented. We have shown you evidence that biological factors are related to sex differences. In the earliest stages of life, girls and boys begin with a different pair of chromosomes in the 23rd position—the sex chromosomes. The SRY gene on the Y chromosome directs the development of the early embryo in a male direction—producing testes rather than ovaries from the rudimentary gonads. The testes secrete hormones that masculinize the developing body as long as the receptors for those hormones are functioning. Hormones continue to act on the body at puberty and beyond to make the sexes different. We have provided evidence that these hormones also masculinize the brain and influence a variety of psychological characteristics.

But there are also social, cultural, and cognitive influences on gender development. From the earliest days of life, boys and girls are treated differently by their family members and everyone else with whom they interact. They are given different names, clothing, toys, books, and other objects, and they are introduced to different activities and experiences. Their parents and others talk to them in different ways about different subject matter, assign them different chores, and have different expectations for them to be self-reliant and competent. Children also see gendered images in books, on television, in movies, and in video games. They learn that boys and girls, and adult men and women, behave differently, have different responsibilities and occupations, and have access to differing spheres of social influence and power.

Children's interactions in peer groups have unique, gendered styles, and the implications of these styles go well beyond childhood. The more frequently and extensively that young children play in these same-sex groups, the more gender-typed their behavior becomes (Martin & Fabes, 2001). Peer groups also lead children to see themselves as belonging to one gender group—the in-group—and children of the other sex as belonging to the other group—the out-group. These loyalties have important consequences for children's prejudices and stereotypes and for the qualities of the adults into which they eventually grow.

In other words, parents, other adults, peers, and the culture at large construct a gendered social reality for children. But children are not passive recipients of this information. Even at a very young age, and increasingly as they grow older, children's own cognitive actions are applied to the gendered information they encounter. Children themselves try to make sense of what they see and hear around them to construct a set of expectations for their own behavior and that of others. They are very active participants in their own gender socialization. Children's identification with their own gender leads them to acquire richer knowledge and behaviors associated with their own sex (Martin, Ruble, & Szkrybalo, 2002) and to remember own-sex characters and activities better than other-sex ones (Signorella, Bigler, & Liben, 1997).

Thus, many factors are involved in the process of gender development. We understand that, at first, it might be overwhelming to think that all these factors are involved. Sometimes students and others find these multiple and interacting explanations frustrating and wish they could simply find the single reason to explain a behavioral outcome. This wish occasionally leads people to believe that some of these explanations or theories are wrong and others are right. Because there is evidence in support of many different explanations, it certainly would be possible to use that evidence to support a favored explanation about the origins of gender-related outcomes and simply ignore the other evidence. Instead, we hope that you are curious to know not which one explanation is right, but why each of them is legitimate, and, more importantly, how genes, hormones, socialization, and the child's own thoughts and actions might work together to lead boys and girls to behave differently and to make different choices.

HOW CAN BIOLOGICAL, SOCIAL, AND COGNITIVE INFLUENCES ALL PLAY A ROLE?

First, behavior is complex, and therefore, no characteristic is determined by a single set of factors. Genes, hormones, social forces, and children's thinking about their social world all account for some (probably different) parts of any particular sex or gender difference. Second, the different theoretical perspectives on gender development generate somewhat different research questions and therefore different types of evidence. In particular, some studies are concerned only with explaining differences between the sexes, whereas other studies are also concerned with explaining variations within each sex. It is possible that some factors account for differences between boys and girls but that other factors account for variations among girls or among boys. Third, the direction of some influences is not always clear. There is little doubt that parents create a gendered world for children, which undoubtedly influences children to behave as they do. But this gendered world may also be constructed partly in response to children's own qualities and to their particular interests.

The Difficulty of Separating Causes

It is difficult to isolate the different influences on gender development because they are generally correlated in typical children. The vast majority of individuals with two X chromosomes and female-typical prenatal hormone exposure are reared as girls, identify as girls, and see themselves as belonging to the same group as other girls and women. They strive to make their behavior consistent with that group, play primarily with girls, are socialized (by parents, peers, teachers, other adults, and the media) as girls, and then at puberty and beyond, experience physical changes largely controlled by estrogen, resulting in a female-typical physical appearance. The reverse is true for the vast majority of individuals with an XY karyotype. These individuals have male-typical hormone exposure and are reared as boys, identify as boys, and are socialized as boys. In other words, the widespread concordance of biological factors, socialization, and cognitions means that, in most people, it is difficult to separate the forces that are responsible for differences between the sexes.

Identifying and Integrating Causes

Nevertheless, there is research that helps to identify the contributions of different influences on development, and it is increasingly clear that biological and social influences work together to affect behavior (Rutter, Moffitt, & Caspi, 2006). Children do not just react to socialization; they sometimes elicit it. Think back to the section in Chapter 10 about the relationship between boys' difficult temperaments and parents' socialization practices with them. We presented evidence that boys receive stricter discipline partly because they are more likely to be temperamentally difficult—to be irritable, prone to anger, and to refuse to comply with parental requests. When parents have difficult children, they tend to become forceful and punitive. But when they do, the child often becomes even more difficult and noncompliant. We showed you that this process happens more often with boys than with girls. One 10-year longitudinal study (Bezirganian & Cohen, 1992) found little average difference between the youngest boys and girls, although some children of both sexes were more difficult than others. Parents did use more forceful discipline with these difficult children, but only boys responded to this punishment and discipline by becoming more noncompliant and difficult, and that was especially so in response to their mothers' discipline. The authors thought that the boys were particularly resistant to being controlled by women (i.e., mothers), in a way that girls were not. Thus, over time, the initially difficult boys were more likely to become noncompliant and increasingly difficult and thereby more likely to receive continued excessive punishment from parents. These findings demonstrate how socialization interacts in complicated ways with children's initial characteristics as well as gendered expectations.

How do we study both the role of biological predispositions and of the environment in understanding gender development? Many studies have offered answers about the interactions of biology and experience by studying people in whom biological and socialization factors are less completely confounded than is typically the case. Illustrative are studies of adopted children and studies of children who have a disorder of sex development such as congenital adrenal hyperplasia (CAH). But there are also studies that use sophisticated new methods for examining how experiences shape gender developmental processes. The research we referred to earlier in this section (Martin & Fabes, 2001), showing that children who play more in same-sex peer groups become more gender-stereotyped over time, provides an example of a study of this kind.

We can combine findings from both these kinds of studies. As you know, there is a well-established sex difference in spatial skills. There is evidence that biological factors are important. Particularly telling is the finding that girls with CAH who are exposed to androgens prenatally have better spatial skills than do other girls (Berenbaum, 2001). But environmental forces are also important. One recent study (Levine, Vasilyeva, Lourenco, Newcombe, & Huttenlocher, 2005) demonstrated that the usual sex difference on spatial tasks held in second- and third-grade children from families of higher socioeconomic status (SES) but not in children of the same age from families of lower SES. The researchers note that lower-SES children have less freedom to explore the environment because of safety concerns (and hence less chance to learn from environmental spaces) and suggest that they may also have less access to toys and games (like interlocking blocks) that promote spatial skills. It may be that when these opportunities are available in higher SES homes, socialization factors lead boys, in particular, to partake in them. These environmental and socialization factors could account for the observed interaction between sex and SES in their data. At the same time, these researchers note that the data do not rule out the possibility that biological factors are relevant. Perhaps—when spatial opportunities are available—boys, more than girls, are biologically predisposed to seize them. Perhaps they need no differential encouragement from society. We look forward to ever-better research strategies that will allow us to learn how biological, social, and cognitive factors interact to produce this sex difference as well as the many others described elsewhere in this book.

FINAL REMARKS

We are now at the end of our examination of the gender development of children and adolescents. As you have surely seen, this has been a very active and diverse field of scientific study for more than a century. Because of the efforts of many dedicated scientists, we have learned many answers to questions about differences between boys and girls and men and women and about the developmental processes that lead to them. But much remains to be investigated and understood. We hope that this book will have given you the background to understand the fascinating gender differences that you have experienced and will continue to experience in your own interests, behaviors, and life choices. In addition, however, we hope that it will lead you to consider joining the scientific enterprise as it continues to explore why boys and girls, men and women, are both so similar and yet so different.

Glossary

2D:4D ratio: The ratio of the index (second) finger to the ring (fourth) finger; it is lower in most boys and men than in most girls and women.

5-α-reductase: The enzyme responsible for converting **testosterone** to **dihydrotestosterone**.

5-α-reductase deficiency (5αRD): A defect in the 5-α-reductase enzyme which prevents the conversion of **testosterone** to **dihydrotestosterone**; boys with this condition thus have feminized genitalia at birth. High doses of testosterone at puberty cause their genitalia to masculinize at that time.

21-hydroxylase (21-OH): An enzyme in the adrenal gland that facilitates the conversion of cholesterol into cortisol and **aldosterone**; people with **congenital adrenal hyperplasia** produce no or very little of this enzyme.

Ablatio penis: A condition in which a normal boy is lacking a penis because of an accident, most commonly a mishandled circumcision.

Activational hormone effects: Effects on a trait (physical or behavioral) produced by hormones that circulate in the body during postnatal life; usually refers to effects of hormones that circulate in the blood after **puberty**.

Activity level: Energy expenditure through movement, consisting of such behaviors as squirming, rolling away, climbing, fidgeting, or running.

Actometer/accelerometer: Devices used to measure the amount of movement people make.

Adolescence: The developmental period associated with **puberty**, and the psychological changes that accompany it.

Adolescent growth spurt: A period of increased rate of growth in the skeleton, the muscles, and many internal organs during the teenage years.

Adrenal glands: Glands that are located on top of the kidneys and produce hormones that regulate many essential functions in the body; they are an important source of **androgens** in both males and females.

Adrenarche: A stage of puberty that involves the production of **androgens** from the **adrenal glands** (and from the ovaries in girls); these androgens are responsible for the onset of sexual hair (i.e., hair that appears after puberty such as pubic, axillary, and beard hair).

Agentic or instrumental characteristics: Characteristics related to competence, confidence, independence, and success at performing tasks. Such characteristics are associated with stereotypic masculinity.

Aggression: Behavior intended to hurt or harm another. Includes physical, verbal, social, and fantasy aggression.

Agreeableness: One of the five factors of personality consisting of compliant, nurturant, and tenderminded characteristics.

Aldosterone: A hormone that acts on the kidneys to regulate the levels of salt and water in the body, which affects blood pressure; most people with **congenital adrenal hyperplasia** have a deficiency in aldosterone.

Allele: Form of a gene.

Alpha bias: A perspective that differences between the sexes are large and significant.

Ambiguous genitalia: External genitalia that are not typical of a boy or of a girl; genitalia that are **virilized (masculinized)** for a girl or **undervirilized (demasculinized)** for a boy.

Amygdala: A structure in the limbic system in the brain that plays a role in emotion.

Anal stage: Second stage in Freud's theory that occurs between 18 months and about 3 years of age when children's libido is centered on the anus and toilet training.

Androgens: A class of hormones that generally cause physical development to proceed in a masculine direction; androgens are produced in large quantity by the testes (primarily in the form of **testosterone**), in small quantity by the ovaries, and in small to moderate quantities by the **adrenal glands**.

Androgen insensitivity syndrome: A genetic condition leading to defective **androgen** receptors, so that individuals with a 46,XY **karyotype** have female-typical sexual differentiation with respect to characteristics that are influenced by androgens.

Androstenedione: A type of **androgen**.

Aneuploidy: An abnormal number of chromosomes; sex chromosome aneuploidy includes **Turner syndrome** (46,X) and **Klinefelter syndrome** (47,XXY).

Anima: A feminine part of everyone's collective unconscious.

Animus: A masculine part of everyone's collective unconscious.

Anorexia: A disorder in which a person is substantially underweight (less than 85% of expected), has fear of gaining weight, a disturbed perception of one's body size, and, for women, ceases to menstruate.

Antisocial behavior: Behavior involving aggression, damage to others or property, and breaking rules or laws.

Asperger's syndrome: A disorder in which children typically have normal language skills and IQs but have the other characteristics of **PDD**s such as stereotyped behaviors and poor social and communicative skills.

Attention deficit hyperactivity disorder (ADHD): A disorder consisting of a pattern of inattention and distractibility, excessive activity, and with the possibility of defiance and disobedience.

Attributions: Assumptions or beliefs about the cause of a phenomenon (e.g., if boys do better on the SATs, what is the reason, and to what do you attribute it?).

Autism: A disorder consisting of social and communicative skill deficits, usually accompanied by lack of language skills and mental retardation.

Autonomy-granting: Permitting children to make their own decisions, to take responsibility for themselves and their actions, and to be independent of parental control.

Autosomes: The first 22 of the 23 pairs of chromosomes that contain most of our genetic material.

Berdache: A term sometimes used to refer to a third gender in Native American culture.

Beta bias: A perspective that sex differences are small, inconsistent, or the result of artifacts such as power differences between males and females.

Biological view of gender development: A theoretical perspective that emphasizes the role that biological factors such as genes and hormones play in sex differences and gender development.

Biomarkers: Physical traits used as indirect indicators of prenatal hormones; for example 2D:4D ratios and otoacoustic emissions.

Bipotentiality: The potential of all fetuses to develop in a feminine or masculine direction.

Breast buds: An elevation of the breast and surrounding area; the earliest sign of breast development in girls.

Bulimia: A disorder consisting of binges of many calories at a time and purging in an attempt to prevent weight gain. Purging may consist of excessive exercise, the use of laxatives or enemas, fasting, or induced vomiting.

Caldecott and Newbery medals: Awards given by the American Library Association. The Caldecott medal is given for most distinguished American picture book for children, and the Newbery Medal is given for the most distinguished contribution to American literature for children. Two or three runners-up are also named and are known as Newbery or Caldecott Honor books.

Cardinal directions: North, south, east, and west.

Cartesian coordinate axes: Two-dimensional (x and y) or three-dimensional (x, y and z) coordinates used in mathematics to represent planes or three-dimensional spaces.

Castration anxiety: A boy's fear that his penis will be removed and he will become like a girl.

Caudate: A part of the brain known primarily for its role in regulating voluntary movements.

Central sulcus: A prominent groove on the surface of the brain that separates the frontal and parietal lobes.

Cerebral cortex: The outer part of the brain primarily involved in higher order thought, such as language and spatial cognition.

Channeling (or shaping): Part of the gender socialization process—the selection of various names, toys, room decorations, other items, and activities differently for boys and girls.

Cloacal exstrophy: A congenital disorder affecting development of the midline of the body; boys with this condition have an absent or poorly formed penis.

Co-rumination: Discussion of interpersonal difficulties and problems extensively with another person, who does the same in return.

COAT: See **OAT**.

Cognitive developmental theory: A term used to refer to both Piaget's theory of cognitive development and Kohlberg's theory of gender development.

Cognitive environmental approach: A theoretical approach that posits both environmental learning mechanisms and children's own cognitions as contributors to gender development.

Cognitive theories: Theoretical perspectives that emphasize the role of children's cognitions and knowledge on their gender development, sometimes referred to as self-socialization.

Collaborative research: A research method in which the participants in the research share in interpreting the findings.

Collective unconscious: Jung's term for images or archetypes that are part of the humanity of every person.

Common language effect size index (CL): The percent of time that a member of one group will outperform a member of the other group. In sex-differences research, the percent of time a male will outperform a female, or vice versa.

Communal or expressive characteristics: Characteristics associated with being kind, caring, and concerned about others. Such characteristics are associated with stereotypic femininity.

Complete androgen insensitivity syndrome (CAIS): A genetic defect in the **androgen** receptor, resulting in inability to use androgens, and thus female-typical physical development of characteristics that are influenced by androgens.

Computation: In arithmetic or mathematics, the correct calculation of an answer to a problem.

Conduct disorder: A disorder in which children show aggression, defiance, and antisocial or criminal behavior including stealing, lying, running away from home, harming animals or people, setting fires, or destruction of property.

Congenital adrenal hyperplasia (CAH): A genetic disorder resulting in excess levels of **androgens** (produced from the adrenal gland) beginning early in gestation and resulting in genital virilization in girls.

Conscientiousness: One of the five factors of personality consisting of being dutiful, competent, and disciplined.

Conservation: The maintenance of an object's physical properties despite changes in form (e.g., quantity of liquid remains the same even it is poured from a short, wide beaker into a tall, narrow one).

Constructed environment: The sense or meaning of the world that is created by the individual.

Corpus callosum: The bundle of fibers that connects the two hemispheres of the **cerebral cortex** and facilitates transmission of information between them.

Cortisol: A hormone that helps to maintain important physiological functions, including maintaining blood sugar levels, helping the body deal with stress, and suppressing inflammation. People with **congenital adrenal hyperplasia** have a deficiency in cortisol, which leads to increased production of **androgens**.

Cultural level of analysis: An analysis used by social constructionist theorists at the level of cultural symbols.

d **statistic:** A measure of effect size that indicates how far apart groups means are in standard deviation units. For sex differences, a common convention is to subtract the female mean from the male mean, so if males score higher *d* is positive, and if females score higher *d* is negative.

Defeminization: A reduction in a trait (physical or behavioral) that is higher in frequency or level in females than in males.

Defensive identification or identification with the aggressor: In psychoanalytic theory, identifying with a powerful person on the basis of fear of punishment.

Delayed puberty: Failure to begin the physical changes of **puberty** well beyond the typical age; girls are usually considered to be delayed if they have not started development by age 13, and boys by age 14.

Demasculinization: A reduction in a trait (physical or behavioral) that is higher in frequency or level in males than in females.

Depression: A disorder consisting of depressed mood, disturbances of sleep, feelings of worthlessness, loss of pleasure in daily activities, and thoughts of suicide.

Developmental or anaclitic identification: In psychoanalytic theory, identifying with a warm, nurturant caretaker. Attachment based on fear of loss of love.

Developmental constructivist theories: Theories in developmental psychology that emphasize the active role of individuals in creating their own knowledge.

Developmental intergroup theory (DIT): A theory developed by Bigler and Liben concerning how children's social stereotypes and prejudices develop as a function of environmental factors and children's cognitive processes.

Differential treatment: A measure of the extent to which parents and others treat boys and girls differently.

Dihydrotestosterone: A form of **testosterone** that is responsible for **masculinization** of the external genitalia; that is, development of the penis, scrotum, and urogenital sinus.

Direct instruction: Parents and others may tell children how to act as boys or girls, or teach them specific gender-related skills such as cooking or woodworking.

Discourse analysis: A variety of qualitative research methods used to analyze language use.

Dishabituation: Recovery of an infant's interest to a change in stimulus demonstrating the infant has detected a difference between a new stimulus and those stimuli that led to **habituation**.

Disorders of sex development (DSDs): Conditions in which one aspect of the process of sexual determination and differentiation is disrupted, usually resulting in discordance between aspects; formerly known as **intersex**.

Distal explanation: An explanation involving distal factors, especially factors that are removed in time; distal explanations of sex differences concern evolutionary forces.

Distribution: A set of scores on some task, measure, or characteristic.

Dominance hierarchy: An ordering of a peer group from the most popular and/or dominant child to the most rejected or dominated child.

Dominant gene: At a given **locus**, an **allele** whose effect dominates over that of the other allele.

Dosage-dependent effects: A concept elaborated by Martin and Fabes, suggesting that the more time that children spend in same-sex peer groups, the greater the effect of the peer group on their gendered behavior and their academic performance.

Double-voice discourse: A style of conflict resolution, more often used by girls, in which a child simultaneously pursues her own goal while being nice to the person with whom she is in conflict over the goal.

Dual pathway gender schema theory: An extension of **gender schema theory** that highlights the role of individual differences and conceptualizes gender development as an outcome of children's attitudes and personal interests.

Dyad: A two-person group.

Dyslexia: A difficulty in the processing of the sounds of language that leads to difficulty in learning to read in children who have normal IQs and adequate instruction.

Early maturing girls: Girls who reach **puberty** earlier than their similar-age peers.

Effect size: A measure of the size of a group difference (e.g., a sex difference).

Effortful control: A temperamental factor consisting of dimensions such as distractibility, attention, and task persistence.

Ego: In psychoanalytic theory, the part of personality that functions in reality and tries to bring satisfaction to the desires of the **id** and the demands of the **superego**; the psychological part of the personality.

Electra complex: A girl's wish to marry her father so that she can have a baby to compensate for not having a penis, accompanied by rivalry with her mother.

Emotional expression: Emotion that is able to be observed or measured by self-report or the reports of others such as parents or teachers.

Emotion-focused coping: A method of coping with emotional distress in which the person attempts to reduce or regulate the intensity of the emotions.

Empathy: Feelings of concern in response to the misfortune or distress of other people.

Encoding: The way that information from the environment is interpreted and entered into memory.

Entity theory of intelligence or ability: The belief that a person has a fixed ability in some domain— they either have it or they do not.

Eros: In psychoanalytic theory, life instincts such as hunger and sex.

Essentialism: A belief that members of categories are alike in important and even invisible ways, and that there is some underlying causal source for those shared qualities, typically assumed to be biological.

Estradiol: A form of **estrogen**.

Estrogens: A class of hormones that are important for bone development in both sexes and for the development of secondary sex characteristics in females.

Ethnography: A qualitative research method, often used in communication studies and anthropology, in which researchers observe people in their natural social setting, attempting not to change or modify the setting, but to become part of it.

Euclidean concepts: Understanding spatial qualities such as angle and distance that can be measured by reference to a coordinated system such as an x- and y-axis system with a defined point of origin; in Piaget and Inhelder's theory, thought to emerge, along with projective concepts, during childhood from the foundation of topological concepts.

Evolution: The principle that species change across time as a result of genetic changes that are transmitted across generations.

Evolutionary (psychology) theory: Theory that focuses on the origins of behavior (including individual differences in behavior) in terms of the adaptive pressures experienced by our ancestors.

Exercise play: Activities such as running, jumping, climbing, chasing, lifting, and pulling.

Exosystem: In Bronfenbrenner's Ecological Theory, the experiences that the child does not take part in directly, but which may impact on the child indirectly.

Expectancy confirmation: A process in which one's behavior is influenced by the verbally and nonverbally expressed expectations of others.

Experiments of nature: Naturally occurring conditions that are as close as we can get to an experimental manipulation of biology (nature's form of an experiment); in this case, conditions in which there is discordance among levels of sexual differentiation.

Experiment of nurture: An environmentally induced condition that is as close as we can get to an experimental manipulation of the social environment (an accidental experiment).

Explicit attributions: The links between social groups and qualities that are expressed directly by others (e.g., parents, peers) in the environment, leading children to internalize stereotypes about those social groups.

External genitalia: The penis and scrotum in males; clitoris, labia, and lower part of the vagina in females.

Externalizing disorders: Disorders involving acting out against others or property, or rule breaking.

Extinction: In learning theory, when behavior does not lead to reinforcement, the behavior eventually diminishes in frequency or rate.

Extroversion: One of the five factors of personality consisting of being outgoing, warm, or sociable.

Factor analysis: A statistical procedure that allows the researcher to see which tests or items appear to measure the same underlying concept or factor.

Felt pressure: The term used by Egan and Perry to refer to the degree to which individuals feel there are demands placed on them to conform to the norms of their own gender group.

Female-typical: A trait (physical or behavioral) that is higher in frequency or level in females than in males.

Feminism: A view that males and females should be seen as equally valuable, and a recognition that females and the feminine have often held lower value than males and the masculine.

Feminist empiricism: A feminist critique of science taking the position that sexist bias should be eliminated from the research process, to the extent that is possible to do so.

Feminist postmodernism: A feminist critique of science that takes the position that science does not really discover the world, but instead that science creates it, and thus that there are multiple versions of reality.

Feminist standpoint epistemology: A feminist critique of science taking the position that knowledge is influenced by the social position of the person producing the knowledge. Thus, if men and women have different social positions, the knowledge they produce will be affected by those positions.

Feminization: An increase in a trait (physical or behavioral) that is higher in frequency or level in females than in males.

Field dependence or independence: Theoretical constructs holding that some people (field dependent) are relatively more affected by the surrounding field when making a judgment whereas others (field independent) are less affected by the surrounding field in making judgments.

Fight-or-flight: A response pattern in which, under conditions of fear or stress, people are physiologically motivated to fight off danger, or to run away.

Fitness: Reproductive success, defined as the number of offspring that live to reproductive age and can reproduce themselves.

Five-factor theory of personality: A widely accepted theoretical view based on many years of research in many different cultures that there are five basic factors that make up the human personality. The five factors are neuroticism, extraversion, openness, agreeableness, and conscientiousness.

Focus groups: A qualitative research method in which there is an informal discussion about a selected topic among a group of participants.

Follicle-stimulating hormone: A hormone that simulates the gonads. In the case of ovaries, it stimulates the follicles leading to the development of a mature egg and ovulation. In the case of testes, it is related to sperm production.

Formal curriculum: The academic subject matter taught at school.

Fraternal twins: Twins resulting from the fertilization of two eggs by two sperm. They develop in utero at the same time, but are no more genetically similar than are other full siblings. Some are same-sex pairs, and some are brother-sister pairs.

Free recall task: A memory task in which people are asked to reproduce previously encountered material.

Frontal lobe: The most anterior (front) of the four lobes of the cerebral cortex; it plays a key role in reasoning, judgment, planning, and regulation of emotion.

Functional magnetic resonance imaging (fMRI): Technology that allows high-resolution pictures of the brain while someone is engaged in mental activity; a picture of the brain at work.

Functional environment: The way that environment is experienced by a particular person or group.

Gametes: Cells involved in sexual reproduction, producing zygotes when fused with gametes from the opposite sex; sperm and ova (egg cells).

GASC: The Gender Attitudes Scale for Children developed by Signorella and Liben to assess children's attitudes towards gender stereotypes.

Gender: Social and cultural aspects of being a male or female person. This can include gender identity, **gender roles**, masculinity and femininity, and other social and cultural processes. Males and females are sometimes referred to as "the genders."

Gender aschematic: A term used by Sandra Bem to describe people for whom gender is not an especially important or salient feature of social life (in contrast to those who are **gender schematic**).

Gender consistency. In Kohlberg's theory, understanding that gender remains unchanged despite superficial changes of appearance (e.g., of hairstyle or clothing); sometimes called sex-category constancy (see **gender constancy**).

Gender constancy: A term used by Kohlberg to refer to children's developing understanding of gender, including understanding **gender identity, gender stability**, and **gender consistency**. Sometimes used to refer to full understanding of all three, sometimes used synonymously with **gender consistency**.

Gender constructivism: A theoretical approach positing that children construct their own knowledge about gender in accord with their developing reasoning skills.

Gender contentedness: The term used by Egan and Perry to refer to the degree to which individuals are satisfied with their own gender.

Gender correlates: Qualities that children believe are related to being male versus female, including both **gender correlations** and **gender stereotypes**.

Gender correlations: Qualities (e.g., occupations, leisure activities) that are statistically associated with gender.

Gender dysphoria (or dysphoric): The state of being unhappy with one's sex.

Gender environmentalism: A theoretical approach positing that environmental factors are the primary causal agents in gender development.

Gender essentialism: Attributing differences between males and females to **essentialism**.

Gender identity: A term used by Kohlberg to refer to a young child's ability to identify himself or herself as a boy or a girl (see **gender constancy**). Gender identity is used by Egan and Perry to refer to an individual's knowledge, understanding, and acceptance of being male or female.

Gender identity disorder: A condition in which a child expresses a persistent desire to be the other sex.

Gender roles: Cultural expectations for people of one sex or the other. May include all components listed under gender stereotypes.

Gender schema or schemata: An internal set of ideas that people have about gender used to organize perception and cognition.

Gender schema theory (GST): A theory of gender development developed by Martin and Halverson in which gender schemas are said to direct children's decisions about behaviors and their interpretation and recall of gender-related information.

Gender schematic: A term used by Sandra Bem to describe people for whom gender is a highly salient feature of social life (see **gender aschematic**).

Gender segregation: The phenomenon in which children play in same sex peer groups, and generally have close friends of the same sex.

Gender stability: In Kohlberg's theory, the term used to refer to a child's understanding that gender remains stable over the life course.

Gender stereotypes: What people believe to be true of males versus females irrespective of the evidence for the presumed differences.

Gender typicality: The term used by Egan and Perry to refer to the degree to which individuals perceive their own qualities as similar to those of others of their gender.

Gene expression: The manifestation of a gene; how genes are manifested depends on a host of factors, including other genes and the environment.

Gene regulation: The process by which genes are turned on and off.

Generalized anxiety disorder: A disorder consisting of high levels of irritability, restlessness, anxiety and worry.

Genetic theories (perspectives, approaches): Theories (perspectives, approaches) that focus on the origins of individual differences in behavior in terms of variations in genes; with respect to sex-related behavior, this refers to genes on the X and Y chromosomes and to sex differences in the expression of genes on the autosomes.

Genital ducts: The precursors to the internal reproductive system: **Wolffian ducts** can become the epididymis, vas deferens (ejaculatory ducts), and seminal vesicles; **Müllerian ducts** can become the uterus, fallopian tubes, and upper part of the vagina.

Genital stage: Final stage in Freud's theory when the person moves into more mature relations with others, and establishes an adult role.

Genotype: A person's genetic constitution; the specific gene variants that a person possesses.

Gonads: The gamete-producing organs: testes in males (produces sperm), ovaries in females (produces eggs).

Gonadal dysgenesis: Abnormal development of the **gonads** (testes or ovaries).

Gonadarche: The aspects of puberty that are governed by the sex hormones (**estrogen** in girls and **testosterone** in boys), resulting in changes in secondary sex characteristics in both sexes and menarche in girls.

Gonadotropins: Hormones that initiate puberty: **luteinizing hormone** (LH) and **follicle-stimulating hormone** (FSH).

Gonadotropin-releasing hormone: A hormone that initiates puberty; it is released by the hypothalamus and acts on the pituitary to release two hormones, **luteinizing** hormone (LH) and **follicle-stimulating hormone** (FSH) which, in turn, stimulate the gonads (ovaries and testes).

Gonadotropin-releasing hormone analog (agonist): The treatment used to stop the physical changes of puberty in children who begin the process at an abnormally early age.

Gray matter: Brain tissue that consists of nerve cell bodies, dendrites, glia (cells that support and nourish the cells) and vasculature (blood supply).

Group-attribute covariation: A statistical association between a social group and some characteristic (e.g., White males and the U.S. presidency) that may lead children to construct some group-related quality to explain the observed association (see also implicit attributions).

Gyri: The parts on the surface of the cerebral cortex that "stick up" as a result of the folding of the brain to fit inside the skull; singular is gyrus.

Habituation: A method in which multiple stimuli of the same kind (e.g., pictures of cats) are shown until the infant stops attending or looking. Of interest is whether the infant recovers attention when a new kind of stimulus is shown (see **dishabituation**).

Having gender versus doing gender: "Having gender" refers to gender as an inherent characteristic of individuals, whereas "doing gender" refers to choosing to enact gender-related behaviors, although the process is subtle, and the person may not be completely aware that they are making such a choice.

Helpless orientation: Children who, when they experience failure, interpret it as meaning they lack ability, and hence give up trying (see the contrast with **mastery orientation**).

Hemispheric specialization: The different functional roles played by the two hemispheres of the cerebral cortex; also called **lateralization**.

Heritable: Transmitted across generations (from parent to offspring) through genes.

Hermeneutics: A philosophical field, originally interpretation of the Bible, now the interpretation of human experience.

Heschl's gyrus: A region of the temporal lobe of the brain that plays an important role in language.

Heterozygous: The condition in which an individual has two different **alleles** at a **locus**.

Hidden curriculum: Subtle gender-related practices that take place at school (e.g., boys taking more advanced placement computer or physical science classes).

Hippocampus: A region of the brain that is crucially important for memory.

Homogeneous and heterogeneous effect sizes: Refers to a calculation in meta-analysis to determine whether all of the effect sizes in a meta-analysis are very similar (homogeneous), or different (heterogeneous). In most cases in the meta-analyses of sex differences, the effect sizes are heterogeneous.

Homozygous: The condition in which an individual has the same two **alleles** at a **locus**.

Hormonal theories (perspectives, approaches): Theories (perspectives, approaches) that focus on the origins of individual differences in behavior in terms of variations in hormones; with respect to sex-related behavior, this refers to the sex hormones.

Hypothalamic-pituitary-gonadal axis: The coordinated action among two regions of the brain (the hypothalamus and the pituitary gland) and the gonads (testes and ovaries); important for the control of pubertal onset.

Hypothalamus: A part of the brain that produces hormones that regulate thirst, hunger, body temperature, sleep, moods, sex drive, and the release of hormones from various glands, primarily the **pituitary** gland.

Id: Unconscious part of personality consisting of basic impulses such as hunger, aggression, and sex; the biological part of the personality.

Identification: On the basis of an attachment with a parent, a child becomes like the parent by internalizing the parent's characteristics.

Idiopathic hypogonadotropic hypogonadism (IHH): A condition caused by a deficiency in **gonadotropin-releasing hormone** from the **hypothalamus** and resulting in **undervirilization** in males and atypical **puberty**.

Illusory correlation: Mistakenly thinking that one has seen some link between two qualities (e.g., being male and driving sports cars) more or less often than one actually has.

Imitation and modeling: Learning based on observing another person's behavior in the environment.

Implicit attributions: The inferences made from observing that some characteristic is associated or correlated with a particular group (e.g., seeing that all U.S. presidents are all male and thus assuming that only men have leadership qualities).

Imposed environment: The environment that is imposed on or selected for a person by others.

Imprinting: The process by which a gene is expressed differently depending on parental origin (whether it comes from the mother or from the father).

In-group bias: The tendency for people to favor their own group.

In-group favoritism: The tendency to believe that members of the group of which one is a member are superior to members of other groups.

In-group/out-group schemas: In Martin and Halverson's **gender schema theory**, the knowledge that children have about their own gender group and about the other gender group that guides gender-related information processing.

Incremental theory of ability: The belief that a person's ability in some domain can increase with practice, hard work, and experience in that domain.

Indirect aggression: Aggression that takes place out of view of the victim of aggression, often involving manipulation of social relationships (i.e., social or relational aggression).

Individual differences: Differences among individuals concerning factors such as skills, abilities, personality characteristics, and developmental timetables.

Inferior frontal gyrus: A region in the frontal lobe of the brain important for language.

Informal curriculum: Activities that take place at school (e.g., athletics or student government).

Information processing: How individuals attend to, encode, and remember material such as events, pictures, or stories.

Interactional level of analysis: An analysis used by social constructionist theorists at the level of social interaction between people.

Intergroup bias: The term used by Egan and Perry to refer to the belief that one's same-sex group is superior to the other-sex group; comparable to **in-group bias**.

Intergroup theory: A theory developed by Tajfel suggesting that individuals divide the world into social groups and then favor their own in-group and respond more negatively to out-groups.

Internalization: Incorporating values into the personality. A term used by psychoanalytic theorists that sometimes overlaps with both identification and introjection.

Internalizing disorders: Disorders involving acting against the self (e.g., depression or anxiety).

Intersex: A term formerly used to describe a disorder of sex development, resulting in one aspect of the process that is discordant with the other aspects.

Intrauterine position (IUP): An animal's position during fetal development as it reflects the sex of its neighboring littermates, denoted in terms of the number of males or females that surround it; for example, an IUP of 2M reflects the fact that the animal developed between two males.

Introjection: A psychoanalytic term generally referring to incorporating parents' values into one's own **superego**.

Intromission: Insertion of the penis into the vagina, a sexual behavior that is typical of male animals, including human males.

IT Scale for children: A projective test of sex-role adoption based on children's beliefs about what a stick figure called "IT," not identified as a boy or girl, liked to do. The test asked the children for IT's preferences for several sex-linked toys, objects, and activities.

Karyotype: A description of a person's chromosomes, designated by the number of sex chromosomes and the composition of the pair of sex chromosomes; typical females have a karyotype of 46,XX, whereas typical males have a karyotype of 46,XY.

Klinefelter syndrome: A sex chromosome **aneuploidy** caused by extra X chromosome in a male, resulting in the **karyotype** of 47,XXY.

Latency stage: Fourth stage in Freud's theory, beginning around the age of 6 and lasting until **puberty** when the child's early personality development is complete and is latent or resting until entering the genital stage.

Lateralization: The different functional roles played by the two hemispheres of the **cerebral cortex**; also called **hemispheric specialization**.

Learning goals: Goals in achievement tasks to acquire new information and develop better skills. In school, children with these goals are likely to be more concerned about what they learn rather than their grades (see the contrast with **performance goals**).

Learning theories: Psychological theories in which learning processes (e.g., reinforcement, punishment) are used to explain behavior.

Libido: In psychoanalytic theory, the energy or force that drives the life instincts.

Limbic system: A part of the brain involved in emotion.

Literary criticism: A field in the humanities involving the interpretation of literary texts.

Locus: The physical location of a gene on a chromosome; plural is loci.

Locus of control: The extent to which people believe the causes of events are internal (they control them; an internal locus of control) or external (events are caused by others or by chance; an external locus of control).

Lordosis: The arching of the back of female nonhuman animals to reflect sexual receptivity.

Luteinizing hormone: A hormone that stimulates the **gonads**.

Macrosystem: A term in Bronfenbrenner's Ecological Theory that refers to the general cultural context of development.

Magnetic resonance imaging (MRI): Technology that allows high-resolution pictures of the brain (and other parts of the body).

Male-typical: A trait (physical or behavioral) that is higher in frequency or level in males than in females.

Masculinity complex: In psychoanalytic theory, a girl or woman's wish to be like a man.

Masculinization: An increase in a trait (physical or behavioral) that is higher in frequency or level in males than in females.

Mastery orientation: Children who, when they experience failure, interpret it as meaning they should work harder, in contrast with **helpless orientation**.

Maternal grandparents: A child's mother's parents.

Mathematical problem solving: Determining the correct procedure to use, and then using the procedure to find a solution to a problem that is often stated in words.

Mean: A measure of group average or central tendency based on adding the scores and dividing by the number of scores in the group. Also known as the arithmetic mean.

Measure of central tendency: A measure indicating the center or the middle of a distribution of scores. Measures of central tendency include the **mean**, the **median**, and the **mode**.

Mechanistic theories: Psychological theories for which a machine serves as a metaphor, thus theories holding that all change, including developmental change, result from factors outside the person.

Median: Middle score in a group.

Membership knowledge: The term used by Egan and Perry to refer to an individual's knowledge of his or her own gender.

Menarche: A girl's first menstrual period.

Mental retardation: An IQ below 70, beginning in childhood, and substantial problems in daily social functioning.

Mental rotation: The ability to rotate—in one's mind—a two-dimensional figure or a three-dimensional object.

Mesosystem: A term in Bronfenbrenner's Ecological Theory that refers to the interactions or connections among the various parts of the environment that affect the child.

Meta-cognition: Reflecting on or thinking about one's own cognitive processes or thoughts.

Meta-analysis: A quantitative review of many studies on a single topic. In sex differences research, a statistical procedure that involves quantitatively pooling the results of several studies of sex differences in a particular behavior (e.g., aggression or self-esteem) to reach a conclusion about whether there seems to be a consistent sex difference in that behavior, and how large it is.

Micropenis: A condition in which a boy is born with a very small, but normally formed, penis.

Microsystem: In Bronfenbrenner's Ecological Theory, the child's actual environment including home, neighborhood, peers, school, etc. It includes the people the child interacts with and the places he or she goes.

Mode: Most common or most frequently obtained score in a group. There may be more than one mode (a bimodal distribution or a multimodal distribution), or the mode may be in a range of scores rather than a single score, or there may be no mode at all.

Modernism: Period after the enlightenment, associated with the development of modern science, which takes the view that there is an objective world to be discovered.

Morality of care: Carol Gilligan's proposition that the morality of girls and women leads to being careful to meet the needs of others with whom one has close relationships, and not to exploit or hurt them. The focus is on the needs of the people.

Morality of justice: The highest level of moral thinking in Kohlberg's theory. The belief that morality leads to treating everyone fairly, as in "do unto others as you would have them do unto you." The focus is on abstract moral principles.

Mosaic karyotype: Situation in which different cell lines have different chromosome compositions.

Motor skills: Skills involved in muscular movement. Gross motor skills consist of movements of the arms, legs, feet, or whole body (e.g., running, throwing). Fine motor skills involve small or fine-tuned movements, often involving the hands and fingers (e.g., cutting with scissors).

Müllerian ducts: One of the two sets of genital ducts; they can become the uterus, fallopian tubes, and upper part of the vagina.

Müllerian inhibiting substance: Also called anti-Müllerian hormone; a hormone produced by the testes during prenatal development which causes the destruction of the **Müllerian ducts** so that a female genital system cannot develop.

Multiple classification: The ability to sort objects or people along two dimensions at the same time (e.g., both color and shape; both gender and occupation).

Narrative review: A review of many studies on a particular topic, in which the reviewer reads the research, organizes it, and comes to conclusions about the findings. Sometimes called a qualitative review.

Narratives: A qualitative research method in which people tell stories of their lives.

Natural selection: The process by which heritable characteristics that are important for survival and reproduction are transmitted across generations.

Negative affectivity: A temperamental factor consisting of dimensions such as intensity, emotionality, fearfulness, anger, and difficulty.

Neo-Freudians: New Freudians, or followers of Freud that often developed variants of **psychoanalytic theory**.

Neonatal: Newborn period. A neonate is a newborn.

Neuroticism: One of the five factors of personality consisting of negative emotions such as anxiety, anger, hostility, depression, and shame.

Normal distribution: A symmetrical distribution of scores in which most of the scores cluster around the **mean**.

Null curriculum: Material that is missing from the academic curriculum (e.g., women's history).

OAT scales: The suite of occupational, activity, and trait (OAT) sex-typing scales developed by Liben and Bigler that includes an attitude measure (AM) and a personal measure (PM) of stereotype endorsement, with forms designed for adults (OAT), children (COAT), and preschoolers (POAT).

Object relations theory: A **psychoanalytic theory** based on children's attachment relations with their early caretakers, who are referred to as objects.

Obsessive-compulsive disorder: A disorder consisting of recurring obsessions (unwanted thoughts) and compulsions (repetitive behaviors).

Occipital lobe: The most posterior (back) of the four lobes of the **cerebral cortex**; it is very important in processing visual information.

Oedipus complex: In psychoanalytic theory, a boy's sexual attraction to and love for his mother, accompanied by rivalry with his father.

Openness: One of the five factors of personality consisting of being open to experiences such as feelings and ideas.

Oppositional defiant disorder: A disorder consisting of a pattern of irritable temperament, defiance, and aggression, but does not usually involve harm to property, stealing, or vandalism.

Oral stage: First stage in Freud's theory between birth and about 18 months of age, when children's **libido** is centered on the mouth and oral activities.

Orbital frontal cortex: A region of the **frontal lobe** involved in emotion.

Organismic theories: Psychological theories for which a living organism serves as a metaphor, thus theories holding that change, including developmental change, is a premise rather than an outcome to be explained.

Organizational hormone effects: Permanent effects on a trait (physical or behavioral) of hormones; usually refers to long-term effects of hormones that are present during prenatal or early postnatal development.

Ossification: Maturing process in skeletal development as cartilage becomes mature bone.

Other-sex schemas: A term in Martin and Halverson's **gender schema theory** used to refer to children's knowledge and beliefs relevant to the other sex.

Otoacoustic emissions: Sounds produced by the ear that are related to hearing sensitivity; they are more common and stronger in females than in males.

Out-group hostility: The tendency to look down on or devalue members of a group of which one is not a member.

Outcome praise (or punishment): Praise (or punishment) that focuses on the outcome achieved (e.g., "I'm proud of the grade you received." "I'm disappointed in how poorly you did.")

Own-sex schemas: A term in Martin and Halverson's **gender schema theory** used to refer to children's knowledge and beliefs relevant to their own sex.

Panic disorder: A disorder consisting of recurrent panic attacks and anxiety associated with experiencing further attacks.

Parental modeling of gender: The extent to which mothers and fathers behave differently in a way that signals gender-related behaviors to children.

Parietal lobe: One of the four lobes of the **cerebral cortex**; it plays a key role in integrating sensory information and in visuospatial processing.

Partial androgen insensitivity syndrome (PAIS): A genetic defect in the **androgen** receptor, resulting in reduced function of the androgen receptor, and thus reduced **masculinization**.

Passionate friendship: Friendships between girls which are typically not sexual, but include many features of passion such as emotional intensity and physical contact such as hugging and holding hands.

Paternal grandparents: A child's father's parents.

Patrilineal: A kinship system in which, in a particular culture, one's family roots are traced through one's father, and children belong to the male lineage.

Penis envy: In psychoanalytic theory, a girl's wish for a penis, which, according to the theory, she sees as superior to the anatomy that she, as a girl, possesses. Usually accompanied by the belief that she has been castrated, for which she typically holds her mother responsible.

Perceptual asymmetries: Differences between the hemispheres in perception and processing reflected in differences in accuracy of performance or reaction time in the left versus right visual fields, left versus right ears, or left versus right hands.

Perceptual speed: The ability to perceive details and shift attention quickly.

Performance goals: Goals in achievement task to look good and do well. In school, the main goal of someone with this orientation is likely to be getting good grades (see the contrast with **mastery goals**).

Person praise (or punishment): Praise (or punishment) that focuses on the person (e.g., "You are a good girl." "I'm disappointed in you.").

Persona: Jung's term for the conscious part of the human personality.

Personal unconscious: Jung's terms for elements of the unconscious that are personal to that individual, such as painful, repressed memories.

Perspective-taking: Children's ability to understand or take another's point of view. This can concern emotions, in which case it may be called *affective perspective-taking.*

Pervasive developmental disorder (PDD): Disorders that involve social skills, communication, and the presence of stereotyped behaviors or interests (e.g., **autism**).

Phallic stage: Third stage in Freud's theory between about 3 and 6 years of age when **libido** is centered on the penis or clitoris, and children experience sexual feelings, leading to an attraction to the parent of the other sex.

Phenotype: An observable or measurable trait; for example, height or spatial ability.

Pheromone: A chemical signal that is emitted by one animal and causes a change in other animals.

Pituitary gland: A part of the brain that regulates the production and use of hormones from other endocrine glands, leading to regulation of a variety of physiological processes.

Planum temporale: A region of the temporal lobe in the brain that is important in language processing and is larger on the left side than on the right side in most people.

POAT: See **OAT.**

Postmodernism: A perspective that knowledge is never objective but is always socially constructed as a function of social time, place, and culture.

Posttraumatic stress disorder: A disorder consisting of a set of characteristic symptoms following the experience of an exceptionally stressful event. The symptoms include recalling the event, avoiding similar situations, anxiety, irritability, sleeplessness, and emotional numbness.

Precocious puberty: The onset of physical changes of **puberty** at a very early age, usually considered to be age 8 in girls and age 9 in boys.

Preferential or preferred looking: A method of measuring infants' sensory and perceptual abilities that compares an infant's looking times to each of two simultaneously presented stimuli. Systematic preference for one stimulus indicates the infant has distinguished between the two on the basis of perceptual or conceptual cues.

Prenatal: Before birth; the period when the fetus is in the womb.

Preoptic area of the anterior hypothalamus: A region of the brain that has a high density of hormone receptors and that is different in size between male and female rats; there is an analogous area in human beings that also differs in size between men and women.

Pretense play: Imaginary play in which the children and their play partners pretend to engage in some activities or roles (e.g., playing house).

Primary sex ratio: The number of males conceived relative to the number of females conceived; the ratio is at least 120:100.

Proactive inhibition (PI): A phenomenon in which learning of new items is diminished by prior learning of items drawn from the same category (e.g., all items of furniture). Learning recovers when items are drawn from a different category (e.g., animals), called **release from PI.**

Probed recall tasks: Measures of memory in which the person is reminded of some aspect of the original memory stimulus (i.e., given a cue) and is asked to provide some additional information about the original stimulus.

Problem-focused coping: A method of coping with emotional distress in which the person tries to get rid of the things that are causing emotional distress.

Process praise (or punishment): Praise (or punishment) that focuses on the process used (the manner of solving a task, or the amount of effort used) to solve a task (e.g., "You worked hard"; "Could you think of a different way to do it?").

Progesterone: A hormone produced by the ovaries.

Projective concepts: Understanding spatial qualities such as "to the right" or "to the left" that change with viewing perspective or vantage point; in Piaget and Inhelder's theory, thought to emerge, along with Euclidean concepts, during childhood from the foundation of **topological concepts**.

Prosocial behavior: Behavior intended to help others.

Proximal explanation: An explanation involving proximal factors, especially factors that are close in time; proximal biological explanations of sex differences involve genes, hormones, and brain structure.

Pseudoconstancy: An appearance that child understands **gender constancy**, but the understanding is discovered to be superficial or flawed when the child is asked to justify the reason for his or her correct answer.

Psychoanalysis: A method of therapy developed by Freud and his followers.

Psychoanalytic theory: Theory associated with Freud and his followers consisting of a theory of personality, and a theory of personality's development through a series of stages.

Psychometricians: Psychological researchers who develop and use quantitative tests of skill, intelligence, and personality.

Pubarche: A stage of puberty that involves the development of sexual hair under the control of **androgens**.

Puberty: The physical changes that take place as a child develops into a sexually mature adult.

Punishment: Anything that follows a behavior and decreases the probability that the preceding behavior will occur in the future.

Receptors: Structures on the surface of a cell that respond to specific substances such as hormones.

Recessive gene: At a given **locus**, an **allele** whose effect is not expressed because it is dominated by the other allele at the locus.

Recognition: A measure of memory in which individuals are shown stimuli (e.g., pictures) and asked to identify those they had seen earlier.

Reinforcement: Anything that follows a behavior and increases the probability that the behavior will occur in the future.

Release from proactive inhibition (PI): See **proactive inhibition**.

Restricted range: Data in which all of the scores on a task are very similar within the tested group.

Retention interval: In memory tasks, the time between initial exposure to material and the time the individual is asked to remember the material.

Rett's syndrome: A disorder in which a child is born normal, but by about 18 months of age begins to show a loss of motor skills, speech, and reasoning, and usually a set of characteristic hand movements such as wringing the hands.

Rhythmic play: A type of physical play done by infants including such activities as foot kicking or arm waving.

Rough and tumble play: Active, physical play, including fun attacks and play fighting.

Rumination: Thinking about, talking about, and dwelling on feelings of distress.

Schema: A set of ideas that people have about a domain that organizes the way that they understand, think about, and remember domain-related information.

Schemata: Traditional plural of **schema**; contemporary scholars may use *schemas* instead.

Secondary sex ratio: The number of males born relative to the number of females born; the ratio is about 105:100.

Secondary sex characteristics: Physical features that differ between the sexes and relate to reproduction, including sexual hair and fully developed genitals.

Secular trend: Change across historical time.

Selected environment: The situations and experiences that one selects for oneself.

Self-concept: Appraisal of one's skills or characteristics in particular areas such as academic capabilities, athletic ability, social skills, or appearance.

Self-efficacy beliefs: Feelings that one is capable or has control over events that happen to them.

Self-esteem: Feelings of self-worth, self-respect, or acceptance.

Self-fulfilling prophecy: A situation in which expectancy confirmation and self-regulation lead to people's behavior confirming stereotypes or other expectations.

Self-reference effect: The process of showing greater attention and memory for self-relevant material.

Self-regulation: Factors involved in choosing or shaping one's own behavior.

Self-sanctions: In social cognitive theory, the **internalization** of sanctions based on learned cultural standards for behavior.

Sensitive period: The time during which an influence has the most effect; for gender development, the time during which hormones are most likely to produce permanent changes to the body and behavior.

Sequential touching: A method in which objects from different categories are placed randomly within an infant's reach, to observe whether infants touch or grasp the objects in a systematic order, thereby implying that the infant categorized the objects.

SERLI: The Sex Role Learning Index developed by Edelbrock and Sugawara to assess sex typing in children. Subscales measure children's knowledge of stereotypes (sex role discrimination or SRD) and their own preferences for masculine and feminine behaviors (sex role preference or SRP).

Sex: The classification of human beings and other organisms into male and female on the basis of chromosomes, reproductive organs, and genital structures. Males and females are often referred to as "the sexes."

Sex chromosomes: One of the 23 pairs of chromosomes (the 23rd pair), X chromosome and Y chromosome; females have two X chromosomes; males have an X chromosome and a Y chromosome.

Sex (sexual) determination: The processes that occur from the time that chromosomal sex is determined until the gonads have differentiated into ovaries or testes (determining gonadal sex).

Sex (sexual) differentiation: The processes that occur from the time that gonadal sex is determined until secondary sex characteristics are fully developed and sexual maturation is completed.

Sex-dimorphic: In the strict sense, existing in two different forms in males and females; in the broad sense, showing sex differences.

Sex hormones: Substances secreted by the gonads that produce physical and psychological sex differences.

Sex-limited inheritance: Sex differences that result from different expression of genes (typically genes on the **autosomes**) in females and males.

Sex-related behaviors: Behaviors that differ in level or frequency in males versus females; in people, these are usually called gender-typed or gendered behaviors.

Sex role identification: A position that children internalize their sex role (or gender role), or the general cultural characteristics associated with masculinity and femininity.

Sex typing or gender typing: The mapping of objects, activities, roles, and traits onto biological sex such that they follow prescriptive cultural stereotypes of gender.

Sexual harassment: Unwanted sexual behavior, including jokes and verbal and physical behavior of a sexual nature.

Sexual identity: A person's self-identity as predominantly heterosexual, homosexual, or bisexual.

Sexual minorities: Individuals who have any sexual experiences that are not exclusively heterosexual, including attraction, fantasy, behavior, and/or a sexual identity that is not heterosexual.

Sexual orientation: Erotic attraction or sexual desire towards persons of the opposite or same sex, or both, referred to respectively as heterosexual, homosexual, and bisexual.

Sexual selection: A special case of natural selection involving characteristics that increase the likelihood that an organism will obtain a mate and reproduce, usually because these characteristics are especially appealing to mates.

Sexually dimorphic nucleus of the preoptic area of the hypothalamus (SDN-POA): A region of the brain that differs greatly in size between male and female rats; it was one of the first regions found to differ between the sexes.

Social cognition: Cognitive skills that have impact on social relationships.

Social cognitive theory: A version of Bandura's **social learning theory** that adds the role of cognitive factors such as thoughts and beliefs to the role of the environment in explaining behavior.

Social construction theory: A postmodern theory of gender that proposes that knowledge can never be removed from social time and place, and that gender norms, roles, and behaviors are socially constructed.

Social impact: In sociometry, the number of times a child is identified as both "liked" and "disliked."

Social learning theory: A learning theory proposed by Bandura that emphasizes complex human social behaviors, and the role of imitation and modeling in learning those behaviors.

Social phobia: A disorder consisting of fears of being evaluated or judged by other people.

Social preference: In **sociometry**, the number of times a child is identified as "liked" minus the number of times the child is identified as "disliked."

Social referencing: The ability of infants to use the facial expressions of others, usually their caretakers, as a source of information.

Social or relational aggression: Behaviors that are directed toward damaging another person's self-esteem, social relationships, or social standing.

Social role theory: A theory proposed by social psychologist Eagly and her colleagues that explains sex differences in behavior and personality as a function of the social roles than males and females typically have played, especially homemaker and breadwinner roles.

Social sex: A person's assigned sex or the sex a person assumes.

Socialization approaches: Theoretical perspectives that emphasize the role of experience in and outside the family on children's gender development.

Sociological theory of Talcott Parsons: A variant of **psychoanalytic theory** that emphasized the necessity of expressive roles being performed by women, and instrumental roles being performed by men, and the importance of socializing children into these roles.

Sociological approach to the study of popularity: A method of identifying and studying popular children in terms of social prominence or status.

Sociometry: A procedure used by researchers to identify which children are liked and disliked by others.

Spatial perception: An individual's ability to identify spatial relations with respect to one's own bodily location or position in relation to something in the external space.

Spatial skills: The ability to encode, generate, retrieve, or mentally manipulate visual spatial images such as patterns or objects.

Spatial visualization: A skill in solving spatial problems that may draw upon many different strategies such as imagery and verbal reasoning.

Specific phobia: A disorder consisting of fear of a specific thing, such as snakes or injury.

Splenium: The posterior (back) part of the **corpus callosum** suggested to be larger and more bulbous in women than in men.

SRY: The sex-determining region of the Y chromosome; the gene that determines whether a fetus differentiates as a male.

Standard normal distribution: A normal distribution in which scores have been transformed to have a mean of 0, and a **standard deviation** of 1. Z-scores are used to refer to the standard normal distribution, in which a z-score of 1 is 1 standard deviation above the mean, a z-score of -2 is 2 standard deviations below the mean, etc.

Standard deviation: A widely used measure of **variability**. In a normal distribution, about 68% of the scores fall within 1 standard deviation above and below the mean.

Stanford-Binet intelligence tests: Measures of general intelligence constructed by Alfred Binet in France in 1905 and modified for use in the United States by Lewis Terman of Stanford University in 1906.

Stereotypes: A person's knowledge, beliefs, and expectations about some human group irrespective of the evidence for the presumed differences.

Stereotype threat: A phenomenon in which people's performance in a domain is diminished by their awareness that others hold negative **stereotypes** about their ability in that domain, because of the group (gendor, ethnicity) to which they belong.

Structural level of analysis: An analysis used by social constructionist theorists at the level of social structure and power relations.

Structural equation modeling: A statistical procedure used to determine whether a particular model fits the data being examined.

Sulci: The grooves on the surface of the **cerebral cortex** that result from the folding of the brain to fit inside the skull; singular is sulcus.

Superego: In psychoanalytic theory, a predominantly unconscious part of the personality consisting of moral values and prohibitions; the social part of the personality.

Surgency: A temperamental factor consisting of dimensions such as activity level, sociability, shyness, approach, high intensity, and impulsivity.

Sworn virgins: A third gender in rural Albania, where celibate women adopt male names and roles.

Sympathy: Expressions of concern in response to the misfortune or distress of other people.

Tanner stages: A measure of changes in **secondary sex characteristics** during **puberty**; Tanner 1 means no development, Tanner 5 means complete development, and Tanner 2, 3, and 4 reflect intermediate (increasing) degrees of development.

Temperament: Individual differences in basic aspects of personality, including such features as activity level, emotionality, self-regulation, and the tendency to approach or avoid new things or new people.

Temporal lobe: One of the four lobes of the **cerebral cortex**; it plays a key role in processing auditory information, including language and memory.

Tend-and-befriend: Proposed by psychologist Shelley Taylor and colleagues, this analogous mechanism to fight-or-flight refers to a pattern of behavior more common in females under conditions of chronic stress.

Tender-mindedness: One of the traits on the agreeableness factor of personality. Tender-mindedness means sympathy and concern for others, similar to **prosocial behavior**.

Testosterone: Hormone produced by the testes; a form of **androgen**.

Thelarche: A stage of **puberty** in girls that involves the development of the breasts under the control of **estrogen**.

Theory: A set of principles that lead to predictions and interpretations about information collected by observation and experimentation.

Theory-of-mind: Young children's developing ability to understand that other people have thoughts, feelings, and wishes—that they have minds.

Third gender: Some cultures include a third gender category beyond male and female, with different expectations for appearance and social roles than for either men or women.

Topological concepts: Understanding spatial qualities such as "next to" or "on" that are maintained even as a hypothetical rubber sheet is stretched and twisted; in Piaget and Inhelder's theory, these topological concepts are thought to be first set of spatial concepts mastered by children.

Transgender or transgendered: Living as a member of the other sex; that is, the sex that was not one's biological birth sex.

Triad: A three-person group.

Triadic reciprocal determinism: The interactive role of behavior, personal cognitions, and perceptions, and the external environment proposed in Bandura's **social cognitive theory**.

Turner Syndrome (TS): A sex chromosome **aneuploidy**, caused by an absent or abnormal second X chromosome, resulting in the **karyotype** 45,XO, or mosaic karyotype.

Undervirilization: Reduced physical masculinization.

Variability: The degree to which a characteristic (or scores measuring it) are spread out or clustered together.

Verbal fluency: A verbal skill requiring a person to generate a list of words, possibly with a common meaning or with a common sound.

Virilization: See **masculinization**.

Visual preference: A way of determining infants' knowledge about visual displays by measuring their preference for looking at one display versus another.

Wayfinding: A term used to refer to finding one's way around the environment.

White matter: Brain tissue that consists of the myelin sheath that covers the axons of neurons, facilitating transmission of nerve impulses.

Wolffian ducts: One of the two sets of genital ducts; they can become the epididymis, vas deferens (ejaculatory ducts), and seminal vesicles.

Womb envy: In psychoanalytic theory, specifally that of Horney, a boy or man's envy at women's ability to have a baby.

X-inactivation: The process by which one of the two X chromosomes is turned off in females during early embryonic development; which X is inactivated is random and varies across cells.

X-linked inheritance: Transmission of genes on the X-chromosome.

X-linked traits: Traits influenced by gene(s) on the X-chromosome; X-linked recessive traits occur more often in males than in females.

Z-scores: Standard deviation units in a standard normal distribution; a z-score of 1 is 1 standard deviation above the mean, a z-score of -2 is 2 standard deviations below the mean, and so on.

Zygote: The product of the fertilization of the egg by the sperm; a fertilized egg.

References

Abramovitch, R., Corter, C. M., & Lando, B. (1979). Sibling interaction in the home. *Child Development, 50*, 997–1003.

Abramovitch, R., Corter, C. M., & Pepler, D. J. (1980). Observations of mixed-sex sibling dyads. *Child Development, 51*, 1268–1271.

Abrams, D., Rutland, A., & Cameron, L. (2003). The development of subjective group dynamics: Children's judgments of normative and deviant in-group and out-group individuals. *Child Development, 74*, 1840–1856.

Achermann, J. C. (2004). Delayed puberty. In O. H. Pescovitz & E. A. Eugster (Eds.), *Pediatric endocrinology: Mechanisms, manifestations, and management* (pp. 334–348). Philadelphia: Lippincott Williams & Wilkins.

Acosta-Alzuru, C., & Kreshel, P. J. (2002). "I'm an American girl . . . Whatever that means": Girls consuming Pleasant Company's American girl identity. *Journal of Communication, 52*, 139–161.

Adams, S., Kuebli, J., Boyle, P. A., & Fivush, R. (1995). Gender differences in parent-child conversations about past emotions: A longitudinal investigation. *Sex Roles, 33*, 309–323.

Adler, P. A. & Adler, P. (1995). Dynamics of inclusion and exclusion in preadolescent cliques. *Social Psychology Quarterly, 58*, 145–162.

Adler, P. A. & Adler, P. (1998). *Peer power: Preadolescent culture and identity*. New Brunswick, NJ: Rutgers University Press.

Adler, P. A., Kless, S. J., & Adler, P. (1992). Socialization to gender roles: Popularity among elementary school boys and girls. *Sociology of Education, 65*, 169–187.

Adolph, K. E. (1997). Learning in the development of infant locomotion. *Monographs of the Society for Research in Child Development, 62* (3, Serial No. 251).

Adolph, K. E. & Avolio, A. M. (2000). Walking infants adapt locomotion to changing body dimensions. *Journal of Experimental Psychology: Human Perception and Performance, 26*, 1148–1166.

Adolph, K. E., Vereijken, B., & Denny, M. A. (1998). Learning to crawl. *Child Development, 69*, 1299–1312.

Ainsworth, M. S. (1993). Attachment as related to mother-infant interaction. *Advances in Infancy Research, 8*, 1–50.

Alexander, G. M. (2003). An evolutionary perspective of sex-typed toy preferences: Pink, blue, and the brain. *Archives of Sexual Behavior, 32*, 7–14.

Alexander, G. M. & Hines, M. (1994). Gender labels and play styles: Their relative contribution to children's selection of playmates. *Child Development, 65*, 869–879.

Alexander, G. M. & Hines, M. (2002). Sex differences in response to children's toys in nonhuman primates (Cercopithecus aethiops sabaeus). *Evolution and Human Behavior, 23*, 467–479.

Allan, K., & Coltrane, S. (1996). Gender display in television commercials: A comparative study of television commercials in the 1950s and 1980s. *Sex Roles, 35*, 185–203.

Allen, A. M. Allen, D. N., & Sigler, G. (1993). Changes in sex-role stereotyping in Caldecott Medal award picture books 1938–1988. *Journal of Research in Childhood Education, 7*, 67–73.

Allen, K. & Ingulsrud, J. E. (1998). What do you want to be when you grow up? An analysis of primary-school textbooks in the People's Republic of China. *Journal of Multilingual and Multicultural Development, 19*, 171–181.

Allen, L. S., Hines, M., Shryne, J. E., & Gorski, R. A. (1989). Two sexually dimorphic cell groups in the human brain. *Journal of Neuroscience, 9*, 497–506.

Allen, M. & Burrell, N. A. (2002). Sexual orientation of the parent: The impact on the child. In M. Allen, R. W. Preiss, B. M. Gayle & N. A. Burrell (Eds.), *Interpersonal communication research: Advances through meta-analysis* (pp. 125–143). Mahwah, NJ: Lawrence Erlbaum Associates.

Almli, C. R., Ball, R. H., & Wheeler, M. E. (2001). Human fetal and neonatal movement patterns: Gender differences and fetal-to-neonatal continuity. *Developmental Psychobiology, 38*, 252–273.

Almqvist, B. (1989). Age and gender differences in children's Christmas requests. *Play and Culture, 2*, 2–19.

Altshuler, J. L. & Ruble, D. N. (1989). Developmental changes in children's awareness of strategies for coping with uncontrollable stress. *Child Development, 60*, 1337–1349.

Ambady, N., Shih, M., Kim, A., & Pittinsky, T. L. (2001). Stereotype susceptibility in children: Effects of identity activation on quantitative performance. *Psychological Science, 12*, 385–390.

American Academy of Pediatrics. (2000). *Joint statement on the impact of entertainment violence on children.* Retrieved August 14, 2005, from: http://www.aap.org/advocacy/releases/jstmtevc.htm.

American Association of University Women Educational Foundation. (1995). *How schools shortchange girls: The AAUW Report*. New York: Marlowe.

American Association of University Women Educational Foundation. (2001). *Hostile hallways*. Washington, DC: Author.

American Psychiatric Association. (1994). *Diagnostic and statistical manual of mental disorders* (4th ed.). Washington, DC: American Psychiatric Association.

American Psychological Association. (1996). Gold medal award for life achievement in psychological science: Eleanor Emmons Maccoby. *American Psychologist, 51*, 757–759.

Anastasi, A. (1992). A century of psychological science. *American Psychologist, 47*, 842–843.

Anderson, C. A. & Bushman, B. J. (2001). Effects of violent video games on aggressive behavior, aggressive cognition, aggressive affect, physiological arousal, and prosocial behavior: A meta-analytic review of the scientific literature. *Psychological Science, 12*, 353–359.

Anderson, C. A., Carnagey, N. L., & Eubanks, J. (2003). Exposure to violent media: The effects of songs with violent lyrics on aggressive thoughts and feelings. *Journal of Personality and Social Psychology, 84*, 960–971.

Anderson, C. A., Carnagey, N. L., Flanagan, M., Benjamin, A. J., Jr., Eubanks, J., & Valentine, J. C. (2004). Violent video games: Specific effects of violent content on aggressive thoughts and behavior. In M. P. Zanna (Ed.), *Advances in experimental social psychology* (Vol. 36, pp. 199–249). San Diego, CA: Elsevier Academic Press.

Anderson, D. A. & Hamilton, M. (2005). Gender role stereotyping of parents in children's picture books: The invisible father. *Sex Roles, 52*, 145–151.

Anderssen, N., Amlie, C., & Ytteroy, E. A. (2002). Outcomes for children with lesbian or gay parents: A review of studies from 1978 to 2000. *Scandinavian Journal of Psychology, 43*, 335–351.

Andersson, G., Hank, K., & Rønsen, M. (2006). Gendering family composition: sex preferences for children and childbearing behavior in the Nordic countries. *Demography, 43*, 255–167.

Andre, T., Whigham, M., Hendrickson, A., & Chambers, S. (1999). Competency beliefs, positive affect, and gender stereotypes of elementary students and their parents about science versus other school subjects. *Journal of Research in Science Teaching, 36*, 719–747.

Angold, A., Costello, E. J., Erkanli, A., & Worthman, C. M. (1999). Pubertal changes in hormone levels and depression in girls. *Psychological Medicine, 29*, 1043–1053.

Antill, J. K., Cotton, S., Russell, G., & Goodnow, J. J. (1996). Measures of children's sex-typing in middle childhood II. *Australian Journal of Psychology, 48*, 35–44.

Antill, J. K., Russell, G., Goodnow, J. J., & Cotton, S. (1993). Measures of children's sex typing in middle childhood. *Australian Journal of Psychology, 45*, 25–33.

APA Task Force on Gender Identity Gender Variance and Intersex Conditions. (2006). *Answers to your questions about transgender individuals and gender identity*. Washington, DC: American Psychological Association.

Aponte, R., French, R., & Sherrill, C. (1990). Motor development of Puerto Rican children: Cross-cultural perspectives. *Perceptual and Motor Skills, 71*, 1200–1202.

Arceneaux, J. M., Cheramie, G. M., & Smith, C. W. (1996). Gender differences in WAIS-R age-corrected scaled scores. *Perceptual and Motor Skills, 83*, 1211–1215.

Arceneaux, J. M., Hill, S. K., Chamberlin, C. M., & Dean, R. S. (1997). Developmental and sex differences in sensory and motor functioning. *International Journal of Neuroscience, 89*, 253–263.

Archer, J. (2000). Sex differences in aggression between heterosexual partners: A meta-analytic review. *Psychological Bulletin, 126*, 651–680.

Archer, J. (2004). Sex differences in aggression in real-world settings: A meta-analytic review. *Review of General Psychology, 8*, 291–322.

Archer, J. & Coyne, S. M. (2005). An integrated review of indirect, relational, and social aggression. *Personality and Social Psychology Review, 9*, 212–230.

Arfai, K., Pitukcheewanont, P. D., Goran, M., J., Tavare, C. J., Heller, L., & Gilsanz, V. (2002). Bone, muscle, and fat: Sex-related differences in prepubertal children. *Radiology, 224*, 338–344.

Aries, E. (1998). Gender differences in interaction: A reexamination. In D. J. Canary & K. Dindia (Eds.), *Sex differences and similarities in communication: Critical essays and empirical investigations of sex and gender in interaction*. (pp. 65–81). Mahwah, NJ: Lawrence Erlbaum Associates.

Arima, A. N. (2003). Gender stereotypes in Japanese television advertisements. *Sex Roles, 49*, 81–90.

Armstrong, J. (2001). Popular series books and the middle class children inhabiting them: Are girls and boys really that frivolous? In S. Lehr (Ed.), *Beauty, brains, and brawn: The construction of gender in children's literature* (pp. 51–55). Portsmouth, NH: Heinemann.

Arnold, A. P. & Breedlove, S. M. (1985). Organizational and activational effects of sex steroids on brain and behavior: A reanalysis. *Hormones and Behavior, 19*, 469–498.

Arnold, D. H. & Doctoroff, G. L. (2003). The early education of socioeconomically disadvantaged children. *Annual Review of Psychology, 54*, 517–545.

Arthur, A. E., Bigler, R. S., Liben, L. S., Gelman, S. A., & Ruble, D. N. (2008). Gender stereotyping and prejudice in young children: A developmental intergroup perspective. In S. R. Levy & M. Killen (Eds.), *Intergroup attitudes and relations in childhood through adulthood* (pp. 66–86). Oxford, UK: Oxford University Press.

Arthur, A. E., Bigler, R. S., & Ruble, D. N. (2004, April). *The effect of gender constancy on preschool children's sex typing.* Poster presented at the Gender Development Research Conference, San Francisco.

Arthur, A. E., Hughes, J. M., Patterson, M. M., & Bigler, R. S. (2006, April). *Power and privilege: Children's reasoning about gender and the presidency.* Poster presented at the Gender Development Research Conference, San Francisco.

Assel, M. A., Landry, S. H., Swank, P., Smith, K. E., & Steelman, L. M. (2003). Precursors to mathematical skills: Examining the roles of visual-spatial skills, executive processes, and parenting factors. *Applied Developmental Science, 7*, 27–38.

Ataca, B. & Sunar, D. (1999). Continuity and change in Turkish urban family life. *Psychology and Developing Societies, 11*, 77–90.

Atwood, M. (1988). *Cat's eye.* New York: Anchor Books: A Division of Random House.

Aubry, S., Ruble, D. N., & Silverman, L. B. (1999). The role of gender knowledge in children's gender-typed preferences. In L. Balter & C. S. Tamis-LeMonda (Eds.), *Child psychology: A handbook of contemporary issues* (pp. 363–390). Philadelphia: Psychology Press/Taylor & Francis.

Aydt, H. & Corsaro, W. A. (2003). Differences in children's construction of gender across culture. *American Behavioral Scientist, 46*, 1306–1325.

Bach, G. R. (1946). Father-fantasies, father-typing and identification in father-separated children. *American Psychologist, 1*, 461.

Bachevalier, J. & Hagger, C. (1991). Sex differences in the development of learning abilities in primates. *Psychoneuroendocrinology, 16*, 177–188.

Baenninger, M. & Newcombe, N. (1995). Environmental input to the development of sex-related differences in spatial and mathematical ability. *Learning and Individual Differences, 7*, 363–379.

Bailey, J. M., Bobrow, D., Wolfe, M., & Mikach, S. (1995). Sexual orientation of adult sons of gay fathers. *Developmental Psychology, 31*, 124–129.

Bailey, J. M. & Oberschneider, M. J. (1997). Sexual orientation and professional dance. *Archives of Sexual Behavior, 26*, 433–444.

Bailey, J. M. & Zucker, K. J. (1995). Childhood sex-typed behavior and sexual orientation: A conceptual analysis and quantitative review. *Developmental Psychology, 31*, 43–55.

Bailey, K. R. (1993). *The girls are the ones with the pointy nails: An exploration of children's conceptions of gender.* London, Ontario: Althouse Press.

Baillargeon, R. H., Zoccolillo, M., Keenan, K., Côté, S., Pérusse, D., Wu, H.-X., et al. (2007). Gender differences in physical aggression: A prospective population-based survey of children before and after 2 years of age. *Developmental Psychology, 43*, 13–26.

Baker, M. A. (1987). Sensory functioning. In M. A. Baker (Ed.), *Sex differences in human performance.* Wiley series on studies in human performance (pp. 5–36). New York: Wiley.

Bandura, A. (1969). Social learning theory of identificatory processes. In D. A. Goslin (Ed.), *Handbook of socialization theory and research* (pp. 213–262). Chicago: Rand McNally.

Bandura, A. (1977). *Social learning theory.* New York: Prentice-Hall.

Bandura, A. (1986). *Social foundations of thought and action: A social cognitive theory.* Upper Saddle River, NJ: Prentice-Hall.

Bandura, A. (1992). Social cognitive theory. In R. Vasta (Ed.), *Six theories of child development: Revised formulations and current issues* (pp. 1–60). Bristol, PA: Jessica Kingsley.

Bandura, A. (1999). Social cognitive theory of personality. In L. A. Pervin & O. P. John (Eds.), *Handbook of personality: Theory and research* (2nd. ed., pp. 154–196). New York: The Guilford Press.

Bandura, A. (2001). Social cognitive theory: An agentic perspective. *Annual Review of Psychology, 52*, 1–26.

Bandura, A. & Huston, A. C. (1961). Identification as a process of incidental learning. *Journal of Abnormal and Social Psychology, 63*, 311–318.

Bandura, A., Ross, D., & Ross, S. A. (1961). Transmission of aggression through imitation of aggressive models. *Journal of Abnormal and Social Psychology, 63*, 575–582.

Bandura, A. & Walters, R. (1963). *Social learning and personality development.* New York: Holt, Rinehart, & Winston.

Bandyopadhyay, M. (2003). Missing girls and son preference in rural India: Looking beyond popular myth. *Health Care for Women International, 24*, 910–926.

Banerjee, R. & Lintern, V. (2000). Boys will be boys: The effect of social evaluation concerns on gender-typing. *Social Development, 9*, 397–408.

Banich, M. T. (2004). *Cognitive neuroscience and neuropsychology*. Boston: Houghton-Mifflin.

Barclay, A. & Cusumano, D. R. (1967). Father absence, cross-sex identity, and field-dependent behavior in male adolescents. *Child Development, 38*, 243–250.

Barner, M. R. (1999). Sex-role stereotyping in FCC-mandated children's educational television. *Journal of Broadcasting and Electronic Media, 43*, 551–564.

Barnett, D., Kidwell, S. L., & Leung, K. H. (1998). Parenting and preschooler attachment among low-income urban African American families. *Child Development, 69*, 1657–1671.

Barnett, R. C. & Hyde, J. S. (2001). Women, men, work, and family. *American Psychologist, 56*, 781–796.

Barry, H., III & Harper, A. S. (1982). Evolution of unisex names. *Names, 30*, 15–22.

Barry, H., III & Harper, A. S. (1995). Increased choice of female phonetic attributes in first names. *Sex Roles, 32*, 809–819.

Barsky, R. D. & Lachman, M. E. (1986). Understanding of horizontality in college women: Effects of two training procedures. *International Journal of Behavioral Development, 9*, 31–43.

Bartlett, F. C. (1932). *Remembering*. London: Cambridge University Press.

Bartlett, N. H., Vasey, P. L., & Bukowski, W. M. (2000). Is gender identity disorder in children a mental disorder? *Sex Roles, 43*, 753–785.

Barton, B. K. & Cohen, R. (2004). Classroom gender composition and children's peer relations. *Child Study Journal, 34*, 29–45.

Bartsch, R. A., Burnett, T., Diller, T. R., & Rankin-Williams, E. (2000). Gender representation in television commercials: Updating an update. *Sex Roles, 43*, 735–743.

Bauer, P. J. (1993). Memory for gender-consistent and gender-inconsistent event sequences by twenty-five-month-old children. *Child Development, 64*, 285–297.

Baum, M. J. (2006). Mammalian animal models of psychosexual differentiation: When is 'translation' to the human situation possible? *Hormones and Behavior, 50*, 579–588.

Baumeister, R. F. (2000). Gender differences in erotic plasticity: The female sex drive as socially flexible and responsive. *Psychological Bulletin, 126*, 347–374.

Baumrind, D. (1986). Sex differences in moral reasoning: Response to Walker's (1984) conclusion that there are none. *Child Development, 57*, 511–521.

Baxter, J. C., Horton, D. L., & Wiley, R. E. (1964). Father identification as a function of mother-father relationship. *Journal of Individual Psychology, 20*, 167–171.

Bayley, N. (1965). Comparisons of mental and motor test scores for ages 1–15 months by sex, birth order, race, geographical location, and education of parents. *Child Development, 36*, 379–412.

Beall, A. E. (1993). A social constructionist view of gender. In A. E. Beall & R. J. Sternberg (Eds.), *The psychology of gender* (pp. 127–147). New York: The Guilford Press.

Beattie, I. R. (2002). Are all "adolescent econometricians" created equal? Racial, class, and gender differences in college enrollment. *Sociology of Education, 75*, 19–43.

Becker, A. E., Burwell, R. A., Herzog, D. B., Hamburg, P., & Gilman, S. E. (2002). Eating behaviours and attitudes following prolonged exposure to television among ethnic Fijian adolescent girls. *British Journal of Psychiatry, 180*, 509–514.

Becker, J. B., Breedlove, S. M., Crews, D., & McCarthy, M. M. (Eds.). (2002). *Behavioral endocrinology*. Cambridge, MA: MIT Press.

Becker, J. R. (1981). Differential treatment of females and males in mathematics classes. *Journal for Research in Mathematics Education, 12*, 40–53.

Bellmore, A. D. & Cillessen, A. H. N. (2003). Children's meta-perceptions and meta-accuracy of acceptance and rejection by same-sex and other-sex peers. *Personal Relationships, 10*, 217–234.

Belsky, J. (1999). Interactional and contextual determinants of attachment security. In J. Cassidy & P. R. Shaver (Eds.), *Handbook of attachment: Theory, research, and clinical applications* (pp. 249–264). New York, NY: Guilford Press.

Belsky, J., Steinberg, L., & Draper, P. (1991). Childhood experience, interpersonal development, and reproductive strategy: and evolutionary theory of socialization. *Child Development, 62*, 647–670.

Bem, S. L. (1981). Gender schema theory: A cognitive account of sex typing. *Psychological Review, 88*, 354–364.

Bem, S. L. (1983). Gender schema theory and its implications for child development: Raising gender-aschematic children in a gender-schematic society. *Signs: Journal of Women in Culture and Society, 8*, 598–616.

Bem, S. L. (1989). Genital knowledge and gender constancy in preschool children. *Child Development, 60*, 649–662.

Bem, S. L. (1998). *An unconventional family*. New Haven, CT: Yale University Press.

Bem, S. L. (2000). Transforming the debate on sexual inequality: From biological difference to institutional andro-centrism. In J. C. Chrisler, C. Golden & P. D. Rozee (Eds.), *Lectures on the psychology of women* (2nd ed., pp. 3–15). New York: McGraw Hill.

Benbow, C. P. (1988). Sex differences in mathematical reasoning ability in intellectually talented preadolescents: Their nature, effects, and possible causes. *Behavioral and Brain Sciences, 11*, 169–232.

Benbow, C. P., Lubinski, D., Shea, D. L., & Eftekhari-Sanjani, H. (2000). Sex differences in mathematical reasoning ability at age 13: Their status 20 years later. *Psychological Science, 11*, 474–480.

Benbow, C. P. & Stanley, J. C. (1980). Sex differences in mathematical ability: Fact or artifact? *Science, 210*, 1262–1264.

Benenson, J. F. (1993). Greater preference among females than males for dyadic interaction in early childhood. *Child Development, 64*, 544–555.

Benenson, J. F. & Alavi, K. (2004). Sex differences in children's investment in same-sex peers. *Evolution and Human Behavior, 25*, 258–266.

Benenson, J. F., Apostoleris, N., & Parnass, J. (1998). The organization of children's same-sex peer relationships. In W. M. Bukowski & A. H. Cillessen (Eds.), *Sociometry then and now: Building on six decades of measuring children's experiences with the peer group.* (pp. 5–23). San Francisco, CA: Jossey-Bass.

Benenson, J. F. & Christakos, A. (2003). The greater fragility of females' versus males' closest same-sex friendships. *Child Development, 74*, 1123–1129.

Benenson, J. F., Liroff, E. R., Pascal, S. J., & Cioppa, G. D. (1997). Propulsion: a behavioural expression of masculinity. *British Journal of Developmental Psychology, 15*, 37–50.

Benenson, J. F., Morganstein, T., & Roy, R. (1998). Sex differences in children's investment in peers. *Human Nature, 9*, 369–390.

Benenson, J. F., Roy, R., Waite, A., Goldbaum, S., Linders, L., & Simpson, A. (2002). Greater discomfort as a proximate cause of sex differences in competition. *Merrill-Palmer Quarterly, 48*, 225–247.

Benjamin, H. (1932). Age and sex differences in the toy preferences of young children. *Journal of Genetic Psychology, 41*, 417–429.

Benjamin, L. T., Jr. (1975). The pioneering work of Leta Stetter Hollingworth in the psychology of women. *Nebraska History, 56*, 493–505.

Bensley, L. & Van Eenwyk, J. (2001). Video games and real-life aggression: Review of the literature. *Journal of Adolescent Health, 29*, 244–257.

Bereaud, S. R. (1975). Sex role images in French children's books. *Journal of Marriage and the Family, 37*, 194–207.

Berenbaum, S. A. (1999). Effects of early androgens on sex-typed activities and interests in adolescents with congenital adrenal hyperplasia. *Hormones and Behavior, 35*, 102–110.

Berenbaum, S. A. (2001). Cognitive function in congenital adrenal hyperplasia. *Endocrinology and Metabolism Clinics of North America, 30*, 173–192.

Berenbaum, S. A. (2002). Prenatal androgens and sexual differentiation of behavior. In E. A. Eugster & O. H. Pescovitz (Eds.), *Developmental endocrinology: From research to clinical practice* (pp. 293–311). Totowa, NJ: Humana Press.

Berenbaum, S. A. (2006). Psychological outcome in children with disorders of sex development: Implications for treatment and understanding typical development. *Annual Review of Sex Research, 17*, in press.

Berenbaum, S. A. & Bailey, J. M. (2003). Effects on gender identity of prenatal androgens and genital appearance: Evidence from girls with congenital adrenal hyperplasia. *Journal of Clinical Endocrinology and Metabolism, 88*, 1102–1106.

Berenbaum, S. A., Duck, S. C., & Bryk, K. (2000). Behavioral effects of prenatal versus postnatal androgen excess in children with 21-hydroxylase-deficient congenital adrenal hyperplasia. *Journal of Clinical Endocrinology and Metabolism, 85*, 727–733.

Berenbaum, S. A. & Hines, M. (1992). Early androgens are related to childhood sex-typed toy preferences. *Psychological Science, 3*, 203–206.

Berenbaum, S. A., Moffat, S., Wisniewski, A. B., & Resnick, S. M. (2003). Neuroendocrinology: Cognitive effects of sex hormones. In M. de Haan & M. H. Johnson (Eds.), *The cognitive neuroscience of development.* (pp. 207–235). New York: Psychology Press.

Berenbaum, S. A. & Resnick, S. M. (1997). Early androgen effects on aggression in children and adults with congenital adrenal hyperplasia. *Psychoneuroendocrinology, 22*, 505–515.

Berenbaum, S. A. & Snyder, E. (1995). Early hormonal influences on childhood sex-typed activity and playmate preferences: Implications for the development of sexual orientation. *Developmental Psychology, 31*, 31–42.

Berglund, E., Eriksson, M., & Westerlund, M. (2005). Communicative skills in relation to gender, birth order, childcare and socioeconomic status in 18-month-old children. *Scandinavian Journal of Psychology, 46*, 485–491.

Berman, P. W. (1980). Are women more responsive than men to the young? A review of developmental and situational variables. *Psychological Bulletin, 88*, 668–695.

Berman, P. W., Monda, L. C., & Myerscough, R. P. (1977). Sex differences in young children's responses to an infant: An observation within a day-care setting. *Child Development, 48*, 711–715.

Berman, P. W., Smith, V. L., & Goodman, V. (1983). Development of sex differences in response to an infant and to the caretaker role. *Journal of Genetic Psychology, 143*, 283–284.

Bernhardt, P. C., Dabbs, J. M., Fielden, J. A., & Lutter, C. D. (1998). Testosterone changes during vicarious experiences of winning and losing among fans at sporting events. *Physiology & Behavior, 65*, 59–62.

Bernzweig, J., Eisenberg, N., & Fabes, R. A. (1993). Children's coping in self- and other-relevant contexts. *Journal of Experimental Child Psychology, 55*, 208–226.

Bertenthal, B. I. & Clifton, R. K. (1998). Perception and action. In D. Kuhn & R. S. Siegler (Eds.), *Handbook of child psychology: Vol. 2. Cognition, Perception, and Language* (5th ed., pp. 51–102). New York: Wiley.

Best, D. L. (2001). Gender concepts: Convergence in cross-cultural research and methodologies. *Cross Cultural Research: The Journal of Comparative Social Science, 35*, 23–43.

Best, D. L. & Williams, J. E. (1993). A cross-cultural viewpoint. In A. E. Beall & R. J. Sternberg (Eds.), *The psychology of gender* (pp. 215–248). New York: The Guilford Press.

Best, D. L. & Williams, J. E. (1997). Sex, gender, and culture. In J. W. Berry, M. H. Segall & C. Kagitcibasi (Eds.), *Handbook of cross-cultural psychology: Vol. 3. Social behavior and applications* (pp. 163–212). Boston: Allyn and Bacon.

Best, R. (1983). *We've all got scars: What boys and girls learn in elementary school.* Bloomington, IN: Indiana University Press.

Bettencourt, B. A. & Kernahan, C. (1997). A meta-analysis of aggression in the presence of violent cues: Effects of gender differences and aversive provocation. *Aggressive Behavior, 23*, 447–456.

Bettencourt, B. A. & Miller, N. (1996). Gender differences in aggression as a function of provocation: A meta-analysis. *Psychological Bulletin, 119*, 422–447.

Bezirganian, S. & Cohen, P. (1992). Sex differences in the interaction between temperament and parenting. *Journal of the American Academy of Child and Adolescent Psychiatry, 31*, 790–801.

Bhanot, R. & Jovanovic, J. (2005). Do parents' academic gender stereotypes influence whether they intrude on their children's homework? *Sex Roles, 52*, 597–607.

Bickham, D. S., Wright, J. C., & Huston, A. C. (2001). Attention, comprehension, and the educational influences of television. In D. G. Singer & J. L. Singer (Eds.), *Handbook of children and the media* (pp. 101–119). Thousand Oaks, CA: Sage.

Biernat, M. & Kobrynowicz, D. (1999). A shifting standards perspective on the complexity of gender stereotypes and gender stereotyping. In W. B. Swann, Jr. & J. H. Langlois (Eds.), *Sexism and stereotypes in modern society: The gender science of Janet Taylor Spence* (pp. 75–106). Washington, DC: American Psychological Association.

Biernat, M. & Vescio, T. K. (2002). She swings, she hits, she's great, she's benched: Implications of gender-based shifting standards for judgment and behavior. *Personality and Social Psychology Bulletin, 28*, 66–77.

Bigler, R. S. (1995). The role of classification skill in moderating environmental influences on children's gender stereotyping: A study of the functional use of gender in the classroom. *Child Development, 66*, 1072–1087.

Bigler, R. S. (1999). Psychological interventions designed to counter sexism in children: Empirical limitations and theoretical foundations. In W. B. Swann, Jr. & J. H. Langlois (Eds.), *Sexism and stereotypes in modern society: The gender science of Janet Taylor Spence* (pp. 129–151). Washington, DC: American Psychological Association.

Bigler, R. S., Jones, L. C., & Lobliner, D. B. (1997). Social categorization and the formation of intergroup attitudes in children. *Child Development, 68*, 530–543.

Bigler, R. S. & Liben, L. S. (1990). The role of attitudes and interventions in gender-schematic processing. *Child Development, 61*, 1440–1452.

Bigler, R. S. & Liben, L. S. (1992). Cognitive mechanisms in children's gender stereotyping: Theoretical and educational implications of a cognitive-based intervention. *Child Development, 63*, 1351–1363.

Bigler, R. S. & Liben, L. S. (2006). A developmental intergroup theory of social stereotypes and prejudice. In R. V. Kail (Ed.), *Advances in child development and behavior* (Vol. 34, pp. 39–89). San Diego, CA: Elsevier.

Bigler, R. S. & Liben, L. S. (2007). Developmental intergroup theory: Explaining and reducing children's social stereotyping and prejudice. *Current Directions in Psychological Science, 16*, 162–166.

Bigler, R. S., Spears Brown, C., & Markell, M. (2001). When groups are not created equal: Effects of group status on the formation of intergroup attitudes in children. *Child Development, 72*, 1151–1162.

Bigner, J. J. (1999). Raising our sons: Gay men as fathers. *Journal of Gay and Lesbian Social Services: Issues in Practice, Policy and Research, 10*, 61–77.

Bijou, S. W. & Baer, D. M. (1961). *Child development: Vol. 1. A systematic and empirical theory*. East Norwalk, CT: Appleton-Century-Crofts.

bin Laden, C. (2004). *Inside the kingdom: My life in Saudi Arabia*. New York: Warner Books.

Bin-Abbas, B., Conte, F. A., Grumbach, M. M., & Kaplan, S. L. (1999). Congenital hypogonadotropic hypogonadism and micropenis: effect of testosterone treatment on adult penile size. Why sex reversal is not indicated. *Journal of Pediatrics, 134*, 579–583.

Biringen, Z., Emde, R. N., Brown, D., Lowe, L., Myers, S., & Nelson, D. (1999). Emotional availability and emotional communication in naturalistic mother-infant interactions: Evidence for gender relations. *Journal of Social Behavior and Personality, 14*, 463–478.

Birnbaum, D. W. & Croll, W. L. (1984). The etiology of children's stereotypes about sex differences in emotionality. *Sex Roles, 10*, 677–691.

Bishop, D. V., Canning, E., Elgar, K., Morris, E., Jacobs, P. A., & Skuse, D. H. (2000). Distinctive patterns of memory function in subgroups of females with Turner syndrome: evidence for imprinted loci on the X-chromosome affecting neurodevelopment. *Neuropsychologia, 38*, 712–721.

Bishop, K. M. & Wahlsten, D. (1997). Sex differences in the human corpus callosum: myth or reality? *Neuroscience and Biobehavioral Reviews, 21*, 581–601.

Bjerregaard, B. (2002). Self-definitions of gang membership and involvement in delinquent activities. *Youth and Society, 34*, 31–54.

Bjorklund, D. F. (2000). *Children's thinking: Developmental function and individual differences* (3rd ed.). Belmont, CA: Wadsworth/Thomson Learning.

Björkqvist, K., Lagerspetz, K. M., & Kaukiainen, A. (1992). Do girls manipulate and boys fight? Developmental trends in regard to direct and indirect aggression. *Aggressive Behavior, 18*, 117–127.

Björkqvist, K., Österman, K., & Kaukiainen, A. (1992). The development of direct and indirect aggressive strategies in males and females. In K. Björkqvist & P. Niemela (Eds.), *Of mice and women: Aspects of female aggression* (pp. 51–64). San Diego, CA: Academic Press.

Björkqvist, K., Österman, K., & Kaukiainen, A. (2000). Social intelligence—empathy = aggression? *Aggression and Violent Behavior, 5*, 191–200.

Björkqvist, K., Österman, K., & Lagerspetz, K. M. J. (1994). Sex differences in covert aggression among adults. *Aggressive Behavior, 20*, 27–33.

Blaise, M. (2005). A feminist poststructuralist study of children "doing" gender in an urban kindergarten classroom. *Early Childhood Research Quarterly, 20*, 85–108.

Blakemore, J. E. O. (1981). Age and sex differences in interaction with a human infant. *Child Development, 52*, 386–388.

Blakemore, J. E. O. (1985). Interaction with a baby by young adults: A comparison of traditional and feminist men and women. *Sex Roles, 13*, 405–411.

Blakemore, J. E. O. (1990). Children's nurturant interactions with their infant siblings: An exploration of gender differences and maternal socialization. *Sex Roles, 22*, 43–57.

Blakemore, J. E. O. (1991). The influence of gender and temperament on children's interaction with a baby. *Sex Roles, 24*, 531–537.

Blakemore, J. E. O. (1992). The influence of age, gender, and having a younger sibling on children's knowledge about babies. *Journal of Genetic Psychology, 153*, 139–153.

Blakemore, J. E. O. (1998). The influence of gender and parental attitudes on preschool children's interest in babies: Observations in natural settings. *Sex Roles, 38*, 73–94.

Blakemore, J. E. O. (2003). Children's beliefs about violating gender norms: Boys shouldn't look like girls, and girls shouldn't act like boys. *Sex Roles, 48*, 411–419.

Blakemore, J. E. O. & Centers, R. (2005). Characteristics of boys' and girls' toys. *Sex Roles, 53*, 619–633.

Blakemore, J. E. O., LaRue, A. A., & Olejnik, A. B. (1979). Sex-appropriate toy preference and the ability to conceptualize toys as sex-role related. *Developmental Psychology, 15*, 339–340.

Blanchard, R. (1997). Birth order and sibling sex ratio in homosexual versus heterosexual males and females. *Annual Review of Sex Research, 8*, 27–67.

Blanchard, R. (2001). Fraternal birth order and the maternal immune hypothesis of male homosexuality. *Hormones and Behavior, 40*, 105–114.

Block, C. E. (2000). Dyadic and gender differences in perceptions of the grandparent-grandchild relationship. *International Journal of Aging and Human Development, 51*, 85–104.

Block, J. & Turula, E. (1963). Identification, ego control, and adjustment. *Child Development, 34*, 945–953.

Block, J. H. (1976). Issues, problems, and pitfalls in assessing sex differences: A critical review of "The Psychology of Sex Differences." *Merrill-Palmer Quarterly, 22*, 283–308.

Block, J. H. (1983). Differential premises arising from differential socialization of the sexes: Some conjectures. *Child Development, 54*, 1335–1354.

Block, R. A., Hancock, P. A., & Zakay, D. (2000). Sex differences in duration judgments: A meta-analytic review. *Memory and Cognition, 28*, 1333–1346.

Bobo, M., Hildreth, B. L., & Durodoye, B. (1998). Changing patterns in career choices among African-American, Hispanic, and Anglo children. *Professional School Counseling, 1*, 37–42.

Bogaert, A. F. (2005a). Gender role/identity and sibling sex ratio in homosexual men. *Journal of Sex and Marital Therapy, 31*, 217–227.

Bogaert, A. F. (2005b). Sibling sex ratio and sexual orientation in men and women: New tests in two national probability samples. *Archives of Sexual Behavior, 34*, 111–116.

Boggiano, A. K. & Barrett, M. (1991). Strategies to motivate helpless and mastery-oriented children: The effect of gender-based expectancies. *Sex Roles, 25*, 487–510.

Bojesen, A. & Gravholt, C. H. (2007). Klinefelter syndrome in clinical practice. *Nature Clinical Practice Urology, 4*, 192–204.

Book, A. S., Starzyk, K. B., & Quinsey, V. L. (2001). The relationship between testosterone and aggression: A meta-analysis. *Aggression and Violent Behavior, 6*, 579–599.

Booth, A., Shelley, G., Mazur, A., Tharp, G., & Kittok, R. (1989). Testosterone, and winning and losing in human competition. *Hormones and Behavior, 23*, 556–571.

Boraas, S. & Rodgers III, W. M. (2003). How does gender play a role in the earnings gap? An update. *Monthly Labor Review, 126*, 9–15.

Born, M. P., Bleichrodt, N., & Van der Flier, H. (1987). Cross-cultural comparison of sex-related differences on intelligence tests: A meta-analysis. *Journal of Cross-Cultural Psychology, 18*, 283–314.

Bornstein, M. H., Hahn, C.-S., & Haynes, O. M. (2004). Specific and general language performance across early childhood: Stability and gender considerations. *First Language, 24*, 267–304.

Boulton, M. J. (1996). A comparison of 8- and 11-year-old girls' and boys' participation in specific types of rough-and-tumble play and aggressive fighting: Implications for functional hypotheses. *Aggressive Behavior, 22*, 271–287.

Bourguignon, J.-P. (2004). Control of the onset of puberty. In O. H. Pescovitz & E. A. Eugster (Eds.), *Pediatric endocrinology: Mechanisms, manifestations, and management.* (pp. 285–298). Philadelphia: Lippincott Williams & Wilkins.

Bradbard, M. R. (1985). Sex differences in adults' gifts and children's toy requests at Christmas. *Psychological Reports, 56*, 969–970.

Bradbard, M. R. & Endsley, R. C. (1983). The effects of sex-typed labeling on preschool children's information-seeking and retention. *Sex Roles, 9*, 247–260.

Bradbard, M. R., Martin, C. L., Endsley, R. C., & Halverson, C. F. (1986). Influence of sex stereotypes on children's exploration and memory: A competence versus performance distinction. *Developmental Psychology, 22*, 481–486.

Bradley, C. B., McMurray, R. G., Harrell, J. S., & Deng, S. (2000). Changes in common activities of 3rd though 10th graders: The CHIC study. *Medicine and Science in Sports and Exercise, 32*, 2071–2078.

Bradley, S. J., Oliver, G. D., Chernick, A. B., & Zucker, K. J. (1998). Experiment of nurture: ablatio penis at 2 months, sex reassignment at 7 months, and a psychosexual follow-up in young adulthood. *Pediatrics, 102*, e9.

Bradley, S. J. & Zucker, K. J. (1990). Gender identity disorder and psychosexual problems in children and adolescents. *Canadian Journal of Psychiatry, 35*, 477–486.

Braungart-Rieker, J., Courtney, S., & Garwood, M. M. (1999). Mother- and father-infant attachment: Families in context. *Journal of Family Psychology, 13*, 535–553.

Braza, F., Braza, P., Carreras, M. R., & Munoz, J. M. (1997). Development of sex differences in preschool children: Social behavior during an academic year. *Psychological Reports, 80*, 179–188.

Breedlove, S. M. (1992). Sexual dimorphism in the vertebrate nervous system. *The Journal of Neuroscience, 12*, 4133–4142.

Brendgen, M., Vitaro, F., Doyle, A. B., Markiewicz, D., & Bukowski, W. M. (2002). Same-sex peer relations and romantic relationships during early adolescence: Interactive links to emotional, behavioral, and academic adjustment. *Merrill-Palmer Quarterly, 48*, 77–103.

Bresnahan, M. J., Inoue, Y., Liu, W. Y., & Nishida, T. (2001). Changing gender roles in prime-time commercials in Malaysia, Japan, Taiwan, and the United States. *Sex Roles, 45*, 117–131.

Bridgeman, B. & Wendler, C. (1991). Gender differences in predictors of college mathematics performance and in college mathematics course grades. *Journal of Educational Psychology, 83*, 275–284.

Brigham, J. C. (1971). Ethnic stereotypes. *Psychological Bulletin, 76*, 15–38.

Brim, O. G., Jr. (1958). Family structure and sex role learning by children: A further analysis of Helen Koch's data. *Sociometry, 21*, 1–16.

Brinn, J., Kraemer, K., Warm, J. S., & Paludi, M. A. (1984). Sex-role preferences in four age levels. *Sex Roles, 11*, 901–910.

Brockmann, H. (2001). Girls preferred? Changing patterns of sex preference in the two German states. *European Sociological Review, 17*, 189–202.

Brody, L. R. (1984). Sex and age variations in the quality and intensity of children's emotional attributions to hypothetical situations. *Sex Roles, 11*, 51–59.

Brody, L. R. (1985). Gender differences in emotional development: A review of theories and research. *Journal of Personality, 53*, 102–149.

Brody, L. R. (1996). Gender, emotional expression, and parent-child boundaries. In R. D. Kavanaugh & B. Zimmerberg (Eds.), *Emotion: Interdisciplinary perspectives* (pp. 139–170). Hillsdale, NJ: Lawrence Erlbaum Associates.

Brody, L. R. (1999). *Gender, emotion, and the family*. Cambridge, MA: Harvard University Press.

Brody, L. R. & Hall, J. A. (2000). Gender, emotion, and expression. In M. Lewis & J. M. Haviland-Jones (Eds.), *Handbook of emotions* (2nd ed., pp. 338–349). New York: The Guilford Press.

Brody, L. R., Lovas, G. S., & Hay, D. H. (1995). Gender differences in anger and fear as a function of situational context. *Sex Roles, 32*, 47–78.

Broidy, L. M., Nagin, D. S., Tremblay, R. E., Bates, J. E., Brame, B., Dodge, K. A., et al. (2003). Developmental trajectories of childhood disruptive behaviors and adolescent delinquency: A six-site, cross-national study. *Developmental Psychology, 39*, 222–245.

Bronfenbrenner, U. (1960). Freudian theories of identification and their derivatives. *Child Development, 31*, 15–40.

Bronfenbrenner, U. (1979). *The ecology of human development*. Cambridge, MA: Harvard University Press.

Bronfenbrenner, U. & Morris, P. A. (1998). The ecology of developmental processes. In R. M. Lerner (Ed.), *Handbook of child psychology: Vol. 1. Theoretical models of human development* (5th ed., pp. 993–1028). New York: Wiley.

Brooks-Gunn, J. (1987). Pubertal processes and girls' psychological adaptation. In R. M. Lerner & T. T. Foch (Eds.), *Biological-psychosocial interactions in early adolescence* (pp. 123–153). Hillsdale, NJ: Erlbaum.

Brooks-Gunn, J., Petersen, A. C., & Compas, B. E. (1995). Physiological processes and the development of childhood and adolescent depression. In I. M. Goodyear (Ed.), *The depressed child and adolescent: Developmental and clinical perspectives* (pp. 91–109). New York: Cambridge University Press.

Brooks-Gunn, J. & Warren, M. P. (1989). Biological and social contributions to negative affect in young adolescent girls. *Child Development, 60*, 40–55.

Brown, D. G. (1956). Sex-role preference in young children. *Psychological Monographs, 70*, 19.

Brown, D. G. (1957). Masculinity-femininity development in children. *Journal of Consulting Psychology, 21*, 197–202.

Brown, D. G. (1962). Sex-role preference in children: Methodological problems. *Psychological Reports, 11*, 477–478.

Brown, L. H. & Roodin, P. A. (2003). Grandparent-grandchild relationships and the life course perspective. In J. Demick & C. Andreoletti (Eds.), *Handbook of adult development* (pp. 459–474). New York: Kluwer Academic/ Plenum.

Brown, P. L. (2006, Dec. 2). Supporting boys or girls when the line isn't clear. *The New York Times*, pp. A1, A11.

Brown, W. M., Hines, M., Fane, B. A., & Breedlove, S. M. (2002). Masculinized finger length patterns in human males and females with congenital adrenal hyperplasia. *Hormones and Behavior, 42*, 380–386.

Browne, B. A. (1998). Gender stereotypes in advertising on children's television in the 1990s: A cross-national analysis. *Journal of Advertising, 27*, 83–96.

Bryden, M. P. (1982). *Laterality: Functional asymmetry in the intact brain*. New York: Academic Press.

Buchanan, C. M., Eccles, J. S., & Becker, J. B. (1992). Are adolescents the victims of raging hormones: evidence for activational effects of hormones on moods and behavior at adolescence. *Psychological Bulletin, 111*, 62–107.

Buck, J. J., Williams, R. M., Hughes, I. A., & Acerini, C. L. (2003). In utero exposure and 2nd to 4th digit length ratio—comparisons between healthy controls and females with classical congenital adrenal hyperplasia. *Human Reproduction, 18*, 976–979.

Buckner, J. P. & Fivush, R. (2000). Gendered themes in family reminiscing. *Memory, 8*, 401–412.

Buhrmester, D. (1996). Need fulfillment, interpersonal competence, and the developmental contexts of early adolescent friendship. In W. M. Bukowski, A. F. Newcomb & W. W. Hartup (Eds.), *The company they keep: Friendship in childhood and adolescence. Cambridge studies in social and emotional development* (pp. 158–185). New York: Cambridge University Press.

Bukowski, W. M., Gauze, C., Hoza, B., & Newcomb, A. F. (1993). Differences and consistency between same-sex and other-sex peer relationships during early adolescence. *Developmental Psychology, 29*, 255–263.

Bumpus, M. F., Crouter, A. C., & McHale, S. M. (2001). Parental autonomy granting during adolescence: Exploring gender differences in context. *Developmental Psychology, 37*, 163–173.

Buntaine, R. L. & Costenbader, V. K. (1997). Self-reported differences in the experience and expression of anger between girls and boys. *Sex Roles, 36*, 625–637.

Burhans, K. K. & Dweck, C. S. (1995). Helplessness in early childhood: The role of contingent worth. *Child Development, 66*, 1719–1738.

Burlage, T. D. (2002, January 13). Shanna Z makes history: A small-town girl with a big-time game. *Fort Wayne Journal Gazette*, p. 1B and 5B.

Burlingame-Lee, L. J. & Canetto, S. S. (2005). Narratives of gender in computer advertisements. In E. Cole & J. H. Daniel (Eds.), *Featuring females: Feminist analyses of media* (pp. 85–99). Washington, DC: American Psychological Association.

Bushman, B. J. & Anderson, C. A. (2001). Media violence and the American public: Scientific facts versus media misinformation. *American Psychologist, 56*, 477–489.

Bushman, B. J. & Huesmann, L. R. (2001). Effects of televised violence on aggression. In D. G. Singer & J. L. Singer (Eds.), *Handbook of children and the media* (pp. 223–254). Thousand Oaks, CA: Sage.

Buss, D. M. (1994). *The evolution of desire: Strategies of human mating*. New York, NY: Basic Books.

Buss, D. M. (2000). Desires in human mating. *Annals of the New York Academy of Sciences, 907*, 39–49.

Buss, D. M. & Kenrick, D. T. (1998). Evolutionary social psychology. In D. T. Gilbert & S. T. Fiske (Eds.), *The handbook of social psychology, Vol. 2* (4th ed., pp. 982–1026). New York: McGraw-Hill.

Bussey, K. & Bandura, A. (1984). Influence of gender constancy and social power on sex-linked modeling. *Journal of Personality and Social Psychology, 47*, 1292–1302.

Bussey, K. & Bandura, A. (1992). Self-regulatory mechanisms governing gender development. *Child Development, 63*, 1236–1250.

Bussey, K. & Bandura, A. (1999). Social cognitive theory of gender development and differentiation. *Psychological Review, 106*, 676–713.

Bussey, K. & Perry, D. G. (1982). Same-sex imitation: The avoidance of cross-sex models or the acceptance of same-sex models? *Sex Roles, 8*, 773–784.

Butler, R. (2000). Making judgments about ability: The role of implicit theories of ability in moderating inferences from temporal and social comparison information. *Journal of Personality and Social Psychology, 78*, 965–978.

Butterfield, S. A. & Loovis, E. M. (1993). Influence of age, sex, balance, and sport participation on development of throwing by children in Grades K-8. *Perceptual and Motor Skills, 76*, 459–464.

Butterfield, S. A. & Loovis, E. M. (1994). Influence of age, sex, balance, and sport participation on development of kicking by children in Grades K-8. *Perceptual and Motor Skills, 79*, 691–697.

Byrnes, J. P., Miller, D. C., & Schafer, W. D. (1999). Gender differences in risk taking: A meta-analysis. *Psychological Bulletin, 125*, 367–383.

Cairns, E. (1990). The relationship between adolescent perceived self-competence and attendance at single-sex secondary school. *British Journal of Educational Psychology, 60*, 207–211.

Caldera, Y. M., Huston, A. C., & O'Brien, M. (1989). Social interactions and play patterns of parents and toddlers with feminine, masculine, and neutral toys. *Child Development, 60*, 70–76.

Calvert, S. L., Kotler, J. A., Zehnder, S. M., & Shockey, E. M. (2003). Gender stereotyping in children's reports about educational and informational television programs. *Media Psychology, 5*, 139–162.

Camarata, S. & Woodcock, R. W. (2006). Sex differences in processing speed: Developmental effects in males and females. *Intelligence, 34*, 231–252.

Cameron, C. (2001). Promise or problem? A review of the literature on men working in early childhood services. *Gender, Work and Organization, 8*, 430–453.

Campbell, A., Shirley, L., & Caygill, L. (2002). Sex-typed preferences in three domains: Do two-year-olds need cognitive variables? *British Journal of Psychology, 93*, 203–217.

Campbell, A., Shirley, L., Heywood, C., & Crook, C. (2000). Infants' visual preference for sex-congruent babies, children, toys and activities: A longitudinal study. *British Journal of Developmental Psychology, 18*, 479–498.

Campbell, D. W. & Eaton, W. O. (1999). Sex differences in the activity level of infants. *Infant and Child Development, 8*, 1–17.

Cannon, W. B. (1932). *The wisdom of the body*. New York: W. W. Norton.

Cantor, J. M., Blanchard, R., Paterson, A. D., & Bogaert, A. F. (2002). How many gay men owe their sexual orientation to fraternal birth order? *Archives of Sexual Behavior, 31*, 63–71.

Caplan, P. J. & Caplan, J. B. (1999). *Thinking critically about research on sex and gender* (2nd ed.). New York: Addison-Wesley Longman.

Capute, A. J., Shapiro, B. K., Ross, A., & Wachtel, R. C. (1985). Normal gross motor development: The influences of race, sex, and socio-economic status. *Developmental Medicine and Child Neurology, 27*, 635–643.

Carey, G. (2003). *Human genetics for the social sciences*. Thousand Oaks, CA: Sage.

Carnagey, N. L. & Anderson, C. A. (2005). The effects of reward and punishment in violent video games on aggressive affect, cognition, and behavior. *Psychological Science, 16*, 882–889.

Carpenter, C. J. (1983). Activity structure and play: Implications for socialization. In M. Liss (Ed.), *Social and cognitive skills* (pp. 117–145). New York: Academic Press.

Carr, M. & Jessup, D. L. (1997). Gender differences in first-grade mathematics strategy use: Social and metacognitive influences. *Journal of Educational Psychology, 89*, 318–328.

Carr, M., Jessup, D. L., & Fuller, D. (1999). Gender differences in first-grade mathematics strategy use: Parent and teacher contributions. *Journal for Research in Mathematics Education, 30*, 20–46.

Carroll, J. L., Volk, K. D., & Hyde, J. S. (1985). Differences between males and females in motives for engaging in sexual intercourse. *Archives of Sexual Behavior, 14*, 131–139.

Carson, J., Burks, V., & Parke, R. D. (1993). Parent-child physical play: Determinants and consequences. In K. MacDonald (Ed.), *Parent-child play: Descriptions and implications* (pp. 197–220). Albany, NY: State University of New York Press.

Carter, D. B. & Levy, G. D. (1988). Cognitive aspects of early sex-role development: The influence of gender schemas on preschoolers' memories and preferences for sex-typed toys and activities. *Child Development, 59*, 782–792.

Carter, D. B. & Levy, G. D. (1991). Gender schemas and the salience of gender: Individual differences in nonreversal discrimination learning. *Sex Roles, 25*, 555–567.

Carter, D. B. & Patterson, C. J. (1982). Sex roles as social conventions: The development of children's conceptions of sex-role stereotypes. *Developmental Psychology, 18*, 812–824.

Carver, K., Joyner, K., & Udry, J. R. (2003). National estimates of adolescent romantic relationships. In P. Florsheim (Ed.), *Adolescent romantic relations and sexual behavior: Theory, research, and practical implications* (pp. 23–56). Mahwah, NJ: Lawrence Erlbaum Associates.

Carver, P., Yunger, J. L., & Perry, D. G. (2003). Gender identity and adjustment in middle childhood. *Sex Roles, 49*, 95–109.

Carver, P. R., Egan, S. K., & Perry, D. G. (2004). Children who question their heterosexuality. *Developmental Psychology, 40*, 43–53.

Casey, M. B., Nuttall, R. L., & Pezaris, E. (1997). Mediators of gender differences in mathematics college entrance test scores: A comparison of spatial skills with internalized beliefs and anxieties. *Developmental Psychology, 33*, 669–680.

Casey, M. B., Nuttall, R. L., Pezaris, E., & Benbow, C. P. (1995). The influence of spatial ability on gender differences in mathematics college entrance test scores across diverse samples. *Developmental Psychology, 31*, 697–705.

Casey, R. J. & Fuller, L. L. (1994). Maternal regulation of children's emotions. *Journal of Nonverbal Behavior, 18*, 57–89.

Caspi, A., Lynam, D., Moffitt, T. E., & Silva, P. A. (1993). Unraveling girls' delinquency: biological, dispositional, and contextual contributions to adolescent misbehavior. *Developmental Psychology, 29*, 19–30.

Cassell, J., Huffaker, D., Tversky, D., & Ferriman, K. (2006). The language of online leadership : Gender and youth engagement on the Internet. *Developmental Psychology, 42*, 436–449.

Cauffman, E. & Steinberg, L. (1996). Interactive effects of menarcheal status and dating on dieting and disordered eating among adolescent girls. *Developmental Psychology, 32*, 631–635.

Centers for Disease Control. (2002). Trends in cigarette smoking among high school students: United States 1991–2001. *Morbidity and Mortality Weekly Report, 51*, 409–412.

Cervantes, C. A. & Callanan, M. A. (1998). Labels and explanations in mother-child emotion talk: Age and gender differentiation. *Developmental Psychology, 34*, 88–98.

Chan, R. W., Brooks, R. C., Raboy, B., & Patterson, C. J. (1998). Division of labor among lesbian and heterosexual parents: Associations with children's adjustment. *Journal of Family Psychology, 12*, 402–419.

Chan, R. W., Raboy, B., & Patterson, C. J. (1998). Psychosocial adjustment among children conceived via donor insemination by lesbian and heterosexual mothers. *Child Development, 69*, 443–457.

Chance, C. & Fiese, B. H. (1999). Gender-stereotyped lessons about emotion in family narratives. *Narrative Inquiry, 9*, 243–255.

Chandler, M. (1988). Doubt and developing theories of mind. In J. W. Astington, P. L. Harris & D. R. Olson (Eds.), *Developing theories of mind.* (pp. 387–413). New York: Cambridge University Press.

Chaplin, T. M., Cole, P. M., & Zahn-Waxler, C. (2005). Parental socialization of emotion expression: Gender differences and relations to child adjustment. *Emotion, 5*, 80–88.

Chappell, K. K. (1996). Mathematics computer software characteristics with possible gender-specific impact: A content analysis. *Journal of Educational Computing Research, 15*, 25–35.

Charlesworth, W. R. & LaFreniere, P. (1983). Dominance, friendship, and resource utilization in preschool children's groups. *Ethology and Sociobiology, 4*, 175–186.

Charman, T., Ruffman, T., & Clements, W. (2002). Is there a gender difference in false belief development? *Social Development, 11*, 1–10.

Chase, C. (1998). Surgical progress is not the answer to intersexuality. *Journal of Clinical Ethics, 9*, 385–392.

Cheng, T. L., Brenner, R. A., Wright, J. L., Sachs, H. C., Moyer, P., & Rao, M. (2003). Community norms on toy guns. *Pediatrics, 111*, 75–79.

Cherland, M. R. (1994). *Private practices: Girls reading fiction and constructing identity*. London: Taylor and Francis.

Cherney, I. D. & Ryalls, B. O. (1999). Gender-linked differences in the incidental memory of children and adults. *Journal of Experimental Child Psychology, 72*, 305–328.

Cheslock, J. (2007). *Who's playing college sports*. East Meadow, NY: Women's Sports Foundation.

Chick, K. A., Heilman-Houser, R. A., & Hunter, M. W. (2002). The impact of child care on gender role development and gender stereotypes. *Early Childhood Education Journal, 29*, 149–154.

Chodorow, N. J. (1978). *The reproduction of mothering*. Los Angeles: University of California Press.

Chodorow, N. J. (1989). *Feminism and psychoanalytic theory*. New Haven, CT: Yale University Press.

Chodorow, N. J. (1994). *Femininities, masculinities, sexualities: Freud and beyond*. Lexington, KY: University Press of Kentucky.

Chodorow, N. J. (1995). Gender as a personal and cultural construction. *Signs, 20*, 516–544.

Chua, S. L., Chen, D.-T., & Wong, A. F. L. (1999). Computer anxiety and its correlates: A meta-analysis. *Computers in Human Behavior, 15*, 609–623.

Cillessen, A. H. N. & Mayeux, L. (2004). From censure to reinforcement: Developmental changes in the association between aggression and social status. *Child Development, 75*, 147–163.

Cioffi, F. (1998). *Freud and the question of pseudoscience*. Chicago: Open Court Publishing Company.

Claes, M. (1998). Adolescents' closeness with parents, siblings, and friends in three countries: Canada, Belgium, and Italy. *Journal of Youth and Adolescence, 27*, 165–184.

Clark, A. S. & Goldman-Rakic, P. S. (1989). Gonadal hormones influence the emergence of cortical function in non-human primates. *Behavioral Neuroscience, 103*, 1287–1295.

Clark, J. E. & Phillips, S. J. (1987). An examination of the contributions of selected anthropometric factors to gender differences in motor skill development. In J. E. Clark & J. H. Humphrey (Eds.), *Advances in motor development research* (Vol. 1, pp. 171–178). New York: AMS Press.

Clark, L. & Tiggemann, M. (2006). Appearance culture in nine- to 12-year-old girls: Media and peer influences on body dissatisfaction. *Social Development, 15*, 628–643.

Clark, M. M. & Galef, B. G. (1998). Effects of intrauterine position on the behavior and genital morphology of litter-bearing rodents. *Developmental Neuropsychology, 14*, 197–211.

Clark, M. M., Vonk, J. M., & Galef, B. G. (1998). Intrauterine position, parenting, and nest-site attachment in male Mongolian gerbils. *Developmental Psychobiology, 32*, 177–181.

Clark, R., Guilmain, J., Saucier, P. K., & Tavarez, J. (2003). Two steps forward, one step back: The presence of female characters and gender stereotyping in award-winning picture books between the 1930s and the 1960s. *Sex Roles, 49*, 439–449.

Clark, R., Lennon, R., & Morris, L. (1993). Of Caldecotts and Kings: Gendered images in recent American children's books by black and non-black illustrators. *Gender and Society, 7*, 227–245.

Clearfield, M. & Nelson, N. (2006). Sex differences in mothers' speech and play behavior with 6-, 9-, and 14-month-old infants. *Sex Roles, 54*, 127–137.

Cleland, F. E. & Gallahue, D. L. (1993). Young children's divergent movement ability. *Perceptual and Motor Skills, 77*, 535–544.

Clutton-Brock, T. (2007). Sexual selection in males and females. *Science, 318*, 1882–1885.

Coats, P. B. & Overman, S. J. (1992). Childhood play experiences of women in traditional and nontraditional professions. *Sex Roles, 26*, 261–271.

Cohen, J. (1969). *Statistical power for the behavioral sciences*. New York: Academic Press.

Cohen-Bendahan, C. C. C., Buitelaar, J. K., van Goozen, S. H. M., & Cohen-Kettenis, P. T. (2004). Prenatal exposure to testosterone and functional cerebral lateralization: A study in same-sex and opposite-sex twin girls. *Psychoneuroendocrinology, 29*, 911–916.

Cohen-Bendahan, C. C. C., Buitelaar, J. K., van Goozen, S. H. M., Orlebeke, J. F., & Cohen-Kettenis, P. T. (2004). Is there an effect of prenatal testosterone on aggression and other behavioral traits? A study comparing same-sex and opposite-sex twin girls. *Hormones and Behavior, 47*, 230–237.

Cohen-Bendahan, C. C. C., Buitelaar, J. K., van Goozen, S. H. M., Orlebeke, J. F., & Cohen-Kettenis, P. T. (2005). Is there an effect of prenatal testosterone on aggression and other behavioral traits? A study comparing same-sex and opposite-sex twin girls. *Hormones and Behavior, 47*, 230–237.

Cohen-Bendahan, C. C. C., van de Beek, C., & Berenbaum, S. A. (2005). Prenatal sex hormone effects on child and adult sex-typed behavior: Methods and findings. *Neuroscience and Biobehavioral Reviews, 29*, 353–384.

Cohen-Kettenis, P. T. (2005). Gender change in 46,XY persons with 5-alpha-reductase-2 deficiency and 17-beta-hydroxysteroid dehydrogenase-3 deficiency. *Archives of Sexual Behavior, 34*, 399–410.

Coie, J. D. & Dodge, K. A. (1998). Aggression and anti-social behavior. In N. Eisenberg (Ed.), *Handbook of child psychology: Vol. 3. Social, emotional, and personality development.* (5th ed., pp. 779–862). New York: Wiley.

Colapinto, J. (2000). *As nature made him: The boy who was raised as a girl.* New York: Harper Collins.

Colapinto, J. (2004). *What were the real reasons behind David Reimer's suicide?* Retrieved January 15, 2007

Colby, A., Kohlberg, L., Gibbs, J., & Lieberman, M. (1983). A longitudinal study of moral judgment. *Monographs of the Society for Research in Child Development, 48*(1–2, Serial No. 200).

Cole, E. R., Zucker, A. N., & Duncan, L. E. (2001). Changing society, changing women (and men). In R. K. Unger (Ed.), *Handbook of the psychology of women and gender* (pp. 410–423). New York: Wiley.

Cole, P. M., Zahn-Waxler, C., & Smith, K. D. (1994). Expressive control during a disappointment: Variations related to preschoolers' behavior problems. *Developmental Psychology, 30*, 835–846.

Cole-Harding, S., Morstad, A. L., & Wilson, J. R. (1988). Spatial ability in members of opposite-sex twin pairs (Abstract). *Behavior Genetics, 18*, 710.

Collaer, M. L. & Hines, M. (1995). Human behavioral sex differences: A role for gonadal hormones during early development? *Psychological Bulletin, 118*, 55–107.

Collins, W. A. (2003). More than myth: The developmental significance of romantic relationships during adolescence. *Journal of Research on Adolescence, 13*, 1–24.

Collins, W. A. & Russell, G. (1991). Mother-child and father-child relationships in middle childhood and adolescence: A developmental analysis. *Developmental Review, 11*, 99–136.

Coltrane, S. (2000). Research on household labor: Modeling and measuring the social embeddedness of routine family work. *Journal of Marriage and the Family, 62*, 1208–1233.

Coltrane, S. & Adams, M. (1997). Children and gender. In T. Arendell (Ed.), *Contemporary parenting: Challenges and issues. Understanding families* (Vol. 9, pp. 219–253). Thousand Oaks, CA: Sage.

Compas, B. E., Malcarne, V. L., & Fondacaro, K. M. (1988). Coping with stressful events in older children and young adolescents. *Journal of Consulting and Clinical Psychology, 56*, 405–411.

Compian, L., Gowen, L. K., & Hayward, C. (2004). Peripubertal girls' romantic and platonic involvement with boys: Associations with body image and depression symptoms. *Journal of Research on Adolescence, 14*, 23–47.

Compian, L. & Hayward, C. (2003). Gender differences in opposite sex relationships: Interactions with puberty. In C. Hayward (Ed.), *Gender differences at puberty* (pp. 77–92). New York: Cambridge University Press.

Comstock, G. (1993). The medium and the society: The role of television in American life. In G. L. Berry & J. K. Asamen (Eds.), *Children & television: Images in a changing sociocultural world* (pp. 117–131). Thousand Oaks, CA: Sage.

Connolly, J., Craig, W., Goldberg, A., & Pepler, D. (1999). Conceptions of cross-sex friendships and romantic relationships in early adolescence. *Journal of Youth and Adolescence, 28*, 481–494.

Connolly, J., Craig, W., Goldberg, A., & Pepler, D. (2004). Mixed-gender groups, dating, and romantic relationships in early adolescence. *Journal of Research on Adolescence, 14*, 185–207.

Cook, H. B. K. (1992). Matrifocality and female aggression in Margariteno society. In K. Björkqvist & P. Niemela (Eds.), *Of mice and women: Aspects of female aggression* (pp. 149–162). San Diego, CA: Academic Press.

Cordua, G. D., McGraw, K. O., & Drabman, R. S. (1979). Doctor or nurse: Children's perception of sex typed occupations. *Child Development, 50*, 590–593.

Cornell, E. H. (1974). Infants' discrimination of photographs of faces following redundant presentations. *Journal of Experimental Child Psychology, 18*, 98–106.

Costa, P., Jr., Terracciano, A., & McCrae, R. R. (2001). Gender differences in personality traits across cultures: Robust and surprising findings. *Journal of Personality and Social Psychology, 81*, 322–331.

Costabile, A., Genta, M. L., Zucchini, E., Smith, P. K., & Harker, R. (1992). Attitudes of parents toward war play in young children. *Early Education and Development, 3*, 356–369.

Crabb, P. B. & Bielawski, D. (1994). The social representation of material culture and gender in children's books. *Sex Roles, 30*, 69–79.

Crick, N. R. (1995). Relational aggression: The role of intent attributions, feelings of distress, and provocation type. *Development and Psychopathology, 7*, 313–322.

Crick, N. R. (1997). Engagement in gender normative versus non-normative forms of aggression: Links to social-psychological adjustment. *Developmental Psychology, 33*, 610–617.

Crick, N. R. & Bigbee, M. A. (1998). Relational and overt forms of peer victimization: A multi-informant approach. *Journal of Consulting and Clinical Psychology, 66*, 337–347.

Crick, N. R., Casas, J. F., & Ku, H. C. (1999). Relational and physical forms of peer victimization in preschool. *Developmental Psychology, 35*, 376–385.

Crick, N. R. & Grotpeter, J. K. (1995). Relational aggression, gender, and social-psychological adjustment. *Child Development, 66*, 710–722.

Crick, N. R. & Grotpeter, J. K. (1996). Children's treatment by peers: Victims of relational and overt aggression. *Development and Psychopathology, 8,* 367–380.

Crick, N. R. & Ladd, G. W. (1990). Children's perceptions of the outcomes of social strategies: Do the ends justify being mean? *Developmental Psychology, 26,* 612–620.

Crick, N. R., Nelson, D. A., Morales, J. R., Cullerton-Sen, C., Casas, J. F., & Hickman, S. E. (2001). Relational victimization in childhood and adolescence: I hurt you through the grapevine. In J. Juvonen & S. Graham (Eds.), *Peer harassment in school: The plight of the vulnerable and victimized* (pp. 196–214). New York: The Guilford Press.

Crick, N. R. & Rose, A. J. (2000). Toward a gender-balanced approach to the study of social-emotional development: A look at relational aggression. In P. H. Miller & E. Kofsky Scholnick (Eds.), *Toward a feminist developmental psychology* (pp. 153–168). Florence, KY: Taylor & Francis/Routledge.

Crick, N. R. & Werner, N. E. (1998). Response decision processes in relational and overt aggression. *Child Development, 69,* 1630–1639.

Cross, S. E. & Madson, L. (1997). Models of the self: Self-construals and gender. *Psychological Bulletin, 122,* 5–37.

Crouter, A. C., Head, M. R., Bumpus, M. F., & McHale, S. M. (2001). Household chores: Under what conditions do mothers lean on daughters? In A. J. Fuligni (Ed.), *Family obligation and assistance during adolescence: Contextual variations and developmental implications* (pp. 23–41). San Francisco, CA: Jossey-Bass/Pfeiffer.

Crouter, A. C., Helms-Erikson, H., Updegraff, K., & McHale, S. M. (1999). Conditions underlying parents' knowledge about children's daily lives in middle childhood: Between-and within-family comparisons. *Child Development, 70,* 246–259.

Crouter, A. C., Manke, B. A., & McHale, S. M. (1995). The family context of gender intensification in early adolescence. *Child Development, 66,* 317–329.

Crowley, K., Callanan, M. A., Tenenbaum, H. R., & Allen, E. (2001). Parents explain more often to boys than to girls during shared scientific thinking. *Psychological Science, 12,* 258–261.

Crum, J. F. & Eckert, H. M. (1985). Play patterns of primary school children. In J. E. Clark & J. H. Humphrey (Eds.), *Motor development: Current selected research* (Vol. 1, pp. 99–114). Princeton, NJ: Princeton Book Company.

Crutchfield, R. S. & Krech, D. (1962). Some guides to the understanding of the history of psychology. In L. Postman (Ed.), *Psychology in the making* (pp. 3–27). New York: Alfred A. Knopf.

Culbertson, F. M. (1997). Depression and gender: An international review. *American Psychologist, 52,* 25–31.

Cushman, P. (2000). Year 13 male students' attitudes to primary school teaching as a career. *New Zealand Journal of Educational Studies, 35,* 223–230.

Dabbs, J. M., Jr., Chang, E. L., Strong, R. A., & Milun, R. (1998). Spatial ability, navigation strategy, and geographic knowledge among men and women. *Evolution and Human Behavior, 19,* 89–98.

Daly, M. & Wilson, M. (1998). The evolutionary social psychology of family violence. In C. B. Crawford & D. L. Krebs (Eds.), *Handbook of evolutionary psychology: Ideas, issues, and applications* (pp. 431–456). Mahwah, NJ: Lawrence Erlbaum Associates.

D'Andrade, R. G. (1966). Sex differences and cultural institutions. In E. E. Maccoby (Ed.), *The development of sex differences* (pp. 174–204). Stanford, CA: Stanford University Press.

Davatzikos, C. & Resnick, S. M. (1998). Sex differences in anatomic measures of interhemispheric connectivity: Correlations with cognition in women but not men. *Cerebral Cortex, 8,* 635–640.

Davenport, M. L. & Calikoglu, A. S. (2004). Turner Syndrome. In O. H. Pescovitz & E. A. Eugster (Eds.), *Pediatric endocrinology: mechanisms, manifestations, and management* (pp. 203–223). Philadelphia: Lippincott Williams & Wilkins.

Davis, A. P. & McDaniel, T. R. (1999). You've come a long way, baby--or have you? Research evaluating gender portrayal in recent Caldecott-winning books. *Reading Teacher, 52,* 532–536.

Davis, J. E. (2001). Transgressing the masculine: African American boys and the failure of schools. In W. Martino & B. Meyenn (Eds.), *What about the boys?: Issues of masculinity in schools* (pp. 140–153). Buckingham, England: Open University Press.

Davis, M. & Emory, E. (1995). Sex differences in neonatal stress reactivity. *Child Development, 66,* 14–27.

Davis, P. J. (1999). Gender differences in autobiographical memory for childhood emotional experiences. *Journal of Personality and Social Psychology, 76,* 498–510.

Davis, T. L. (1995). Gender differences in masking negative emotions: Ability or motivation? *Developmental Psychology, 31,* 660–667.

Davison, K. K. & Susman, E. J. (2001). Are hormone levels and cognitive ability related during early adolescence? *International Journal of Behavioral Development, 25,* 416–428.

Dawson, T. L. (2002). New tools, new insights: Kohlberg's moral judgment stages revisited. *International Journal of Behavioral Development, 26,* 154–166.

Day, R. D., Peterson, G. W., & McCracken, C. (1998). Predicting spanking of younger and older children by mothers and fathers. *Journal of Marriage and the Family, 60*, 79–94.

De Bellis, M. D., Keshavan, M. S., Beers, S. R., Hall, J., Frustaci, K., Masalehdan, A., et al. (2001). Sex differences in brain maturation during childhood and adolescence. *Cerebral Cortex, 11*, 552–557.

de Lacoste-Utamsing, C., & Holloway, R. L. (1982). Sexual dimorphism in the corpus callosum. *Science, 216*, 1431–1432.

De Lisi, R. & Cammarano, D. M. (1996). Computer experience and gender differences in undergraduate mental rotation performance. *Computers in Human Behavior, 12*, 351–361.

De Lisi, R. & McGillicuddy-De Lisi, A. V. (2002). Sex differences in mathematical abilities and achievement. In A. V. McGillicuddy-De Lisi & R. De Lisi (Eds.), *Biology, society, and behavior: The development of sex differences in cognition* (pp. 155–181). Westport, CT: Ablex Publishing.

De Lisi, R. & Wolford, J. L. (2002). Improving children's mental rotation accuracy with computer game playing. *Journal of Genetic Psychology, 163*, 272–282.

de Silva, W. I. (1993). Influence of son preference on the contraceptive use and fertility of Sri Lankan women. *Journal of Biosocial Science, 25*, 319–331.

De Vries, G. J., Rissman, E. F., Simerly, R. B., Yang, L. -Y., Scordalakes, E. M., Auger, C. J., et al. (2002). A model system for study of sex chromosome effects on sexually dimorphic neural and behavioral traits. *Journal of Neuroscience, 22*, 9005–9014.

Deaux, K. (1984). From individual differences to social categories: Analysis of a decade's research on gender. *American Psychologist, 39*, 105–116.

Deaux, K. & Kite, M. (1993). Gender stereotypes. In F. L. Denmark & M. A. Paludi (Eds.), *Psychology of women: A handbook of issues and theories* (pp. 107–139). Westport, CT: Greenwood Press/Greenwood Publishing Group.

Deliyanni-Kouimtzi, K. (1992). "Father is out shopping because mother is at work..." Greek primary school reading texts as an example of educational policy for gender equality. *Gender and Education, 4*, 67–79.

DeLoache, J. S., Cassidy, D. J., & Carpenter, C. J. (1987). The three bears are all boys: Mothers' gender labeling of neutral picture book characters. *Sex Roles, 17*, 163–178.

Delucia, L. A. (1963). The toy preference test: A measure of sex-role identification. *Child Development, 34*, 107–117.

DePaulo, B. M., Epstein, J. A., & Wyer, M. M. (1993). Sex differences in lying: How women and men deal with the dilemma of deceit. In M. Lewis & C. Saarni (Eds.), *Lying and deception in everyday life* (pp. 126–147). New York: The Guilford Press.

DePaulo, B. M. & Kashy, D. A. (1998). Everyday lies in close and casual relationships. *Journal of Personality and Social Psychology, 74*, 63–79.

Dessens, A. B., Slijper, F. M. E., & Drop, S. L. S. (2005). Gender dysphoria and gender change in chromosomal females with congenital adrenal hyperplasia. *Archives of Sexual Behavior, 34*, 389–397.

Deutsch, F. M. (1999). *Halving it all: How equally shared parenting works.* Cambridge, MA: Harvard University Press.

Deutsch, F. M. (2001). Equally shared parenting. *Current Directions in Psychological Science, 10*, 25–28.

Deutsch, F. M., Servis, L. J., & Payne, J. D. (2001). Paternal participation in child care and its effects on children's self-esteem and attitudes toward gendered roles. *Journal of Family Issues, 22*, 1000–1024.

DeVries, R. (1974). Relationships among Piagetian, IQ, and achievement assessments. *Child Development, 45*, 746–756.

Dewing, P., Shi, T., Horvath, S., & Vilain, E. (2003). Sexually dimorphic gene expression in mouse brain precedes gonadal differentiation. *Molecular Brain Research, 118*, 82–90.

Diamond, F. B. & Bercu, B. B. (2004). Normative laboratory results. In O. H. Pescovitz & E. A. Eugster (Eds.), *Pediatric endocrinology: Mechanisms, manifestations, and management* (pp. 780–825). Philadelphia: Lippincott Williams & Wilkins.

Diamond, L. M. (1998). Development of sexual orientation among adolescent and young adult women. *Developmental Psychology, 34*, 1085–1095.

Diamond, L. M. (2000). Passionate friendships among adolescent sexual-minority women. *Journal of Research on Adolescence, 10*, 191–209.

Diamond, L. M. (2002). "Having a girlfriend without knowing it": Intimate friendships among adolescent sexual-minority women. *Journal of Lesbian Studies, 6*, 5–16.

Diamond, L. M. (2003a). Love matters: Romantic relationships among sexual-minority adolescents. In P. Florsheim (Ed.), *Adolescent romantic relations and sexual behavior: Theory, research, and practical implications.* (pp. 85–107). Mahwah, NJ:: Lawrence Erlbaum Associates.

Diamond, L. M. (2003b). New paradigms for research on heterosexual and sexual-minority development. *Journal of Clinical Child and Adolescent Psychology, 32*, 490–498.

Diamond, L. M. (2006). What we got wrong about sexual identity development: Unexpected findings from a longitudinal study of young women. In A. M. Omoto & H. S. Kurtzman (Eds.), *Sexual orientation and mental health: Examining identity and development in lesbian, gay, and bisexual people. Contemporary perspectives on lesbian, gay, and bisexual psychology* (pp. 73–94). Washington, DC: American Psychological Association.

Diamond, L. M. (2008). Female bisexuality from adolescence to adulthood: Results from a 10-year longitudinal study. *Developmental Psychology, 44*, 5–14.

Diamond, L. M. & Lucas, S. (2004). Sexual-minority and heterosexual youths' peer relationships: Experiences, expectations, and implications for well-being. *Journal of Research on Adolescence, 14*, 313–340.

Diamond, L. M. & Savin-Williams, R. C. (2003). The intimate relationships of sexual-minority youths. In G. R. Adams & M. D. Berzonsky (Eds.), *Blackwell handbook of adolescence* (pp. 393–412). Malden, MA: Blackwell Publishing.

Diamond, M. & Sigmundson, H. K. (1997). Sex reassignment at birth: A long term review and clinical implications. *Archives of Pediatric and Adolescent Medicine, 151*, 298–304.

Dickhaeuser, O. & Stiensmeier-Pelster, J. (2003). Gender differences in the choice of computer courses: Applying an expectancy-value model. *Social Psychology of Education, 6*, 173–189.

Dickstein, E. B. & Seymour, M. W. (1977). Effect of the addition of neutral items on IT Scale scores. *Developmental Psychology, 13*, 79–80.

Diehl, L. A. (1986). The paradox of G. Stanley Hall: Foe of coeducation and educator of women. *American Psychologist, 41*, 868–878.

Diekman, A. B. & Eagly, A. H. (2000). Stereotypes as dynamic constructs: Women and men of the past, present, and future. *Personality and Social Psychology Bulletin, 26*, 1171–1188.

Diekman, A. B. & Murnen, S. K. (2004). Learning to be little women and little men: The inequitable gender equality of nonsexist children's literature. *Sex Roles, 50*, 373–385.

Dietz, T. L. (1998). An examination of violence and gender role portrayals in video games: Implications for gender socialization and aggressive behavior. *Sex Roles, 38*, 425–442.

DiPietro, J. A. (1981). Rough and tumble play: A function of gender. *Developmental Psychology, 17*, 50–58.

Dishion, T. J. & McMahon, R. J. (1998). Parental monitoring and the prevention of child and adolescent problem behavior: A conceptual and empirical formulation. *Clinical Child and Family Psychology Review, 1*, 61–75.

Dittmann, R. W., Kappes, M. H., Kappes, M. E., Borger, D., Stegner, H., Willig, R. H., et al. (1990). Congenital adrenal hyperplasia I: Gender-related behaviors and attitudes in female patients and their sisters. *Psychoneuroendocrinology, 15*, 401–420.

Dittmar, H., Halliwell, E., & Ive, S. (2006). Does Barbie make girls want to be thin? The effect of experimental exposure to images of dolls on the body image of 5- to 8-year-old girls. *Developmental Psychology, 42*, 283–292.

Dobbs, J., Arnold, D. H., & Doctoroff, G. L. (2004). Attention in the preschool classroom: The relationships among child gender, child misbehavior, and types of teacher attention. *Early Child Development and Care, 174*, 281–295.

Dohrmann, R. (1975). A gender profile of children's educational TV. *Journal of Communication, 25*, 56–65.

Dorn, L. D., Dahl, R. E., Woodward, R., & Biro, F. (2006a). Defining the boundaries of early adolescence: A user's guide to assessing pubertal status and pubertal timing in research with adolescents. *Applied Developmental Science, 10*, 30–56.

Dorn, L. D., Dahl, R. E., Woodward, R., & Biro, F. (2006b). Defining the boundaries of early adolescence: A user's guide to assessing pubertal status and pubertal timing in research with adolescents. *Applied Developmental Science, 10*, 30–56.

Dorn, L. D., Hitt, S. F., & Rotenstein, D. (1999). Biopsychological and cognitive differences in children with premature vs. on-time adrenarche. *Archives of Pediatrics and Adolescent Medicine, 153*, 137–146.

Dornbusch, S. M. (1966). Afterword. In E. E. Maccoby (Ed.), *The development of sex differences* (pp. 205–219). Stanford, CA: Stanford University Press.

Downs, A. C. (1983). Letters to Santa Claus: Elementary school-age children's sex-typed toy preferences in a natural setting. *Sex Roles, 9*, 159–163.

Downs, R. M. & Liben, L. S. (1991). The development of expertise in geography: A cognitive-developmental approach to geographic education. *Annals of the Association of American Geographers, 81*, 304–327.

Drees, D. E. & Phye, G. D. (2001). Gender representation in children's language arts computer software. *Journal of Educational Research, 95*, 49–55.

Dreves, C. & Jovanovic, J. (1998). Male dominance in the classroom: Does it explain the gender difference in young adolescents' science ability perceptions? *Applied Developmental Science, 2*, 90–98.

Drew, L. M., Richard, M. H., & Smith, P. K. (1998). Grandparenting and its relationship to parenting. *Clinical Child Psychology and Psychiatry, 3*, 465–480.

Driesen, N. R. & Raz, N. (1995). The influence of sex, age, and handedness on corpus callosum morphology: A meta-analysis. *Psychobiology, 23*, 240–247.

Dubas, J. S. (2001). How gender moderates the grandparent-grandchild relationship: A comparison of kin-keeper and kin-selector theories. *Journal of Family Issues, 22*, 478–492.

Duffy, J., Warren, K., & Walsh, M. (2001). Classroom interactions: Gender of teacher, gender of student, and classroom subject. *Sex Roles, 45*, 579–593.

Duke, L. (2002). Get real!: Cultural relevance and resistance to the mediated feminine ideal. *Psychology and Marketing, 19*, 211–233.

Dunn, J., Bretherton, I., & Munn, P. (1987). Conversations about feeling states between mothers and their young children. *Developmental Psychology, 23*, 132–139.

Dunn, J. & Hughes, C. (2001). "I got some swords and you're dead!": Violent fantasy, antisocial behavior, friendship, and moral sensibility in young children. *Child Development, 72*, 491–505.

Dunn, J. & Kendrick, C. (1981). Social behavior of young siblings in the family context: Differences between same-sex and different-sex dyads. *Child Development, 52*, 1265–1273.

Dunn, J. & Kendrick, C. (1982). The speech of two- and three-year-olds to infant siblings: "Baby talk" and the context of communication. *Journal of Child Language, 9*, 579–595.

Dunn, J., Slomkowski, C., & Beardsall, L. (1994). Sibling relationships from the preschool period through middle childhood and early adolescence. *Developmental Psychology, 30*, 315–324.

Dunn, S. & Morgan, V. (1987). Nursery and infant school play patterns: Sex-related differences. *British Educational Research Journal, 13*, 271–281.

Durston, S., Hulshoff Pol, H. E., Casey, B. J., Giedd, J. N., Buitelaar, J. K., & van Engeland, H. (2001). Anatomical MRI of the developing human brain: what have we learned? *Journal of the American Academy of Child & Adolescent Psychiatry, 40*, 1012–1020.

Dutro, E. (2002). 'But that's a girls' book!' Exploring gender boundaries in children's reading practices. *Reading Teacher, 55*, 376–384.

Dweck, C. S. (2002a). The development of ability conceptions. In A. Wigfield & J. S. Eccles (Eds.), *Development of achievement motivation* (pp. 57–88). San Diego, CA: Academic Press.

Dweck, C. S. (2002b). Messages that motivate: How praise molds students' beliefs, motivation, and performance (in surprising ways). In J. Aronson (Ed.), *Improving academic achievement: Impact of psychological factors on education* (pp. 37–60). San Diego, CA: Academic Press.

Dwyer, C. A. & Johnson, L. M. (1997). Grades, accomplishments, and correlates. In W. W. Willingham & N. S. Cole (Eds.), *Gender and fair assessment* (pp. 127–156). Mahwah, NJ: Lawrence Erlbaum Associates.

Eagly, A. H. (1987). *Sex differences in social behavior: A social-role interpretation.* Hillsdale, NJ: Lawrence Erlbaum Associates.

Eagly, A. H. (1995). The science and politics of comparing women and men. *American Psychologist, 50*, 145–158.

Eagly, A. H. (1997). Sex differences in social behavior: Comparing social role theory and evolutionary psychology. *American Psychologist, 52*, 1380–1383.

Eagly, A. H. & Chrvala, C. (1986). Sex differences in conformity: Status and gender role interpretations. *Psychology of Women Quarterly, 10*, 203–220.

Eagly, A. H. & Crowley, M. (1986). Gender and helping behavior: A meta-analytic review of the social psychological literature. *Psychological Bulletin, 100*, 283–308.

Eagly, A. H. & Steffen, V. J. (1984). Gender stereotypes stem from the distribution of women and men into social roles. *Journal of Personality and Social Psychology, 46*, 735–754.

Eagly, A. H. & Steffen, V. J. (1986a). Gender and aggressive behavior: A meta-analytic review of the social psychological literature. *Psychological Bulletin, 100*, 309–330.

Eagly, A. H. & Steffen, V. J. (1986b). Gender stereotypes, occupational roles, and beliefs about part-time employees. *Psychology of Women Quarterly, 10*, 252–262.

Eagly, A. H. & Wood, W. (1999). The origins of sex differences in human behavior: Evolved dispositions versus social roles. *American Psychologist, 54*, 408–423.

Eagly, A. H., Wood, W., & Diekman, A. B. (2000). Social role theory of sex differences and similarities: A current appraisal. In T. Eckes & H. M. Trautner (Eds.), *The developmental social psychology of gender* (pp. 123–174). Mahwah, NJ: Lawrence Erlbaum Associates.

Eals, M. & Silverman, I. (1994). The hunter-gatherer theory of spatial sex differences: Proximate factors mediating the female advantage in recall of object arrays. *Ethology and Sociobiology, 15*, 95–105.

Eaton, S. (2003, April 18). FWCS sued over student's battering. *Fort Wayne Journal Gazette*, p. 1C & 4C.

Eaton, W. O. & Enns, L. R. (1986). Sex differences in human motor activity level. *Psychological Bulletin, 100*, 19–28.

Eaton, W. O. & Yu, A. P. (1989). Are sex differences in child motor activity level a function of sex differences in maturational status? *Child Development, 60*, 1005–1011.

Eccles, J. S., Freedman-Doan, C., Frome, P., Jacobs, J., & Yoon, K. S. (2000). Gender-role socialization in the family: A longitudinal approach. In T. Eckes & H. M. Trautner (Eds.), *The developmental social psychology of gender* (pp. 333–360). Mahwah, NJ: Lawrence Erlbaum Associates.

Eccles, J. S. & Harold, R. D. (1991). Gender differences in sport involvement: Applying the Eccles' expectancy-value model. *Journal of Applied Sport Psychology, 3*, 7–35.

Eccles, J. S., Wigfield, A., Flanagan, C. A., Miller, C., Reuman, D. A., & Yee, D. (1989). Self-concepts, domain values, and self-esteem: Relations and changes at early adolescence. *Journal of Personality, 57*, 283–310.

Eccles, J. S., Wigfield, A., & Schiefele, U. (1998). Motivation to succeed. In N. Eisenberg (Ed.), *Handbook of child psychology: Vol. 3. Social, emotional, and personality development.* (5th ed., pp. 1017–1095). New York: Wiley.

Edelbrock, C. S. & Sugawara, A. I. (1978). Acquisition of sex-typed preferences in preschool-aged children. *Developmental Psychology, 14*, 614–623.

Eder, D. (1985). The cycle of popularity: Interpersonal relations among female adolescents. *Sociology of Education, 58*, 154–165.

Eder, D. & Kinney, D. A. (1995). The effect of middle school extracurricular activities on adolescents' popularity and peer status. *Youth and Society, 26*, 298–324.

Eder, D. & Parker, S. (1987). The cultural production and reproduction of gender: The effect of extracurricular activities on peer-group culture. *Sociology of Education, 60*, 200–213.

Edwards, C. P. (2000). Children's play in cross-cultural perspective: A new look at the Six Cultures study. *Cross Cultural Research: The Journal of Comparative Social Science, 34*, 318–338.

Edwards, C. P. (2002). Behavioral sex differences in children of diverse cultures: The case of nurturance to infants. In M. E. Pereira & L. A. Fairbanks (Eds.), *Juvenile primates: Life history, development, and behavior* (pp. 327–338). Chicago: University of Chicago Press.

Edwards, R., Mauthner, M., & Hadfield, L. (2005). Children's sibling relationships and gendered practices: Talk, activity and dealing with change. *Gender and Education, 17*, 499–513.

Egan, S. K. & Perry, D. G. (2001). Gender identity: A multidimensional analysis with implications for psychosocial adjustment. *Developmental Psychology, 37*, 451–463.

Eggleston, E. J. (1997). Boys' talk: Exploring gender discussions with New Zealand male youth gang members. *Caribbean Journal of Criminology and Social Psychology, 2*, 100–114.

Ehrensaft, M. K. (2005). Interpersonal relationships and sex differences in the development of conduct problems. *Clinical Child and Family Psychology Review, 8*, 39–63.

Ehrhardt, A. A. & Baker, S. W. (1974). Fetal androgens, human central nervous system differentiation and behavior sex differences. In R. C. Friedman, R. M. Richart & R. L. Van de Wiele (Eds.), *Sex differences in behavior* (pp. 33–51). New York: Wiley.

Ehrlich, S. B., Levine, S. C., & Goldin-Meadow, S. (2006). The importance of gesture in children's spatial reasoning. *Developmental Psychology, 42*, 1259–1268.

Einon, D. & Potegal, M. (1994). Temper tantrums in young children. In M. Potegal & J. F. Knutson (Eds.), *The dynamics of aggression: Biological and social processes in dyads and groups* (pp. 157–194). Hillsdale, NJ: Lawrence Erlbaum Associates.

Eisenberg, A. R. (1988). Grandchildren's perspectives on relationships with grandparents: The influence of gender across generations. *Sex Roles, 19*, 205–217.

Eisenberg, N., Cumberland, A., & Spinrad, T. L. (1998). Parental socialization of emotion. *Psychological Inquiry, 9*, 241–273.

Eisenberg, N. & Fabes, R. A. (1994). Mothers' reactions to children's negative emotions: Relations to children's temperament and anger behavior. *Merrill-Palmer Quarterly, 40*, 138–156.

Eisenberg, N. & Fabes, R. A. (1998). Prosocial development. In N. Eisenberg (Ed.), *Handbook of child psychology: Vol. 3. Social, emotional, and personality development.* (5th ed., pp. 701–778). New York: Wiley.

Eisenberg, N., Fabes, R. A., & Murphy, B. C. (1996). Parents' reactions to children's negative emotions: Relations to children's social competence and comforting behavior. *Child Development, 67*, 2227–2247.

Eisenberg, N., Martin, C. L., & Fabes, R. A. (1996). Gender development and gender effects. In D. C. Berliner & R. C. Calfee (Eds.), *Handbook of educational psychology* (pp. 358–396). New York: Macmillan Library Reference.

Eisenberg, N., Spinrad, T. L., & Sadovsky, A. (2006). Empathy-related responding in children. In M. Killen & J. G. Smetana (Eds.), *Handbook of moral development.* (pp. 517–549). Mahwah, NJ: Lawrence Erlbaum Associates.

Eisenberg, N., Wolchik, S. A., Hernandez, R., & Pasternack, J. F. (1985). Parental socialization of young children's play: A short-term longitudinal study. *Child Development, 56,* 1506–1513.

Ekstrom, R. B., French, J. W., & Harman, H. H. (1976). *Manual for kit of factor-referenced cognitive tests.* Princeton, NJ: Educational Testing Service.

Eldridge, K. A. & Christenson, A. (2002). Demand-withdraw communication during couple conflict: A review and analysis. In P. Noller & J. A. Sweeney (Eds.), *Understanding marriage* (pp. 289–322). New York: Cambridge University Press.

Eliot, J. (1987). *Models of psychological space, psychometric, developmental, and experimental approaches.* New York: Springer-Verlag.

Ellis, A. L. & Mitchell, R. W. (2000). Sexual orientation. In L. T. Szuchman & F. Muscarella (Eds.), *Psychological perspectives on human sexuality* (pp. 196–231). New York: Wiley.

Ellis, B. J. (2004). Timing of pubertal maturation in girls: An integrated life history approach. *Psychological Bulletin, 130,* 920–958.

Else-Quest, N. M., Hyde, J. S., Goldsmith, H. H., & Van Hulle, C. A. (2006). Gender differences in temperament: A meta-analysis. *Psychological Bulletin, 132,* 33–72.

Eme, R. F. & Kavanaugh, L. (1995). Sex differences in conduct disorder. *Journal of Clinical Child Psychology, 24,* 406–426.

Emmerich, W. (1959). Parental identification in young children. *Genetic Psychology Monographs, 60,* 257–308.

Emmerich, W., Goldman, K. S., Kirsh, B., & Sharabany, R. (1977). Evidence for a transitional phase in the development of gender constancy. *Child Development, 48,* 930–936.

Emmett, W. C. (1949). Evidence of a space factor at 11 and earlier. *British Journal of Psychology, 2,* 3–16.

Endsley, R. C. (1967). Effects of concealing "IT" on sex role preferences of preschool children. *Perceptual and Motor Skills, 24,* 998.

England, A. O. (1947). Cultural milieu and parental identification. *Nervous Child, 6,* 301–305.

Entwisle, D. R., Alexander, K. L., & Olson, L. S. (2007). Early schooling: The handicap of being poor and male. *Sociology of Education, 80,* 114–138.

Epstein, D., Kehily, M., Mac an Ghaill, M., & Redman, P. (2001). Boys and girls come out to play: Making masculinities and femininities in school playgrounds. *Men and Masculinities, 4,* 158–172.

Erden, F. & Wolfgang, C. H. (2004). An exploration of the differences in prekindergarten, kindergarten, and first grade teachers' beliefs related to discipline when dealing with male and female students. *Early Child Development and Care, 174,* 3–11.

Ericsson, K. A. & Charness, N. (1994). Expert performance: Its structure and acquisition. *American Psychologist, 49,* 725–747.

Ernst, M., Maheu, F., Schroth, E., Hardin, J., Golan, L. G., Cameron, J., et al. (2007). Amygdala function in adolescents with congenital adrenal hyperplasia: A model for the study of early steroid abnormalities. *Neuropsychologia, 45,* 2104–2113.

Eron, L. D. (1992). Gender differences in violence: Biology and/or socialization? In K. Björkqvist & P. Niemela (Eds.), *Of mice and women: Aspects of female aggression* (pp. 89–97). San Diego, CA, US: Academic Press.

Eron, L. D., Huesmann, L. R., Lefkowitz, M. M., & Walder, L. O. (1972). Does television violence cause aggression? *American Psychologist, 27,* 253–263.

Eron, L. D., Huesmann, L. R., Lefkowitz, M. M., & Walder, L. O. (1996). Does television violence cause aggression? In D. F. Greenberg (Ed.), *Criminal careers, Vol. 2. The international library of criminology, criminal justice and penology* (pp. 311–321). Brookfield, VT: Dartmouth Publishing Company Limited.

Esbensen, F.-A., Deschenes, E. P., & Winfree, L. T., Jr. (1999). Differences between gang girls and gang boys: Results from a multisite survey. *Youth and Society, 31,* 27–53.

Etaugh, C., Grinnell, K., & Etaugh, A. (1989). Development of gender labeling: Effect of age of pictured children. *Sex Roles, 21,* 769–773.

Etaugh, C. & Liss, M. B. (1992). Home, school, and playroom: Training grounds for adult gender roles. *Sex Roles, 26,* 129–147.

Eugenides, J. (2002). *Middlesex.* New York: Farrar, Strauss and Giroux.

Evans, E. D., Rutberg, J., Sather, C., & Turner, C. (1991). Content analysis of contemporary teen magazines for adolescent females. *Youth and Society, 23,* 99–120.

Evans, E. M., Schweingruber, H., & Stevenson, H. W. (2002). Gender differences in interest and knowledge acquisition: The United States, Taiwan, and Japan. *Sex Roles, 47,* 153–167.

Evans, K. (2001). *The lost daughters of China.* New York: Jeremy P. Tarcher/Putnam.

Evans, L. & Davies, K. (2000). No sissy boys here: A content analysis of the representation of masculinity in elementary school reading textbooks. *Sex Roles, 42,* 255–270.

Eveleth, P. B. & Tanner, J. M. (1990). *Worldwide variation in human growth*. New York: Cambridge University Press.

Fabes, R. A., Eisenberg, N., Karbon, M., Bernzweig, J., Speer, A. L., & Carlo, G. (1994). Socialization of children's vicarious emotional responding and prosocial behavior: Relations with mothers' perceptions of children's emotional reactivity. *Developmental Psychology, 30*, 44–55.

Fabes, R. A., Martin, C. L., & Hanish, L. D. (2003). Young children's play qualities in same, other, and mixed sex peer groups. *Child Development, 74*, 921–932.

Fabes, R. A., Martin, C. L., Hanish, L. D., Anders, M. C., & Madden-Derdich, D. A. (2003). Early school competence: The roles of sex-segregated play and effortful control. *Developmental Psychology, 39*, 848–858.

Fabes, R. A., Shepard, S. A., Guthrie, I. K., & Martin, C. L. (1997). Roles of temperamental arousal and gender-segregated play in young children's social adjustment. *Developmental Psychology, 33*, 693–702.

Fagot, B. I. (1977). Consequences of moderate cross-gender behavior in preschool children. *Child Development, 48*, 902–907.

Fagot, B. I. (1978). The influence of sex of child on parental reactions to toddler children. *Child Development, 49*, 459–465.

Fagot, B. I. (1981). Continuity and change in play styles as a function of sex of child. *International Journal of Behavioral Development, 4*, 37–43.

Fagot, B. I. (1984). Teacher and peer reactions to boys' and girls' play styles. *Sex Roles, 11*, 691–702.

Fagot, B. I. (1985a). Beyond the reinforcement principle: Another step toward understanding sex role development. *Developmental Psychology, 21*, 1097–1104.

Fagot, B. I. (1985b). Changes in thinking about early sex role development. *Developmental Review, 5*, 83–98.

Fagot, B. I. (1995). Psychosocial and cognitive determinants of early gender-role development. *Annual Review of Sex Research*, 1–31.

Fagot, B. I. & Hagan, R. (1985). Aggression in toddlers: Responses to the assertive acts of boys and girls. *Sex Roles, 12*, 341–351.

Fagot, B. I. & Hagan, R. (1991). Observations of parent reactions to sex-stereotyped behaviors: Age and sex effects. *Child Development, 62*, 617–628.

Fagot, B. I., Hagan, R., Leinbach, M. D., & Kronsberg, S. (1985). Differential reactions to assertive and communicative acts of toddler boys and girls. *Child Development, 56*, 1499–1505.

Fagot, B. I. & Leinbach, M. D. (1989). The young child's gender schema: Environmental input, internal organization. *Child Development, 60*, 663–672.

Fagot, B. I. & Leinbach, M. D. (1995). Gender knowledge in egalitarian and traditional families. *Sex Roles, 32*, 513–526.

Fagot, B. I., Leinbach, M. D., & Hagan, R. (1986). Gender labeling and the adoption of sex-typed behaviors. *Developmental Psychology, 22*, 440–443.

Fagot, B. I., Leinbach, M. D., & O' Boyle, C. (1992). Gender labeling, gender stereotyping, and parenting behaviors. *Developmental Psychology, 28*, 225–230.

Fagot, B. I. & Patterson, G. R. (1969). An in vivo analysis of reinforcing contingencies for sex-role behaviors in the preschool child. *Developmental Psychology, 1*, 563–568.

Fagot, B. I., Rodgers, C. S., & Leinbach, M. D. (2000). Theories of gender socialization. In T. Eckes & H. M. Trautner (Eds.), *The developmental social psychology of gender* (pp. 65–89). Mahwah, NJ: Lawrence Erlbaum Associates.

Faisel, A. & Ahmed, T. (1996). Underestimation of malnutrition among Pakistani infants weighed with clothes on. *Eastern Mediterranean Health Journal, 2*, 255–260.

Farris, C. S. (1992). The gender of child discourse: Same-sex peer socialization through language use in a Taiwanese preschool. *Journal of Linguistic Anthropology, 1*, 198–224.

Fausto Sterling, A. (1993). The five sexes: Why male and female are not enough. *The Sciences, 33*, 20–25.

Fausto Sterling, A. (2000). The five sexes, revisited. *Sciences, 40*, 18–23.

Federal Bureau of Investigation. (2006). *Crime in the United States 2005: Uniform crime reports*. Washington, DC: United States Department of Justice.

Feingold, A. (1988). Cognitive gender differences are disappearing. *American Psychologist, 43*, 95–103.

Feingold, A. (1994). Gender differences in personality: A meta-analysis. *Psychological Bulletin, 116*, 429–456.

Feingold, A. & Mazzella, R. (1998). Gender differences in body image are increasing. *Psychological Science, 9*, 190–195.

Feiring, C. (1999). Other-sex friendship networks and the development of romantic relationships in adolescence. *Journal of Youth and Adolescence, 28*, 495–512.

Feldman, R., Weller, A., Zagoory-Sharon, O., & Levine, A. (2007). Evidence for a neuroendocrinological foundation of human affiliation: Plasma oxytocin levels across pregnancy and the postpartum period predict mother-infant bonding. *Psychological Science, 18*, 965–970.

Feldman, S. S. & Nash, S. C. (1978). Interest in babies during young adulthood. *Child Development, 49*, 617–622.

Feldman, S. S. & Nash, S. C. (1979a). Changes in responsiveness to babies during adolescence. *Child Development, 50*, 942–949.

Feldman, S. S. & Nash, S. C. (1979b). Sex differences in responsiveness to babies among mature adults. *Developmental Psychology, 15*, 430–436.

Feldman, S. S., Nash, S. C., & Cutrona, C. (1977). The influence of age and sex on responsiveness to babies. *Developmental Psychology, 13*, 675–676.

Felson, R. B. & Trudeau, L. (1991). Gender differences in mathematics performance. *Social Psychology Quarterly, 54*, 113–126.

Feng, J., Spence, I., & Pratt, J. (2007). Playing an action video game reduces gender differences in spatial cognition. *Psychological Science, 18*, 850–855.

Fennema, E. (1990). Teachers' beliefs and gender differences in mathematics. In E. Fennema & G. C. Leder (Eds.), *Mathematics and gender* (pp. 169–187). New York: Teachers College Press.

Fenner, J., Heathcote, D., & Jerrams-Smith, J. (2000). The development of wayfinding competency: Asymmetrical effects of visuo-spatial and verbal ability. *Journal of Environmental Psychology, 20*, 165–175.

Fenson, L., Dale, P. S., Reznick, J. S., Bates, E., Thal, D. J., & Pethick, S. J. (1994). Variability in early communicative development. *Monographs of the Society for Research in Child Development, 59*(5, Serial No. 242).

Finders, M. J. (1996). Queens and teen zines: Early adolescent females reading their way toward adulthood. *Anthropology and Education Quarterly, 27*, 71–89.

Finders, M. J. (1997). *Just girls: Hidden literacies and life in junior high.* New York: Teachers College Press.

Finegan, J.-A. K., Niccols, G. A., Zacher, J. E., & Hood, J. E. (1991). The Play Activity Questionnaire: A parent report measure of children's play preferences. *Archives of Sexual Behavior, 20*, 393–408.

Fingerhut, L. A. & Warner, M. (1997). *Injury chartbook. Health, United States, 1997–97.* Hyattsville, MD: National Center for Health Statistics.

Fingerman, K. L. (2004). The role of offspring and in-laws in grandparents' ties to their grandchildren. *Journal of Family Issues, 25*, 1026–1049.

Finkelstein, J. W., Susman, E. J., Chinchilli, V. M., Kunselman, S. J., D'Arcangelo, M. R., Schwab, J., et al. (1997). Estrogen or testosterone increases self-reported aggressive behaviors in hypogonadal adolescents. *Journal of Clinical Endocrinology and Metabolism, 82*, 2433–2438.

Fisch, S. M. (2002). Vast wasteland or vast opportunity? Effects of educational television on children's academic knowledge, skills, and attitudes. In J. Bryant & D. Zillmann (Eds.), *Media effects: Advances in theory and research* (2nd ed., pp. 397–426). Mahwah, NJ: Lawrence Erlbaum Associates.

Fischer, A. H. & Manstead, A. S. R. (2000). The relation between gender and emotion in different cultures. In A. H. Fischer (Ed.), *Gender and emotion: Social psychological perspectives.* (pp. 71–94). New York: Cambridge University Press.

Fisher-Thompson, D. (1993). Adult toy purchases for children: Factors affecting sex-typed toy selection. *Journal of Applied Developmental Psychology, 14*, 385–406.

Fisher-Thompson, D., Sausa, A. D., & Wright, T. F. (1995). Toy selection for children: Personality and toy request influences. *Sex Roles, 33*, 239–255.

Fiske, S. T. (1998). Stereotyping, prejudice, and discrimination. In D. T. Gilbert, S. T. Fiske & G. Lindzey (Eds.), *The handbook of social psychology* (4th ed., Vol. 2, pp. 357–414). Boston: McGraw-Hill.

Fitch, R. H. & Denenberg, V. H. (1998). A role for ovarian hormones in sexual differentiation of the brain. *Behavioral and Brain Sciences, 21*, 311–352.

Fivush, R. (1989). Exploring sex differences in the emotional content of mother-child conversations about the past. *Sex Roles, 20*, 675–691.

Fivush, R. (1998). Gendered narratives: Elaboration, structure, and emotion in parent-child reminiscing across the preschool years. In C. P. Thompson & D. J. Herrmann (Eds.), *Autobiographical memory: Theoretical and applied perspectives* (pp. 79–103). Mahwah, NJ: Lawrence Erlbaum Associates.

Fivush, R. (2000). Accuracy, authority, and voice: Feminist perspectives on autobiographical memory. In P. H. Miller & E. Kofsky Scholnick (Eds.), *Toward a feminist developmental psychology* (pp. 85–105). Florence, KY: Taylor & Francis/Routledge.

Fivush, R., Brotman, M. A., Buckner, J. P., & Goodman, S. H. (2000). Gender differences in parent-child emotion narratives. *Sex Roles, 42*, 233–253.

Fivush, R. & Buckner, J. P. (2000). Gender, sadness, and depression: The development of emotional focus through gendered discourse. In A. H. Fischer (Ed.), *Gender and emotion: Social psychological perspectives.* Studies in emotion and social interaction. Second series (pp. 232–253). New York, NY: Cambridge University Press.

Flaks, D. K., Ficher, I., Masterpasqua, F., & Joseph, G. (1995). Lesbians choosing motherhood: A comparative study of lesbian and heterosexual parents and their children. *Developmental Psychology, 31,* 105–114.

Flam, F. (1993). Random samples: Why map Y? *Science, 251,* 679.

Flammer, A., Alsaker, F. D., & Noack, P. (1999). Time use by adolescents in an international perspective. I: The case of leisure activities. In F. D. Alsaker & A. Flammer (Eds.), *The adolescent experience: European and American adolescents in the 1990s.* Research monographs in adolescence (pp. 33–60). Mahwah, NJ: Lawrence Erlbaum Associates.

Flannagan, D. (1996). Mothers' and kindergartners' talk about interpersonal relationships. *Merrill-Palmer Quarterly, 42,* 519–536.

Flannagan, D., Baker-Ward, L., & Graham, L. (1995). Talk about preschool: Patterns of topic discussion and elaboration related to gender and ethnicity. *Sex Roles, 32,* 1–15.

Flannagan, D. & Perese, S. (1998). Emotional references in mother-daughter and mother-son dyads' conversations about school. *Sex Roles, 39,* 353–367.

Flannery, D. J., Huff, C. R., & Manos, M. (1998). Youth gangs: A developmental perspective. In T. P. Gullotta & G. R. Adams (Eds.), *Delinquent violent youth: Theory and interventions.* Advances in adolescent development (Vol. 9, pp. 175–204). Thousand Oaks, CA: Sage Publications.

Flynn, J. R. (1998). Israeli military IQ tests: Gender differences small: IQ gains large. *Journal of Biosocial Science, 30,* 541–553.

Fogel, A., Melson, G. F., Toda, S., & Mistry, J. (1987). Young children's responses to unfamiliar infants: The effects of adult involvement. *International Journal of Behavioral Development, 10,* 37–50.

Forastieri, V., Andrade, C. P., Souza, A. L., Silva, M. S., El-Hani, C. N., Moreira, L. M., et al. (2002). Evidence against a relationship between dermatoglyphic asymmetry and male sexual orientation. *Human Biology, 74,* 861–870.

Foster, V., Kimmel, M., & Skelton, C. (2001). "What about the boys?" An overview of the debates. In W. Martino & B. Meyenn (Eds.), *What about the boys?: Issues of masculinity in schools* (pp. 1–23). Buckingham, England: Open University Press.

Fouts, G. & Vaughan, K. (2002). Television situation comedies: male weight, negative references, and audience reactions. *Sex Roles, 46,* 439–442.

Fredricks, J. A. & Eccles, J. S. (2002). Children's competence and value beliefs from childhood through adolescence: Growth trajectories in two male-sex-typed domains. *Developmental Psychology, 38,* 519–533.

Freedman-Doan, C., Wigfield, A., Eccles, J. S., Blumenfeld, P., Arbreton, A., & Harold, R. D. (2000). What am I best at? Grade and gender differences in children's beliefs about ability improvement. *Journal of Applied Developmental Psychology, 21,* 379–402.

Freeman, H. & Brown, B. B. (2001). Primary attachment to parents and peers during adolescence: Differences by attachment style. *Journal of Youth and Adolescence, 30,* 653–674.

Freeman, J. (2003). Gender differences in gifted achievement in Britain and the U.S. *Gifted Child Quarterly, 47,* 202–211.

Freeman, J. G. (1996). An exploratory study of a gender equity program for secondary school students. *Gender and Education, 8,* 289–300.

French, D. C., Jansen, E. A., & Pidada, S. (2002). United States and Indonesian children's and adolescents' reports of relational aggression by disliked peers. *Child Development, 73,* 1143–1150.

Freud, S. (1927). Some psychological consequences of the anatomical distinction between the sexes. *International Journal of Psychoanalysis, 8,* 133–142.

Frey, C. & Hoppe-Graff, S. (1994). Serious and playful aggression in Brazilian girls and boys. *Sex Roles, 30,* 249–268.

Frey, K. S. & Ruble, D. N. (1992). Gender constancy and the "cost" of sex-typed behavior: A test of the conflict hypothesis. *Developmental Psychology, 28,* 714–721.

Friedman, L. (1995). The space factor in mathematics: Gender differences. *Review of Educational Research, 65,* 22–50.

Frodi, A. M. & Lamb, M. E. (1978). Sex differences in responsiveness to infants: A developmental study of psychophysiological and behavioral responses. *Child Development, 49,* 1182–1188.

Frodi, A. M., Murray, A. D., Lamb, M. E., & Steinberg, J. (1984). Biological and social determinants of responsiveness to infants in 10-to-15-year-old girls. *Sex Roles, 10,* 639–649.

Fry, D. P. (1992). Female aggression among the Zapotec of Oaxaca, Mexico. In K. Björkqvist & P. Niemela (Eds.), *Of mice and women: Aspects of female aggression* (pp. 187–199). San Diego, CA: Academic Press.

Fuchs, D. & Thelen, M. H. (1988). Children's expected interpersonal consequences of communicating their affective state and reported likelihood of expression. *Child Development, 59*, 1314–1322.

Fulton, R. & Anderson, S. W. (1992). The Amerindian "Man-Woman": Gender, liminality, and cultural continuity. *Current Anthropology, 33*, 603–610.

Funk, J. B. & Buchman, D. D. (1996). Children's perceptions of gender differences in social approval for playing electronic games. *Sex Roles, 35*, 219–232.

Funk, J. B., Buchman, D. D., & Germann, J. N. (2000). Preference for violent electronic games, self-concept and gender differences in young children. *American Journal of Orthopsychiatry, 70*, 233–241.

Furman, W. (1999). Friends and lovers: The role of peer relationships in adolescent romantic relationships. In W. A. Collins & B. Laursen (Eds.), *Relationships as developmental contexts. The Minnesota symposia on child psychology* (Vol. 30, pp. 133–154). Mahwah, NJ: Lawrence Erlbaum Associates.

Furman, W. & Buhrmester, D. (1992). Age and sex differences in perceptions of networks of personal relationships. *Child Development, 63*, 103–115.

Furnham, A. & Mak, T. (1999). Sex-role stereotyping in television commercials: A review and comparison of fourteen studies done on five continents over 25 years. *Sex Roles, 41*, 413–437.

Furnham, A., Reeves, E., & Budhani, S. (2002). Parents think their sons are brighter than their daughters: Sex differences in parental self-estimations and estimations of their children's multiple intelligences. *Journal of Genetic Psychology, 163*, 24–39.

Furnham, A. & Thomas, C. (2004). Parents' gender and personality and estimates of their own and their children's intelligence. *Personality and Individual Differences, 37*, 887–903.

Furstenberg, F. F., Jr. (1988). Good dads-bad dads: Two faces of fatherhood. In A. J. Cherlin (Ed.), *The changing American family and public policy* (pp. 193–218). Washington, DC: Urban Institute Press.

Gabb, J. (2004). Sexuality education: How children of lesbian mothers 'learn' about sexuality. *Sex Education, 4*, 19–34.

Gailey, C. W. (1996). Mediated messages: Gender, class, and cosmos in home video games. In P. M. Greenfield & R. R. Cocking (Eds.), *Interacting with video. Advances in applied developmental psychology* (Vol. 11, pp. 9–23). Westport, CT: Ablex Publishing.

Galea, L. A. & Kimura, D. (1993). Sex differences in route-learning. *Personality and Individual Differences, 14*, 53–65.

Galen, B. R. & Underwood, M. K. (1997). A developmental investigation of social aggression among children. *Developmental Psychology, 33*, 589–600.

Gallagher, A. M. & De Lisi, R. (1994). Gender differences in Scholastic Aptitude Test: Mathematics problem solving among high-ability students. *Journal of Educational Psychology, 86*, 204–211.

Gallagher, A. M., De Lisi, R., Holst, P. C., McGillicuddy-De Lisi, A. V., Morely, M., & Cahalan, C. (2000). Gender differences in advanced mathematical problem solving. *Journal of Experimental Child Psychology, 75*, 165–190.

Gallas, K. (1994). *The languages of learning: How children talk, write, dance, draw, and sing their understanding of the world*. New York: Teachers College Press.

Gallas, K. (1997). Bad boys and silent girls: What children know about language and power. *Women and Language, 20*, 63–70.

Gallas, K. (1998). *"Sometimes I can be anything." Power, gender, and identity in a primary classroom*. The practitioner inquiry series. New York: Teachers College Press.

Galsworthy, M. J., Dionne, G., Dale, P. S., & Plomin, R. (2000). Sex differences in early verbal and non-verbal cognitive development. *Developmental Science, 3*, 206–215.

Galton, F., Sir. (1883). *Inquiries into human faculty and its development*. London: Macmillan.

Galton, F., Sir. (1894). *Natural inheritance*. London: Macmillan.

Garai, J. E. & Scheinfeld, A. (1968). Sex differences in mental and behavioral traits. *Genetic Psychology Monographs, 77*, 169–299.

Garber, J. (2000). Development and depression. In A. J. Sameroff & M. Lewis (Eds.), *Handbook of developmental psychopathology* (2nd ed., pp. 467–490). New York: Kluwer Academic/Plenum.

Garber, J., Keiley, M. K., & Martin, N. C. (2002). Developmental trajectories of adolescents' depressive symptoms: Predictors of change. *Journal of Consulting and Clinical Psychology, 70*, 79–95.

Gard, M. (2001). "I like smashing people, and I like getting smashed myself": Addressing issues of masculinity in physical education and sport. In W. Martino & B. Meyenn (Eds.), *What about the boys?: Issues of masculinity in schools* (pp. 222–234). Buckingham, England: Open University Press.

Garner, A., Sterk, H. M., & Adams, S. (1998). Narrative analysis of sexual etiquette in teenage magazines. *Journal of Communication, 48*, 59–78.

Garrett, C. S., Ein, P. L., & Tremaine, L. (1977). The development of gender stereotyping of adult occupations in elementary school children. *Child Development, 48*, 507–512.

Gatewood, J. D., Wills, A., Shetty, S., Xu, J., Arnold, A. P., Burgoyne, P. S., et al. (2006). Sex chromosome complement and gonadal sex influence aggressive and parental behaviors in mice. *Journal of Neuroscience, 26*, 2335–2342.

Gaub, M. & Carlson, C. L. (1997). Gender differences in ADHD: A meta-analysis and critical review. *Journal of the American Academy of Child and Adolescent Psychiatry, 36*, 1036–1045.

Gaulin, S. J. C. (1995). Does evolutionary theory predict sex differences in the brain? In M. S. Gazzaniga (Ed.), *The cognitive neurosciences.* (pp. 1211–1225). Cambridge, MA: The MIT Press.

Gaulin, S. J. C. & Fitzgerald, R. W. (1989). Sexual selection for spatial-learning ability. *Animal Behaviour, 37*, 322–331.

Gaulin, S. J. C. & McBurney, D. H. (2004). *Evolutionary psychology* (2nd ed.). Upper Saddle River, NJ: Prentice Hall.

Gauthier, A. H., Smeeding, T. M., & Furstenberg, F. F., Jr. (2004). Are parents investing less time in children? Trends in selected industrialized countries. *Population and Development Review, 30*, 647–671.

Gazzaniga, M. S. (1967). The split brain in man. *Scientific American, 217*, 24–29.

Gazzaniga, M. S. (1970). *The bisected brain.* New York: Appleton-Century-Crofts.

Ge, X., Brody, G. H., Conger, R. D., Simons, R. L., & Murry, V. M. (2002). Contextual amplification of pubertal transition effects on deviant peer affiliation and externalizing behavior among African American children. *Developmental Psychology, 38*, 42–54.

Geary, D. C. (1998). *Male, female: The evolution of human sex differences.* Washington, DC: American Psychological Association.

Geary, D. C. (1999). Evolution and developmental sex differences. *Current Directions in Psychological Science, 8*, 115–120.

Geary, D. C. (2000). Evolution and proximate expression of human paternal investment. *Psychological Bulletin, 126*, 55–77.

Geary, D. C. & Bjorklund, D. F. (2000). Evolutionary developmental psychology. *Child Development, 71*, 57–65.

Geary, D. C., Saults, S. J., Liu, F., & Hoard, M. K. (2000). Sex differences in spatial cognition, computational fluency, and arithmetical reasoning. *Journal of Experimental Child Psychology, 77*, 337–353.

Geddes, P. & Thomson, J. A. (1897). *The evolution of sex.* New York: Charles Scribner's Sons.

Gelman, S. A. (2003). *The essential child: Origins of essentialism in everyday thought.* New York: Oxford University Press.

Gelman, S. A., Taylor, M. G., & Nguyen, S. P. (2004). Mother-child conversations about gender. *Monographs of the Society for Research in Child Development, 69*(1, Serial No. 275).

Gentry, M., Gable, R. K., & Rizza, M. G. (2002). Students' perceptions of classroom activities: Are there grade-level and gender differences? *Journal of Educational Psychology, 94*, 539–544.

Gerald, D. E. & Hussar, W. J. (2003). *Projections of Education Statistics to 2013* (No. NCES 2004–013). Washington, DC: US Department of Education: Institute of Education Sciences.

Gerbner, G., Gross, L., Morgan, M., Signorielli, N., & Shanahan, J. (2002). Growing up with television: Cultivation processes. In J. Bryant & D. Zillmann (Eds.), *Media effects: Advances in theory and research* (2nd ed., pp. 43–67). Mahwah, NJ: Lawrence Erlbaum Associates.

Gergen, K. J. (1985). The social constructionist movement in modern psychology. *American Psychologist, 40*, 266–275.

Gergen, K. J. (2001). Psychological science in a postmodern context. *American Psychologist, 56*, 803–813.

Gergen, M. (2001). *Feminist reconstructions in psychology: Narrative, gender, and performance.* Thousand Oaks, CA: Sage.

Gergen, M., Chrisler, J. C., & LoCicero, A. (1999). Innovative methods: Resources for research, publishing, and teaching. *Psychology of Women Quarterly, 23*, 431–456.

Gershon, J. (2002). A meta-analytic review of gender differences in ADHD. *Journal of Attention Disorders, 5*, 143–154.

Gervais, J., Tremblay, R. E., Desmarais-Gervais, L., & Vitaro, F. (2000). Children's persistent lying, gender differences, and disruptive behaviours: A longitudinal perspective. *International Journal of Behavioral Development, 24*, 213–221.

Gibbons, J. L. (2000). Gender development in cross-cultural perspective. In T. Eckes & H. M. Trautner (Eds.), *The developmental social psychology of gender* (pp. 389–415). Mahwah, NJ: Lawrence Erlbaum Associates.

Gibbs, A. C. & Wilson, J. F. (1999). Sex differences in route learning by children. *Perceptual and Motor Skills, 88*, 590–594.

Gibbs, J. C., Arnold, K. D., & Burkhart, J. E. (1984). Sex differences in the expression of moral judgment. *Child Development, 55*, 1040–1043.

Giedd, J. N. (2004). Structural magnetic resonance imaging of the adolescent brain. *Annals of the New York Academy of Sciences, 1021*, 77–85.

Giedd, J. N., Blumenthal, J., Jeffries, N. O., Castellanos, F. X., Liu, H., Zijdenbos, A., et al. (1999). Brain development during childhood and adolescence: a longitudinal MRI study. *Nature Neuroscience, 2*, 861–863.

Gilbert, K. (1998). The body, young children and popular culture. In N. Yelland (Ed.), *Gender in early childhood* (pp. 55–71). London: Taylor and Francis/Routledge.

Giles, J. W. & Heyman, G. D. (2005). Young children's beliefs about the relationship between gender and aggressive behavior. *Child Development, 76*, 107–121.

Gillett-Netting, R. & Perry, A. (2005). Gender and nutritional status at the household level among Gwembe Valley Tonga children, 0–10 years. *American Journal of Human Biology, 17*, 372–375.

Gilligan, C. (1977). In a different voice: Women's conceptions of self and of morality. *Harvard Educational Review, 47*, 481–517.

Gilligan, C. (1982). *In a different voice: Psychological theory and women's development*. Cambridge, MA: Harvard University Press.

Gilligan, C. (1994). In a different voice: Women's conceptions of self and of morality. In B. Puka (Ed.), *Caring voices and women's moral frames: Gilligan's view. Moral development: A compendium* (Vol. 6, pp. 1–37). New York: Garland Publishing.

Gilligan, C., Lyons, N. P., & Hanmer, T. J. (Eds.). (1990). *Making connections: The relational worlds of adolescent girls at Emma Willard School*. Cambridge, MA: Harvard University Press.

Ginsburg, H. P., Klein, A., & Starkey, P. (1998). The development of children's mathematical thinking: Connecting research with practice. In I. A. Sigel & K. A. Renninger (Eds.), *Handbook of child psychology: Vol. 4. Child psychology in practice* (5th ed., pp. 401–476). New York: Wiley.

Giordano, P. C., Manning, W. D., & Longmore, M. A. (2006). Adolescent romantic relationships: An emerging portrait of their nature and developmental significance. In A. C. Crouter & A. Booth (Eds.), *Romance and sex in adolescence and emerging adulthood: Risks and opportunities.* (pp. 127–150). Mahwah, NJ: Lawrence Erlbaum Associates.

Glass, T. E. (2000). Where are all the women superintendents? *School Administrator, 57*, 28–32.

Gleason, J. B. & Ely, R. (2002). Gender differences in language development. In A. McGillicuddy-De Lisi & R. De Lisi (Eds.), *Biology, society, and behavior: The development of sex differences in cognition* (Vol. 21, pp. 127–154). Westport, CT: Ablex Publishing.

Glos, J. & Goldin, S. (1998). An interview with Brenda Laurel (Purple Moon). In J. Cassell & H. Jenkins (Eds.), *From Barbie to Mortal Kombat: Gender and computer games* (pp. 90–114). Cambridge, MA: The MIT Press.

Gogtay, N., Giedd, J. N., Lusk, L., Hayashi, K. M., Greenstein, D., Vaituzis, A. C., et al. (2004). Dynamic mapping of human cortical development during childhood through early adulthood. *Proceedings of the National Academy of Sciences, 101*, 8174–8179.

Goldstein, J. H. (1994). Sex differences in toy play and use of video games. In J. H. Goldstein (Ed.), *Toys, play, and child development* (pp. 110–129). New York: Cambridge University Press.

Goldstein, J. H. (1995). Aggressive toy play. In A. D. Pellegrini (Ed.), *The future of play theory: A multidisciplinary inquiry into the contributions of Brian Sutton-Smith* (pp. 127–147). Albany, NY: State University of New York Press.

Goldstein, J. H. (1998). Immortal kombat: War toys and violent video games. In J. H. Goldstein (Ed.), *Why we watch: The attractions of violent entertainment* (pp. 53–68). New York: Oxford University Press.

Goldstein, J. M., Seidman, L. J., Horton, N. J., Makris, N., Kennedy, D. N., Caviness, V. S., et al. (2001). Normal sexual dimorphism of the adult human brain assessed by in vivo magnetic resonance imaging. *Cerebral Cortex, 11*, 490–497.

Golombok, S., Perry, B., Burston, A., Murray, C., Mooney-Somers, J., Stevens, M., et al. (2003). Children with lesbian parents: A community study. *Developmental Psychology, 39*, 20–33.

Golombok, S. & Tasker, F. (1996). Do parents influence the sexual orientation of their children? Findings from a longitudinal study of lesbian families. *Developmental Psychology, 32*, 3–11.

Good, C. D., Johnsrude, I., Ashburner, J., Henson, R. N. A., Friston, K. J., & Frackowiak, R. S. J. (2001). Cerebral asymmetry and the effects of sex and handedness on brain structure: A voxel-based morphometric analysis of 465 normal adult human brains. *NeuroImage, 14*, 685–700.

Goodwin, M. H. (1990). *He-said-she-said: Talk as social organization among Black children*. Bloomington, IN: Indiana University Press.

Goodwin, M. H. (1995). Co-construction in girls' hopscotch. *Research on Language and Social Interaction, 28*, 261–281.

Goodwin, M. H. (2002). Exclusion in girls' peer groups: Ethnographic analysis of language practices on the playground. *Human Development, 45*, 392–415.

Goodwin, M. P. & Roscoe, B. (1990). Sibling violence and agonistic interactions among middle adolescents. *Adolescence, 25*, 451–467.

Goodwin, S. A. & Fiske, S. T. (2001). Power and gender: The double-edged sword of ambivalence. In R. K. Unger (Ed.), *Handbook of the psychology of women and gender* (pp. 358–366). New York: Wiley.

Gorard, S., Rees, G., & Salisbury, J. (1999). Reappraising the apparent underachievement of boys at school. *Gender and Education, 11*, 441–454.

Gorski, R. A., Gordon, J. H., Shryne, J. E., & Southam, A. M. (1978). Evidence for a morphological sex difference within the medial preoptic area of the rat brain. *Brain Research, 148*, 333–346.

Gottman, J. M. (1983). How children become friends. *Monographs of the Society for Research in Child Development, 48*(3, Serial No. 201).

Gottman, J. M. (1986). The world of coordinated play: Same- and cross-sex friendship in young children. In J. M. Gottman & J. G. Parker (Eds.), *Conversations of friends: Speculations on affective development. Studies in emotion and social interaction* (pp. 139–191). New York: Cambridge University Press.

Gottman, J. M. & Carrère, S. (1994). Why can't men and women get along? Developmental roots and marital inequities. In D. J. Canary & L. Stafford (Eds.), *Communication and relational maintenance* (pp. 203–229). San Diego, CA: Academic Press.

Gottman, J. M., Katz, L. F., & Hooven, C. (1996). Parental meta-emotion philosophy and the emotional life of families: Theoretical models and preliminary data. *Journal of Family Psychology, 10*, 243–268.

Gottman, J. M. & Notarius, C. I. (2002). Marital research in the 20th century and a research agenda for the 21st century. *Family Process, 41*, 159–197.

Government of India. (1990). *The lesser child: The girl in India.* New Dehli: Department of Women and Child Development, Ministry of Human Resource Development, with assistance from UNICEF.

Gow, J. (1996). Reconsidering gender roles on MTV: Depictions in the most popular music videos of the early 1990s. *Communication Reports, 9*, 151–161.

Goy, R. W., Bercovitch, F. B., & McBrair, M. C. (1988). Behavioral masculinization is independent of genital masculinization in prenatally androgenized female rhesus macaques. *Hormones and Behavior, 22*, 552–571.

Goy, R. W. & McEwen, B. S. (1980). *Sexual differentiation of the brain.* Cambridge: MIT Press.

Graham, S., Taylor, A. Z., & Hudley, C. (1998). Exploring achievement values among ethnic minority early adolescents. *Journal of Educational Psychology, 90*, 606–620.

Graham, T. & Ickes, W. (1997). When women's intuition isn't greater than men's. In W. J. Ickes (Ed.), *Empathic accuracy* (pp. 117–143). New York: The Guilford Press.

Gralinski, J. H. & Kopp, C. B. (1993). Everyday rules for behavior: Mothers' requests to young children. *Developmental Psychology, 29*, 573–584.

Grauerholz, E. & Pescosolido, B. A. (1989). Gender representation in children's literature 1900–1984. *Gender and Society, 3*, 113–125.

Graunt, J. (1662). *Natural and political observations mentioned in a following index, and made upon the bills of mortality.* London: Thomas Roycroft for John Martin, James Allestry, and Thomas Dicas.

Green, C. S. & Bavelier, D. (2003). Action video game modifies visual selective attention. *Nature, 423*, 534–537.

Greener, S. & Crick, N. R. (1999). Normative beliefs about prosocial behavior in middle childhood: What does it mean to be nice? *Social Development, 8*, 349–363.

Greenfield, P. M., Camaioni, L., Ercolani, P., Weiss, L., Lauber, B. A., & Perucchini, P. (1996). Cognitive socialization by computer games in two cultures: Inductive discovery or mastery of an iconic code? In P. M. Greenfield & R. R. Cocking (Eds.), *Interacting with video. Advances in applied developmental psychology* (Vol. 11, pp. 141–167). Westport, CT: Ablex Publishing.

Greenfield, P. M., deWinstanley, P., Kilpatrick, H., & Kaye, D. (1996). Action video games and informal education: Effects on strategies for dividing visual attention. In P. M. Greenfield & R. R. Cocking (Eds.), *Interacting with video. Advances in applied developmental psychology* (Vol. 11, pp. 187–205). Westport, CT: Ablex Publishing.

Greenfield, P. M. & Yan, Z. (2006). Children, adolescents, and the Internet : A new field of inquiry in developmental psychology. *Developmental Psychology, 42*, 391–394.

Greeno, C. G. & Maccoby, E. E. (1986). How different is the "different voice"? *Signs, 11*, 310–316.

Greever, E. A., Austin, P., & Welhousen, K. (2000). "William's Doll" revisited. *Language Arts, 77*, 324–330.

Grieshaber, S. (1998). Constructing the gendered infant. In N. Yelland (Ed.), *Gender in early childhood* (pp. 15–35). Florence, KY: Taylor & Francis/Routledge.

Griffiths, M. (1997). Computer game playing in early adolescence. *Youth and Society, 29*, 223–237.

Grimshaw, G. M., Sitarenios, G., & Finegan, J. A. (1995). Mental rotation at 7 years: Relations with prenatal testosterone levels and spatial play experience. *Brain and Cognition, 29*, 85–100.

Groesz, L. M., Levine, M. P., & Murnen, S. K. (2002). The effect of experimental presentation of thin media images on body satisfaction: A meta-analytic review. *International Journal of Eating Disorders, 31*, 1–16.

Grön, G., Wunderlich, A. P., Spitzer, M., Tomczak, R., & Riepe, M. W. (2000). Brain activation during human navigation: gender-different neural networks as substrate of performance. *Nature Neuroscience, 3*, 404–408.

Gross, P. R. & Levitt, N. (1994). *Higher superstition: The academic left and its quarrels with science.* Baltimore, MD: Johns Hopkins University Press.

Grumbach, M. M. & Auchus, R. J. (1999). Estrogen: Consequences and implications of human mutations in synthesis and action. *Journal of Clinical Endocrinology and Metabolism, 84*, 4677–4694.

Grumbach, M. M., Hughes, I. A., & Conte, F. A. (2003). Disorders of sex differentiation. In P. R. Larsen, H. M. Kronenberg, S. Melmed & K. S. Polonsky (Eds.), *Williams textbook of endocrinology* (pp. 842–1002). Philadelphia: W. B. Saunders.

Grusec, J. E. (1992). Social learning theory and developmental psychology: The legacies of Robert Sears and Albert Bandura. *Developmental Psychology, 28*, 776–786.

Grusec, J. E. (1994). Social learning theory and developmental psychology: The legacies of Robert R. Sears and Albert Bandura. In R. D. Parke, P. A. Ornstein, J. J. Rieser & C. Zahn-Waxler (Eds.), *A century of developmental psychology* (pp. 473–497). Washington, DC: The American Psychological Association.

Grusec, J. E. & Brinker, D. B. (1972). Reinforcement for imitation as a social learning determinant with implications for sex-role development. *Journal of Personality and Social Psychology, 21*, 149–158.

Guerilla Girls. (2002). *The estrogen bomb card.* Retrieved January 18, 2008, from: http://www.guerrillagirls.com/posters/spiritus.shtml.

Guillet, E., Sarrazin, P., & Fontayne, P. (2000). "If it contradicts my gender role, I'll stop": Introducing survival analysis to study the effects of gender typing on the time of withdrawal from sport practice: A 3-year study. *European Review of Applied Psychology, 50*, 417–421.

Gutierrez-Lobos, K., Woelfl, G., Scherer, M., Anderer, P., & Schmidl Mohl, B. (2000). The gender gap in depression reconsidered: The influence of marital and employment status on the female/male ratio of treated incidence rates. *Social Psychiatry and Psychiatric Epidemiology, 35*, 202–210.

Haight, W. L., Parke, R. D., & Black, J. E. (1997). Mothers' and fathers' beliefs about and spontaneous participation in their toddlers' pretend play. *Merrill-Palmer Quarterly, 43*, 271–290.

Hall, C. S., Lindzey, G., & Campbell, J. B. (1998). *Theories of personality* (4th ed.). New York: Wiley.

Hall, G. S. (1883). The contents of children's minds on entering school. *Princeton Review, 2*, 249–272.

Hall, G. S. (1905). *Adolescence.* New York: D. Appleton.

Hall, G. S. (1906). *Youth: Its education, regimen, and hygiene.* New York: D. Appleton.

Hall, G. S. (1965). Coeducation in high school. In C. Strickland, E. & C. Burgess (Eds.), *Health, growth and heredity: G. Stanley Hall on natural education* (pp. 179–187). New York: Teachers College Press.

Hall, J. A. (1978). Gender effects in decoding nonverbal cues. *Psychological Bulletin, 85*, 845–857.

Hall, J. A., Carter, J. D., & Horgan, T. G. (2000). Gender differences in nonverbal communication of emotion. In A. H. Fischer (Ed.), *Gender and emotion: Social psychological perspectives.* Studies in emotion and social interaction. Second series (pp. 97–117). New York: Cambridge University Press.

Hall, J. A. Y. & Kimura, D. (1994). Dermatoglyphic asymmetry and sexual orientation in men. *Behavioral Neuroscience, 108*, 1203–1206.

Hall, M. & Keith, R. A. (1964). Sex-role preference among children of upper and lower social class. *Journal of Social Psychology, 62*, 101–110.

Hallingby, L. (1987). Sesame Street no kid treat. *New Directions for Women, 16*, 7.

Hallingby, L. (1993). Sesame Street still no kid treat. *New Directions for Women, 22*, 13.

Halpern, C. T., Udry, J. R., Campbell, B., & Suchindran, C. (1999). Effects of body fat on weight concerns, dating, and sexual activity: A longitudinal analysis of Black and White adolescent girls. *Developmental Psychology, 35*, 721–736.

Halpern, D. F. (1997). Sex differences in intelligence: Implications for education. *American Psychologist, 52*, 1091–1102.

Halpern, D. F. (2000). *Sex differences in cognitive abilities* (3rd ed.). Mahwah, NJ: Lawrence Erlbaum Associates.

Halpern, D. F., Benbow, C. P., Geary, D. C., Gur, R. C., Hyde, J. S., & Gernsbacher, M. A. (2007). The science of sex differences in science and mathematics. *Psychological Science in the Public Interest, 8*, 1–51.

Halpern, D. F. & LaMay, M. L. (2000). The smarter sex: A critical review of sex differences in intelligence. *Educational Psychology Review, 12*, 229–246.

Hamann, S. (2005). Sex differences in the responses of the human amygdala. *Neuroscientist, 11*, 288–293.

Hamann, S. & Canli, T. (2004). Individual differences in emotional processing. *Current Opinion in Neurobiology, 14*, 233–238.

Hamann, S., Herman, R. A., Nolan, C. L., & Wallen, K. (2004). Men and women differ in amygdala response to visual sexual stimuli. *Nature Neuroscience, 7*, 411–416.

Hamburg, D. A. & Lunde, D. T. (1966). Sex hormones in the development of sex differences in behavior. In E. E. Maccoby (Ed.), *The development of sex differences* (pp. 1–24). Stanford, CA: Stanford University Press.

Hamilton, D. L. & Rose, T. L. (1980). Illusory correlation and the maintenance of stereotypic beliefs. *Journal of Personality and Social Psychology, 39*, 832–845.

Hamilton, D. L. & Trolier, T. K. (1986). Stereotypes and stereotyping: An overview of the cognitive approach. In J. F. Dovidio & S. L. Gaertner (Eds.), *Prejudice, discrimination, and racism.* (pp. 127–163). San Diego, CA: Academic Press.

Hamilton, M. C., Anderson, D., Broaddus, M., & Young, K. (2006). Gender stereotyping and under-representation of female characters in 200 popular children's picture books: A twenty-first century update. *Sex Roles, 55*, 757–765.

Hammer, M. & McFerran, J. (1988). Preference for sex of child: A research update. *Individual Psychology: Journal of Adlerian Theory, Research and Practice, 44*, 481–491.

Hampson, E. (2002). Sex differences in human brain and cognition: The influence of sex steroids in early and adult life. In J. B. Becker, S. M. Breedlove, D. Crews & M. M. McCarthy (Eds.), *Behavioral endocrinology* (pp. 579–628). Cambridge, MA: MIT Press.

Hampson, E. (2007). Endocrine contributions to sex differences in visuospatial perception and cognition. In J. B. Becker, K. J. Berkley, N. Geary, E. Hampson, J. Herman & E. Young (Eds.), *Sex differences in the brain: From genes to behavior*. New York: Oxford University Press.

Hampson, E., Rovet, J. F., & Altmann, D. (1998). Spatial reasoning in children with congenital adrenal hyperplasia due to 21-hydroxylase deficiency. *Developmental Neuropsychology, 14*, 299–320.

Hanson, S. & Pratt, G. (1995). *Gender, work, and space*. New York: Routledge.

Hare-Mustin, R. T. & Marecek, J. (1988). The meaning of difference: Gender theory, postmodernism, and psychology. *American Psychologist, 43*, 455–464.

Harre, N. (2000). Risk evaluation, driving, and adolescents: A typology. *Developmental Review, 20*, 206–226.

Harris, K. M. & Morgan, S. P. (1991). Fathers, sons, and daughters: Differential paternal involvement in parenting. *Journal of Marriage and the Family, 53*, 531–544.

Harris, L. J. (1978). Sex differences in spatial ability: Possible environmental, genetic, and neurological factors. In M. Kinsbourne (Ed.), *Asymmetrical functions of the brain* (pp. 405–522). London: Cambridge University Press.

Harrison, K. & Hefner, V. (2006). Media exposure, current and future body ideals, and disordered eating among pre-adolescent girls: A longitudinal panel study. *Journal of Youth and Adolescence, 35*, 146–156.

Hartley, R. E., Lynn, D. B., Sutton-Smith, B., & Lansky, L. M. (1964). Sex role identification: A symposium. *Merrill-Palmer Quarterly, 10*, 3–50.

Hartung, C. M. & Widiger, T. A. (1998). Gender differences in the diagnosis of mental disorders: Conclusions and controversies of the DSM-IV. *Psychological Bulletin, 123*, 260–278.

Hartung, C. M., Willcutt, E. G., Lahey, B. B., Pelham, W. E., Loney, J., Stein, M. A., et al. (2002). Sex differences in young children who meet criteria for attention deficit hyperactivity disorder. *Journal of Clinical Child and Adolescent Psychology, 31*, 453–464.

Hartup, W. W., French, D. C., Laursen, B., Johnston, M. K., & Ogawa, J. R. (1993). Conflict and friendship relations in middle childhood: Behavior in a closed-field situation. *Child Development, 64*, 445–454.

Hassett, J. M., Siebert, E. R., & Wallen, K. (2004). Sexually differentiated toy preferences in rhesus monkeys. *Hormones and Behavior, 46*, 91.

Hastings, P. D., McShane, K. E., Parker, R., & Ladha, F. (2007). Ready to make nice: Parental socialization of young sons' and daughters' prosocial behaviors with peers. *Journal of Genetic Psychology, 168*, 177–200.

Hastings, P. D., Rubin, K. H., & DeRose, L. (2005). Links among gender, inhibition, and parental socialization in the development of prosocial behavior. *Merrill-Palmer Quarterly, 51*, 467–493.

Hatchell, H. (1998). Girls' entry into higher secondary sciences. *Gender and Education, 10*, 375–386.

Haughton, D. & Haughton, J. (1996). Using a mixture model to detect son preference in Vietnam. *Journal of Biosocial Science, 28*, 355–365.

Hay, D. F., Castle, J., Stimson, C. A., & Davies, L. (1995). The social construction of character in toddlerhood. In M. Killen & D. Hart (Eds.), *Morality in everyday life: Developmental perspectives* (pp. 23–51). New York: Cambridge University Press.

Hayes, R. L. (1994). The legacy of Lawrence Kohlberg: Implications for counseling and human development. *Journal of Counseling and Development, 72*, 261–267.

Hayes, S. C. & et al. (1981). The development of the display and knowledge of sex related motor behavior in children. *Child Behavior Therapy, 3*, 1–24.

Hedges, L. V. & Nowell, A. (1995). Sex differences in mental test scores, variability, and numbers of high-scoring individuals. *Science, 269*, 41–45.

Hegarty, M., Montello, D. R., Richardson, A. E., Ishikawa, T., & Lovelace, K. (2006). Spatial abilities at different scales: Individual differences in aptitude-test performance and spatial-layout learning. *Intelligence, 34*, 151–176.

Heilbrun, A. B., Jr. (1965a). An empirical test of the modeling theory of sex-role learning. *Child Development, 36*, 789–799.

Heilbrun, A. B., Jr. (1965b). The measurement of identification. *Child Development, 36*, 111–127.

Heilbrun, A. B., Jr. (1965c). Sex differences in identification learning. *Journal of Genetic Psychology, 106*, 185–193.

Helleday, J., Edman, G., Ritzén, E. M., & Siwers, B. (1993). Personality characteristics and platelet MAO activity in women with congenital adrenal hyperplasia (CAH). *Psychoneuroendocrinology, 18*, 343–354.

Hellendoorn, J. & Harinck, F. J. H. (1997). War toy play and aggression in Dutch kindergarten children. *Social Development, 6*, 340–354.

Helwig, A. A. (2002). Sex and developmental differences by complexity of functions of occupational aspirations of school children across ten years. *Psychological Reports, 90*, 597–605.

Henderson, B. A. & Berenbaum, S. A. (1997). Sex-typed play in opposite-sex twins. *Developmental Psychobiology, 31*, 115–123.

Herbert, J. & Stipek, D. (2005). The emergence of gender differences in children's perceptions of their academic competence. *Journal of Applied Developmental Psychology, 26*, 276–295.

Herlitz, A., Nilsson, L.-G., & Baeckman, L. (1997). Gender differences in episodic memory. *Memory and Cognition, 25*, 801–811.

Herman-Giddens, M. E., Slora, E. J., Wasserman, R. C., Bourdony, C. J., Bhapkar, M. V., Koch, G. G., et al. (1997). Secondary sexual characteristics and menses in young girls seen in office practice: a study from the Pediatric Research in Office Settings network. *Pediatrics, 99*, 505–512.

Herrett-Skjellum, J. & Allen, M. (1996). Television programming and sex stereotyping: A meta-analysis. In B. R. Burleson (Ed.), *Communication yearbook* (pp. 157–185). Thousand Oaks, CA: Sage.

Hetherington, E. M. (1965). A developmental study of the effects of sex of the dominant parent on sex-role preference, identification, and imitation in children. *Journal of Personality and Social Psychology, 2*, 188–194.

Hewlett, B. S. (1989). Multiple caretaking among African Pygmies. *American Anthropologist, 91*, 186–191.

Hewlett, B. S. (1991). *Intimate fathers: The nature and context of Aka Pygmy paternal infant care*. Ann Arbor, MI: The University of Michigan Press.

Hewlett, B. S. (1992). Husband-wife reciprocity and the father-infant relationship among Aka Pygmies. In B. S. Hewlett (Ed.), *Father-child relations: Cultural and biosocial contexts. Foundations of human behavior* (pp. 153–176). Hawthorne, NY: Aldine de Gruyter.

Hewlett, B. S. (2000). Culture, history, and sex: Anthropological contributions to conceptualizing father involvement. *Marriage and Family Review, 29*, 59–73.

Heyward, C. B. (1995). Catching up: Gender values at a Canadian independent school for girls, 1978–93. *Gender and Education, 7*, 189–203.

Hibbard, D. R. & Buhrmester, D. (1998). The role of peers in the socialization of gender-related social interaction styles. *Sex Roles, 39*, 185–202.

Hier, D. B. & Crowley, W. F. (1982). Spatial ability in androgen-deficient men. *New England Journal of Medicine, 302*, 1202–1205.

Hill, J. P. & Lynch, M. E. (1983). The intensification of gender-related role expectations during early adolescence. In J. Brooks-Gunn & A. C. Peterson (Eds.), *Girls at puberty: Biological and psychosocial perspectives* (pp. 201–228). New York: Plenum.

Hill, S. A. (2002). Teaching and doing gender in African American families. *Sex Roles, 47*, 493–506.

Hill, W. F. (1960). Learning theory and the acquisition of values. *Psychological Review, 67*, 317–331.

Hillman, J. S. (1974). An analysis of male and female roles in two periods of children's literature. *Journal of Educational Research, 68*, 84–88.

Hilton, J. M. & Macari, D. P. (1997). Grandparent involvement following divorce: A comparison in single-mother and single-father families. *Journal of Divorce and Remarriage, 28*, 203–224.

Hines, M., Ahmed, F., & Hughes, I. A. (2003). Psychological outcomes and gender-related development in complete androgen insensitivity syndrome. *Archives of Sexual Behavior, 32*, 93–101.

Hines, M., Brook, C., & Conway, G. S. (2004). Androgen and psychosexual development: Core gender identity, sexual orientation, and recalled gender role behavior in women and men with congenital adrenal hyperplasia (CAH). *Journal of Sex Research, 41*, 75–81.

Hines, M., Fane, B. A., Pasterski, V. L., Mathews, G. A., Conway, G. S., & Brook, C. (2003). Spatial abilities following prenatal androgen abnormality: Targeting and mental rotations performance in individuals with congenital adrenal hyperplasia. *Psychoneuroendocrinology, 28*, 1010–1026.

Hines, M., Golombok, S., Rust, J., Johnston, K. J., Golding, J., & Avon Longitudinal Study of Parents and Children Study Team. (2002). Testosterone during pregnancy and gender role behavior of preschool children: A longitudinal, population study. *Child Development, 73*, 1678–1687.

Hines, M. & Kaufman, F. R. (1994). Androgen and the development of human sex-typical behavior: Rough-and-tumble play and sex of preferred playmates in children with congenital adrenal hyperplasia (CAH). *Child Development, 65*, 1042–1053.

Hines, N. J. & Fry, D. P. (1994). Indirect modes of aggression among women of Buenos Aires, Argentina. *Sex Roles, 30*, 213–236.

Hoffman, C. D. & Teyber, E. C. (1985). Naturalistic observations of sex differences in adult involvement with girls and boys of different ages. *Merrill Palmer Quarterly, 31*, 93–97.

Hoffman, K. L. & Edwards, J. N. (2004). An integrated theoretical model of sibling violence and abuse. *Journal of Family Violence, 19*, 185–200.

Hoffman, L. W. & Youngblade, L. M. (1999). *Mothers at work: Effects on children's well-being*. New York: Cambridge University Press.

Holland, A. & Andre, T. (1994). Athletic participation and the social status of adolescent males and females. *Youth and Society, 25*, 388–407.

Hollingworth, H. L. (1943). *Leta Stetter Hollingworth*. Lincoln, NE: University of Nebraska Press.

Hollingworth, L. S. (1914a). *Functional periodicity: An experimental study of the mental and motor abilities of women during menstruation*. New York: Teachers College.

Hollingworth, L. S. (1914b). Variability as related to sex differences in achievement. *American Journal of Sociology, 19*, 510–530.

Hollingworth, L. S. (1916). Sex differences in mental traits. *Psychological Bulletin, 13*, 377–384.

Hollingworth, L. S. (1918). Comparison of the sexes in mental traits. *Psychological Bulletin, 15*, 427–432.

Hollingworth, L. S. (1919). Comparison of the sexes in mental traits. *Psychological Bulletin, 16*, 371–373.

Hollingworth, L. S. (1928). *The psychology of the adolescent*. New York: D. Appelton.

Hollingworth, L. S. & Montague, H. (1914). The comparative variability of the sexes at birth. *American Journal of Sociology, 20*, 335–370.

Holmes, J. (2006). Do community factors have a differential impact on the health outcomes of boys and girls? Evidence from rural Pakistan. *Health Policy and Planning, 21*, 231–240.

Holzman, M. (1992). Do we really need "leadership"? *Educational Leadership, 49*, 36–40.

Hopf, D. & Hatzichristou, C. (1999). Teacher gender-related influences in Greek schools. *British Journal of Educational Psychology, 69*, 1–18.

Horgan, D. (1995). *Achieving gender equity: Strategies for the classroom*. Boston, MA: Allyn and Bacon.

Horney, K. (1935). The problem of feminine masochism. *The Psychoanalytic Review, 22*, 241–257.

Horney, K. (2000). *The unknown Karen Horney: Essays on gender, culture, and psychoanalysis*. New Haven, CT: Yale University Press.

Hornstein, G. A. (1992). The return of the repressed: Psychology's problematic relations with psychoanalysis, 1909–1960. *American Psychologist, 47*, 254–263.

Horowitz, F. D. & Paden, L. Y. (1973). The effectiveness of environmental intervention programs. In B. M. Caldwell & H. N. Ricciuti (Eds.), *Review of child development research* (Vol. 3, pp. 331–401). Chicago: University of Chicago Press.

Hortacsu, N., Bastug, S. S., & Muhammetberdiev, O. B. (2001). Desire for children in Turkmenistan and Azerbaijan: Son preference and perceived instrumentality for value satisfaction. *Journal of Cross Cultural Psychology, 32*, 309–321.

Hossain, Z. & Roopnarine, J. L. (1993). Division of household labor and child care in dual-earner African-American families with infants. *Sex Roles, 29*, 571–583.

Hothersall, D. (1995). *History of psychology* (3rd ed.). New York: McGraw-Hill.

Howes, C. (1988). Same- and cross-sex friends: Implications for interaction and social skills. *Early Childhood Research Quarterly, 3*, 21–37.

Howes, C. (1996). The earliest friendships. In W. M. Bukowski, A. F. Newcomb & W. W. Hartup (Eds.), *The company they keep: Friendship in childhood and adolescence* (pp. 66–86). New York: Cambridge University Press.

Howes, C. & Phillipsen, L. (1992). Gender and friendship: Relationships within peer groups of young children. *Social Development, 1*, 230–242.

Hoyenga, K. B. & Hoyenga, K. T. (1993). *Gender-related differences: Origins and outcomes*. Needham Heights, MA: Allyn & Bacon.

Hsu, J. (2005). Marital quality, sex-typed parenting, and girls' and boys' expression of problem behaviors. In P. A. Cowan, C. P. Cowan, J. C. Ablow, V. K. Johnson & J. R. Measelle (Eds.), *The family context of parenting in children's adaptation to elementary school* (pp. 139–162). Mahwah, NJ: Lawrence Erlbaum Associates.

Hubbard, J. A. (2001). Emotion expression processes in children's peer interaction: The role of peer rejection, aggression, and gender. *Child Development, 72*, 1426–1438.

Huesmann, L. R., Guerra, N. G., Zelli, A., & Miller, L. S. (1992). Differing normative beliefs about aggression for boys and girls. In K. Björkqvist & P. Niemelae (Eds.), *Of mice and women: Aspects of female aggression* (pp. 77–87). San Diego, CA: Academic Press.

Huesmann, L. R., Lagerspetz, K., & Eron, L. D. (1984). Intervening variables in the TV violence-aggression relation: Evidence from two countries. *Developmental Psychology, 20*, 746–775.

Huesmann, L. R. & Miller, L. S. (1994). Long-term effects of repeated exposure to media violence in childhood. In L. R. Huesmann (Ed.), *Aggressive behavior: Current perspectives* (pp. 153–186). New York: Plenum Press.

Huesmann, L. R., Moise, J. F., & Podolski, C. L. (1997). The effects of media violence on the development of antisocial behavior. In D. M. Stoff & J. Breiling (Eds.), *Handbook of antisocial behavior* (pp. 181–193). New York: Wiley.

Huesmann, L. R., Moise-Titus, J., Podolski, C. L., & Eron, L. D. (2003). Longitudinal relations between children's exposure to TV violence and their aggressive and violent behavior in young adulthood: 1977–1992. *Developmental Psychology, 39*, 201–221.

Hughes, C. & Dunn, J. (1998). Understanding mind and emotion: Longitudinal associations with mental-state talk between young friends. *Developmental Psychology, 34*, 1026–1037.

Hughes, I. A. & Deeb, A. (2006). Androgen resistance. *Best Practice and Research Clinical Endocrinology and Metabolism, 20*, 577–598.

Hughes, I. A., Houk, C., Ahmed, F., Lee, P. A., & LWPES/ESPE Consensus Group. (2006). Consensus statement on management of intersex disorders. *Archives of Disease in Childhood, 91*, 554–563.

Hull, E. M., Franz, J. R., Snyder, A. M., & Nishita, J. K. (1980). Perinatal progesterone and learning, social and reproductive behavior in rats. *Physiology and Behavior, 24*, 251–256.

Humphreys, A. P. & Smith, P. K. (1987). Rough and tumble, friendship, and dominance in schoolchildren: Evidence for continuity and change with age. *Child Development, 58*, 201–212.

Huston, A. C. (1983). Sex-typing. In E. M. Hetherington (Ed.), *Handbook of child psychology. Vol. 4. Socialization, personality and social development* (4th ed., pp. 387–468). New York: Wiley.

Huston, A. C., Greer, D., Wright, J. C., Ross, W., & Ross, R. (1984). Children's comprehension of televised formal features with masculine and feminine connotations. *Developmental Psychology, 20*, 707–716.

Huston, A. C. & Wright, J. C. (1996). Television and socialization of young children. In T. M. MacBeth (Ed.), *Tuning in to young viewers: Social science perspectives on television* (pp. 37–60). Thousand Oaks, CA: Sage.

Huston, A. C., Wright, J. C., Marquis, J., & Green, S. B. (1999). How young children spend their time: Television and other activities. *Developmental Psychology, 35*, 912–925.

Huttenlocher, J., Haight, W., Bryk, A., Seltzer, M., & Lyons, T. (1991). Early vocabulary growth: Relation to language input and gender. *Developmental Psychology, 27*, 236–248.

Hyde, J. S. (1984a). Children's understanding of sexist language. *Developmental Psychology, 20*, 697–706.

Hyde, J. S. (1984b). How large are gender differences in aggression? A developmental meta-analysis. *Developmental Psychology, 20*, 722–736.

Hyde, J. S. (1986a). Gender differences in aggression. In J. S. Hyde, & M. C. Linn (Eds.), *The psychology of gender: Advances through meta-analysis* (pp. 51–66). Baltimore: Johns Hopkins University Press.

Hyde, J. S. (1986b). Introduction: Meta-analysis and the psychology of gender. In J. S. Hyde, & M. C. Linn (Eds.), *The psychology of gender: Advances through meta-analysis* (pp. 1–13). Baltimore: Johns Hopkins University Press.

Hyde, J. S. (1994). Can meta-analysis make feminist transformations in psychology? *Psychology of Women Quarterly, 18*, 451–462.

Hyde, J. S. (2005). The gender similarities hypothesis. *American Psychologist, 60*, 581–592.

Hyde, J. S., Fennema, E., & Lamon, S. J. (1990). Gender differences in mathematics performance: A meta-analysis. *Psychological Bulletin, 107*, 139–155.

Hyde, J. S., Fennema, E., Ryan, M., Frost, L. A., & Hopp, C. (1990). Gender comparisons of mathematics attitudes and affect: A meta-analysis. *Psychology of Women Quarterly, 14*, 299–324.

Hyde, J. S. & Linn, M. C. (1988). Gender differences in verbal ability: A meta-analysis. *Psychological Bulletin, 104*, 53–69.

Hyde, J. S. & McKinley, N. M. (1997). Gender differences in cognition: Results from meta-analyses. In P. J. Caplan, M. Crawford, J. S. Hyde & J. T. E. Richardson (Eds.), *Gender differences in human cognition* (pp. 30–51). New York: Oxford University Press.

Ickes, W., Gesn, P. R., & Graham, T. (2000). Gender differences in empathic accuracy: Differential ability or differential motivation? *Personal Relationships, 7*, 95–109.

Iijima, M., Arisaka, O., Minamoto, F., & Arai, Y. (2001). Sex differences in children's free drawings: A study on girls with congenital adrenal hyperplasia. *Hormones and Behavior, 40*, 99–104.

Imperato-McGinley, J., Peterson, R. E., Gautier, T., & Sturla, E. (1979). Androgens and the evolution of male gender identity among male pseudohermaphrodites with 5-alpha-reductase deficiency. *New England Journal of Medicine, 300*, 1233–1237.

Imperato-McGinley, J., & Zhu, Y. S. (2002). Androgens and male physiology the syndrome of 5alpha-reductase-2 deficiency. *Molecular and Cellular Endocrinology, 198*, 51–59.

Inhelder, B. & Jean, P. (1969). *The early growth of logic in the child.* New York: Norton.

Isaacs, S. (1933). *Social development in young children.* New York: Harcourt Brace.

Isgor, C. & Sengelaub, D. R. (2003). Effects of neonatal gonadal steroids on adult CA3 pyramidal neuron dendritic morphology and spatial memory in rats. *Journal of Neurobiology, 55*, 179–190.

Ittyerah, M. & Mahindra, K. (1990). Moral development and its relation to perspective taking ability. *Psychology and Developing Societies, 2*, 203–216.

Jacklin, C. N., DiPietro, J. A., & Maccoby, E. E. (1984). Sex-typing behavior and sex-typing pressure in child/parent interaction. *Archives of Sexual Behavior, 13*, 413–425.

Jacklin, C. N. & Maccoby, E. E. (1978). Social behavior at thirty-three months in same-sex and mixed-sex dyads. *Child Development, 49*, 557–569.

Jacklin, C. N., Maccoby, E. E., Doering, C. H., & King, D. R. (1984). Neonatal sex-steroid hormones and muscular strength of boys and girls in the first three years. *Developmental Psychobiology, 17*, 301–310.

Jackson, C. & Bisset, M. (2005). Gender and school choice: Factors influencing parents when choosing single-sex or co-educational independent schools for their children. *Cambridge Journal of Education, 35*, 195–211.

Jacobs, J. E. & Eccles, J. S. (1992). The impact of mothers' gender-role stereotypic beliefs on mothers' and children's ability perceptions. *Journal of Personality and Social Psychology, 63*, 932–944.

Jacobson, N. S. (1989). The politics of intimacy. *The Behavior Therapist, 12*, 29–32.

Jaffee, S. & Hyde, J. S. (2000). Gender differences in moral orientation: A meta-analysis. *Psychological Bulletin, 126*, 703–726.

James, A. N. & Richards, H. C. (2003). Escaping stereotypes: Educational attitudes of male alumni of single-sex and coed schools. *Psychology of Men and Masculinity, 4*, 136–148.

James, T. W. & Kimura, D. (1997). Sex differences in remembering the locations of objects in an array: Location-shifts versus location-exchanges. *Evolution and Human Behavior, 18*, 155–163.

Jessee, P. O., Strickland, M., & Jessee, J. E. (1994). Infant and toddler interactions with a new infant in a group environment. *Early Child Development and Care, 100*, 57–68.

Jimenez, E. & Lockheed, M. E. (1989). Enhancing girls' learning through single-sex education: Evidence and a policy conundrum. *Educational Evaluation and Policy Analysis, 11*, 117–142.

Jimenez-Castellanos, J., Carmona, A., Catalina-Herrera, C. J., & Vinuales, M. (1996). Skeletal maturation of wrist and hand ossification centers in normal Spanish boys and girls: A study using the Greulich-Pyle method. *Acta Anatomica (Basel), 155*, 206–211.

Jodl, K. M., Michael, A., Malanchuk, O., Eccles, J. S., & Sameroff, A. (2001). Parents' roles in shaping early adolescents' occupational aspirations. *Child Development, 72*, 1247–1265.

Johnson, B. T. & Eagly, A. H. (2000). Quantitative synthesis of social psychological research. In H. T. Reis & C. M. Judd (Eds.), *Handbook of research methods in social and personality psychology* (pp. 496–528). New York: Cambridge University Press.

Johnson, E. S. & Meade, A. C. (1987). Developmental patterns of spatial ability: An early sex difference. *Child Development, 58*, 725–740.

Johnson, J. & Ettema, J. (1982). *Positive images: Breaking stereotypes with children's television.* Beverly Hills, CA: Sage Publications.

Johnson, K. L. & Tassinary, L. G. (2005). Perceiving sex directly and indirectly: Meaning in motion and morphology. *Psychological Science, 16*, 890–897.

Johnson, L. D., O'Malley, P. M., & Bachman, J. G. (2002). *Monitoring the future: National results on adolescent drug use.* Bethesda, MD: National Institute on Drug Abuse.

Johnson, M. M. (1963). Sex role learning in the nuclear family. *Child Development, 34*, 319–333.

Johnston, K. E., Bittinger, K., Smith, A., & Madole, K. L. (2001). Developmental changes in infants' and toddlers' attention to gender categories. *Merrill-Palmer Quarterly, 47*, 563–584.

Jones, D. C. & Costin, S. E. (1995). Friendship quality during preadolescence and adolescence: The contributions of relationship orientations, instrumentality, and expressivity. *Merrill-Palmer Quarterly, 41*, 517–535.

Jones, E. (1910). Psycho-analysis and education. *Journal of Educational Psychology, 1*, 497–520.

Jones, E. (1933). The phallic phase. *International Journal of Psycho-Analysis, 14*, 1–33.

Jones, L. & Smart, T. (1995). Confidence and mathematics: A gender issue? *Gender and Education, 7*, 157–166.

Jones, M. G., Howe, A., & Rua, M. J. (2000). Gender differences in students' experiences, interests, and attitudes toward science and scientists. *Science Education, 84*, 180–192.

Jordan, E. & Cowan, A. (1995). Warrior narratives in the kindergarten classroom: Renegotiating the social contract? *Gender and Society, 9*, 727–743.

Juraska, J. M. (1991). Sex differences in "cognitive" regions of the rat brain. *Psychoneuroendocrinology, 16*, 105–119.

Jürgensen, M., Hiort, O., Holterhus, P. M., & Thyen, U. (2007). Gender role behavior in children with XY karyotype and disorders of sex development. *Hormones and Behavior, 51*, 443–453.

Jussim, L. & Eccles, J. S. (1992). Teacher expectations: Construction and reflection of student achievement. *Journal of Personality and Social Psychology, 63*, 947–961.

Jussim, L. J. & Eccles, J. S. (1995). Are teacher expectations biased by students' gender, social class, or ethnicity? In Y. T. Lee, L. J. Jussim & C. R. McCauley (Eds.), *Stereotype accuracy: Toward appreciating group differences* (pp. 245–271). Washington: American Psychological Association.

Kafai, Y. B. (1996). Gender differences in children's constructions of video games. In P. M. Greenfield & R. R. Cocking (Eds.), *Interacting with video. Advances in applied developmental psychology* (Vol. 11, pp. 39–66). Westport, CT: Ablex Publishing.

Kafai, Y. B. (1998). Video game designs by girls and boys: Variability and consistency of gender differences. In J. Cassell & H. Jenkins (Eds.), *From Barbie to Mortal Kombat: Gender and computer games* (pp. 90–114). Cambridge, MA: The MIT Press.

Kafai, Y. B. & Sutton, S. (1999). Elementary school students' computer and Internet use at home: Current trends and issues. *Journal of Educational Computing Research, 21*, 345–362.

Kagan, J. (1958). The concept of identification. *Psychological Review, 65*, 296–305.

Kagan, J. (1964). Acquisition and significance of sex typing and sex role identity. In M. Hoffman & L. Hoffman (Eds.), *Review of child development research* (Vol. 1, pp. 137–167). New York: Russell Sage.

Kail, R. V. & Levine, L. E. (1976). Encoding processes and sex-role preferences. *Journal of Experimental Child Psychology, 21*, 256–263.

Kallai, J., Karadi, K., & Kovacs, B. (2000). Influences of fear and anxiety on organization of way-finding and spatial orientation. *Review of Psychology, 7*, 27–35.

Kamins, M. L. & Dweck, C. S. (1999). Person versus process praise and criticism: Implications for contingent self-worth and coping. *Developmental Psychology, 35*, 835–847.

Kane, E. W. (2006). "No way my boys are going to be like that!": Parents' responses to children's gender nonconformity. *Gender and Society, 20*, 149–176.

Kaplowitz, P. B. & Oberfield, S. E. (1999). Reexamination of the age limit for defining when puberty is precocious in girls in the United States: implications for evaluation and treatment. Drug and Therapeutics and Executive Committees of the Lawson Wilkins Pediatric Endocrine Society. *Pediatrics, 104*, 936–941.

Kaplowitz, P. B., Slora, E. J., Wasserman, R. C., Pedlow, S. E., & Herman-Giddens, M. E. (2001). Earlier onset of puberty in girls: relation to increased body mass index and race. *Pediatrics, 108*, 347–353.

Karapetsas, A. B. & Vlachos, F. M. (1997). Sex and handedness in development of visuomotor skills. *Perceptual and Motor Skills, 85*, 131–140.

Karbon, M., Fabes, R. A., Carlo, G., & Martin, C. L. (1992). Preschoolers' beliefs about sex and age differences in emotionality. *Sex Roles, 27*, 377–390.

Karraker, K. H., Vogel, D. A., & Lake, M. A. (1995). Parents' gender-stereotyped perceptions of newborns: The eye of the beholder revisited. *Sex Roles, 33*, 687–701.

Katz, P. A. (1986). Modification of children's gender-stereotyped behavior: General issues and research considerations. *Sex Roles, 14*, 591–602.

Katz, P. A. (1996). Raising feminists. *Psychology of Women Quarterly, 20*, 323–340.

Katz, P. A. & Walsh, P. V. (1991). Modification of children's gender-stereotyped behavior. *Child Development, 62*, 338–351.

Katzev, A. R., Warner, R. L., & Acock, A. C. (1994). Girls or boys? Relationship of child gender to marital instability. *Journal of Marriage and the Family, 56*, 89–100.

Kaufman, G. (1999). The portrayal of men's family roles in television commercials. *Sex Roles, 41*, 439–458.

Kazura, K. (2000). Fathers' qualitative and quantitative involvement: An investigation of attachment, play, and social interactions. *Journal of Men's Studies, 9*, 41–57.

Keehn, J. D. (1996). *Master builders of modern psychology: From Freud to Skinner*. New York: New York University Press.

Keenan, K. & Shaw, D. (1997). Developmental and social influences on young girls' early problem behavior. *Psychological Bulletin, 121*, 95–113.

Keillor, G. (1993). *The book of guys*. New York: Viking.

Keller, C. (2001). Effect of teachers' stereotyping on students' stereotyping of mathematics as a male domain. *Journal of Social Psychology, 141*, 165–173.

Kelly, A. (1988). Gender differences in teacher-pupil interactions: A meta-analytic review. *Research in Education, 39*, 1–23.

Kelly, L. (1993). What little girls and boys are made of: The gendering of childhood. *Educational and Child Psychology, 10*, 12–21.

Kemp, D. T. (2002). Otoacoustic emissions, their origin in cochlear function, and use. *British Medical Bulletin, 63*, 223–241.

Kendrick, C. & Dunn, J. (1982). Protest or pleasure? The response of first-born children to interactions between their mothers and infant siblings. *Journal of Child Psychology and Psychiatry and Allied Disciplines, 23*, 117–129.

Kennedy, E. (1995). Correlates of perceived popularity among peers: A study of race and gender differences among middle school students. *Journal of Negro Education, 64*, 186–195.

Kenrick, D. T. & Luce, C. L. (2000). An evolutionary life-history model of gender differences and similarities. In T. Eckes & H. M. Trautner (Eds.), *The developmental social psychology of gender* (pp. 35–63). Mahwah, NJ: Lawrence Erlbaum Associates.

Kerns, K. A. & Berenbaum, S. A. (1991). Sex differences in spatial ability in children. *Behavior Genetics, 21*, 383–396.

Kerr, D. C. R., Lopez, N. L., Olson, S. L., & Sameroff, A. J. (2004). Parental discipline and externalizing behavior problems in early childhood: The roles of moral regulation and child gender. *Journal of Abnormal Child Psychology, 32*, 369–383.

Kesler, S. R. (2007). Turner Syndrome. *Child and Adolescent Psychiatric Clinics of North America, 16*, 709–722.

Khanna, S. K. (1997). Traditions and reproductive technology in an urbanizing north Indian village. *Social Science and Medicine, 44*, 171–180.

Kier, C. & Lewis, C. (1998). Preschool sibling interaction in separated and married families: Are same-sex pairs or older sisters more sociable? *Journal of Child Psychology and Psychiatry and Allied Disciplines, 39*, 191–201.

Killen, M., Lee-Kim, J., McGlothlin, H., & Stangor, C. (2002). How children and adolescents evaluate gender and racial exclusion. *Monographs of the Society for Research in Child Development, 67*(4, Serial No. 271).

Killen, M. & McKown, C. (2005). How integrative approaches to intergroup attitudes advance the field. *Journal of Applied Developmental Psychology, 26*, 616–622.

Kimball, M. M. (1985). Television and sex-role attitudes. In T. M. Williams (Ed.), *The impact of television: A natural experiment in three communities* (pp. 265–302). New York: Academic Press.

Kimball, M. M. (1989). A new perspective on women's math achievement. *Psychological Bulletin, 105*, 198–214.

Kimball, M. M. (2001). Gender similarities and differences as feminist contradictions. In R. K. Unger (Ed.), *Handbook of psychology of women and gender* (pp. 66–83). New York: Wiley.

Kimmel, M. S. & Mahler, M. (2003). Adolescent masculinity, homophobia, and violence: Random school shootings, 1982–2001. *American Behavioral Scientist, 46*, 1439–1458.

Kimura, D. (1999). *Sex and cognition*. Cambridge, MA: The MIT Press.

Kinder, M. (Ed.). (1999). *Kids' media culture*. Durham, NC: Duke University Press.

Kinman, J. R. & Henderson, D. L. (1985). An analysis of sexism in Newbery Medal Award books from 1977 to 1984. *Reading Teacher, 38*, 885–889.

Kiriti, T. W. & Tisdell, C. (2005). Family size, economics and child gender preference: A case study in the Nyeri district of Kenya. *International Journal of Social Economics, 32*, 492–509.

Kirsch, S. J. & Olczak, P. V. (2001). Rating comic book violence: Contributions of gender and trait hostility. *Social Behavior and Personality, 29*, 833–836.

Kite, M. (2001). Changing times, changing gender roles: Who do we want women and men to be? In R. K. Unger (Ed.), *Handbook of psychology of women and gender* (pp. 215–227). New York: Wiley.

Klebanov, P. K. & Ruble, D. N. (1994). Toward an understanding of women's experience of menstrual cycle symptoms. In V. J. Adesso, D. M. Reddy & R. Fleming (Eds.), *Psychological perspectives on women's health* (pp. 183–221). Washington, DC: Taylor & Francis.

Klein, M. (1928). Early stages of the Oedipus conflict. *International Journal of Psycho-Analysis, 9*, 167–180.

Klein, M. W. (1995). *The American street gang. Its nature, prevalence, and control*. New York: Oxford University Press.

Kleinfeld, J. A. (1998). *The myth that schools shortchange girls: Social science in the service of deception*. Washington, DC: The Women's Freedom Network.

Kling, K. C., Hyde, J. S., Showers, C. J., & Buswell, B. N. (1999). Gender differences in self-esteem: A meta-analysis. *Psychological Bulletin, 125*, 470–500.

Klinger, L. J., Hamilton, J. A., & Cantrell, P. J. (2001). Children's perceptions of aggressive and gender-specific content in toy commercials. *Social Behavior and Personality, 29*, 11–20.

Klinnert, M. D., Emde, R. N., Butterfield, P., & Campos, J. J. (1986). Social referencing: The infant's use of emotional signals from a friendly adult with mother present. *Developmental Psychology, 22*, 427–432.

Klugman, K. (1999). A bad hair day for G. I. Joe. In B. L. Clark & M. R. Higonnet (Eds.), *Girls, boys, books, toys* (pp. 169–182). Baltimore. MD: The Johns Hopkins University Press.

Klump, K. L., Perkins, P. S., Burt, S. A., McGue, M., & Iacono, W. G. (2007). Puberty moderates genetic influences on disordered eating. *Psychological Medicine, 37*, 627–634.

Knickmeyer, R., Baron-Cohen, S., Fane, B. A., Wheelwright, S., Mathews, G. A., Conway, G. S., et al. (2006). Androgens and autistic traits: A study of individuals with congenital adrenal hyperplasia. *Hormones and Behavior, 50*, 148–153.

Knickmeyer, R. C., Wheelwright, S., Taylor, K., Raggatt, P., Hackett, G., & Baron-Cohen, S. (2005). Gender-typed play and amniotic testosterone. *Developmental Psychology, 41*, 517–528.

Knight, G. P., Fabes, R. A., & Higgins, D. A. (1996). Concerns about drawing causal inferences from meta-analyses: An example in the study of gender differences in aggression. *Psychological Bulletin, 119*, 410–421.

Knobloch, S., Callison, C., Chen, L., Fritzsche, A., & Zillmann, D. (2005). Children's sex-stereotyped self-socialization through selective exposure to entertainment: Cross-cultural experiments in Germany, China, and the United States. *Journal of Communication, 55*, 122 - 138.

Knudson-Martin, C., & Mahoney, A. R. (2005). Moving beyond gender: Processes that create relationship equality. *Journal of Marital and Family Therapy, 31*, 235–246.

Koblinsky, S. G., Cruse, D. F., & Sugawara, A. I. (1978). Sex role stereotypes and children's memory for story content. *Child Development, 49*, 452–458.

Koch, J. (2003). Gender issues in the classroom. In W. M. Reynolds & G. E. Miller (Eds.), *Handbook of psychology: Educational psychology* (Vol. 7, pp. 259–281). New York: Wiley.

Kochanska, G. (2001). Emotional development in children with different attachment histories: The first three years. *Child Development, 72*, 474–490.

Kochanska, G. & Aksan, N. (2004). Development of mutual responsiveness between parents and their young children. *Child Development, 75*, 1657–1676.

Koehler, M. S. (1990). Classrooms, teachers, and gender differences in mathematics. In E. Fennema & G. C. Leder (Eds.), *Mathematics and gender* (pp. 128–148). New York: Teachers College Press.

Kohlberg, L. (1966). A cognitive developmental analysis of children's sex role concepts and attitudes. In E. E. Maccoby (Ed.), *The development of sex differences* (pp. 82–172). Stanford, CA: Stanford University Press.

Kohlberg, L. & Kramer, R. (1969). Continuities and discontinuities in childhood and adult moral development. *Human Development, 12*, 3–120.

Kohlberg, L. & Puka, B. (1994). *Kohlberg's original study of moral development.* New York: Garland Publishing.

Koivula, N. (1999). Sport participation: Differences in motivation and actual participation due to gender typing. *Journal of Sport Behavior, 22*, 360–380.

Koivula, N. (2001). Perceived characteristics of sports categorized as gender-neutral, feminine and masculine. *Journal of Sport Behavior, 24*, 377–393.

Kornreich, J. L., Hearn, K. D., Rodriguez, G., & O'Sullivan, L. F. (2003). Sibling influence, gender roles, and the sexual socialization of urban early adolescent girls. *Journal of Sex Research, 40*, 101–110.

Kortenhaus, C. M. & Demarest, J. (1993). Gender role stereotyping in children's literature: An update. *Sex Roles, 28*, 219–232.

Kosfeld, M., Heinrichs, M., Zak, P. J., Fischbacher, U., & Fehr, E. (2005). Oxytocin increases trust in humans. *Nature, 435*, 673–676.

Kotler, J. A., Wright, J. C., & Huston, A. C. (2001). Television use in families with children. In J. Bryant & J. A. Bryant (Eds.), *Television and the American family* (2nd ed., pp. 33–48). Mahwah, NJ: Lawrence Erlbaum Associates.

Kovalev, V. A., Kruggel, F., & von Cramon, D. Y. (2003). Gender and age effects in structural brain asymmetry as measured by MRI texture analysis. *NeuroImage, 19*, 895–905.

Kowalski, K. & Kanitkar, K. (2002, April). *Kindergartner's naturally occurring discourse concerning ethnicity and gender.* Paper presented at the Southwest Society for Research in Human Development, Austin, TX.

Kramer, J. H., Delis, D. C., Kaplan, E., O'Donnell, L., & Prifitera, A. (1997). Developmental sex differences in verbal learning. *Neuropsychology, 11*, 577–584.

Kuebli, J., Butler, S., & Fivush, R. (1995). Mother-child talk about past emotions: Relations of maternal language and child gender over time. *Cognition and Emotion, 9*, 265–283.

Kuebli, J. & Fivush, R. (1992). Gender differences in parent-child conversations about past emotions. *Sex Roles, 27*, 683–698.

Kuhn, D., Nash, S. C., & Brucken, L. (1978). Sex role concepts of two- and three-yr-olds. *Child Development, 49*, 445–451.

Kuiper, N. A. & Rogers, T. B. (1979). Encoding of personal information: Self-other differences. *Journal of Personality and Social Psychology, 37*, 499–514.

Kulik, L. (2002). The impact of social background on gender-role ideology: Parent's versus children's attitudes. *Journal of Family Issues, 23*, 53–73.

Kunkel, D. (1998). Policy battles over defining children's educational television. *The Annals of the American Academy of Political and Social Science, 557*, 39–53.

Kunkel, D. & Gantz, W. (1993). Assessing compliance with industry self-regulation of television advertising to children. *Journal of Applied Communication Research, 21*, 148–162.

Kunkel, D. & Roberts, D. (1991). Young minds and marketplace values: Issues in children's television advertising. *Journal of Social Issues, 47*, 57–72.

Kuznar, L. A. (1997). *Reclaiming a scientific anthropology*. Walnut Creek, CA: Altamira Press.

Kyratzis, A. (2001a). Children's gender indexing in language: From the separate worlds hypothesis to considerations of culture, context, and power. *Research on Language and Social Interaction, 34*, 1–13.

Kyratzis, A. (2001b). Emotion talk in preschool same-sex friendship groups: Fluidity over time and context. *Early Education and Development, 12*, 359–392.

Kyratzis, A. & Guo, J. (2001). Preschool girls' and boys' verbal conflict strategies in the United States and China. *Research on Language and Social Interaction, 34*, 45–74.

LaFontana, K. M. & Cillessen, A. H. N. (2002). Children's perceptions of popular and unpopular peers: A multimethod assessment. *Developmental Psychology, 38*, 635–647.

LaFrance, M., Hecht, M. A., & Paluck, E. L. (2003). The contingent smile: A meta-analysis of sex differences in smiling. *Psychological Bulletin, 129*, 305–334.

LaFreniere, P., Strayer, F. F., & Gauthier, R. (1984). The emergence of same-sex affiliative preferences among preschool peers: A developmental/ethological perspective. *Child Development, 55*, 1958–1965.

Lahey, B. B., McBurnett, K., & Loeber, R. (2000). Are attention-deficit/hyperactivity disorder and oppositional defiant disorder developmental precursors to conduct disorder? In A. J. Sameroff & M. Lewis (Eds.), *Handbook of developmental psychopathology* (2nd ed., pp. 431–446). New York: Kluwer Academic/Plenum.

Lahn, B. T. & Page, D. C. (1997). Functional coherence of the human Y chromosome. *Science, 278*, 675–680.

Laidler, K. J. & Hunt, G. (2001). Accomplishing femininity among the girls in the gang. *British Journal of Criminology, 41*, 658–678.

Lamb, M. E. (1978). Interactions between eighteen-month-olds and their preschool-aged siblings. *Child Development, 49*, 51–59.

Lamb, M. E., Frodi, A. M., Frodj, M., & Hwang, C. P. (1982). Characteristics of maternal and paternal behavior in traditional and nontraditional Swedish families. *International Journal of Behavioral Development, 5*, 131–141.

Landis, T. Y. (1982). Interaction between text and prior knowledge in children's memory for prose. *Child Development, 53*, 811–814.

Langerman, D. (1990). Books and boys: Gender preferences and book selection. *School Library Journal, 36*, 132–136.

Langlois, J. H. & Downs, A. C. (1980). Mothers, fathers, and peers as socialization agents of sex-typed play behaviors in young children. *Child Development, 51*, 1237–1247.

Lantz, C. D. & Schroeder, P. J. (1999). Endorsement of masculine and feminine gender roles: Differences between participation in and identification with the athletic role. *Journal of Sport Behavior, 22*, 545–557.

Largo, R. H., Caflisch, J. A., Hug, F., Muggli, K., Molnar, A. A., & Molinari, L. (2001). Neuromotor development from 5 to 18 years. Part 2: Associated movements. *Developmental Medicine and Child Neurology, 43*, 444–453.

Largo, R. H., Caflisch, J. A., Hug, F., Muggli, K., Molnar, A. A., Molinari, L., et al. (2001). Neuromotor development from 5 to 18 years. Part 1: Timed performance. *Developmental Medicine and Child Neurology, 43*, 436–443.

Larkin, J. (1994). Walking through walls: The sexual harassment of high school girls. *Gender and Education, 6*, 263–280.

Larson, M. S. (2003). Gender, race, and aggression in television commercials that feature children. *Sex Roles, 48*, 67–75.

Larson, R. & Pleck, J. (1999). Hidden feelings: Emotionality in boys and men. In D. Bernstein (Ed.), *Gender and motivation. Nebraska symposium on motivation, Vol. 45* (pp. 25–74). Lincoln, NE: University of Nebraska Press.

Lauzen, M. M. & Dozier, D. M. (2002). You look mahvelous: An examination of gender and appearance comments in the 1999–2000 prime-time season. *Sex Roles, 46*, 429–437.

Lawton, C. A. (1994). Gender differences in way-finding strategies: Relationship to spatial ability and spatial anxiety. *Sex Roles, 30*, 765–779.

Lawton, C. A. (1996). Strategies for indoor wayfinding: The role of orientation. *Journal of Environmental Psychology, 16*, 137–145.

Lawton, C. A., Charleston, S. I., & Zieles, A. S. (1996). Individual- and gender-related differences in indoor wayfinding. *Environment and Behavior, 28*, 204–219.

Layman, C. (2007). Hypogonadotropic hypogonadism. *Endocrinology and Metabolism Clinics of North America, 36*, 283–296.

Leahey, T. H. (1994). *A history of modern psychology* (2nd ed.). Upper Saddle River, NJ: Prentice-Hall.

Leaper, C. (1991). Influence and involvement in children's discourse: Age, gender, and partner effects. *Child Development, 62*, 797–811.

Leaper, C. (1994a). Exploring the consequences of gender segregation on social relationships. In C. Leaper (Ed.), *Childhood gender segregation: Causes and consequences.* New directions for child development, No. 65 (pp. 67–86). San Francisco: Jossey Bass.

Leaper, C. (2000a). Gender, affiliation, assertion, and the interactive context of parent-child play. *Developmental Psychology, 36*, 381–393.

Leaper, C. (2000b). The social construction and socialization of gender during development. In P. H. Miller, & E. Kofsky Scholnick (Eds.), *Toward a feminist developmental psychology* (pp. 127–152). New York: Taylor & Francis/Routledge.

Leaper, C. (2002). Parenting girls and boys. In M. H. Bornstein (Ed.), *Handbook of parenting* (2nd ed., pp. 189–225). Mahwah, NJ: Lawrence Erlbaum, Associates.

Leaper, C. (Ed.). (1994b). *Childhood gender segregation: Causes and consequences.* San Francisco, CA: Jossey-Bass.

Leaper, C., Anderson, K. J., & Sanders, P. (1998). Moderators of gender effects on parents' talk to their children: A meta-analysis. *Developmental Psychology, 34*, 3–27.

Leaper, C., Breed, L., Hoffman, L., & Perlman, C. A. (2002). Variations in the gender-stereotyped content of children's television cartoons across genres. *Journal of Applied Social Psychology, 32*, 1653–1662.

Leaper, C., Carson, M., Baker, C., Holliday, H., & Myers, S. (1995). Self-disclosure and listener verbal support in same-gender and cross-gender friends' conversations. *Sex Roles, 33*, 387–404.

Leaper, C. & Gleason, J. B. (1996). The relationship of play activity and gender to parent and child sex-typed communication. *International Journal of Behavioral Development, 19*, 689–703.

Leaper, C. & Smith, T. E. (2004). A meta-analytic review of gender variations in children's language use: Talkativeness, affiliative speech, and assertive speech. *Developmental Psychology, 40*, 993–1027.

Leaper, C., Tenenbaum, H. R., & Shaffer, T. G. (1999). Communication patterns of African American girls and boys from low-income, urban background. *Child Development, 70*, 1489–1503.

Lease, A. M., Kennedy, C. A., & Axelrod, J. L. (2002). Children's social constructions of popularity. *Social Development, 11*, 87–109.

Lee, P. A. & Kerrigan, J. R. (2004). Precocious puberty. In O. H. Pescovitz & E. A. Eugster (Eds.), *Pediatric endocrinology: Mechanisms, manifestations, and management.* (pp. 316–333). Philadelphia: Lippincott Williams & Wilkins.

Lee, V. E. & Marks, H. M. (1990). Sustained effects of the single-sex secondary school experience on attitudes, behaviors, and values in college. *Journal of Educational Psychology, 82*, 578–592.

Lee, V. E. & Marks, H. M. (1992). Who goes where? Choice of single-sex and coeducational independent secondary schools. *Sociology of Education, 65*, 226–253.

Lee, Y.-C. & Jessee, P. O. (1997). Taiwanese infants' and toddlers' interactions with a baby in a group setting. *Early Child Development and Care, 134*, 75–87.

Lehr, S. (2001). The hidden curriculum: Are we teaching young girls to wait for the prince. In S. Lehr (Ed.), *Beauty, brains, and brawn: The construction of gender in children's literature* (pp. 1–20). Portsmouth, NH: Heinemann.

Leichty, M. M. (1960). The effect of father-absence during early childhood upon the Oedipal situation as reflected in young adults. *Merrill-Palmer Quarterly, 6*, 212–217.

Leinbach, M. D. & Fagot, B. I. (1986). Acquisition of gender labels: A test for toddlers. *Sex Roles, 15*, 655–666.

Leinbach, M. D. & Fagot, B. I. (1993). Categorical habituation to male and female faces: Gender schematic processing in infancy. *Infant Behavior and Development, 16*, 317–332.

Leinbach, M. D., Hort, B. E., & Fagot, B. I. (1997). Bears are for boys: Metaphorical associations in young children's gender stereotypes. *Cognitive Development, 12*, 107–130.

Lemish, D. (1998). "Girls can wrestle too": Gender differences in the consumption of a television wrestling series. *Sex Roles, 38*, 833–849.

Lennon, R. & Eisenberg, N. (1987). Gender and age differences in empathy and sympathy. In N. Eisenberg & J. Strayer (Eds.), *Empathy and its development. Cambridge studies in social and emotional development* (pp. 195–217). New York: Cambridge University Press.

Lenroot, R. K. & Giedd, J. N. (2006). Brain development in children and adolescents: Insights from anatomical magnetic resonance imaging. *Neuroscience and Biobehavioral Reviews, 30,* 718–729.

Lenroot, R. K., Gogtay, N., Greenstein, D. K., Wells, E. M., Wallace, G. L., Clasen, L. S., et al. (2007). Sexual dimorphism of brain developmental trajectories during childhood and adolescence. *NeuroImage, 15,* 1065–1073.

Leonard, D. K. & Jiang, J. (1999). Gender bias and the college predictions of the SATs: A cry of despair. *Research in Higher Education, 40,* 375–407.

Lepowsky, M. (1994). Women, men, and aggression in an egalitarian society. *Sex Roles, 30,* 199–211.

LeVay, S. (1993). *The sexual brain.* Cambridge, MA: MIT Press.

Leve, L. D. & Fagot, B. I. (1997). Gender-role socialization and discipline processes in one- and two-parent families. *Sex Roles, 36,* 1–21.

Leventhal, T. & Brooks-Gunn, J. (2004). A randomized study of neighborhood effects on low-income children's educational outcomes. *Developmental Psychology, 40,* 488–507.

Lever, J. (1976). Sex differences in the games children play. *Social Problems, 23,* 478–487.

Leveroni, C. L. & Berenbaum, S. A. (1998). Early androgen effects on interest in infants: Evidence from children with congenital adrenal hyperplasia. *Developmental Neuropsychology, 14,* 321–340.

Levin, H. & Sears, R. R. (1956). Identification with parents as a determinant of doll play aggression. *Child Development, 27,* 135–153.

Levine, M. P. & Smolak, L. (1998). The mass media and disordered eating: Implications for primary prevention. In W. Vandereycken & G. Noordenbos (Eds.), *The prevention of eating disorders* (pp. 23–56). New York: New York University Press.

LeVine, R. A., LeVine, S. E., & Schnell, B. (2001). "Improve the women": Mass schooling, female literacy, and worldwide social change. *Harvard Educational Review, 71,* 1–50.

Levine, S. C., Huttenlocher, J., Taylor, A., & Langrock, A. (1999). Early sex differences in spatial skill. *Developmental Psychology, 35,* 940–949.

Levine, S. C., Vasilyeva, M., Lourenco, S. F., Newcombe, N. S., & Huttenlocher, J. (2005). Socioeconomic status modifies the sex difference in spatial skill. *Psychological Science, 16,* 841–845.

Levy, G. D. (1989). Developmental and individual differences in preschoolers' recognition memories: The influences of gender schematization and verbal labeling of information. *Sex Roles, 21,* 305–324.

Levy, G. D. & Carter, D. B. (1989). Gender schema, gender constancy, and gender-role knowledge: The roles of cognitive factors in preschoolers' gender-role stereotype attributions. *Developmental Psychology, 25,* 444–449.

Levy, G. D., Sadovsky, A. L., & Troseth, G. L. (2000). Aspects of young children's perceptions of gender-typed occupations. *Sex Roles, 42,* 993–1006.

Levy, G. D., Taylor, M. G., & Gelman, S. A. (1995). Traditional and evaluative aspects of flexibility in gender roles, social conventions, moral rules, and physical laws. *Child Development, 66,* 515–531.

Levy, J. (1974). Psychobiological implications of bilateral asymmetry. In S. J. Dimond & J. G. Beaumont (Eds.), *Hemisphere function in the human brain* (pp. 121–183). New York: Wiley.

Levy, S. R. & Killen, M. (Eds.). (2008). *Intergroup attitudes and relations in childhood through adulthood.* Oxford, UK: Oxford University Press.

Lewin, M. (1984). "Rather worse than folly?" Psychology measures femininity and masculinity. In M. Lewin (Ed.), *In the shadow of the past: Psychology portrays the sexes* (pp. 155–178). New York: Columbia University Press.

Lewis, C. & Lamb, M. E. (2003). Fathers' influences on children's development: The evidence from two-parent families. *European Journal of Psychology of Education, 18,* 211–228.

Lewis, M., Stanger, C., & Sullivan, M. W. (1989). Deception in 3-year-olds. *Developmental Psychology, 25,* 439–443.

Liben, L. S. (1975). Long-term memory for pictures related to seriation, horizontality, and verticality concepts. *Developmental Psychology, 11,* 795–806.

Liben, L. S. (1977). Memory in the context of cognitive development: The Piagetian approach. In R. V. Kail & J. W. Hagen (Eds.), *Perspectives on the development of memory and cognition* (pp. 297–331). Hillsdale, NJ: Lawrence Erlbaum Associates.

Liben, L. S. (1978). Performance on Piagetian spatial tasks as a function of sex, field dependence, and training. *Merrill-Palmer Quarterly, 24,* 97–110.

Liben, L. S. & Bigler, R. S. (1987). Reformulating children's gender schemata. In L. S. Liben & M. L. Signorella (Eds.), *New directions for child development: Children's gender schemata* (pp. 89–105). San Francisco: Jossey-Bass.

Liben, L. S. & Bigler, R. S. (2002). The developmental course of gender differentiation: Conceptualizing, measuring, and evaluating constructs and pathways. *Monographs of the Society for Research in Child Development, 67*(2, Serial No. 269).

Liben, L. S., Bigler, R. S., & Krogh, H. R. (2001). Pink and blue collar jobs: Children's judgments of job status and job aspirations in relation to sex of worker. *Journal of Experimental Child Psychology, 79,* 346–363.

Liben, L. S., Bigler, R. S., & Krogh, H. R. (2002). Language at work: Children's gendered interpretations of occupational titles. *Child Development, 73,* 810–828.

Liben, L. S., Bigler, R. S., Shechner, T., & Arthur, A. E. (2006, April). *Preschoolers' sex typing of self and others: Toward coordinated lifespan measures.* Poster presented at the Gender Development Research Conference, San Francisco.

Liben, L. S. & Golbeck, S. L. (1980). Sex differences in performance on Piagetian spatial tasks: Differences in competence or performance? *Child Development, 51,* 594–597.

Liben, L. S. & Golbeck, S. L. (1984). Performance on Piagetian horizontality and verticality tasks: Sex-related differences in knowledge of relevant physical phenomena. *Developmental Psychology, 20,* 595–606.

Liben, L. S., Myers, L. J., & Kastens, K. A. (in press). Locating oneself on a map in relation to person qualities and map characteristics. In C. Freska, N. Newcombe, & P. Gardenfors (Eds.), *Spatial cognition VI.* Heidelberg: Springer-Verlag.

Liben, L. S. & Signorella, M. L. (1980). Gender-related schemata and constructive memory in children. *Child Development, 51,* 11–18.

Liben, L. S., Susman, E. J., Finkelstein, J. W., Chinchilli, V. M., Kunselman, S., Schwab, J., et al. (2002). The effects of sex steroids on spatial performance: A review and an experimental clinical investigation. *Developmental Psychology, 38,* 236–253.

Lieberman, M., Doyle, A.-B., & Markiewicz, D. (1999). Developmental patterns in security of attachment to mother and father in late childhood and early adolescence: Associations with peer relations. *Child Development, 70,* 202–213.

Lieberson, S. & Bell, E. O. (1992). Children's first names: An empirical study of social taste. *American Journal of Sociology, 98,* 511–554.

Lightfoot-Klein, H., Chase, C., Hammond, T., & Goldman, R. (2000). Genital surgery on children below the age of consent. In L. T. Szuchman & F. Muscarella (Eds.), *Psychological perspectives on human sexuality.* (pp. 440–479). Hoboken, NJ: John Wiley & Sons.

Lincoln, E. A. (1927). *Sex differences in the growth of American children.* Baltimore, MD: Warwick and York.

Lincoln, E. A. (1931). The reliability of the Lincoln Hollow Square Form Board and a comparison of Hollow Square scores with Stanford Binet mental ages. *Journal of Applied Psychology, 15,* 79–81.

Lincoln, E. A. (1934). The insignificance of significant differences. *Journal of Experimental Education, 2,* 288–290.

Lincoln, E. A. (1936). Stanford-Binet IQ changes in the Harvard growth study. *Journal of Applied Psychology, 20,* 236–242.

Lincoln, E. A. & Workman, L. L. (1935). *Testing and the uses of test results.* New York: Macmillan.

Lindahl, L. B. & Heimann, M. (1997). Social proximity in early mother-infant interactions: Implications for gender differences? *Early Development and Parenting, 6,* 83–88.

Lindahl, L. B. & Heimann, M. (2002). Social proximity in Swedish mother-daughter and mother-son interactions in infancy. *Journal of Reproductive and Infant Psychology, 20,* 37–42.

Lindroos, M. (1995). The production of "girl" in an educational setting. *Gender and Education, 7,* 143–155.

Lindsey, E. W. & Mize, J. (2000). Parent-child physical and pretense play: Links to children's social competence. *Merrill-Palmer Quarterly, 46,* 565–591.

Lindsey, E. W. & Mize, J. (2001). Contextual differences in parent-child play: Implications for children's gender role development. *Sex Roles, 44,* 155–176.

Linn, M. C. & Petersen, A. C. (1985). Emergence and characterization of sex differences in spatial ability: A meta-analysis. *Child Development, 56,* 1479–1498.

Linn, M. C. & Petersen, A. C. (1986). A meta-analysis of gender differences in spatial ability: Implications for mathematics and science achievement. In J. S. Hyde & M. C. Linn (Eds.), *The psychology of gender: Advances through meta-analysis* (pp. 67–101). Baltimore, MD: Johns Hopkins University Press.

Lippa, R. (2002). Gender-related traits of heterosexual and homosexual men and women. *Archives of Sexual Behavior, 31,* 83–98.

Lippa, R. A. (2002). *Gender, nature, and nurture.* Mahwah, NJ: Lawrence Erlbaum Associates.

Lippman, W. (1922). *Public opinion.* New York: Harcourt.

Lirgg, C. D. (1991). Gender differences in self-confidence in physical activity: A meta-analysis of recent studies. *Journal of Sport and Exercise Psychology, 13,* 294–310.

Liss, M., O'Connor, C., Morosky, E., & Crawford, M. (2001). What makes a feminist? Predictors and correlates of feminist social identity in college women. *Psychology of Women Quarterly, 25,* 124–133.

Litvack-Miller, W., McDougall, D., & Romney, D. M. (1997). The structure of empathy during middle childhood and its relationship to prosocial behavior. *Genetic, Social, and General Psychology Monographs, 123*, 303–324.

Lobel, A. (1979). *Frog and Toad are friends*. New York: HarperCollins.

Lobel, T. E. & Menashri, J. (1993). Relations of conceptions of gender-role transgressions and gender constancy to gender-typed toy preferences. *Developmental Psychology, 29*, 150–155.

Lockheed, M. E. (1986). Reshaping the social order: The case of gender segregation. *Sex Roles, 14*, 617–628.

Loehlin, J. C. & Martin, N. G. (2000). Dimensions of psychological masculinity-femininity in adult twins from opposite-sex and same-sex pairs. *Behavior Genetics, 30*, 19–28.

Loehlin, J. C. & McFadden, D. (2003). Otoacoustic emissions, auditory evoked potentials, and traits related to sex and sexual orientation. *Archives of Sexual Behavior, 32*, 115–127.

Logan, J. P. & Scollay, S. (1999). The gender equity role of educational administration: Where are we? Where do we want to go? *Journal of School Leadership, 9*, 97–124.

Lollis, S., Ross, H., & Leroux, L. (1996). An observational study of parents' socialization of moral orientation during sibling conflicts. *Merrill-Palmer Quarterly, 42*, 475–494.

Lombardo, W. K., Cretser, G. A., & Roesch, S. C. (2001). For crying out loud: The differences persist into the '90s. *Sex Roles, 45*, 529–547.

Loovis, E. M. & Butterfield, S. A. (1993). Influence of age, sex, balance, and sport participation on development of catching by children Grades K-8. *Perceptual and Motor Skills, 77*, 1267–1273.

Loovis, E. M. & Butterfield, S. A. (1995). Influence of age, sex, balance, and sport participation on development of sidearm striking by children Grades K-8. *Perceptual and Motor Skills, 81*, 595–600.

Loovis, E. M. & Butterfield, S. A. (2000). Influence of age, sex and balance on mature skipping by children in grades K-8. *Perceptual and Motor Skills, 90*, 974–978.

Lorber, J. (1991). Dismantling Noah's ark. In J. Lorber & S. A. Farrell (Eds.), *The social construction of gender* (pp. 355–369). Thousand Oaks, CA: Sage Publications.

Lorber, J. (1994). *Paradoxes of gender*. New Haven, CT: Yale University Press.

Luecke-Aleksa, D., Anderson, D. R., Collins, P. A., & Schmitt, K. L. (1995). Gender constancy and television viewing. *Developmental Psychology, 31*, 773–780.

Lundberg, S. & Rose, E. (2002). The effects of sons and daughters on men's labor supply and wages. *Review of Economics and Statistics, 84*, 251–268.

Lundberg, S. & Rose, E. (2003). Child gender and the transition to marriage. *Demography, 40*, 333–349.

Lundberg, S. & Rose, E. (2004). Investments in sons and daughters: Evidence from the consumer expenditure survey. In A. Kalil & T. DeLeire (Eds.), *Family investments in children's potential: Resources and parenting behaviors that promote success*. (pp. 163–180). Mahwah, NJ: Lawrence Erlbaum Associates.

Lundberg, U. (1983). Sex differences in behaviour pattern and catecholamine and cortisol excretion in 3–6 year old day-care children. *Biological Psychology, 16*, 109–117.

Luria, Z. (1986). A methodological critique. *Signs, 11*, 316–321.

Lutz, S. E. & Ruble, D. N. (1994). Children and gender prejudice: Context, motivation, and the development of gender conceptions. In R. Vasta (Ed.), *Annals of child development: A research annual* (Vol. 10, pp. 131–166). Bristol, PA: Jessica Kingsley.

Lynch, J. (2002). Parents' self-efficacy beliefs, parents' gender, children's reader self-perceptions, reading achievement and gender. *Journal of Research in Reading, 25*, 54–67.

Lynn, D. B. (1962). Sex-role and parental identification. *Child Development, 33*, 555–564.

Lytton, H. & Romney, D. M. (1991). Parents' differential socialization of boys and girls: A meta-analysis. *Psychological Bulletin, 109*, 267–296.

Ma, X. (1999). A meta-analysis of the relationship between anxiety toward mathematics and achievement in mathematics. *Journal for Research in Mathematics Education, 30*, 520–540.

Ma, X. & Kishor, N. (1997a). Assessing the relationship between attitude toward mathematics and achievement in mathematics: A meta-analysis. *Journal for Research in Mathematics Education, 28*, 26–47.

Ma, X. & Kishor, N. (1997b). Attitude toward self, social factors, and achievement in mathematics: A meta-analytic review. *Educational Psychology Review, 9*, 89–120.

Maccoby, E. E. (1966a). *The development of sex differences*. Stanford, CA: Stanford University Press.

Maccoby, E. E. (1966b). Sex differences in intellectual functioning. In E. E. Maccoby (Ed.), *The development of sex differences* (pp. 25–55). Stanford, CA: Stanford University Press.

Maccoby, E. E. (1988). Gender as a social category. *Developmental Psychology, 24*, 755–765.

Maccoby, E. E. (1989). Eleanor E. Maccoby. In G. Lindzey (Ed.), *A history of psychology in autobiography*. Stanford, CA: Stanford University Press.

Maccoby, E. E. (1990). Gender and relationships: A developmental account. *American Psychologist, 45*, 513–520.

Maccoby, E. E. (1998). *The two sexes: Growing up apart, coming together.* Cambridge, MA: Belknap Press/Harvard University Press.

Maccoby, E. E. (2000). Perspectives on gender development. *International Journal of Behavioral Development, 24,* 398–406.

Maccoby, E. E. & Jacklin, C. N. (1974). *The psychology of sex differences.* Stanford, CA: Stanford University Press.

Maccoby, E. E. & Jacklin, C. N. (1987). Gender segregation in childhood. In H. W. Reese (Ed.), *Advances in child development and behavior* (Vol. 20, pp. 239–287). San Diego, CA: Academic Press.

Maccoby, E. E., Snow, M. E., & Jacklin, C. N. (1984). Children's dispositions and mother-child interaction at 12 and 18 months: A short-term longitudinal study. *Developmental Psychology, 20,* 459–472.

MacDonald, K. (1992). A time and a place for everything: A discrete systems perspective on the role of children's rough-and-tumble play in educational settings. *Early Education and Development, 3,* 334–355.

Madson, L. & Hessling, R. M. (1999). Does alternating between masculine and feminine pronouns eliminate perceived gender bias in text? *Sex Roles, 41,* 559–575.

Mageo, J. M., Fulton, R., & Anderson, S. W. (1992). Male transvestism and cultural change in Samoa: The Amerindian "Man-Woman": Gender, Liminality, and Cultural Continuity. *American Ethnologist, 19,* 443–459.

Maguire, E. A., Spiers, H. J., Good, C. D., Hartley, T., Frackowiak, R. S., & Burgess, N. (2003). Navigation expertise and the human hippocampus: a structural brain imaging analysis. *Hippocampus, 13,* 250–259.

Maher, J. K. & Childs, N. M. (2003). A longitudinal content analysis of gender roles in children's television advertisements: A 27 year review. *Journal of Current Issues and Research in Advertising, 25,* 71–81.

Majeres, R. L. (1997). Sex differences in phonetic processing: Speed of identification of alphabetical sequences. *Perceptual and Motor Skills, 85,* 1243–1251.

Majeres, R. L. (1999). Sex differences in phonological processes: Speeded matching and word reading. *Memory and Cognition, 27,* 246–253.

Major, B., Barr, L., Zubek, J., & Babey, S. H. (1999). Gender and self-esteem: A meta-analysis. In W. B. Swann, Jr. & J. H. Langlois (Eds.), *Sexism and stereotypes in modern society: The gender science of Janet Taylor Spence* (pp. 223–253). Washington, DC: American Psychological Association.

Maki, P. M. & Resnick, S. M. (2001). Effects of estrogen on patterns of brain activity at rest and during cognitive activity: Our view of neuroimaging studies. *NeuroImage, 14,* 789–801.

Malatesta, C. Z., Culver, C., Tesman, J. R., & Shepard, B. (1989). The development of emotion expression during the first two years of life. *Monographs of the Society for Research in Child Development, 54*(1–2, Serial No. 219).

Malatesta, C. Z. & Haviland, J. M. (1982). Learning display rules: The socialization of emotion expression in infancy. *Child Development, 53,* 991–1003.

Malina, R. M. (1986). Growth of muscle tissue and muscle mass. In F. Falkner & J. M. Tanner (Eds.), *Human growth: A comprehensive treatise. Vol. 2: Postnatal growth and neurobiology* (pp. 77–99). New York: Plenum Press.

Malinowski, J. C. (2001). Mental rotation and real-world wayfinding. *Perceptual and Motor Skills, 92,* 19–30.

Malinowski, J. C. & Gillespie, W. T. (2001). Individual differences in performance on a large-scale, real-world way-finding task. *Journal of Environmental Psychology, 21,* 73–82.

Mandara, J., Murray, C., & Joyner, T. (2005). The impact of fathers' absence on African American adolescents' gender role development. *Sex Roles, 53,* 207–220.

Mandler, J. M. & Bauer, P. J. (1988). The cradle of categorization: Is the basic level basic? *Cognitive Development, 3,* 247–264.

Manning, J. T., Stewart, A., Bundred, P. E., & Trivers, R. L. (2004). Sex and ethnic differences in 2nd to 4th digit ratio of children. *Early Human Development, 80,* 161–168.

Manstead, A. S. R. (1992). Gender differences in emotion. In A. Gale & M. W. Eysenck (Eds.), *Handbook of individual differences: Biological perspectives* (pp. 355–387). New York: Wiley.

Marcon, R. A. & Freeman, G. (1996). Linking gender-related toy preferences to social structure: Changes in children's letters to Santa since 1978. *Journal of Psychological Practice, 2,* 1–10.

Marcus, D. E. & Overton, W. F. (1978). The development of cognitive gender constancy and sex role preferences. *Child Development, 49,* 434–444.

Marecek, J., Kimmel, E. B., Crawford, M., & Hare-Mustin, R. T. (2003). Psychology of women and gender. In D. K. Freedheim (Ed.), *Handbook of psychology: History of psychology, Vol. 1* (pp. 249–268). New York: Wiley.

Markee, N. L., Pedersen, E. L., Murray, C. I., & Stacey, P. B. (1994). What role do fashion dolls play in socialization of children? *Perceptual and Motor Skills, 79,* 187–190.

Markovits, H., Benenson, J., & Dolenszky, E. (2001). Evidence that children and adolescents have internal models of peer interactions that are gender differentiated. *Child Development, 72,* 879–886.

Marleau, J. D. & Saucier, J. F. (2002). Preference for a first-born boy in Western societies. *Journal of Biosocial Science, 34,* 13–27.

Marshall, W. A. & Tanner, J. M. (1986). Puberty. In F. Falkner & J. M. Tanner (Eds.), *Human growth: A comprehensive treatise. Vol. 2: Postnatal growth and neurobiology* (pp. 171–209). New York: Plenum Press.

Martin, C. L. (1987). A ratio measure of sex stereotyping. *Journal of Personality and Social Psychology, 52*, 489–499.

Martin, C. L. (1989). Children's use of gender-related information in making social judgments. *Developmental Psychology, 25*, 80–88.

Martin, C. L. (2000). Cognitive theories of gender development. In T. Eckes & H. M. Trautner (Eds.), *The developmental social psychology of gender* (pp. 91–121). Mahwah, NJ: Lawrence Erlbaum Associates.

Martin, C. L., Eisenbud, L., & Rose, H. (1995). Children's gender-based reasoning about toys. *Child Development, 66*, 1453–1471.

Martin, C. L. & Fabes, R. A. (2001). The stability and consequences of young children's same-sex peer interactions. *Developmental Psychology, 37*, 431–446.

Martin, C. L., Fabes, R. A., Evans, S. M., & Wyman, H. (1999). Social cognition on the playground: Children's beliefs about playing with girls versus boys and their relations to sex segregated play. *Journal of Social and Personal Relationships, 16*, 751–771.

Martin, C. L. & Halverson, C. F. (1981). A schematic processing model of sex typing and stereotyping in children. *Child Development, 52*, 1119–1134.

Martin, C. L. & Halverson, C. F. (1983). The effects of sex-typing schemas on young children's memory. *Child Development, 54*, 563–574.

Martin, C. L. & Ruble, D. (2004). Children's search for gender cues: Cognitive perspectives on gender development. *Current Directions in Psychological Science, 13*, 67–70.

Martin, C. L., Ruble, D. N., & Szkrybalo, J. (2002). Cognitive theories of early gender development. *Psychological Bulletin, 128*, 903–933.

Martin, C. L., Wood, C. H., & Little, J. K. (1990). The development of gender stereotype components. *Child Development, 61*, 1891–1904.

Martin, J. A., King, D. R., Maccoby, E. E., & Jacklin, C. N. (1984). Secular trends and individual differences in toilet-training progress. *Journal of Pediatric Psychology, 9*, 457–467.

Martin, J. A., Maccoby, E. E., & Jacklin, C. N. (1981). Mothers' responsiveness to interactive bidding and nonbidding in boys and girls. *Child Development, 52*, 1064–1067.

Martin, J. L. & Ross, H. S. (2005). Sibling aggression: Sex differences and parents' reactions. *International Journal of Behavioral Development, 29*, 129–138.

Matthews, B. (2004). Promoting emotional literacy, equity and interest in science lessons for 11–14 year olds: The 'Improving Science and Emotional Development' project. *International Journal of Science Education, 26*, 281–308.

Maughan, B., Rowe, R., Messer, J., Goodman, R., & Meltzer, H. (2004). Conduct Disorder and Oppositional Defiant Disorder in a national sample: Developmental epidemiology. *Journal of Child Psychology and Psychiatry, 4*, 609–621.

Maxson, C. L. & Klein, M. W. (1995). Investigating gang structures. *Journal of Gang Research, 3*, 33–40.

Maxson, C. L. & Whitlock, M. L. (2002). Joining the gang: Gender differences in risk factors for gang membership. In C. R. Huff (Ed.), *Gangs in America* (3rd ed., pp. 19–35). Thousand Oaks, CA: Sage.

Mayhew, D. R., Ferguson, S. A., Desmond, K. J., & Simpson, H. M. (2001). *Trends in fatal crashes involving female drivers, 1975–1998*. Arlington, VA: Insurance Institute for Highway Safety.

Mazur, A. & Booth, A. (1998). Testosterone and dominance in men. *Behavioral and Brain Sciences, 21*, 353–397.

Mazur, T. (2005). Gender dysphoria and gender change in androgen insensitivity or micropenis. *Archives of Sexual Behavior, 34*, 411–421.

McAndrew, F. T., King, J. C., & Honoroff, L. R. (2002). A sociobiological analysis of namesaking patterns in 322 American families. *Journal of Applied Social Psychology, 32*, 851–864.

McBride, B. A. & Darragh, J. (1995). Interpreting the data on father involvement: Implications for parenting programs for men. *Families in Society, 76*, 490–497.

McBride-Chang, C. & Jacklin, C. N. (1993). Early play arousal, sex-typed play, and activity level as precursors to later rough-and-tumble play. *Early Education and Development, 4*, 99–108.

McCarthy, D. (1954). Language development in children. In L. Carmichael (Ed.), *Manual of Child Psychology* (2nd ed., pp. 492–630). New York: Wiley.

McCaul, K. D., Gladue, B. A., & Joppa, M. (1992). Winning, losing, mood, and testosterone. *Hormones and Behavior, 26*, 486–504.

McCauley, E., Kay, T., Ito, J., & Treder, R. (1987). The Turner Syndrome: Cognitive deficits, affective discrimination and behavior problems. *Child Development, 58*, 464–473.

McClintock, M. K. & Herdt, G. (1996). Rethinking puberty: The development of sexual attraction. *Current Directions in Psychological Science, 5*, 178–183.

McClure, E. B. (2000). A meta-analytic review of sex differences in facial expression processing and their development in infants, children, and adolescents. *Psychological Bulletin, 126*, 424–453.

McConaghy, M. J. (1979). Gender permanence and the genital basis of gender: Stages in the development of constancy of gender identity. *Child Development, 50*, 1223–1226.

McCord, J., McCord, W., & Thurber, E. (1962). Some effects of paternal absence on male children. *Journal of Abnormal and Social Psychology, 64*, 361–369.

McCrae, R. R. & Costa, P. T., Jr. (1997). Personality trait structure as a human universal. *American Psychologist, 52*, 509–516.

McCrae, R. R. & Costa, P. T., Jr. (1999). A Five-Factor theory of personality. In L. A. Pervin & O. P. John (Eds.), *Handbook of personality: Theory and research* (2nd ed., pp. 139–153). New York: The Guilford Press.

McDaniel, M. A. (2005). Big-brained people are smarter: A meta-analysis of the relationship between in vivo brain volume and intelligence. *Intelligence, 33*, 337–346.

McDonald, D. L. & McKinney, J. P. (1994). Steady dating and self-esteem in high school students. *Journal of Adolescence, 17*, 557–564.

McDougall, J., DeWit, D. J., & Ebanks, G. E. (1999). Parental preferences for sex of children in Canada. *Sex Roles, 41*, 615–626.

McFadden, D. (1998). Sex differences in the auditory system. *Developmental Neuropsychology, 14*, 261–298.

McFadden, D. & Mishra, R. (1993). On the relation between hearing sensitivity and otoacoustic emissions. *Hearing Research, 71*, 208–213.

McFadden, D. & Pasanen, E. G. (1998). Comparison of the auditory systems of heterosexuals and homosexuals: Click-evoked otoacoustic emissions. *Proceedings of the National Academy of Sciences, 95*, 2709–2713.

McFadyen-Ketchum, S. A., Bates, J. E., Dodge, K. A., & Pettit, G. S. (1996). Patterns of change in early childhood aggressive-disruptive behavior: Gender differences in predictions from early coercive and affectionate mother-child interactions. *Child Development, 67*, 2417–2433.

McGivern, R. F., Huston, J. P., Byrd, D., King, T., Siegle, G. J., & Reilly, J. (1997). Sex differences in visual recognition memory: Support for a sex-related difference in attention in adults and children. *Brain and Cognition, 34*, 323–336.

McGlone, J. (1980). Sex differences in human brain asymmetry: A critical survey. *Behavioral and Brain Sciences, 3*, 215–263.

McGraw, K. O. & Wong, S. P. (1992). A common language effect size statistic. *Psychological Bulletin, 111*, 361–365.

McGuffey, C. S. & Rich, B. L. (1999). Playing in the gender transgression zone: Race, class, and hegemonic masculinity in middle childhood. *Gender and Society, 13*, 608–627.

McGuinness, D. & Morley, C. (1991). Sex differences in the development of visuo-spatial ability in pre-school children. *Journal of Mental Imagery, 15*, 143–150.

McHale, S. M., Crouter, A. C., & Tucker, C. J. (1999). Family context and gender role socialization in middle childhood: Comparing girls to boys and sisters to brothers. *Child Development, 70*, 990–1004.

McHale, S. M., Crouter, A. C., & Whiteman, S. D. (2003). The family contexts of gender development in childhood and adolescence. *Social Development, 12*, 125–148.

McHale, S. M., Kim, J. -Y., Whiteman, S., & Crouter, A. C. (2004). Links between sex-typed time use in middle childhood and gender development in early adolescence. *Developmental Psychology, 40*, 868–881.

McHale, S. M., Shanahan, L., Updegraff, K. A., Crouter, A. C., & Booth, A. (2004). Developmental and individual differences in girls' sex-typed activities in middle childhood and adolescence. *Child Development, 75*, 1575–1593.

McHale, S. M., Updegraff, K. A., Helms-Erikson, H., & Crouter, A. C. (2001). Sibling influences on gender development in middle childhood and early adolescence: A longitudinal study. *Developmental Psychology, 37*, 115–125.

McIntyre, M. H., Cohn, B. A., & Ellison, P. T. (2006). Sex dimorphism in digital formulae of children. *American Journal of Physical Anthropology, 129*, 143–150.

McKown, C. & Weinstein, R. S. (2002). Modeling the role of child ethnicity and gender in children's differential response to teacher expectations. *Journal of Applied Social Psychology, 32*, 159–184.

McNair, S., Kirova-Petrova, A., & Bhargava, A. (2001). Computers and young children in the classroom: Strategies for minimizing gender bias. *Early Childhood Education Journal, 29*, 51–55.

McPhaul, M. J. (2002). Molecular defects of the androgen receptor. *Recent Progress in Hormone Research, 57*, 181–194.

Meehan, A. M. & Janik, L. M. (1990). Illusory correlation and the maintenance of sex role stereotypes in children. *Sex Roles, 22*, 83–95.

Mehl, M. R., Vazire, S., Ramirez-Esparza, N., Slatcher, R. B., & Pennebaker, J. W. (2007). Are women really more talkative than men? *Science, 317*, 82.

Melson, G. F. & Fogel, A. (1982). Young children's interest in unfamiliar infants. *Child Development, 53*, 693–700.

Melson, G. F. & Fogel, A. (1989). Children's ideas about animal young and their care: A reassessment of gender differences in the development of nurturance. *Anthrozoos, 2*, 265–273.

Melson, G. F. & Fogel, A. (1996). Parental perceptions of their children's involvement with household pets: A test of a specificity model of nurturance. *Anthrozoos, 9*, 95–106.

Melson, G. F., Fogel, A., & Toda, S. (1986). Children's ideas about infants and their care. *Child Development, 57*, 1519–1527.

Mendez, L. M. R. & Knoff, H. M. (2003). Who gets suspended from school and why: A demographic analysis of schools and disciplinary infractions in a large school district. *Education and Treatment of Children, 26*, 30–51.

Mendle, J., Turkheimer, E., & Emery, R. E. (2007). Detrimental psychological outcomes associated with early pubertal timing in adolescent girls. *Developmental Review, 27*, 151–171.

Merke, D. P., Fields, J. D., Keil, M. F., Vaituzis, A. C., Chrousos, G. P., & Giedd, J. N. (2003). Children with classic congenital adrenal hyperplasia have decreased amygdala volume: Potential prenatal and postnatal hormonal effects. *Journal of Clinical Endocrinology and Metabolism, 88*, 1760–1765.

Merskin, D. (2002). Boys will be boys: A content analysis of gender and race in children's advertisements on the Turner Cartoon Network. *Journal of Current Issues and Research in Advertising, 24*, 51–58.

Messner, M. A. (1990). Boyhood, organized sports, and the construction of masculinities. *Journal of Contemporary Ethnography, 18*, 416–444.

Messner, M. A. (2000). Barbie girls versus sea monsters: Children constructing gender. *Gender and Society, 14*, 765–784.

Meyenn, B. & Parker, J. (2001). Naughty boys at school: Perspectives on boys and discipline. In W. Martino & B. Meyenn (Eds.), *What about the boys?: Issues of masculinity in schools* (pp. 169–185). Buckingham, England: Open University Press.

Meyer-Bahlburg, H. F. L. (1998). Gender assignment in intersexuality. *Journal of Psychology and Human Sexuality, 10*, 1–21.

Meyer-Bahlburg, H. F. L. (2005a). Gender identity outcome in female-raised 46,XY persons with penile agenesis, cloacal exstrophy of the bladder, or penile ablation. *Archives of Sexual Behavior, 34*, 423–438.

Meyer-Bahlburg, H. F. L. (2005b). Introduction: Gender dysphoria and gender change in persons with intersexuality. *Archives of Sexual Behavior, 34*, 371–373.

Meyer-Bahlburg, H. F. L., Dolezal, C., Baker, S., Carlson, A. D., Obeid, J. S., & New, M. I. (2004). Prenatal androgenization affects gender-related behavior but not gender identity in 5–12-year-old girls with congenital adrenal hyperplasia. *Archives of Sexual Behavior, 33*, 94–104.

Meyer-Bahlburg, H. F. L., Dolezal, C., Baker, S. W., Ehrhardt, A. A., & New, M. I. (2006). Gender development in women with congenital adrenal hyperplasia as a function of disorder severity. *Archives of Sexual Behavior, 35*, 667–684.

Meyer-Bahlburg, H. F. L., Gruen, R. S., New, M. I., Bell, J. J., Morishima, A., Shimshi, M., et al. (1996). Gender change from female to male in classical congenital adrenal hyperplasia. *Hormones and Behavior, 30*, 319–332.

Migeon, C. J., Berkovitz, G., & Brown, T. (1994). Sexual differentiation and ambiguity. In M. S. Kappy, R. M. Blizzard & C. J. Migeon (Eds.), *Diagnosis and Treatment of Endocrine Disorders in Childhood and Adolescence*. Springfield, IL: Charles C. Thomas.

Migeon, C. J., Wisniewski, A. B., & Gearhart, J. P. (2001). Syndromes of abnormal sex differentiation: A guide for patients and their families. Baltimore: Johns Hopkins Hospital. http://www.hopkinschildrens.org/intersex.

Miles, T. R., Haslum, M. N., & Wheeler, T. J. (1998). Gender ratio in dyslexia. *Annals of Dyslexia, 48*, 27–55.

Miller, C. L. (1983). Developmental changes in male/female voice classification by infants. *Infant Behavior and Development, 6*, 313–330.

Miller, C. L. (1987). Qualitative differences among gender-stereotyped toys: Implications for cognitive and social development in girls and boys. *Sex Roles, 16*, 473–487.

Miller, J. (2002). The girls in the gang: What we've learned from two decades of research. In C. R. Huff (Ed.), *Gangs in America* (3rd ed., pp. 175–197). Thousand Oaks, CA: Sage.

Miller, J. L. & Levy, G. D. (1996). Gender role conflict, gender-typed characteristics, self-concepts, and sport socialization in female athletes and nonathletes. *Sex Roles, 35*, 111–122.

Miller, L. M., Schweingruber, H., & Brandenburg, C. L. (2001). Middle school students' technology practices and preferences: Re-examining gender differences. *Journal of Educational Multimedia and Hypermedia, 10*, 125–140.

Milloy, M. (2003). The guy teacher. *NEA Today, 22*, 22–31.

Mills, C. J., Ablard, K. E., & Stumpf, H. (1993). Gender differences in academically talented young students' mathematical reasoning: Patterns across age and subskills. *Journal of Educational Psychology, 85*, 340–346.

Mills, R. S. & Rubin, K. H. (1992). A longitudinal study of maternal beliefs about children's social behaviors. *Merrill-Palmer Quarterly, 38*, 494–512.

Mills, T. L., Wakeman, M. A., & Fea, C. B. (2001). Adult grandchildren's perceptions of emotional closeness and consensus with their maternal and paternal grandparents. *Journal of Family Issues, 22*, 427–455.

Milne, A. A. (1974). *Winnie-the-Pooh*. New York: Dell Publishing Co: A Yearling Book.

Minton, H. L. (2000). Psychology and gender at the turn of the century. *American Psychologist, 55*, 613–615.

Mintz, S. (1998). From patriarchy to androgyny and other myths: Placing men's family roles in historical perspective. In A. Booth & A. C. Crouter (Eds.), *Men in families: When do they get involved? What difference does it make?* (pp. 3–30). Mahwah, NJ: Lawrence Erlbaum Associates.

Mischel, W. (1966). A social learning view of sex differences in behavior. In E. E. Maccoby (Ed.), *The development of sex differences* (pp. 56–81). Stanford, CA: Stanford University Press.

Mischel, W. (1970). Sex-typing and socialization. In P. H. Mussen (Ed.), *Carmichael's manual of child psychology* (3rd ed., Vol. 2, pp. 3–72). New York: Wiley.

Moffat, S. D., Hampson, E., & Hatzipantelis, M. (1998). Navigation in a "virtual" maze: Sex differences and correlation with psychometric measures of spatial ability in humans. *Evolution and Human Behavior, 19*, 73–87.

Moffitt, T. E., Caspi, A., Rutter, M., & Silva, P. A. (2001). *Sex differences in antisocial behaviour: Conduct disorder, delinquency, and violence in the Dunedin Longitudinal Study*. New York: Cambridge University Press.

Moller, L. C., Hymel, S., & Rubin, K. H. (1992). Sex typing in play and popularity in middle childhood. *Sex Roles, 26*, 331–353.

Moller, L. C. & Serbin, L. A. (1996). Antecedents of toddler gender segregation: Cognitive consonance, gender-typed toy preferences and behavioral compatibility. *Sex Roles, 35*, 445–460.

Mondschein, E. R., Adolph, K. E., & Tamis-LeMonda, C. S. (2000). Gender bias in mothers' expectations about infant crawling. *Journal of Experimental Child Psychology, 77*, 304–316.

Money, J. (1973). Gender role, gender identity, core gender identity: Usage and definition of terms. *Journal of the American Academy of Psychoanalysis, 1*, 397–402.

Money, J. & Ehrhardt, A. A. (1972). *Man and woman, boy and girl: Differentiation and dimorphism of gender identity from conception to maturity*. Baltimore, MD: Johns Hopkins University Press.

Money, J., Hampson, J. G., & Hampson, J. L. (1955). Hermaphroditism: Recommendations concerning assignment of sex, change of sex, and psychologic management. *Bulletin of Johns Hopkins Hospital, 97*, 284–300.

Money, J., Hampson, J. G., & Hampson, J. L. (1957). Imprinting and the establishment of gender role. *Archives of Neurology and Psychiatry, 77*, 333–336.

Montello, D. R., Lovelace, K. L., Golledge, R. G., & Self, C. M. (1999). Sex-related differences and similarities in geographic and environmental spatial abilities. *Annals of the Association of American Geographers, 89*, 515–534.

Montgomery, K. C. (2000). Children's media culture in the new millennium. *The Future of Children: Children and Computer Technology, 10*, 145–167.

Morahan-Martin, J. (1998). The gender gap in Internet use: Why men use the Internet more than women--A literature review. *CyberPsychology and Behavior, 1*, 3–10.

Morgan, M. & Shanahan, J. (1997). Two decades of cultivation research: An appraisal and meta-analysis. In B. R. Burleson (Ed.), *Communication yearbook* (pp. 1–46). Thousand Oaks, CA: Sage.

Morgan, V. & Dunn, S. (1988). Chameleons in the classroom: Visible and invisible children in nursery and infant classrooms. *Educational Review, 40*, 3–12.

Morisset, C. E., Barnard, K. E., & Booth, C. L. (1995). Toddlers' language development: Sex differences within social risk. *Developmental Psychology, 31*, 851–865.

Morrongiello, B. A. & Dawber, T. (1998). Toddlers' and mothers' behaviors in an injury-risk situation: Implications for sex differences in childhood injuries. *Journal of Applied Developmental Psychology, 19*, 625–639.

Morrongiello, B. A. & Dawber, T. (1999). Parental influences on toddlers' injury-risk behaviors: Are sons and daughters socialized differently? *Journal of Applied Developmental Psychology, 20*, 227–251.

Morrongiello, B. A. & Dawber, T. (2000). Mothers' responses to sons and daughters engaging in injury-risk behaviors on a playground: Implications for sex differences in injury rates. *Journal of Experimental Child Psychology, 76*, 89–103.

Morrongiello, B. A. & Hogg, K. (2004). Mothers' reactions to children misbehaving in ways that can lead to injury: Implications for gender differences in children's risk taking and injuries. *Sex Roles, 50*, 103–118.

Morse, J., Bower, A., Healy, R., Barnes, S., Berestein, L., Locke, L. A., et al. (2002, April 1). Women on a binge. *Time, 159*, 56–61.

Morse, J. F. (2002). Ignored but not forgotten: The work of Helen Bradford Thompson Woolley. *NWSA Journal, 14*, 121–147.

Mueller, C. M. & Dweck, C. S. (1998). Praise for intelligence can undermine children's motivation and performance. *Journal of Personality and Social Psychology, 75*, 33–52.

Mueller, M. M., Wilhelm, B., & Elder, G. H., Jr. (2002). Variations in grandparenting. *Research on Aging, 24*, 360–388.

Mullen, M. K. (1994). Earliest recollections of childhood: A demographic analysis. *Cognition, 52*, 55–79.

Mullis, I. V. S., Martin, M. O., Gonzalez, E. J., Gregory, K. D., Garden, R. A., O'Connor, K. M., et al. (2000). *TIMSS international mathematics report*. Boston, MA: The International Association for the Evaluation of Educational Achievement.

Munroe, R. L., Hulefeld, R., Rodgers, J. M., Tomeo, D. L., & Yamazaki, S. K. (2000). Aggression among children in four cultures. *Cross-Cultural Research: The Journal of Comparative Social Science, 34*, 3–25.

Munroe, R. L. & Munroe, R. H. (1997). Logoli childhood and the cultural reproduction of sex differentiation. In T. S. Weisner & C. Bradley (Eds.), *African families and the crisis of social change* (pp. 299–314). Westport, CT: Bergin & Garvey/Greenwood.

Murchison, C. (Ed.). (1931). *A handbook of child psychology*. Worcester, MA: Clark University Press.

Muris, P., Merckelbach, H., Mayer, B., & Prins, E. (2000). How serious are common childhood fears? *Behaviour Research and Therapy, 38*, 217–228.

Murnen, S. K. & Smolak, L. (2000). The experience of sexual harassment among grade-school students: Early socialization of female subordination? *Sex Roles, 43*, 1–17.

Mussen, P. & Distler, L. (1959). Masculinity, identification, and father-son relationships. *Journal of Abnormal and Social Psychology, 59*, 350–356.

Mussen, P. & Rutherford, E. (1963). Parent-child relations and parental personality in relation to young children's sex-role preferences. *Child Development, 34*, 589–607.

Mustanski, B. S., Bailey, J. M., & Kaspar, S. (2002). Dermatoglyphics, handedness, sex, and sexual orientation. *Archives of Sexual Behavior, 31*, 113–132.

Mwangi, M. W. (1996). Gender roles portrayed in Kenyan television commercials. *Sex Roles, 34*, 205–214.

Nash, S. C. & Feldman, S. S. (1981). Sex-related differences in the relationship between sibling status and responsivity to babies. *Sex Roles, 7*, 1035–1042.

Nathanson, A. I., Wilson, B. J., McGee, J., & Sebastian, M. (2002). Counteracting the effects of female stereotypes on television via active mediation. *Journal of Communication, 52*, 922–937.

National Basketball Association. (2005). Player profile: David Robinson. Retrieved January 22, 2008, from: http://www.nba.com/playerfile/david_robinson/bio.html

National Center for Education Statistics. (2002). *Digest of education statistics*. Washington, DC: U.S. Department of Education.

National Center for Health Statistics. (2000). *Centers for disease control growth charts: United States*. Hyattsville, MD: U.S. Department of Health and Human Services.

National Center for Health Statistics. (2001). *Body measurements: Average height for men and women ages 20+*. Hyattsville, MD: U.S. Department of Health and Human Services.

National Center on Addiction and Substance Abuse. (2002). *Teen tipplers: America's underage drinking epidemic*. New York: CASA: The National Center on Addiction and Substance Abuse at Columbia University.

National Federation of State High School Associations. (2006). *NFHS 2005–2006 high school athletics participation survey*. Indianapolis, IN: Author.

Nell, V. (2002). Why young men drive dangerously: Implications for injury prevention. *Current Directions in Psychological Science, 11*, 75–79.

Nelson, A. (2005). Children's toy collections in Sweden -- A less gender-typed country? *Sex Roles, 52*, 93–102.

Nelson, D. A., Robinson, C. C., & Hart, C. H. (2005). Relational and physical aggression of preschool-age children: Peer status linkages across informants. *Early Education and Development, 16*, 115–139.

Neto, F. & Furnham, A. (2005). Gender-role portrayals in children's television advertisements. *International Journal of Adolescence and Youth, 12*, 69–90.

Newcomb, A. F. & Bagwell, C. L. (1995). Children's friendship relations: A meta-analytic review. *Psychological Bulletin, 117*, 306–347.

Newcomb, A. F., Bukowski, W. M., & Pattee, L. (1993). Children's peer relations: A meta-analytic review of popular, rejected, neglected, controversial, and average sociometric status. *Psychological Bulletin, 113*, 99–128.

Newcombe, N. S. (2007). Taking science seriously: Straight thinking about spatial sex differences. In S. J. Ceci & W. M. Williams (Eds.), *Why aren't more women in science: Top researchers debate the evidence*. (pp. 69–77). Washington, DC: American Psychological Association.

Newcombe, N. S., Mathason, L., & Terlecki, M. (2002). Maximization of spatial competence: More important than finding the cause of sex differences. In A. V. McGillicuddy-De Lisi & R. De Lisi (Eds.), *Biology, society, and behavior: The development of sex differences in cognition* (pp. 183–206). Westport, CT: Ablex Publishing.

Newson, J. & Newson, E. (1976). *Seven years old in the home environment*. Oxford, England: John Wiley & Sons.

Newson, J. & Newson, E. (1987). Family and sex roles in middle childhood. In D. J. Hargreaves & A. M. Colley (Eds.), *The psychology of sex roles* (pp. 142–158). Washington: Hemisphere Publishing Corp.

Nguyen, T. V., Maynard, L. M., Towne, B., Roche, A. F., Wisemandle, W., Li, J., et al. (2001). Sex differences in bone mass acquisition during growth: The Fels longitudinal study. *Journal of Clinical Densitometry, 4*, 147–158.

NICHD Early Child Care Research Network. (2004). Trajectories of physical aggression from toddlerhood to middle childhood. *Monographs of the Society for Research in Child Development, 69*(4, Serial No. 278).

Nichols, S. L. & Good, T. L. (1998). Students' perceptions of fairness in school settings: A gender analysis. *Teachers College Record, 100*, 369–401.

Nicolopoulou, A. (1997). Worldmaking and identity formation in children's narrative play-acting. In B. Cox & C. Lightfoot (Eds.), *Sociogenic perspectives in internalization* (pp. pp. 157–187). Hillsdale, NJ: Lawrence Erlbaum.

Nigro, G. N. & Snow, A. L. (1992). Sex, lies, and smiling faces: A brief report on gender differences in 3-year-olds' deceptions. In S. J. Ceci & M. D. Leichtman (Eds.), *Cognitive and social factors in early deception* (pp. 63–68). Hillsdale, NJ: Lawrence Erlbaum Associates.

Nilges, L. M. & Spencer, A. F. (2002). The pictorial representation of gender and physical activity level in Caldecott medal winning children's literature (1940–1999): A relational analysis of physical culture. *Sport, Education, and Society, 7*, 135–150.

Nobes, G. & Smith, M. (2000). The relative extent of physical punishment and abuse by mothers and fathers. *Trauma Violence and Abuse, 1*, 47–66.

Noguera, P. A. (2003). The trouble with Black boys: The role and influence of environmental and cultural factors on the academic performance of African American males. *Urban Education, 38*, 431–459.

Nolen-Hoeksema, S. (2001). Gender differences in depression. *Current Directions in Psychological Science, 10*, 173–176.

Nopoulos, P., Flaum, M., O'Leary, D. S., & Andreasen, N. C. (2000). Sexual dimorphism in the human brain: Evaluation of tissue volume, tissue composition and surface anatomy using magnetic resonance imaging. *Psychiatry Research, 98*, 1–13.

Nordenström, A., Servin, A., Bohlin, G., Larsson, A., & Wedell, A. (2002). Sex-typed toy play behavior correlates with the degree of prenatal androgen exposure assessed by CYP21 genotype in girls with congenital adrenal hyperplasia. *Journal of Clinical Endocrinology and Metabolism, 87*, 5119–5124.

Norton, K. I., Olds, T. S., Olive, S., & Dank, S. (1996). Ken and Barbie at life size. *Sex Roles, 34*, 287–294.

O'Brien, M., Huston, A. C., & Risley, T. R. (1983). Sex-typed play of toddlers in a day care center. *Journal of Applied Developmental Psychology, 4*, 1–9.

Ochman, J. M. (1996). The effects of nongender-role stereotyped, same-sex role models in storybooks on the self-esteem of children in grade three. *Sex Roles, 35*, 711–736.

O'Connell, A. N. (1990). Eleanor Emmons Maccoby. In A. N. O'Connell & N. F. Russo (Eds.), *Women in psychology: A bio-bibliographic sourcebook* (pp. 230–237). New York: Greenwood Press.

Oetzel, R. M. (1966). Annotated bibliography. In E. E. Maccoby (Ed.), *The development of sex differences* (pp. 223–321). Stanford, CA: Stanford University Press.

Okagaki, L. & Frensch, P. A. (1994). Effects of video game playing on measures of spatial performance: Gender effects in late adolescence. *Journal of Applied Developmental Psychology, 15*, 33–58.

O'Keefe, J. J., Carr, A., & McQuaid, P. (1998). Conduct disorder in girls and boys: The identification of distinct psychological profiles. *Irish Journal of Psychology, 19*, 368–385.

Okpala, C. O. (1996). Gender-related differences in classroom interaction. *Journal of Instructional Psychology, 23*, 275–285.

Oliva, A. & Arranz, E. (2005). Sibling relationships during adolescence. *European Journal of Developmental Psychology, 2*, 253–270.

Oliver, M. B. & Green, S. (2001). Development of gender differences in children's responses to animated entertainment. *Sex Roles, 45*, 67–88.

Oliver, M. B. & Hyde, J. S. (1993). Gender differences in sexuality: A meta-analysis. *Psychological Bulletin, 114*, 29–51.

Olson, E. (1994). Female voices of aggression in Tonga. *Sex Roles, 30*, 237–248.

Orenstein, P. (1995). *Schoolgirls: Young women, self-esteem, and the confidence gap*. New York: Anchor Books.

Oser, F. K. (1990). Kohlberg's educational legacy. *New Directions for Child Development, 47*, 81–87.

Osman, B. B. (2000). Learning disabilities and the risk of psychiatric disorders in children and adolescents. In L. L. Greenhill (Ed.), *Learning disabilities: Implications for psychiatric treatment*. Review of psychiatry series (Vol. 19, No. 5, pp. 33–57). Washington, DC: American Psychiatric Press.

Österman, K., Björkqvist, K., Lagerspetz, K. M. J., Kaukiainen, A., Landau, S. F., Fraczek, A., et al. (1998). Cross-cultural evidence of female indirect aggression. *Aggressive Behavior, 24*, 1–8.

Ostrov, J. M. & Keating, C. F. (2004). Gender differences in preschool aggression during free play and structured interactions: An observational study. *Social Development, 13*, 255–277.

Otberg, N., Finner, A. M., & Shapiro, J. (2007). Androgenetic alopecia. *Endocrinology and Metabolism Clinics of North America, 36*, 379–398.

Ott, E. M. (1989). Effects of the male-female ratio at work: Policewomen and male nurses. *Psychology of Women Quarterly, 13*, 41–57.

Overfield, T. (1985). *Biologic variation in health and illness.* Menlo Park, CA: Addison-Wesley Publishing Company.

Overton, W. F. (1984). World views and their influence on psychological theory and research: Kuhn-Lakatos-Laudan. In H. W. Reese (Ed.), *Advances in child development and behavior* (Vol. 18, pp. 191–226). New York: Academic Press.

Overton, W. F. (1998). Developmental psychology: Philosophy, concepts, and methodology. In R. M. Lerner (Ed.), *Handbook of child psychology: Vol. 1. Theoretical models of human development* (5th ed., pp. 107–188). New York: Wiley.

Overton, W. F. (2006). Developmental psychology: Philosophy, concepts, and methodology. In R. M. Lerner (Ed.), *Handbook of child psychology: Vol. 1. Theoretical models of human development* (6th ed., pp. 18–88). Hoboken, NJ: Wiley.

Owens, L., Shute, R., & Slee, P. (2000). "I'm in and you're out . . ." Explanations for teenage girls' indirect aggression. *Psychology, Evolution and Gender, 2*, 19–46.

Owens, L., Slee, P., & Shute, R. (2000). "It hurts a hell of a lot . . .": The effects of indirect aggression on teenage girls. *School Psychology International, 21*, 359–376.

Paik, H. (2001). The history of children's use of electronic media. In D. G. Singer & J. L. Singer (Eds.), *Handbook of children and the media* (pp. 7–27). Thousand Oaks, CA: Sage.

Paik, H. & Comstock, G. (1994). The effects of television violence on antisocial behavior: A meta-analysis. *Communication Research, 21*, 516–546.

Paquette, D. (2004). Theorizing the father-child relationship: Mechanisms and developmental outcomes. *Human Development, 47*, 193–219.

Paquette, J. A. & Underwood, M. K. (1999). Gender differences in young adolescents' experiences of peer victimization: Social and physical aggression. *Merrill-Palmer Quarterly, 45*, 242–266.

Parke, R. D. (2002). Fathers and families. In M. H. Bornstein (Ed.), *Handbook of parenting: Vol. 3: Being and becoming a parent* (2nd ed., pp. 27–73). Mahwah, NJ: Lawrence Erlbaum Associates.

Parke, R. D. & Buriel, R. (1998). Socialization in the family: Ethnic and ecological perspectives. In W. Damon & N. Eisenberg (Eds.), *Handbook of child psychology: Vol 3. Social, emotional, and personality development* (5th ed., pp. 463–552). New York: Wiley.

Parkhurst, J. T. & Hopmeyer, A. (1998). Sociometric popularity and peer-perceived popularity: Two distinct dimensions of peer status. *Journal of Early Adolescence, 18*, 125–144.

Parsad, B. & Glover, D. (2002). *Tenure status of postsecondary instructional faculty and staff: 1992 -1998* (No. 2002–210). Washington, DC: U.S. Department of Education National Center for Education Statistics.

Parsons, T. (1958). Social structure and the development of personality: Freud's contribution to the integration of psychology and sociology. *Journal for the Study of Interpersonal Processes, 21*, 321–340.

Parsons, T. & Bales, R. F. (1955). *Family, socialization and interaction process.* Glencoe, IL: Free Press.

Pasterski, V. L., Geffner, M. E., Brain, C., Hindmarsh, P., Brook, C., & Hines, M. (2005). Prenatal hormones and postnatal socialization by parents as determinants of male-typical toy play in girls with Congenital Adrenal Hyperplasia. *Child Development, 76*, 264–278.

Pasterski, V. L., Hindmarsh, P., Geffner, M. E., Brook, C., Brain, C., & Hines, M. (2007). Increased aggression and activity level in 3- to 11-year-old girls with congenital adrenal hyperplasia (CAH). *Hormones and Behavior, 52*, 368–374.

Paterson, J. E., Field, J., & Pryor, J. (1994). Adolescents' perceptions of their attachment relationships with their mothers, fathers, and friends. *Journal of Youth and Adolescence, 23*, 579–600.

Paterson, S. B. & Lach, M. A. (1990). Gender stereotypes in children's books: Their prevalence and influence on cognitive and affective development. *Gender and Education, 2*, 185–198.

Patterson, C. J. (1992). Children of lesbian and gay parents. *Child Development, 63*, 1025–1042.

Patterson, C. J. (1995). Sexual orientation and human development: An overview. *Developmental Psychology, 31*, 3–11.

Patterson, C. J. (1998). The family lives of children born to lesbian mothers. In C. J. Patterson & A. R. D'Augelli (Eds.), *Lesbian, gay, and bisexual identities in families: Psychological perspectives* (pp. 154–176). New York: Oxford University Press.

Patterson, C. J., Sutfin, E. L., & Fulcher, M. (2004). Division of labor among lesbian and heterosexual parenting couples: Correlates of specialized versus shared patterns. *Journal of Adult Development, 11*, 179–189.

Paus, T. (2005). Mapping brain maturation and cognitive development during adolescence. *Trends in Cognitive Sciences, 9*, 60–68.

Pawlby, S. J., Mills, A., & Quinton, D. (1997). Vulnerable adolescent girls: Opposite-sex relationships. *Journal of Child Psychology and Psychiatry, 38*, 909–920.

Pearson, G. H. J. (1931). The psychosexual development of the child. *Mental Hygiene, 14*, 685–713.

Pecora, N. (1992). Superman/superboys/supermen: The comic book hero as socializing agent. In S. Craig (Ed.), *Men, masculinity, and the media*. Research on men and masculinities series (Vol. 1, pp. 61–77). Thousand Oaks, CA: Sage.

Pedersen, E. L. & Markee, N. L. (1991). Fashion dolls: Representation of ideals of beauty. *Perceptual and Motor Skills, 73*, 93–94.

Peirce, K. (1990). A feminist theoretical perspective on the socialization of teenage girls through Seventeen magazine. *Sex Roles, 23*, 491–500.

Pellegrini, A. D. (1988). Elementary-school children's rough-and-tumble play and social competence. *Developmental Psychology, 24*, 802–806.

Pellegrini, A. D. (1990). Elementary school children's playground behavior: Implications for children's social-cognitive development. *Children's Environment Quarterly, 7*, 8–16.

Pellegrini, A. D. (1993). Boys' rough-and-tumble play, social competence and group composition. *British Journal of Developmental Psychology, 11*, 237–248.

Pellegrini, A. D. (1994). The rough play of adolescent boys of differing sociometric status. *International Journal of Behavioral Development, 17*, 525–540.

Pellegrini, A. D. (1995). A longitudinal study of boys' rough-and-tumble play and dominance during early adolescence. *Journal of Applied Developmental Psychology, 16*, 77–93.

Pellegrini, A. D. (2002). Perceptions of playfighting and real fighting: Effects of sex and participant status. In J. L. Roopnarine (Ed.), *Conceptual, social-cognitive, and contextual issues in the fields of play* (pp. 223–233). Westport, CT: Ablex Publishing.

Pellegrini, A. D. (2003). Perceptions and functions of play and real fighting in early adolescence. *Child Development, 74*, 1522–1533.

Pellegrini, A. D. & Long, J. D. (2003). A sexual selection theory longitudinal analysis of sexual segregation and integration in early adolescence. *Journal of Experimental Child Psychology, 85*, 257–278.

Pellegrini, A. D. & Smith, P. K. (1998). Physical activity play: The nature and function of a neglected aspect of play. *Child Development, 69*, 577–598.

Pepper, S. C. (1942). *World hypotheses*. Berkeley, CA: University of California Press.

Perry, D. G. & Bussey, K. (1979). The social learning theory of sex differences: Imitation is alive and well. *Journal of Personality and Social Psychology, 37*, 1699–1712.

Perry, D. G., Perry, L. C., & Weiss, R. J. (1989). Sex differences in the consequences that children anticipate for aggression. *Developmental Psychology, 25*, 312–319.

Perry, D. G., White, A. J., & Perry, L. C. (1984). Does early sex typing result from children's attempts to match their behavior to sex role stereotypes? *Child Development, 55*, 2114–2121.

Pettit, G. S., Bakshi, A., Dodge, K. A., & Coie, J. D. (1990). The emergence of social dominance in young boys' play groups: Developmental differences and behavior correlates. *Developmental Psychology, 26*, 1017–1025.

Pfister, O. (1918). Psychoanalysis and the study of children and youth. *American Journal of Psychology, 26*, 130–141.

Phoenix, C. H., Goy, R. W., Gerall, A. A., & Young, W. C. (1959). Organizing action of prenatally administered testosterone propionate on the tissues mediating mating behavior in the female guinea pig. *Endocrinology, 65*, 369–382.

Piaget, J. (1965). *The moral judgment of the child*. New York: Free Press.

Piaget, J. (1970). Piaget's theory. In P. H. Mussen (Ed.), *Carmichael's manual of child psychology* (3rd ed., Vol. 2, pp. 703–732). New York: Wiley.

Piaget, J. & Inhelder, B. (1956). *The child's conception of space*. New York: Norton (Originally published in 1948 as *La representation de l'espace chez l'enfant*. Paris, France: Presses Universitaires de France).

Pine, K. J. & Nash, A. (2002). Dear Santa: The effects of television advertising on young children. *International Journal of Behavioral Development, 26*, 529–539.

Pitcher, E. G. & Schultz, L. H. (1983). *Boys and girls at play: The development of sex roles*. New York: Praeger.

Pleck, J. H. (1997). Paternal involvement: Levels, sources, and consequences. In M. E. Lamb (Ed.), *The role of the father in child development* (3rd ed., pp. 66–103). New York: Wiley.

Pollard, M. S. & Morgan, S. P. (2002). Emerging parental gender indifference? Sex composition of children and the third birth. *American Sociological Review, 67*, 600–613.

Pollatou, E., Karadimou, K., & Gerodimos, V. (2005). Gender differences in musical aptitude, rhythmic ability and motor performance in preschool children. *Early Child Development and Care, 175*, 361–369.

Pomerantz, E. M., Altermatt, E. R., & Saxon, J. L. (2002). Making the grade but feeling distressed: Gender differences in academic performance and internal distress. *Journal of Educational Psychology, 94*, 396–404.

Pomerantz, E. M. & Eaton, M. M. (2000). Developmental differences in children's conceptions of parental control: "They love me, but they make me feel incompetent." *Merrill-Palmer Quarterly, 46*, 140–167.

Pomerantz, E. M. & Ruble, D. N. (1998). The role of maternal control in the development of sex differences in child self-evaluative factors. *Child Development, 69*, 458–478.

Pomerleau, A., Bolduc, D., Malcuit, G., & Cossette, L. (1990). Pink or blue: Environmental gender stereotypes in the first two years of life. *Sex Roles, 22*, 359–367.

Pooler, W. S. (1991). Sex of child preferences among college students. *Sex Roles, 25*, 569–576.

Porter, L. S., Marco, C. A., Schwartz, J. E., Neale, J. M., Shiffman, S., & Stone, A. A. (2000). Gender differences in coping: A comparison of trait and momentary assessments. *Journal of Social and Clinical Psychology, 19*, 480–498.

Potts, R., Huston, A. C., & Wright, J. C. (1986). The effects of television form and violent content on boys' attention and social behavior. *Journal of Experimental Child Psychology, 41*, 1–17.

Poulin-Dubois, D., Serbin, L. A., Eichstedt, J. A., Sen, M. G., & Beissel, C. F. (2002). Men don't put on make-up: Toddlers' knowledge of the gender stereotyping of household activities. *Social Development, 11*, 166–181.

Poulin-Dubois, D., Serbin, L. A., Kenyon, B., & Derbyshire, A. (1994). Infants' intermodal knowledge about gender. *Developmental Psychology, 30*, 436–442.

Power, T. G. & Parke, R. D. (1986). Patterns of early socialization: Mother- and father-infant interaction in the home. *International Journal of Behavioral Development, 9*, 331–341.

Powlishta, K. K. (1995). Intergroup processes in childhood: Social categorization and sex role development. *Developmental Psychology, 31*, 781–788.

Powlishta, K. K. & Maccoby, E. E. (1990). Resource utilization in mixed-sex dyads: The influence of adult presence and task type. *Sex Roles, 23*, 223–240.

Prentice, D. A. & Carranza, E. (2002). What women and men should be, shouldn't be, are allowed to be, and don't have to be: The contents of prescriptive gender stereotypes. *Psychology of Women Quarterly, 26*, 269–281.

Probst, R., Lonsbury-Martin, B. L., & Martin, G. K. (1991). A review of otoacoustic emissions. *Journal of the Acoustical Society of America, 89*, 2027–2067.

Pryor, S. E. & Achilles, C. M. (1998). Gender equity in the classroom: Are preservice teachers in the know? *Professional Educator, 21*, 63–72.

Pryzgoda, J. & Chrisler, J. C. (2000). Definitions of gender and sex: The subtleties of meaning. *Sex Roles, 43*, 553–569.

Purcell, P. & Stewart, L. (1990). Dick and Jane in 1989. *Sex Roles, 22*, 177–185.

Putallaz, M., Hellstern, L., Sheppard, B. H., Grimes, C. L., & Glodis, K. A. (1995). Conflict, social competence, and gender: Maternal and peer contexts. *Early Education and Development, 6*, 433–447.

Putz, D. A., Gaulin, S. J. C., Sporter, R. J., & McBurney, D. H. (2004). Sex hormones and finger length. What does 2D:4D indicate? *Evolution and Human Behavior, 25*, 182–199.

Puzzanchera, C., Stahl, A. L., Finnegan, T. A., Tierney, N., & Snyder, H. N. (2003). *Juvenile court statistics 1998.* Washington, DC: National Center for Juvenile Justice: Office of Juvenile Justice and Delinquency Prevention.

Pyle, W. J. (1976). Sexism in children's literature. *Theory into Practice, 15*, 116–119.

Quadagno, D. M., Briscoe, R., & Quadagno, J. S. (1977). Effects of perinatal gonadal hormones on selected nonsexual behavior patterns: A critical assessment of the non-human and human literature. *Psychological Bulletin, 84*, 62–80.

Quatman, T. & Watson, C. M. (2001). Gender differences in adolescent self-esteem: An exploration of domains. *Journal of Genetic Psychology, 162*, 93–117.

Quetelet, L. A. J. (1830/1969). *A treatise on man and the development of his faculties* (R. Knox, Trans.). Gainesville, FL: Scholars Facsimiles and Reprints. (Original work published 1830; translated 1842).

Quigley, C. A., De Bellis, A., Marschke, K. B., el-Awady, M. K., Wilson, E. M., & French, F. S. (1995). Androgen receptor defects: Historical, clinical, and molecular perspectives. *Endocrine Reviews, 16*, 271–321.

Quinn, P. C. (2005). Young infants' categorization of humans versus nonhuman animals: Roles for knowledge access and perceptual process. In L. Gershkoff-Stowe & D. H. Rakison (Eds.), *Building object categories in developmental time* (pp. 107–130). Mahwah, NJ: Lawrence Erlbaum Associates.

Rabinowicz, T., Dean, D. E., Petetot, J. M., & de Courten-Myers, G. M. (1999). Gender differences in the human cerebral cortex: More neurons in males; More processes in females. *Journal of Child Neurology, 14*, 98–107.

Radke-Yarrow, M. & Kochanska, G. (1990). Anger in young children. In N. L. Stein & B. Leventhal (Eds.), *Psychological and biological approaches to emotion* (pp. 297–310). Hillsdale, NJ, England: Lawrence Erlbaum.

Raz, N., Gunning-Dixon, F., Head, D., Rodrique, K. M., Williamson, A., & Acker, J. D. (2004). Aging, sexual dimorphism, and hemispheric asymmetry of the cerebral cortex: Replicability of regional differences in volume. *Neurobiology of Aging, 25*, 377–396.

Reay, D. (2001). "Spice girls," "nice girls," "girlies," and "tomboys": Gender discourses, girls' cultures and femininities in the primary classroom. *Gender and Education, 13*, 153–166.

Rebelsky, F. (1964). Adult perception of the horizontal. *Perceptual and Motor Skills, 19*, 371–374.

Reed, T. & Brown, M. (2001). The expression of care in the rough and tumble play of boys. *Journal of Research in Childhood Education, 15*, 104–116.

Reeder, H. M. (2003). The effect of gender role orientation on same- and cross-sex friendship formation. *Sex Roles, 49*, 143–152.

Reese, E. & Fivush, R. (1993). Parental styles of talking about the past. *Developmental Psychology, 29*, 596–606.

Reese, E., Haden, C. A., & Fivush, R. (1996). Mothers, fathers, daughters, sons: Gender differences in autobiographical reminiscing. *Research on Language and Social Interaction, 29*, 27–56.

Reese, L. (1994). Gender equity and texts. *Social Studies Review, 33*, 12–15.

Reid, P. T., Tate, C. S., & Berman, P. W. (1989). Preschool children's self-presentations in situations with infants: Effects of sex and race. *Child Development, 60*, 710–714.

Reilly, J. M. & Woodhouse, C. R. (1989). Small penis and the male sexual role. *Journal of Urology, 142*, 569–571.

Reiner, W. G. & Gearhart, J. P. (2004). Discordant sexual identity in some genetic males with cloacal exstrophy assigned to female sex at birth. *New England Journal of Medicine, 350*, 333–341.

Reinisch, J. M. (1981). Prenatal exposure to synthetic progestins increases potential for aggression in humans. *Science, 211*, 1171–1173.

Reinisch, J. M. & Sanders, S. A. (1992). Prenatal hormonal contributions to sex differences in human cognitive and personality development. In A. A. Gerall, H. Moltz & I. L. Ward (Eds.), *Handbook of behavioral neurology: Vol. 11. Sexual differentiation* (pp. 221–243). New York: Plenum Press.

Reis, H. T. & Wright, S. (1982). Knowledge of sex-role stereotypes in children aged 3 to 5. *Sex Roles, 8*, 1049–1056.

Reskin, B. (1993). Sex segregation in the workplace. *Annual Review of Sociology, 19*, 241–270.

Resnick, S. M. (1982). *Psychological functioning in individuals with congenital adrenal hyperplasia: Early hormonal influences on cognition and personality.* Unpublished doctoral dissertation, University of Minnesota, Minneapolis.

Resnick, S. M. (2006). Sex differences in regional brain structure and function. In P. W. Kaplan (Ed.), *Neurologic disease in women* (pp. 15–26). New York: Demos Medical Publications.

Resnick, S. M., Berenbaum, S. A., Gottesman, I. I., & Bouchard, T. J. (1986). Early hormonal influences on cognitive functioning in congenital adrenal hyperplasia. *Developmental Psychology, 22*, 191–198.

Resnick, S. M., Gottesman, I. I., & McGue, M. (1993). Sensation seeking in opposite-sex twins: An effect of prenatal hormones? *Behavior Genetics, 23*, 323–329.

Reynolds, K. (1994). Toys for boys and girls. *Science Scope, 17*, 64.

Rheingold, H. L. & Cook, K. V. (1975). The contents of boys' and girls' rooms as an index of parents' behavior. *Child Development, 46*, 459–463.

Richards, M. H., Crowe, P. A., Larson, R., & Swarr, A. (1998). Developmental patterns and gender differences in the experience of peer companionship during adolescence. *Child Development, 69*, 154–163.

Richards, M. H. & Larson, R. (1989). The life space and socialization of the self: Sex differences in the young adolescent. *Journal of Youth and Adolescence, 18*, 617–626.

Richardson, D. R. & Green, L. R. (1999). Social sanction and threat explanations of gender effects on direct and indirect aggression. *Aggressive Behavior, 25*, 425–434.

Richardson, J. G. & Simpson, C. H. (1982). Children, gender, and social structure: An analysis of the contents of letters to Santa Claus. *Child Development, 53*, 429–436.

Rieger, G., Linsenmeier, J. A. W., Gygax, L., & Bailey, J. M. (2008). Sexual orientation and childhood gender nonconformity: Evidence from home videos. *Developmental Psychology, 44*, 46–58.

Riger, S. (1992). Epistemological debates, feminist voices: Science, social values, and the study of women. *American Psychologist, 47*, 730–740.

Riordan, C. (1994). Single-gender schools: Outcomes for African and Hispanic Americans. *Research in Sociology of Education and Socialization, 10*, 177–205.

Risman, B. J. & Myers, K. (1997). As the twig is bent: Children reared in feminist households. *Qualitative Sociology, 20*, 229–252.

Ritzén, E. M. (2003). Early puberty: What is normal and when is treatment indicated? *Hormone Research, 60*, 31–34.

Roberts, W. L. (1999). The socialization of emotional expression: Relations with prosocial behaviour and competence in five samples. *Canadian Journal of Behavioural Science, 31*, 72–85.

Robinson, C. C. & Morris, J. T. (1986). The gender-stereotyped nature of Christmas toys received by 36-, 48-, and 60-month-old children: A comparison between nonrequested vs. requested toys. *Sex Roles, 15*, 21–32.

Robinson, E. F. (1946). Doll play as a function of the doll family constellation. *Child Development, 17*, 99–119.

Robinson, K. H. (1992). Class-room discipline: Power, resistance and gender. A look at teacher perspectives. *Gender and Education, 4*, 273–287.

Robinson, N. M., Abbott, R. D., Berninger, V. W., & Busse, J. (1996). Structure of abilities in math-precocious young children: Gender similarities and differences. *Journal of Educational Psychology, 88*, 341–352.

Robinson, T. N., Saphir, M. N., Kraemer, H. C., Varady, A., & Haydel, K. F. (2001). Effects of reducing television viewing on children's requests for toys: A randomized controlled trial. *Journal of Developmental and Behavioral Pediatrics, 22*, 179–184.

Rodgers, C. S., Fagot, B. I., & Winebarger, A. (1998). Gender-typed toy play in dizygotic twin pairs: A test of hormone transfer theory. *Sex Roles, 39*, 173–184.

Rodkin, P. C., Farmer, T. W., Pearl, R., & Van Acker, R. (2000). Heterogeneity of popular boys: Antisocial and prosocial configurations. *Developmental Psychology, 36*, 14–24.

Roger, A. & Duffield, J. (2000). Factors underlying persistent gendered option choices in school science and technology in Scotland. *Gender and Education, 12*, 367–383.

Rogers, L. & Walsh, J. (1982). Shortcomings of the psychomedical research of John Money and co-workers into sex differences in behavior: Social and political implications. *Sex Roles, 8*, 269–281.

Rogers, M. F. (1999). *Barbie culture*. Thousand Oaks, CA: Sage.

Rogers, T. B., Kuiper, N. A., & Kirker, W. S. (1977). Self-reference and the encoding of personal information. *Journal of Personality and Social Psychology, 35*, 677–688.

Roggman, L. A. (2004). Do fathers just want to have fun? Commentary on theorizing the father-child relationship. *Human Development, 47*, 228–236.

Rohner, R. P. & Veneziano, R. A. (2001). The importance of father love: History and contemporary evidence. *Review of General Psychology, 5*, 382–405.

Rome-Flanders, T. & Cronk, C. (1995). A longitudinal study of infant vocalizations during mother-infant games. *Journal of Child Language, 22*, 259–274.

Roof, R. L. & Havens, M. D. (1992). Testosterone improves maze performance and induces development of a male hippocampus in females. *Brain Research, 572*, 310–313.

Roopnarine, J. L., Ahmeduzzaman, M., Hossain, Z., & Riegraf, N. B. (1992). Parent-infant rough play: Its cultural specificity. *Early Education and Development, 3*, 298–311.

Roopnarine, J. L., Fouts, H. N., Lamb, M. E., & Lewis-Elligan, T. Y. (2005). Mothers' and fathers' behaviors toward their 3- to 4-month-old infants in lower, middle, and upper socioeconomic African American families. *Developmental Psychology, 41*, 723–732.

Rose, A. J., Carlson, W., & Waller, E. M. (2007). Prospective associations of co-rumination with friendship and emotional adjustment: Considering the socioemotional trade-offs of co-rumination. *Developmental Psychology, 43*, 1019–1031.

Rose, A. J. & Rudolph, K. D. (2006). A review of sex differences in peer relationship processes: Potential trade-offs for the emotional and behavioral development of girls and boys. *Psychological Bulletin, 132*, 98–131.

Rose, A. J., Swenson, L. P., & Waller, E. M. (2004). Overt and relational aggression and perceived popularity: Developmental differences in concurrent and prospective relations. *Developmental Psychology, 40*, 378–387.

Rose, R. J., Kaprio, J., Winter, T., Dick, D. M., Viken, R. J., Pulkkinen, L., et al. (2002). Femininity and fertility in sisters with twin brothers: Prenatal androgenization? Cross-sex socialization? *Psychological Science, 13*, 263–267.

Rose, R. J., Viken, R. J., Dick, D. M., Bates, J. E., Pulkkinen, L., & Kaprio, J. (2003). It does take a village: Nonfamilial environments and children's behavior. *Psychological Science, 14*, 273–277.

Rosen, W. D., Adamson, L. B., & Bakeman, R. (1992). An experimental investigation of infant social referencing: Mothers' messages and gender differences. *Developmental Psychology, 28*, 1172–1178.

Rosenberg, B. G. & Sutton-Smith, B. (1968). Family interaction effects on masculinity-femininity. *Journal of Personality and Social Psychology, 8*, 117–120.

Rosenberg, R. (1982). *Beyond separate spheres: The intellectual roots of modern feminism*. New Haven, CT: Yale University Press.

Rosenbluth, S. (1997). Is sexual orientation a matter of choice? *Psychology of Women Quarterly, 21*, 595–610.

Ross, D. (1972). *G. Stanley Hall: The psychologist as prophet*. Chicago: University of Chicago Press.

Ross, H., Tesla, C., Kenyon, B., & Lollis, S. (1990). Maternal intervention in toddler peer conflict: The socialization of principles of justice. *Developmental Psychology, 26*, 994–1003.

Ross, J., Roeltgen, D., & Zinn, A. (2006). Cognition and the sex chromosomes: Studies in Turner Syndrome. *Hormone Research, 65*, 47–56.

Ross, J. L., Roeltgen, D., Kushner, H., Wei, F., & Zinn, A. R. (2000). The Turner syndrome-associated neurocognitive phenotype maps to distal Xp. *American Journal of Human Genetics, 67*, 672–681.

Rosser, S. V. & Miller, P. H. (2000). Feminist theories: Implications for developmental psychology. In P. H. Miller & E. Kofsky Scholnick (Eds.), *Toward a feminist developmental psychology* (pp. 11–28). New York: Taylor & Francis/Routledge.

Rossi, A. S. (1981). On the reproduction of mothering: A methodological debate. *Signs, 6*, 492–500.

Rossiter, M. W. (1982). *Women scientists in America: Struggles and strategies to 1940*. Baltimore, MD: The Johns Hopkins University Press.

Rothbart, M. K. & Bates, J. E. (1998). Temperament. In W. Damon & N. Eisenberg (Eds.), *Handbook of child psychology: Vol 3. Social, emotional, and personality development.* (5th ed., pp. 105–176). Hoboken, NJ: John Wiley & Sons.

Rovet, J. F. (1990). The cognitive and neuropsychological characteristics of females with Turner Syndrome. In D. B. Berch & G. B. Bender (Eds.), *Sex chromosome abnormalities and human behavior* (pp. 38–77). New York: American Association for the Advancement of Science.

Rovet, J. F., Netley, C., Keenan, M., Bailey, J., & Stewart, D. (1996). The psychoeducational profile of boys with Klinefelter syndrome. *Journal of Learning Disabilities, 29*, 180–196.

Rovinelli, L. & Whissell, C. (1998). Emotion and style in 30-second television advertisements targeted at men, women, boys, and girls. *Perceptual and Motor Skills, 86*, 1048–1050.

Rowe, R., Maughan, B., Worthman, C. M., Costello, E. J., & Angold, A. (2004). Testosterone, antisocial behavior, and social dominance in boys: Pubertal development and biosocial interaction. *Biological Psychiatry, 55*, 546–552.

Royer, J. M., Tronsky, L. N., Chan, Y., Jackson, S. J., & Marchant, H., III. (1999). Math-fact retrieval and the cognitive mechanism underlying gender differences in math test performance. *Contemporary Educational Psychology, 24*, 181–266.

Royer, J. M., Tronsky, L. N., Marchant, H., III., & Jackson, S. J. (1999). Reply to the commentaries on the math-fact retrieval hypothesis. *Contemporary Educational Psychology, 24*, 286–300.

Rubin, J. Z., Provenzano, F. J., & Luria, Z. (1974). The eye of the beholder: Parents' views on sex of newborns. *American Journal of Orthopsychiatry, 44*, 512–519.

Rubin, K. H., Bukowski, W. M., & Parker, J. G. (1998). Peer interactions, relationships, and groups. In N. Eisenberg (Ed.), *Handbook of child psychology: Vol. 3. Social, emotional, and personality development.* (5th ed., pp. 619–700). New York: Wiley.

Rubin, K. H. & Mills, R. S. (1990). Maternal beliefs about adaptive and maladaptive social behaviors in normal, aggressive, and withdrawn preschoolers. *Journal of Abnormal Child Psychology, 18*, 419–435.

Rubinow, D. R. & Schmidt, P. J. (2006). Gonadal steroid regulation of mood: The lessons of premenstrual syndrome. *Frontiers in Neuroendocrinology, 27*, 210–216.

Ruble, D. N., Balaban, T., & Cooper, J. (1981). Gender constancy and the effects of sex-typed televised toy commercials. *Child Development, 52*, 667–673.

Ruble, D. N. & Martin, C. L. (1998). Gender development. In W. Damon & N. Eisenberg (Eds.), *Handbook of child psychology: Vol 3. Social, emotional, and personality development.* (5th ed., pp. 933–1016). Hoboken, NJ: John Wiley & Sons.

Ruble, D. N., Martin, C. L., & Berenbaum, S. A. (2006). Gender development. In N. Eisenberg (Ed.), *Handbook of child psychology: Vol. 3. Social, emotional, and personality development.* (6th ed., pp. 858–932). Hoboken, NJ: Wiley.

Ruble, D. N. & Stangor, C. (1986). Stalking the elusive schema: Insights from developmental and social-psychological analyses of gender schemas. *Social Cognition, 4*, 227–261.

Ruble, D. N., Taylor, L. J., Cyphers, L., Greulich, F. K., Lurye, L. E., & Shrout, P. E. (2007). The role of gender constancy in early gender development. *Child Development, 78*, 1121–1136.

Russell, A. & Saebel, J. (1997). Mother-son, mother-daughter, father-son, and father-daughter: Are they distinct relationships? *Developmental Review, 17*, 111–147.

Russell, G. M. & Bohan, J. S. (1999). Hearing voices: The uses of research and the politics of change. *Psychology of Women Quarterly, 23*, 403–418.

Rust, J., Golombok, S., Hines, M., Johnston, K., Golding, J., & Alspac Study Team. (2000). The role of brothers and sisters in the gender development of preschool children. *Journal of Experimental Child Psychology, 77*, 292–303.

Rust, P. C. (1993). "Coming out" in the age of social constructionism: Sexual identity formation among lesbian and bisexual women. *Gender and Society, 7*, 50–77.

Rust, P. C. (2000). Bisexuality: A contemporary paradox for women. *Journal of Social Issues, 56*, 205–221.

Rust, P. C. (2003). Finding a sexual identity and community: Therapeutic implications and cultural assumptions in scientific models of coming out. In L. D. Garnets & D. C. Kimmel (Eds.), *Psychological perspectives on lesbian, gay, and bisexual experiences* (2nd ed., pp. 227–269). New York: Columbia University Press.

Rutland, A. (1999). The development of national prejudice, in-group favouritism and self-stereotypes in British children. *British Journal of Social Psychology, 38*, 55–70.

Rutland, A., Cameron, L., Milne, A., & McGeorge, P. (2005). Social norms and self-presentation: Children's implicit and explicit intergroup attitudes. *Child Development, 76*, 451–466.

Rutter, M., Caspi, A., Fergusson, D., Horwood, L. J., Goodman, R., Maughan, B., et al. (2004). Sex differences in developmental reading disability: New findings from four epidemiological studies. *Journal of the American Medical Association, 291*, 2007–2012.

Rutter, M., Giller, H., & Hagell, A. (1998). *Antisocial behavior by young people*. New York: Cambridge University Press.

Rutter, M., Moffitt, T. E., & Caspi, A. (2006). Gene-environment interplay and psychopathology: Multiple varieties but real effects. *Journal of Child Psychology and Psychiatry, 47*, 226–261.

Ryan, B. C. & Vandenbergh, J. G. (2002). Intrauterine position effects. *Neuroscience and Biobehavioral Reviews, 26*, 665–678.

Saarni, C., Mumme, D. L., & Campos, J. J. (1998). Emotional development: Action, communication, and understanding. In N. Eisenberg (Ed.), *Handbook of child psychology: Vol. 3. Social, emotional, and personality development.* (5th ed., pp. 237–309). New York: Wiley.

Sadker, D. (1999). Gender equity: Still knocking at the classroom door. *Educational Leadership, 56*, 22–26.

Sadker, D. (2000). Gender equity: Still knocking at the classroom door. *Equity and Excellence in Education, 33*, 80–83.

Sadker, D. (2002). An educator's primer on the gender war. *Phi Delta Kappan, 84*, 235–240,244.

Sadker, M. & Sadker, D. (1993). Fair and square: Creating a nonsexist classroom. *Instructor, 102*, 44–46,67–68.

Sadker, M. & Sadker, D. (1994). *Failing at fairness: How American schools cheat girls*. New York: Charles Scribner's Sons.

Sadker, M., Sadker, D., Fox, L., & Salata, M. (1994). Gender equity in the classroom: The unfinished agenda. *College Board Review, 170*, 14–21.

Sahlstein, E. & Allen, M. (2002). Sex differences in self-esteem: A meta-analytic assessment. In M. Allen & R. W. Preiss (Eds.), *Interpersonal communication research: Advances through meta-analysis.* LEA's communication series (pp. 59–72). Mahwah, NJ: Lawrence Erlbaum Associates.

Salkever, S. G. (1990). *Finding the mean: Theory and practice in Aristotelian political philosophy*. Princeton, NJ: Princeton University Press.

Salomone, R. C. (2006). Single-sex programs: Resolving the research conundrum. *Teachers College Record, 108*, 778–802.

Saluja, G., Early, D. M., & Clifford, R. M. (2002). *Demographic characteristics of early childhood teachers and structural elements of early care and education in the United States*. Washington, DC.: Office of Educational Research and Improvement.

Saminy, K. K. & Liu, J. (1997). A comparative study of selected United States and Japanese first-grade mathematics textbooks. *Focus on Learning Problems in Mathematics, 19*, 1–13.

Sandberg, J. F. & Hofferth, S. L. (2001). Changes in children's time with parents: United States, 1981–1997. *Demography, 38*, 423.

Sanders, J. S., Koch, J., & Urso, J. (1997a). *Gender equity, Vol. 1: Instructional activities for teacher educators in mathematics, science, and technology*. Mahwah, NJ: Lawrence Erlbaum Associates.

Sanders, J. S., Koch, J., & Urso, J. (1997b). *Gender equity, Vol. 2: Sources and resources for education students*. Mahwah, NJ: Lawrence Erlbaum Associates.

Sanford, N. (1955). The dynamics of identification. *Psychological Review, 62*, 106–117.

Sanson, A. & Di Muccio, C. (1993). The influence of aggressive and neutral cartoons and toys on the behaviour of preschool children. *Australian Psychologist, 28*, 93–99.

Sanson, A., Prior, M., Smart, D., & Oberklaid, F. (1993). Gender differences in aggression in childhood: Implications for a peaceful world. *Australian Psychologist, 28*, 86–92.

Santos, P., Guerra, S., Ribiero, J. C., Duarte, J. A., & Mota, J. (2003). Age and gender-related physical activity. *Journal of Sports Medicine and Physical Fitness, 43*, 85–89.

Sartorio, A., Lafortuna, C. L., Pogliaghi, S., & Trecate, L. (2002). The impact of gender, body dimension and body composition on hand-grip strength in healthy children. *Journal of Endocrinological Investigation, 25*, 431–435.

Satake, E. & Amato, P. P. (1995). Mathematics anxiety and achievement among Japanese elementary school students. *Educational and Psychological Measurement, 55*, 1000–1007.

Saunders, T. J. (1995). Plato on women in the laws. In A. Powell (Ed.), *The Greek world* (pp. 591–609). New York: Routledge.

Savin-Williams, R. C. (1979). Dominance hierarchies in groups of early adolescents. *Child Development, 50,* 923–935.

Savin-Williams, R. C. (1998). *And then I became gay.* New York: Routledge.

Savin-Williams, R. C. (2003). Are adolescent same-sex romantic relationships on our radar screen? In P. Florsheim (Ed.), *Adolescent romantic relations and sexual behavior: Theory, research, and practical implications.* (pp. 325–336). Mahwah, NJ: Lawrence Erlbaum Associates.

Savin-Williams, R. C. (2004). Boy-on-boy sexuality. In N. Way & J. Y. Chu (Eds.), *Adolescent boys: Exploring diverse cultures of boyhood.* (pp. 271–292). New York: New York University Press.

Schanen, C. (2002). *The genetics of Rett Syndrome.* Retrieved June 28, 2002, from: http://www.rettsyndrome.org/main/genetics_of_rett_syndrome.htm

Schau, C. G. & Scott, K. P. (1984). Impact of gender characteristics of instructional materials: An integration of the research literature. *Journal of Educational Psychology, 76,* 183–193.

Schmitz, S. (1997). Gender-related strategies in environmental development: Effects of anxiety on wayfinding in and representation of a three-dimensional maze. *Journal of Environmental Psychology, 17,* 215–228.

Schmitz, S. (1999). Gender differences in acquisition of environmental knowledge related to wayfinding behavior, spatial anxiety and self-estimated environmental competencies. *Sex Roles, 41,* 71–93.

Schober, J. M., Carmichael, P. A., Hines, M., & Ransley, P. G. (2002). The ultimate challenge of cloacal exstrophy. *Journal of Urology, 167,* 300–304.

Schonert-Reichl, K. A., & Beaudoin, K. (1998). Social cognitive development and psychopathology during adolescence. In R. E. Muuss & H. D. Porton (Eds.), *Adolescent behavior and society: A book of readings* (5th ed., pp. 368–372). New York: McGraw-Hill.

Schultz, D. P. & Schultz, S. E. (1992). *A history of modern psychology* (5th ed.). New York: Harcourt Brace Jovanovich.

Schulz, J. J. & Schulz, L. (1999). The darkest of ages: Afghan women under the Taliban. *Peace and Conflict: Journal of Peace Psychology, 5,* 237–254.

Schumacher, P. & Morahan-Martin, J. (2001). Gender, Internet and computer attitudes and experiences. *Computers in Human Behavior, 17,* 95–110.

Searl, M. N. (1938). A note on the relation between physical and psychical differences in boys and girls. *International Journal of Psycho Analysis, 19,* 50–62.

Sears, R. R. (1950). Personality. *Annual Review of Psychology, 1,* 105–118.

Sears, R. R. (1957). Identification as a form of behavior development. In D. B. Harris (Ed.), *The concept of development* (pp. 149–161). Minneapolis: The University of Minnesota Press.

Sears, R. R. (1985). Psychoanalysis and behavior theory: 1907–1965. In S. Koch & D. E. Leary (Eds.), *A century of psychology as science* (pp. 208–220). Washington, DC: American Psychological Association.

Sears, R. R., Maccoby, E. E., & Levin, H. (1957). *Patterns of child rearing.* Evanston, IL: Row, Peterson.

Sears, R. R., Rau, L., & Alpert, R. (1965). *Identification and child rearing.* Stanford, CA: Stanford University Press.

Sebanc, A. M., Pierce, S. L., Cheatham, C. L., & Gunnar, M. R. (2003). Gendered social worlds in preschool: Dominance, peer acceptance and assertive social skills in boys' and girls' peer groups. *Social Development, 12,* 91–106.

Sell, R. L. (1997). Defining and measuring sexual orientation: A review. *Archives of Sexual Behavior, 26,* 643–658.

Seminara, S. B., Messager, S., Chatzidaki, E. E., Thresher, R. R., Acierno, J. S., Shagoury, J. K., et al. (2003). The GPR54 gene as a regulator of puberty. *New England Journal of Medicine, 349,* 1614–1627.

Sendak, M. (1988). *Where the wild things are.* New York: Harper Trophy.

Serbin, L. A., Connor, J. M., Burchardt, C. J., & Citron, C. C. (1979). Effects of peer presence on sex-typing of children's play behavior. *Journal of Experimental Child Psychology, 27,* 303–309.

Serbin, L. A., Moller, L. C., Gulko, J., Powlishta, K. K., & Colburne, K. A. (1994). The emergence of gender segregation in toddler playgroups. In C. Leaper (Ed.), *Childhood gender segregation: Causes and consequences* (pp. 7–17). San Francisco: Jossey Bass.

Serbin, L. A., O'Leary, K. D., Kent, R. N., & Tonick, I. J. (1973). A comparison of teacher response to the preacademic and problem behavior of boys and girls. *Child Development, 44,* 796–804.

Serbin, L. A., Poulin-Dubois, D., Colburne, K. A., Sen, M. G., & Eichstedt, J. A. (2001). Gender stereotyping in infancy: Visual preferences for and knowledge of gender-stereotyped toys in the second year. *International Journal of Behavioral Development, 25,* 7–15.

Serbin, L. A., Poulin-Dubois, D., & Eichstedt, J. A. (2002). Infants' response to gender-inconsistent events. *Infancy, 3,* 531–542.

Serbin, L. A., Powlishta, K. K., & Gulko, J. (1993). The development of sex typing in middle childhood. *Monographs of the Society for Research in Child Development, 58*(2, Serial No. 232).

Serbin, L. A. & Sprafkin, C. (1986). The salience of gender and the process of sex typing in three- to seven-year-old children. *Child Development, 57*, 1188–1199.

Serbin, L. A., Sprafkin, C., Elman, M., & Doyle, A. B. (1984). The early development of sex differentiated patterns of social influence. *Canadian Journal of Social Science, 14*, 350–363.

Serbin, L. A., Zelkowitz, P., Doyle, A. B., Gold, D., & Wheaton, B. (1990). The socialization of sex-differentiated skills and academic performance: A mediational model. *Sex Roles, 23*, 613–628.

Servin, A., Bohlin, G., & Berlin, L. (1999). Sex differences in 1-, 3-, and 5-year-olds' toy-choice in a structured play-session. *Scandinavian Journal of Psychology, 40*, 43–48.

Servin, A., Nordenström, A., Larsson, A., & Bohlin, G. (2003). Prenatal androgens and gender-typed behavior: A study of girls with mild and severe forms of congenital adrenal hyperplasia. *Developmental Psychology, 39*, 440–450.

Shakin, M., Shakin, D., & Sternglanz, S. H. (1985). Infant clothing: Sex labeling for strangers. *Sex Roles, 12*, 955–964.

Shanahan, K. J., Hermans, C. M., & Hyman, M. R. (2003). Violent commercials in television programs for children. *Journal of Current Issues and Research in Advertising, 25*, 63–69.

Shapleske, J., Rossell, S. L., Woodruff, P. W. R., & David, A. S. (1999). The planum temporale: A systematic, quantitative review of its structural, functional and clinical significance. *Brain Research Reviews, 29*, 26–49.

Shaywitz, B. A., Shaywitz, S. E., Pugh, K. R., Constable, R. T., Skudlarski, P., Fulbright, R. K., et al. (1995). Sex differences in the functional organization of the brain for language. *Nature, 373*, 607–609.

Shea, D. L., Lubinski, D., & Benbow, C. P. (2001). Importance of assessing spatial ability in intellectually talented young adolescents: A 20-year longitudinal study. *Journal of Educational Psychology, 93*, 604–614.

Shechner, T., Liben, L. S., & Bigler, R. S. (2006, April). *Extending American sex-typing measures to another culture and linguistic context.* Paper presented at the Gender Development Conference, San Francisco, CA.

Sheldon, A. (1992). Conflict talk: Sociolinguistic challenges to self-assertion and how young girls meet them. *Merrill-Palmer Quarterly, 38*, 95–117.

Sheldon, A. (1997). Talking power: Girls, gender enculturation and discourse. In R. Wodak (Ed.), *Gender and discourse* (pp. 225–244). Thousand Oaks, CA: Sage Publications.

Sheldon, J. P. (2004). Gender stereotypes in educational software for young children. *Sex Roles, 51*, 433–444.

Shell, R. & Eisenberg, N. (1990). The role of peers' gender in children's naturally occurring interest in toys. *International Journal of Behavioral Development, 13*, 373–388.

Shepard, R. N. & Metzler, J. (1971). Mental rotation of three-dimensional objects. *Science, 171*, 701–703.

Shepardson, D. P. & Pizzini, E. L. (1992). Gender bias in female elementary teachers' perceptions of the scientific ability of students. *Science Education, 76*, 147–153.

Sher, M. A. & Lansky, L. M. (1968). The IT Scale for Children: Effects of variations in the sex-specificity of the IT figure. *Merrill-Palmer Quarterly, 14*, 322–330.

Sherif, M., Harvey, O. J., White, B. J., Hood, W. R., & Sherif, C. W. (1954/1961). *Intergroup conflict and cooperation: The Robber's Cave experiment.* Norman, OK: University Book Exchange.

Sherman, J. D., Honegger, S. D., McGivern, J. L., & Lemke, M. (2003). *Comparative indictors of education in the United States and other G8 countries: 2002* (No. NCES 2003–026). Washington, DC: US Department of Education: Institute of Education Sciences.

Shields, S. (1975). Functionalism, Darwinism, and the psychology of women. *American Psychologist, 30*, 739–754.

Shipman, K. L., Zeman, J., Nesin, A. E., & Fitzgerald, M. (2003). Children's strategies for displaying anger and sadness: What works with whom? *Merrill-Palmer Quarterly, 49*, 100–122.

Shirley, L. J. & Campbell, A. (2000). Same-sex preference in infancy. *Psychology, Evolution and Gender, 2*, 3–18.

Sholl, M. J. (1989). The relation between horizontality and rod-and-frame and vestibular navigational performance. *Journal of Experimental Psychology: Learning, Memory, and Cognition, 15*, 110–125.

Sholl, M. J., Acacio, J. C., Makar, R. O., & Leon, C. (2000). The relation of sex and sense of direction to spatial orientation in an unfamiliar environment. *Journal of Environmental Psychology, 20*, 17–28.

Sholl, M. J. & Bartels, G. P. (2002). The role of self-to-object updating in orientation-free performance on spatial-memory tasks. *Journal of Experimental Psychology: Learning, Memory, and Cognition, 28*, 422–436.

Sigel, I. E. & Cocking, R. R. (1977). *Cognitive development from childhood to adolescence: A constructivist perspective.* New York: Holt Rinehart and Winston.

Signorella, M. L. (1987). Gender schemata: Individual differences and context effects. In L. S. Liben & M. L. Signorella (Eds.), *New directions for child development: Children's gender schemata* (pp. 23–37). San Francisco: Jossey Bass.

Signorella, M. L., Bigler, R. S., & Liben, L. S. (1993). Developmental differences in children's gender schemata about others: A meta-analytic review. *Developmental Review, 13*, 147–183.

Signorella, M. L., Bigler, R. S., & Liben, L. S. (1997). A meta-analysis of children's memories for own-sex and other-sex information. *Journal of Applied Developmental Psychology, 18*, 429–445.

Signorella, M. L. & Liben, L. S. (1984). Recall and reconstruction of gender-related pictures: Effects of attitude, task difficulty, and age. *Child Development, 55*, 393–405.

Signorella, M. L. & Liben, L. S. (1985). Assessing children's gender-related attitudes. *Psychological Documents, 15*, 7.

Signorielli, N. (2001). Television's gender role images and contribution to stereotyping: Past, present, future. In D. G. Singer & J. L. Singer (Eds.), *Handbook of children and the media* (pp. 341–358). Thousand Oaks, CA: Sage.

Signorielli, N., McLeod, D., & Healy, E. (1994). Gender stereotypes in MTV commercials: The beat goes on. *Journal of Broadcasting and Electronic Media, 38*, 91–101.

Silverman, I. (2003). Gender differences in resistance to temptation: Theories and evidence. *Developmental Review, 23*, 219–259.

Silverman, I. & Eals, M. (1992). Sex differences in spatial abilities: Evolutionary theory and data. In J. H. Barkow & L. Cosmides (Eds.), *The adapted mind: Evolutionary psychology and the generation of culture* (pp. 533–549). London: Oxford University Press.

Simpson, J. L., de la Cruz, F., Swerdloff, R. S., Samango-Sprouse, C., Skakkebaek, N. E., Graham, J. M., et al. (2003). Klinefelter syndrome: Expanding the phenotype and identifying new research directions. *Genetics in Medicine, 5*, 460–468.

Singh, K., Vaught, C., & Mitchell, E. W. (1998). Single-sex classes and academic achievement in two inner-city schools. *Journal of Negro Education, 67*, 157–167.

Sisk, C. L. & Zehr, J. L. (2005). Pubertal hormones organize the adolescent brain and behavior. *Frontiers in Neuroendocrinology, 26*, 163–174.

Skeels, H. M., Updegraff, R., Wellman, B. L., & Williams, H. M. (1938). A study of environmental stimulation: An orphanage preschool project. *University of Iowa Studies: Studies in Child Welfare, 15*.

Skoric, M. & Furnham, A. (2002). Gender role stereotyping in television advertisements: A comparative study of British and Serbian television. In S. P. Shohov (Ed.), *Advances in psychology research* (Vol. 10, pp. 123–142). Huntington, NY: Nova Science.

Skowronski, J. J. & Thompson, C. P. (1990). Reconstructing the dates of personal events: Gender differences in accuracy. *Applied Cognitive Psychology, 4*, 371–381.

Skrypnek, B. J. & Snyder, M. (1982). On the self-perpetuating nature of stereotypes about women and men. *Journal of Experimental Social Psychology, 18*, 277–291.

Skuse, D. H., James, R. S., Bishop, D. V. M., Coppins, B., Dalton, P., Aamodt-Leeper, G., et al. (1997). Evidence from Turner's syndrome of an imprinted X-linked locus affecting cognitive function. *Nature, 387*, 705–708.

Slaby, R. G. & Frey, K. S. (1975). Development of gender constancy and selective attention to same-sex models. *Child Development, 46*, 849–856.

Slaughter-Defoe, D. T., Addae, W. A., & Bell, C. (2002). Toward the future schooling of girls: Global status, issues, and prospects. *Human Development, 45*, 34–53.

Smail, P. J., Reyes, F. I., Winter, J. S. D., & Faiman, C. (1981). The fetal hormone environment and its effect on the morphogenesis of the genital system. In S. J. Kogan & E. S. E. Hafez (Eds.), *Pediatric andrology* (pp. 9–19). The Hague, Netherlands: Martinus Nijhoff.

Small, M. Y. & Morton, M. E. (1983). Spatial visualization training improves performance in organic chemistry. *Journal of College Science Teaching, 13*, 41–43.

Smith, I. M. (1948). Measuring spatial ability in school pupils. *Occupational Psychology, 22*, 150–159.

Smith, J. & Russell, G. (1984). Why do males and females differ? Children's beliefs about sex differences. *Sex Roles, 11*, 1111–1120.

Smith, P. K. (1994). The war play debate. In J. H. Goldstein (Ed.), *Toys, play, and child development* (pp. 67–84). New York: Cambridge University Press.

Smith, P. K. & Connolly, K. (1980). *The ecology of preschool behavior.* Cambridge: Cambridge University Press.

Smith, P. K. & Drew, L. M. (2002). Grandparenthood. In M. H. Bornstein (Ed.), *Handbook of parenting: Vol. 3: Being and becoming a parent* (2nd ed., pp. 141–172). Mahwah, NJ: Lawrence Erlbaum Associates.

Smith, P. K., Hunter, T., Carvalho, A. M., & Costabile, A. (1992). Children's perceptions of playfighting, playchasing and real fighting: A cross-national interview study. *Social Development, 1*, 211–229.

Smith, P. K., Smees, R., Pellegrini, A. D., & Menesini, E. (2002). Comparing pupil and teacher perceptions for playful fighting, serious fighting, and positive peer interaction. In J. L. Roopnarine (Ed.), *Conceptual, social-cognitive, and contextual issues in the fields of play* (pp. 235–245). Westport, CT: Ablex Publishing.

Smith, T. E. & Leaper, C. (2006). Self-perceived gender typicality and the peer context during adolescence. *Journal of Research on Adolescence, 16*, 91–103.

Smuts, B. (1995). The evolutionary origins of patriarchy. *Human Nature, 6*, 1–32.

Snow, M. E., Jacklin, C. N., & Maccoby, E. E. (1983). Sex-of-child differences in father-child interaction at one year of age. *Child Development, 54*, 227–232.

Snow, W. G. & Weinstock, J. (1990). Sex differences among non-brain-damaged adults on the Wechsler Adult Intelligence Scales: A review of the literature. *Journal of Clinical and Experimental Neuropsychology, 12*, 873–886.

Snyder, T. D., Dillow, S. A., & Hoffman, C. M. (2007). *Digest of education statistics, 2006* (No. NCES 2007–017). Washington, DC: U.S. Department of Education National Center for Education Statistics.

Snyder, T. D. & Tan, A. G. (2005). *Digest of education statistics, 2004* (No. NCES 2006005). Washington, DC: U.S. Department of Education National Center for Education Statistics.

Sobieraj, S. (1998). Taking control: Toy commercials and the social construction of patriarchy. In L. H. Bowker (Ed.), *Masculinities and violence* (pp. 15–28). Thousand Oaks, CA,: Sage.

Sokal, A. & Bricmont, J. (1999). *Fashionable nonsense: Postmodern intellectuals' abuse of science*. New York: Picador USA.

Solomon, G. B. & Bredemeier, B. J. L. (1999). Children's moral conceptions of gender stratification in sport. *International Journal of Sport Psychology, 30*, 350–368.

Solomon, S. E., Rothblum, E. D., & Balsam, K. F. (2005). Money, housework, sex, and conflict: Same-sex couples in civil unions, those not in civil unions, and heterosexual married siblings. *Sex Roles, 52*, 561–575.

Sommers-Flanagan, R., Sommers-Flanagan, J., & Davis, B. (1993). What's happening on music television? A gender role content analysis. *Sex Roles, 28*, 745–753.

Sorby, S. A. & Baartmans, B. J. (1996). A course for the development of 3D spatial visualization skills. *Engineering Design Graphics Journal, 60*, 13–20.

Sorby, S. A. & Baartmans, B. J. (2000). The development and assessment of a course for enhancing the 3-D spatial visualization skills of first year engineering students. *Journal of Engineering Education, 89*, 301–307.

Speiser, P. W. (2001a). Congenital adrenal hyperplasia owing to 21-hydroxylase deficiency. *Endocrinology and Metabolism Clinics of North America, 30*, 31–59.

Speiser, P. W. (Ed.). (2001b). Congenital adrenal hyperplasia. *Endocrinology and Metabolism Clinics of North America, 30*, 1–244.

Spence, J. T. (1984). Masculinity, femininity, and gender-related traits: A conceptual analysis and critique of current research. In B. A. Maher & W. B. Maher (Eds.), *Progress in experimental personality research* (Vol. 13, pp. 1–97). New York: Academic Press.

Spence, J. T. (1993). Gender-related traits and gender ideology: Evidence for a multifactorial theory. *Journal of Personality and Social Psychology, 64*, 624–635.

Spence, J. T. & Hall, S. K. (1996). Children's gender-related self-perceptions, activity preferences, and occupational stereotypes: A test of three models of gender constructs. *Sex Roles, 35*, 659–692.

Spencer, S. J., Steele, C. M., & Quinn, D. M. (1999). Stereotype threat and women's math performance. *Journal of Experimental Social Psychology, 35*, 4–28.

Sperry, R. W. (1964). The great cerebral commissure. *Scientific American, 210*, 42–52.

Spinrad, T. L., Losoya, S. H., Eisenberg, N., Fabes, R. A., Shepard, S. A., Cumberland, A., et al. (1999). The relations of parental affect and encouragement to children's moral emotions and behaviour. *Journal of Moral Education, 28*, 323–337.

Sport Canada. (1998). *Sport participation in Canada*. Ottawa, ON: Culture Statistics Program: Statistics Canada.

Springer, S. P. & Deutsch, G. (1998). *Left brain, right brain: Perspectives from cognitive neuroscience*. New York: W. H. Freeman.

Sroufe, L. A., Bennett, C., Englund, M., Urban, J., & Shulman, S. (1993). The significance of gender boundaries in preadolescence: Contemporary correlates and antecedents of boundary violation and maintenance. *Child Development, 64*, 455–466.

St. Peter, S. (1979). Jack went up the hill...but where was Jill? *Psychology of Women Quarterly, 4*, 256–260.

Stables, A. (1990). Differences between pupils from mixed and single-sex schools in their enjoyment of school subjects and in their attitudes to science and to school. *Educational Review, 42*, 221–230.

Stacey, J. & Biblarz, T. J. (2001). (How) does the sexual orientation of parents matter? *American Sociological Review, 66*, 159–183.

Stafford, R. E. (1961). Sex differences in spatial visualization as evidence of sex-linked inheritance. *Perceptual and Motor Skills, 13*, 428.

Stanley, S. M., Markman, H. J., St Peters, M., & Leber, B. D. (1995). Strengthening marriages and preventing divorce: New directions in prevention research. *Family Relations: Journal of Applied Family and Child Studies, 44*, 392–401.

Statistics, N. C. f. H. (2001). *Body measurements: Average height for men and women ages 20+.* Hyattsville, MD: U. S. Department of Health and Human Services.

Stattin, H. & Klackenberg-Larsson, I. (1991). The short- and long-term implications for parent-child relations of parents' prenatal preferences for their child's gender. *Developmental Psychology, 27*, 141–147.

Steele, C. M. (1997). A threat in the air: How stereotypes shape intellectual identity and performance. *American Psychologist, 52*, 613–629.

Steele, C. M. & Aronson, J. (1995). Stereotype threat and the intellectual test performance of African Americans. *Journal of Personality and Social Psychology, 69*, 797–811.

Steffen, V. J. & Eagly, A. H. (1985). Implicit theories about influence style: The effects of status and sex. *Personality and Social Psychology Bulletin, 11*, 191–205.

Steinbacher, R. & Gilroy, F. (1990). Sex selection technology: A prediction of its use and effect. *Journal of Psychology, 124*, 283–288.

Steinberg, L. & Morris, A. S. (2001). Adolescent development. *Annual Review of Psychology, 52*, 83–110.

Steiner, M., Dunn, E., & Born, L. (2003). Hormones and mood: From menarche to menopause and beyond. *Journal of Affective Disorders, 74*, 67–83.

Stennes, L. M., Burch, M. M., Sen, M. G., & Bauer, P. J. (2005). A Longitudinal study of gendered vocabulary and communicative action in young children. *Developmental Psychology, 41*, 75–88.

Sternglanz, S. H. & Serbin, L. A. (1974). Sex role stereotyping in children's television programs. *Developmental Psychology, 10*, 710–715.

Stetsenko, A., Little, T. D., Gordeeva, T., Grasshof, M., & Oettingen, G. (2000). Gender effects in children's beliefs about school performance: A cross-cultural study. *Child Development, 71*, 517–527.

Stevens, M., Golombok, S., Beveridge, M., & Alspac Study Team. (2002). Does father absence influence children's gender development?: Findings from a general population study of preschool children. *Parenting: Science and Practice, 2*, 47–60.

Stewart, R. B. (1983a). Sibling attachment relationships: Child-infant interaction in the strange situation. *Developmental Psychology, 19*, 192–199.

Stewart, R. B. (1983b). Sibling interaction: The role of the older child as teacher for the younger. *Merrill-Palmer Quarterly, 29*, 47–68.

Stewart, R. B. & Marvin, R. S. (1984). Sibling relations: The role of conceptual perspective-taking in the ontogeny of sibling caregiving. *Child Development, 55*, 1322–1332.

Stice, E., Spangler, D., & Agras, W. S. (2001). Exposure to media-portrayed thin-ideal images adversely affects vulnerable girls: A longitudinal experiment. *Journal of Social and Clinical Psychology, 20*, 270–288.

Stouthamer-Loeber, M. (1986). Lying as a problem behavior in children: A review. *Clinical Psychology Review, 6*, 267–289.

Straus, M. A. (1999). The controversy over domestic violence by women: A methological, theoretical, and sociology of science analysis. In X. B. Arriaga & S. Oskamp (Eds.), *Violence in intimate relationships* (pp. 17–44). Thousand Oaks, CA: Sage.

Straus, M. A. (2001). Physical aggression in the family: prevalence rates, links to non-family violence, and implications for primary prevention of societal violence. In M. Martinez (Ed.), *Prevention and control of aggression and the impact on its victims.* New York: Kluwer Academic.

Straus, M. A. & Stewart, J. H. (1999). Corporal punishment by American parents: National data on prevalence, chronicity, severity, and duration, in relation to child and family characteristics. *Clinical Child and Family Psychology Review, 2*, 55–70.

Streicher, H. W. (1974). The girls in the cartoons. *Journal of Communication, 24*, 125–129.

Strickland, C., E. & Burgess, C. (1965). G. Stanley Hall: Prophet of naturalism. In C. Strickland, E. & C. Burgess (Eds.), *Health, growth, and heredity: G. Stanley Hall on natural education* (pp. 1–26). New York: Teachers College Press.

Strough, J. & Marie Covatto, A. (2002). Context and age differences in same- and other-gender peer preferences. *Social Development, 11*, 346–361.

Stumpf, H. (1995). Gender differences in performance on tests of cognitive abilities: Experimental design issues and empirical results. *Learning and Individual Differences, 7*, 275–287.

Stumpf, H. & Jackson, D. N. (1994). Gender-related differences in cognitive abilities: Evidence from a medical school admissions testing program. *Personality and Individual Differences, 17*, 335–344.

Subrahmanyam, K. & Greenfield, P. M. (1994). Effect of video game practice on spatial skills in girls and boys. *Journal of Applied Developmental Psychology, 15*, 13–32.

Subrahmanyam, K. & Greenfield, P. M. (1998). Computer games for girls: What makes them play? In J. Cassell & H. Jenkins (Eds.), *From Barbie to Mortal Kombat: Gender and computer games* (pp. 46–71). Cambridge, MA: The MIT Press.

Subrahmanyam, K., Greenfield, P. M., Kraut, R., & Gross, E. (2001). The impact of computer use on children's and adolescents' development. *Journal of Applied Developmental Psychology, 22*, 7–30.

Subrahmanyam, K., Kraut, R., Greenfield, P. M., & Gross, E. (2001). New forms of electronic media: The impact of interactive games and the internet on cognition, socialization, and behavior. In D. G. Singer & J. L. Singer (Eds.), *Handbook of children and the media* (pp. 73–99). Thousand Oaks, CA: Sage.

Subrahmanyam, K., Smahel, D., & Greenfield, P. M. (2006). Connecting developmental constructions to the Internet : Identity presentation and sexual exploration in online teen chat rooms. *Developmental Psychology, 42*, 395–406.

Subrahmanyan, L. & Bozonie, H. (1996). Gender equity in middle school science teaching: Being "equitable" should be the goal. *Middle School Journal, 27*, 3–10.

Sulin, R. A. & Dooling, D. J. (1974). Intrusion of a thematic idea in retention of prose. *Journal of Experimental Psychology, 103*, 255–262.

Sun, L. C. & Roopnarine, J. L. (1996). Mother-infant, father-infant interaction and involvement in childcare and household labor among Taiwanese families. *Infant Behavior and Development, 19*, 121–129.

Susman, E. J., Inoff-Germain, G., Nottelmann, E. D., Loriaux, D. L., Cutler, G. B., & Chrousos, G. P. (1987). Hormones, emotional dispositions, and aggressive attributes in young adolescents. *Child Development, 58*, 1114–1134.

Susman, E. J. & Rogol, A. D. (2004). Puberty and psychological development. In R. M. Lerner & L. Steinberg (Eds.), *Handbook of adolescent psychology* (pp. 15–44). Hoboken, NJ: Wiley.

Sutherland, M. B. (1999). Gender equity in success at school. *International Review of Education, 45*, 431–443.

Sutton-Smith, B. (1986). *Toys as culture.* New York: Gardner Press.

Sutton-Smith, B. (1988). War toys and childhood aggression. *Play and Culture, 1*, 57–69.

Swetkis, D., Gilroy, F. D., & Steinbacher, R. (2002). Firstborn preference and attitudes toward using sex selection technology. *Journal of Genetic Psychology, 163*, 228–238.

Symons, C. S. & Johnson, B. T. (1997). The self-reference effect in memory: A meta-analysis. *Psychological Bulletin, 121*, 371–394.

Tabs, E. D. (2002). *The gender and racial/ethnic composition of postsecondary instructional faculty and staff, 1992 -1998* (No. NCES 2002 - 160). Washington, DC: U.S. Department of Education National Center for Education Statistics.

Tajfel, H., Billig, M. G., Bundy, R. P., & Flament, C. (1971). Social categorization and intergroup behaviour. *European Journal of Social Psychology, 1*, 149–178.

Tajfel, H. & Turner, J. C. (1986). The social identity theory of intergroup behavior. In S. Worchel & W. G. Austin (Eds.), *Psychology of intergroup relations* (2nd ed., pp. 7–24). Chicago: Nelson-Hall.

Tamres, L. K., Janicki, D., & Helgeson, V. S. (2002). Sex differences in coping behavior: A meta-analytic review and an examination of relative coping. *Personality and Social Psychology Review, 6*, 2–30.

Tannen, D. (1994a). *Gender and discourse.* New York: Oxford University Press.

Tannen, D. (1994b). *Talking from 9 to 5.* New York: Morrow.

Tanner, J. M. (1978). *Foetus into man: Physical growth from conception to maturity.* Cambridge, MA: Harvard University Press.

Taranger, J., Bruning, B., Claesson, I., Karlberg, P., Landstrom, T., & Lindstrom, B. (1976). Skeletal development from birth to 7 years. *Acta Paediatrica Scandinavica. Supplementum*, 98–108.

Tasker, F. L. & Golombok, S. (1997). *Growing up in a lesbian family: Effects on child development.* New York: The Guilford Press.

Tavris, C. & Wade, C. (1984). *The longest war: Sex differences in perspective.* New York: Harcourt Brace Jovanovich.

Taylor, M. G. (1996). The development of children's beliefs about social and biological aspects of gender differences. *Child Development, 67*, 1555–1571.

Taylor, S. E., Klein, L. C., Lewis, B. P., Gruenewald, T. L., Gurung, R. A. R., & Updegraff, J. A. (2000). Biobehavioral responses to stress in females: Tend-and-befriend, not fight-or-flight. *Psychological Review, 107*, 411–429.

Teichner, G., Ames, E. W., & Kerig, P. K. (1997). The relation of infant crying and the sex of the infant to parents' perceptions of the infant and themselves. *Psychology: A Journal of Human Behavior, 34*, 59–60.

Tenenbaum, H. R. & Leaper, C. (2003). Parent-child conversations about science: The socialization of gender inequities? *Developmental Psychology, 39*, 34–47.

Tenenbaum, H. R., Snow, C. E., Roach, K. A., & Kurland, B. (2005). Talking and reading science: Longitudinal data on sex differences in mother–child conversations in low-income families. *Journal of Applied Developmental Psychology, 26*, 1–19.

Terman, L. M., Johnson, W., Kuznets, G., & McNemar, O. (1946). Psychological sex differences. In L. Carmichael (Ed.), *Manual of child psychology* (pp. 954–1000). New York: Wiley.

Terman, L. M. & Miles, C. C. (1936). *Sex and personality: studies in masculinity and femininity*. New York: McGraw-Hill.

Terman, L. M. & Tyler, L. E. (1954). Psychological sex differences. In L. Carmichael (Ed.), *Manual of Child Psychology* (2nd ed., pp. 1064–1114). New York: Wiley.

The Association of Medical Colleges. (2003). *Applicants to U.S. medical schools increase: Women the majority for the first time*. Washington, DC: Author.

Thomas, H. & Jamison, W. (1975). On the acquisition of understanding that still water is horizontal. *Merrill-Palmer Quarterly, 21*, 31–44.

Thomas, H., Jamison, W., & Hummel, D. D. (1973). Observation is insufficient for discovering that the surface of still water is invariantly horizontal. *Science, 181*, 173–174.

Thomas, J. R. & French, K. E. (1985). Gender differences across age in motor performance: A meta-analysis. *Psychological Bulletin, 98*, 260–282.

Thompson, C. (1942). Cultural pressures in the psychology of women. *Psychiatry, 5*, 331–339.

Thompson, C. (1943). "Penis envy" in women. *Psychiatry: Journal for the Study of Interpersonal Processes, 6*, 123–125.

Thompson, C. (1953). Towards a psychology of women. *Pastoral Psychology, 4*, 29–38.

Thompson, C. (1971). *On women*. New York: A Mentor Book from New American Library.

Thompson, D. L. (2001). Deconstructing Harry: Casting a critical eye on the witches and wizards of Hogwarts. In S. Lehr (Ed.), *Beauty, brains, and brawn: The construction of gender in children's literature* (pp. 42–50). Portsmouth, NH: Heinemann.

Thompson, H. B. (1903). *The mental traits of sex*. Chicago: University of Chicago Press.

Thompson, K. M. & Haninger, K. (2001). Violence in E-rated video games. *JAMA: Journal of the American Medical Association, 286*, 591–598.

Thompson, R. B. & Moore, K. (2000). Collaborative speech in dyadic problem solving: Evidence for preschool gender differences in early pragmatic development. *Journal of Language and Social Psychology, 19*, 248–255.

Thompson, S. K. (1975). Gender labels and early sex role development. *Child Development, 46*, 339–347.

Thompson, T. L. & Zerbinos, E. (1995). Gender roles in animated cartoons: Has the picture changed in 20 years? *Sex Roles, 32*, 651–673.

Thompson, T. L. & Zerbinos, E. (1997). Television cartoons: Do children notice it's a boy's world? *Sex Roles, 37*, 415–432.

Thomsen, S. R., McCoy, J. K., & Williams, M. (2001). Internalizing the impossible: Anorexic outpatients' experiences with women's beauty and fashion magazines. *Eating Disorders: The Journal of Treatment and Prevention, 9*, 49–64.

Thomsen, S. R., Weber, M. M., & Brown, L. B. (2002). The relationship between reading beauty and fashion magazines and the use of pathogenic dieting methods among adolescent females. *Adolescence, 37*, 1–18.

Thorne, B. (1993). *Gender play: Girls and boys in school*. New Brunswick, NJ: Rutgers University Press.

Thorne, B. & Luria, Z. (1986). Sexuality and gender in children's daily worlds. *Social Problems, 33*, 176–190.

Thornton, A. & Young-DeMarco, L. (2001). Four decades of trends in attitudes toward family issues in the United States: The 1960s through the 1990s. *Journal of Marriage and the Family, 63*, 1009–1037.

Tiedemann, J. (2000). Gender-related beliefs of teachers in elementary school mathematics. *Educational Studies in Mathematics, 41*, 191–207.

Tilghman, S. M. (1999). The sins of the fathers and mothers: Genomic imprinting in mammalian development. *Cell, 96*, 185–193.

Titus, J. J. (1993). Gender messages in education foundation textbooks. *Journal of Teacher Education, 44*, 38–44.

Tomada, G. & Schneider, B. H. (1997). Relational aggression, gender, and peer acceptance: Invariance across culture, stability over time, and concordance among informants. *Developmental Psychology, 33*, 601–609.

Travis, L. L. & Sigman, M. D. (2000). A developmental approach to autism. In A. J. Sameroff & M. Lewis (Eds.), *Handbook of developmental psychopathology* (2nd ed., pp. 641–655). New York: Kluwer Academic/Plenum.

Trecker, J. L. (1971). Women in U.S. history high school textbooks. *Social Education, 35*, 249–260.

Trent, L. M. Y., Cooney, G., Russell, G., & Warton, P. M. (1996). Significant others' contribution to early adolescents' perceptions of their competence. *British Journal of Educational Psychology, 66*, 95–107.

Trivers, R. L. (1972). Parental investment and sexual selection. In B. Campbell (Ed.), *Sexual selection and the descent of man, 1871–1971* (pp. 136–179). Chicago: Aldine-Atherton.

Trusty, J. & Dooley-Dickey, K. (1993). Alienation from school: An exploratory analysis of elementary and middle school students' perceptions. *Journal of Research and Development in Education, 26*, 232–242.

Tsai, L. Y. (1998). *Pervasive developmental disorders*. Washington, DC: National Information Center for Children and Youth with Disabilities.

Tschantz, J. & Markowitz, J. (2003). *Gender and special education: Current state data collection*. Alexandria, VA: National Association of State Directors of Special Education.

Tsouroufli, M. (2002). Gender and teachers' classroom practice in a secondary school in Greece. *Gender and Education, 14*, 135–147.

Tucker, C. J., McHale, S. M., & Crouter, A. C. (2003). Dimensions of mothers' and fathers' differential treatment of siblings: Links with adolescents' sex-typed personal qualities. *Family Relations, 52*, 82–89.

Turiel, E. (1998). The development of morality. In N. Eisenberg (Ed.), *Handbook of child psychology: Vol. 3. Social, emotional, and personality development.* (5th ed., pp. 863–932). New York: Wiley.

Turner, C. W. & Goldsmith, D. (1976). Effects of toy guns and airplanes on children's antisocial free play behavior. *Journal of Experimental Child Psychology, 21*, 303–315.

Turner, P. J., Gervai, J., & Hinde, R. A. (1993). Gender-typing in young children: Preferences, behaviour and cultural differences. *British Journal of Developmental Psychology, 11*, 323–342.

Turner-Bowker, D. M. (1996). Gender stereotyped descriptors in children's picture books: Does "curious Jane" exist in the literature? *Sex Roles, 35*, 461–488.

Twenge, J. M. (1997a). Attitudes toward women, 1970–1995: A meta-analysis. *Psychology of Women Quarterly, 21*, 35–51.

Twenge, J. M. (1997b). Changes in masculine and feminine traits over time: A meta-analysis. *Sex Roles, 36*, 305–325.

Twenge, J. M. (1999). Mapping gender: The multifactorial approach and the organization of gender-related attributes. *Psychology of Women Quarterly, 23*, 485–502.

Twenge, J. M. (2001). Changes in women's assertiveness in response to status and roles: A cross-temporal meta-analysis, 1931–1993. *Journal of Personality and Social Psychology, 81*, 133–145.

Twenge, J. M. & Nolen-Hoeksema, S. (2002). Age, gender, race, socioeconomic status, and birth cohort difference on the children's depression inventory: A meta-analysis. *Journal of Abnormal Psychology, 111*, 578–588.

Twenge, J. M. & Zucker, A. N. (1999). What is a feminist? Evaluations and stereotypes in closed- and open-ended responses. *Psychology of Women Quarterly, 23*, 591–605.

Tyrka, A. R., Graber, J. A., & Brooks-Gunn, J. (2000). The development of disordered eating: Correlates and predictors of eating problems in the context of adolescence. In A. J. Sameroff & M. Lewis (Eds.), *Handbook of developmental psychopathology* (2nd ed., pp. 607–624). New York: Kluwer Academic/Plenum.

Tyson, P. & Tyson, R. L. (1990). *Psychoanalytic theories of development: An integration*. New Haven, CT.: Yale University Press.

U.S. Department of Education. (2006). *The condition of education 2006* (No. NCES 2006–071). Washington, DC: National Center for Education Statistics.

U.S. Department of Labor. (2005). Highlights of women's earnings in 2004. *(Bureau of Labor Statistics Report 987)*.

U.S. Department of Labor. (2006). Highlights of women's earnings in 2005. *(Bureau of Labor Statistics Report 995)*.

Udry, J. R. (1994). The nature of gender. *Demography, 31*, 561–573.

Udry, J. R. (2000). Biological limits of gender construction. *American Sociological Review, 65*, 443–457.

Udry, J. R., Morris, N. M., & Kovenock, J. (1995). Androgen effects on women's gendered behavior. *Journal of Biosocial Science, 27*, 359–368.

Uhlenberg, P. & Hammill, B. G. (1998). Frequency of grandparent contact with grandchild sets: Six factors that make a difference. *Gerontologist, 38*, 276–285.

Ullian, D. Z. (1976). The development of conceptions of masculinity and femininity. In *Exploring sex differences*. Oxford, England: Academic Press.

Underwood, M. K. (2003). *Social aggression among girls*. New York: The Guilford Press.

Underwood, M. K., Galen, B. R., & Paquette, J. A. (2001). Top ten challenges for understanding gender and aggression in children: Why can't we all just get along? *Social Development, 10*, 248–266.

Underwood, M. K., Hurley, J. C., Johanson, C. A., & Mosley, J. E. (1999). An experimental, observational investigation of children's responses to peer provocation: Developmental and gender differences in middle childhood. *Child Development, 70*, 1428–1446.

Underwood, M. K., Schockner, A. E., & Hurley, J. C. (2001). Children's responses to same- and other-gender peers: An experimental investigation with 8-, 10-, and 12-year-olds. *Developmental Psychology, 37*, 362–372.

Underwood, M. K., Scott, B. L., Galperin, M. B., Bjornstad, G. J., & Sexton, A. M. (2004). An observational study of social exclusion under varied conditions: Gender and developmental differences. *Child Development, 75*, 1538–1555.

Ungar, S. B. (1982). The sex-typing of adult and child behavior in toy sales. *Sex Roles, 8*, 251–260.

Unger, R. K. (1979). Toward a redefinition of sex and gender. *American Psychologist, 34*, 1085–1094.

Unger, R. K. (1998). *Resisting gender: Twenty-five years of feminist psychology*. Thousand Oaks, CA: Sage.

UNICEF. (2004). *UNICEF global database on child malnutrition*. Retrieved September 17, 2004, from: http://www.childinfo.org/eddb/malnutrition/index.htm

United Nations. (2000). *The world's women 2000: Trends and statistics*. New York: United Nations Publications.

University of California Museum of Paleontology. (2006). *Understanding evolution for teachers*. Retrieved January 18, 2008, from: http://evolution.berkeley. edu/evosite/evo101/IIIENaturalSelection.shtml.

Updegraff, K. A., McHale, S. M., & Crouter, A. C. (1996). Gender roles in marriage: What do they mean for girls' and boys' school achievement? *Journal of Youth and Adolescence, 25*, 73–88.

Updegraff, K. A., McHale, S. M., & Crouter, A. C. (2000). Adolescents' sex-typed friendship experiences: Does having a sister versus a brother matter? *Child Development, 71*, 1597–1610.

Updegraff, K. A., McHale, S. M., Crouter, A. C., & Kupanoff, K. (2001). Parents' involvement in adolescents' peer relationships: A comparison of mothers' and fathers' roles. *Journal of Marriage and the Family, 63*, 655–668.

Uray, N. & Burnaz, S. (2003). An analysis of the portrayal of gender roles in Turkish television advertisements. *Sex Roles, 48*, 77–87.

Urberg, K. A. (1982). The development of the concepts of masculinity and femininity in young children. *Sex Roles, 8*, 659–668.

Van Balen, F. (2005). The choice for sons or daughters. *Journal of Psychosomatic Obstetrics and Gynecology, 26*, 229–320.

Vandenberg, S. G. & Kuse, A. R. (1978). Mental rotations, a group test of three-dimensional spatial visualization. *Perceptual and Motor Skills, 47*, 599–604.

Vandenbergh, J. G. (1983). Pheromonal regulation of puberty. In J. G. Vandenbergh (Ed.), *Pheromones and reproduction in mammals* (pp. 95–112). New York: Academic.

Varney, W. (2000). Playing with "war fare". *Peace Review, 12*, 385–391.

Vasey, M. W. & Ollendick, T. H. (2000). Anxiety. In A. J. Sameroff & M. Lewis (Eds.), *Handbook of developmental psychopathology* (2nd ed., pp. 511–529). New York: Kluwer Academic/Plenum.

Vederhus, L. & Krekling, S. (1996). Sex differences in visual spatial ability in 9-year-old children. *Intelligence, 23*, 33–43.

Veniegas, R. C. & Conley, T. D. (2000). Biological research on women's sexual orientations: Evaluating the scientific evidence. *Journal of Social Issues, 56*, 267–282.

Vezeau, C., Bouffard, T., & Chouinard, R. (2000). The impact of single-sex versus coeducational school environment on girls' general attitudes, self-perceptions and performance in mathematics. *Journal of Research and Development in Education, 34*, 50–59.

Vilhjalmsson, R. & Kristjansdottir, G. (2003). Gender differences in physical activity in older children and adolescents: The central role of organized sport. *Social Science and Medicine, 56*, 363–374.

Vingerhoets, A., Cornelius, R. R., Van Heck, G. L., & Becht, M. C. (2000). Adult crying: A model and review of the literature. *Review of General Psychology, 4*, 354–377.

Vingerhoets, A. & Scheirs, J. (2000). Sex differences in crying: Empirical findings and possible explanations. In A. H. Fischer (Ed.), *Gender and emotion: Social psychological perspectives* (pp. 143–165). New York: Cambridge University Press.

Voyer, D. (1996). On the magnitude of laterality effects and sex differences in functional lateralities. *Laterality, 1*, 51–83.

Voyer, D., Voyer, S., & Bryden, M. P. (1995). Magnitude of sex differences in spatial abilities: A meta-analysis and consideration of critical variables. *Psychological Bulletin, 117*, 250–270.

Waber, B. (1973). *Lyle the crocodile*. New York: Houghton Mifflin.

Wade, C. & Tavris, C. (1999). Gender and culture. In L. A. Peplau, S. C. DeBro, R. C. Veniegas, & P. L. Taylor (Eds.), *Gender culture and ethnicity: Current research about women and men* (pp. 15–22). Mountain View, CA: Mayfield.

Wager, T. D., Phan, K. L., Liberzon, I., & Taylor, S. F. (2003). Valence, gender, and lateralization of functional brain anatomy in emotion: A meta-analysis of findings from neuroimaging. *NeuroImage, 19*, 513–531.

Wagner, M. E., Schubert, H. J. P., & Schubert, D. S. P. (1993). Sex-of-sibling effects: Part I. Gender role, intelligence, achievement, and creativity. In H. W. Reese (Ed.), *Advances in child development and behavior* (Vol. 24, pp. 181–214). San Diego, CA: Academic Press.

Wainright, J. L. & Patterson, C. J. (2008). Peer relations among adolescents with female same-sex parents. *Developmental Psychology, 44*, 117–126.

Walker, L. J. (1984). Sex differences in the development of moral reasoning: A critical review. *Child Development, 55*, 677–691.

Walker, L. J. (1986). Sex differences in the development of moral reasoning: A rejoinder to Baumrind. *Child Development, 57*, 522–526.

Walker, S. (2005). Gender differences in the relationship between young children's peer-related social competence and individual differences in theory of mind. *Journal of Genetic Psychology, 166*, 297–312.

Walker, S., Irving, K., & Berthelsen, D. (2002). Gender influences on preschool children's social problem-solving strategies. *Journal of Genetic Psychology, 163*, 197–210.

Wallen, K. (1996). Nature needs nurture: The interaction of hormonal and social influences on the development of behavioral sex differences in rhesus monkeys. *Hormones and Behavior, 30*, 364–378.

Wallen, K. (2005). Hormonal influences on sexually differentiated behavior in nonhuman primates. *Frontiers in Neuroendocrinology, 26*, 7–26.

Wallen, K. & Baum, M. J. (2002). Masculinization and defeminization in altricial and precocial mammals: Comparative aspects of steroid hormone action. In D. W. Pfaff, A. P. Arnold, A. M. Etgen, S. E. Fahrbach, & R. T. Rubin (Eds.), *Hormones, brain and behavior* (Vol. 4, pp. 385–423). New York: Academic Press.

Walsh, M., Hickey, C., & Duffy, J. (1999). Influence of item content and stereotype situation on gender differences in mathematical problem solving. *Sex Roles, 41*, 219–240.

Wang, J., Horlick, M., Thornton, J. C., Levine, L. S., Heymsfield, S. B., & Pierson, R. N. J. (1999). Correlations between skeletal muscle mass and bone mass in children 6–18 years: Influences of sex, ethnicity, and pubertal status. *Growth, Development, and Aging, 63*, 99–109.

Ward, L. M. & Friedman, K. (2006). Using TV as a guide: Associations between television viewing and adolescents' sexual attitudes and behavior. *Journal of Research on Adolescence, 16*, 133–156.

Ward, S. L., Newcombe, N., & Overton, W. F. (1986). Turn left at the church, or three miles north: A study of direction giving and sex differences. *Environment and Behavior, 18*, 192–213.

Warrington, M. & Younger, M. (2000). The other side of the gender gap. *Gender and Education, 12*, 493–508.

Warrington, M. & Younger, M. (2001). Single-sex classes and equal opportunities for girls and boys: Perspectives through time from a mixed comprehensive school in England. *Oxford Review of Education, 27*, 339–356.

Wason-Ellam, L. (1997). If only I was like Barbie. *Language Arts, 74*, 430–437.

Waters, P. L. & Cheek, J. M. (1999). Personality development. In V. J. Derlega, B. A. Winstead, & W. H. Jones (Eds.), *Personality: Contemporary theory and research* (2nd ed., pp. 126–161). Chicago: Nelson Hall.

Watson, C. M., Quatman, T., & Edler, E. (2002). Career aspirations of adolescent girls: Effects of achievement level, grade, and single-sex school environment. *Sex Roles, 46*, 323–335.

Watson, J. B. (1913). Psychology as the behaviorist views it. *Psychological Review, 20*, 158–177.

Watson, M. W. & Peng, Y. (1992). The relation between toy gun play and children's aggressive behavior. *Early Education and Development, 3*, 370–389.

Weasel, J. (2001, February 4). Son's antics show he's just 'all boy'. *Fort Wayne Journal Gazette*, p. 3.

Wedell, A., Thilén, A., Ritzén, E. M., Stengler, B., & Luthman, H. (1994). Mutational spectrum of the steroid 21-hydroxylase gene in Sweden: Implications for genetic diagnosis and association with disease manifestation. *Journal of Clinical Endocrinology and Metabolism, 78*, 1145–1152.

Wehren, A. & De Lisi, R. (1983). The development of gender understanding: Judgments and explanations. *Child Development, 54*, 1568–1578.

Weichold, K., Silbereisen, R. K., & Schmitt-Rodermund, E. (2003). Short-and long-term consequences of early versus late physical maturation in adolescents. In C. Hayward (Ed.), *Puberty and psychopathology* (pp. 241–276). Cambridge, MA: Cambridge University Press.

Weinberg, M. K., Tronick, E. Z., Cohn, J. F., & Olson, K. L. (1999). Gender differences in emotional expressivity and self-regulation during early infancy. *Developmental Psychology, 35*, 175–188.

Weinberg, R., Tenenbaum, G., McKenzie, A., Jackson, S., Anshel, M., Grove, R., et al. (2000). Motivation for youth participation in sport and physical activity: Relationships to culture, self-reported activity levels, and gender. *International Journal of Sport Psychology, 31*, 321–346.

Weinberger, J. (1996). A longitudinal study of children's early literacy experiences at home and later literacy development at home and school. *Journal of Research in Reading, 19*, 14–24.

Weinburgh, M. (1995). Gender differences in student attitudes toward science: A meta-analysis of the literature from 1970 to 1991. *Journal of Research in Science Teaching, 32*, 387–398.

Weinraub, M., Clemens, L. P., Sockloff, A., Ethridge, T., Gracely, E., & Myers, B. (1984). The development of sex role stereotypes in the third year: Relationships to gender labeling, gender identity, sex-typed toy preference, and family characteristics. *Child Development, 55*, 1493–1503.

Weinraub, M., Horvath, D. L., & Gringlas, M. B. (2002). Single parenthood. In M. H. Bornstein (Ed.), *Handbook of parenting: Vol. 3: Being and becoming a parent* (2nd ed., pp. 109–140). Mahwah, NJ: Lawrence Erlbaum Associates.

Weisner, T. S. & Wilson-Mitchell, J. E. (1990). Nonconventional family life-styles and sex typing in six-year-olds. *Child Development, 61*, 1915–1933.

Weitzman, L. J., Eifler, D., Hokada, E., & Ross, C. (1972). Sex-role socialization in picture books for preschool children. *American Journal of Sociology, 77*, 1125–1150.

Weitzman, L. J. & Rizzo, D. (1975). Sex bias in textbooks. *Today's Education, 64*, 49–52.

Welch, R. L., Huston-Stein, A., Wright, J. C., & Plethal, R. (1979). Subtle sex-role cues in children's commercials. *Journal of Communication, 29*, 202–209.

Wellman, B. L. (1933). Sex differences. In C. Murchison (Ed.), *A handbook of child psychology* (pp. 626–649). Worcester, MA: Clark University Press.

Wellman, B. L. & Skeels, H. M. (1938). Decreases in IQ of children under an unfavorable environment. *Psychological Bulletin, 35*, 715.

Wellman, H. M., Cross, D., & Watson, J. (2001). Meta-analysis of theory-of-mind development: The truth about false belief. *Child Development, 72*, 655–684.

Welty, E. (1982). *Delta wedding*. London: Virago Press.

Wen, X. (1993). Effect of son preference and population policy on sex ratios at birth in two provinces of China. *Journal of Biosocial Science, 25*, 509–521.

Westen, D. (1990). Psychoanalytic approaches to personality. In L. A. Pervin (Ed.), *Handbook of personality: Theory and research* (pp. 21–65). New York: The Guilford Press.

Wheaton, B. (2000). "New lads"? Masculinities and the "new sport" participant. *Men and Masculinities, 2*, 434–456.

Whissell, C. M. (1996). Predicting the size and direction of sex differences in measures of emotion and personality. *Genetic, Social, and General Psychology Monographs, 122*, 253–284.

White, S. H. (1992). G. Stanley Hall: From philosophy to developmental psychology. *Developmental Psychology, 28*, 25–34.

Whiteley, P. (1996). The gender balance of physics textbooks: Caribbean and British books, 1985–91. *Physics Education, 31*, 169–174.

Whitley, B. E., Jr. (1997). Gender differences in computer-related attitudes and behavior: A meta-analysis. *Computers in Human Behavior, 13*, 1–22.

Wigfield, A., Battle, A., Keller, L. B., & Eccles, J. S. (2002). Sex differences in motivation, self-concept, career aspiration, and career choice: Implications for cognitive development. In A. McGillicuddy-De Lisi & R. De Lisi (Eds.), *Biology, society, and behavior: The development of sex differences in cognition. Advances in applied developmental psychology*, (Vol. 21, pp. 93–124). Westport, CT: Ablex Publishing.

Wigfield, A. & Eccles, J. S. (1994). Children's competence beliefs, achievement values, and general self-esteem: Change across elementary and middle school. *Journal of Early Adolescence, 14*, 107–138.

Wigfield, A., Eccles, J. S., Mac Iver, D., Reuman, D. A., & Midgley, C. (1991). Transitions during early adolescence: Changes in children's domain-specific self-perceptions and general self-esteem across the transition to junior high school. *Developmental Psychology, 27*, 552–565.

Wild, H. A., Barrett, S. E., Spence, M. J., O'Toole, A. J., Cheng, Y. D., & Brooke, J. (2000). Recognition and sex categorization of adults' and children's faces: Examining performance in absence of sex-stereotyped cues. *Journal of Experimental Child Psychology, 77*, 269–291.

Wilgenbusch, T. & Merrell, K. W. (1999). Gender differences in self-concept among children and adolescents: A meta-analysis of multidimensional studies. *School Psychology Quarterly, 14*, 101–120.

Wilkinson, S. (1999). Focus groups: A feminist method. *Psychology of Women Quarterly, 23*, 221–244.

Wilkinson, S. (2001). Theoretical perspectives on women and gender. In R. K. Unger (Ed.), *Handbook of the psychology of women and gender* (pp. 17–28). New York: Wiley.

Willard, H. F. (2000). The sex chromosomes and X chromosome inactivation. In C. R. Scriver, A. L. Beaudet, W. S. Sly, D. Valle, B. Childs, & B. Vogelstein (Eds.), *The metabolic and molecular bases of inherited disease*. New York: McGraw-Hill.

Willemsen, T. M. (1998). Widening the gender gap: Teenage magazines for girls and boys. *Sex Roles, 38*, 851–861.

Williams, C. L. (2002). Hormones and cognition in nonhuman animals. In J. B. Becker, S. M. Breedlove, D. Crews, & M. M. McCarthy (Eds.), *Behavioral endocrinology* (pp. 527–577). Cambridge, MA: MIT Press.

Williams, C. L., Barnett, A. M., & Meck, W. H. (1990). Organizational effects of early gonadal secretions on sexual differentiation in spatial memory. *Behavioral Neuroscience, 104*, 84–97.

Williams, C. L. & Meck, W. H. (1991). The organizational effects of gonadal steroids on sexually dimorphic spatial ability. *Psychoneuroendocrinology*. Special Issue: Neuroendocrine effects on brain development and cognition, *16*, 155–176.

Williams, J. E., Bennett, S. M., & Best, D. L. (1975). Awareness and expression of sex stereotypes in young children. *Developmental Psychology, 11*, 635–642.

Williams, J. E. & Best, D. L. (1990). *Measuring sex stereotypes: A multination study* (Rev. ed.). Thousand Oaks, CA: Sage.

Williams, J. E. & Morland, J. K. (1976). *Race, color, and the young child*. Chapel Hill, NC: University of North Carolina Press.

Williams, J. E., Satterwhite, R. C., & Best, D. L. (1999). Pancultural gender stereotypes revisited: The five factor model. *Sex Roles, 40*, 513–525.

Williams, S., Connolly, J., & Segal, Z. V. (2001). Intimacy in relationships and cognitive vulnerability to depression in adolescent girls. *Cognitive Therapy and Research, 25*, 477–496.

Williams, S. W. & Blunk, E. M. (2003). Sex differences in infant-mother attachment. *Psychological Reports, 92*, 84–88.

Williams, T. J., Pepitone, M. E., Christensen, S. E., Cooke, B. M., Huberman, A. D., Breedlove, N. J., et al. (2000). Finger-length ratios and sexual orientation. *Nature, 404*, 455–456.

Williams, T. M. (1985). *The impact of television: A natural experiment in three communities*. New York: Academic Press.

Williamson, N. E. (1976). Sex preferences, sex control, and the status of women. *Signs, 1*, 847–862.

Willoughby, T. (2008). A short-term longitudinal study of Internet and computer game use by adolescent boys and girls: Prevalence, frequency of use, and psychosocial predictors. *Developmental Psychology, 44*, 195–204.

Wills, R., Kilpatrick, S., & Hutton, B. (2006). Single-sex classes in co-educational schools. *British Journal of Sociology of Education, 27*, 277–291.

Wilson, B. J., Smith, S. L., Potter, W. J., Kunkel, D., Linz, D., Colvin, C. M., et al. (2002). Violence in children's television programming: Assessing the risks. *Journal of Communication, 52*, 5–35.

Wilson, M. I. & Daly, M. (1996). Male sexual proprietariness and violence against wives. *Current Directions in Psychological Science, 5*, 2–7.

Winkvist, A. & Akhtar, H. Z. (2000). God should give daughters to rich families only: Attitudes towards childbearing among low-income women in Punjab, Pakistan. *Social Science and Medicine, 51*, 73–81.

Winstead, B. A., Derlega, V. J., & Unger, R. K. (1999). Sex and gender. In V. J. Derlega, B. A. Winstead, & W. H. Jones (Eds.), *Personality: Contemporary theory and research* (pp. 257–281). Chicago: Nelson-Hall.

Wintre, M. G., Polivy, J., & Murray, M. A. (1990). Self-predictions of emotional response patterns: Age, sex, and situational determinants. *Child Development, 61*, 1124–1133.

Wisniewski, A. B., Migeon, C. J., Meyer-Bahlburg, H. F. L., Gearhart, J. P., Berkovitz, G. D., Brown, T. R., et al. (2000). Complete androgen insensitivity syndrome: Long-term medical, surgical, and psychosexual outcome. *Journal of Clinical Endocrinology and Metabolism, 85*, 2664–2669.

Witelson, S. F., Glezer, I. I., & Kigar, D. L. (1995). Women have greater density of neurons in posterior temporal cortex. *Journal of Neuroscience, 15*, 3418–3428.

Witkin, H. A. (1949). Sex differences in perception. *Transactions of the New York Academy of Sciences, 12*, 22–26.

Witkin, H. A. & Goodenough, D. R. (1981). *Cognitive styles: Essence and origins*. New York: International Universities Press.

Witt, S. D. (1996). Traditional or androgynous: An analysis to determine gender role orientation of basal readers. *Child Study Journal, 26*, 303–318.

Wizemann, T. M. & Pardue, M.-L. (Eds.). (2001). *Exploring the biological contributions to human health: Does sex matter?* Washington, DC: National Academy Press.

Wolf, T. M. (1973). Effects of live modeled sex-inappropriate play behavior in a naturalistic setting. *Developmental Psychology, 9*, 120–123.

Wood, W. & Eagly, A. H. (2002). A cross-cultural analysis of the behavior of women and men: Implications for the origins of sex differences. *Psychological Bulletin, 128*, 699–727.

Woodward, L. J., Fergusson, D. M., & Horwood, L. J. (1999). Effects of single-sex and coeducational secondary schooling on children's academic achievement. *Australian Journal of Education, 43*, 142–156.

Woolley, C. S. (1998). Estrogen-mediated structural and functional synaptic plasticity in the female rat hippocampus. *Hormones and Behavior, 34*, 140–148.

Woolley, H. T. (1910). Psychological literature: A review of the recent literature on the psychology of sex. *Psychological Bulletin, 7*, 335–342.

Woolley, H. T. (1914). The psychology of sex. *Psychological Bulletin, 11*, 353–379.

Woolley, H. T. (1915). A new scale of mental and physical measurements for adolescents. *Journal of Educational Psychology, 6*, 521–550.

Woolley, H. T. & Fisher, C. R. (1914). Mental and physical traits of working children. *Psychological Monographs, 18*, 247.

Wooten, B. H. (1997). Gender differences in occupational employment. *Monthly Labor Review, 120*, 15–24.

Worthy, J., Moorman, M., & Turner, M. (1999). What Johnny likes to read is hard to find in school. *Reading Research Quarterly, 34*, 12–27.

Wright, J. C., Huston, A. C., Vandewater, E. A., Bickham, D. S., Scantlin, R. M., Kotler, J. A., et al. (2001). American children's use of electronic media in 1997: A national survey. *Journal of Applied Developmental Psychology, 22*, 31–47.

Wright, P. H. (1998). Toward an expanded orientation to the study of sex differences in friendship. In D. J. Canary & K. Dindia (Eds.), *Sex differences and similarities in communication: Critical essays and empirical investigations of sex and gender in interaction.* (pp. 41–63). Mahwah, NJ: Lawrence Erlbaum Associates.

Wu, T., Mendola, P., & Buck, G. M. (2002). Ethnic differences in the presence of secondary sex characteristics and menarche among US girls: the Third National Health and Nutrition Examination Survey, 1988–1994. *Pediatrics, 110*, 752–757.

Xie, H., Li, Y., Boucher, S. M., Hutchins, B. C., & Cairns, B. D. (2006). What makes a girl (or a boy) popular (or unpopular)? African American children's perceptions and developmental differences. *Developmental Psychology, 42*, 599–612.

Yanowitz, K. L. & Weathers, K. J. (2004). Do boys and girls act differently in the classroom? A content analysis of student characters in educational psychology textbooks. *Sex Roles, 51*, 101–107.

Yelland, N. (1998). *Gender in early childhood.* New York: Taylor & Francis/Routledge.

Yelland, N. & Grieshaber, S. (1998). Blurring the edges. In N. Yelland (Ed.), *Gender in early childhood* (pp. 1–11). Florence, KY: Taylor & Francis/Routledge.

Yeung, W. J., Sandberg, J. F., Davis-Kean, P. E., & Hofferth, S. L. (2001). Children's time with fathers in intact families. *Journal of Marriage and the Family, 63*, 136–154.

Yoder, J. D. & Berendsen, L. L. (2001). "Outsider within" the firehouse: African American and White women firefighters. *Psychology of Women Quarterly, 25*, 27–36.

Yogman, M. W. (1981). Games fathers and mothers play with their infants. *Infant Mental Health Journal, 2*, 241–248.

Young, A. (2000). *Women who become men.* New York: Berg.

Younger, B. A. & Fearing, D. D. (1999). Parsing items into separate categories: Developmental change in infant categorization. *Child Development, 70*, 291–303.

Younger, M. & Warrington, M. (1996). Differential achievement of girls and boys at GCSE: Some observations from the perspective of one school. *British Journal of Sociology of Education, 17*, 299–313.

Younger, M. & Warrington, M. (2002). Single-sex teaching in a co-educational comprehensive school in England: An evaluation based upon students' performance and classroom interactions. *British Educational Research Journal, 28*, 353–374.

Younger, M., Warrington, M., & Williams, J. (1999). The gender gap and classroom interactions: Reality and rhetoric? *British Journal of Sociology of Education, 20*, 325–341.

Yount, K. M. (2001). Excess mortality of girls in the Middle East in the 1970s and 1980s: Patterns, correlates and gaps in research. *Population Studies, 55*, 291–308.

Yount, K. M. (2004). Maternal resources, proximity of services, and curative care of boys and girls in Minya, Egypt 1995–97. *Population Studies, 58*, 345–355.

Yücel, M., Stuart, G. W., Maruff, P., Velakoulis, D., Crowe, S. F., Savage, G., et al. (2001). Hemispheric and gender-related differences in the gross morphology of the anterior cingulate/paracingulate cortex in normal volunteers: An MRI morphometric study. *Cerebral Cortex, 11*, 17–25.

Yunger, J. L., Carver, P. R., & Perry, D. G. (2004). Does gender identity influence children's psychological well-being? *Developmental Psychology, 40*, 572–582.

Zahn-Waxler, C. (1993). Warriors and worriers: Gender and psychopathology. *Development and Psychopathology, 5*, 79–89.

Zahn-Waxler, C., Cole, P. M., Welsh, J. D., & Fox, N. A. (1995). Psychophysiological correlates of empathy and prosocial behaviors in preschool children with behavior problems. *Development and Psychopathology, 7*, 27–48.

Zahn-Waxler, C. & Polanichka, N. (2004). All things interpersonal: Socialization and female aggression. In M. Putallaz & K. L. Bierman (Eds.), *Aggression, antisocial behavior, and violence among girls: A developmental perspective.* Duke series in child development and public policy (pp. 48–68). New York: Guilford.

Zarbatany, L., Ghesquiere, K., & Mohr, K. (1992). A context perspective on early adolescents' friendship expectations. *Journal of Early Adolescence, 12*, 111–126.

Zarbatany, L., McDougall, P., & Hymel, S. (2000). Gender-differentiated experience in the peer culture: Links to intimacy in preadolescence. *Social Development, 9*, 62–79.

Zarbatany, L. & Pepper, S. (1996). The role of the group in peer group entry. *Social Development, 5*, 251–260.

Zeman, J. & Garber, J. (1996). Display rules for anger, sadness, and pain: It depends on who is watching. *Child Development, 67*, 957–973.

Zeman, J. & Shipman, K. (1997). Social-contextual influences on expectancies for managing anger and sadness: The transition from middle childhood to adolescence. *Developmental Psychology, 33*, 917–924.

Zemore, S. E., Fiske, S. T., & Kim, H. J. (2000). Gender stereotypes and the dynamics of social interaction. In T. Eckes & H. M. Trautner (Eds.), *The developmental social psychology of gender* (pp. 207–241). Mahwah, NJ: Lawrence Erlbaum Associates.

Zimmer-Gembeck, M. J. (2002). The development of romantic relationships and adaptions in the system of peer relationships. *Journal of Adolescent Health, 31*, 216–225.

Zimmer-Gembeck, M. J., Siebenbruner, J., & Collins, W. A. (2001). Diverse aspects of dating: Associations with psychosocial functioning from early to middle adolescence. *Journal of Adolescence, 24*, 313–336.

Zittleman, K. & Sadker, D. (2002). Gender bias in teacher education texts: New (and old) lessons. *Journal of Teacher Education, 53*, 168–180.

Zolotow, C. (1972). *William's doll*. New York: Harper and Row.

Zucker, K. J. (1999). Intersexuality and gender identity differentiation. *Annual Review of Sex Research, 10*, 1–69.

Zucker, K. J. (2000). Gender identity disorder. In A. J. Sameroff, M. Lewis, & S. M. Miller (Eds.), *Handbook of developmental psychopathology* (2nd ed., pp. 671–686). New York: Kluwer Academic/Plenum.

Zucker, K. J., Bradley, S. J., Oliver, G., Blake, J., Fleming, S., & Hood, J. (1996). Psychosexual development of women with congenital adrenal hyperplasia. *Hormones and Behavior, 30*, 300–318.

Zucker, K. J., Wilson-Smith, D. N., Kurita, J. A., & Stern, A. (1995). Children's appraisals of sex-typed behavior in their peers. *Sex Roles, 33*, 703–725.

Zuk, M. (2002). *Sexual selection: What we can and can't learn about sex from animals*. Berkeley: University of California Press.

Zuo, J. & Tang, S. (2000). Breadwinner status and gender ideologies of men and women regarding family roles. *Sociological Perspectives, 43*, 29–43.

Author Index

E

Subject Index

Page numbers followed by f indicate figures; those followed by t indicate tables.